Bartholomew
CONCISE
WORLD ATLAS

Bartholomew
CONCISE
WORLD ATLAS

This edition published in 1999
by HarperCollins Publishers for
Bookmart Limited
Desford Road, Enderby
Leicester LE9 5AD

HarperCollins Publishers
77-85 Fulham Palace Road, London W6 8JB

First published by Bartholomew 1991

Revised 1998

Printed in Singapore by Imago

ISBN 0 261 67211 8

LH 10074

CONTENTS

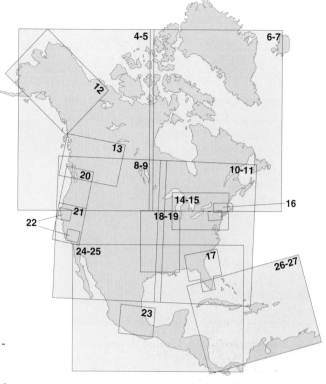

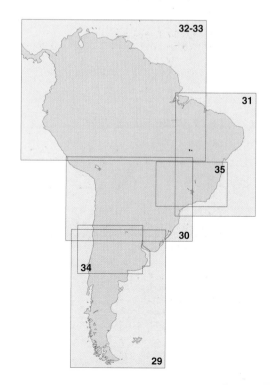

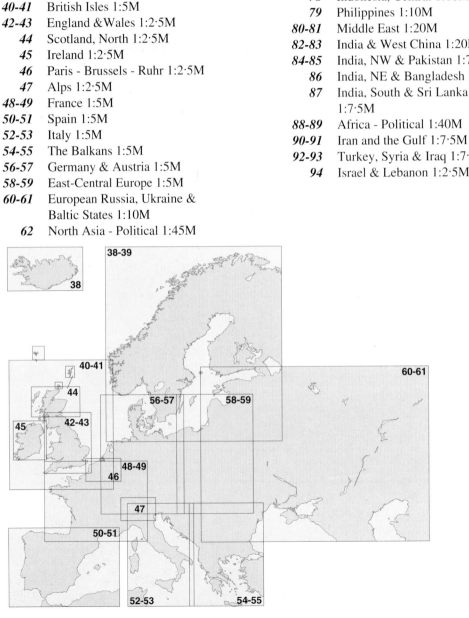

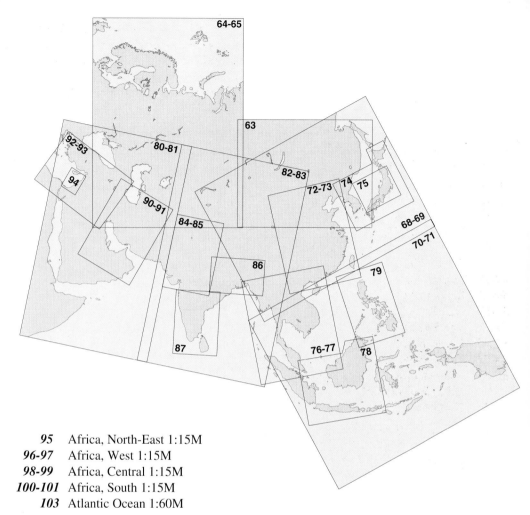

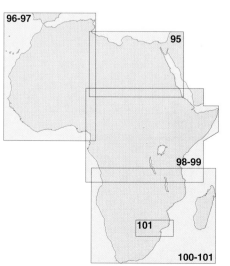

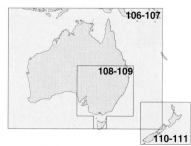

The statistics used for the area and population, and as the basis for languages and religions, are from the latest available sources. The order of the different languages and religions reflect their relative importance within the country; generally all languages and religions over one or two percent of adherents are mentioned.
Membership of international organizations is shown by abbreviations. The full forms are as follows:-

Aladi	Latin American Integration Association	G7	'Group of Seven' industrialised nations
ANZUS	Australia, New Zealand, United States Security Treaty	Mercosur	Common Market of the Southern Cone
ASEAN	Association of Southeast Asian Nations	NAFTA	North American Free Trade Area
CACM	Central American Common Market	NATO	North Atlantic Treaty Organization
Caricom	Caribbean Community	OAS	Organization of American States
CEEAS	Economic Community of Central African States	OAU	Organization of African Unity
CIS	Commonwealth of Independent States	OECD	Organization for Economic Cooperation and Development
Col. Plan	Colombo Plan	OPEC	Organization of Petroleum Exporting Countries
Comm.	Commonwealth	OSCE	Organization for Security and Cooperation in Europe
ECOWAS	Economic Community of West African States	SADC	Southern African Development Community
EEA	European Economic Area	UN	United Nations
EFTA	European Free Trade Association	WEU	Western European Union
EU	European Union		

AFGHANISTAN
Republic

AREA	652,225 sq km (251,825 sq miles)
POPULATION	18,879,000
CAPITAL	Kabul
LANGUAGE	Dari, Pushtu, Uzbek, Turkmen
RELIGION	Sunni Muslim, Shi'a Muslim, Hindu, Sikh and Jewish minorities
CURRENCY	Afghani (AFA)
ORGANIZATIONS	Col. Plan, UN

ALBANIA
Republic

AREA	28,748 sq km (11,100 sq miles)
POPULATION	3,414,000
CAPITAL	Tirana (Tiranë)
LANGUAGE	Albanian (Gheg, Tosk), Greek
RELIGION	Sunni Muslim, Greek Orthodox, Roman Catholic
CURRENCY	lek (ALL)
ORGANIZATIONS	Council of Europe, OSCE, UN

ALGERIA
Republic

AREA	2,381,741 sq km (919,595 sq miles)
POPULATION	27,325,000
CAPITAL	Algiers (Alger, El Djezaïr)
LANGUAGE	Arabic, French, Berber
RELIGION	Sunni Muslim, Roman Catholic
CURRENCY	Algerian dinar (DZD)
ORGANIZATIONS	Arab League, OAU, OPEC, UN

AMERICAN SAMOA
US Territory

AREA	197 sq km (76 sq miles)
POPULATION	53,000
CAPITAL	Pago Pago
LANGUAGE	Samoan, English
RELIGION	Protestant, Roman Catholic
CURRENCY	US dollar (USD)

ANDORRA
Principality

AREA	465 sq km (180 sq miles)
POPULATION	65,000
CAPITAL	Andorra la Vella
LANGUAGE	Catalan, Spanish, French
RELIGION	Roman Catholic
CURRENCY	French franc (FRF), Spanish peseta (ESP)
ORGANIZATIONS	Council of Europe, OSCE, UN

ANGOLA
Republic

AREA	1,246,700 sq km (481,354 sq miles)
POPULATION	10,674,000
CAPITAL	Luanda
LANGUAGE	Portuguese, Local languages
RELIGION	Roman Catholic, Protestant, Traditional beliefs
CURRENCY	kwanza (AOK)
ORGANIZATIONS	OAU, SADC, UN

ANGUILLA
UK Territory

AREA	155 sq km (60 sq miles)
POPULATION	8,000
CAPITAL	The Valley
LANGUAGE	English
RELIGION	Protestant, Roman Catholic
CURRENCY	East Caribbean Dollar (XCD)

ANTIGUA and BARBUDA
Monarchy

AREA	442 sq km (171 sq miles)
POPULATION	65,000
CAPITAL	St John's (on Antigua)
LANGUAGE	English, Creole
RELIGION	Protestant, Roman Catholic
CURRENCY	East Caribbean dollar (XCD)
ORGANIZATIONS	Caricom, Comm., OAS, UN

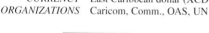

ARGENTINA
Republic

AREA	2,766,889 sq km (1,068,302 sq miles)
POPULATION	34,180,000
CAPITAL	Buenos Aires
LANGUAGE	Spanish, Italian, Amerindian languages
RELIGION	Roman Catholic, Protestant, Jewish
CURRENCY	Argentinian peso (ARP)
ORGANIZATIONS	Aladi, Mercosur, OAS, UN

ARMENIA
Republic

AREA	29,800 sq km (11,506 sq miles)
POPULATION	3,548,000
CAPITAL	Yerevan
LANGUAGE	Armenian, Azeri, Russian
RELIGION	Armenian Orthodox, Roman Catholic, Shi'a Muslim
CURRENCY	dram
ORGANIZATIONS	CIS, OSCE, UN

ARUBA
Netherlands Territory

AREA	193 sq km (75 sq miles)
POPULATION	69,000
CAPITAL	Oranjestad
LANGUAGE	Dutch, Papiamento, English
RELIGION	Roman Catholic, Protestant
CURRENCY	Aruban florin

AUSTRALIA
Federation

AREA	7,682,300 sq km (2,966,153 sq miles)
POPULATION	17,843,000
CAPITAL	Canberra
LANGUAGE	English, Italian, Greek, Aboriginal languages
RELIGION	Protestant, Roman Catholic, Greek Orthodox, Aboriginal beliefs
CURRENCY	Australian dollar (AUD)
ORGANIZATIONS	ANZUS, Col. Plan, Comm., OECD, UN

AUSTRIA
Republic

AREA	83,855 sq km (32,377 sq miles)
POPULATION	8,031,000
CAPITAL	Vienna (Wien)
LANGUAGE	German, Serbo-Croat, Turkish
RELIGION	Roman Catholic, Protestant
CURRENCY	Schilling (ATS)
ORGANIZATIONS	Council of Europe, EEA, EU, OECD, OSCE, UN

AZERBAIJAN
Republic

AREA	86,600 sq km (33,436 sq miles)
POPULATION	7,472,000
CAPITAL	Baku (Bakı)
LANGUAGE	Azeri, Armenian, Russian, Lezgian
RELIGION	Shi'a Muslim, Sunni Muslim, Russian and Armenian Orthodox
CURRENCY	Azerbaijan manat
ORGANIZATIONS	CIS, OSCE, UN

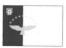

AZORES
Portuguese Territory

AREA	2,247 sq km (868 sq miles)
POPULATION	237,800
CAPITAL	Ponta Delgada
LANGUAGE	Portuguese
RELIGION	Roman Catholic, Protestant
CURRENCY	Portuguese escudo (PTE)

THE BAHAMAS
Monarchy

AREA	19,939 sq km (5,382 sq miles)
POPULATION	272,000
CAPITAL	Nassau
LANGUAGE	English, Creole, French Creole
RELIGION	Protestant, Roman Catholic
CURRENCY	Bahamian dollar (BSD)
ORGANIZATIONS	Caricom, Comm., OAS, UN

BAHRAIN
Monarchy

AREA	691 sq km (267 sq miles)
POPULATION	549,000
CAPITAL	Manama (Al Manāmah)
LANGUAGE	Arabic, English
RELIGION	Shi'a Muslim, Sunni Muslim, Christian
CURRENCY	Bahraini dinar (BHD)
ORGANIZATIONS	Arab League, UN

BANGLADESH
Republic

AREA	143,998 sq km (55,598 sq miles)
POPULATION	117,787,000
CAPITAL	Dhaka (Dhākā, Dacca)
LANGUAGE	Bengali, Bihari, Hindi, English, Local languages
RELIGION	Sunni Muslim, Hindu, Buddhist, Christian
CURRENCY	taka (BDT)
ORGANIZATIONS	Col. Plan, Comm., UN

BARBADOS
Monarchy

AREA	430 sq km (166 sq miles)
POPULATION	261,000
CAPITAL	Bridgetown
LANGUAGE	English, Creole (Bajan)
RELIGION	Protestant, Roman Catholic
CURRENCY	Barbados dollar (BBD)
ORGANIZATIONS	Caricom, Comm., OAS, UN

BELARUS
Republic

AREA	207,600 sq km (80,155 sq miles)
POPULATION	10,355,000
CAPITAL	Minsk
LANGUAGE	Belorussian, Russian, Ukrainian
RELIGION	Belorussian Orthodox, Roman Catholic
CURRENCY	Belarus rouble
ORGANIZATIONS	CIS, OSCE, UN

BELGIUM
Monarchy

AREA	30,520 sq km (11,784 sq miles)
POPULATION	10,080,000
CAPITAL	Brussels (Bruxelles/Brussel)
LANGUAGE	Dutch (Flemish), French, German (all official), Italian,
RELIGION	Roman Catholic , Protestant
CURRENCY	Belgian franc (BEF)
ORGANIZATIONS	Council of Europe, EEA, EU, NATO, OECD, OSCE, UN, WEU

BELIZE
Monarchy

AREA	22,965 sq km (8,867 sq miles)
POPULATION	211,000
CAPITAL	Belmopan
LANGUAGE	English, Creole, Spanish, Mayan
RELIGION	Roman Catholic, Protestant, Hindu
CURRENCY	Belizean dollar (BZD)
ORGANIZATIONS	Caricom, Comm., OAS, UN

BENIN
Republic

AREA	112,620 sq km (43,483 sq miles)
POPULATION	5,246,000
CAPITAL	Porto Novo
LANGUAGE	French, Fon, Yoruba, Adja, Local languages
RELIGION	Traditional beliefs, Roman Catholic, Sunni Muslim
CURRENCY	CFA franc (W Africa) (XOF)
ORGANIZA-	ECOWAS, OAU, UN

BERMUDA
UK Territory

AREA	54 sq km (21 sq miles)
POPULATION	63,000
CAPITAL	Hamilton
LANGUAGE	English
RELIGION	Protestant, Roman Catholic
CURRENCY	Bermuda dollar (BMD)

BHUTAN
Monarchy

AREA	46,620 sq km (18,000 sq miles)
POPULATION	1,614,000
CAPITAL	Thimphu
LANGUAGE	Dzongkha, Nepali, Assamese, English
RELIGION	Buddhist, Hindu, Sunni Muslim
CURRENCY	ngultrum (BTN), Indian rupee (INR)
ORGANIZATIONS	Col. Plan, UN

BOLIVIA
Republic

AREA	1,098,581 sq km (424,164 sq miles)
POPULATION	7,237,000
CAPITAL	La Paz
LANGUAGE	Spanish, Quechua, Aymara
RELIGION	Roman Catholic, Protestant, Baha'i
CURRENCY	boliviano (BOB)
ORGANIZATIONS	Aladi, OAS, UN

BOSNIA-HERZEGOVINA
Republic

AREA	51,130sq km (19,741 sq miles)
POPULATION	3,527,000
CAPITAL	Sarajevo
LANGUAGE	Serbo-Croat
RELIGION	Sunni Muslim, Serbian Orthodox, Roman Catholic, Protestant
CURRENCY	Bosnia-Herzegovina dinar
ORGANIZATIONS	OSCE, UN

BOTSWANA
Republic

AREA	581,370 sq km (224,468 sq miles)

POPULATION	1,443,000
CAPITAL	Gaborone
LANGUAGE	English (official), Setswana, Shona, Local languages
RELIGION	Traditional beliefs, Protestant, Roman Catholic
CURRENCY	pula (BWP)
ORGANIZATIONS	Comm., OAU, SADC, UN

BRAZIL
Republic

AREA	8,511,965 sq km (3,286,488 sq miles)
POPULATION	153,725,000
CAPITAL	Brasília
LANGUAGE	Portuguese, German, Japanese, Italian, Amerindian languages
RELIGION	Roman Catholic, Spiritist, Protestant
CURRENCY	real (BRC)
ORGANIZATIONS	Aladi, Mercosur, OAS, UN

BRUNEI
Monarchy

AREA	5,765 sq km (2,226 sq miles)
POPULATION	280,000
CAPITAL	Bandar Seri Begawan
LANGUAGE	Malay, English, Chinese
RELIGION	Sunni Muslim, Buddhist, Christian
CURRENCY	dollar (ringgit) (BND)
ORGANIZATIONS	ASEAN, Comm, UN

BULGARIA
Republic

AREA	110,994 sq km (42,855 sq miles)
POPULATION	8,443,000
CAPITAL	Sofia (Sofiya)
LANGUAGE	Bulgarian, Turkish, Romany, Macedonian
RELIGION	Bulgarian Orthodox, Sunni Muslim
CURRENCY	lev (BGL)
ORGANIZATIONS	Council of Europe, OSCE, UN

BURKINA
Republic

AREA	274,200 sq km (105,869 sq miles)
POPULATION	9,889,000
CAPITAL	Ouagadougou
LANGUAGE	French, Moré (Mossi), Fulani,

BURKINA *continued*

Local languages
RELIGION Traditional beliefs, Sunni Muslim, Roman Catholic
CURRENCY CFA franc (W Africa) (XOF)
ORGANIZATIONS ECOWAS, OAU, UN

BURUNDI
Republic

AREA 27,835 sq km (10,747 sq miles)
POPULATION 6,209,000
CAPITAL Bujumbura
LANGUAGE Kirundi (Hutu, Tutsi), French
RELIGION Roman Catholic, Trad. beliefs, Protestant, Sunni Muslim
CURRENCY Burundi franc (BIF)
ORGANIZATIONS CEEAC, OAU, UN

CAMBODIA
Monarchy

AREA 181,000 sq km (69,884 sq miles)
POPULATION 9,968,000
CAPITAL Phnom Penh
LANGUAGE Khmer, Vietnamese
RELIGION Buddhist, Roman Catholic, Sunni Muslim
CURRENCY riel (KHR)
ORGANIZATIONS Col. Plan, UN

CAMEROON
Republic

AREA: 475,442 sq km(183,569 sq miles)
POPULATION: 12,871,000
CAPITAL: Yaoundé
LANGUAGE: French, English, Fang, Bamileke, many local languages
RELIGION: Trad. beliefs, Roman Catholic, Sunni Muslim, Protestant
CURRENCY: CFA franc (C Africa) (XAF)
ORGANIZATIONS: CEEAC, Comm, OAU, UN

CANADA
Federation

AREA 9,970,610 sq km (3,849,674 sq miles)
POPULATION 29,248,000
CAPITAL Ottawa

LANGUAGE English, French, Amerindian languages, Inuktitut (Eskimo)
RELIGION Roman Catholic, Protestant, Greek Orthodox, Jewish
CURRENCY Canadian dollar (CAD)
ORGANIZATIONS Col. Plan, Comm., G7, NAFTA, NATO, OAS, OECD, OSCE, UN

CAPE VERDE
Republic

AREA 4,033 sq km (1,557 sq miles)
POPULATION 381,000
CAPITAL Praia
LANGUAGE Portuguese, Portuguese Creole
RELIGION Roman Catholic, Protestant, Traditional beliefs
CURRENCY Cape Verde escudo (CVE)
ORGANIZATIONS ECOWAS, OAU, UN

CAYMAN ISLANDS
UK Territory

AREA 259 sq km (100 sq miles)
POPULATION 30,000
CAPITAL George Town
LANGUAGE English
RELIGION Protestant, Roman Catholic
CURRENCY Cayman Islands dollar (KYD)

CENTRAL AFRICAN REPUBLIC
Republic

AREA 622,436 sq km (240,324 sq miles)
POPULATION 3,235,000
CAPITAL Bangui
LANGUAGE French, Sango, Banda, Baya, Local languages
RELIGION Protestant, Roman Catholic, Traditional beliefs, Sunni Muslim
CURRENCY CFA franc (C Africa) (XAF)
ORGANIZATIONS CEEAC, OAU, UN

CHAD
Republic

AREA 1,284,000 sq km (495,755 sq miles)
POPULATION 6,183,000
CAPITAL Ndjamena
LANGUAGE Arabic, French, local languages
RELIGION Sunni Muslim, Traditional beliefs,

Roman Catholic
CURRENCY   CFA franc (C Africa) (XAF)
ORGANIZATIONS   CEEAC, OAU, UN

CHILE
Republic

AREA	756,945 sq km (292,259 sq miles)
POPULATION	13,994,000
CAPITAL	Santiago
LANGUAGE	Spanish, Amerindian languages
RELIGION	Roman Catholic, Protestant
CURRENCY	Chilean peso (CLP)
ORGANIZATIONS	Aladi, OAS, UN

CHINA
Republic

AREA	9,560,900 sq km (3,691,484 sq miles)
POPULATION	1,208,841,000
CAPITAL	Beijing (Peking)
LANGUAGE	Chinese (Mandarin official), many regional languages
RELIGION	Confucian, Taoist, Buddist, Sunni Muslim, Roman Catholic
CURRENCY	yuan (CNY)
ORGANIZATIONS	UN

CHRISTMAS ISLAND
Australian Territory

AREA	135 sq km (52 sq miles)
POPULATION	2,000
CAPITAL	The Settlement
LANGUAGE	English
RELIGION	Buddhist, Sunni Muslim, Protestant, Roman Catholic
CURRENCY	Australian dollar (AUD)

COCOS ISLANDS
Australian Territory

AREA	14 sq km (5 sq miles)
POPULATION	1,000
CAPITAL	Home Island
LANGUAGE	English
RELIGION	Sunni Muslim, Christian
CURRENCY	Australian dollar (AUD)

COLOMBIA
Republic

AREA	1,141,748 (440,831 sq miles)
POPULATION	34,520,000
CAPITAL	Bogotá
LANGUAGE	Spanish, Amerindian languages
RELIGION	Roman Catholic, Protestant
CURRENCY	Colombian peso (COP)
ORGANIZATIONS	Aladi, OAS, UN

COMOROS
Republic

AREA	1,862 sq km (719 sq miles)
POPULATION	630,000
CAPITAL	Moroni
LANGUAGE	Comorian, French, Arabic
RELIGION	Sunni Muslim, Roman Catholic
CURRENCY	Comoro franc (KMF)
ORGANIZATIONS	Arab League, OAU, UN

CONGO
Republic

AREA	342,000 sq km (132,047 sq miles)
POPULATION	2,516,000
CAPITAL	Brazzaville
LANGUAGE	French (official), Kongo, Monokutuba, local languages
RELIGION	Roman Catholic, Protestant, Traditional beliefs, Sunni Muslim and Muslim minorities
CURRENCY	CFA franc (C Africa) (XAF)
ORGANIZATIONS	CEEAC, OAU, UN

COOK ISLANDS
New Zealand Territory

AREA	293 sq km (113 sq miles)
POPULATION	19,000
CAPITAL	Avarua on Rarotonga
LANGUAGE	English, Maori
RELIGION	Protestant, Roman Catholic
CURRENCY	New Zealand dollar (NZD)

COSTA RICA
Republic

AREA	51,100 sq km (19,730 sq miles)

COSTA RICA *continued*

POPULATION	3,011,000
CAPITAL	San José
LANGUAGE	Spanish
RELIGION	Roman Catholic, Protestant
CURRENCY	Costa Rican colón (CRC)
ORGANIZATIONS	CACM, OAS, UN

CÔTE D'IVOIRE
Republic

AREA	322,463 sq km (124,504 sq miles)
POPULATION	13,965,000
CAPITAL	Yamoussoukro
LANGUAGE	French (official), Akan, Kru, Gur, Local languages
RELIGION	Traditional beliefs, Sunni Muslim, Roman Catholic
CURRENCY	CFA franc (W Africa) (XOF)
ORGANIZATIONS	ECOWAS, OAU, UN

CROATIA
Republic

AREA	56,538 sq km (21,829 sq miles)
POPULATION	4,504,000
CAPITAL	Zagreb
LANGUAGE	Serbo-Croat
RELIGION	Roman Catholic, Orthodox, Sunni Muslim
CURRENCY	kuna
ORGANIZATIONS	OSCE, UN

CUBA
Republic

AREA	110,860 sq km (42,803 sq miles)
POPULATION	10,960,000
CAPITAL	Havana (Habana)
LANGUAGE	Spanish
RELIGION	Roman Catholic, Protestant
CURRENCY	Cuban peso (CUP)
ORGANIZATIONS	UN

CYPRUS
Republic

AREA	9,251 sq km (3,572 sq miles)
POPULATION	734,000
CAPITAL	Nicosia
LANGUAGE	Greek, Turkish, English
RELIGION	Greek (Cypriot) Orthodox, Sunni Muslim
CURRENCY	Cyprus pound (CYP)
ORGANIZATIONS	Comm., Council of Europe, OSCE, UN

CZECH REPUBLIC
Republic

AREA	78,864 sq km (30,450 sq miles)
POPULATION	10,333,000
CAPITAL	Prague (Praha)
LANGUAGE	Czech, Moravian, Slovak
RELIGION	Roman Catholic, Protestant
CURRENCY	Czech crown or koruna (CEK)
ORGANIZATIONS	Council of Europe, OSCE, UN

DENMARK
Monarchy

AREA	43,075 sq km (16,631 sq miles)
POPULATION	5,205,000
CAPITAL	Copenhagen (København)
LANGUAGE	Danish
RELIGION	Protestant, Roman Catholic
CURRENCY	Danish krone (DKK)
ORGANIZATIONS	Council of Europe, EEA, EU, NATO, OECD, OSCE, UN

DJIBOUTI
Republic

AREA	23,200 sq km (8,958 sq miles)
POPULATION	566,000
CAPITAL	Djibouti
LANGUAGE	Somali, French, Arabic, Issa, Afar
RELIGION	Sunni Muslim, Roman Catholic
CURRENCY	Djibouti franc (DJF)
ORGANIZATIONS	Arab League, OAU, UN

DOMINICA
Republic

AREA	750 sq km (290 sq miles)
POPULATION	71,000
CAPITAL	Roseau
LANGUAGE	English, French creole
RELIGION	Roman Catholic, Protestant
CURRENCY	East Caribbean dollar (XCD)
ORGANIZATIONS	Caricom, Comm., OAS, UN

DOMINICAN REPUBLIC
Republic

AREA	48,442 sq km (18,704 sq miles)
POPULATION	7,769,000
CAPITAL	Santo Domingo
LANGUAGE	Spanish, French creole
RELIGION	Roman Catholic, Protestant
CURRENCY	Dominican peso (DOP)
ORGANIZATIONS	OAS, UN

ECUADOR
Republic

AREA	272,045 sq km (105,037 sq miles)
POPULATION	11,221,000
CAPITAL	Quito
LANGUAGE	Spanish, Quechua, Amerindian languages
RELIGION	Roman Catholic, Protestant
CURRENCY	sucre (ECS)
ORGANIZATIONS	Aladi, OAS, UN

EGYPT
Republic

AREA	1,000,250 sq km (386,199 sq miles)
POPULATION	58,326,000
CAPITAL	Cairo (El Qâhira)
LANGUAGE	Arabic, French
RELIGION	Sunni Muslim, Coptic Christian
CURRENCY	Egyptian pound (EGP)
ORGANIZATIONS	Arab League, OAU, UN

EL SALVADOR
Republic

AREA	21,041 sq km (8,124 sq miles)
POPULATION	5,641,000
CAPITAL	San Salvador
LANGUAGE	Spanish
RELIGION	Roman Catholic, Protestant
CURRENCY	El Salvador colón (SVC)
ORGANIZATIONS	CACM, OAS, UN

EQUATORIAL GUINEA
Republic

AREA	28,051 sq km (10,831 sq miles)
POPULATION	389,000
CAPITAL	Malabo
LANGUAGE	Spanish, Fang
RELIGION	Roman Catholic, Traditional beliefs
CURRENCY	CFA franc (C Africa) (XAF)
ORGANIZATIONS	CEEAC, OAU, UN

ERITREA
Republic

AREA	117,400 sq km (45,328 sq miles)
POPULATION	3,437,000
CAPITAL	Asmara (Āsmera)
LANGUAGE	Tigrinya, Arabic, Tigre, English
RELIGION	Sunni Muslim, Coptic Christian
CURRENCY	Ethiopian birr (ETB)
ORGANIZATIONS	OAU, UN

ESTONIA
Republic

AREA	45,200 sq km (17,452 sq miles)
POPULATION	1,541,000
CAPITAL	Tallinn
LANGUAGE	Estonian, Russian
RELIGION	Protestant, Russian Orthodox
CURRENCY	kroon (EKR)
ORGANIZATIONS	Council of Europe, OSCE, UN

ETHIOPIA
Republic

AREA	1,133,880 sq km (437,794 sq miles)
POPULATION	54,938,000
CAPITAL	Addis Ababa (Ādīs Ābeba)
LANGUAGE	Amharic (official), Oromo, Local languages
RELIGION	Ethiopian Orthodox, Sunni Muslim, Traditional beliefs
CURRENCY	birr (ETB)
ORGANIZATIONS	OAU, UN

FAEROES
Danish Territory

AREA	1,399 sq km (540 sq miles)
POPULATION	47,000
CAPITAL	Tórshavn
LANGUAGE	Danish, Faeroese
RELIGION	Protestant
CURRENCY	Danish krone (DKK)

FALKLAND ISLANDS
UK Territory

AREA	12,170 sq km (4,699 sq miles)
POPULATION	2,000
CAPITAL	Stanley
LANGUAGE	English
RELIGION	Protestant, Roman Catholic
CURRENCY	Falkland Islands pound (FKP)

FIJI
Republic

AREA	18,330 sq km (7,077 sq miles)
POPULATION	771,000
CAPITAL	Suva
LANGUAGE	English, Fijian, Hindi
RELIGION	Protestant, Hindu, Roman Catholic, Sunni Muslim
CURRENCY	Fiji dollar (FJD)
ORGANIZATIONS	Col. Plan, UN

FINLAND
Republic

AREA	338,145 sq km (130,559 sq miles)
POPULATION	5,095,000
CAPITAL	Helsinki
LANGUAGE	Finnish, Swedish
RELIGION	Protestant, Finnish (Greek) Orthodox
CURRENCY	markka (finnmark) (FIM)
ORGANIZATIONS	Council of Europe, EEA, EU, OECD, OSCE, UN

FRANCE
Republic

AREA	543,965 sq km (210,026 sq miles)
POPULATION	57,747,000
CAPITAL	Paris
LANGUAGE	French, French dialects, Arabic, German (Alsatian), Breton
RELIGION	Roman Catholic, Protestant, Sunni Muslim
CURRENCY	French franc (FRF)
ORGANIZATIONS	Council of Europe, EEA, EU, G7, NATO, OECD, OSCE, UN, WEU

FRENCH GUIANA
French Territory

AREA	90,000 sq km (34,749 sq miles)
POPULATION	141,000
CAPITAL	Cayenne
LANGUAGE	French, French creole
RELIGION	Roman Catholic, Protestant
CURRENCY	French franc (FRF)

FRENCH POLYNESIA
French Territory

AREA	3,265 sq km (1,261 sq miles)
POPULATION	215,000
CAPITAL	Papeete
LANGUAGE	French, Polynesian languages
RELIGION	Protestant, Roman Catholic, Mormon
CURRENCY	Pacific franc (CFP)

GABON
Republic

AREA	267,667 sq km (103,347 sq miles)
POPULATION	1,283,000
CAPITAL	Libreville
LANGUAGE	French, Fang, Local languages
RELIGION	Roman Catholic, Protestant, Traditional beliefs
CURRENCY	CFA franc (C Africa) (XAF)
ORGANIZATIONS	CEEAC, OAU, OPEC, UN,

THE GAMBIA
Republic

AREA	11,295 sq km (4,361 sq miles)
POPULATION	1,081,000
CAPITAL	Banjul
LANGUAGE	English (official), Malinke, Fulani, Wolof
RELIGION	Sunni Muslim, Protestant
CURRENCY	dalasi (GMD)
ORGANIZATIONS	Comm., ECOWAS, OAU, UN

GEORGIA
Republic

AREA	69,700 sq km (26,911 sq miles)
POPULATION	5,450,000

CAPITAL	Tbilisi
LANGUAGE	Georgian, Russian, Armenian, Azeri, Ossetian, Abkhaz
RELIGION	Georgian Orthodox, Russian Orthodox, Shi'a Muslim
CURRENCY	lari
ORGANIZATIONS	CIS, OSCE, UN

GERMANY
Republic

AREA	357,868 sq km (138,174 sq miles)
POPULATION	81,410,000
CAPITAL	Berlin
LANGUAGE	German, Turkish
RELIGION	Protestant, Roman Catholic Sunni Muslim
CURRENCY	Deutschmark (DM)
ORGANIZATIONS	Council of Europe, EEA, EU, G7, NATO, OECD, OSCE, UN, WEU

GHANA
Republic

AREA	238,537 sq km (92,100 sq miles)
POPULATION	16,944,000
CAPITAL	Accra
LANGUAGE	English (official), Hausa, Akan, Local languages
RELIGION	Protestant, Roman Catholic, Sunni Muslim, Traditional beliefs
CURRENCY	cedi (GHC)
ORGANIZATIONS	Comm., ECOWAS, OAU, UN

GIBRALTAR
UK Territory

AREA	6.5 sq km (2.5 sq miles)
POPULATION	28,000
CAPITAL	Gibraltar
LANGUAGE	English, Spanish
RELIGION	Roman Catholic, Protestant, Sunni Muslim
CURRENCY	Gibraltar pound (GIP)

GREECE
Republic

AREA	131,957 sq km (50,949 sq miles)
POPULATION	10,426,000
CAPITAL	Athens (Athínai)
LANGUAGE	Greek, Macedonian
RELIGION	Greek Orthodox, Sunni Muslim
CURRENCY	drachma (GRD)
ORGANIZATIONS	Council of Europe, EEA, EU, NATO, OECD, OSCE, UN, WEU

GREENLAND
Danish Territory

AREA	2,175,600 sq km (840,004 sq miles)
POPULATION	58,000
CAPITAL	Nuuk (Godthåb)
LANGUAGE	Greenlandic, Danish
RELIGION	Protestant
CURRENCY	Danish krone (DKK)

GRENADA
Monarchy

AREA	378 sq km (146 sq miles)
POPULATION	92,000
CAPITAL	St George's
LANGUAGE	English, Creole
RELIGION	Roman Catholic, Protestant
CURRENCY	East Caribbean dollar (XCD)
ORGANIZATIONS	Caricom, Comm., OAS, UN

GUADELOUPE
French Territory

AREA	1,780 sq km (687 sq miles)
POPULATION	421,000
CAPITAL	Basse-Terre
LANGUAGE	French, French Creole
RELIGION	Roman Catholic, Hindu
CURRENCY	French franc (FRF)

GUAM
US Territory

AREA	541 sq km (209 sq miles)
POPULATION	146,000
CAPITAL	Agaña
LANGUAGE	Chamorro, English, Tagalog
RELIGION	Roman Catholic
CURRENCY	US dollar (USD)

GUATEMALA
Republic

AREA	108,890 sq km (42,043 sq miles)
POPULATION	10,322,000
CAPITAL	Guatemala City (Guatemala)
LANGUAGE	Spanish, Mayan languages
RELIGION	Roman Catholic, Protestant
CURRENCY	quetzal (GTQ)
ORGANIZATIONS	CACM, OAS, UN

GUERNSEY
UK Territory

AREA	79 sq km (31 sq miles)
POPULATION	64,000
CAPITAL	St Peter Port
LANGUAGE	English, French
RELIGION	Protestant, Roman Catholic
CURRENCY	pound sterling (GBP)

GUINEA
Republic

AREA	245,857 sq km (94,926 sq miles)
POPULATION	6,501,000
CAPITAL	Conakry
LANGUAGE	French, Fulani, Malinke, Local languages
RELIGION	Sunni Muslim, Traditional beliefs, Roman Catholic
CURRENCY	Guinea franc (GNF)
ORGANIZATIONS	ECOWAS, OAU, UN

GUINEA-BISSAU
Republic

AREA	36,125 sq km (13,948 sq miles)
POPULATION	1,050,000
CAPITAL	Bissau
LANGUAGE	Portuguese, Portuguese Creole, Local languages
RELIGION	Traditional beliefs, Sunni Muslim, Roman Catholic
CURRENCY	Guinea-Bissau peso (GWP)
ORGANIZATIONS	ECOWAS, OAU, UN

GUYANA
Republic

AREA	214,969 sq km (83,000 sq miles)
POPULATION	825,000
CAPITAL	Georgetown
LANGUAGE	English, Creole, Hindi, Amerindian languages,
RELIGION	Protestant, Hindu, Roman Catholic, Sunni Muslim
CURRENCY	Guyana dollar (GYD)
ORGANIZATIONS	Caricom, Comm., OAS, UN

HAITI
Republic

AREA	27,750 sq km (10,714 sq miles)
POPULATION	7,041,000
CAPITAL	Port-au-Prince
LANGUAGE	French, French Creole
RELIGION	Roman Catholic, Protestant, Voodoo
CURRENCY	gourde (HTG)
ORGANIZATIONS	OAS, UN

HONDURAS
Republic

AREA	112,088 sq km (43,277 sq miles)
POPULATION	5,770,000
CAPITAL	Tegucigalpa
LANGUAGE	Spanish, Amerindian languages
RELIGION	Roman Catholic, Protestant
CURRENCY	lempira (HNL)
ORGANIZATIONS	CACM, OAS, UN

Hong Kong
reverted to China 1 July 1997

AREA	1,075 sq km (415 sq miles)
POPULATION	6,061,000
LANGUAGE	Chinese (Cantonese official, Mandarin), English (official)
RELIGION	Buddhist, Taoist, Protestant
CURRENCY	Hong Kong dollar (HKD)

HUNGARY
Republic

AREA	93,030 sq km (35,919 sq miles)
POPULATION	10,261,000
CAPITAL	Budapest
LANGUAGE	Hungarian, Romany, German, Slovak
RELIGION	Roman Catholic, Protestant
CURRENCY	forint (HUF)
ORGANIZATIONS	Council of Europe, OSCE, UN

ICELAND
Republic

AREA	102,820 sq km (39,699 sq miles)
POPULATION	266,000
CAPITAL	Reykjavík
LANGUAGE	Icelandic
RELIGION	Protestant, Roman Catholic
CURRENCY	króna (ISK)
ORGANIZATIONS	Council of Europe, EEA, EFTA, NATO, OECD, OSCE, UN

INDIA
Republic

AREA	3,287,263 sq km (1,269,219 sq miles)
POPULATION	918,570,000
CAPITAL	New Delhi
LANGUAGE	Hindi, English (official), many regional languages
RELIGION	Hindu, Sunni Muslim, Sikh, Christian, Buddhist
CURRENCY	Indian rupee (INR)
ORGANIZATIONS	Col. Plan, Comm., UN

INDONESIA
Republic

AREA	1,919,445 sq km (741,102 sq miles)
POPULATION	193,017,000
CAPITAL	Jakarta
LANGUAGE	Indonesian (official), many local languages
RELIGION	Sunni Muslim, Protestant, Roman Catholic, Hindu, Buddhist
CURRENCY	rupiah (IDR)
ORGANIZATIONS	ASEAN, Col. Plan, OPEC, UN

IRAN
Republic

AREA	1,648,000 sq km (636,296 sq miles)
POPULATION	59,778,000
CAPITAL	Tehran
LANGUAGE	Farsi (Persian), Azeri, Kurdish, Regional languages
RELIGION	Shi'a Muslim, Sunni Muslim, Baha'i, Christian, Zoroastrian
CURRENCY	Iranian rial (IRR)
ORGANIZATIONS	Col. Plan, OPEC, UN

IRAQ
Republic

AREA	438,317 sq km (169,235 sq miles)
POPULATION	19,925,000
CAPITAL	Baghdad
LANGUAGE	Arabic, Kurdish, Turkmen
RELIGION	Shi'a Muslim, Sunni Muslim, Roman Catholic
CURRENCY	Iraqi dinar (IQD)
ORGANIZATIONS	Arab League, OPEC, UN

IRELAND, REPUBLIC OF
Republic

AREA	70,282 sq km (27,136 sq miles)
POPULATION	3,571,000
CAPITAL	Dublin (Baile Átha Cliath)
LANGUAGE	English, Irish
RELIGION	Roman Catholic, Protestant
CURRENCY	punt or Irish pound (IEP)
ORGANIZATIONS	Council of Europe, EEA, EU, OECD, OSCE, UN

ISLE OF MAN
UK Territory

AREA	572 sq km (221 sq miles)
POPULATION	73,000
CAPITAL	Douglas
LANGUAGE	English
RELIGION	Protestant, Roman Catholic
CURRENCY	pound sterling (GBP)

ISRAEL
Republic

AREA	20,770 sq km (8,019 sq miles)
POPULATION	5,383,000
CAPITAL	Jerusalem
LANGUAGE	Hebrew, Arabic, Yiddish, English
RELIGION	Jewish, Sunni Muslim, Christian, Druze
CURRENCY	shekel (ILS)
ORGANIZATIONS	UN

ITALY
Republic

AREA	301,245 sq km (116,311 sq miles)
POPULATION	57,193,000
CAPITAL	Rome (Roma)
LANGUAGE	Italian, Italian dialects
RELIGION	Roman Catholic
CURRENCY	Italian lira (ITL)
ORGANIZATIONS	Council of Europe, EEA, EU, G7, NATO, OECD, OSCE, UN, WEU

JAMAICA
Monarchy

AREA	10,911 sq km (4,244 sq miles)
POPULATION	2,429,000
CAPITAL	Kingston
LANGUAGE	English, Creole
RELIGION	Protestant, Roman Catholic, Rastafarian
CURRENCY	Jamaican dollar (JMD)
ORGANIZATIONS	Caricom, Comm., OAS, UN

JAPAN
Monarchy

AREA	377,727 sq km (145,841 sq miles)
POPULATION	124,961,000
CAPITAL	Tokyo (Tōkyō)
LANGUAGE	Japanese
RELIGION	Shintoist, Buddhist, Christian
CURRENCY	yen (JPY)
ORGANIZATIONS	Col. Plan, G7, OECD, UN

JERSEY
UK Territory

AREA	116 sq km (45 sq miles)
POPULATION	86,800
CAPITAL	St Helier
LANGUAGE	English, French
RELIGION	Protestant, Roman Catholic
CURRENCY	pound sterling (GBP)

JORDAN
Monarchy

AREA	89,206 sq km (34,443 sq miles)
POPULATION	5,198,000
CAPITAL	Amman ('Ammān)
LANGUAGE	Arabic
RELIGION	Sunni Muslim, Christian, Shi'a Muslim
CURRENCY	Jordanian dinar (JOD)
ORGANIZATIONS	Arab League, UN

KAZAKHSTAN
Republic

AREA	2,717,300 sq km (1,049,155 sq miles)
POPULATION	17,027,000
CAPITAL	Alma-Ata (Almaty)
LANGUAGE	Kazakh, Russian, German, Ukrainian, Uzbek, Tatar
RELIGION	Sunni Muslim, Russian Orthodox, Protestant
CURRENCY	tanga
ORGANIZATIONS	CIS, OSCE, UN

KENYA
Republic

AREA	582,646 sq km (224,961 sq miles)
POPULATION	27,343,000
CAPITAL	Nairobi
LANGUAGE	Swahili (official), English, many local languages
RELIGION	Roman Catholic, Protestant, Traditional beliefs
CURRENCY	Kenya shilling (KES)
ORGANIZATIONS	Comm., OAU, UN

KIRIBATI
Republic

AREA	717 sq km (277 sq miles)
POPULATION	77,000
CAPITAL	Bairiki
LANGUAGE	I-Kiribati (Gilbertese), English
RELIGION	Roman Catholic, Protestant, Baha'i, Mormon
CURRENCY	Australian dollar (AUD)
ORGANIZATIONS	Comm.

KUWAIT
Monarchy

AREA	17,818 sq km (6,880 sq miles)
POPULATION	1,620,000
CAPITAL	Kuwait City (Al Kuwayṭ)
LANGUAGE	Arabic
RELIGION	Sunni Muslim, Shi'a Muslim, other

Muslim, Christian, Hindu
CURRENCY Kuwaiti dinar (KWD)
ORGANIZATIONS Arab League, OPEC, UN

KYRGYZSTAN
Republic

AREA 198,500 sq km (76,641 sq miles)
POPULATION 4,596,000
CAPITAL Bishkek
LANGUAGE Kirghiz, Russian, Uzbek
RELIGION Sunni Muslim, Russian Orthodox
CURRENCY Kyrgyzstan som
ORGANIZATIONS CIS, OSCE, UN

LAOS
Republic

AREA 236,800 sq km (91,429 sq miles)
POPULATION 4,742,000
CAPITAL Vientiane (Viangchan)
LANGUAGE Lao, local languages
RELIGION Buddhist, Traditional beliefs,
Roman Catholic, Sunni Muslim
CURRENCY kip (LAK)
ORGANIZATIONS Col. Plan, UN

LATVIA
Republic

AREA 63,700 sq km (24,595 sq miles)
POPULATION 2,548,000
CAPITAL Riga
LANGUAGE Latvian, Russian
RELIGION Protestant, Roman Catholic
Russian Orthodox
CURRENCY lat
ORGANIZATIONS Council of Europe, OSCE, UN

LEBANON
Republic

AREA 10,452 sq km (4,036 sq miles)
POPULATION 2,915,000
CAPITAL Beirut (Beyrouth)
LANGUAGE Arabic, French, Armenian
RELIGION Shi'a, Sunni and other Muslim,
Protestant, Roman Catholic
CURRENCY Lebanese pound (LBP)
ORGANIZATIONS Arab League, UN

LESOTHO
Monarchy

AREA 30,355 sq km (11,720 sq miles)
POPULATION 1,996,000
CAPITAL Maseru
LANGUAGE Sesotho, English, Zulu
RELIGION Roman Catholic, Protestant,
Traditional beliefs
CURRENCY loti (LSL), South African rand (ZAR)
ORGANIZATIONS Comm., OAU, SADC, UN

LIBERIA
Republic

AREA 111,369 sq km (43,000 sq miles)
POPULATION 2,941,000
CAPITAL Monrovia
LANGUAGE English, Creole,
many local languages
RELIGION Traditional beliefs, Sunni Muslim,
Protestant, Roman Catholic
CURRENCY Liberian dollar (LRD)
ORGANIZATIONS ECOWAS, OAU, UN

LIBYA
Republic

AREA 1,759,540 sq km (679,362 sq miles)
POPULATION 5,225,000
CAPITAL Tripoli (Țarābulus)
LANGUAGE Arabic, Berber
RELIGION Sunni Muslim, Roman Catholic
CURRENCY Libyan dinar (LYD)
ORGANIZATIONS Arab League, OAU

LIECHTENSTEIN
Monarchy

AREA 160 sq km (62 sq miles)
POPULATION 30,000
CAPITAL Vaduz
LANGUAGE German
RELIGION Roman Catholic, Protestant
CURRENCY Franken (Swiss franc) (CHF)
ORGANIZATIONS Council of Europe, EEA, EFTA,
OSCE, UN

LITHUANIA
Republic

AREA	65,200 sq km (25,174 sq miles)
POPULATION	3,721,000
CAPITAL	Vilnius
LANGUAGE	Lithuanian, Russian, Polish
RELIGION	Roman Catholic, Protestant, Russian Orthodox
CURRENCY	litas
ORGANIZATIONS	Council of Europe, OSCE, UN

LUXEMBOURG
Monarchy

AREA	2,586 sq km (998 sq miles)
POPULATION	401,000
CAPITAL	Luxembourg
LANGUAGE	Letzeburgish (Luxembourgian), German, French, Portuguese
RELIGION	Roman Catholic, Protestant
CURRENCY	Luxembourg franc (LUF)
ORGANIZATIONS	Council of Europe, EEA, EU, NATO, OECD, OSCE, UN, WEU

MACAU
Portuguese Territory

AREA	17 sq km (7 sq miles)
POPULATION	398,000
CAPITAL	Macau
LANGUAGE	Chinese (Cantonese), Portuguese
RELIGION	Buddhist, Roman Catholic, Protestant
CURRENCY	pataca (MOP)

MACEDONIA
Republic

AREA	25,713 sq km (9,928 sq miles)
POPULATION	2,142,000
CAPITAL	Skopje
LANGUAGE	Macedonian, Albanian, Serbo-Croat, Turkish, Romany
RELIGION	Macedonian Orthodox, Sunni Muslim, Roman Catholic
CURRENCY	denar
ORGANIZATIONS	OSCE, UN

MADAGASCAR
Republic

AREA	587,041 sq km (226,658 sq miles)
POPULATION	14,303,000
CAPITAL	Antananarivo
LANGUAGE	Malagasy, French
RELIGION	Traditional beliefs, Roman Catholic, Protestant, Sunni Muslim
CURRENCY	Malagasy franc (MGF)
ORGANIZATIONS	OAU, UN

MADEIRA
Portuguese Territory

AREA	794 sq km (307 sq miles)
POPULATION	253,000
CAPITAL	Funchal
LANGUAGE	Portuguese
RELIGION	Roman Catholic, Protestant
CURRENCY	Portuguese escudo (PTE)

MALAWI
Republic

AREA	118,484 sq km (45,747 sq miles)
POPULATION	10,843,000
CAPITAL	Lilongwe
LANGUAGE	English (official), Chichewa, Lomwe, local languages
RELIGION	Protestant, Roman Catholic, Traditional beliefs, Sunni Muslim
CURRENCY	kwacha (MWK)
ORGANIZATIONS	Comm., OAU, SADC, UN

MALAYSIA
Federation

AREA	332,965 sq km (128,559 sq miles)
POPULATION	19,489,000
CAPITAL	Kuala Lumpur
LANGUAGE	Malay, English, Chinese, Tamil, local languages
RELIGION	Sunni Muslim, Buddhist, Hindu, Christian, Traditional beliefs
CURRENCY	Malaysian dollar or ringgit (MYR)
ORGANIZATIONS	ASEAN, Col. Plan, Comm., UN

MALDIVES
Republic

AREA	298 sq km (115 sq miles)
POPULATION	246,000
CAPITAL	Male
LANGUAGE	Divehi (Maldivian)
RELIGION	Sunni Muslim
CURRENCY	rufiyaa (MVR)
ORGANIZATIONS	Col. Plan, Comm., UN

MALI
Republic

AREA	1,240,140 sq km (478,821 sq miles)
POPULATION	10,462,000
CAPITAL	Bamako
LANGUAGE	French, Bambara, many local languages
RELIGION	Sunni Muslim, Traditional beliefs, Roman Catholic
CURRENCY	CFA franc (W Africa) (XOF)
ORGANIZATIONS	ECOWAS, OAU, UN

MALTA
Republic

AREA	316 sq km (122 sq miles)
POPULATION	364,000
CAPITAL	Valletta
LANGUAGE	Maltese, English
RELIGION	Roman Catholic
CURRENCY	Maltese lira (MTL)
ORGANIZATIONS	Comm., Council of Europe, OSCE, UN

MARSHALL ISLANDS
Republic

AREA	181 sq km (70 sq miles)
POPULATION	52,000
CAPITAL	Dalap-Uliga-Darrit
LANGUAGE	Marshallese, English
RELIGION	Protestant, Roman Catholic
CURRENCY	US dollar (USD)
ORGANIZATIONS	UN

MARTINIQUE
French Territory

AREA	1,079 sq km (417 sq miles)
POPULATION	375,000
CAPITAL	Fort-de-France
LANGUAGE	French, French Creole
RELIGION	Roman Catholic, Protestant, Hindu,
CURRENCY	Traditional beliefs
ORGANIZATIONS	French franc (FRF)

MAURITANIA
Republic

AREA	1,030,700 sq km (397,955 sq miles)
POPULATION	2,211,000
CAPITAL	Nouakchott
LANGUAGE	Arabic, French, local languages
RELIGION	Sunni Muslim
CURRENCY	ouguiya (MRO)
ORGANIZATIONS	Arab League, ECOWAS, OAU, UN

MAURITIUS
Republic

AREA	2,040 sq km (788 sq miles)
POPULATION	1,104,000
CAPITAL	Port Louis
LANGUAGE	English, French Creole, Hindi, Indian languages
RELIGION	Hindu, Roman Catholic, Sunni Muslim, Protestant
CURRENCY	Mauritian rupee (MUR)
ORGANIZATIONS	Comm., OAU, SADC, UN

MAYOTTE
French Territory

AREA	373 sq km (144 sq miles)
POPULATION	110,000
CAPITAL	Dzaoudzi
LANGUAGE	Mahorian (Swahili), French
RELIGION	Sunni Muslim, Roman Catholic
CURRENCY	French franc (FRF)

MEXICO
Republic

AREA	1,972,545 sq km (761,604 sq miles)

MEXICO *continued*

POPULATION	93,008,000
CAPITAL	México City
LANGUAGE	Spanish, Amerindian languages
RELIGION	Roman Catholic, Protestant
CURRENCY	Mexican peso (MXP)
ORGANIZATIONS	Aladi, NAFTA, OAS, OECD, UN

MICRONESIA, FEDERATED STATES OF
Republic

AREA	701 sq km (271 sq miles)
POPULATION	121,000
CAPITAL	Palikir
LANGUAGE	English, Trukese, Pohnpeian, local languages
RELIGION	Protestant, Roman Catholic
CURRENCY	US dollar (USD)
ORGANIZATIONS	UN

MOLDOVA
Republic

AREA	33,700 sq km (13,012 sq miles)
POPULATION	4,350,000
CAPITAL	Chişinău (Kishinev)
LANGUAGE	Romanian, Russian, Ukrainian, Gagauz
RELIGION	Moldovan Orthodox, Russian Orthodox
CURRENCY	Moldovan leu
ORGANIZATIONS	Council of Europe, OSCE, UN

MONACO
Monarchy

AREA	1.95 sq km (0.75 sq miles)
POPULATION	31,000
CAPITAL	Monaco
LANGUAGE	French, Monegasque, Italian
RELIGION	Roman Catholic
CURRENCY	French franc (FRF)
ORGANIZATIONS	OSCE, UN

MONGOLIA
Republic

AREA	1,565,000 sq km (604,250 sq miles)
POPULATION	2,363,000
CAPITAL	Ulan Bator (Ulaanbaatar)
LANGUAGE	Khalkha (Mongolian), Kazakh, Local languages
RELIGION	Buddhist, Sunni Muslim, Traditional beliefs
CURRENCY	tugrik (MNT)
ORGANIZATIONS	UN

MONTSERRAT
UK Territory

AREA	100 sq km (39 sq miles)
POPULATION	11,000
CAPITAL	Plymouth
LANGUAGE	English
RELIGION	Protestant, Roman Catholic
CURRENCY	East Caribbean dollar (XCD)
ORGANIZATIONS	Caricom

MOROCCO
Monarchy

AREA	446,550 sq km (172,414 sq miles)
POPULATION	26,590,000
CAPITAL	Rabat
LANGUAGE	Arabic, Berber, French, Spanish
RELIGION	Sunni Muslim, Roman Catholic
CURRENCY	Moroccan dirham (MAD)
ORGANIZATIONS	Arab League, UN

MOZAMBIQUE
Republic

AREA	799,380 sq km (308,642 sq miles)
POPULATION	15,527,000
CAPITAL	Maputo
LANGUAGE	Portuguese, Makua, Tsonga, many local languages
RELIGION	Traditional beliefs, Roman Catholic, Sunni Muslim
CURRENCY	metical (MZM)
ORGANIZATIONS	Comm., OAU, SADC, UN

MYANMAR
Republic

AREA	676,577 sq km (261,228 sq miles)
POPULATION	45,555,000
CAPITAL	Rangoon (Yangon)
LANGUAGE	Burmese, Shan, Karen, Local languages

RELIGION Buddhist, Sunni Muslim, Protestant,
Roman Catholic
CURRENCY kyat (BUK)
ORGANIZATIONS Col. Plan, UN

NAMIBIA
Republic

AREA 824,292 sq km (318,261 sq miles)
POPULATION 1,500,000
CAPITAL Windhoek
LANGUAGE English, Afrikaans, German,
Ovambo, local languages
RELIGION Protestant, Roman Catholic
CURRENCY Namibian dollar
ORGANIZATIONS Comm., OAU, SADC, UN

NAURU
Republic

AREA 21 sq km (8 sq miles)
POPULATION 11,000
CAPITAL Yaren
LANGUAGE Nauruan, Gilbertese, English
RELIGION Protestant, Roman Catholic
CURRENCY Australian dollar (AUD)
ORGANIZATIONS Comm. (special member)

NEPAL
Monarchy

AREA 147,181 sq km (56,827 sq miles)
POPULATION 21,360,000
CAPITAL Kathmandu
LANGUAGE Nepali, Maithili, Bhojpuri, English,
many local languages
RELIGION Hindu, Buddhist, Sunni Muslim
CURRENCY Nepalese rupee (NPR)
ORGANIZATIONS Col. Plan, UN

NETHERLANDS
Monarchy

AREA 41,526 sq km (16,033 sq miles)
POPULATION 15,380,000
CAPITAL Amsterdam
LANGUAGE Dutch, Frisian, Turkish
RELIGION Roman Catholic, Protestant,
Sunni Muslim
CURRENCY Dutch guilder (NLG)
ORGANIZATIONS Council of Europe, EEA, EU,
NATO, OECD, OSCE, UN, WEU

NETHERLANDS ANTILLES
Netherlands Territory

AREA 800 sq km (309 sq miles)
POPULATION 197,000
CAPITAL Willemstad
LANGUAGE Dutch, Papiamento
RELIGION Roman Catholic, Protestant
CURRENCY Dutch guilder (NLG)

NEW CALEDONIA
French Territory

AREA 19,058 sq km (7,358 sq miles)
POPULATION 178,000
CAPITAL Nouméa
LANGUAGE French, Local languages
RELIGION Roman Catholic, Protestant,
Sunni Muslim
CURRENCY Pacific franc

NEW ZEALAND
Monarchy

AREA 270,534 sq km (104,454 sq miles)
POPULATION 3,493,000
CAPITAL Wellington
LANGUAGE English, Maori
RELIGION Protestant, Roman Catholic
CURRENCY New Zealand dollar (NZD)
ORGANIZATIONS ANZUS, Col. Plan, Comm., OECD,
UN

NICARAGUA
Republic

AREA 130,000 sq km (50,193 sq miles)
POPULATION 4,401,000
CAPITAL Managua
LANGUAGE Spanish, Amerindian languages
RELIGION Roman Catholic, Protestant
CURRENCY córdoba (NIO)
ORGANIZATIONS CACM, OAS, UN

NIGER
Republic

AREA 1,267,000 sq km (489,191 sq miles)
POPULATION 8,846,000
CAPITAL Niamey

NIGER *continued*

LANGUAGE	French (official), Hausa, Fulani, Local languages
RELIGION	Sunni Muslim, Protestant, Roman Catholic, Traditional beliefs
CURRENCY	CFA franc (W Africa) (XOF)
ORGANIZATIONS	ECOWAS, OAU, UN

NIGERIA
Republic

AREA	923,768 sq km (356,669 sq miles)
POPULATION	108,467,000
CAPITAL	Abuja
LANGUAGE	English, Creole, Hausa, Yoruba, Ibo, Fulani
RELIGION	Sunni Muslim Protestant, Roman Catholic, Traditional beliefs
CURRENCY	naira (NGN)
ORGANIZATIONS	Comm., ECOWAS, OAU, OPEC, UN

NIUE
New Zealand Territory

AREA	258 sq km (100 sq miles)
POPULATION	2,000
CAPITAL	Alofi
LANGUAGE	English, Polynesian (Niuean)
RELIGION	Protestant, Roman Catholic
CURRENCY	New Zealand dollar (NZD)

NORFOLK ISLAND
Australian Territory

AREA	35 sq km (14 sq miles)
POPULATION	2,000
CAPITAL	Kingston
LANGUAGE	English
RELIGION	Protestant, Roman Catholic
CURRENCY	Australian dollar (AUD)

NORTH KOREA
Republic

AREA	120,538 sq km (46,540 sq miles)
POPULATION	23,483,000
CAPITAL	P'yŏngyang
LANGUAGE	Korean
RELIGION	Traditional beliefs, Chondoist, Buddhist, Confucian, Taoist
CURRENCY	North Korean won (KPW)
ORGANIZATIONS	UN

NORTHERN MARIANA ISLANDS
US Territory

AREA	477 sq km (184 sq miles)
POPULATION	47,000
CAPITAL	Saipan
LANGUAGE	English, Chamorro, Tagalog, Local languages
RELIGION	Roman Catholic, Protestant
CURRENCY	US dollar (USD)

NORWAY
Monarchy

AREA	323,878 sq km (125,050 sq miles)
POPULATION	4,325,000
CAPITAL	Oslo
LANGUAGE	Norwegian
RELIGION	Protestant, Roman Catholic
CURRENCY	Norwegian krone (NOK)
ORGANIZATIONS	Council of Europe, EEA, EFTA, NATO, OECD, OSCE, UN

OMAN
Monarchy

AREA	271,950 sq km (105,000 sq miles)
POPULATION	2,077,000
CAPITAL	Muscat (Masqaṭ)
LANGUAGE	Arabic, Baluchi, Farsi, Swahili, Indian languages
RELIGION	Ibadhi Muslim, Sunni Muslim
CURRENCY	Omani rial (OMR)
ORGANIZATIONS	Arab League, UN

PAKISTAN
Republic

AREA	803,940 sq km (310,403 sq miles)
POPULATION	126,610,000
CAPITAL	Islamabad
LANGUAGE	Urdu (official), Punjabi, Sindhi, Pushtu, English
RELIGION	Sunni Muslim, Shi'a Muslim, Christian, Hindu
CURRENCY	Pakistan rupee (PKR)
ORGANIZATIONS	Col. Plan, Comm., UN

PALAU
Republic

AREA	497 sq km (192 sq miles)
POPULATION	17,000
CAPITAL	Koror
LANGUAGE	Palauan, English
RELIGION	Roman Catholic, Protestant, Traditional beliefs
CURRENCY	US dollar (USD)
ORGANIZATIONS	UN

PANAMA
Republic

AREA	77,082 sq km (29,762 sq miles)
POPULATION	2,563,000
CAPITAL	Panama City (Panamá)
LANGUAGE	Spanish, English Creole, Amerindian languages
RELIGION	Roman Catholic, Protestant, Sunni Muslim, Baha'i
CURRENCY	balboa (PAB)
ORGANIZATIONS	OAS, UN

PAPUA NEW GUINEA
Monarchy

AREA	462,840 sq km (178,704 sq miles)
POPULATION	4,205,000
CAPITAL	Port Moresby
LANGUAGE	English (official), Tok Pisin (Pidgin), many local languages
RELIGION	Protestant, Roman Catholic, Traditional beliefs
CURRENCY	kina (PGK)
ORGANIZATIONS	Col. Plan, Comm., UN

PARAGUAY
Republic

AREA	406,752 sq km (157,048 sq miles)
POPULATION	4,700,000
CAPITAL	Asunción
LANGUAGE	Spanish, Guaraní
RELIGION	Roman Catholic, Protestant
CURRENCY	guaraní (PYG)
ORGANIZATIONS	Aladi, Mercosur, OAS, UN

PERU
Republic

AREA	1,285,216 sq km (496,225 sq miles)
POPULATION	23,088,000
CAPITAL	Lima
LANGUAGE	Spanish, Quechua, Aymara
RELIGION	Roman Catholic, Protestant
CURRENCY	sol (PES)
ORGANIZATIONS	Aladi, OAS, UN

PHILIPPINES
Republic

AREA	300,000 sq km (115,831 sq miles)
POPULATION	67,038,000
CAPITAL	Manila
LANGUAGE	English, Filipino (Tagalog), Cebuano, many local languages
RELIGION	Roman Catholic, Aglipayan, Sunni Muslim, Protestant
CURRENCY	Philippine peso (PHP)
ORGANIZATIONS	ASEAN, Col. Plan, UN

PITCAIRN ISLANDS
UK Territory

AREA	45 sq km (17 sq miles)
POPULATION	71
CAPITAL	Adamstown
LANGUAGE	English
RELIGION	Protestant
CURRENCY	New Zealand dollar (NZD)

POLAND
Republic

AREA	312,683 sq km (120,728 sq miles)
POPULATION	38,544,000
CAPITAL	Warsaw (Warszawa)
LANGUAGE	Polish, German
RELIGION	Roman Catholic, Polish Orthodox
CURRENCY	złoty (PLZ)
ORGANIZATIONS	Council of Europe, OSCE, UN,

PORTUGAL
Republic

AREA	88,940 sq km (34,340 sq miles)
POPULATION	9,830,000
CAPITAL	Lisbon (Lisboa)
LANGUAGE	Portuguese
RELIGION	Roman Catholic, Protestant
CURRENCY	Portuguese escudo (PTE)
ORGANIZATIONS	Council of Europe, EEA, EU, NATO, OECD, OSCE, UN, WEU

PUERTO RICO
US Territory

AREA	9,104 sq km (3,515 sq miles)
POPULATION	3,646,000
CAPITAL	San Juan
LANGUAGE	Spanish, English
RELIGION	Roman Catholic, Protestant
CURRENCY	US dollar (USD)

QATAR
Monarchy

AREA	11,437 sq km (4,416 sq miles)
POPULATION	540,000
CAPITAL	Doha (Ad Dawhah)
LANGUAGE	Arabic, Indian languages
RELIGION	Sunni Muslim, Christian, Hindu
CURRENCY	Qatar riyal (QAR)
ORGANIZATIONS	Arab League, OPEC, UN

RÉUNION
French Territory

AREA	2,551 sq km (985 sq miles)
POPULATION	644,000
CAPITAL	St-Denis
LANGUAGE	French, French Creole
RELIGION	Roman Catholic
CURRENCY	French franc (FRF)

ROMANIA
Republic

AREA	237,500 sq km (91,699 sq miles)
POPULATION	22,736,000
CAPITAL	Bucharest (Bucureşti)
LANGUAGE	Romanian, Hungarian
RELIGION	Romanian Orthodox, Roman Catholic, Protestant
CURRENCY	Romanian leu (ROL)
ORGANIZATIONS	Council of Europe, OSCE, UN

RUSSIAN FEDERATION
Republic

AREA	17,075,400 sq km (6,592,849 sq miles)
POPULATION	147,997,000
CAPITAL	Moscow (Moskva)
LANGUAGE	Russian, Tatar, Ukrainian, many local languages
RELIGION	Russian Orthodox, Sunni Muslim, Other Christian, Jewish
CURRENCY	Russian rouble
ORGANIZATIONS	CIS, Council of Europe, OSCE, UN

RWANDA
Republic

AREA	26,338 sq km (10,169 sq miles)
POPULATION	7,750,000
CAPITAL	Kigali
LANGUAGE	Kinyarwanda (Bantu), French
RELIGION	Roman Catholic, Traditional beliefs, Protestant, Sunni Muslim
CURRENCY	Rwanda franc (RWF)
ORGANIZATIONS	CEEAC, OAU, UN

ST HELENA
UK Territory

AREA	122 sq km (47 sq miles)
POPULATION	5,302
CAPITAL	Jamestown
LANGUAGE	English
RELIGION	Protestant, Roman Catholic
CURRENCY	pound sterling (GBP)

ST KITTS and NEVIS
Monarchy

AREA	261 sq km (101 sq miles)
POPULATION	41,000
CAPITAL	Basseterre
LANGUAGE	English, Creole
RELIGION	Protestant, Roman Catholic
CURRENCY	East Caribbean dollar (XCD)
ORGANIZATIONS	Caricom, Comm., OAS, UN

ST LUCIA
Monarchy

AREA	616 sq km (238 sq miles)
POPULATION	141,000
CAPITAL	Castries
LANGUAGE	English, French Creole
RELIGION	Roman Catholic, Protestant
CURRENCY	East Caribbean dollar (XCD)
ORGANIZATIONS	Caricom, Comm., OAS, UN

ST PIERRE and MIQUELON
French Territory

AREA	242 sq km (93 sq miles)
POPULATION	6,000
CAPITAL	St-Pierre
LANGUAGE	French
RELIGION	Roman Catholic
CURRENCY	French franc (FRF)

ST VINCENT and THE GRENADINES
Monarchy

AREA	389 sq km (150 sq miles)
POPULATION	111,000
CAPITAL	Kingstown
LANGUAGE	English, Creole
RELIGION	Protestant, Roman Catholic
CURRENCY	East Caribbean dollar (XCD)
ORGANIZATIONS	Caricom, Comm., OAS, UN

SAN MARINO
Republic

AREA	61 sq km (24 sq miles)
POPULATION	25,000
CAPITAL	San Marino
LANGUAGE	Italian
RELIGION	Roman Catholic
CURRENCY	Italian lira (ITL), San Marino coinage
ORGANIZATIONS	Council of Europe, OSCE, UN

SÃO TOMÉ and PRÍNCIPE
Republic

AREA	964 sq km (372 sq miles)
POPULATION	130,000

CAPITAL	São Tomé
LANGUAGE	Portuguese, Portuguese Creole
RELIGION	Roman Catholic, Protestant
CURRENCY	dobra (STD)
ORGANIZATIONS	CEEAC, OAU, UN

SAUDI ARABIA
Monarchy

AREA	2,200,000 sq km (849,425 sq miles)
POPULATION	17,451,000
CAPITAL	Riyadh (Ar Riyāḍ)
LANGUAGE	Arabic
RELIGION	Sunni Muslim, Shi'a Muslim
CURRENCY	Saudi riyal (SAR)
ORGANIZATIONS	Arab League, OPEC, UN

SENEGAL
Republic

AREA	196,720 sq km (75,954 sq miles)
POPULATION	8,102,000
CAPITAL	Dakar
LANGUAGE	French (official), Wolof, Fulani, local languages
RELIGION	Sunni Muslim, Roman Catholic, Traditional beliefs
CURRENCY	CFA franc (W Africa) (XOF)
ORGANIZATIONS	ECOWAS, OAU, UN

SEYCHELLES
Republic

AREA	455 sq km (176 sq miles)
POPULATION	74,000
CAPITAL	Victoria
LANGUAGE	Seychellois (Seselwa, French Creole), English
RELIGION	Roman Catholic, Protestant
CURRENCY	Seychelles rupee (SCR)
ORGANIZATIONS	Comm., OAU, UN

SIERRA LEONE
Republic

AREA	71,740 sq km (27,699 sq miles)
POPULATION	4,402,000
CAPITAL	Freetown
LANGUAGE	English, Creole, Mende, Temne, local languages
RELIGION	Traditional beliefs, Sunni Muslim,

SIERRA LEONE *continued*

	Protestant, Roman Catholic
CURRENCY	leone (SLL)
ORGANIZATIONS	Comm., ECOWAS, OAS, UN

SINGAPORE
Republic

AREA	639 sq km (247 sq miles)
POPULATION	2,930,000
CAPITAL	Singapore
LANGUAGE	Chinese, English, Malay, Tamil
RELIGION	Buddhist, Taoist, Sunni Muslim, Christian, Hindu
CURRENCY	Singapore dollar (SGD)
ORGANIZATIONS	ASEAN, Col. Plan, Comm., UN

SLOVAKIA
Republic

AREA	49,035 sq km (18,933 sq miles)
POPULATION	5,347,000
CAPITAL	Bratislava
LANGUAGE	Slovak, Hungarian, Czech
RELIGION	Roman Catholic, Protestant, Orthodox
CURRENCY	Slovak crown or koruna
ORGANIZATIONS	Council of Europe, OSCE, UN

SLOVENIA
Republic

AREA	20,251 sq km (7,819 sq miles)
POPULATION	1,942,000
CAPITAL	Ljubljana
LANGUAGE	Slovene, Serbo-Croat
RELIGION	Roman Catholic, Protestant
CURRENCY	tólar (SLT)
ORGANIZATIONS	Council of Europe, OSCE, UN

SOLOMON ISLANDS
Monarchy

AREA	28,370 sq km (10,954 sq miles)
POPULATION	366,000
CAPITAL	Honiara
LANGUAGE	English, Solomon Islands Pidgin, many local languages
RELIGION	Protestant, Roman Catholic

CURRENCY	Solomon Islands dollar (SBD)
ORGANIZATIONS	Comm., UN

SOMALIA
Republic

AREA	637,657sq km (246,201 sq miles)
POPULATION	9,077,000
CAPITAL	Mogadishu (Muqdisho)
LANGUAGE	Somali, Arabic (official)
RELIGION	Sunni Muslim
CURRENCY	Somali shilling (SOS)
ORGANIZATIONS	Arab League, OAU, UN

SOUTH AFRICA
Republic

AREA	1,219,080 sq km (470,689 sq miles)
POPULATION	39,659,000
CAPITAL	Pretoria (administrative), Cape Town (legislative)
LANGUAGE	Afrikaans, English, nine local languages (all official)
RELIGION	Protestant, Roman Catholic, Sunni Muslim, Hindu
CURRENCY	rand (ZAR)
ORGANIZATIONS	Comm., OAU, SADC, UN

SOUTH KOREA
Republic

AREA	99,274 sq km (38,330 sq miles)
POPULATION	44,453,000
CAPITAL	Seoul (Sŏul)
LANGUAGE	Korean
RELIGION	Buddhist, Protestant, Roman Catholic, Confucian, Traditional beliefs
CURRENCY	won (KRW)
ORGANIZATIONS	Col. Plan, UN

SPAIN
Monarchy

AREA	504,782 sq km (194,897 sq miles)
POPULATION	39,193,000
CAPITAL	Madrid
LANGUAGE	Spanish (Castilian), Catalan, Galician, Basque
RELIGION	Roman Catholic

CURRENCY   Spanish peseta (ESP)
ORGANIZATIONS   Council of Europe, EEA, EU,
              NATO, OECD, OSCE, UN, WEU

SRI LANKA
Republic

AREA   65,610 sq km (25,332 sq miles)
POPULATION   17,865,000
CAPITAL   Colombo
LANGUAGE   Sinhalese, Tamil, English
RELIGION   Buddhist, Hindu, Sunni Muslim,
              Roman Catholic
CURRENCY   Sri Lanka rupee (LKR)
ORGANIZATIONS   Col. Plan, Comm., UN

SUDAN
Republic

AREA   2,505,813 sq km (967,500 sq miles)
POPULATION   27,361,000
CAPITAL   Khartoum
LANGUAGE   Arabic, Dinka, Nubian, Beja, Nuer,
              local languages
RELIGION   Sunni Muslim,Traditional beliefs,
              Roman Catholic, Protestant
CURRENCY   Sudanese dinar (SDD)
ORGANIZATIONS   Arab League, OAU, UN

SURINAM
Republic

AREA   163,820 sq km (63,251 sq miles)
POPULATION   418,000
CAPITAL   Paramaribo
LANGUAGE   Dutch, Surinamese (Sranan Tongo),
              English, Hindi, Javanese
RELIGION   Hindu, Roman Catholic,
              Protestant, Sunni Muslim
CURRENCY   Surinam guilder (SRG)
ORGANIZATIONS   Caricom, OAS, UN

SWAZILAND
Monarchy

AREA   17,364 sq km (6,704 sq miles)
POPULATION   879,000
CAPITAL   Mbabane
LANGUAGE   Swazi (Siswati), English
RELIGION   Protestant, Roman Catholic,
              Traditional beliefs

CURRENCY   emalangeni (SZE)
ORGANIZATIONS   Comm., OAU, SADC, UN

SWEDEN
Monarchy

AREA   449,964 sq km (173,732 sq miles)
POPULATION   8,794,000
CAPITAL   Stockholm
LANGUAGE   Swedish
RELIGION   Protestant, Roman Catholic
CURRENCY   krona (SED)
ORGANIZATIONS   Council of Europe, EEA, EU,
              OECD, OSCE, UN

SWITZERLAND
Federation

AREA   41,293 sq km (15,943 sq miles)
POPULATION   6,994,000
CAPITAL   Bern (Berne)
LANGUAGE   German, French, Italian, Romansch
RELIGION   Roman Catholic, Protestant
CURRENCY   Swiss franc (CHF)
ORGANIZATIONS   Council of Europe, EFTA, OECD,
              OSCE

SYRIA
Republic

AREA   185,180 sq km (71,498 sq miles)
POPULATION   13,844,000
CAPITAL   Damascus (Dimashq, Esh Sham)
LANGUAGE   Arabic, Kurdish, Armenian
RELIGION   Sunni Muslim, other Muslim,
              Christian
CURRENCY   Syrian pound (SYP)
ORGANIZATIONS   Arab League, UN

TAIWAN
Republic

AREA   36,179 sq km (13,969 sq miles)
POPULATION   21,074,000
CAPITAL   Taipei (T'ai-pei)
LANGUAGE   Chinese (Mandarin official, Fukien,
              Hakka), local languages
RELIGION   Buddhist, Taoist,
              Confucian, Christian
CURRENCY   New Taiwan dollar (TWD)
ORGANIZATIONS   none listed

TAJIKISTAN
Republic

AREA	143,100 sq km (55,251 sq miles)
POPULATION	5,751,000
CAPITAL	Dushanbe
LANGUAGE	Tajik, Uzbek, Russian
RELIGION	Sunni Muslim
CURRENCY	Tajik rouble
ORGANIZATIONS	CIS, OSCE, UN

TANZANIA
Republic

AREA	945,087 sq km (364,900 sq miles)
POPULATION	28,846,000
CAPITAL	Dodoma
LANGUAGE	Swahili, English, Nyamwezi, many local languages
RELIGION	Roman Catholic, Sunni Muslim, Traditional beliefs, Protestant
CURRENCY	Tanzanian shilling (TZS)
ORGANIZATIONS	Comm., OAU, SADC, UN

THAILAND
Monarchy

AREA	513,115 sq km (198,115 sq miles)
POPULATION	59,396,000
CAPITAL	Bangkok (Krung Thep)
LANGUAGE	Thai, Lao, Chinese, Malay, Mon-Khmer languages
RELIGION	Buddhist, Sunni Muslim
CURRENCY	baht (THB)
ORGANIZATIONS	ASEAN, Col. Plan, UN

TOGO
Republic

AREA	56,785 sq km (21,925 sq miles)
POPULATION	3,928,000
CAPITAL	Lomé
LANGUAGE	French, Ewe, Kabre, many local languages
RELIGION	Traditional beliefs, Roman Catholic, Sunni Muslim, Protestant
CURRENCY	CFA franc (West Africa) (XOF)
ORGANIZATIONS	ECOWAS, OAU, UN

TOKELAU
New Zealand Territory

AREA	10 sq km (4 sq miles)
POPULATION	2,000
CAPITAL	none; each island has its own administration centre
LANGUAGE	English, Tokelauan
RELIGION	Protestant, Roman Catholic
CURRENCY	New Zealand dollar (NZD)

TONGA
Monarchy

AREA	748 sq km (289 sq miles)
POPULATION	98,000
CAPITAL	Nuku'alofa
LANGUAGE	Tongan, English
RELIGION	Protestant, Roman Catholic, Mormon
CURRENCY	pa'anga (TOP)
ORGANIZATIONS	Comm.

TRINIDAD and TOBAGO
Republic

AREA	5,130 sq km (1,981 sq miles)
POPULATION	1,257,000
CAPITAL	Port of Spain
LANGUAGE	English, Creole, Hindi,
RELIGION	Roman Catholic, Hindu, Protestant, Sunni Muslim
CURRENCY	Trinidad and Tobago dollar (TTD)
ORGANIZATIONS	Caricom, Comm., OAS, UN

TUNISIA
Republic

AREA	164,150 sq km (63,379 sq miles)
POPULATION	8,733,000
CAPITAL	Tunis
LANGUAGE	Arabic, French
RELIGION	Sunni Muslim
CURRENCY	Tunisian dinar (TND)
ORGANIZATIONS	Arab League, OAU, UN

TURKEY
Republic

AREA	779,452 sq km (300,948 sq miles)
POPULATION	61,183,000

CAPITAL	Ankara
LANGUAGE	Turkish, Kurdish
RELIGION	Sunni Muslim, Shi'a Muslim
CURRENCY	Turkish lira (TRL)
ORGANIZATIONS	Council of Europe, NATO, OECD, OSCE, UN

TURKMENISTAN
Republic

AREA	488,100 sq km (188,456 sq miles)
POPULATION	4,010,000
CAPITAL	Ashkhabad (Ashgabat)
LANGUAGE	Turkmen, Russian
RELIGION	Sunni Muslim
CURRENCY	Turkmen manat
ORGANIZATIONS	CIS, OSCE, UN

TURKS and CAICOS ISLANDS
UK Territory

AREA	430 sq km (166 sq miles)
POPULATION	14,000
CAPITAL	Grand Turk
LANGUAGE	English
RELIGION	Protestant
CURRENCY	US dollar (USD)

TUVALU
Monarchy

AREA	25 sq km (10 sq miles)
POPULATION	9,000
CAPITAL	Funafuti
LANGUAGE	Tuvaluan, English (official)
RELIGION	Protestant
CURRENCY	Tuvalu dollar (Australian dollar)
ORGANIZATIONS	Comm. (special member)

UGANDA
Republic

AREA	241,038 sq km (93,065 sq miles)
POPULATION	20,621,000
CAPITAL	Kampala
LANGUAGE	English, Swahili (official), Luganda, many local languages
RELIGION	Roman Catholic, Protestant, Sunni Muslim, Traditional beliefs
CURRENCY	Uganda shilling (UGS)
ORGANIZATIONS	Comm., OAU, UN

UKRAINE
Republic

AREA	603,700 sq km (233,090 sq miles)
POPULATION	51,910,000
CAPITAL	Kiev (Kiyev)
LANGUAGE	Ukrainian, Russian, regional languages
RELIGION	Ukrainian Orthodox, Roman Catholic
CURRENCY	karbovanets
ORGANIZATIONS	CIS, OSCE, UN

UNITED ARAB EMIRATES (UAE)
Federation

AREA	77,700 sq km (30,000 sq miles)
POPULATION	1,861,000
CAPITAL	Abu Dhabi (Abū Ẓabī)
LANGUAGE	Arabic (official), English, Hindi, Urdu, Farsi
RELIGION	Sunni Muslim, Shi'a Muslim
CURRENCY	UAE dirham (AED)
ORGANIZATIONS	Arab League, OPEC, UN

UNITED KINGDOM (UK)
Monarchy

AREA	244,082 sq km (94,241 sq miles)
POPULATION	58,091,000
CAPITAL	London
LANGUAGE	English, south Indian languages, Chinese, Welsh, Gaelic
RELIGION	Protestant, Roman Catholic, Muslim, Sikh, Hindu, Jewish
CURRENCY	pound sterling (GBP)
ORGANIZATIONS	Col. Plan, Comm., Council of Europe, EEA, EU, G7, NATO, OECD, OSCE, UN, WEU

ENGLAND
Constituent Country

AREA	130,423 sq km (50,357 sq miles)
POPULATION	48,532,700
CAPITAL	London

NORTHERN IRELAND
Constituent Region

AREA	14,121 sq km (5,452 sq miles)
POPULATION	1,631,800
CAPITAL	Belfast

SCOTLAND
Constituent Country

AREA	78,772 sq km (30,414 sq miles)
POPULATION	5,120,200
CAPITAL	Edinburgh

WALES
Principality

AREA	20,766 sq km (8,018 sq miles)
POPULATION	2,906,500
CAPITAL	Cardiff

UNITED STATES OF AMERICA (USA)
Republic

AREA	9,809,386 sq km (3,787,425 sq miles)
POPULATION	260,560,000
CAPITAL	Washington D.C.
LANGUAGE	English, Spanish, Amerindian languages
RELIGION	Protestant, Roman Catholic, Sunni Muslim, Jewish, Mormon
CURRENCY	US dollar (USD)
ORGANIZATIONS	ANZUS, Col. Plan, G7, NAFTA, NATO, OAS, OECD, OSCE, UN

ALABAMA
State

AREA	135,775 sq km (52,423 sq miles)
POPULATION	4,136,000
CAPITAL	Montgomery

ALASKA
State

AREA	1,700,130 sq km (656,424 sq miles)
POPULATION	587,000
CAPITAL	Juneau

ARIZONA
State

AREA	295,274 sq km (114,006 sq miles)
POPULATION	3,832,000
CAPITAL	Phoenix

ARKANSAS
State

AREA	137,741 sq km (53,182 sq miles)
POPULATION	2,399,000
CAPITAL	Little Rock

CALIFORNIA
State

AREA	423,999 sq km (163,707 sq miles)
POPULATION	30,867,000
CAPITAL	Sacramento

COLORADO
State

AREA	269,618 sq km (104,100 sq miles)
POPULATION	3,470,000
CAPITAL	Denver

CONNECTICUT
State

AREA	14,359 sq km (5,544 sq miles)
POPULATION	3,281,000
CAPITAL	Hartford

DELAWARE
State

AREA	6,446 sq km (2,489 sq miles)
POPULATION	689,000
CAPITAL	Dover

DISTRICT OF COLUMBIA
Federal District

AREA	76 sq km (68 sq miles)
POPULATION	589,000
CAPITAL	Washington D.C.

FLORIDA
State

AREA	170,312 sq km (65,758 sq miles)
POPULATION	13,488,000
CAPITAL	Tallahassee

GEORGIA
State

AREA	153,951 sq km (59,441 sq miles)
POPULATION	6,751,000
CAPITAL	Atlanta

HAWAII
State

AREA	28,314 sq km (10,932 sq miles)
POPULATION	1,160,000
CAPITAL	Honolulu

IDAHO
State

AREA	216,456 sq km (83,574 sq miles)
POPULATION	1,067,000
CAPITAL	Boise

ILLINOIS
State

AREA	150,007 sq km (57,918 sq miles)
POPULATION	11,631,000
CAPITAL	Springfield

INDIANA
State

AREA	94,327 sq km (36,420 sq miles)
POPULATION	5,662,000
CAPITAL	Indianapolis

IOWA
State

AREA	145,754 sq km (56,276 sq miles)
POPULATION	2,812,000
CAPITAL	Des Moines

KANSAS
State

AREA	213,109 sq km (82,282 sq miles)
POPULATION	2,523,000
CAPITAL	Topeka

KENTUCKY
State

AREA	104,664 sq km (40,411 sq miles)
POPULATION	3,755,000
CAPITAL	Frankfort

LOUISIANA
State

AREA	134,273 sq km (51,843 sq miles)
POPULATION	4,287,000
CAPITAL	Baton Rouge

MAINE
State

AREA	91,652 sq km (35,387 sq miles)
POPULATION	1,235,000
CAPITAL	Augusta

MARYLAND
State

AREA	32,134 sq km (12,407 sq miles)
POPULATION	4,908,000
CAPITAL	Annapolis

MASSACHUSETTS
State

AREA	27,337 sq km (10,555 sq miles)
POPULATION	5,998,000
CAPITAL	Boston

MICHIGAN
State

AREA	250,737 sq km (96,810 sq miles)
POPULATION	9,437,000
CAPITAL	Lansing

MINNESOTA
State

AREA	225,181 sq km (86,943 sq miles)
POPULATION	4,480,000
CAPITAL	St Paul

MISSISSIPPI
State

AREA	125,443 sq km (48,434 sq miles)
POPULATION	2,614,000
CAPITAL	Jackson

MISSOURI
State

AREA	180,545 sq km (69,709 sq miles)
POPULATION	5,193,000
CAPITAL	Jefferson City

MONTANA
State

AREA	380,847 sq km (147,046 sq miles)
POPULATION	824,000
CAPITAL	Helena

NEBRASKA
State

AREA	200,356 sq km (77,358 sq miles)
POPULATION	1,606,000
CAPITAL	Lincoln

NEVADA
State

AREA	286,367 sq km (110,567 sq miles)
POPULATION	1,327,000
CAPITAL	Carson City

NEW HAMPSHIRE
State

AREA	24,219 sq km (9,351 sq miles)
POPULATION	1,111,000
CAPITAL	Concord

NEW JERSEY
State

AREA	22,590 sq km (8,722 sq miles)
POPULATION	7,789,000
CAPITAL	Trenton

NEW MEXICO
State

AREA	314,937 sq km (121,598 sq miles)
POPULATION	1,581,000
CAPITAL	Sante Fe

NEW YORK
State

AREA	141,090 sq km (54,475 sq miles)
POPULATION	18,119,000
CAPITAL	Albany

NORTH CAROLINA
State

AREA	139,396 sq km (53,821 sq miles)
POPULATION	6,843,000
CAPITAL	Raleigh

NORTH DAKOTA
State

AREA	183,123 sq km (70,704 sq miles)
POPULATION	638,000
CAPITAL	Bismarck

OHIO
State

AREA	116,104 sq km (44,828 sq miles)
POPULATION	11,016,000
CAPITAL	Columbus

OKLAHOMA
State

AREA	181,048 sq km (69,903 sq miles)
POPULATION	3,212,00
CAPITAL	Oklahoma City

OREGON
State

AREA	254,819 sq km (98,386 sq miles)
POPULATION	2,977,000
CAPITAL	Salem

PENNSYLVANIA
State

AREA	119,290 sq km (46,058 sq miles)
POPULATION	12,009,000
CAPITAL	Harrisburg

RHODE ISLAND
State

AREA	4,002 sq km (1,545 sq miles)
POPULATION	1,005,000
CAPITAL	Providence

SOUTH CAROLINA
State

AREA	82,898 sq km (32,007 sq miles)
POPULATION	3,603,000
CAPITAL	Columbia

SOUTH DAKOTA
State

AREA	199,742 sq km (77,121 sq miles)
POPULATION	711,000
CAPITAL	Pierre

TENNESSEE
State

AREA	109,158 sq km (42,146 sq miles)
POPULATION	5,024,000
CAPITAL	Nashville

TEXAS
State

AREA	695,673 sq km (268,601 sq miles)
POPULATION	17,656,000
CAPITAL	Austin

UTAH
State

AREA	219,900 sq km (84,904 sq miles)
POPULATION	1,813,000
CAPITAL	Salt Lake City

VERMONT
State

AREA	24,903 sq km (9,615 sq miles)
POPULATION	570,000
CAPITAL	Montpelier

VIRGINIA
State

AREA	110,771 sq km (42,769 sq miles)
POPULATION	6,377,000
CAPITAL	Richmond

WASHINGTON
State

AREA	184,674 sq km (71,303 sq miles)
POPULATION	5,136,000
CAPITAL	Olympia

WEST VIRGINIA
State

AREA	62,758 sq km (24,231 sq miles)
POPULATION	1,812,000
CAPITAL	Charleston

WISCONSIN
State

AREA	169,652 sq km (65,503 sq miles)
POPULATION	5,007,000
CAPITAL	Madison

WYOMING
State

AREA	253,347 sq km (97,818 sq miles)
POPULATION	466,000
CAPITAL	Cheyenne

URUGUAY
Republic

AREA	176,215 sq km (68,037 sq miles)
POPULATION	3,167,000
CAPITAL	Montevideo
LANGUAGE	Spanish
RELIGION	Roman Catholic, Protestant, Jewish
CURRENCY	Uruguayan peso (UYP)
ORGANIZATIONS	Aladi, Mercosur, OAS, UN

UZBEKISTAN
Republic

AREA	447,400 sq km (172,742 sq miles)
POPULATION	22,349,000
CAPITAL	Tashkent
LANGUAGE	Uzbek, Russian, Tajik, Kazakh
RELIGION	Sunni Muslim, Russian Orthodox
CURRENCY	Uzbekistan som
ORGANIZATIONS	CIS, OSCE, UN

VANUATU
Republic

AREA	12,190 sq km (4,707 sq miles)
POPULATION	165,000
CAPITAL	Port-Vila
LANGUAGE	English, Bislama (English Creole), French (all official)
RELIGION	Protestant, Roman Catholic, Traditional beliefs
CURRENCY	vatu (VUV)
ORGANIZATIONS	Comm., UN

VATICAN CITY
Ecclesiastical State

AREA	0.44 sq km (0.17 sq miles)
POPULATION	1,000
LANGUAGE	Italian, Latin
RELIGION	Roman Catholic
CURRENCY	Italian lira (ITL)
ORGANIZATIONS	OSCE

VENEZUELA
Republic

AREA	912,050 sq km (352,144 sq miles)
POPULATION	21,177,000
CAPITAL	Caracas
LANGUAGE	Spanish, Amerindian languages
RELIGION	Roman Catholic, Protestant
CURRENCY	bolívar (VEB)
ORGANIZATIONS	Aladi, OAS, OPEC, UN

VIETNAM
Republic

AREA	329,565 sq km (127,246 sq miles)
POPULATION	72,509,000
CAPITAL	Hanoi
LANGUAGE	Vietnamese, Thai, Khmer, Chinese, many local languages
RELIGION	Buddhist, Taoist, Roman Catholic, Cao Dai, Hoa Hao
CURRENCY	dong (VND)
ORGANIZATIONS	ASEAN, UN

VIRGIN ISLANDS (UK)
UK Territory

AREA	153 sq km (59 sq miles)
POPULATION	18,000
CAPITAL	Road Town
LANGUAGE	English
RELIGION	Protestant, Roman Catholic
CURRENCY	US dollar (USD)

VIRGIN ISLANDS (USA)
US Territory

AREA	352 sq km (136 sq miles)
POPULATION	104,000
CAPITAL	Charlotte Amalie
LANGUAGE	English, Spanish
RELIGION	Protestant, Roman Catholic
CURRENCY	US dollar (USD)

WALLIS and FUTUNA
French Territory

AREA	274 sq km (106 sq miles)
POPULATION	14,000
CAPITAL	Mata-Utu
LANGUAGE	French, Polynesian (Wallisian, Futunian)
RELIGION	Roman Catholic
CURRENCY	Pacific franc

WESTERN SAHARA
Territory

AREA	266,000 sq km (102,703 sq miles)
POPULATION	272,000
CAPITAL	Laâyoune
LANGUAGE	Arabic
RELIGION	Sunni Muslim
CURRENCY	Moroccan dirham
ORGANIZATIONS	OAU

WESTERN SAMOA
Monarchy

AREA	2,831 sq km (1,093 sq miles)
POPULATION	164,000
CAPITAL	Apia
LANGUAGE	Samoan, English
RELIGION	Protestant, Roman Catholic, Mormon
CURRENCY	tala (dollar) (WST)
ORGANIZATIONS	Comm., UN

YEMEN
Republic

AREA	527,968 sq km (203,850 sq miles)
POPULATION	13,873,000
CAPITAL	Sana (Şan'ā')
LANGUAGE	Arabic
RELIGION	Sunni Muslim, Shi'a Muslim
CURRENCY	Yemeni dinar and rial
ORGANIZATIONS	Arab League, UN

YUGOSLAVIA
Republic

AREA	102,173 sq km (39,449 sq miles)
POPULATION	10,515,000
CAPITAL	Belgrade (Beograd)
LANGUAGE	Serbo-Croat, Albanian, Hungarian
RELIGION	Serbian Orthodox, Montenegrin Orthodox, Sunni Muslim
CURRENCY	Yugoslav dinar (YUD)
ORGANIZATIONS	OSCE, UN (suspended)

Zaire, now

DEMOCRATIC REPUBLIC OF CONGO

AREA	2,345,410 sq km (905,568 sq miles)
POPULATION	42,552,000
CAPITAL	Kinshasa
LANGUAGE	French, Lingala, Swahili, Kongo, many local languages
RELIGION	Roman Catholic, Protestant, Sunni Muslim, Traditional beliefs
CURRENCY	zaïre (ZRZ)
ORGANIZATIONS	CEEAC, OAU, UN

ZAMBIA
Republic

AREA	752,614 sq km (290,586 sq miles)
POPULATION	9,196,000
CAPITAL	Lusaka
LANGUAGE	English, Bemba, Nyanja, Tonga, many local languages
RELIGION	Protestant, Roman Catholic, Traditional beliefs, Sunni Muslim
CURRENCY	kwacha (ZMK)
ORGANIZATIONS	Comm., OAU, SADC, UN

ZIMBABWE
Republic

AREA	390,759 sq km (150,873 sq miles)
POPULATION	11,150,000
CAPITAL	Harare
LANGUAGE	English (official), Shona, Ndebele
RELIGION	Protestant, Roman Catholic, Traditional beliefs
CURRENCY	Zimbabwe dollar (ZWD)
ORGANIZATIONS	Comm., OAU, SADC, UN

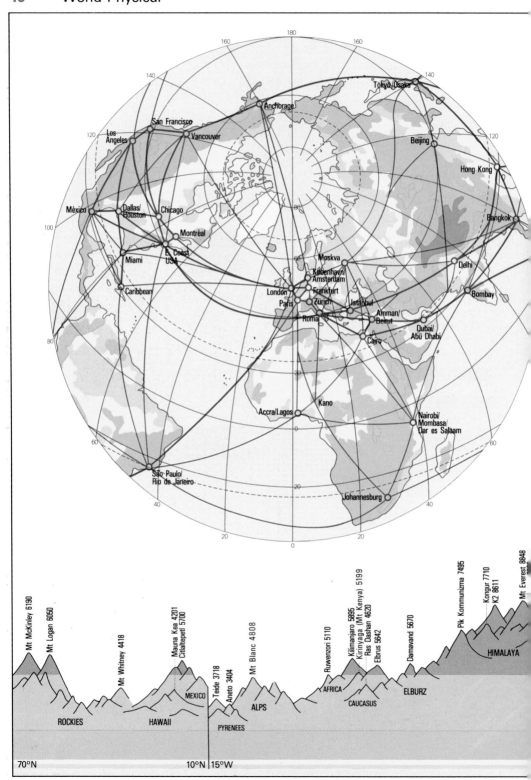

180
160   160
140   140
120   120
100   100
80   80
60   60
40   40
20   20
0

Tokyo/Osaka
Anchorage
San Francisco
Los Angeles
Vancouver
Beijing
Hong Kong
México
Dallas/Houston
Chicago
Montréal
Bangkok
Miami
E. Coast USA
Moskva
Delhi
København/Amsterdam
Frankfurt
Caribbean
London
Paris
Zürich
Istanbul
Bombay
Roma
Amman/Beirut
Dubai/Abū Dhabi
Cairo
Kano
Accra/Lagos
Nairobi/Mombasa/Dar es Salaam
São Paulo/Rio de Janeiro
Johannesburg

Mt McKinley 6190
Mt Logan 6050
Mt Whitney 4418
Mauna Kea 4201
Citlaltepetl 5700
MEXICO
Teide 3718
Aneto 3404
Mt Blanc 4808
Ruwenzori 5110
Kilimanjaro 5895
Kirinyaga (Mt Kenya) 5199
Ras Dashan 4620
Elbrus 5642
Damavand 5670
Pik Kommunizma 7495
Kongur 7710
K2 8611
Mt Everest 8848
HIMALAYA
AFRICA
CAUCASUS
ELBURZ
ROCKIES
HAWAII
PYRENEES
ALPS

70°N
10°N | 15°W

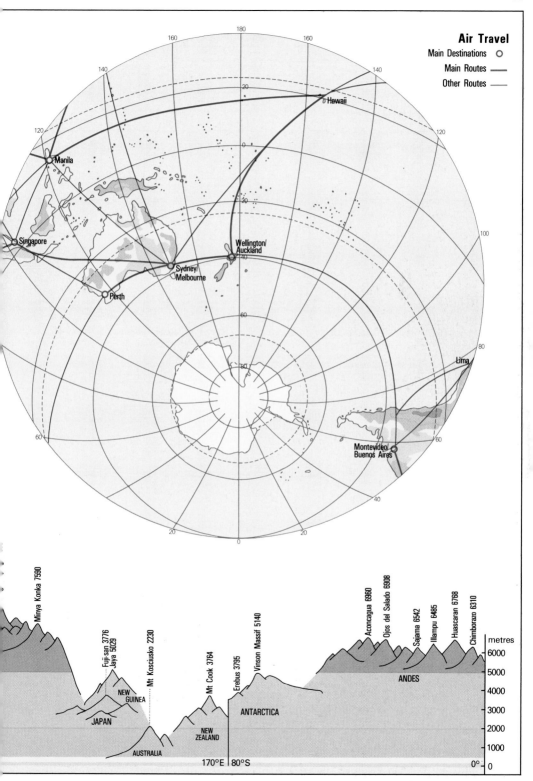

Air Travel

Main Destinations ⊙
Main Routes ━━━
Other Routes ───

Hawaii

Manila

Singapore

Perth

Sydney/
Melbourne

Wellington/
Auckland

Lima

Montevideo/
Buenos Aires

Minya Konka 7590

Fuji-san 3776
Jaya 5029

Mt Kosciusko 2230

Mt Cook 3764

Erebus 3795

Vinson Massif 5140

Aconcagua 6960
Ojos del Salado 6908
Sajama 6542
Illampu 6485
Huascaran 6768
Chimborazo 6310

NEW
GUINEA

JAPAN

AUSTRALIA

NEW
ZEALAND

ANTARCTICA

ANDES

170°E 80°S

metres
6000
5000
4000
3000
2000
1000
0° 0

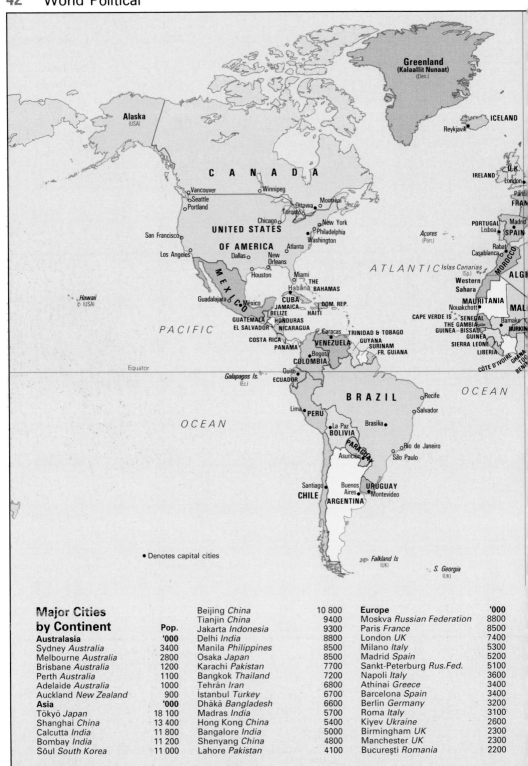

Greenland (Kalaallit Nunaat) (Den.)

ICELAND

Alaska (USA)

Reykjavik

CANADA

IRELAND U.K.
London
Paris
FRAN

Vancouver
Seattle
Portland
Winnipeg
Ottawa Montréal
Toronto

Chicago
New York
Philadelphia
Washington

UNITED STATES
OF AMERICA
Atlanta

PORTUGAL Madrid
Lisboa SPAIN

San Francisco

Acores (Port.)

Rabat
Casablanca MOROCCO

Los Angeles
Dallas
New Orleans

ATLANTIC Islas Canarias (Sp.) ALGI

Houston
Miami

Western Sahara

Hawaii (USA)

Guadalajara
México
MEXICO

THE BAHAMAS
Habana CUBA
JAMAICA DOM. REP.
BELIZE HAITI
GUATEMALA HONDURAS
EL SALVADOR NICARAGUA

MAURITANIA
Nouakchott MAL

CAPE VERDE IS SENEGAL
THE GAMBIA Bamako
GUINEA-BISSAU BURKIN
GUINEA
SIERRA LEONE
LIBERIA

PACIFIC

COSTA RICA
PANAMA

Caracas TRINIDAD & TOBAGO
VENEZUELA GUYANA
SURINAM
FR. GUIANA
Bogotá
COLOMBIA

CÔTE D'IVOIRE GHANA
BENI

Equator

Galapagos Is. (Ec.)

Quito
ECUADOR

BRAZIL
Recife

OCEAN

Lima
PERU
La Paz
BOLIVIA
Salvador

Brasilia

OCEAN

PARAGUAY
Asunción

Rio de Janeiro
São Paulo

Santiago
CHILE

Buenos
Aires
ARGENTINA

URUGUAY
Montevideo

• Denotes capital cities

Falkland Is (UK)

S. Georgia (UK)

Major Cities by Continent

Australasia	Pop. '000
Sydney *Australia*	3400
Melbourne *Australia*	2800
Brisbane *Australia*	1200
Perth *Australia*	1100
Adelaide *Australia*	1000
Auckland *New Zealand*	900
Asia	**'000**
Tōkyō *Japan*	18 100
Shanghai *China*	13 400
Calcutta *India*	11 800
Bombay *India*	11 200
Sŏul *South Korea*	11 000
Beijing *China*	10 800
Tianjin *China*	9400
Jakarta *Indonesia*	9300
Delhi *India*	8800
Manila *Philippines*	8500
Osaka *Japan*	8500
Karachi *Pakistan*	7700
Bangkok *Thailand*	7200
Tehrān *Iran*	6800
İstanbul *Turkey*	6700
Dhākā *Bangladesh*	6600
Madras *India*	5700
Hong Kong *China*	5400
Bangalore *India*	5000
Shenyang *China*	4800
Lahore *Pakistan*	4100

Europe	'000
Moskva *Russian Federation*	8800
Paris *France*	8500
London *UK*	7400
Milano *Italy*	5300
Madrid *Spain*	5200
Sankt-Peterburg *Rus.Fed.*	5100
Napoli *Italy*	3600
Athinai *Greece*	3400
Barcelona *Spain*	3400
Berlin *Germany*	3200
Roma *Italy*	3100
Kiyev *Ukraine*	2600
Birmingham *UK*	2300
Manchester *UK*	2300
Bucureşti *Romania*	2200

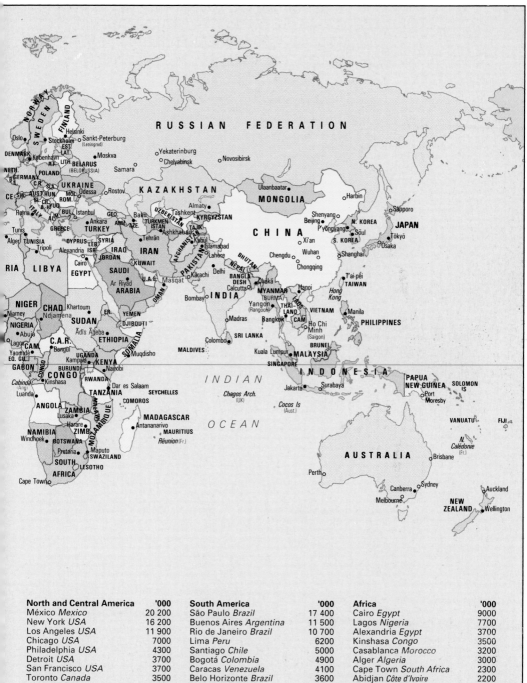

North and Central America	'000	South America	'000	Africa	'000
México *Mexico*	20 200	São Paulo *Brazil*	17 400	Cairo *Egypt*	9000
New York *USA*	16 200	Buenos Aires *Argentina*	11 500	Lagos *Nigeria*	7700
Los Angeles *USA*	11 900	Rio de Janeiro *Brazil*	10 700	Alexandria *Egypt*	3700
Chicago *USA*	7000	Lima *Peru*	6200	Kinshasa *Congo*	3500
Philadelphia *USA*	4300	Santiago *Chile*	5000	Casablanca *Morocco*	3200
Detroit *USA*	3700	Bogotá *Colombia*	4900	Alger *Algeria*	3000
San Francisco *USA*	3700	Caracas *Venezuela*	4100	Cape Town *South Africa*	2300
Toronto *Canada*	3500	Belo Horizonte *Brazil*	3600	Abidjan *Côte d'Ivoire*	2200
Dallas *USA*	3400	Pôrto Alegre *Brazil*	3100	Tarābulus *Libya*	2100
Guadalajara *Mexico*	3200	Recife *Brazil*	2500	Adīs Ābeba *Ethiopia*	1900
Houston *USA*	3000	Brasília *Brazil*	2400	Khartoum *Sudan*	1900
Monterrey *Mexico*	3000	Salvador *Brazil*	2400	Dar es Salaam *Tanzania*	1700
Montréal *Canada*	3000	Fortaleza *Brazil*	2100	Johannesburg *South Africa*	1700
Washington *USA*	2900	Curitiba *Brazil*	2000	Luanda *Angola*	1700
Boston *USA*	2800	Guayaquil *Ecuador*	1700	Maputo *Mozambique*	1600

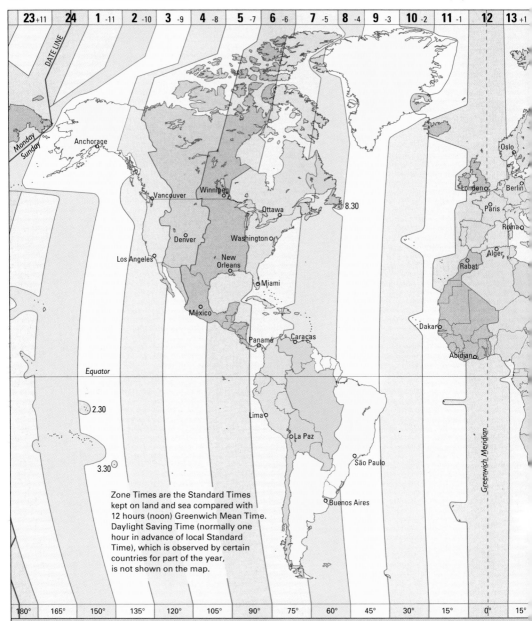

| 23 +11 | 24 | 1 -11 | 2 -10 | 3 -9 | 4 -8 | 5 -7 | 6 -6 | 7 -5 | 8 -4 | 9 -3 | 10 -2 | 11 -1 | 12 | 13 +1 |

DATE LINE

Monday
Sunday

Anchorage

Oslo

Vancouver   Winnipeg   London   Berlin

Ottawa   8.30   Paris

Denver   Washington   Roma

Los Angeles   New Orleans   Alger

Rabat

Miami

México   Dakar

Panamá   Caracas   Abidjan

Equator

2.30   Lima

La Paz

3.30   São Paulo

Zone Times are the Standard Times
kept on land and sea compared with
12 hours (noon) Greenwich Mean Time.
Daylight Saving Time (normally one
hour in advance of local Standard
Time), which is observed by certain
countries for part of the year,
is not shown on the map.

Buenos Aires

Greenwich Meridian

| 180° | 165° | 150° | 135° | 120° | 105° | 90° | 75° | 60° | 45° | 30° | 15° | 0° | 15° |

Journey Times

Sail	Steam	Steam	Supertanker
(via Cape)	(via Cape)	(via Suez)	(via Cape)
164 days	43 days	30 days	28 days

Singapore ←

1:105M

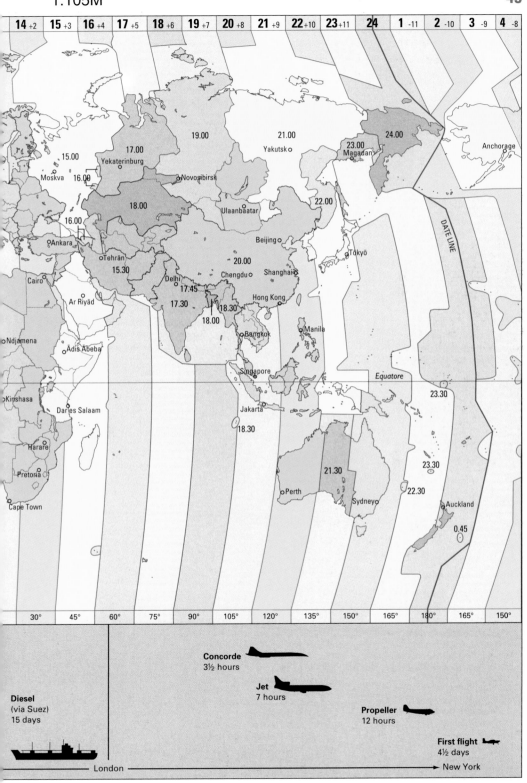

| 14 +2 | 15 +3 | 16 +4 | 17 +5 | 18 +6 | 19 +7 | 20 +8 | 21 +9 | 22 +10 | 23 +11 | 24 | 1 -11 | 2 -10 | 3 -9 | 4 -8 |

15.00

19.00   21.00

17.00   24.00

Yekaterinburg   Yakutsk   23.00   Anchorage
Magadan

Moskva   16.00

Novosibirsk

18.00   22.00

Ulaanbaatar

16.00

DATE LINE

Ankara

Tehrān   Beijing

15.30   20.00

Cairo   Chengdu   Shanghai   Tōkyō

Delhi
Ar Riyād   17.45

17.30   18.30   Hong Kong

18.00

Ndjamena   Manila

Bangkok

Ädis Abeba

Kinshasa   Singapore   Equatore

Dar es Salaam   23.30

Jakarta

Harare   18.30

23.30

Pretoria   21.30

22.30

Cape Town   Perth   Sydney   Auckland

0.45

| 30° | 45° | 60° | 75° | 90° | 105° | 120° | 135° | 150° | 165° | 180° | 165° | 150° |

Concorde
3½ hours

Jet
7 hours

Diesel
(via Suez)
15 days

Propeller
12 hours

First flight
4½ days

London →   → New York

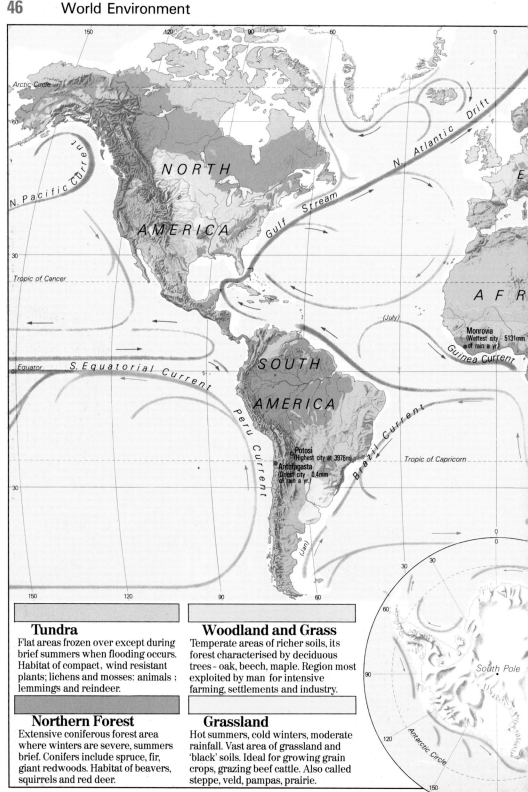

150   120   90   60   0

Arctic Circle

60

N. Pacific Current

NORTH

AMERICA

N. Atlantic Drift

Gulf Stream

30

Tropic of Cancer

A F R

Monrovia
(Wettest city - 5131mm
of rain a yr.)

(July)

Guinea Current

Equator   S. Equatorial Current

SOUTH

AMERICA

Peru Current

Potosi
(Highest city at 3976m)

Antofagasta
(Driest city - 0.4mm
of rain a yr.)

Brazil Current

Tropic of Capricorn

30

(Jan)

150   120   90   60

30   30

60

90

South Pole

120

Antarctic Circle

150

Tundra

Flat areas frozen over except during brief summers when flooding occurs. Habitat of compact, wind resistant plants; lichens and mosses: animals ; lemmings and reindeer.

Northern Forest

Extensive coniferous forest area where winters are severe, summers brief. Conifers include spruce, fir, giant redwoods. Habitat of beavers, squirrels and red deer.

Woodland and Grass

Temperate areas of richer soils, its forest characterised by deciduous trees - oak, beech, maple. Region most exploited by man for intensive farming, settlements and industry.

Grassland

Hot summers, cold winters, moderate rainfall. Vast area of grassland and 'black' soils. Ideal for growing grain crops, grazing beef cattle. Also called steppe, veld, pampas, prairie.

Scrub
Areas of long, hot, dry summers and short warm winters where crop growing and grazing have destroyed original tree cover. Now habitat of evergreen scrub–vines and olives.

Desert
Environment includes bare mountains, rocky waste, sand dunes. Plants (wiry grass, thorn bushes, cacti) and animals (lizards, camels) must be well adapted to extremes of heat and drought.

Savanna
Habitat supports tall coarse grasses with thorny, flat-topped trees. Grazed by giraffes and zebras. Drought is common and plants are adapted to recover quickly from ravages of fire.

Rainforest
Hot and wet–without marked seasons. Habitat of luxuriant trees, lianas, monkeys and tigers. Five vegetation layers– high trees, tree canopy, open canopy, shrubs, ground herbs.

Places with extreme climatic conditions

Continental shelf

Ice shelf

Ocean Circulation

Surface currents-warm

Surface currents-cold

Noril'sk
(Coolest city with -10.9°C mean annual temp.)

Al Aziziyah
(Highest recorded temp. of 57.8°C)

Jericho
(Lowest city at -270m)

Djibouti
(Warmest city with 30°C mean annual temp.)

Vostok Station
(Lowest recorded temp. of -88.3°C)

ASIA

AUSTRALIA

Kuro-Shio

N Equatorial Current

Monsoon Drift

Indian Counter Current

Equatorial Current

West Wind Drift

(July)

(Jan)

(July)

(July)

(Jan)

(July)

(Jan)

BOUNDARIES

━━━━━	International
━ ━ ━ ━	International under Dispute
· · · · · ·	Cease Fire Line
━━━━━	Autonomous or State/ Administrative
━ ━ ━ ━	Maritime (National)
━ ━ ━ ━	International Date Line

COMMUNICATIONS

══════ ━ ━	Motorway/Under Construction
━━━━━	Major/Other Road
━ ━ ━ ━	Under Construction
· · · · · ·	Track
⇉═══⇇	Road Tunnel
─ ─ ─ ─ ─	Car Ferry
━━━━━	Main/Other Railway
─ ─ ─ ─	Under Construction
─ ─ ─ ─ ─	Rail Ferry
→─ ─ ─ ─←	Rail Tunnel
┴┴┴┴┴	Canal
⊕ ✈	International/Other Airport

LANDSCAPE FEATURES

Glacier, Ice Cap
Marsh, Swamp
Sand Desert, Dunes
Freshwater
Saltwater
Seasonal
Salt Pan

OTHER FEATURES

∼∼∼∼→	River/Seasonal
≍	Pass, Gorge
⬭	Dam, Barrage
∼∼∼	Waterfall, Rapid
━━━━━	Aqueduct
∼∿∿∿∼	Reef
.217 ▲4231	Spot Height, Depth/ Summit, Peak
⌣	Well
Δ ▲	Oil/Gas Field
─ Gas / Oil ─	Oil/Natural Gas Pipeline
Gemsbok Nat. Pk	National Park
.·UR	Historic Site

LETTERING STYLES

CANADA	Independent Nation
FLORIDA	State, Province or Autonomous Region
Gibraltar (U.K.)	Sovereignty of Dependent Territory
Lothian	Administrative Area
LANGUEDOC	Historic Region
Loire ***Vosges***	Physical Feature or Physical Region

TOWNS AND CITIES

Square symbols denote capital cities

▣	◉	**New York**	Major City
■	●	**Montréal**	City
▢	○	Ottawa	Small City
▪	•	**Québec**	Large Town
▫	○	St John's	Town
▫	○	Yorkton	Small Town
▫	○	Jasper	Village
			Built-up-area

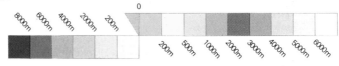

Depth	Sea Level	Height
	0	

8000m 6000m 4000m 2000m 200m   200m 500m 1000m 2000m 3000m 4000m 5000m 6000m

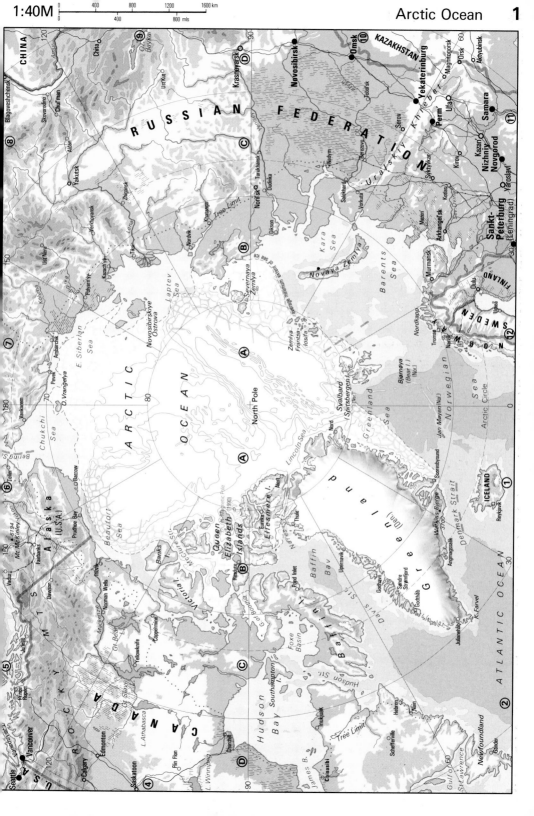

1:40M

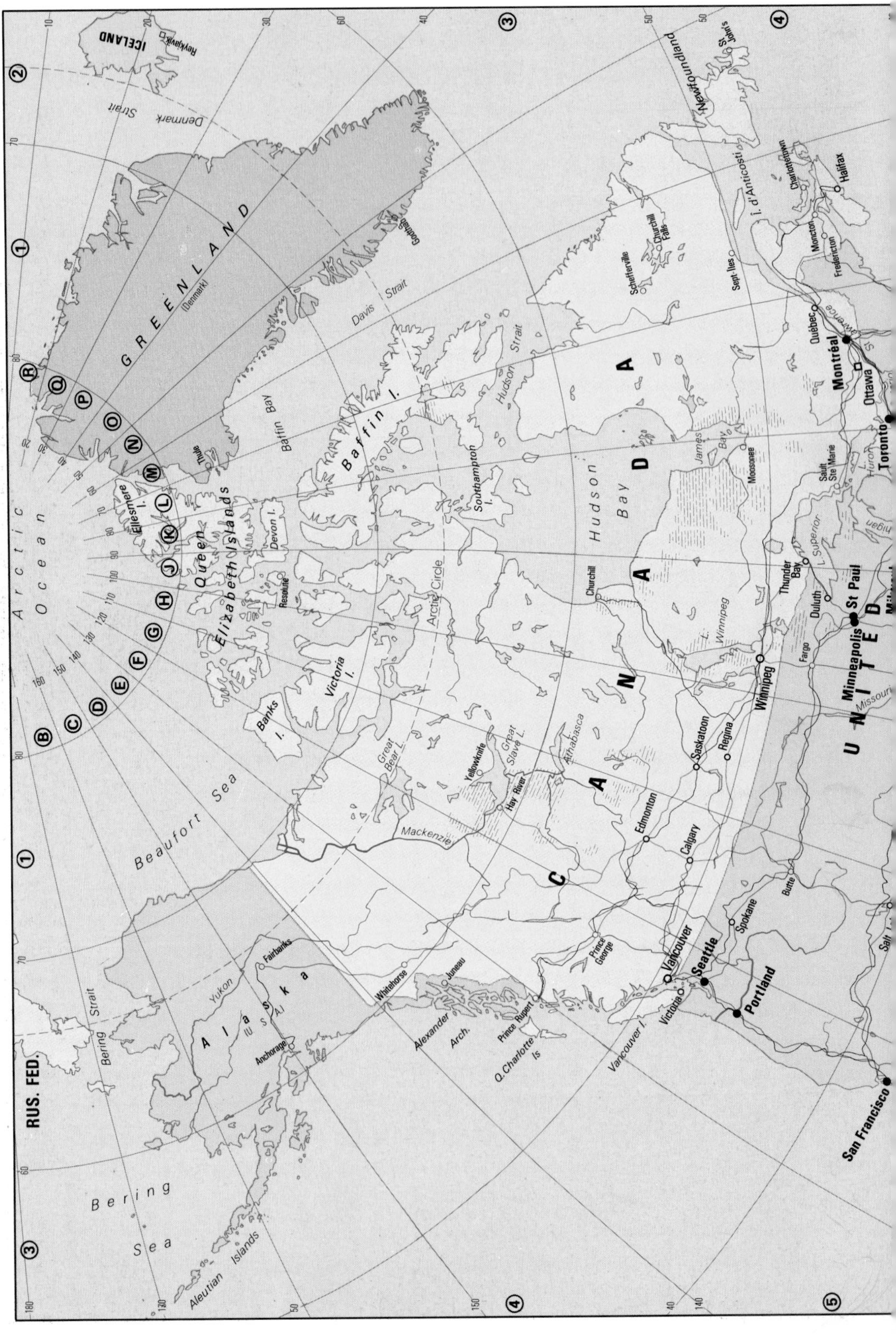

ICELAND
Reykjavík
Denmark Strait
GREENLAND
(Denmark)
Godthåb
Thule
Arctic Ocean
Davis Strait
Baffin Bay
Baffin I.
Ellesmere I.
Devon I.
Queen Elizabeth Islands
Resolute
Victoria I.
Banks I.
Beaufort Sea
Southampton I.
Hudson Strait
Hudson Bay
James Bay
Arctic Circle
Churchill
Great Bear L.
Great Slave L.
Yellowknife
Hay River
Mackenzie
L. Athabasca
L. Winnipeg
CANADA
Schefferville
Churchill Falls
Newfoundland
St John's
I. d'Anticosti
Sept-Iles
Charlottetown
Halifax
Moncton
Fredericton
Québec
Montréal
Ottawa
Toronto
St Lawrence
Moosonee
Sault Ste Marie
L. Huron
L. Superior
Thunder Bay
Duluth
St Paul
Minneapolis
Fargo
Winnipeg
Regina
Saskatoon
Edmonton
Calgary
Missouri
UNITED
Butte
Spokane
Seattle
Portland
Vancouver
Victoria
Vancouver I.
Prince George
Prince Rupert
Q.Charlotte Is
Alexander Arch.
Juneau
Whitehorse
Fairbanks
Anchorage
Yukon
Alaska
(U.S.A.)
Bering Strait
RUS. FED.
Bering Sea
Aleutian Islands
San Francisco
Salt L.

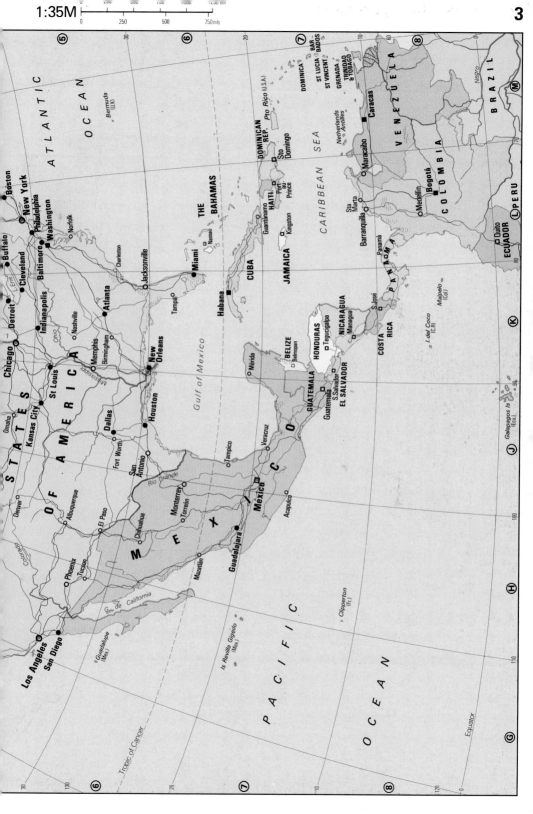

0   250   500   750 mls

ATLANTIC OCEAN

Bermuda (U.K.)

Boston
New York
Philadelphia
Washington
Norfolk
Baltimore
Cleveland
Buffalo
Erie
Detroit
Indianapolis
Nashville
Memphis
Birmingham
Atlanta
Charleston
Jacksonville
Ohio
Chicago
St Louis
Kansas City
Omaha
Denver
Albuquerque
UNITED STATES OF AMERICA
Colorado
Phoenix
Tucson
El Paso
Chihuahua
Mississippi
New Orleans
Houston
Dallas
Fort Worth
San Antonio
Rio Grande
Monterrey
Torreón
Guadalajara
Mazatlán
MEXICO
México
Acapulco
Veracruz
Tampico
Mérida

Tampa
Miami
THE BAHAMAS
Nassau
Habana
CUBA
Guantánamo
Kingston
JAMAICA

Gulf of Mexico

Los Angeles
San Diego
G. de California
ªGuadalupe (Mex.)
Is Revilla Gigedo (Mex.)

Tropic of Cancer

PACIFIC OCEAN

Clipperton (Fr.)

Galapagos Is (Ecu.)

Equator

DOMINICAN REP.
HAITI
Port-au-Prince
Sto Domingo
Pto Rico (U.S.A.)
Netherlands Antilles
DOMINICA
ST LUCIA
ST VINCENT
GRENADA
BARBADOS
TRINIDAD & TOBAGO

CARIBBEAN SEA

BELIZE
Belmopan
GUATEMALA
Guatemala
EL SALVADOR
S.Salvador
HONDURAS
Tegucigalpa
NICARAGUA
Managua
COSTA RICA
S.José
PANAMA
Panamá
I. del Coco (C.R.)
Malpelo (Col.)

Sta Marta
Barranquilla
Maracaibo
Caracas
VENEZUELA
Medellín
Bogotá
COLOMBIA
BRAZIL
Negro
Quito
ECUADOR
PERU

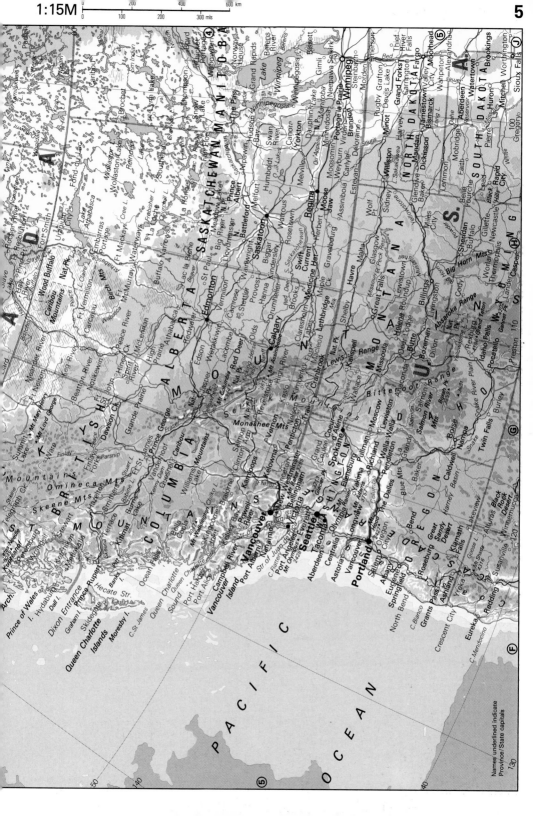

1:15M

200   400   600 km
100   200   300 mils

PACIFIC

OCEAN

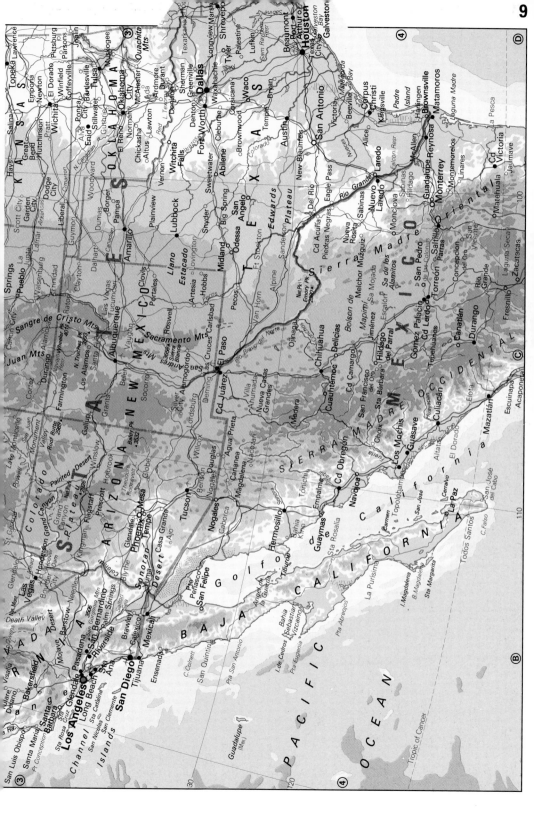

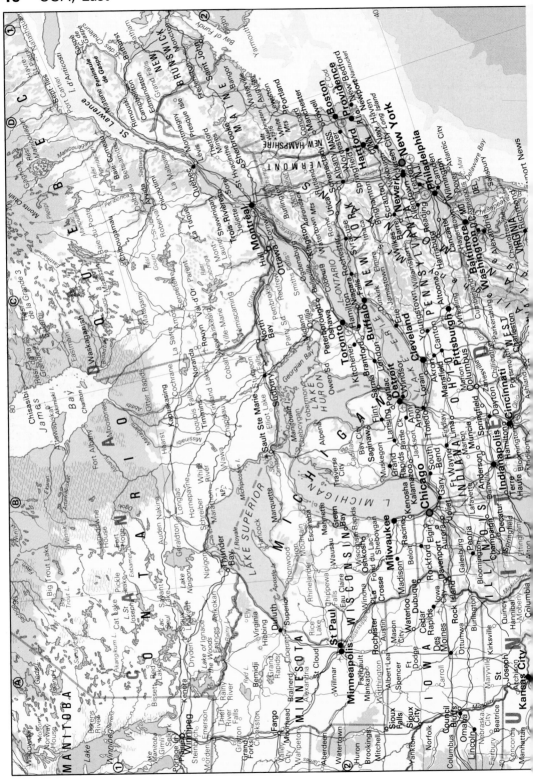

1:12.5M

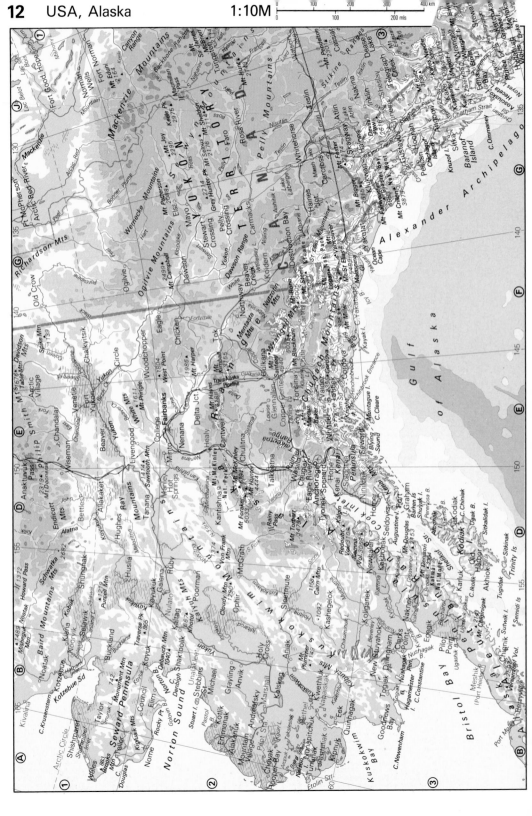

1:7.5M

100   200   300 km

50   100   150 mls

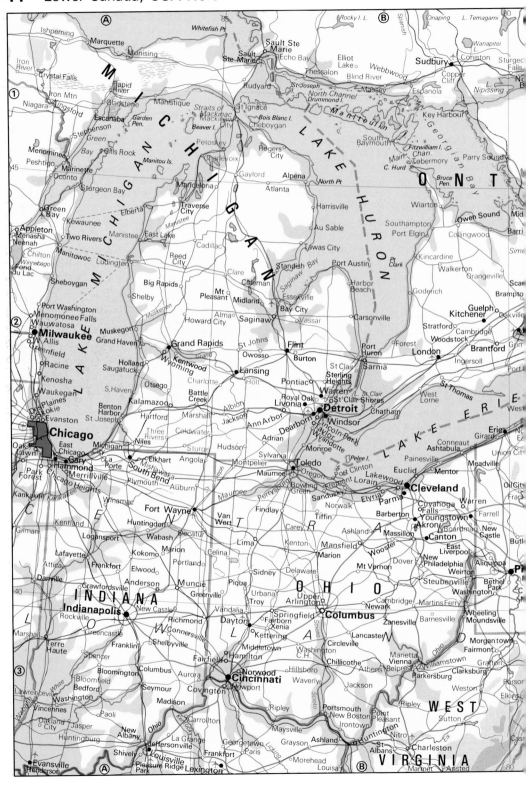

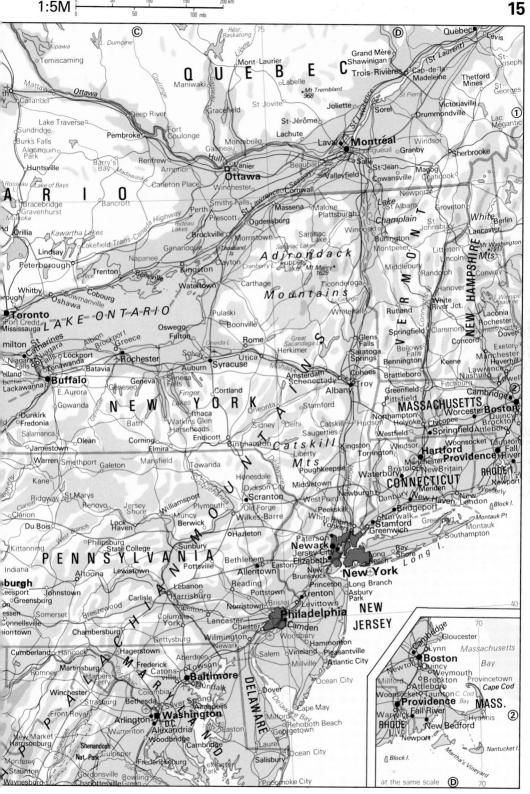

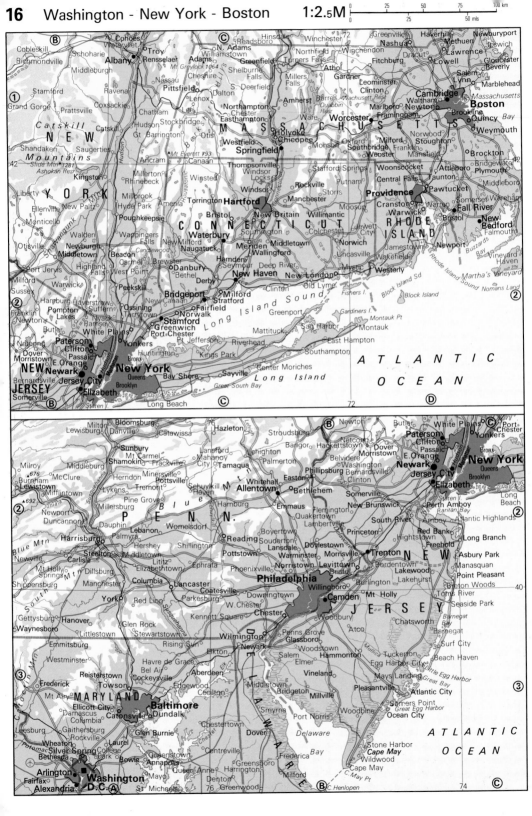

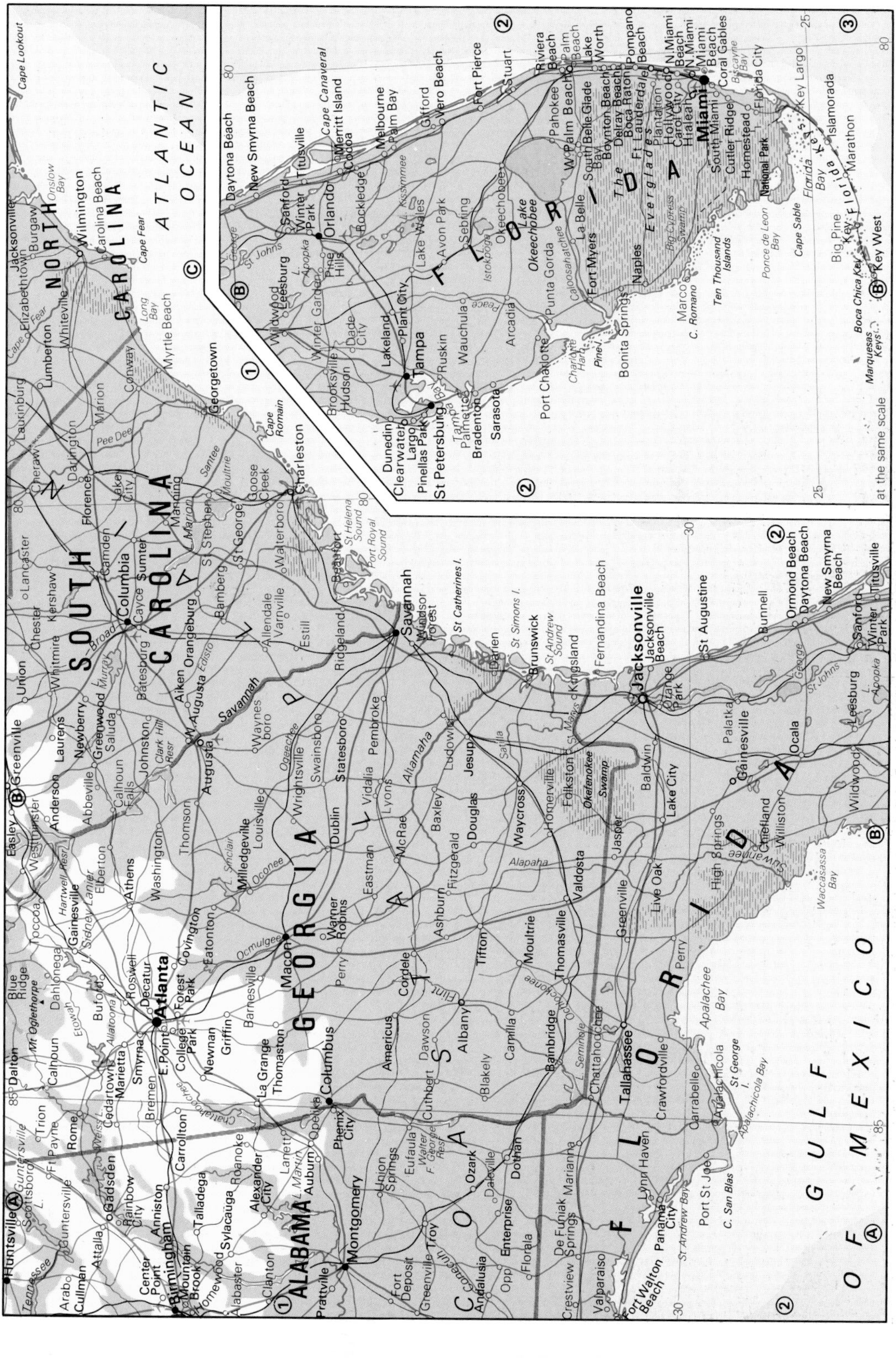
NORTH CAROLINA
SOUTH CAROLINA
GEORGIA
FLORIDA
ALABAMA
ATLANTIC OCEAN
GULF OF MEXICO
Atlanta
Columbia
Savannah
Charleston
Jacksonville
Tallahassee
Montgomery
Birmingham
Macon
Augusta
Columbus
Wilmington
Orlando
Tampa
St Petersburg
Miami
Key West
Okeechobee
Lake Okeechobee
The Everglades
Cape Canaveral
Cape Fear
Cape Lookout
Cape Romain
Apalachee Bay
Florida Keys
at the same scale

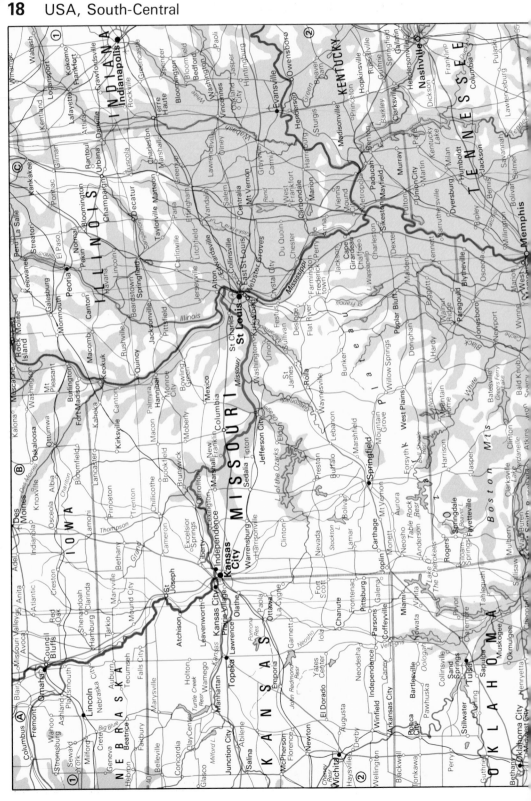

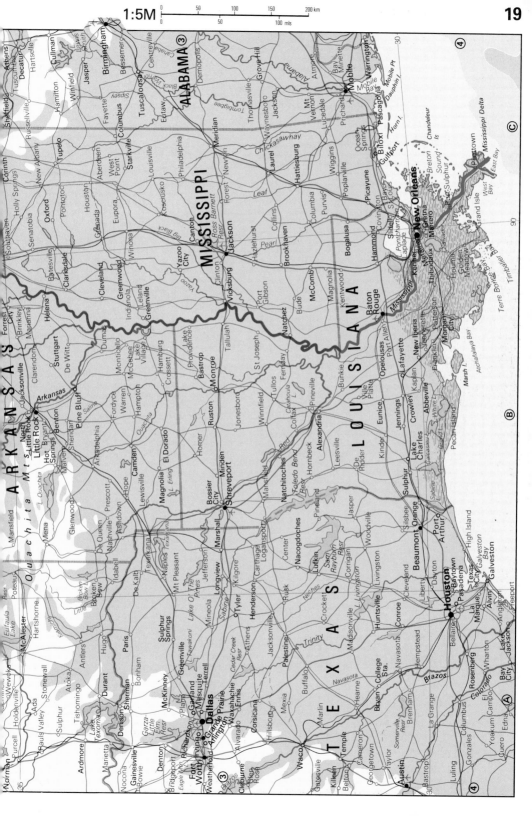

1:5M

0 50 100 150 200 km
0 50 100 mls

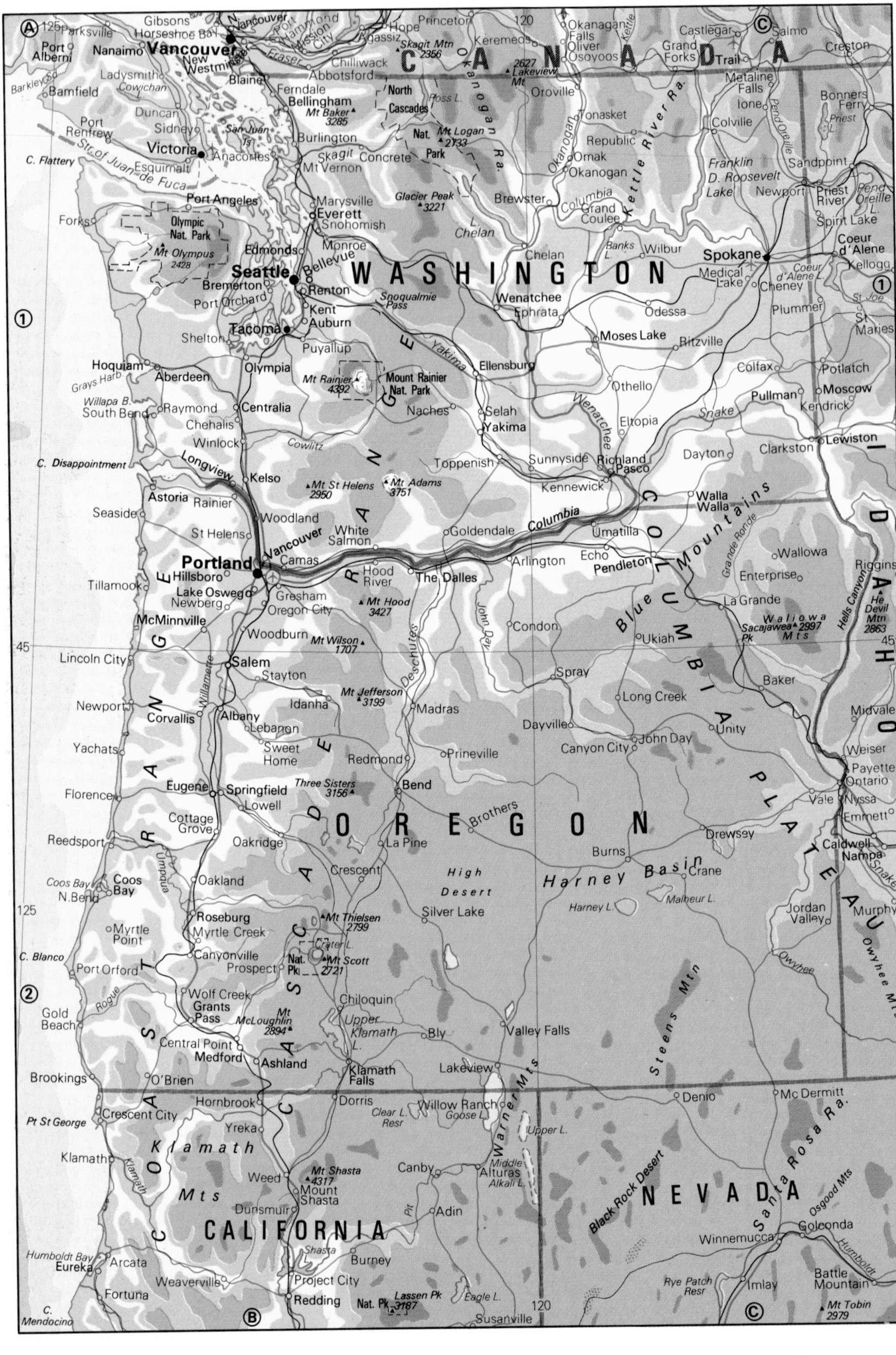

CANADA

WASHINGTON

OREGON

CALIFORNIA

NEVADA

IDAHO

Parksville, Gibsons, Horseshoe Bay, Vancouver, Hope, Princeton, Okanagan Falls, Keremeos, Castlegar, Salmo
Port Alberni, Nanaimo, Ladysmith, New Westm, Blaine, Agassiz, Chilliwack, Oliver, Osoyoos, Grand Forks, Trail, Creston
Bamfield, Duncan, Cowichan, Ferndale, Bellingham, Abbotsford, North Cascades, Mt Baker 3285, Oroville, Tonasket, Republic, Colville, Metaline Falls, Bonners Ferry, Priest
Barkley S, Port Renfrew, Sidney, San Juan Is, Anacortes, Burlington, Concrete, Nat. Park, Mt Logan 2733, Okanogan, Omak, Franklin D. Roosevelt Lake, Newport, Priest River, Sandpoint
Victoria, Esquimalt, Port Angeles, Mt Vernon, Glacier Peak 3221, Brewster, Columbia, Grand Coulee, Spokane, Coeur d'Alene, Coeur d'Alene L.
C. Flattery, St. of Juan de Fuca, Marysville, Everett, Snohomish, L Chelan, Chelan, Banks L, Wilbur, Medical Lake, Cheney, Kellogg, St Maries
Forks, Olympic Nat. Park, Mt Olympus 2428, Edmonds, Bellevue, Seattle, Bremerton, Renton, Kent, Auburn, Snoqualmie Pass, Wenatchee, Ephrata, Odessa, Plummer, St Joe
Hoquiam, Aberdeen, Shelton, Olympia, Tacoma, Puyallup, Yakima, Ellensburg, Moses Lake, Ritzville, Colfax, Moscow, Kendrick
Grays Harb, Raymond, South Bend, Chehalis, Centralia, Mt Rainier 4392, Mount Rainier Nat. Park, Naches, Selah, Othello, Eltopia, Pullman, Potlatch, Lewiston
Willapa B, Winlock, Cowlitz, Toppenish, Yakima, Sunnyside, Richland, Pasco, Dayton, Clarkston, Snake
C. Disappointment, Longview, Kelso, Mt St Helens 2950, Mt Adams 3751, Goldendale, Kennewick, Walla Walla, Umatilla, Wallowa
Astoria, Rainier, Woodland, White Salmon, Columbia, Arlington, Echo, Pendleton, Enterprise, Riggins
Seaside, St Helens, Vancouver, Camas, Hood River, The Dalles, Umatilla, La Grande, Hells Canyon, He Devil Mtn 2863
Portland, Hillsboro, Lake Oswego, Gresham, Oregon City, Mt Hood 3427, Condon, Ukiah, Blue Mountains, Grande Ronde, Wallowa Mts, Sacajawea 2997 Pk, Baker
Tillamook, Newberg, McMinnville, Woodburn, Mt Wilson 1707, John Day, Dayville, Long Creek, Unity, Midvale, Weiser
Lincoln City, Salem, Stayton, Mt Jefferson 3199, Madras, Spray, Canyon City, John Day, Payette, Ontario
Newport, Corvallis, Albany, Lebanon, Idanha, Redmond, Prineville, Dayville, Nyssa, Emmett
Yachats, Sweet Home, Three Sisters 3156, Bend, Brothers, Burns, Crane, Drewsey, Caldwell, Nampa, Murphy
Florence, Eugene, Springfield, Lowell, La Pine, Harney Basin, Harney L, Malheur L, Jordan Valley, Owyhee Mts
Reedsport, Cottage Grove, Oakridge, Crescent, High Desert, Silver Lake, Steens Mtn, Vale
Coos Bay, N.Bend, Oakland, Roseburg, Myrtle Creek, Canyonville, Prospect, Crater L., Chiloquin, Upper Klamath, Bly, Valley Falls, Owyhee
Myrtle Point, Wolf Creek, Grants Pass, Mt Thielsen 2799, Mt Scott 2721, Bly, McDermitt, Santa Rosa Ra.
Gold Beach, Central Point, Medford, Ashland, Mt McLoughlin 2894, Klamath Falls, Lakeview, Denio, Osgood Mts
Brookings, O'Brien, Hornbrook, Dorris, Clear L. Resr, Willow Ranch, Goose L., Warner Mts, Black Rock Desert, Winnemucca, Golconda
Pt St George, Crescent City, Yreka, Canby, Upper L., Middle Alturas, Alkali L., Rye Patch Resr, Imlay, Battle Mountain
Klamath, Klamath Mts, Weed, Mt Shasta 4317, Mount Shasta, Adin, Mt Tobin 2979
Humboldt Bay, Eureka, Arcata, Fortuna, Weaverville, Dunsmuir, Shasta, Burney, Project City, Redding, Nat. Pk, Lassen Pk 3187, Eagle L., Susanville
C. Mendocino, Coast Range, Cascade Range, Umpqua, Rogue, Klamath, Deschutes, Columbia Plateau, Owyhee

50 100 150 200 km
50 100 mls

Map labels (California / Nevada region):

Humboldt Bay, Arcata, Eureka, Fortuna, Weaverville, Dunsmuir, Shasta, Adin, Burney, Project City, Redding, Nat. Pk. Lassen Pk 3187, Chester, Eagle L., Susanville, Winnemucca, Golconda, Emigrant Pass, Rye Patch Resr, Imlay, Battle Mountain, Mt Tobin 2979

Garberville, Cummings, Fort Bragg, Red Bluff, Almanor, Honey L., Lovelock, Eastgate, Austin, Summit Mtn 3188

Ukiah, Lakeport, Pt Arena, Healdsburg, Paradise, Chico, Oroville, Quincy, Feather Mid. Fork, Reno, Sparks, Fernley, Fallon, Pyramid L., Humboldt L., Mt Jefferson 3642, Monitor Ra., Wildcat Pk 3203

Grass Valley, Marysville, Yuba City, Roseville, Colfax, Auburn, Placerville, Tahoe City, Lake Tahoe, S. Lake Tahoe, Virginia City, Silver City, Carson City, Stewart, Yerington, Schurz, Gabbs, Walker L., Hawthorne, Mt Grant 3426, Warm Springs, Tonopah

Woodland, Davis, Vacaville, Fairfield, Vallejo, Napa, Sonoma, Carmichael, **Sacramento**, Sutter Creek, San Andreas, Galt, Lodi, Bridgeport, Mono L., Coaldale, Boundary Peak 4005, Goldfield, Piper Pk 2880

San Rafael, Berkeley, **San Francisco**, **Oakland**, Alameda, Daly City, San Mateo, Redwood City, Sunnyvale, Santa Clara, Los Gatos, Gilroy, Hayward, Livermore, **Stockton**, Oakdale, Modesto, Turlock, Sonora, El Portal, Yosemite Nat. Park, White Mtn Peak 4342, Bishop, Big Pine, Beatty

Santa Rosa, Bodega Head, Petaluma, Concord, Antioch, Gustine, Merced, Madera, Pinedale, Kings Canyon Nat. Park, Independence, Lone Pine, Owens L., Keeler, Telescope Peak 3368, Death Valley Range, Panamint Range

Santa Cruz, Watsonville, Monterey Bay, Pt Pinos, Monterey, **San Jose**, Los Banos, Fresno, Pine Flat Resr, Sequoia Nat. Park, Mt Whitney 4418, Exeter

Salinas, Gonzales, King City, Hanford, Lemoore, Visalia, Tulare, Earlimart, Porterville, Inyokern

Coalinga, Paso Robles, Wasco, Delano, Johannesburg

Morro Bay, San Luis Obispo, Grover City, Oildale, Bakersfield, Arvin, Mojave, Barstow, Yermo

Santa Maria, Lompoc, Santa Barbara, Santa Paula, Fillmore, Lancaster, Tehachapi Pass, Tehachapi Mts, Mojave Desert, Victorville

Pt Conception, Santa Barbara Chan, Ventura, Oxnard, Burbank, Glendale, Beverly Hills, Pasadena, Santa Monica, Mt San Antonio 3068, San Bernardino, Redlands, Beaumont, San Jacinto Peak 3301

San Miguel, Santa Cruz, Santa Rosa, **Los Angeles**, Torrance, Long Beach, Huntington Beach, Laguna Beach, Anaheim, Santa Ana, Pomona, Riverside, Palm Springs, Palomar Mtn 1871

Channel Islands, Santa Catalina, San Clemente, Gulf of Santa Catalina, Oceanside, Carlsbad, Vista, Escondido, Ramona

San Diego, Chula Vista, National City, El Cajon, La Mesa, Tijuana, Tecate, Descanso

PACIFIC OCEAN

State labels: C O A S T R A N G E S, Sacramento Valley, S I E R R A N E V A D A, San Joaquin Valley, Diablo Range, Santa Lucia Range, N E V A D A, Shoshone Mts, Stillwater Ra., Monitor Ra., Mojave Desert

Inset — USA, Hawaii:

PACIFIC OCEAN

Kauai, Hanalei, Lihue, Mana, Niihau, Kauai Channel, Kaena Pt, Kahuku Pt, Wahiawa, Kailua, Oahu, Pearl City, Pearl Harbor, Honolulu, Kaiwi Channel, Molokai, Kaunakakai, Kalaupapa, Lanai, Lanai City, Wailuku, Hana, Maui, Kahoolawe, Kealaikahiki Channel, Alenuihaha Channel, Kapaau, Waimea, Mauna Kea 4201, Hakalau, Hilo, Pahoa, Kailua, Mauna Loa 4169, Kilauea Crater 1243, Hawaii Volcanoes Nat. Park, Miloli'i, Naalehu, Ka Lae (South Cape), **Hawaii**

USA, Hawaii

100 200 km
50 100 mls

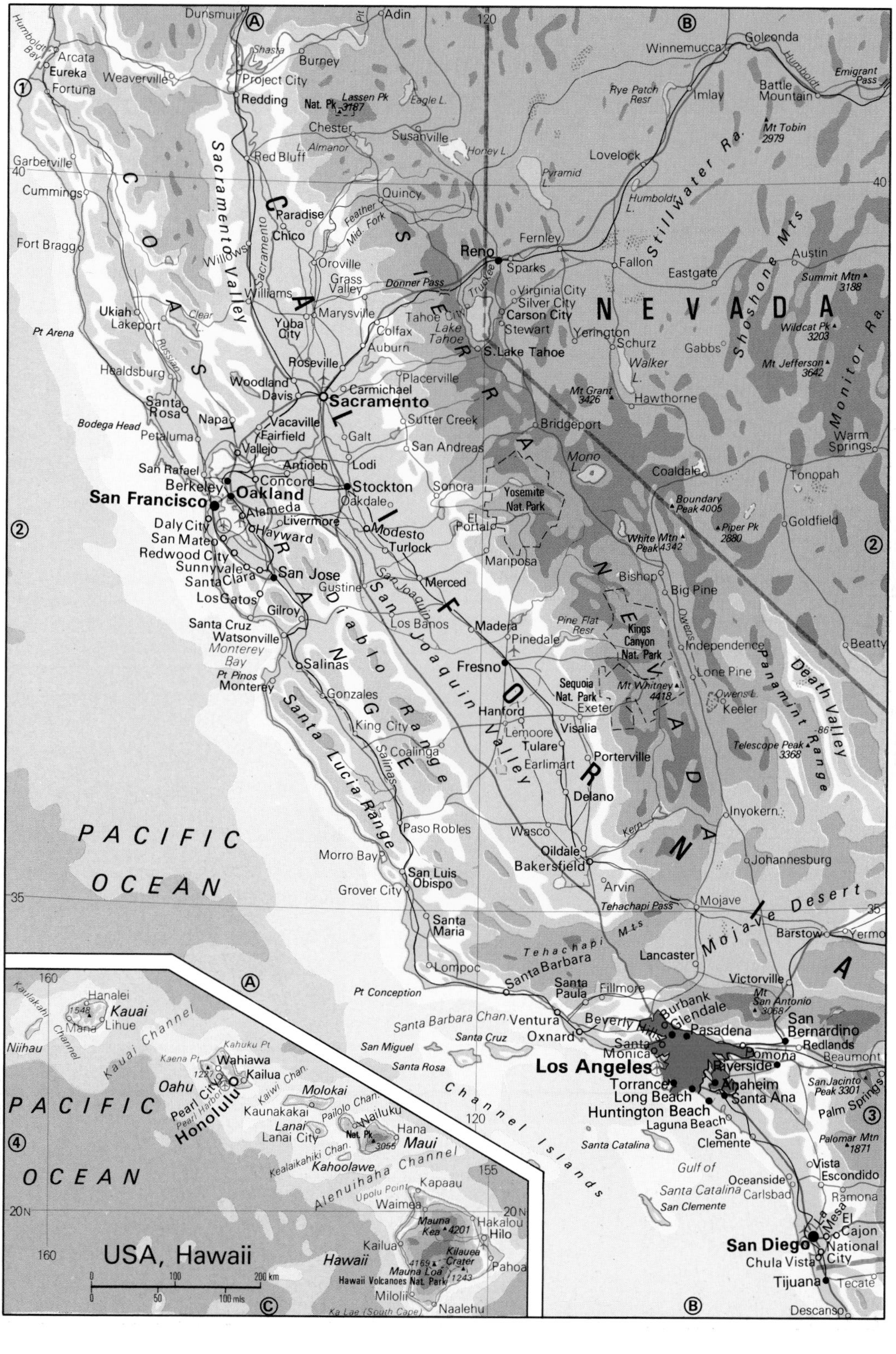

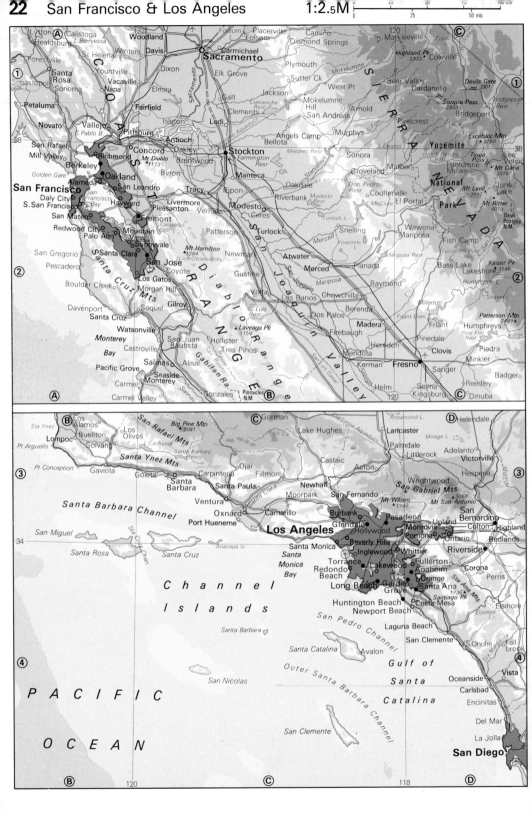

1:2.5M

0   25   50 mls

San Francisco & Los Angeles map (page 22)

Lytton, Calistoga, L. Berryessa, Woodland, Folsom, Placerville, Folsom, Markleeville, Topaz, Highland Pk 3333, Coleville
Healdsburg, St Helena, Winters, Davis, Carmichael, Camino, Diamond Springs
Forestville, Yountville, **Sacramento**, Plymouth, Bear Valley, Dardanelle, Devils Gate 2301
Sebastopol, Santa Rosa, Sonoma, Napa, Vacaville, Elmira, Elk Grove, Sutter Ck, West Pt, Mokelumne, Sonora Pass 2933, Bridgeport, Bridgeport Resr
Petaluma, Fairfield, Galt, Jackson, Mokelumne Hill, Arnold, Pinecrest
Novato, Vallejo, Pittsburg, Isleton, Lodi, Clements, San Andreas, Murphys, Excelsior Mtn 3790
San Rafael, Concord, Oakley, Brentwood, Antioch, Bellota, Angels Camp, L. Eleanor, Hetch Hetchy, Tioga Pass, Lee Vining, Tuolumne Mdws, Mt Dana 3978
Mill Valley, Berkeley, Richmond, Byron, Stockton, Farmington Resr, Melones Resr, Sonora, Matber, Groveland, **Yosemite**, Mt Lyell 3997, June Lake
Golden Gate, Oakland, San Leandro, Tracy, Manteca, Oakdale, Don Pedro Resr, Coulterville, **National**, Mt Ritter 4010, Devil Postpile N.M.
San Francisco, Daly City, Hayward, Fremont, Ripon, Riverbank, Modesto Resr, El Portal, **Park**, Wawona
S. San Francisco, San Mateo, Pleasanton, Livermore, Vernalis, Ceres, McClure, Mariposa, Fish Camp
Redwood City, Palo Alto, Mountain View, Sunnyvale, Patterson, Turlock, Snelling, Yosemite, Bass Lake, Kaiser Pk 3146, Lakeshore, Huntington L.
San Gregorio, Santa Clara, Mt Hamilton 1284 Lick Observatory, Newman, Atwater, Merced, Planada, Raymond
Pescadero, San Jose, Coyote, Gustine, Merced, Mariposa, Chowchilla, Madera, Friant, Pine Flat Resr, Humphreys, Patterson Mtn 2489, Piedra
Boulder Creek, Los Gatos, Volta, Los Banos, Berenda, Firebaugh, Herndon, Clovis, Minkler
Davenport, Morgan Hill, Gilroy, S. Luis Resr, Dos Palos, Mendota, Kerman, Sanger, Badger
Santa Cruz, Soquel, Laveaga Pk 1154, Helm, Selma, Reedley, Fresno
Watsonville, San Juan Bautista, Hollister, Tres Pinos, Kingsburg, Dinuba
Monterey Bay, Castroville, Alisal, Gonzales, Pinnacles N.M.
Pacific Grove, Monterey, Seaside, Salinas
Carmel, Carmel Valley

Sta Ynez, Los Alamos, Buellton, Los Olivos, Big Pine Mtn 2081, Gorman, Rosamond L., Helendale
Lompoc, Solvang, San Rafael Mts, Piru Ck, Lake Hughes, Lancaster, Mirage L., Adelanto
Pt Arguello, Gaviota, Santa Ynez Mts, Ojai, Fillmore, Castaic, Palmdale, Littlerock, Victorville
Pt Conception, Goleta, Santa Barbara, Carpinteria, Santa Paula, Moorpark, Newhall, Acton, Wrightwood, Hesperia
Santa Barbara Channel, Ventura, Santa Clara, Camarillo, San Fernando, San Gabriel Mts 3068, Mt San Antonio, San Bernardino
San Miguel, Oxnard, Port Hueneme, Burbank, Pasadena, Upland, Colton, Highland
Santa Rosa, Santa Cruz, Anacapa Is, **Los Angeles**, Glendale, Hollywood, Monrovia, Pomona, Ontario, Redlands
Santa Cruz Chan., Santa Monica, Beverly Hills, Inglewood, Whittier, Riverside
Channel, Santa Monica Bay, Torrance, Fullerton, Corona, Perris
Islands, Redondo Beach, Lakewood, Anaheim, Orange, Santa Ana, Elsinore
Santa Barbara, Long Beach, Garden Grove, Santiago Pk 1736, Fallbrook
Huntington Beach, Newport Beach, Costa Mesa
Laguna Beach, **Gulf of Santa Catalina**, San Clemente
Santa Catalina, Avalon, S Onofre, Oceanside, Vista
San Nicolas, Outer Santa Barbara Channel, Carlsbad, Encinitas
PACIFIC OCEAN, San Clemente, Del Mar, La Jolla, **San Diego**

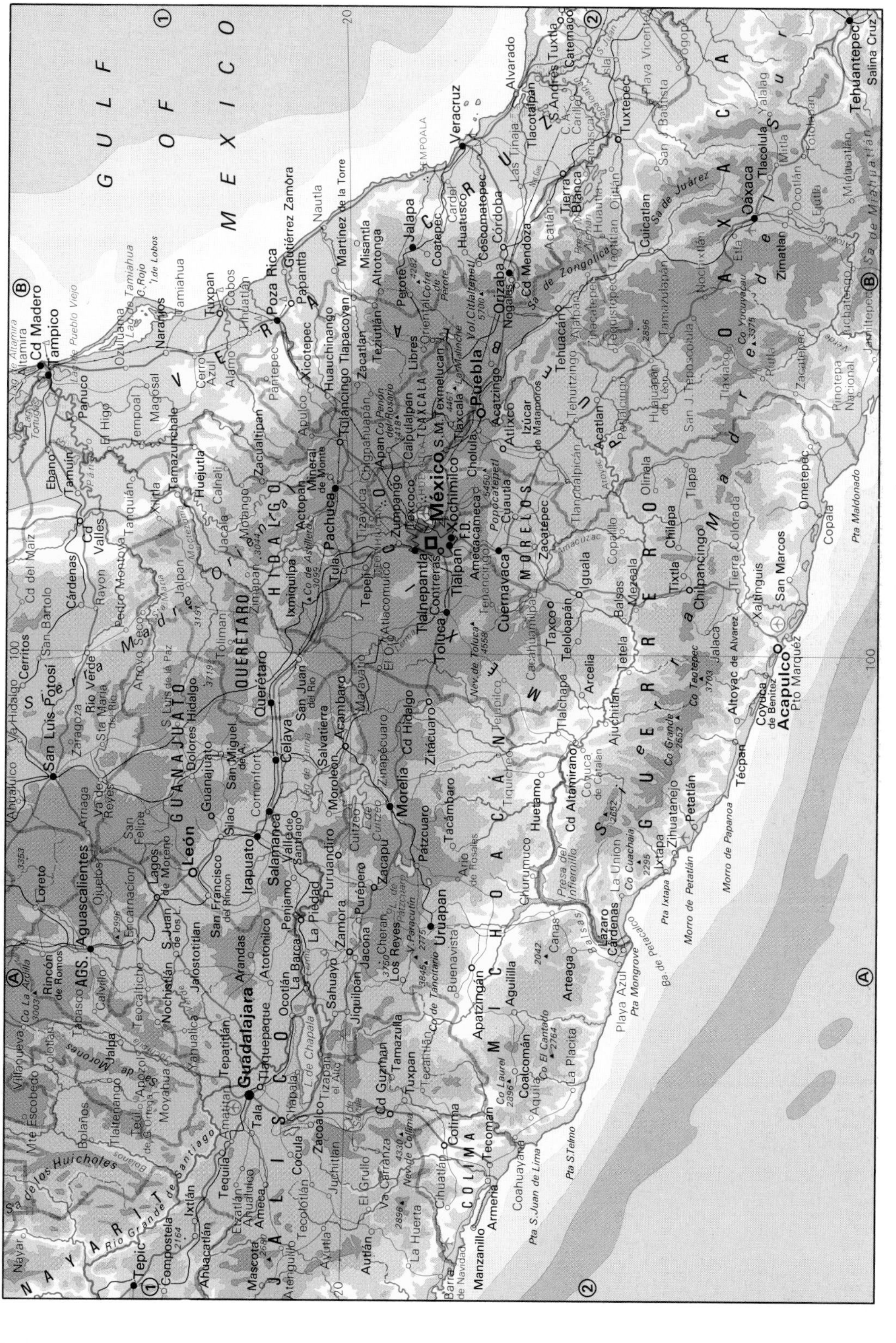

200 km
50 100 100 mls

GULF OF MEXICO

NAYARIT **JALISCO** **COLIMA** **MICHOACÁN** **GUERRERO** **OAXACA** **PUEBLA** **MORELOS** **TLAXCALA** **HIDALGO** **QUERÉTARO** **GUANAJUATO** **AGS.** **S. L. P.**

Sa. Madre del Sur
Sa. Madre Oriental

Tepic
Compostela
Ixtlán
Ahuacatlán
Amatlán
Tequila
Tala
Tlaquepaque
Guadalajara
Tepatitlán
Atotonilco
Ocotlán
La Barca
Zamora
Jacona
Los Reyes
Sahuayo
Jiquilpan
Uruapan
Apatzingán
Coalcomán
Aquila
La Placita
Playa Azul
Lázaro Cárdenas
La Unión
Zihuatanejo
Ixtapa
Petatlán
Técpan
Acapulco
Pto Marqués
San Marcos
Ometepec
Pinotepa Nacional

Manzanillo
Tecomán
Colima
Armería
Autlán
El Grullo
La Huerta
Cihuatlán

Aguascalientes
Loreto
León
Silao
Irapuato
Salamanca
Celaya
Querétaro
San Juan del Río
Morelia
Pátzcuaro
Zitácuaro
Toluca
México
Xochimilco
Puebla
Tlaxcala
Cholula
Atlixco
Izúcar de Matamoros
Cuernavaca
Taxco
Iguala
Chilpancingo
Tierra Colorada

Pachuca
Tula
Tulancingo
Huachinango
Teziutlán
Jalapa
Veracruz
Córdoba
Orizaba
Cd Mendoza
Tehuacán
Oaxaca
Tehuantepec
Salina Cruz

San Luis Potosí
Cerritos
Cd del Maíz
Cd Valles
Tamazunchale
Huejutla
Pánuco
Tampico
Cd Madero
Tuxpan
Poza Rica
Papantla

Martínez de la Torre

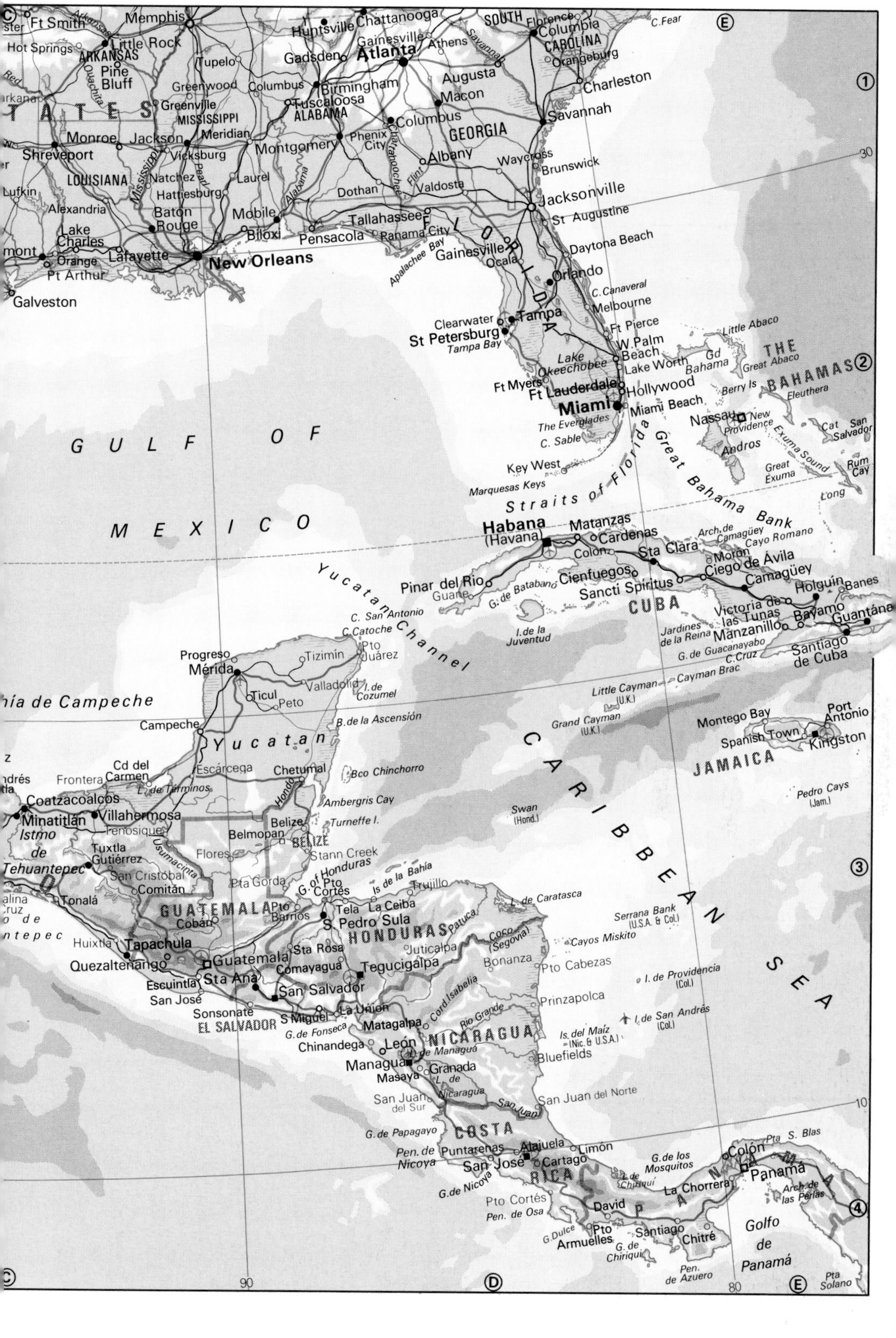

C
Ft Smith
Memphis
Huntsville Chattanooga
SOUTH
Florence
Columbia
C. Fear
E
Hot Springs
Little Rock
Gainesville
Athens
Orangeburg
①
ARKANSAS
Gadsden
Atlanta
CAROLINA
Pine
Bluff
Tupelo
Columbus
Birmingham
Augusta
Charleston
Greenwood
Tuscaloosa
Macon
Greenville
ALABAMA
Savannah
Monroe Jackson
MISSISSIPPI
Montgomery
Columbus
30
Shreveport
Vicksburg
Meridian
GEORGIA
Waycross
Brunswick
LOUISIANA
Natchez
Laurel
Dothan
Valdosta
Jacksonville
Lufkin
Hattiesburg
Tallahassee
St Augustine
Alexandria
Baton
Rouge
Mobile
Pensacola
Panama City
Gainesville
Daytona Beach
Lake
Charles
Orange
Biloxi
Apalachee Bay
Ocala
Orlando
Pt Arthur
New Orleans
FLORIDA
C. Canaveral
Galveston
Melbourne
Clearwater
Tampa
Ft Pierce
St Petersburg
Tampa Bay
W. Palm
Beach
Little Abaco
THE
Lake
Okeechobee
Lake Worth
Gd
Bahama
Great Abaco
BAHAMAS
②
GULF   OF
Ft Myers
Ft Lauderdale
Hollywood
Berry Is
Eleuthera
The Everglades
Miami
Miami Beach
Nassau
New
Providence
Cat
San
Salvador
C. Sable
Andros
Great
Exuma
Exuma Sound
Rum
Cay
MEXICO
Key West
Marquesas Keys
Straits of Florida
Great Bahama Bank
Long
Habana
(Havana)
Matanzas
Arch. de
Camagüey
Cayo Romano
Cárdenas
Colón
Sta Clara
Morón
Ciego de Ávila
Camagüey
Pinar del Río
Cienfuegos
Sancti Spíritus
Holguín
Banes
Guane
G. de Batabanó
CUBA
Victoria de
las Tunas
Bayamo
Guantána
C. San Antonio
I. de la
Juventud
Manzanillo
Santiago
de Cuba
Jardines
de la Reina
G. de Guacanayabo
C. Cruz
Progreso
Tizimín
Pto
Juárez
Little Cayman
Cayman Brac
Mérida
I. de
Cozumel
Montego Bay
Port
Antonio
hía de Campeche
Ticul
Peto
Valladolid
Grand Cayman
(U.K.)
Spanish Town
Kingston
Campeche
Yucatan
B. de la Ascensión
JAMAICA
andrés
Escárcega
Chetumal
Bco Chinchorro
Pedro Cays
(Jam.)
③
Frontera
Cd del
Carmen
Ambergris Cay
Coatzacoalcos
I. de Términos
Turneffe I.
Swan
(Hond.)
Minatitlán
Istmo
Villahermosa
Tenosique
Belize
Belmopan
BELIZE
Stann Creek
de
Tuxtla
Gutiérrez
Flores
CARIBBEAN
Tehuantepec
San Cristóbal
Comitán
Pta Gorda
G. of
Honduras
Is. de la Bahía
Trujillo
I. de Caratasca
alina
ruz
Tonalá
GUATEMALA
Pto
Barrios
S. Pedro Sula
La Ceiba
Cayos Miskito
Serrana Bank
(U.S.A. & Col.)
Tela
Huixtla
Tapachula
Cobán
Coco
(Segovia)
Pto Cabezas
SEA
I. de Providencia
(Col.)
Quezaltenango
Guatemala
Sta Rosa
HONDURAS
Juticalpa
Patuca
Escuintla
STA ANA
Comayagua
Tegucigalpa
Río Grande
San José
San Salvador
Bonanza
④
Sonsonate
S Miguel
La Unión
Cord. Isabelia
Prinzapolca
I. del Maíz
(Nic. & U.S.A.)
I. de San Andrés
(Col.)
EL SALVADOR
Matagalpa
Chinandega
León
NICARAGUA
Bluefields
Managua
L. de Managua
Masaya
Granada
L. de
Nicaragua
San Juan
del Sur
San Juan
San Juan del Norte
10
G. de Papagayo
COSTA
Pen. de
Nicoya
Puntarenas
Alajuela
Cartago
Limón
G. de los
Mosquitos
Pta S. Blas
Colón
San José
G. de
Chiriquí
La Chorrera
Panamá
Arch. de
las Perlas
E
RICA
David
Golfo
de
Panamá
Pta
Solano
Pto Cortés
Pen. de Osa
G. Dulce
Pto
Armuelles
G. de
Chiriquí
Santiago
Chitré
Pen.
de Azuero

90
D
80
E

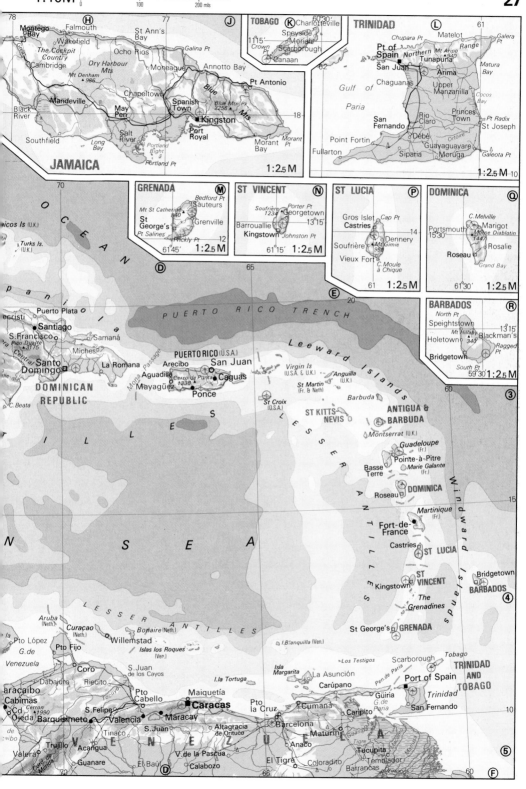

1:10M

0   100   200 mls

TOBAGO
Charlotteville
Speyside
Moriah
Scarborough
Canaan
Crown

TRINIDAD
Chupara Pt   Matelot   Galera Pt
Pt of   Northern   Mt Aripo   Range
Spain   Tunapuna   940
San Juan   Arima   Matura
Chaguanas   Upper   Bay
Manzanilla   Cocos
Gulf of   Bay
Paria   Princes
San   Town
Fernando   Rio   Pt Radix
Claro   St Joseph
Point Fortin   Débé
Fullarton   Guayaguayare
Siparia   Moruga   Galeota Pt
1:2.5M

JAMAICA
Montego   Falmouth   St Ann's
Bay   Wakefield   Bay
The Cockpit   Ocho Rios
Country   Dry Harbour   Galina Pt
Cambridge   Mts   Moneague   Annotto Bay
Mt Denham   Pt Antonio
▲986   Chapeltown   Blue   Blue Mtn Pk
Spanish   Mtn   2256
Mandeville   Town   Mts
May   Kingston
Pen   Port   18
Black   Royal
River   Salt   Morant
Southfield   River   Bay   Morant
Long   Portland   Pt
Bay   Bight   Portland Pt
1:2.5M

GRENADA
Bedford Pt
Mt St Catherine   Sauteurs
840
St   Grenville
George's
Pt Salines
Hickly Pt   12
61°45'   1:2.5M

ST VINCENT
Soufrière   Porter Pt
1234   Georgetown
13°15'
Barrouallie
Kingstown   Johnston Pt
61°15'   1:2.5M

ST LUCIA
Gros Islet   Cap Pt
Castries
14
Mt   Dennery
Gimie
Soufrière   950
Vieux Fort   C.Moule
à Chique
61   1:2.5M

DOMINICA
C.Melville
Portsmouth   Marigot
15°30'   Morne Diablotin
1447
Rosalie
Roseau
Grand Bay
61°30'   1:2.5M

BARBADOS
North Pt
Speightstown   13°15'
Mt Hillab   Blackman's
Holetown   340
Ragged
Bridgetown   Pt
South Pt
59°30'   1:2.5M

O C E A N

icos Is (U.K.)
Turks Is.
(U.K.)

P U E R T O   R I C O   T R E N C H

20

L e e w a r d   I s l a n d s

escristi
Santiago
Puerto Plata
S.Francisco   Samaná
Pico Duarte   Miches
▲3175
Central   La Romana
Santo   **DOMINICAN**   Aguadilla   Cerro de Punta
Domingo   **REPUBLIC**   Mayagüez   1338
C.Beata   Ponce

PUERTO RICO (U.S.A.)
Arecibo   San Juan
Caguas

Mona Passage

Virgin Is   Anguilla
(U.S.A. & U.K.)   (U.K.)
St Martin
(Fr. & Neth)
St Croix   Barbuda
(U.S.A.)
St Kitts   **ANTIGUA &**
Nevis   **BARBUDA**
Montserrat (U.K.)
Guadeloupe
(Fr.)
Pointe-à-Pitre
Basse   Marie Galante
Terre   (Fr.)
Roseau   **DOMINICA**
15
Martinique
(Fr.)
Fort-de-
France
Castries   **ST LUCIA**

W i n d w a r d   I s l a n d s

60

3

C A R I B B E A N   S E A

L E S S E R   A N T I L L E S

Aruba
(Neth.)   Curaçao
Pto López   (Neth.)   Bonaire (Neth.)
G.de
Venezuela   Pto Fijo
Willemstad   Islas los Roques
Coro   (Ven.)
S.Juan   I.Blanquilla (Ven.)
Dabajuro   de los Cayos
aracaibo   Riecito   I.la Tortuga
Cabimas   Maiquetía
Cd   Cerrón   S.Felipe   Pto
Ojeda   ▲1990   Cabello
Barquisimeto   Valencia   **Caracas**
Valera   Maracay   Pto
Trujillo   S.Juan   la Cruz
Acarigua   Tinaco   Altagracia
Guanare   de Orituco   **Barcelona**
El Baúl   V.de la Pascua   El Tigre   Maturín
Calabozo   Coloradito

Kingstown   **ST VINCENT**   Bridgetown
The   **BARBADOS**
Grenadines
4
St George's   **GRENADA**

Tobago
Scarborough   **TRINIDAD**
Los Testigos   **AND**
Isla   Pen de Paria   **TOBAGO**
Margarita   Port of Spain
La Asunción   Güiria   Trinidad
Carúpano   G.de   San Fernando
Cumaná   Paria
Carípito   10
Anaco   Tucupita
Tembladon
Barrancas
5
66   60   F

V E N E Z U E L A

65

H   J   K   L
M   N   P   Q
D   E   R
D   F

1:40M

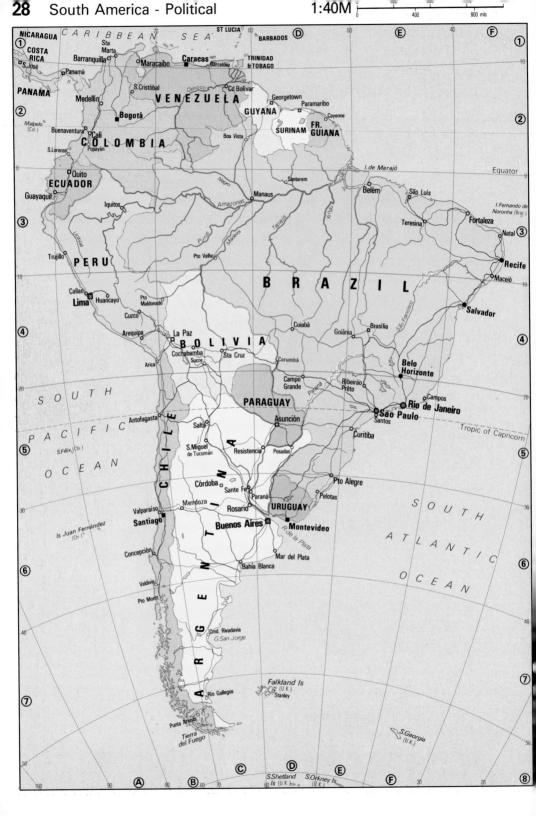

400   800 mls

NICARAGUA
**COSTA
RICA**
S.José
PANAMA
Panamá
Barranquilla
Sta
Marta
Maracaibo
S.Cristóbal
Medellín
Bogotá
Buenaventura
Cali
Popayán
S.Lorenzo
COLOMBIA
Quito
ECUADOR
Guayaquil
Iquitos
Trujillo
PERU
Callao
Lima
Huancayo
Pto
Maldonado
Cuzco
Arequipa
La Paz
BOLIVIA
Cochabamba
Sucre
Sta Cruz
Arica
Antofagasta
S.Félix (Chi.)
Valparaíso
Santiago
Concepción
Valdivia
Pto Montt
Mendoza
CHILE
Salta
S.Miguel
de Tucumán
Córdoba
Sante Fe
Rosario
Buenos Aires
Mar del Plata
Bahía Blanca
ARGENTINA
Cmd. Rivadavia
G.San Jorge
Rio Gallegos
Punta Arenas
Tierra
del Fuego

CARIBBEAN SEA
ST LUCIA
BARBADOS
Caracas
Barcelona
**TRINIDAD
& TOBAGO**
Cd Bolívar
Orinoco
VENEZUELA
Georgetown
Paramaribo
GUYANA
Cayenne
SURINAM
**FR.
GUIANA**
Boa Vista
Negro
Santarem
Manaus
Amazonas
I. de Marajó
Belém
São Luís
*I.Fernando de
Noronha (Braz.)*
Teresina
Fortaleza
Natal
Recife
Maceió
Salvador
Purús
Pto Velho
Madeira
Tapajós
Xingu
B R A Z I L
Cuiabá
Goiânia
Brasília
São Francisco
Belo
Horizonte
Corumbá
Campo
Grande
Campos
PARAGUAY
Paraná
Ribeirão
Prêto
São Paulo
Santos
Rio de Janeiro
Asunción
Curitiba
Resistencia
Posadas
Paraná
Pto Alegre
Pelotas
URUGUAY
R.de la Plata
Montevideo

Equator

S O U T H
P A C I F I C
O C E A N
Is Juan Fernández
(Chi.)

Tropic of Capricorn

S O U T H
A T L A N T I C
O C E A N

Falkland Is
(U.K.)
Stanley

S.Georgia
(U.K.)

S.Shetland
Is (U.K.)
S.Orkney Is.
(U.K.)

Malpelo
(Col.)

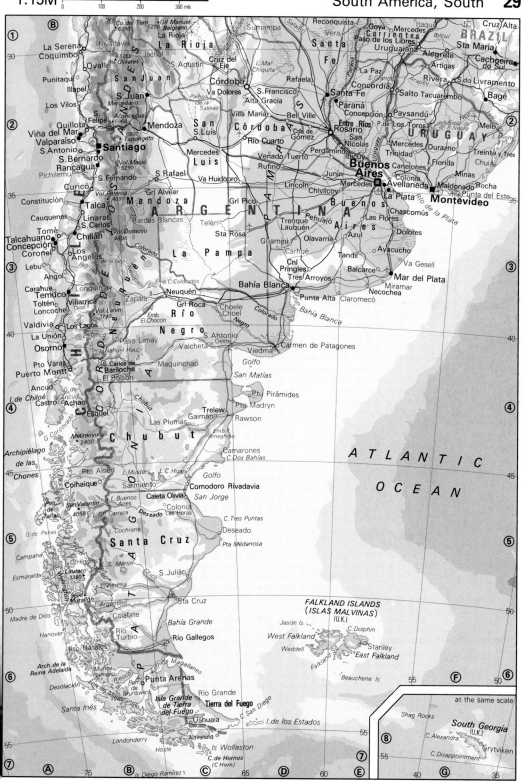

1:15M

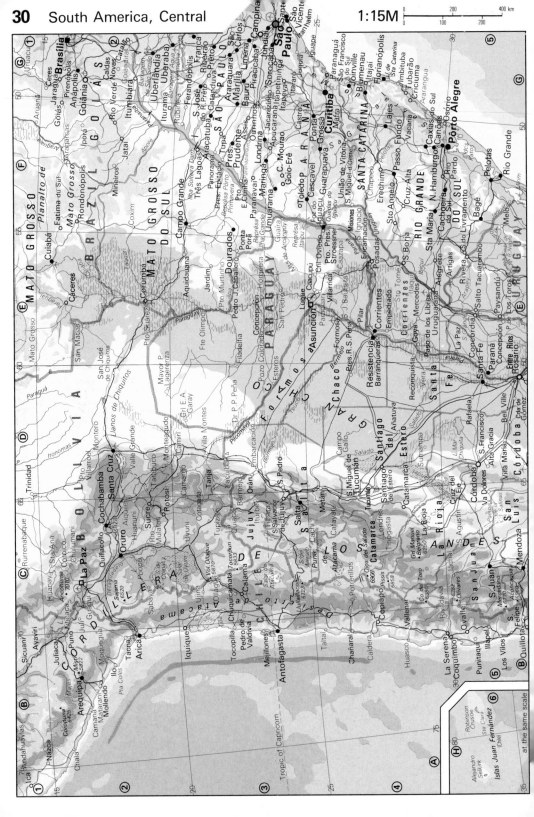

1:15M

200   400 km
100   200

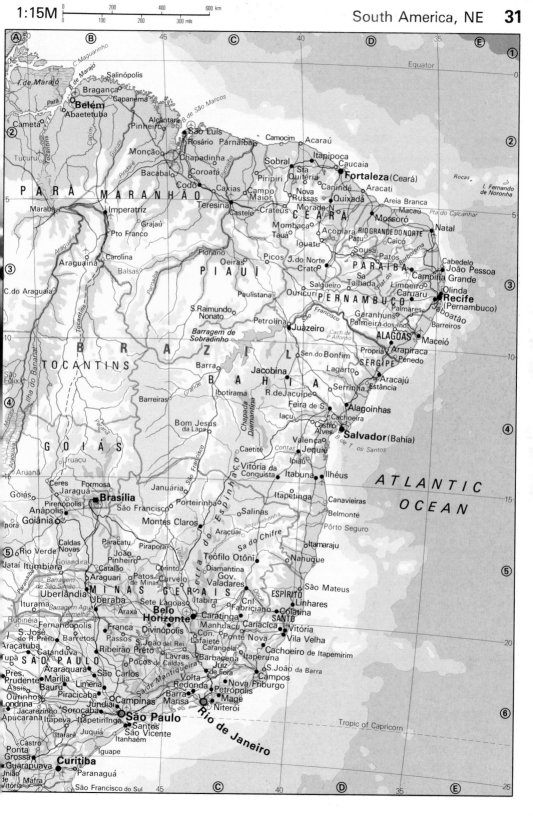

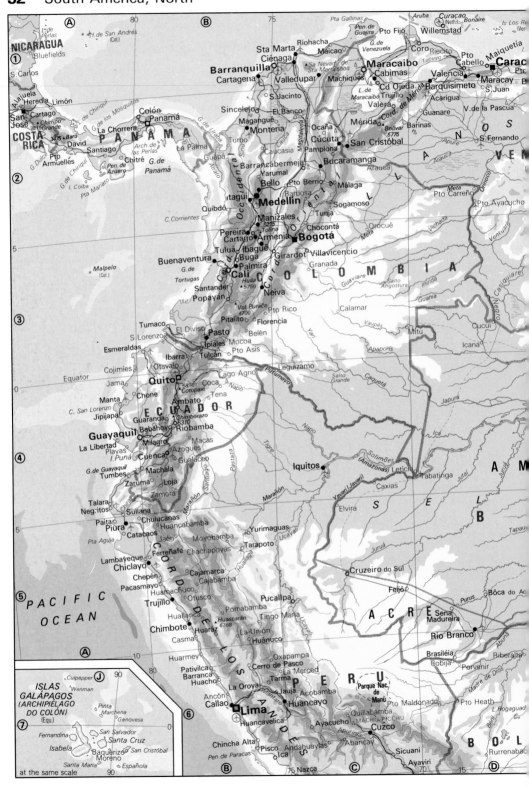

ISLAS
GALÁPAGOS
(ARCHIPIÉLAGO
DO COLÓN)
(Equ.)

at the same scale

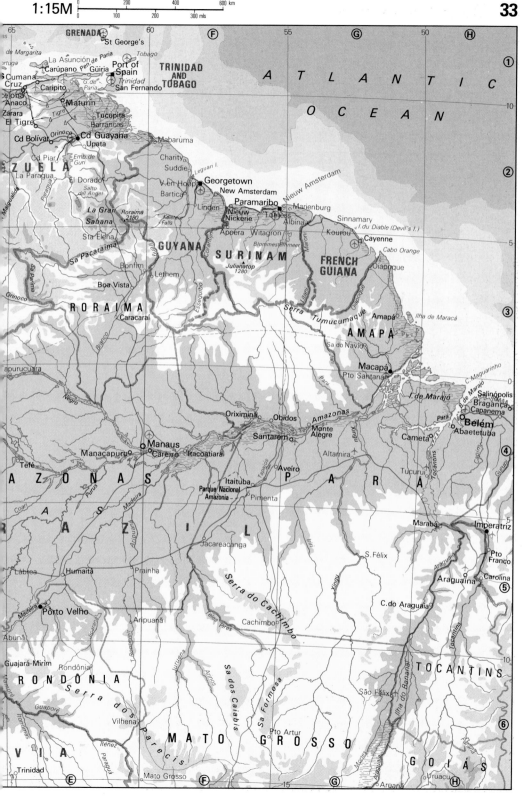

1:15M

0   200   400   600 km

0   100   200   300 mls

GRENADA
St George's
de Margarita
Portuga   La Asunción   Pen. de Paria   Tobago
Carúpano   Güiria
Cumaná   Trinidad   Port of
Cruz   Spain
celona   Caripito   G. de   TRINIDAD
Anaco   Paria   Trinidad   San Fernando   AND
Zarara   Maturín   TOBAGO
El Tigre   Tucupita
Tigre   Barrancas
Cd Bolívar   Orinoco   Mabaruma
Cd Guayana
Upata
ZUELA   Charity
Cd Piar   Emb. de   Suddie
Guri   Leguan I.
La Paragua   El Dorado   V-en Hoop   Georgetown
Paragua   Salto   Bartica   New Amsterdam
del Angel   Linden   Paramaribo
La Gran   Roraima   Nieuw Amsterdam
Sabana   2180   Nieuw   Marienburg
Kaieteur   Nickerie   Totness   Sinnamary
Sta Elena   Falls   Albina   I. du Diable (Devil's I.)
Apoera   Witagron   Kourou   Cayenne
Sa Pacaraima   Bonfim   GUYANA   SURINAM   Cabo Orange
Julianatop   Blommesteinmeer   Oiapoque
Sa Parima   Lethem   1280   FRENCH
Orinoco   GUIANA
RORAIMA   Serra Tumucumaque   Amapá
Caracaraí   AMAPÁ   Ilha de Maracá
apurucuara   Sa do Navio
Macapá   C. Maguarinho
Negro   Branco   Pto Santana   0
I. de Marajó   Salinópolis
Bragança
Oriximiná   Obidos   Amazonas   Pará   Capanema
Manaus   Santarém   Monte   Cametá   Belém
Manacapuru   Careiro   Alegre   Abaetetuba
Tefé   Itacoatiara   Altamira   Tucuruí
A   Aveiro   P   A   R   Á
Z   Purus   Itaituba   Tapajós   Pimenta
O   Parque Nacional   Xingu
Madeira   Amazônia
N   Coari   B   R   A   Z   I   L   Marabá
A   Jacareacanga   Imperatriz
S   S.Félix   Pto
Labrea   Humaitá   Prainha   Franco
Madeira   Araguaína   Carolina
Pôrto Velho   Aripuanã   Serra do Cachimbo   Araguaia
Abunã   Cachimbo   C. do Araguaia   TOCANTINS
Guajará-Mirim   Rondônia   Sa dos Caiabis
RONDÔNIA   Serra dos Parecis   Sa Formosa
Guaporé   São Félix
VIA   Vilhena   MATO   Pto Artur
Trinidad   GROSSO   GOIÁS
Mato Grosso   Aruanã
E   F   G   H

65   60   F   55   G   50   H
①
ATLANTIC   10
OCEAN
②

③

④

⑤

⑥

ANOTLANTIC

OCEAN

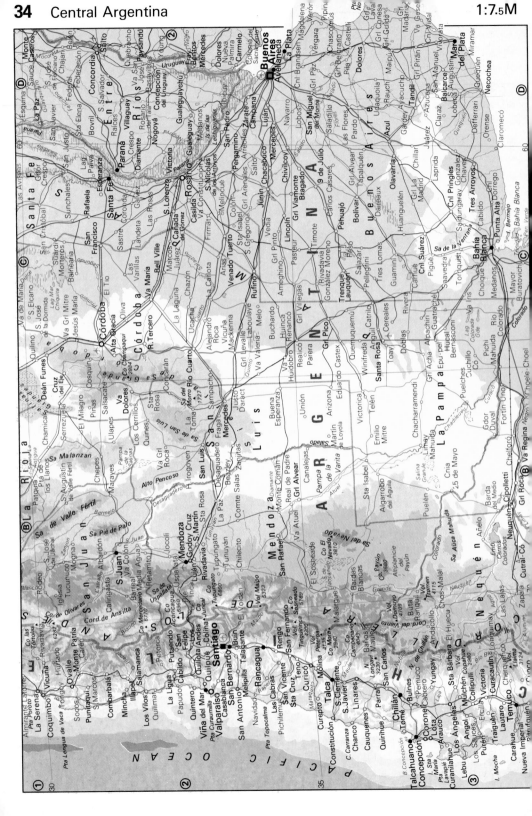

100   200   300 km
0   50   100   150 mils

Tropic of Capricorn

ATLANTIC OCEAN

Rio de Janeiro
Belo Horizonte
São Paulo
Brasília
DISTRITO FEDERAL

ESPÍRITO SANTO
MINAS GERAIS
SÃO PAULO

Vitória · Vila Velha · Colatina · Linhares
Conceição da Barra · São Mateus
Campos · Macaé · Cabo Frio
Niterói · Petrópolis · Nova Friburgo · Teresópolis
Juiz de Fora · Barbacena · Volta Redonda
Montes Claros · Teófilo Otóni · Governador Valadares
Uberaba · Uberlândia · Araguari · Patos de Minas
Ribeirão Prêto · Franca · Campinas · Sorocaba
Santos · São Vicente · Jundiaí · Taubaté
Anápolis · Goiânia
Presidente Prudente · Marília · Bauru · Araçatuba
Londrina · Maringá · Apucarana

ARCTIC OCEAN

Greenland (Den.)

ICELAND

Jan Mayen (Nor.)

NORWEGIAN SEA

FINLAND

RUSSIAN FEDERATION

Sankt-Peterburg (Leningrad)

Murmansk

Arkhangel'sk

O. Kolguyev

O. Onezhskoye Oz.

Ladozhskoye Oz.

Vyborg

Oulu

Tampere

Helsinki

Vaasa

Åland

ESTONIA

Tallinn

LATVIA

Riga

LITHUANIA

Vilnius

BELARUS (BELORUSSIA)

Minsk

Kaliningrad RUS. FED.

Gdansk

Baltic Sea

N O R W A Y

S W E D E N

Narvik

Vesterålen

Lofoten

Sundsvall

Umeå

Gulf of Bothnia

Stockholm

Gotland

Öland

Norrköping

Vänern

Göteborg

Vättern

Jönköping

Bornholm

Rostock

Trondheim

Oslo

Bergen

Stavanger

Ålborg

DENMARK

København

Malmö

Hamburg

NORTH SEA

Shetland

Færøyar (Den.)

Orkney

Aberdeen

Newcastle

Edinburgh

Glasgow

Manchester

Liverpool

Birmingham

UNITED KINGDOM OF GREAT BRITAIN AND NORTHERN IRELAND

Belfast

Dublin

IRELAND

Cork

Arctic Circle

ATLANTIC OCEAN

Reykjavik

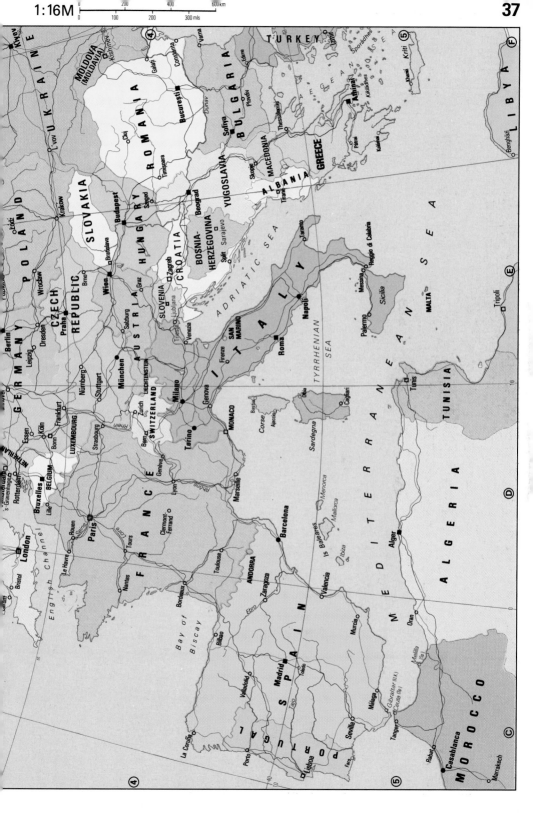

200   400   600 km
100   200   300 mls

TURKEY

MOLDOVA
(MOLDAVIA)
Kishinev
Galati
Constanta
Varna
Edirne
Izmir
Sporádhes
Kriti
Khaniá

U K R A I N E
L'vov
Kiyev

P O L A N D
Kraków
Wroclaw

R O M A N I A
Cluj
Timisoara
Bucuresti
Dunav

B U L G A R I A
Sofiya
Plovdiv

Beograd
YUGOSLAVIA
MACEDONIA
Skopje

G R E E C E
Thessaloníki
ALBANIA
Tiranë
Kérkira
Pátrai
Kalamai
Athínai

LIBYA
Benghazi

SLOVAKIA
Budapest
Bratislava
Szeged

H U N G A R Y
Graz

CROATIA
Zagreb
BOSNIA-
HERZEGOVINA
Sarajevo
Split

A D R I A T I C S E A

A E G E A N

S E A

SLOVENIA
Ljubljana

CZECH
REPUBLIC
Praha
Brno

AUSTRIA
Wien
Salzburg

Taranto

Reggio di Calabria
Messina
Sicilia
Palermo

M E D I T E R R A N E A N S E A

GERMANY
Berlin
Dresden
Leipzig
Nürnberg
Stuttgart
München
Frankfurt
Köln
Essen
Bonn

NETHERLANDS
's Gravenhage
Rotterdam

LUXEMBOURG
Strasbourg

BELGIUM
Bruxelles
Lille

London
Bristol
Cardiff

English Channel
Le Havre
Rouen

F R A N C E
Paris
Tours
Nantes
Clermont-
Ferrand
Lyon
Bordeaux
Toulouse
Marseille

LIECHTENSTEIN
SWITZERLAND
Zürich
Bern
Genève

Torino
Milano
Genova
MONACO

I T A L Y
Trieste
Venezia
Firenze
SAN
MARINO
Roma
Napoli

TYRRHENIAN
SEA

Corse
Bastia
Ajaccio
Sardegna
Cagliari
Olbia

MALTA

Tunis
TUNISIA
Tripoli

A L G E R I A
Alger
Oran

Bay of
Biscay

ANDORRA
Zaragoza
Barcelona

Balears
Is
Menorca
Mallorca
Ibiza
Valencia
Murcia

S P A I N
Madrid
Valladolid
Bilbao
Toledo

P O R T U G A L
Lisboa
Porto
La Coruña
Faro
Sevilla
Málaga

Gibraltar (U.K.)
Ceuta (Sp.)
Tánger
Melilla (Sp.)

M O R O C C O
Casablanca
Rabat
Marrakech

Ebro
Tajo

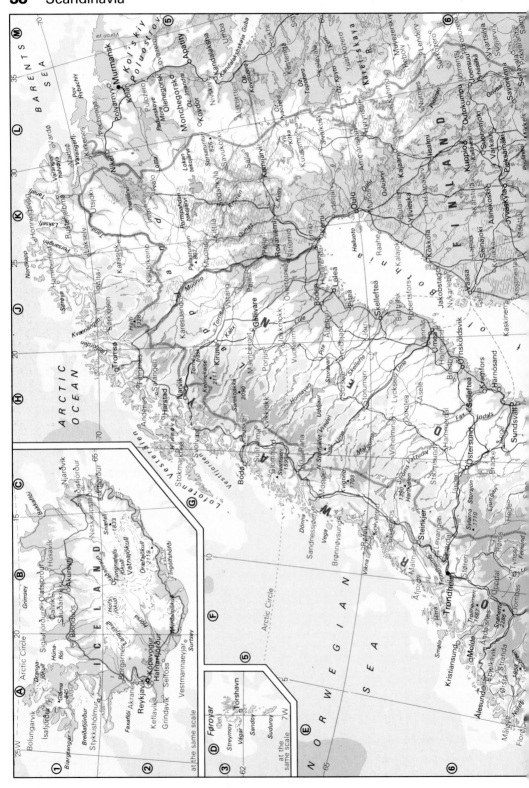

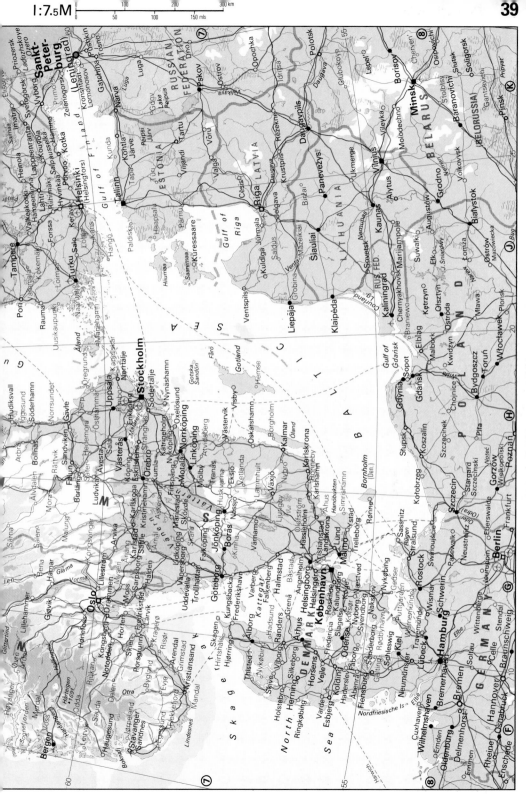

1:5M

0   50   100 mls

NORWAY

Nordhordland
Bergen
Sotra
Sunnhordland
Haugesund
Benfjo
Stord
Skolde
Leirvik
Karmø
Daler

Herma Ness
Isbister
St Magnus B.
Unst
Fetlar
Whalsay
Lerwick
Foula
Shetland

NORTH SEA

Fair Isle
Sumburgh Hd

Westray
Rousay
Sanday
Stronsay
Kirkwall
Stromness
Scapa Flow
Hoy
Orkney
Duncansby Hd

Sule Skerry
Stack Skerry
Sule Stack
N. Rona
Sula Sgeir

C. Wrath
Thurso
Wick
Helmsdale
Dornoch Firth
Ben Hope
927
Ben More
Assynt
998

Burt of Lewis
Stornoway
Lewis
Flannan Is
Harris
N. Uist
S. Uist
Barra
St Kilda

The Minch
Outer Hebrides

Ullapool
Dingwall
Inverness
L. Ness
Fort Augustus
Moray Firth
Elgin
Spey
Banff
Fraserburgh
Peterhead
Buchan Ness
Aberdeen
Dee
Stonehaven
Ben Macdui
1309
Braemar
Montrose
Arbroath
Pitlochry
Don
Firth of Tay
St Andrews
Perth
Kirkcaldy
Firth of Forth
Edinburgh
Berwick-upon-Tweed
St Abbs Hd
Galashiels
Hawick
Moffat
White Coomb
822
Nith
Dumfries
Merrick
843
Ayr
Kilmarnock
Irvine
Arran
F. of Clyde
Girvan
Stranraer
Larne
Belfast

Portree
Kyle of Lochalsh
Skye
Mallaig
Fort William
Ben Nevis
1344
Rum
Mull
Coll
Tiree
F. of Lorn
Oban
L. Awe
Jura
Colonsay
Islay
Campbeltown
Rathlin I.

SCOTLAND
GRAMPIAN MTS
L. Lomond
Stirling
Glasgow
Motherwell
Paisley
Greenock
Clyde

N IRELAND
Coleraine
Ballymena
Omagh
L. Neagh
Ballycastle
Londonderry
L. Foyle
Tory I.
Malin Hd
Donegal
Errigal
752
Rossan Pt
Aran I.

Newcastle upon Tyne
S. Shields
Gateshead
Sunderland
Blyth
Morpeth
Alnwick
Holy I.
Cheviot Hills
Carlisle
Solway Firth
Kirkcudbright
Durham
Hartlepool
Penn

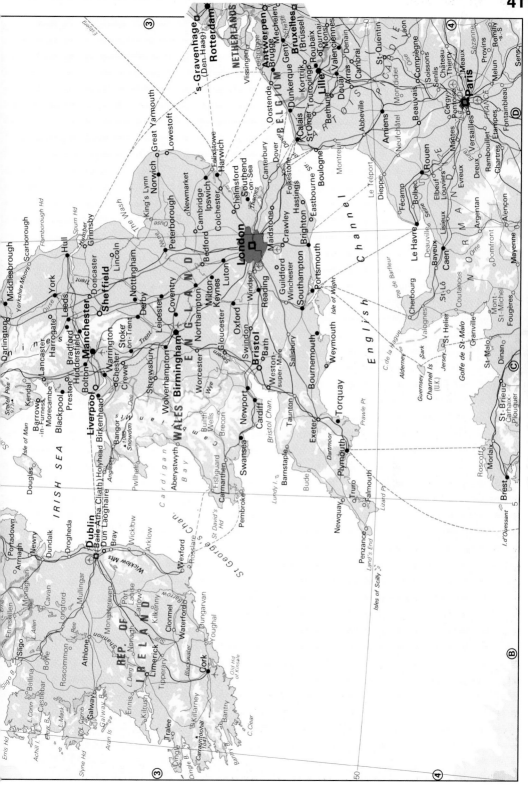

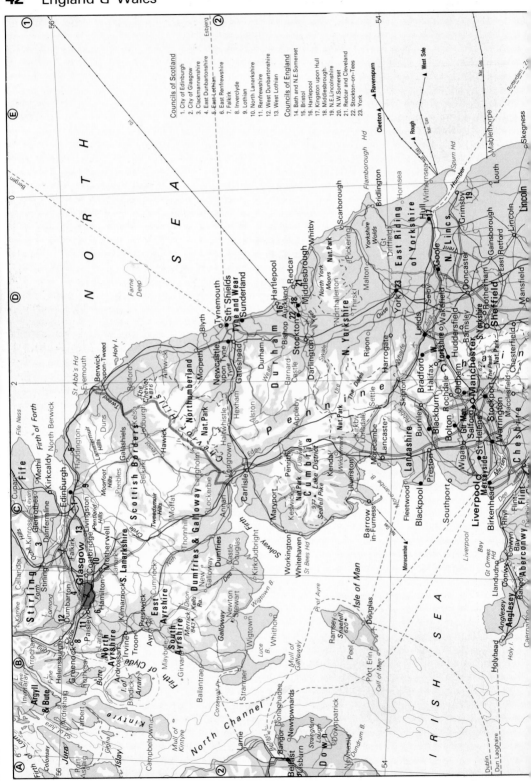

Councils of Scotland
1. City of Edinburgh
2. City of Glasgow
3. Clackmannanshire
4. East Dunbartonshire
5. East Lothian
6. East Renfrewshire
7. Falkirk
8. Inverclyde
9. Lothian
10. North Lanarkshire
11. Renfrewshire
12. West Dunbartonshire
13. West Lothian

Councils of England
14. Bath and N.E. Somerset
15. Bristol
16. Hartlepool
17. Kingston upon Hull
18. Middlesbrough.
19. N.E. Lincolnshire
20. N.W. Somerset
21. Redcar and Cleveland
22. Stockton-on-Tees
23. York

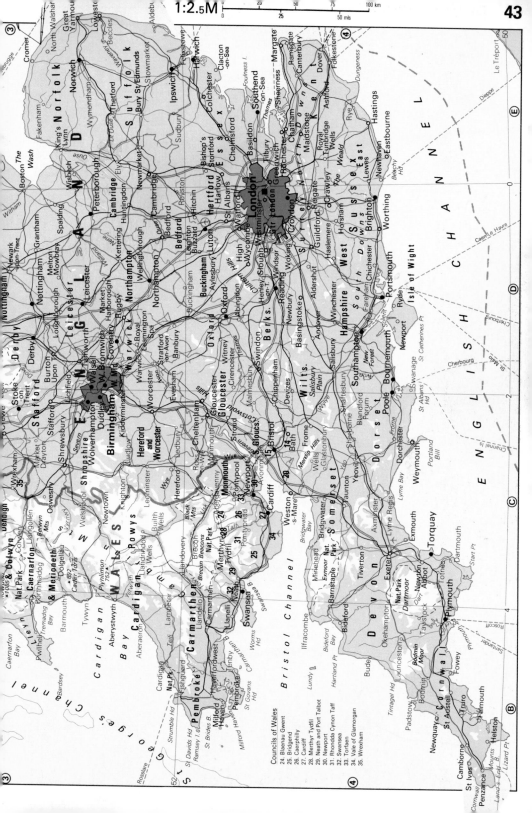

1:2.5M

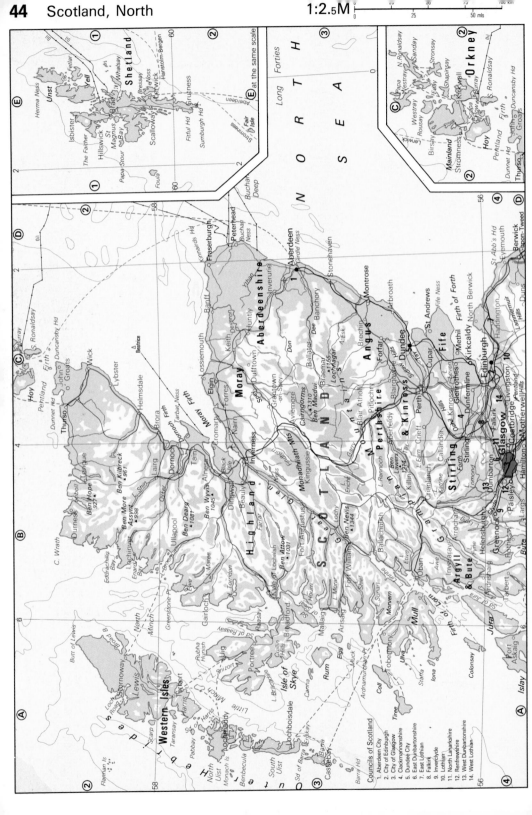

Councils of Scotland
1. Aberdeen City
2. City of Edinburgh
3. City of Glasgow
4. Clackmannanshire
5. Dundee City
6. East Dunbartonshire
7. East Lothian
8. Falkirk
9. Inverclyde
10. Lothian
11. North Lanarkshire
12. Renfrewshire
13. West Dunbartonshire
14. West Lothian

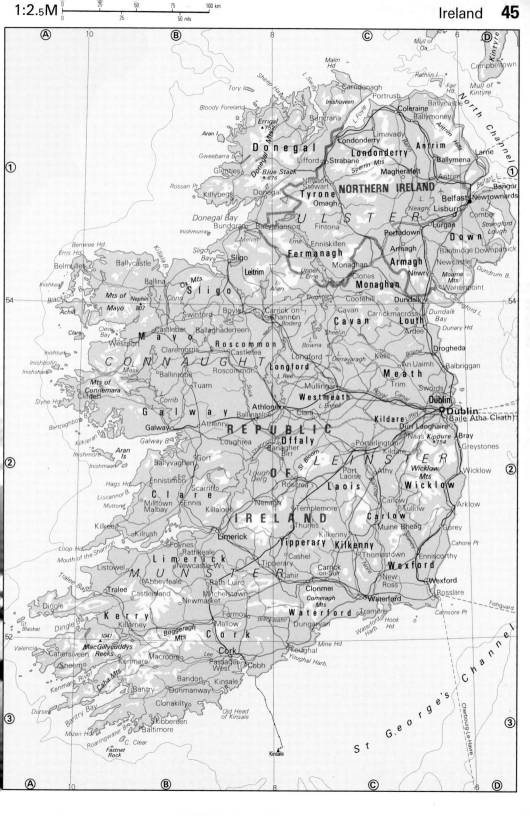

1:2.5M

1:2.5M

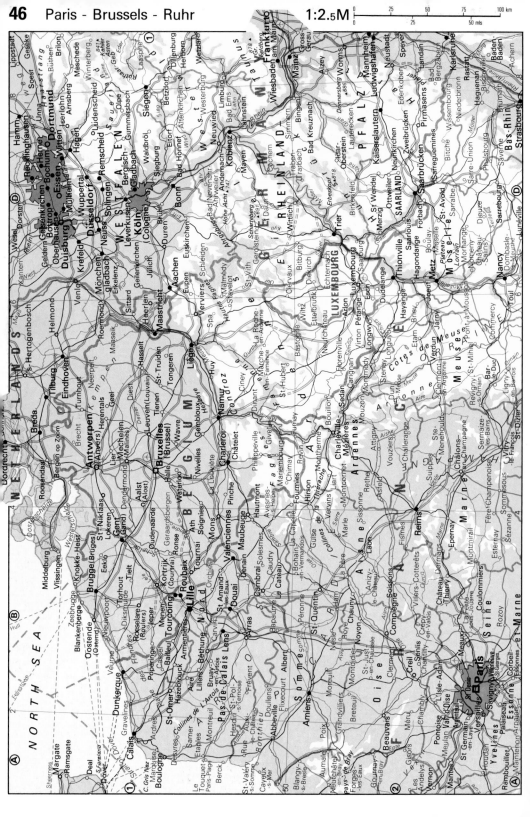

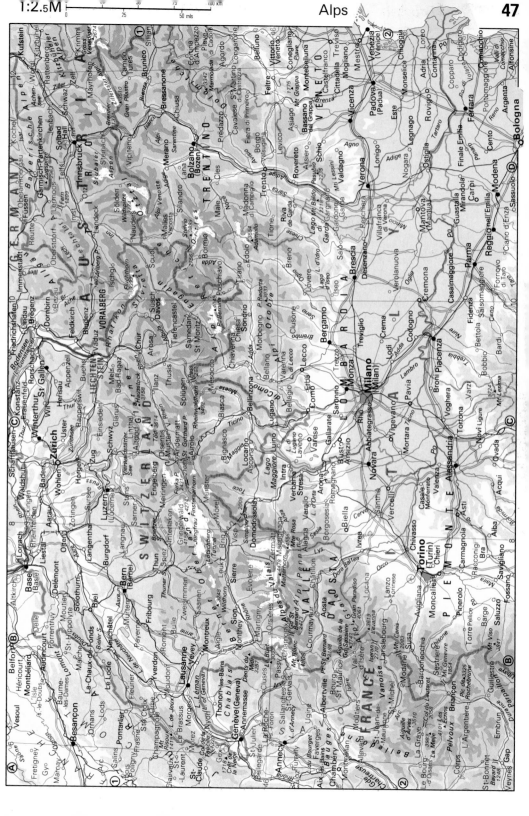

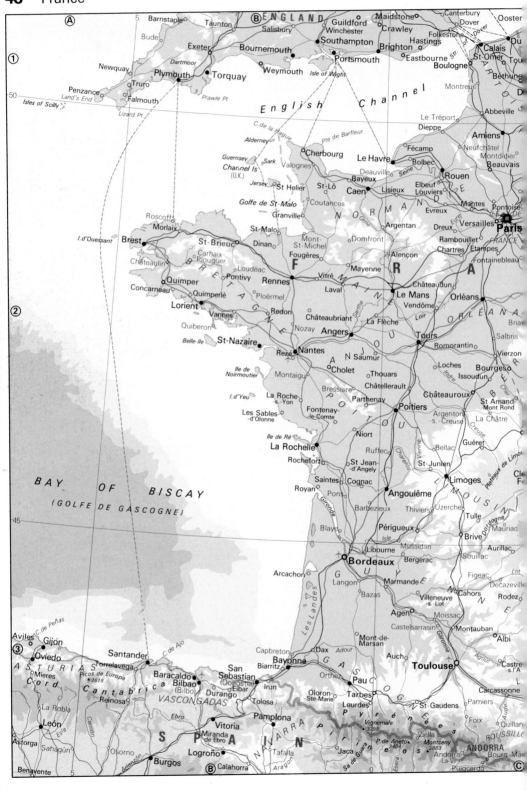

48 France

A ① B ② ③

ENGLAND

Barnstaple
Bude
Taunton
Salisbury
Guildford
Winchester
Maidstone
Crawley
Canterbury
Dover
Ooster
Newquay
Exeter
Bournemouth
Southampton
Brighton
Hastings
Folkestone
Calais
St-Omer
Tou
Dartmoor
Plymouth
Torquay
Weymouth
Portsmouth
Eastbourne
Boulogne
Béthune
D
Penzance
Truro
Isle of Wight
Montreuil
Lizard Pt
Falmouth
Prawle Pt
Abbeville
Isles of Scilly

English Channel

50
Land's End

C. de la Hague
Pte de Barfleur
Le Tréport
Dieppe
Amiens
Alderney
Cherbourg
Le Havre
Fécamp
Neufchâtel
Montdidier
Beauvais
Guernsey
Sark
Valognes
Deauville
Bolbec
Rouen
Channel Is
(U.K.)
St Hélier
St-Lô
Bayeux
Seine
Elbeuf
Louviers
Jersey
Caen
Lisieux
Mantes
Golfe de St-Malo
Coutances
Evreux
Versailles
Pontoise
Paris
Granville
Argentan
Dreux
FRANCE
Roscoff
Mont-
St-Michel
Domfront
Rambouillet
Chartres
Etampes
Fontainebleau
Morlaix
St-Malo
Dinan
Fougères
Alençon
R
A
Brest
St-Brieuc
Mayenne
Châteaudun
Châteaulin
Carhaix-
Plouguer
Loudéac
Pontivy
Rennes
Vitré
Le Mans
Orléans
Quimper
Ploërmel
Laval
Vendôme
ORLÉANA
Concarneau
Quimperlé
Redon
Châteaubriant
La Flèche
Tours
Romorantin
Bria
Lorient
Vannes
Nozay
Angers
Loir
Loches
Bourges
Salbris
Vierzon
Quiberon
Belle-Ile
St-Nazaire
Rezé
Nantes
Saumur
Cholet
Thouars
Châtellerault
Châteauroux
St Amand-
Mont Rond
Issoudun
La Châtre
B
Ile de
Noirmoutier
Montaigu
Bressuire
Parthenay
Poitiers
Argenton
-s.-Creuse
Creuse
I.d'Yeu
La Roche-
-s.-Yon
Fontenay-
le-Comte
Niort
Bellac
Guéret
Les Sables-
d'Olonne
Ile de Ré
La Rochelle
Ruffec
St Jean-
d'Angely
St-Junien
Limoges
Cl
F
Rochefort
Cognac
Angoulême
Uzerche
Tulle
Royan
Pons
Blaye
Barbezieux
Thiviers
Brive
Aurillac
Souillac
Périgueux
Mussidan
Libourne
Bergerac
Figeac
Décazevill
Bordeaux
Marmande
Cahors
Rodez
Arcachon
Langon
Bazas
Villeneuve
-s.-Lot
Agen
Moissac
Albi
Castelsarrasin
Montauban
Mont-de-
Marsan
Auch
Toulouse
Castre
-s.l'A
Capbreton
Dax
Adour
Bayonne
Biarritz
Pau
Tarbes
Carcassonne
Orthez
Oloron-
Ste-Marie
Lourdes
St-Gaudens
Pamiers
Irun
Tolosa
Vignemale
Foix
Quillan
Pamplona
Jaca
P. de Aneto
Viella
ANDORRA
Andorra-
-La-V.
ROUSSILLO
Bourg-Ma

BAY OF BISCAY
(GOLFE DE GASCOGNE)

45

ASTURIAS
Aviles
Gijón
Oviedo
Santander
C. de Ajo
San
Sebastian
(Donostia)
Mieres
Torrelavega
Baracaldo
Bilbao
(Bilbo)
Eibar
Durango
Reinosa
VASCONGADAS
León
La Robla
Picos de Europa
2615
Cord
Cantabrica
S P A I N
Vitoria
NAVARRA
Burgos
Benavente
Astorga
Sahagún
Osorno
Logroño
Calahorra
Tafalla
Aragón

C

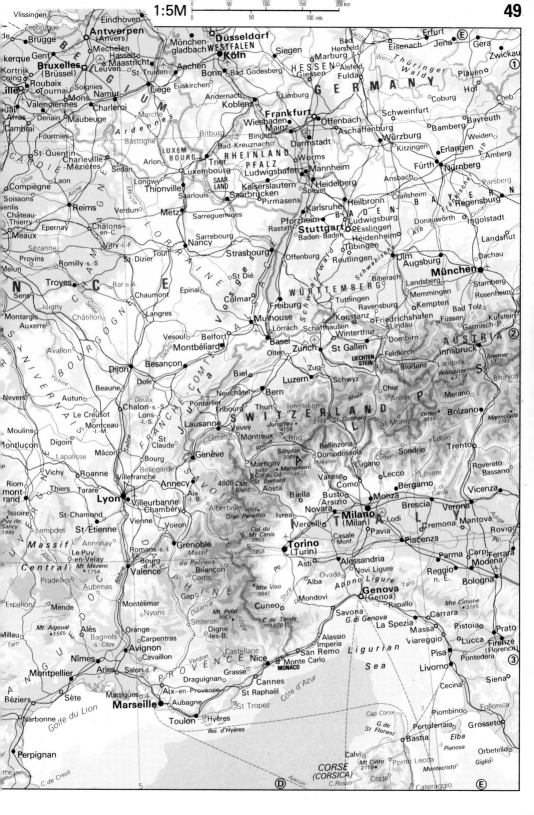

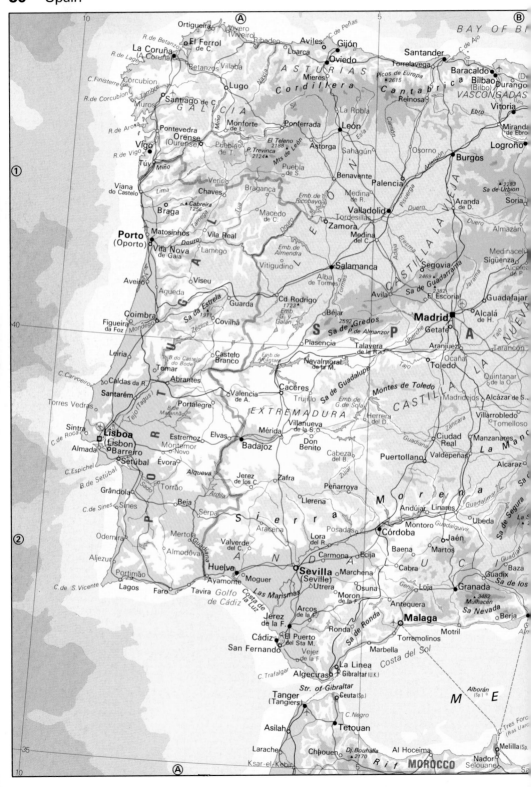

30
100
150
200 km
50
100 mls

CAY
Capbreton
Mont-de-Marsin
Dax
Auch
Albi
C
Montpellier
Nîmes
Arles
Salon-d.-P.
D
San
Biarritz
Bayonne
Adour
Toulouse
Garonne
Castres-s.l'A
Martigues
Aix-en-Provence
Aubagne
sebastian
Orthez
Pau
Tarn
Agout
Béziers
Sète
Marseille
bar
Irun
Oloron-Ste-Marie
Tarbes
St-Gaudens
Pamiers
Carcassonne
Narbonne
Golfe du Lion
Toulon
Hyères
Tolosa
Lourdes
Foix
Aude
Quillan
Golfe du Lion
Pamplona
Pyrénées
Vignemale
3298
Viella
o Vielha
Monteny
2883
ANDORRA
ROUSSILLON
Perpignan
NAVARRA
Jaca
P. de Aneto
3404
Andorra-
La-V.
Bourg-Madame
C. de Creus
Tafalla
Aragón
Sa de Guara
Puigcerdá
Figueras
(Figueres)
Costa Brava
Calahorra
Huesca
Sa del Codi
Ter
Alfaro
Barbastro
Segre
Vich
(Vic)
Gerona
(Girona)
Tarazona
CATALUÑA
San Feliu de G.
Alagón
Lérida
(Lleida)
Sabadell
Granollers
Tudela
(Tutera)
Zaragoza
Cinca
Tarrasa
Mataró
Badalona
Costa Brava
Calatayud
Emb. de
Mequinenza
Valls
Barcelona
Daroca
Caspe
Reus
Villanueva-y-G.
(Vilanova i la Geltrú)
Monreal
del C.
ARAGÓN
Ebro
Tarragona
Sa de Albarracín
Sa de Gudar
Alcañiz
Golfo
de
San Jorge
Jiloca
Guadalope
Tortosa
C. de Tortosa
Amposta
Teruel
2019
Peñarroya
Vinaroz
Benicarló
de Cuenca
Sarrión
Torreblanca
Cuenca
N
Castellon de la P.
Is Columbretes
40
C. de Caballeria
Menorca
C. Formentor
Ciudadela
Mahón
Emb. de
Alarcón
Segorbe
Villarreal
C. Binibeca
Motilla
del P.
Utiel
Turia
Sagunto
Golfo de
Mallorca
1445
Mayor
Alcudia
Capdepera
La Roda
Cabriel
VALENCIA
VALENCIA
Palma
de Mallorca
Manacor
Albacete
Júcar
Alcira
Játiva
Valencia
Santañy
C. de Salinas
Cabrera
Almansa
Gandia
Ibiza
Onteniente
Denia
ISLAS BALEARES
caraz
Villena
Alcoy
C. de la Nao
S. Antonio
Abad
Ibiza
(BALEARIC ISLANDS)
(Sp.)
Hellín
Benidorm
Elda
MURCIA
Segura
Cieza
Villena
Alicante
Formentera
Caravaca
Elche
Orihuela
Totana
Murcia
Costa Blanca
Lorca
C. de Palos
Cartagena
Hüercal
Overa
G. de
Mazarrón
Aguilas
bres
Vera
meria
C. de Gata
Bejaia
(Bougie)
Dellys
Alger
(Algiers)
Harrach
Cherchell
Tizi Ouzou
Djurdjura
Kherrata
Soummam
Boufarik
Ténès
Blida
Bouira
Beni
Mansour
Sétif
Miliana
Médéa
Bir
Rabalou
Isser
Bj bou
Arréridj
Khemis
Bosquet
Dahra
Ech Cheliff
Cheliff
M'Sila
Mts du Hodna
Arzew
C. Ferrat
Massif de l'Ouarsenis
Ksar El
Boukhari
Spisseb
Mostaganem
A
L
G
E
R
I
A
Chott
el Hodna
Barika
Mers el Kebir
Sig
Relizane
Mina
Aïn
Oussera
Aïn el
Hadjel
Oran
O Tlélat
Mohammadia
Mascara
Ouassel
Bou Saâda
Beni-Saf
Aïn
Témouchent
Tiaret
Plat. du Sersou
Z. Chergui
Monts des
Ouled Nail
hazaouet
Sidi-bel-Abbés
Frenda
C
M E D I T E R R A N E A N   S E A
35
5
1
2
3

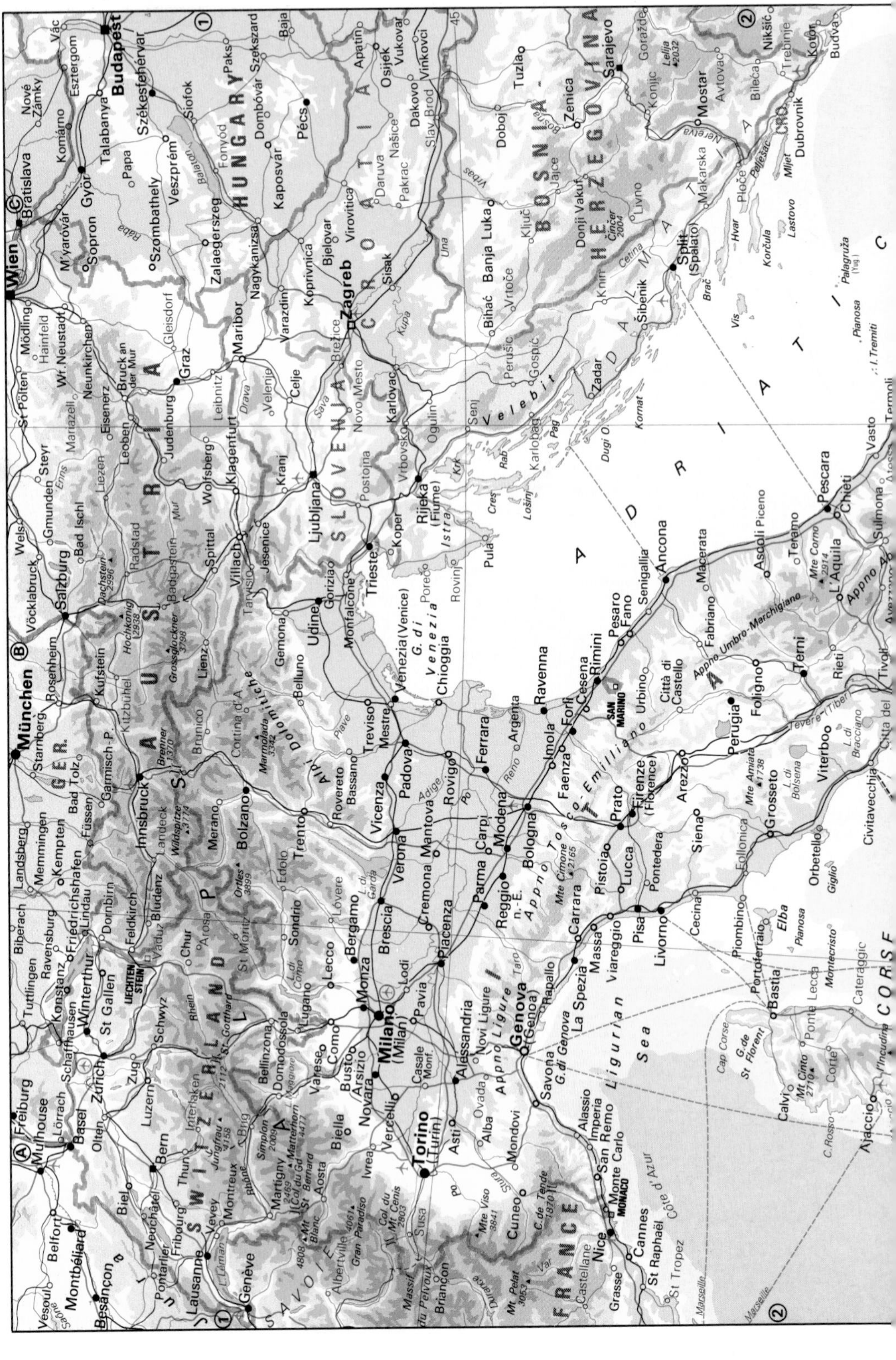

A map of Italy and surrounding regions (northern Italy, the Adriatic, and neighbouring countries).

Countries and regions: HUNGARY, CROATIA, BOSNIA-HERZEGOVINA, SLOVENIA, AUSTRIA, GER., SWITZERLAND, FRANCE, ITALY, MONACO, LIECHTENSTEIN, CORSE

Selected cities and places:

Budapest, Wien, Bratislava, Vác, Esztergom, Komárno, Nové Zámky, Mödling, Wr. Neustadt, Hainfeld, Neunkirchen, St. Pölten, Mariazell, Bruck an der Mur, Leoben, Judenburg, Graz, Leibnitz, Wolfsberg, Klagenfurt, Villach, Spittal, Győr, Talabanya, Mór, Székesfehérvár, Siófok, Papa, Veszprém, Fonyód, Balaton, Zalaegerszeg, Nagykanizsa, Kaposvár, Pécs, Baja, Szekszárd, Dombóvár, Osijek, Vukovar, Apatin, Vinkovci, Dakowo, Daruva, Našice, Pakrac, Sisak, Bjelovar, Virovitica, Zagreb, Varazdin, Brezice, Koprivnica, Krapina, Sava, Novo Mesto, Karlovac, Una, Bihać, Banja Luka, Doboj, Tuzla, Zenica, Sarajevo, Goražde, Foča, Konjic, Mostar, Avtovac, Bileća, Nikšić, Trebinje, Kotor, Budva, Dubrovnik, Makarska, Ploče, Split (Spalato), Hvar, Korčula, Lastovo, Mljet, Brač, Šibenik, Zadar, Pag, Rab, Senj, Ogulin, Gospić, Otočac, Vrbovsko, Rijeka (Fiume), Koper, Trieste, Gorizia, Monfalcone, Pula, Rovinj, Poreč, Cres, Lošinj, Velebit, Dugi, Kornat, Pianosa, Tremiti, Pescara, Chieti, L'Aquila, Teramo, Ascoli Piceno, Ancona, Senigallia, Fano, Pesaro, Rimini, Macerata, Fabriano, Città di Castello, Urbino, Perugia, Foligno, Terni, Rieti, Tivoli, Viterbo, Spoleto, Arezzo, Siena, Firenze (Florence), Prato, Pistoia, Lucca, Pisa, Livorno, Grosseto, Orbetello, Elba, Piombino, Cecina, Pontedera, Empoli, Bologna, Modena, Parma, Reggio n.E., Ferrara, Ravenna, Forlì, Cesena, Faenza, Imola, Argenta, Rovigo, Padova, Venezia (Venice), Mestre, Treviso, Vicenza, Verona, Mantova, Cremona, Piacenza, Brescia, Bergamo, Lecco, Como, Monza, Milano (Milan), Pavia, Lodi, Alessandria, Novara, Vercelli, Biella, Ivrea, Torino (Turin), Asti, Cuneo, Mondovi, Alba, Ovada, Savona, Genova (Genoa), Rapallo, La Spezia, Massa, Carrara, Viareggio, Imperia, Alassio, San Remo, Monte Carlo, MONACO, Nice, Cannes, Antibes, St. Raphaël, St. Tropez, Grasse, Marseille, Bastia, Calvi, Ajaccio, Corte, Bastelica, Varese, Novi Ligure, Carpi, Belluno, Cortina d'A., Bolzano, Merano, Trento, Bressanone, Bruneck, Rovereto, Bassano, Udine, Gemona, Tolmezzo, Innsbruck, Kufstein, Rosenheim, München, Starnberg, Garmisch-P., Bad Tölz, Füssen, Kempten, Memmingen, Landsberg, Augsburg, Biberach, Ravensburg, Friedrichshafen, Lindau, Bregenz, Dornbirn, Feldkirch, Vaduz, Chur, St. Moritz, St. Gallen, Winterthur, Zürich, Schaffhausen, Konstanz, Singen, Tuttlingen, Freiburg, Lörrach, Mulhouse, Basel, Olten, Luzern, Zug, Schwyz, Interlaken, Thun, Bern, Biel, Neuchâtel, Fribourg, Lausanne, Montreux, Genève, Sion, Brig, Aosta, Martigny, Albertville, Briançon, Gap, Susa

Seas and water: G. di Venezia, ADRIATIC SEA, Ligurian Sea, G. di Genova, L. di Como, L. di Garda, L. Maggiore, L. di Bolsena, L. di Bracciano, Lago Trasimeno

Mountains (selected with heights): Mt. Blanc 4808, Matterhorn 4477, Jungfrau 4158, Gran Paradiso 4061, Mte Viso 3841, Mte Rosa 4638, Mt Cenis 3610, Ortles 3905, Marmolada 3342, Grossglockner 3798, Hochkönig 2938, Dachstein 2996, Mte Cimone 2165, Mte Amiata 1738, Mte Corno 2914, Appennino, Dolomiti (Alpi), Mte Cinto 2710, Gotthard

Grid references: (1), (2), (A), (B), (C)

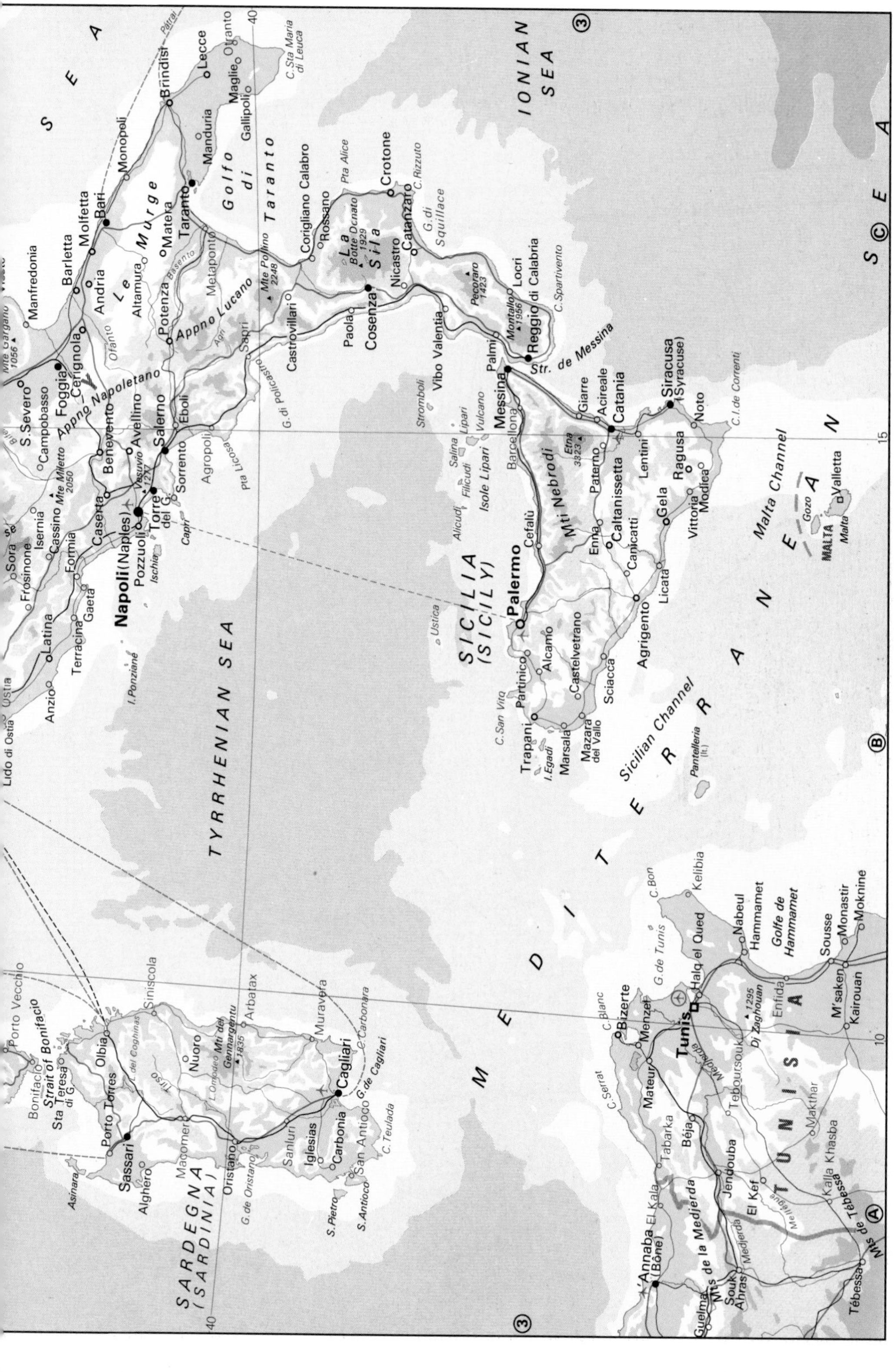

200 km
50
100 mls
40

IONIAN SEA

③

A DRIATIC SEA

Brindisi
Lecce
Maglie
Otranto
Monopoli
C. Sta Maria di Leuca
Gallipolio
Manduria
Bari
Molfetta
Barletta
Le Murge
Taranto
Golfo di Taranto
Andria
Altamura
Matera
Cerignola
Foggia
Manfredonia
Mte Gargano 1056
S. Severo
Potenza
Appno Lucano
Metaponto
Basento
Agri
Sinni
Mte Pollino 2248
Castrovillari
Corigliano Calabro
Rossano
Campobasso
Benevento
Appno Napoletano
Mte Miletto 2050
Caserta
Avellino
Salerno
Sorrento
Eboli
Agropoli
Sapri
G. di Policastro
Paola
Cosenza
La Sila
Botte Donato 1929
Nicastro
Catanzaro
G. di Squillace
C. Rizzuto
Crotone
Pra Alice
Isernia
Cassino
Formia
Torre del G.
Pozzuoli
Napoli (Naples)
Vesuvio 1277
Capri
Ischia
I. Ponziane
Sora
Frosinone
Latina
Terracina
Gaeta
Anzio
Lido di Ostia
Ustica
C. San Vito
Trapani
I. Egadi
Marsala
Mazara del Vallo
Castelvetrano
Sciacca
Agrigento
SICILIA (SICILY)
Alcamo
Partinico
Palermo
Cefalù
Mti Nebrodi
Etna 3323 a
Paterno
Enna
Caltanissetta
Caltanissetta
Canicatti
Licata
Gela
Vittoria
Ragusa
Modica
Noto
Siracusa (Syracuse)
Catania
Acireale
Giarre
Lentini
Barcellona
Messina
Reggio di Calabria
Str. de Messina
Palmi
Locri
Montalto 1956
C. Spartivento
Pecoraro 1423
Vibo Valentia
Stromboli
Salina
Lipari
Filicudi
Vulcano
Isole Lipari
Alicudi
Usica
TYRRHENIAN SEA

C. de Correnti
Malta Channel
Gozo
MALTA
Valletta
Malta
MEDITERRANEAN SEA
Pantelleria (It.)
Sicilian Channel

③
B
A

SARDEGNA (SARDINIA)
Porto Torres
Sassari
Alghero
Asinara
Porto Vecchio
Bonifacio
Strait of Bonifacio
Sta Teresa di G.
Siniscola
Olbia
Arbatax
Nuoro
Muravera
Mte del Gennargentu 1835
C. di Monte Santu
Arzana
Macomer
Oristano
G. di Oristano
Sanluri
Iglesias
Carbonia
San Antioco
S. Pietro
C. Teulada
Cagliari
G. de Cagliari
C. Carbonara

TUNISIA
Tunis
Bizerte
Menzel
Mateur
Nabeul
Hammamet
Golfe de Hammamet
Sousse
Monastir
Moknine
Kelibia
C. Bon
G. de Tunis
Halq el Oued
Enfida
M'saken
Kairouan
Dj Zaghouan 1295
C. Blanc
C. Serrat
Tabarka
Béja
Jendouba
Medjerda
El Kef
Kalla Khasba
Makthar
Maktar
Mts de la Medjerda
'Annaba (Bône)
Guelma
Souk Ahras
El Kala
Medjerda
Tébessa
Mts de Tébessa

③
A

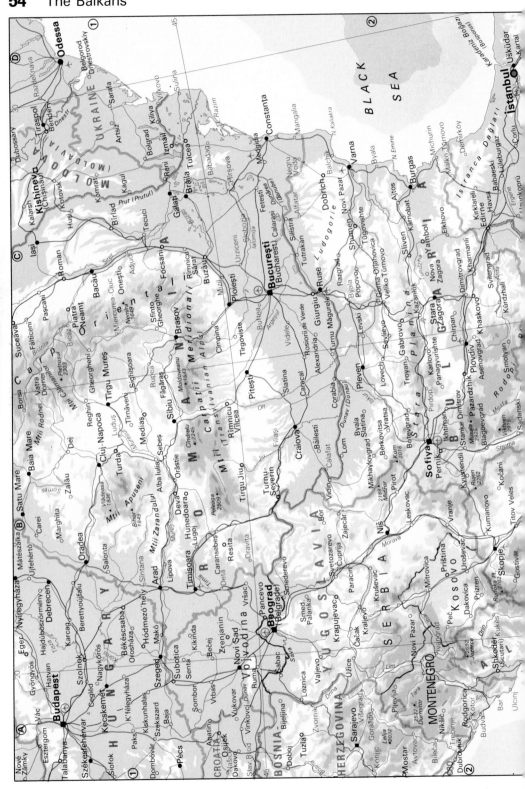

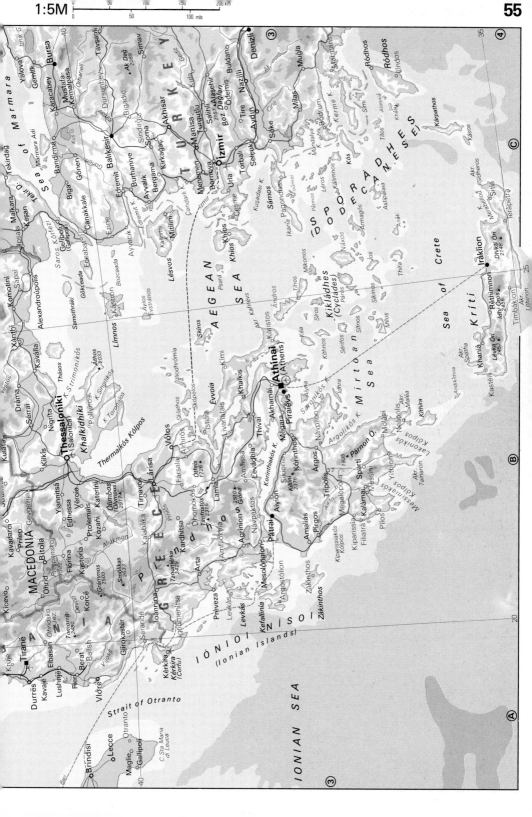

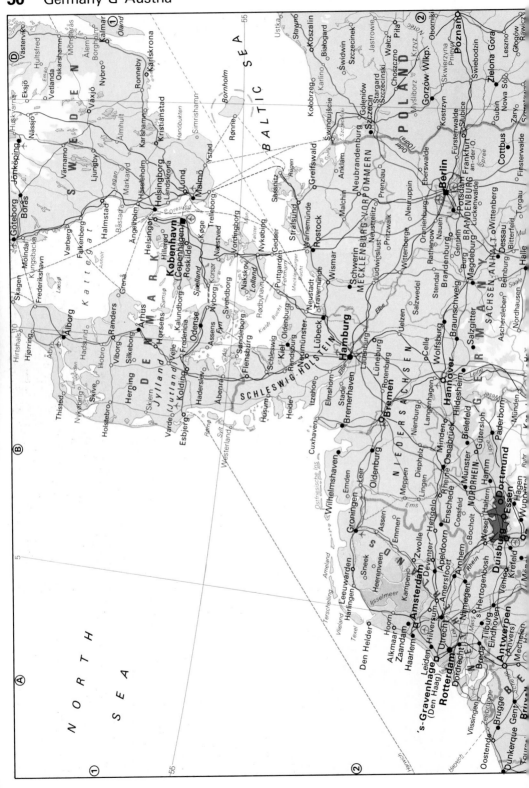

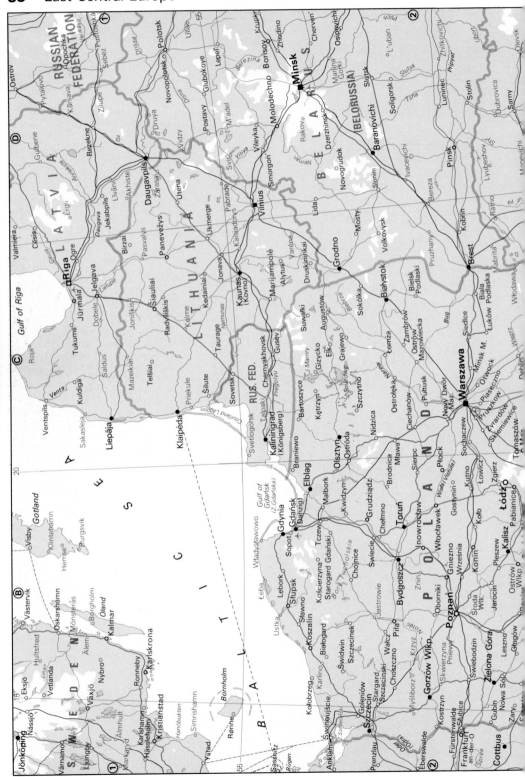

Map labels

RUSSIAN FEDERATION

Opochka
Pustoshka
Velikaya
Ostrov
Pytalovo
Sebez
Zilupe
Rezekne
Gubene
Balvi
Aluksne
Ilgirli
Valmiera
Cesis
Roja
Ogre
Gulf of Riga
Riga
Jurmala
Jelgava
Dobele
Bielupe
Tukums
Kuldiga
Saldus
Venta
Mazeikiai
Telsiai
Ventspils
Sakasleja
Liepāja
Kuršansava
Druya
Postavy
Glubokoye
Lepel
Berezina
Borisov
Zhodino
Cherven
Pluch
Minsk
Marina Gorki
Smolevichi
Osipovichi
Luban
Slutsk
Soligorsk
Tsna
Sluch
Stolin
Lyubeshov
Dubrovica
Sarny
Ubort
Olevsk
Novopolotsk
Polotsk
Ullab
Molodechno
Vileyka
Rakovo
Dzerzhinsk
B E L A R U S (BELORUSSIA)
Baranovichi
Pinsk
Ivacevichi
Bereza
Kobrin
Brest
Mabrita
Wlodawa
Ratno
Turiya
Daugavpils
Zarasai
Utena
Smorgon'
Negrudok
Lida
Slonim
Mosty
Volkovysk
Pruzhany
Druskininkai
Grodno
Bielsk Podlaski
Biala Podlaska
Siedlce
Luków

L A T V I A
Egli
Livani
Jekabpils
Daugava
Akhiste
Birzai
Pasvalys
Panevezys
Radviliskis
Siauliai
Jonava
Kaisiadorys
Vilnius
Kaunas (Kovno)
Kedainiai
Kelme
Taurage
Nemunas
Marijampolé
Alytus
Vareña
Priekule
Šilute
Courland Lagoon
Svetlogorsk
Sovetsk
Talpaki
Chernyakhovsk
Pregolyu
Kaliningrad (Königsberg)
Braniewo
Bartoszyce
Ketrzyn
Giżycko
Elk
Grajewo
Lomza
Ostrów Mazowiecka
Zambrów
Bialystok
Sokólka
Augustów
Suwalki
Gusev
Marny

L I T H U A N I A

RUS. FED.

Klaipéda
Gdynia
Sopot
Gdansk (Danzig)
Gulf of Gdansk (Z Gdańska)
Wladyslawowo
Leba
Ustka
Slupsk
Lebork
Slawno
Koszalin
Kolobrzeg
Bialogard
Karlino
Swidwin
Szczecinek
Walcz
Jastrowie
Pila
Noteć
Chojnice
Tuchola
Bory Tucholskie
Starogard Gdański
Tczew
Swiecie
Bydgoszcz
Inowroclaw
Gniezno
Poznań
Września
Środa Wlkp.
Jarocin
Pleszew
Ostrów Wlkp.
Kalisz
Pabianice
Łódz
Zgierz
Kolo
Konin
Kutno
Lowicz
Sochaczew
Warszawa
Pruszków
Otwock
Piaseczno
Zyrardów
Skierniewice
Tomaszów Maz.
Nowy Dwór Maz.
Minsk M.
Ciechanów
Pultusk
Plońsk
Plock
Wloclawek
Gostynin
Sierpc
Mlawa
Nidzica
Dzialdowo
Brodnica
Grudziadz
Kwidzyn
Chelmno
Toruń
Malbork
Elblag
Ostróda
Olsztyn
Szczytno
Ostrolęka

P O L A N D

Gorzów Wlkp.
Skwierzyna
Miedzyrzecz
Pniewy
Swiebodzin
Zielona Góra
Nowa Sól
Glogów
Leszno
Poborniki
Wyszlborz
Choszczno
Stargard Szczecinski
Goleniów
Szczecin
Swinoujscie
Kolobrzeg
Kostrzyn
Slubice
Frankfurt an-der-O
Eberswalde
Prenzlau
Anklam
Fürstenwalde
Gubin
Zary
Spree
Cottbus
Odra (Oder)

SWEDEN
Jönköping
Nässjö
Varnamo
Ljungby
Eksjö
Vetlanda
Almhult
Markaryd
Hässleholm
Ljungby
Karlshamn
Ronneby
Nybro
Vaxjö
Kalmar
Oland
Borgholm
Monsterås
Oskarshamn
Hultsfred
Vastervik
Visby
Klintehamn
Hemse
Burgsvik
Gotland
Gulf of Riga
B A L T I C   S E A
Bornholm
Rönne
Sassnitz
Rügen
Bugen
Hanobukten
Simrishamn
Ystad
Kristianstad
Karlskrona

B E L A R U S

Minsk

50   100   150   200 km
0   50   100 mls

Novograd
Novovolynskiy
Polonnye
Starokonstantinov
Kostopol'
Korec
Slavuta
Shepetovka
Kremenets
Bazaliya
Dunayevtsy
Kamenets-Podol'skiy
Khotin
Yedintsy
Ryskany
Iasi
Roman
Bacău
Onești
Adjud
Tecuci
Focșani
Buzău
Ploiești
Rîmnicu Sărat

Lutsk
Rovno
Dubno
Brody
Ternopol'
Chortkov
Kolomya
Chernovtsy
Storozhinets
Rădăuți
Suceava
Fălticeni
Botoșani
Dorohoi
Piatra-Neamț
Mercurea-Ciuc
Gheorgheni
Miercurea
Sfîntu Gheorghe
Brașov
Cîmpina

Kivercy
Vladimir Volynskiy
Zolochev
L'vov
Berezhany
Ivano-Frankovsk
Nadvornaya
Yasinya
Borsa
Vatra Dornei
Mții Rodnei
Reghin
Tîrnăveni
Sibiu
Mediaș
Sebeș
Făgăraș
Rîmnicu Vîlcea

Kovel'
Chelm
Lublin
Krasnystaw
Zamość
Tomaszów Lubelski
Jarosław
Przemyśl
Sambor
Drogobych
Borislav
Stryy
Kalush
Khust
Svalyava
Mukachevo
Uzhgorod
Baia Mare
Sighetu Marmației
Satu Mare
Carei
Zalău
Dej
Cluj-Napoca
Turda
Alba Iulia
Orăștie
Deva
Hunedoara
Tîrgu Jiu

Krasnik
Stalowa Wola
Tarnobrzeg
Mielec
Dębica
Rzeszów
Jasło
Nowy Sącz
Bardejov
Prešov
Michalovce
Košice
Kisvárda
Nyíregyháza
Mátészalka
Marghita
Oradea
Salonta
Arad
Timișoara
Lugoj
Reșița
Caransebeș
Deta

Kielce
Skarżysko-Kamienna
Starachowice
Ostrowiec
Sandomierz
Tarnów
Kraków
Bochnia
Zakopane
Ružomberok
Banská Bystrica
Zvolen
Lučenec
Rožňava
Miskolc
Kazincbarcika
Ózd
Eger
Mezőkövesd
Hajdúböszörmény
Debrecen
Berettyóújfalu
Karcag
Szolnok
Békéscsaba
Orosháza
Hódmezővásárhely
Makó
Szeged
Szentes
Subotica
Kikinda
Becej
Zrenjanin
Novi Sad

Częstochowa
Radomsko
Zawiercie
Dąbrowa-Górn
Sosnowiec
Katowice
Bytom
Gliwice
Zabrze
Chorzów
Bielsko-Biała
Cieszyn
Żywiec
Myślenice
Martin
Žilina
Čadca
Trenčín
Piešťany
Nitra
Nové Zámky
Komárno
Győr
Talabánya
Salgótarján
Gyöngyös
Hatvan
Vác
Budapest
Cegléd
Kecskemét
Kiskunfélegyháza
Kiskunhalas
Szekszárd
Baja
Sombor
Apatin
Vukovar
Vrbas

Opole
Kędzierzyn
Ostrava
Opava
Hranice
Přerov
Zlín
Trnava
Bratislava
Wien (Vienna)
Sopron
Mosonmagyaróvár
Székesfehérvár
Veszprém
Siófok
Dombóvár
Pécs
Osijek
Đakovo

Wrocław (Breslau)
Brzeg
Nysa
Kłodzko
Olomouc
Prostějov
Vyškov
Brno
Břeclav
Hodonín
Szombathely
Zalaegerszeg
Nagykanizsa
Kaposvár
Vinkovci
Slav. Brod
Daruvar
Našice
Pakrac

Legnica
Jelenia Góra
Jablonec n.N.
Mladá Boleslav
Hradec Králové
Pardubice
Kolín
Kutná Hora
Svitavy
Jihlava
Znojmo
Třebíč
Hollabrunn
Stockerau
Mödling
Wiener Neustadt
Maribor
Varaždin
Koprivnica
Bjelovar
Virovitica

Görlitz
Zittau
Ústí n.L.
Liberec
Praha (Prague)
Kladno
Benešov
Beroun
Tábor
Písek
České Budějovice
Třebon
Gmünd
Freistadt
Linz
Steyr
Enns
Krems
St. Pölten
Hainfeld
Neunkirchen
Gleisdorf
Graz
Leibnitz
Celje
Velenje
Kranj
Ljubljana
Novo Mesto
Karlovac
Sisak
Zagreb
Rijeka (Fiume)

Wałbrzych
Świdnica
Dzierżoniów
Bielawa

Bautzen
Bolesławiec
Wołów

UKRAINE
POLAND
SLOVAKIA
HUNGARY
AUSTRIA
ROMANIA
CROATIA
SLOVENIA
VOJVODINA
Carpații Orientali
Carpații Meridionali
Mții (Transylvanian Alps)
Beskidy Zachodnie
Mții Apuseni
Mții Zarandului
Podol'skaya Vozv.

Dunăre
Drava
Sava
Tisza
Mureș
Someș
Danube
Bug
Wisła
Odra
San
Prut (Prutul)
Dnestr
Siret

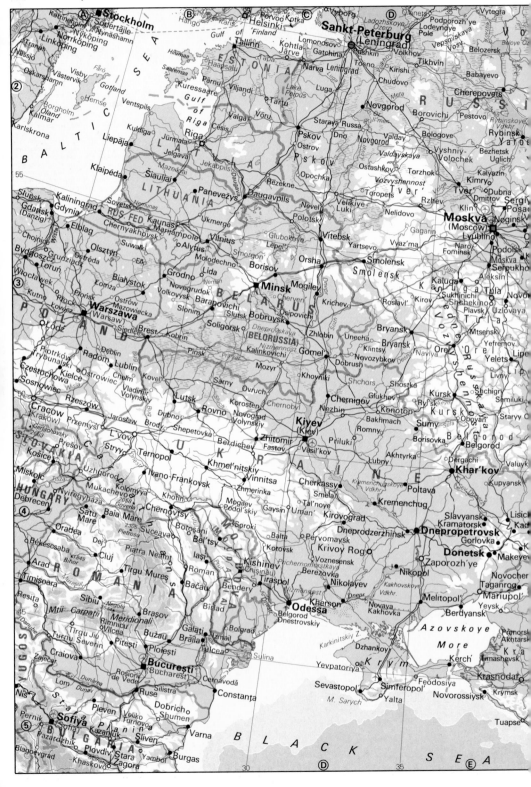

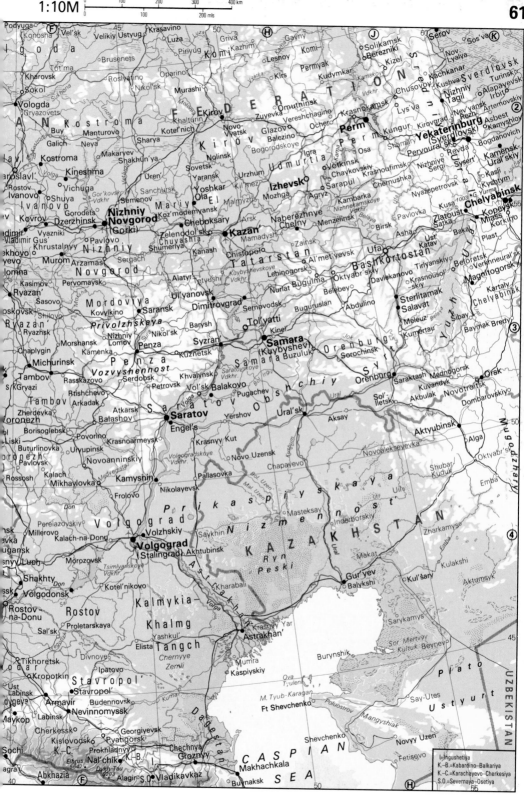

1:10M

100   200   300   400 km
100   200 mls

RUSSIAN FEDERATION

Vologda · Gryazaovets · Kostroma · Buy · Manturovo · Galich · Neya · Makaryev · Shakhun'ya · Tot'ma · Sokol · Kharovsk · Roslyatino · Oparino · Murashi · Kotel'nich · Khalturin · Kirov · Omutninsk · Solikamsk · Berezniki · Kizel · Serov · Sos'va · Nov. Lyalya · Kachkanar · Kushva · Turinsk · Nizhniy Tagil · Alapayevsk · Artemovskiy

Kostroma · Makaryev · Sharya · Nolinsk · Novo-Vyatsk · Glazov · Balezino · Ocher · Krasnokamsk · Chusovoy · Nev'yansk · Asbest · Kamyshlov · Sverdlovsk · **Yekaterinburg** · Bogdanovich

Ivanovo · Vichuga · Kineshma · Yaransk · Sovetsk · Urzhum · Izhevsk · Sarapul · Agryz · Chaykovskiy · Krasnoufimsk · Nyazepetrovsk · Kusa · Zlatoust · **Chelyabinsk**

Shuya · Kovrov · Dzerzhinsk · **Nizhniy Novgorod (Gorki)** · Cheboksary · **Kazan'** · Naberezhnyye Chelny · Mamadysh · Menzelinsk · Birsk · Asha · Satka · Bakal · Miass · Kopeysk · Korkino

Vladimir · Vyazniki · Pavlovo · Zelenodol'sk · Chuvashia · **Tatarstan** · Al'met'yevsk · **Bashkortostan** · **Ufa** · Plast

Murom · Arzamas · Sergach · Kanash · Lebedinoye · Bugul'ma · Belebey · Sterlitamak · Salavat · Beloretsk · Verkhneural'sk · **Magnitogorsk**

Kasimov · Pervomaysk · Alatyr · Tetyushi · Al'met'yevsk · Nurlat · Buguruslan · Abdulino · Davlekanovo · Kumertau · Baymak · Bredy · Kartaly · **Chelyabinsk**

Ryazan' · Sasovo · Ul'yanovsk · Dimitrovgrad · Sernovodsk · **Orenburg** · Sorochinsk · **Orenburg** · Meleuz · Sibay

Ryazhsk · Shilovo · Saransk · Kovylkino · **Privolzhskaya** · Barysh · Tol'yatti · **Samara** · Buzuluk · Saraktash · Mednogorsk · Orsk

Chaplygin · Morshansk · Nizhniy Lomov · Penza · Syzran' · Kinel · **Samara (Kuybyshev)** · Kuvandyk · Akbulak · Novotroitsk · Dombarovskiy

Michurinsk · Kamenka · **Penza** · Kuznetsk · Khvalynsk · **Vozvyshennost'** · Pugachev · Sol'-Iletsk · Alga

Tambov · Rasskazovo · Serdobsk · Petrovsk · Vol'sk · Balakovo · **Saratov** · **Obshchiy Syrt** · Ural'sk · **Aktyubinsk** · **Mugodzhary**

Zherdevka · Rtishchevo · Arkadak · Atkarsk · Balashov · Yershov · Aksay · Novoalekseyevka

Borisoglebsk · Povorino · Krasnoarmeysk · **Saratov** · Engel's · Krasnyy Kut · Novo Uzensk · Chapayevo · **KAZAKHSTAN**

Buturlinovka · Uryupinsk · Novoanninskiy · Pallasovka · Shubar Kuduk · Emba

Pavlovsk · Kalach · Mikhaylovka · Kamyshin · Nikolayevsk · Masteksay · Inderborskiy

Rossosh · Frolovo · **Prikaspiyskaya** · Saykhin · **Nizmennost'** · Zharkamys

Perelazovskiy · Millerovo · Kalach-na-Donu · **Volgograd** · Volzhskiy · **Ryn Peski** · Makat

Lugansk · Morozovsk · Kotel'nikovo · **Volgograd (Stalingrad)** · Akhtubinsk · Gur'yev · Balykshi · Kul'sary · Aktumsyk

Shakhty · Volgodonsk · **Kalmykia-Khalmg Tangch** · Kharabali · Krasnyy Yar · Sarykamys

Rostov-na-Donu · Proletarskaya · Sal'sk · Yashkul' · Elista · Astrakhan' · Burynshik

Tikhoretsk · Divnoye · Ipatovo · Chernyye Zemli · Mumra · Kaspiyskiy · **Plato Ustyurt** · **UZBEKISTAN**

Kropotkin · **Stavropol'** · Ova T;ulen'i · Sor Mertvyy Kultuk Beyneu · Say-Utes

Ust Labinsk · Budennovsk · Nevinnomyssk · M. Tyub-Karagan · Ft Shevchenko · Poluostrov Mangyshlak · Novyy Uzen · Fetisovo

Armavir · Labinsk · Georgiyevsk · Pyatigorsk · Cherkessk · Kislovodsk · Prokhladnyy · Nal'chik · **Chechnya** · Groznyy · Makhachkala · Shevchenko

Maykop · Elbrus 5642 · Dykh Tau 5204 · **K.-C.** · **K.-B.** · Alagir · Vladikavkaz · Buynaksk

Sochi · Abkhazia · **Dagestan** · **CASPIAN SEA**

I=Ingushetiya
K.-B.=Kabardino-Balkariya
K.-C.=Karachayevo-Cherkesiya
S.O.=Severnaya-Osetiya

1:45M

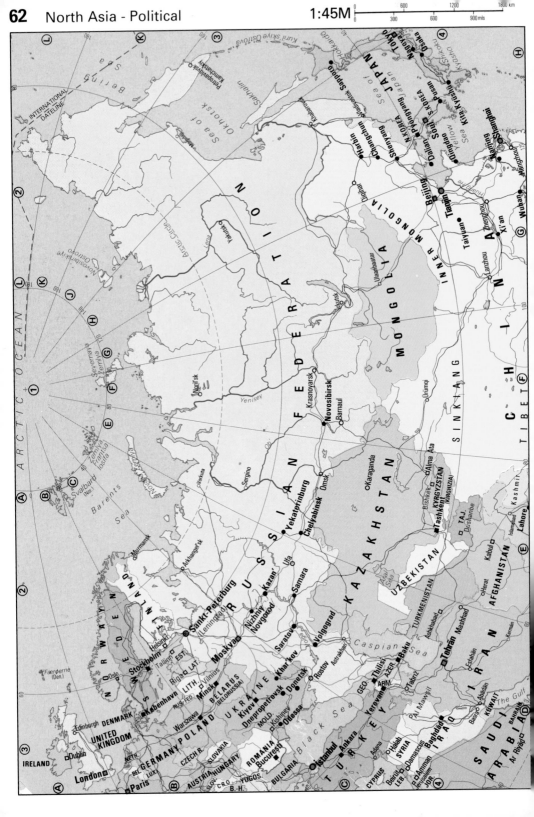

200 400 600 800 km
0
200 400 mls
0

SAKHALIN

Yuzhno-Sakhalinsk

KOREA SOUTH

Pusan

Taegu

P'yŏngyang

NORTH KOREA

Dalian

Beijing

Tianjin Tientsin

Harbin

Changchun

Shenyang

Vladivostok

Nakhodka

SEA OF JAPAN

YELLOW SEA

Sikhote Alin'

Khabarovsk

Komsomol'sk

Nikolayevsk

C H I N A

M O N G O L I A

Ulaanbaatar

Da Hinggan Ling

Khrebet Stanovoy

Yakutsk

R U S S I A N   F E D E R A T I O N

S r e d n e   S i b i r s k o y e   P l o s k o g o r ' y e

Bratsk

Irkutsk

Angarsk

Ulan Ude

Chita

Baykal

Krasnoyarsk

Novokuznetsk

Biysk

A L T A Y

Ba

Arctic Circle

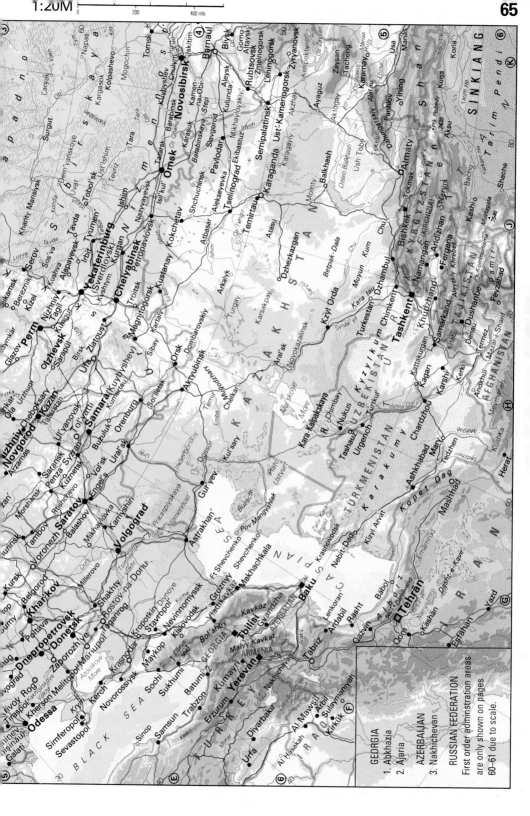

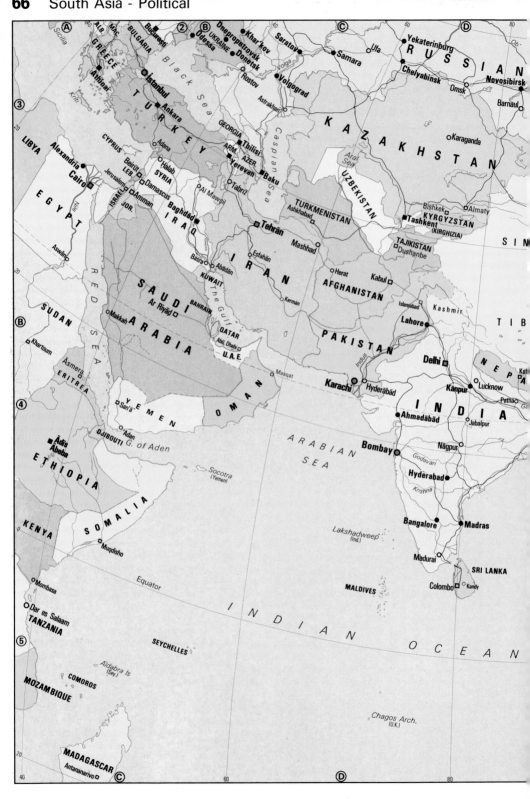

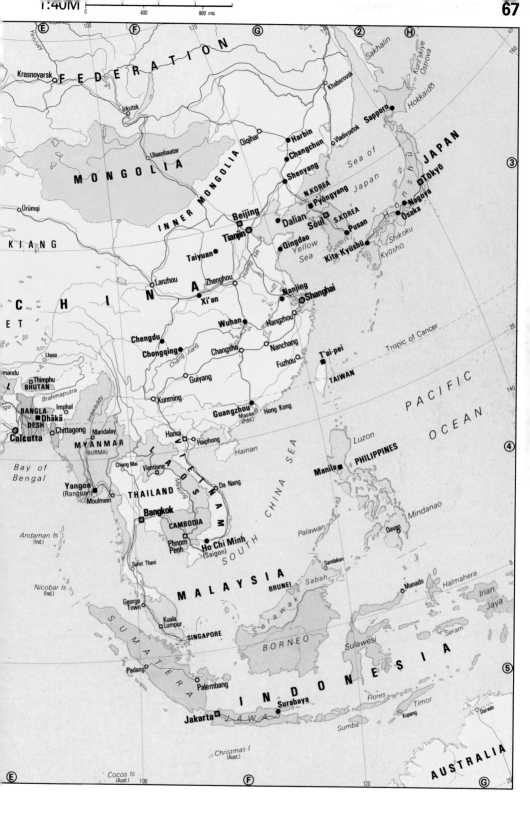

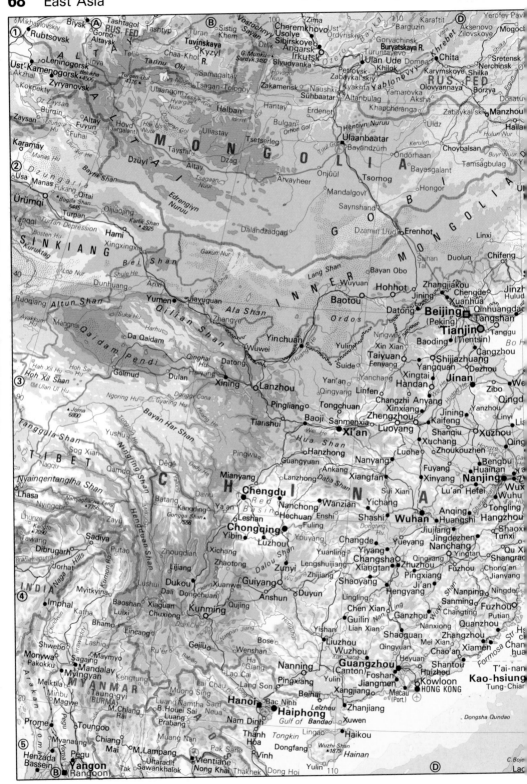

1:20M

200 400 600 800 km
0   200   400 mls

SEA OF OKHOTSK

Skovorodino
Zeya
Tugur
Ekimchan
Pelimy
Moskva
Okha
Opala
Mys Lopatka
Nikolayevsk-na-Amure
Bogorodskoye
Paramushir

Svobodnyy
Komsomol'sk
na-Amure
Tymovskoye
Aleksandrovsk-Sakhalinskiy
Onekotan
Shiashkotan

Belogorsk
Blagoveshchensk
Pobedino
SAKHALIN
Rasshua

Khabarovsk
Uglegorsk
Poronaysk
Simushir

Birobidzhan
Vanino
Zaliv
Terpeniya
Kuril'skiye Ostrova
(Kuril Islands)

Harbin
Korsakov
Mys Aniva
Iturup
(Rus.Fed.
admin/claimed
by Japan)
Vityaz Depth
10542

Changchun
Abashiri
Kunashir
Shikotan
Nemuro

Sapporo
HOKKAIDŌ
Erimo-misaki

Hakodate

SEA OF JAPAN

Aomori
Hachinohe

NORTH KOREA
Akita
Morioka

P'yŏngyang
Sendai

Sŏul (Seoul)
SOUTH KOREA
Niigata
Fukushima

YELLOW SEA
Tōkyō
Yokohama

Shanghai
Ōsaka
Nagoya

Kyōto
Kōbe

Fukuoka
Kita-Kyūshū
SHIKOKU

Kagoshima
Miyazaki

EAST CHINA SEA

Ramapo Deep
10374

PACIFIC OCEAN

Ogasawara Gunto
(Bonin Islands)
(Jap.)

Fleming Deep
8651

Okinawa
RYŪKYŪ RETTO

T'ai-pei
TAIWAN (FORMOSA)
(China Nat. Rep.)

Tropic of Cancer

MARIANAS

Northern
Mariana
Islands

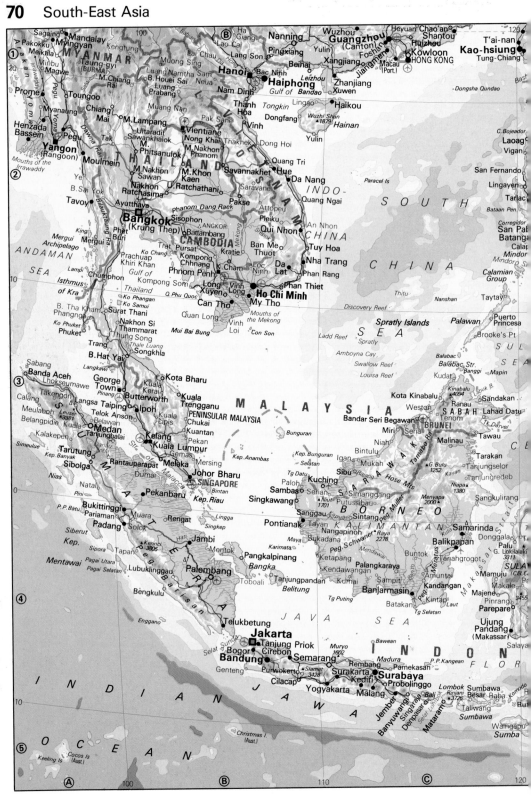

1:10M

100 200 300 400 km
100 200 mls

SOUTH CHINA SEA

GULF OF TONGKIN

Shanghai
Songjiang
Nanking
Wuxi
Suzhou
Changzhou
Ma'anshan
Wuhu
Xuancheng
Hangzhou
Jiaxing
Wuxing
Shaoxing
Ningbo
Zhoushan Qundao
Linhai
Huangyan
Wenling
Wenzhou
Lishui
Ningde
Fuding

Zhejiang
Jinhua
Qu Xian
Shangrao
Pucheng

TAIWAN
Chi-lung (Keelung)
T'ai-pei
Hsin-chu
Chia-i Nat.Rep.China
T'ai-tung
Ping-tung
Kao-hsiung
Fang-liao
Heng-ch'un

FORMOSA STRAIT (TAIWAN HAI-HSIA)
Quanzhou
Xiamen (Amoy)
Kinmen
Jinjiang
Dongshan

Fujian
Nanping
Sanming
Sha Xian
Yong'an
Zhangping
Zhangzhou
Zhao'an
Shantou (Swatow)
Chao'an
Lufeng
Huilai

Jingdezhen
Nanchang
Fengcheng
Fuzhou
Linchuan
Guangze

Jiangxi
Ji'an
Pingxiang
Zhuzhou

Hubei
Wuhan
Hanyang
Huangshi
Anqing
Jiujiang
Huangshi

Changsha
Xiangtan
Yiyang
Changde
Dayong

Hunan
Shaoyang
Hengyang
Hongjiang
Lingling
Chaling
Leiyang
Guidong

Guizhou
Guiyang
Zunyi
Kaili
Anshun
Zhenyuan
Xifeng

Sichuan
Chengdu
Chongqing (Chungking)
Neijiang
Zigong
Yibin
Luzhou
Fuling
Wanxian

Chuzhou
Zhuzhou
Ganzhou
Xinfeng

Guangdong
Shaoguan
Heyuan
Huizhou
Guangzhou (Canton)
Foshan
Zhongshan
Macau
Kowloon
HONG KONG
Shenzhen
Jiangmen
Yangjiang
Maoming
Zhanjiang
Lianjiang
Leizhou

Guangxi
Liuzhou
Nanning
Wuzhou
Guilin
Beihai
Qinzhou
Lingshan
Hepu

VIETNAM
Hanoi
Haiphong
Hadong
Lang Son
Ha Giang
Cao Bang

Yunnan
Kunming
Qujing
Mile
Gejiu
Mengzi
Kaiyuan

LAOS

Daxue Shan
Qionglai Shan

Red River
Black River

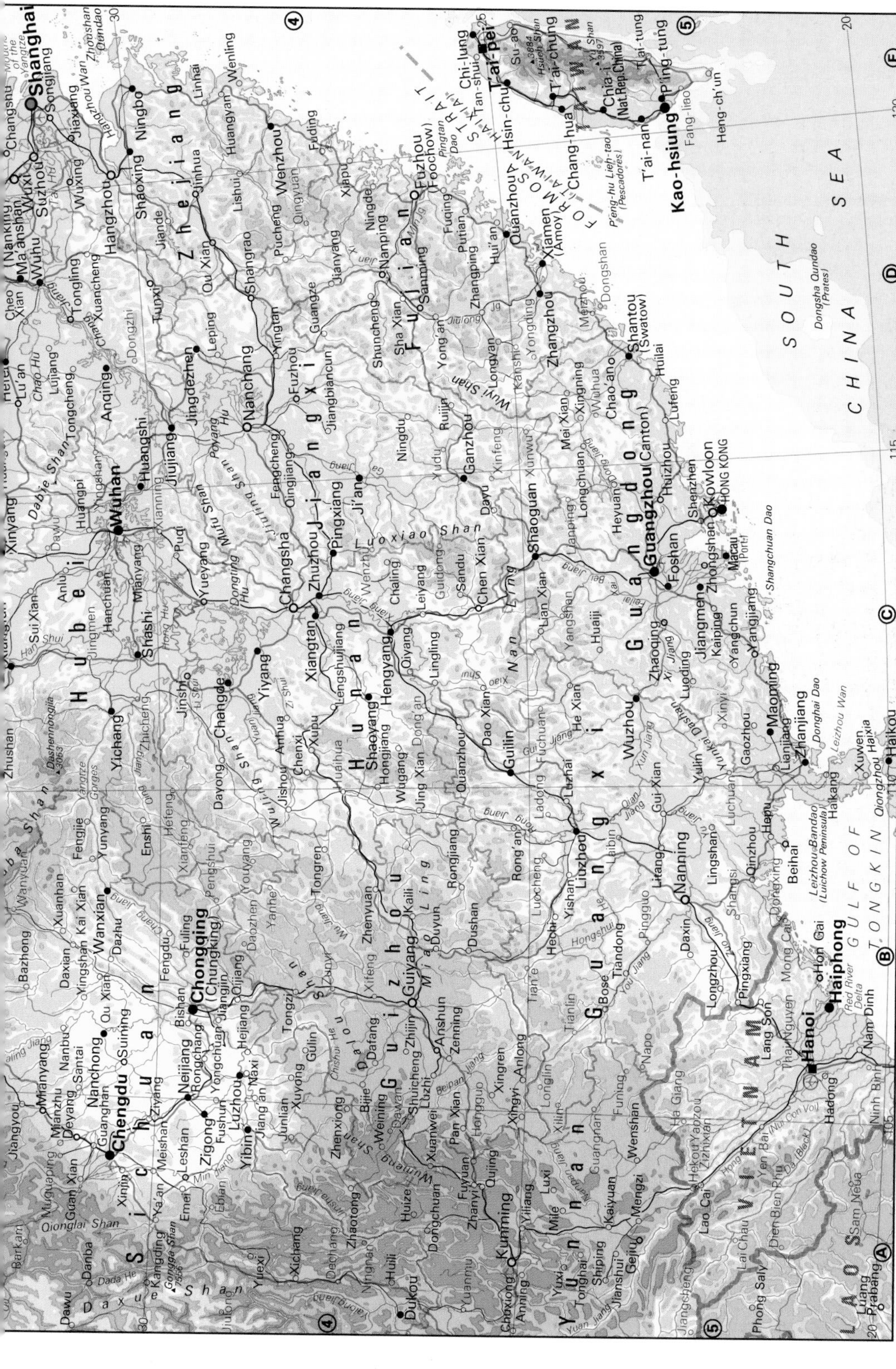

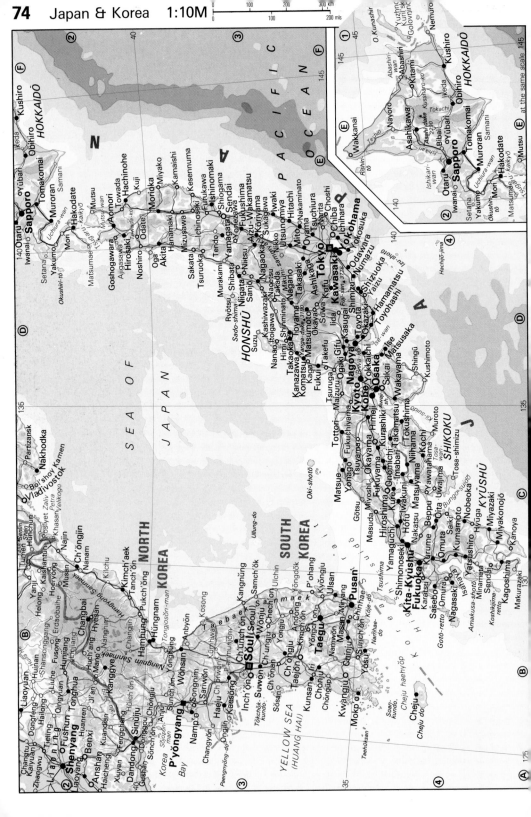

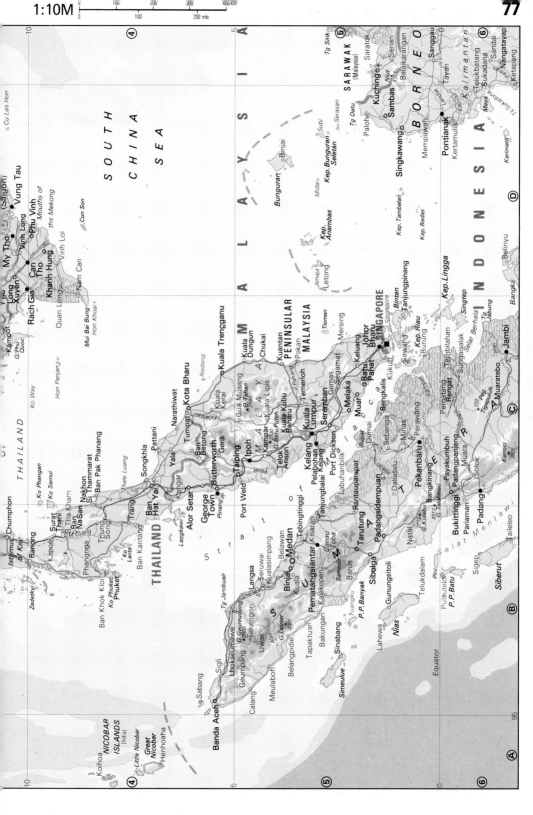

1:10M

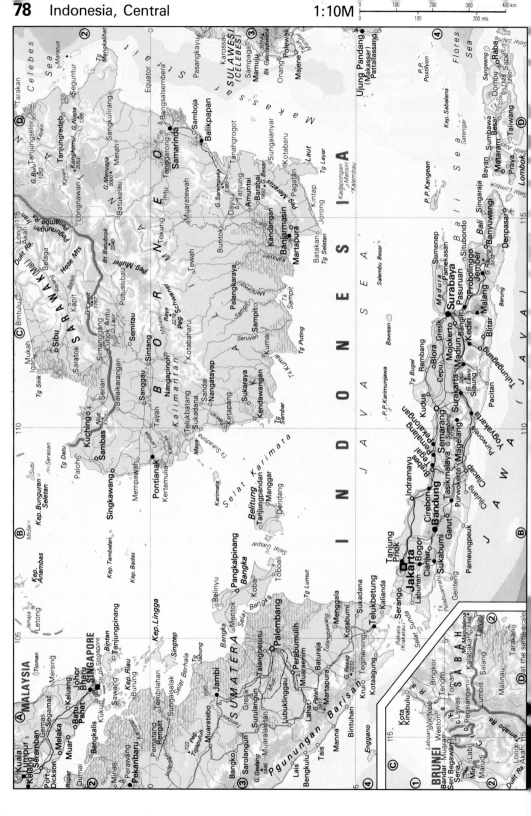

1:10M

1:10M

0   100   200   300   400 km

0   100   200 mls

Ⓐ   120   Ⓑ   125   Ⓒ

① *Dongsha*   *PACIFIC*   ①
Qundao

Luzon   *Batan*
Strait   *Islands*
20   *Basco*   *OCEAN*   20

Balintang Channel

② *Babuyan Islands*   ②

Babuyan Channel   *Cape Engaño*

Cape Bojeador   *Aparri*
Laoago   *2234*
Banguod   Tuguegarao   *P*
Vigan   *H*
Santiago   Ilagan   *I*
San   Solano   *L*   ②
Fernando   *Mt Pulog*2929   *LUZON*   *I*
La Trinidad   Bayombang   *P*
Baguio   San   *P*
Lingayen   Dagupan   *Baler*   *I*
San Carlos   Jose   *N*
Camiling   Cabanatuan   *E*
Tarlac   Gapan

SOUTH   Angeles   San Fernando   *Polillo*
San Antonio   Malolos   *Islands*   ② *S*
CHINA   Olongapo   Quezon City   *Lamon*   15
15   Manila   *Bay*   *Calagua Islands*   *E*
Cavite   *Laguna*   Jose Pañganiban   *A*
Corregidor   Santa Cruz   Daet
SEA   San Pablo   Lucban   *Catanduanes*
Lipao   Lucena
Lubang   Batangas   Sipocot
Islands   Boac   Naga   *Virac*
Calapan   Iriga   *Mayon*
2585   *2421*
③ *MINDORO*   Sablayan   *Mt Halcon*   Legazpi   ③
Mt Baco   Sorsogon   Gubat
2488   *Burias*   Bulan   *Catarman*
Mindoro Strait   *Sibuyan*   Masbate
Busuanga   Romblon   Calbayog   *Oras*
Calamian   San Jose   *Sibuyan*   *Masbate*   *SAMAR*
Group   *Tablas*   *Sea*   Catbalogan
Culion   Kalibo   Roxas   *Visayan*   San
Linapacan Strait   Pandan   *Sea*   Isidro   Carigara
El   *PANAY*   Bogo   Ormoc   Tacloban
Nido   *Cuyo*   Cadiz   Escalante   Burauen   *Guiuan*
Islands   Iloilo   Silay   Baybay   *Leyte*
Dalanganem   Bacolod   Danao   *Gulf*
Taytay   *Islands*   La Carlota   Lapu-Lapu   *Dinagat*
Dumaran   Binalbagan   Cebu
Roxas   Maasin
Cleopatra   *Bohol*   Surigao   *Siargao*
*Needle*1593   *Cagayan*   Sipalay   Tagbilaran
④ *Islands*   Bais   *Bohol Sea*
Puerto   Tanjay   *10497*
Princesa   Dumaguete   *Siquijor*   *10265*
Aborlan   Lazi   *Camiguin*
1798   Siaton   Butuan
Tubbataha   Dipolog   Gingoog
Mt   *Reefs*   Dapitan   Cagayan   *Diuat Mts*
Mantalingajan 2054   Manukan   Oroquieta   de Oro   *Lianga*
Brooke's   Liloy   Iligan   *Malaybalay*   Bislig
Point   *SULU SEA*   *Mt Ozamiz*   Marawi   *MINDANAO*
Balabac   Pagadian   *Mt Apo*2954
2560
Balabac Strait   Cotabato   Davao   Mati
Banggi   Zamboanga   *Datu*   Digos
Kudat   Isabela   *Piang*
Mapin   *Pangutaran*   *Basilan*   General   Lais
Bandau   *Group*   *Moro*   Santos   *Cape San Agustin*
Kota   *Mt Palin* 1216   *Gulf*
Kinabulu   Ranau   Jolo   *Jolo*
Sandakan   Parang   *Samales*
Mt Melfu 2000   *Group*   *CELEBES*
⑤ *SABAH*   Lahad   *Tapul*   *Tinaca Point*   ⑤
Kinabalu 4094   Datu   *Group*   *Kepulauan*
Tenom   *1606*   *Tawitawi*   *Kawio*
Tomani   *Mt Magdalena* 1346   *Tawitawi*   *SEA*
Kalabakan   *Bum Bum*   *Group*   *Karakelong*
120   Ⓑ   125   Ⓒ

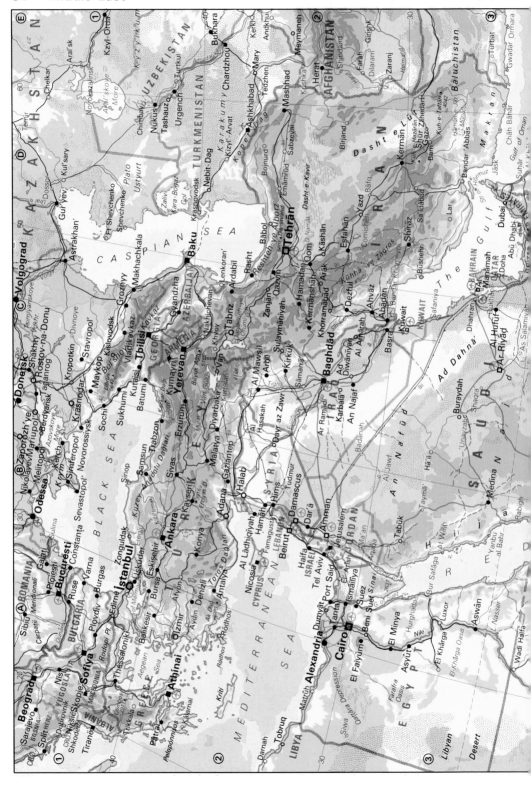

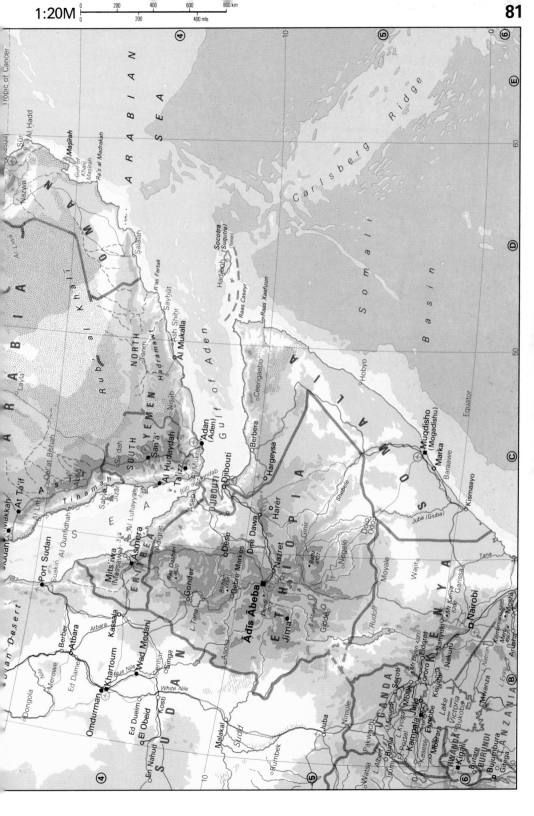

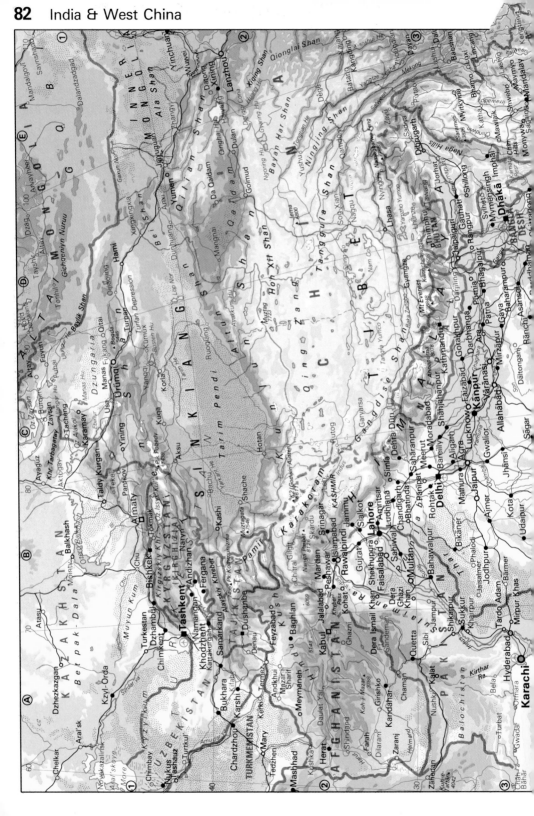

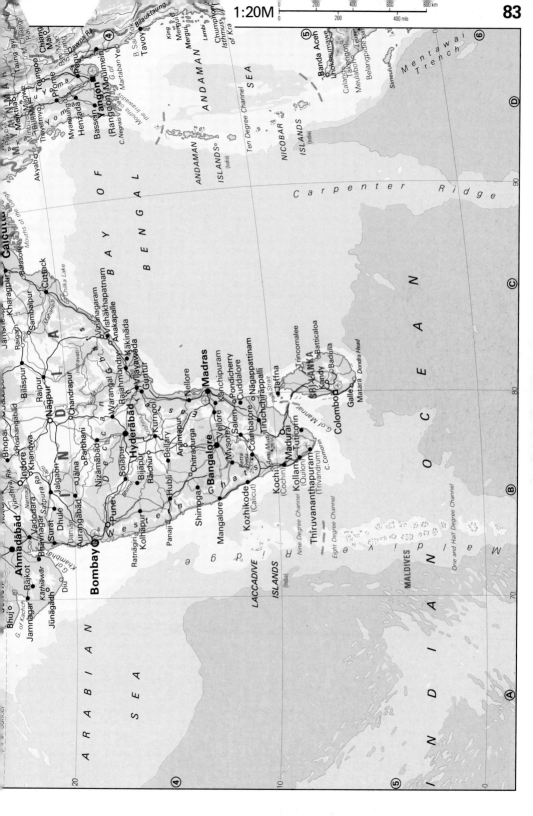

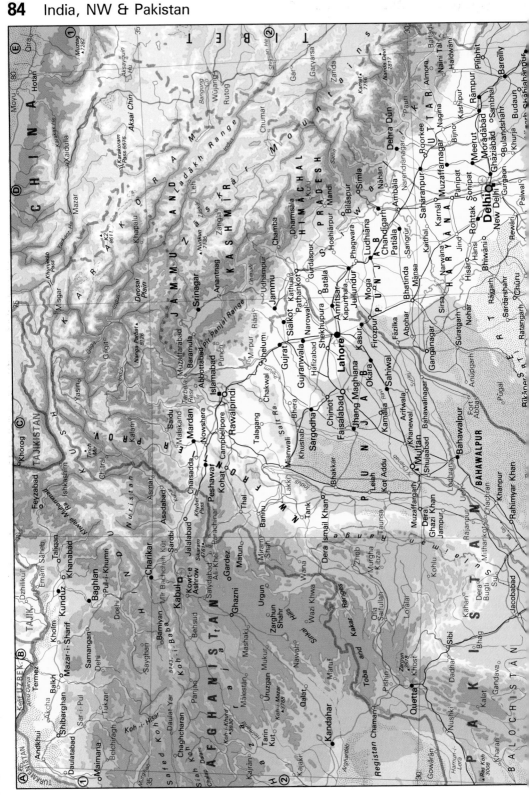

1:7.5M

100   200   300 km
50   100   150 mls

④ ⑤

P R A D E S H

Ganga Ganges

Kānpur
Hāthras
Firozābād
Etāwah
Mainpuri
Auraiya
Kālpi
Hamīrpur
Rāth
Mahoba
Charkhāri
Chhatarpur
Tikamgarh
Panna
Nainpur
Seoni
Tirodi
Tumsar
Bhandāra
Chāndrapur

Mathura
Bharatpur
Agra
Morena
Gwalior
Datia
Jhānsi
Lalitpur
Bina
Etawa
Garhākota
Sāgar
Damoh
Sihora
Jabalpur
Narsimhāpur
Chhindwāra
Betul
Nāgpur
Wardha
Umred
Hinganghāt
Kāmthi
Rājur
Adilābād
Belampalliⁿ Maṇcherāl

Alwar
Jaipur
Dausa
Daulpur
Hindaun
Sheopur
Shivpuri
Guna
Sironj
Vidisha
Bhopāl
Hoshangābād
Harda
Achalpur
Amrāvati
Washim
Pusad
Hingoli
Nizāmābād
Jagtial
Karimnagar

Sīkar
Kishangarh
Ajmer
Beāwar
Makrāna
Nāgaur
Didwāna
Ladnūn
Merta
Tonk
Toda
Devli
Bundi
Kota
Rājgarh
Agar
Shājapur
Ujjain
Dewās
Mhow
Indore
Dhār
Barwāni
Khandwa
Khargon
Sendwha
Sanawad
Burhānpur
Bhusāwal
Akot
Akola
Khāmgaon
Kāranja
Mehekar
Parbhani
Pārli
Bīr
Udgir

Sujāngarh
Nāgaur
Kekri
Bhilwāra
Chittaurgarh
Rāmpura
Nimach
Mandsaur
Jaora
Ratlām
Jhābua
Barwāni
Barwāh
Dhūle
Amalner
Jalgaon
Dhule
Chālisgaon
Malkāpur
Buldāna
Aurangābād
Jālna
Ahmadnagar

Bīlāra
Sojat
Sādri
Pāli
Jālor
Sādri
Sirohi
Udaipur
Dungarpur
Bānswāra
Sātpura Range
Nandurbār
Malegaon
Deolāli
Mānmād
Kopargaon
Sangamner
Pune (Poona)

Jodhpur
Bālotra
Bārmer
Devikot
Pokaran
Phalodi
Shergarh
Jaisalmer
Rāmgarh
Pātan
Rādhanpur
Mahesāna
Kadi
Khed Brahma
Siddhapur
Himatnagar
Gandhinagar
Ahmadābād
Nadiād
Godhra
Dābhoi
Rājpipla
Vadodara
Petlād
Bharūch
Sūrat
Navsāri
Valsād
Silvassa
Daman (G.D.&D.)
Kalyān
Thāne
Bombay
Alibāg

R Ā J A S T H Ā N

M A D H Y A

P R A D E S H

M A H Ā R Ā S H T R A

G U J A R Ā T

T H A R

Nāgar Parkar

Palanpur
Dhrāngadhra
Morbi
Surendranagar
Wānkāner
Rājkot
Jasdan
Gondal
Dhorāji
Junāgadh
Porbandar
Māngral
Verāval
Diu (Goa, Daman & Diu)
Gir Hills
Amreli
Kundla
Pālitāna
Bhāvnagar
Botād
Jambusar
Kāvi
Dholka
Kheda

KHAIRPUR

Sukkur
Rohri
Khairpur
Sanghar
Nawābshah
Sartanahu
Tando Adam
Mirpur Khas
Umarkot
Nāckot
Chāchro

S I N D H

Larkāna
Shadādkot
Dadu
Sehwān
Kotri
Hyderābād
Tando Muhammad Khān
Badin
Tatta

Khuzdār
Wad
Nāgha Kalat
Bela
Uthal
Khirthar Range
Central Makran Range
Makran Coast Range
Sonmiāni Bay
Korangi
Karachi
Sonmiāni
Mouths of the Indus
Keti Bandar
Shāh Bandar
Lakhpat
Kori
Rann of Kachchh
Bhuj
Mandvi
Okha
G. of Kachchh
Jāmnagar
Navlakhi
Dwārka
Gulf of Khambhat

Tropic of Cancer

A R A B I A N

S E A

③ ④ Ⓑ Ⓒ Ⓓ

25
20
20
70
75

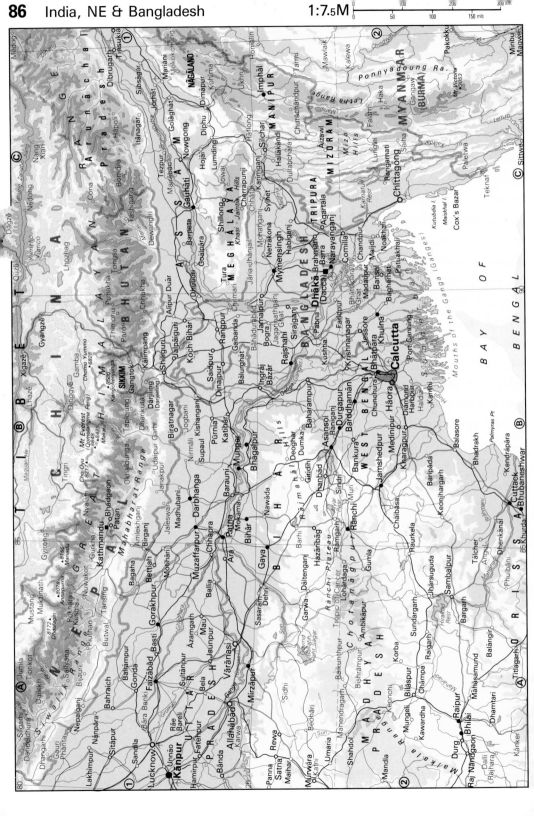

1:7.5M

100 200 300 km
50 100 150 mls

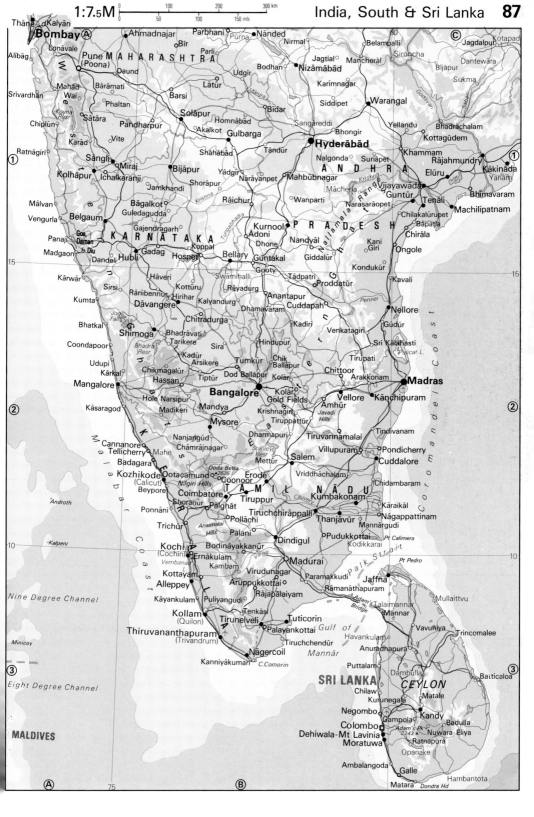

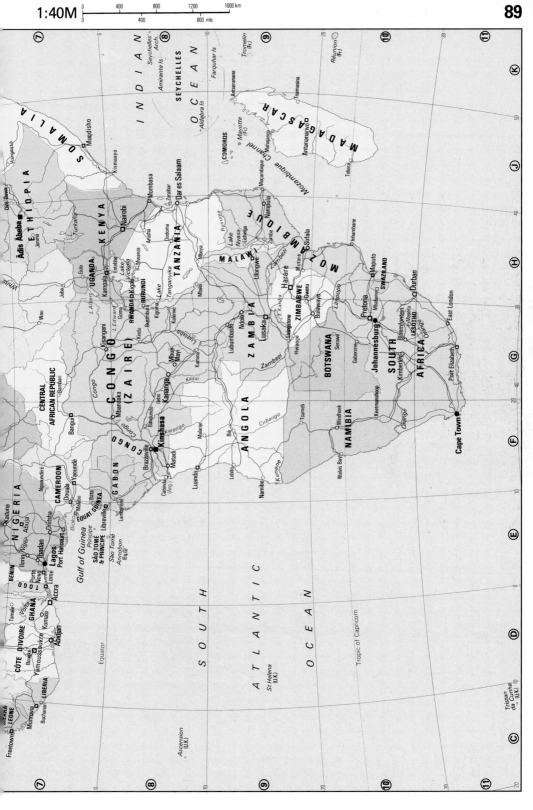

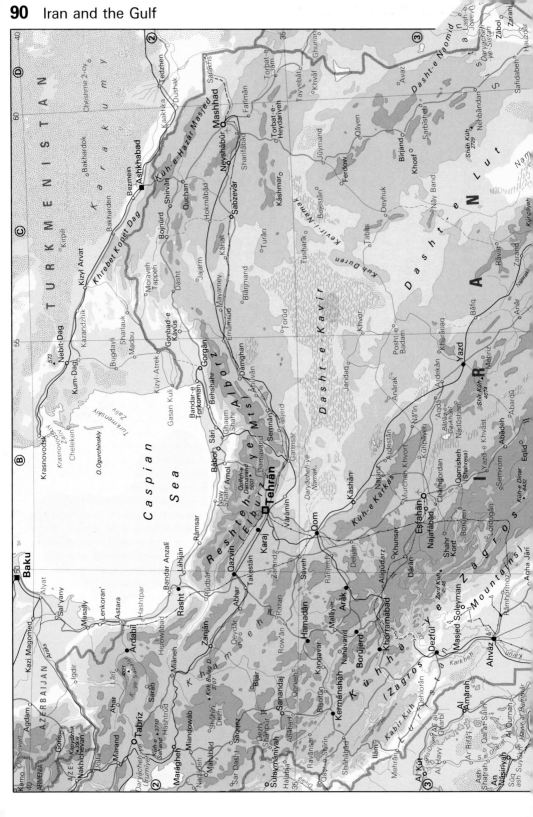

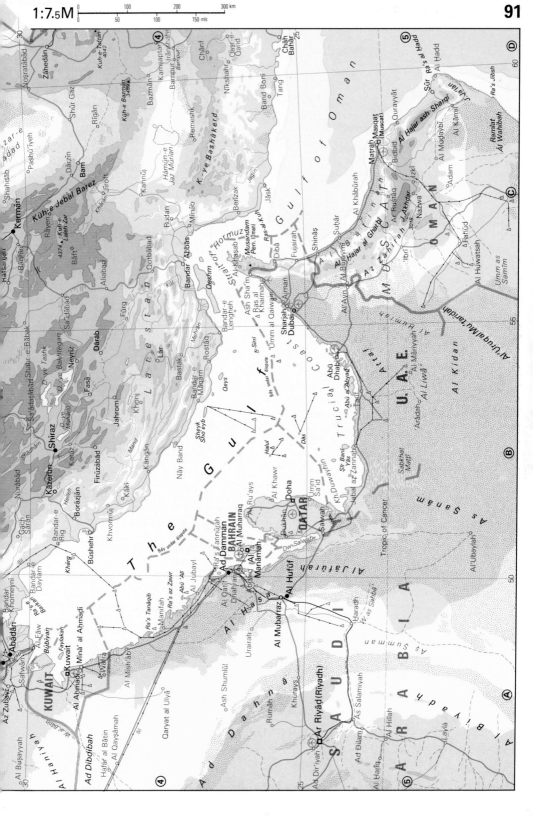

1:7.5M

100   200   300 km
50   100   150 mls

30

Gulf of Oman

Kermān

Bandar 'Abbās

Strait of Hormuz

Qeshm

Musandam Pen. (Oman)

Dibā

Fujairah

Matrah Masqat (Muscat)

Sūr

Ra's al Hadd

Al Hadd

Al Hajar ash Sharqī

Quryāt

Ra's Jibsh

Ramlat Al Wahībah

Al Kāmil

Al Mudaybī

Bidbid

Al Ḥajar al Gharbī

Al Akhḍar

Nazwā

Ibrī

Adam

Faḥūd

Al Huwatsah

Umm as Samīm

OMAN

MUSCAT AND OMAN

Al Buraymī

'Ibrī

Al Ḥajar al Gharbī

Ash Shām

Ras al Khaimah

Umm al Qaiwain

Sharjah Ajmān

Dubai

Abu Dhabi

U.A.E.

Al Māhnyah

Al Liwā'

Al Kidan

As Sanām

Trucial Coast

Qatar

Doha

BAHRAIN

Al Manāmah

Al Muharraq

Ad Dammām

Al Hufūf

Al Mubarraz

Al Hasa

SAUDI ARABIA

Ar Riyād (Riyadh)

KUWAIT

Kuwait

Abādān

The Gulf

Laristan

Shiraz

Kāzerūn

Būshehr

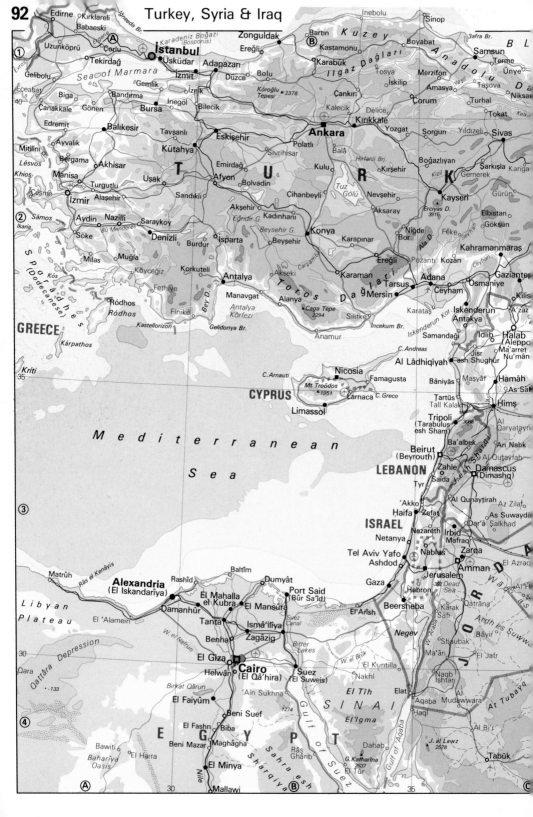

① ② ③ ④

Ⓐ Ⓑ Ⓒ

Edirne Kırklareli
Uzunköprü Babaeski
Iğneada Br.
Karadeniz Boğazı
(Bosporus)
Corlu
Tekirdağ İstanbul
Üsküdar
İzmit Adapazarı
Düzce Bolu
Köroğlu
Tepesi 2378
Gemlik İznik
Bandırma İnegöl Bilecik
Gönen Bursa Eskişehir
Biga
Çanakkale
Edremit Balıkesir Tavşanlı
Ayvalık Kütahya
Mitilini Bergama Akhisar Emirdağ
Lésvos Manisa Afyon Bolvadin
Khios Turgutlu Uşak Sandıklı
Çeşme İzmir Alaşehir
Sámos Aydın Nazilli Saraykoy Akşehir
Ikaria Söke Denizli Eğridir G. Kadınhanı
Milas Burdur İsparta Beyşehir G.
Muğla Korkuteli Beyşehir
Köyceğiz Antalya
Fethiye Bey D. Manavgat
Finike Alanya
Kastellorizon Akseki

Zonguldak Ereğli
Bartın Boyabat
Karabük Kastamonu
İlgaz Dağları
Tosya İskilip
Çankırı
Kalecik
Delice
Kırıkkale
Ankara
Polatlı Yozgat Sorgun
Balâ
Sivrihisar Kulu Hirfanlı Brj.
Kırşehir Boğazlıyan
Cihanbeyli
Tuz Gölü Nevşehir Kayseri
Aksaray Erciyas D.
3916
Konya Niğde Feke
Bor Ala D.
Karapınar
Karaman Ereğli Pozantı Kozan
Tarsus Adana
Mersin Ceyhan
Toros Dağları Osmaniye
Caga Tepe Karataş İskenderun
2294 Silifke Antakya
Anamur İncekum Br. Samandağı

Sinop
İnebolu
Kuzey
Bartın Boyabat
Anadolu Samsun
Terme
Ünye
Niksa
Merzifon
Amasya Taşova
Çorum Turhal
Tokat Kelkit
Yıldızeli
Sivas
Şarkışla Kanga
Gemerek
Gürün
Kahramanmaraş
Gaziantep
Kilis
A'zaz
Halab
(Aleppo)
Ma'arret
Nu'mân

GREECE
Ródhos
Ródhos
Kárpathos
Kríti

Mediterranean Sea

CYPRUS
C. Arnauti
Nicosia
Mt. Troödos Famagusta
1951 C. Greco
Larnaca
Limassol

C. Andreas
Al Lâdhiqiyah
Jisr
ash Shughûr
Idlib
Ma'arret
Nu'mân

Bâniyâs Maşyâf
Tartûs Hamâh
Tall Kalakh As-Sal
Ḥimş
Tripoli
(Tarabulus
esh Sham) Al
Qaryatayn
Ba'albek
An Nabk
Beirut Al Qutayfah
(Beyrouth)
Zahle
LEBANON Damascus
Tyr Saida (Dimashq)

'Akko Al Qunayṭirah
Haifa Az Zilaf
Zefat
Irbid As Suwaydâ
ISRAEL Dar'â Ṣalkhad
Nazareth Mafraq
Netanya
Nablus Zarqa
Tel Aviv Yafo Amman
Ashdod
Jerusalem
Gaza Dead
Hebron Sea
Beersheba Karak
Şâfi
Negev

Matrûh
Râs el Kenâyis
Baltîm
Rashîd Dumyât
Alexandria Port Said
(El Iskandariya) (Bûr Sa'îd)
El Mahalla
el Kubra El Mansûra
Damanhûr El 'Arîsh
El 'Alamein Tanta İsmâ'ilîya
Libyan Benha Zagazig Suez
Plateau Canal
Bitter
Lakes
El Giza
Qattâra Depression Helwân Cairo Suez
(El Qâ'hira) (El Suweis)
-133 'Ain Sukhna Nakhl
Qara Birkat Qârûn
El Faiyûm El Tîh
Beni Suef SINAI
El Fashn 1274 El 'Igma
Bawiti Biba Râs
Beni Mazar Maghâgha Ghârib
Baharîya El Harra G. Katharîna
Oasis El Minya 2637
Sahara esh El Tûr
Sharqiya
Nile Dahab
Mallawi
EGYPT

JORDAN
El Azraq
Wâdi
Qâtrâna
Ardh es Suwwe
Ma'ân
El Jafr
Shaubak Bâyir
Naqb
Ishtar
Elat
Aqaba Mudawwara
Haql At Tubayq
J. al Lawz
2578 Tabûk

Gulf of Suez
Gulf of 'Aqaba

40 35 30 35
30

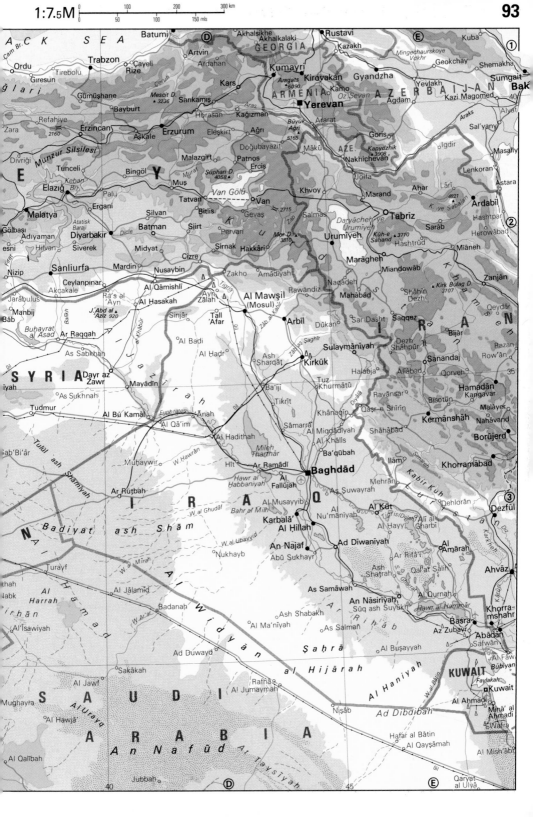

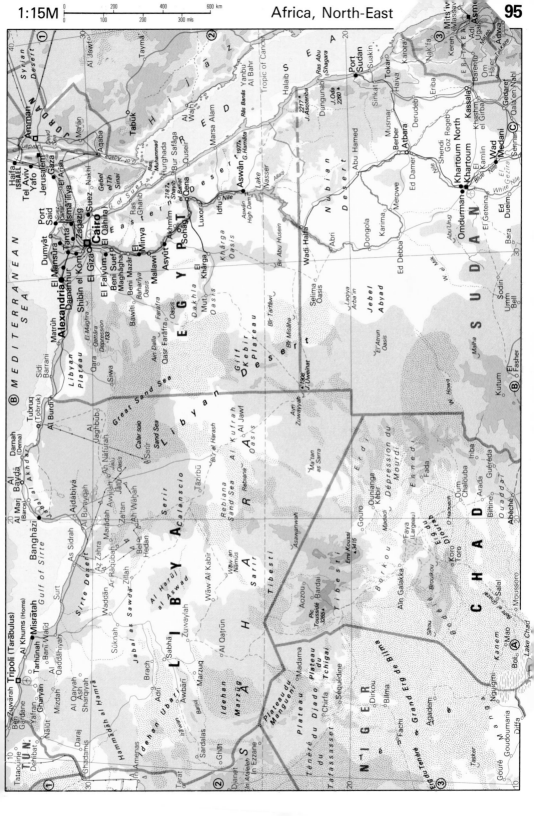

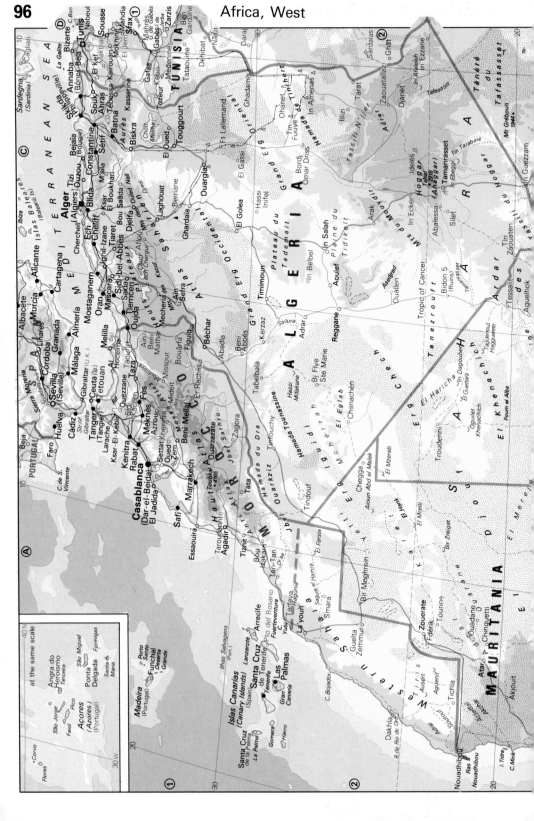

1:15M

0 200 400 600 km
0 100 200 300 mils

NIGER · MALI · NIGERIA · CAMEROON · EQUATORIAL GUINEA · S. TOME & PRINCIPE · BENIN · TOGO · GHANA · BURKINA · CÔTE D'IVOIRE · LIBERIA · SIERRA LEONE · GUINEA · GUINEA BISSAU · THE GAMBIA · SENEGAL · CAPE VERDE

GULF OF GUINEA · Bight of Biafra · Bight of Benin · Mouths of the R. Niger

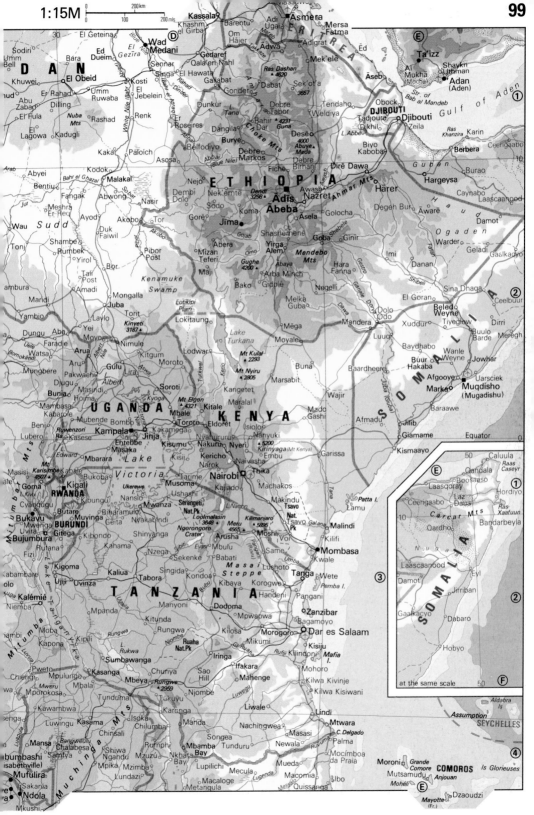

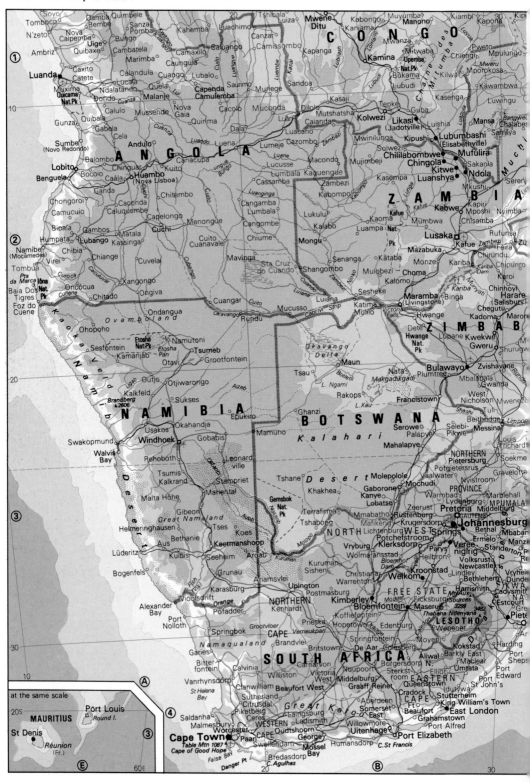

at the same scale

MAURITIUS

Port Louis
Round I.

③

St Denis
Réunion
(Fr.)

60E

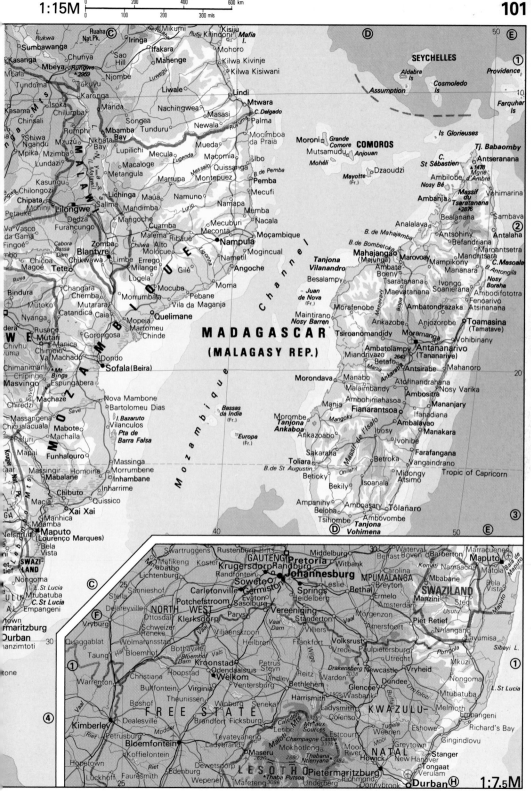

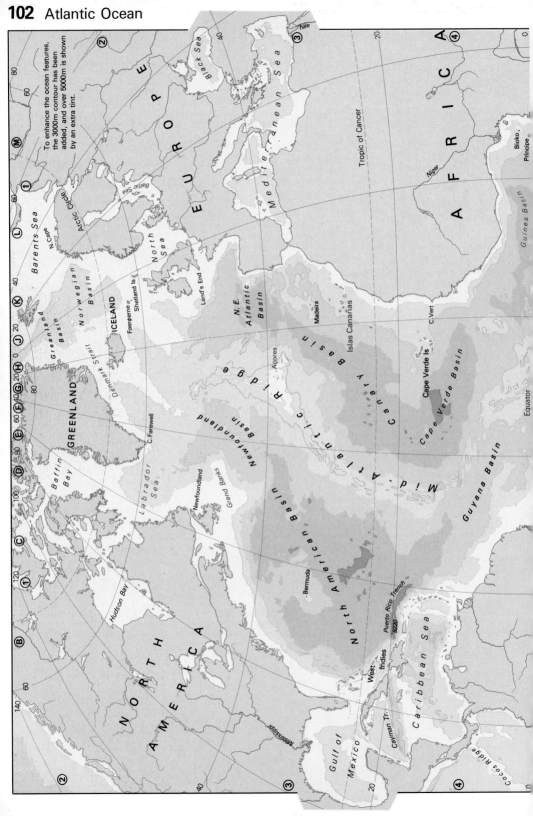

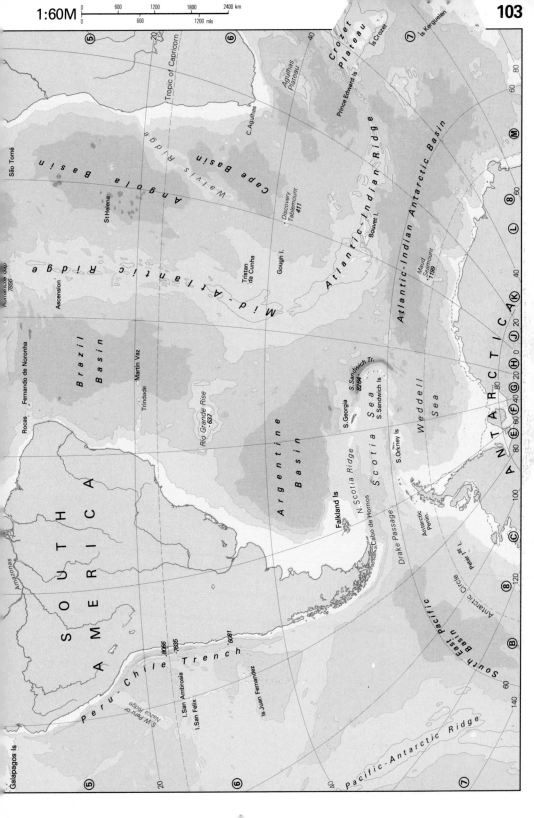

1:60M

600   1200   1800   2400 km
600   1200 mls

⑤   20   ⑥   Crozet Plateau   40   Is Kerguelen   ⑦

Tropic of Capricorn

Agulhas Plateau

C. Agulhas   Prince Edward Is   Atlantic - Indian Ridge   Ⓜ

São Tomé   Cape Basin   Atlantic - Indian Antarctic Basin   80

Angola Basin   Walvis Ridge   60   ⑧   60

St Helena   Discovery Tablemount 411   Ⓛ

Ascension   Tristan da Cunha   Gough I.   Bouvet I.   Maud Seamount 1989   40   Ⓚ

Mid-Atlantic Ridge   Ⓙ   20

Romanche Gap 7856

Fernando de Noronha   Brazil Basin   Martin Vaz   S. Sandwich Tr. 8264   Ⓗ   20   80

Rocas   Trindade   Rio Grande Rise 637   S.Georgia   S.Sandwich Is   Weddell Sea   Ⓖ   40   Ⓕ   60   Ⓔ   80

Argentine Basin   Scotia Sea   S.Orkney Is   ANTARCTICA

SOUTH   Falkland Is   N.Scotia Ridge   Cabo de Hornos   Antarctic Penin.   Ⓒ   100

Amazonas   ⑧   Peter I st I.   120   Antarctic Circle

AMERICA   Drake Passage   East Pacific   ⑧

8066   7635   6081   South East Basin   Ⓑ   140

Peru - Chile Trench   i.San Ambrosia   i.San Felix   Is Juan Fernandez   60

S.W.Peru or Nazca Ridge

Galapagos Is   ⑤   20   ⑥   40   Pacific - Antarctic Ridge   ⑦

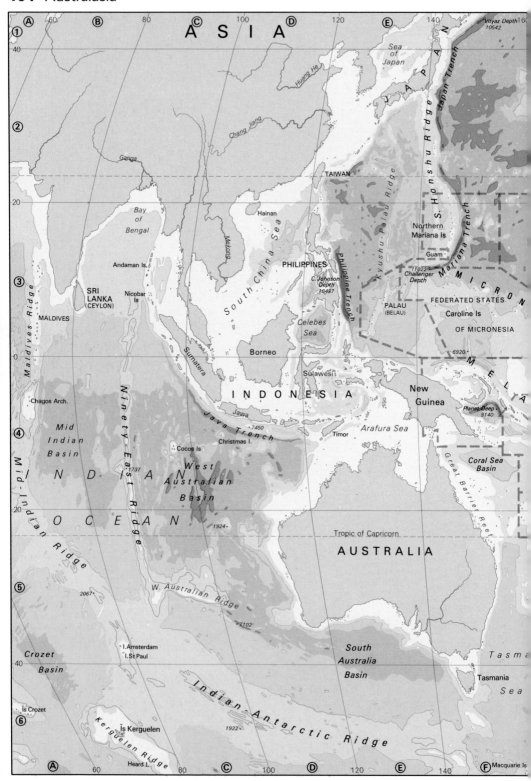

ⒶⒷⒸⒹⒺ

① ② ③ ④ ⑤ ⑥

ASIA

Sea of Japan

J A P A N

Huang He

Chang Jiang

Ganga

Vityaz Depth 160
10542

40

20

TAIWAN

Hainan

Bay of Bengal

Andaman Is.

MALDIVES

SRI LANKA (CEYLON)

Nicobar Is

Chagos Arch.

Maldives Ridge

Mid Indian Basin

Mid-Indian Ridge

Mekong

South China Sea

PHILIPPINES

C. Johnson Depth
10497

Philippine Trench

Celebes Sea

Borneo

Sulawesi

I N D O N E S I A

Sumatera

Ninety-East Ridge

Java Trench

•7450

Jawa

Cocos Is

Christmas I.

•1737

West Australian Basin

I N D I A N

O C E A N

•1924

•2067

W. Australian Ridge

•7102

I. Amsterdam
I. St Paul

Crozet Basin

40

Is Crozet

Kerguelen Ridge

Îs Kerguelen

Heard I.

Indian-Antarctic Ridge

•1922

Kyushu-Palau Ridge

S. Honshu Ridge

Japan Trench

Northern Mariana Is

Guam

Challenger Depth

Mariana Trench

M I C R O N

Federated States

Caroline Is

OF MICRONESIA

PALAU (BELAU)

11022
Challenger Depth

•6920

M E L A

New Guinea

Timor

Arafura Sea

Planet Deep
9140

Great Barrier Reef

Coral Sea Basin

Tropic of Capricorn

A U S T R A L I A

South Australia Basin

T a s m a

Tasmania

Sea

60 80 100 120 140 160

ⒶⒸⒹⒺⒻ Macquarie Is

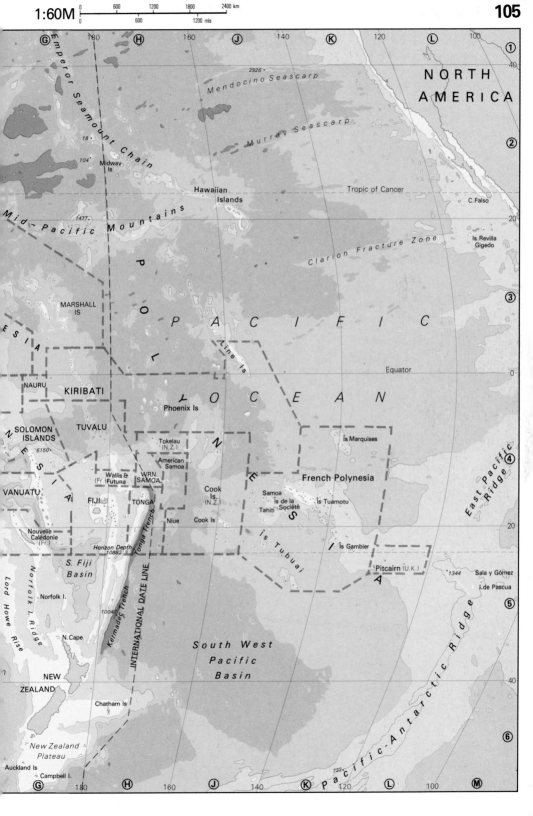

1:60M

0   600   1200   1800   2400 km
0   600   1200 mls

NORTH AMERICA

2926 ·
Mendocino Seascarp

Murray Seascarp

Tropic of Cancer

C.Falso

18 ·
104 · Midway Is

Hawaiian Islands

Is Revilla Gigedo

1477 ·
Mid-Pacific Mountains

Clarion Fracture Zone

P A C I F I C

Emperor Seamount Chain

MARSHALL IS

P O L Y N E S I A

Equator

Line Is

NAURU

KIRIBATI

O C E A N

East Pacific Ridge

SOLOMON ISLANDS

TUVALU

Phoenix Is

6150 ·

Tokelau (N.Z.)

Is Marquises

American Samoa

French Polynesia

Wallis & (Fr.) Futuna

WRN. SAMOA

VANUATU

FIJI

TONGA

Cook Is. (N.Z.)

Samoa
Is de la Société
Is Tuamotu
Tahiti

Nouvelle Calédonie (Fr.)

Niue   Cook Is

Is Tubuai

Is Gambier

Horizon Depth 10882 ·

S. Fiji Basin

Tonga Trench

INTERNATIONAL DATE LINE

Pitcairn (U.K.)   · 1344   Sala y Gómez
I.de Pascua

Norfolk I.

Norfolk I. Ridge

10047 ·

Kermadec Trench

N.Cape

South West Pacific Basin

Lord Howe Rise

NEW ZEALAND

Chatham Is

732 ·

New Zealand Plateau

Pacific-Antarctic Ridge

Auckland Is

Campbell I.

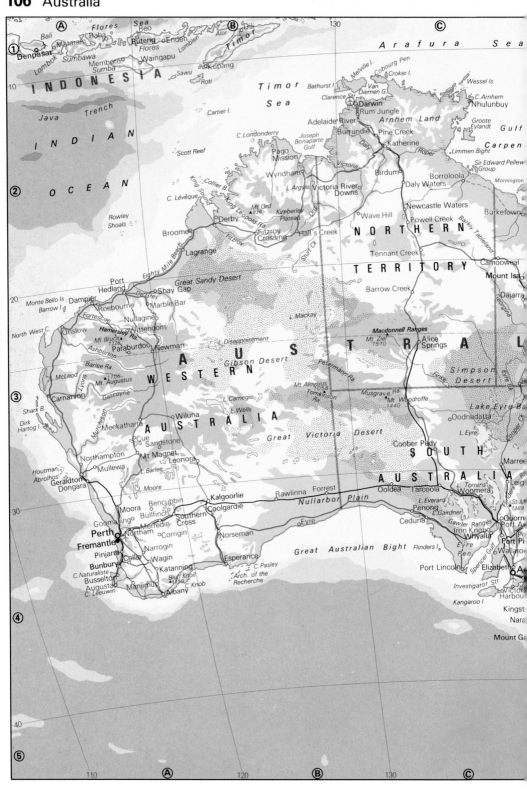

A ① Flores Sea Reo
Bali Maletsai Raba Ruteng Endeh B Dili Alor
Denpasar Flores Lomblen Timor C
Lombok Sumbawa Memberoo Waingapu Kupang
Sumba

INDONESIA Sawu Roti

Java Trench 10

INDIAN Cartier I.

OCEAN ②

Rowley Shoals

Scott Reef

Monte Bello Is
Barrow I.

North West C.

③

Shark B.
Dirk Hartog I.

Houtman Abrolhos

④

⑤

A R A F U R A   S e a

130   C

Timor Sea

Melville I. Cobourg Pen
Bathurst I. Van Croker I. Wessel Is
Clarence Str. Diemen G. C. Arnhem Nhulunbuy
Darwin Rum Jungle
Adelaide River Arnhem Land Groote
C. Londonderry Burrundie Pine Creek Eylandt Gulf
Joseph Katherine Roper Limmen Bight Carpen
Bonaparte Gulf Daly Sir Edward Pellew
Pago Victoria Birdum Borroloola Group Mornington
Mission Daly Waters
Wyndham
L. Argyle Victoria River Newcastle Waters Burketown
C. Lévêque Downs
Mt Ord Qld Wave Hill Powell Creek
▲936 Kimberley Barkly Tableland Carnoowedl
Derby King Leopold Ra Plateau NORTHERN Mount Isa
Broome Fitzroy Hall's Creek 0
Crossing Sturt Ck
Lagrange Tennant Creek TERRITORY
Eighty Mile Beach Fitzroy Dajarra
Port Great Sandy Desert Barrow Creek
Hedland Shay Gap L. Mackay Georgina
Dampier Roebourne Marble Bar Macdonnell Ranges
Onslow Nullagine Mt Zeil Alice Simpson
Fortescue Wittenoom ▲1510 Springs
Hamersley Ra. A U S T R A L Desert
Mt Bruce L. Disappointment Petermann Ra
Ashburton 1236 Paraburdoo Newman Mt Aloysius I
Barlee Ra. Gibson Desert 1058 Musgrave Ra
McLeod Mt ▲1106 Tomkinson Mt Woodroffe Lake Eyre Ba
Carnarvon Augustus WESTERN Ra 1440
Lyons Gascoyne L. Carnegie Oodnadatta
Murchison L. Wells Great Victoria Desert L. Eyre
Meekatharra Wiluna AUSTRALIA Coober Pedy SOUTH
Cue Sandstone Marree
Northampton Mt Magnet Leonora AUSTRALIA
Geraldton Mullewa L. Barlee Oodea Tarcoola L. Torrens Leigh
Dongara L. Moore Rawlinna Forrest Penong St M
L. Everard Woomera 1189
Moora Bencubbin Kalgoorlie Nullarbor Plain Ceduna L. Gairdner Quorn
Goomalling Bullfinch Coolgardie Eyre Penong Gawler Ranges Port A
Perth Merredin Southern Iron Knobo Whyalla
Fremantle Northam Cross Eyre Port Pi
Narrogin Corrigin Norseman Port Lincoln Pen Elizabeth Wallaro
Pinjarra Wagin Great Australian Bight Flinders I. A
Collie Esperance Investigator Str.
Bunbury Katanning C. Pasley Spencer Gulf
C. Naturaliste Busselton Bluff Knoll Arch. of the Kingst
Augusta Manjimup ▲1110 Recherche Kangaroo I. Nara
C. Leeuwin C. Kriob Albany Victor
Harbou

Mount Ga

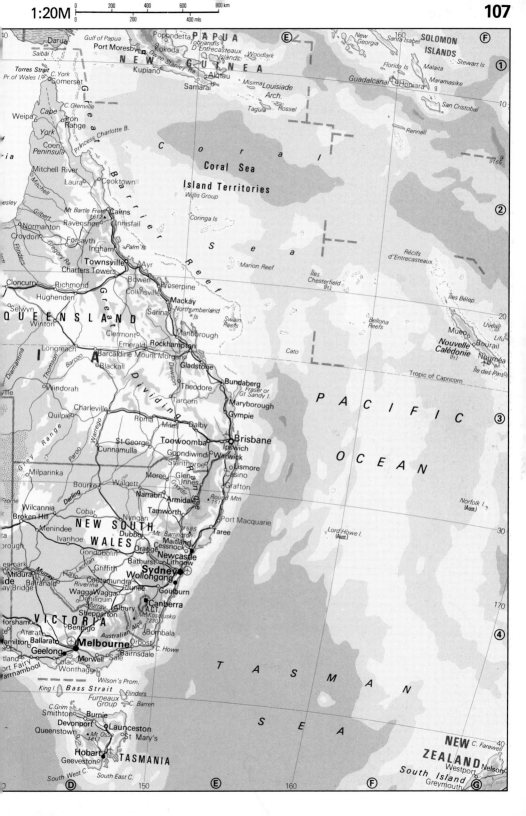

200   400   600   800 km

200   400 mls

PAPUA

Gulf of Papua   Popondetta   Tobriands Is.   New   160   SOLOMON
Saibai I.   D'Entrecasteaux   Georgia   Santa Isabel   ISLANDS
Daru   Port Moresby   Kokoda   Woodlark   Stewart Is.   ①
Torres Strait   **NEW GUINEA**   Owen Stanley Ra.   Alotau   Florida Is.   Malaita
Pr. of Wales I.   Kupiano   Misima   Louisiade   Guadalcanal   Honiara   Maramasike
Somerset   Samarai   Arch.   10   San Cristobal
C. York   Rossel   Rennell
Cape   C. Grenville   Tagula
Weipa   York   Iron   Récifs
Coen   Range   C   d'Entrecasteaux
Peninsula   Princess Charlotte B.   o   r   a   ②
Mitchell River   r   l

Coral Sea
Laura   a   **Island Territories**
Cooktown   l   Willis Group
Mitchell   Mt Bartle Frere   Cairns   Coringa Is.   Récifs   Îles Bélep
1612   Innisfail   S   d'Entrecasteaux
Normanton   Ravenshoe   e   Îles Chesterfield   Uvéa
Croydon   Forsayth   Ingham   B   a   (Fr.)   Lifu
Palm Is.   a   Muea   Bourail
Townsville   r   Marion Reef   **Nouvelle**   Nouméa
Charters Towers   Ayr   r   Îles   **Calédonie**   Île des Pins
Cloncurry   Bowen   i   Chesterfield   (Fr.)
Richmond   Collinsville   Proserpine   e   (Fr.)   Tropic of Capricorn
Hughenden   Mackay   r   Bellona
QUEENSLAND   Sarina   Northumberland Is.   Reefs   20
Selwyn   Swain   Cato
Winton   Clermont   Reefs
Emerald   Marlborough   **PACIFIC**   ③
Longreach   Barcaldine   Rockhampton
Windorah   Blackall   Mount Morgan   **OCEAN**
Charleville   Gladstone
Quilpie   Roma   Theodore   Bundaberg   Fraser or
Taroom   Gt Sandy I.
Milparinka   Miles   Dalby   Maryborough
St George   Toowoomba   Gympie
Bourke   Cunnamulla   Dalby   **Brisbane**   Norfolk I.
Wilcannia   Goondiwindi   Ipswich   (Aust.)
Broken Hill   Walgett   Stanthorpe   Warwick
Menindee   Narrabri   Glen   Lismore   Lord Howe I.   30
Ivanhoe   Moree   Innes   Casino   (Aust.)
Cobar   Armidale   Grafton
Nyngan   Tamworth   Round Mtn
NEW SOUTH   Port Macquarie
Dubbo   Mt Barrington   Taree
WALES   Orange   1585
Gondobolin   Maitland
Griffith   Bathurst   Cessnock
Hay   Lachlan   Lithgow   Newcastle
Murray   Cootamundra   **Sydney**
Balranald   Junee   **Wollongong**
Wagga Wagga   Goulburn
Deniliquin   Albury   **Canberra**
Shepparton   A.C.T.   170
VICTORIA   Mt Kosciusko   ④
Bendigo   2230
Ararat   Australian   Bombala
Ballarat   Alps   Orbost
Melbourne   Bairnsdale   C. Howe
Geelong   Morwell   Sale
Colac   Wonthaggi   **TASMAN**
Warrnambool   Wilson's Prom.
King I.   **Bass Strait**   Flinders   **SEA**
Furneaux
Group   C. Barren
Smithton   Burnie
Devonport   Launceston   **NEW**   C. Farewell
Queenstown   St Mary's   **ZEALAND**   Nelson
Mt Ossa   Westport
Hobart   1617   **South Island**   40
Geeveston   **TASMANIA**   Greymouth
South West C.   South East C.   150   160

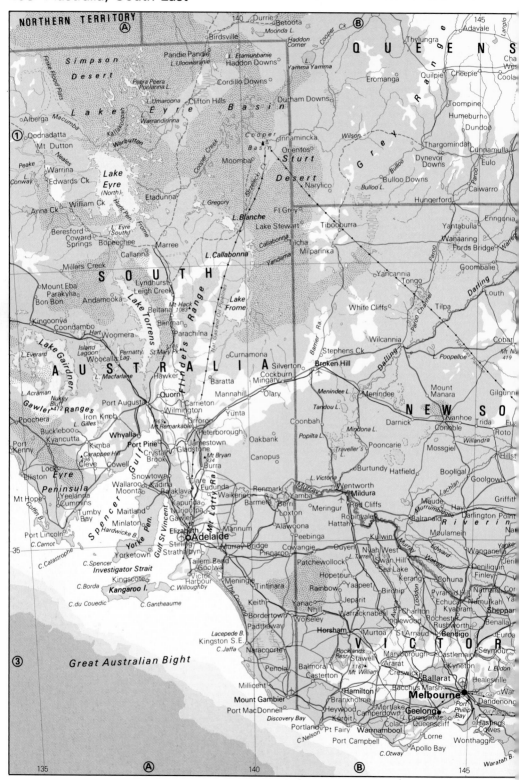

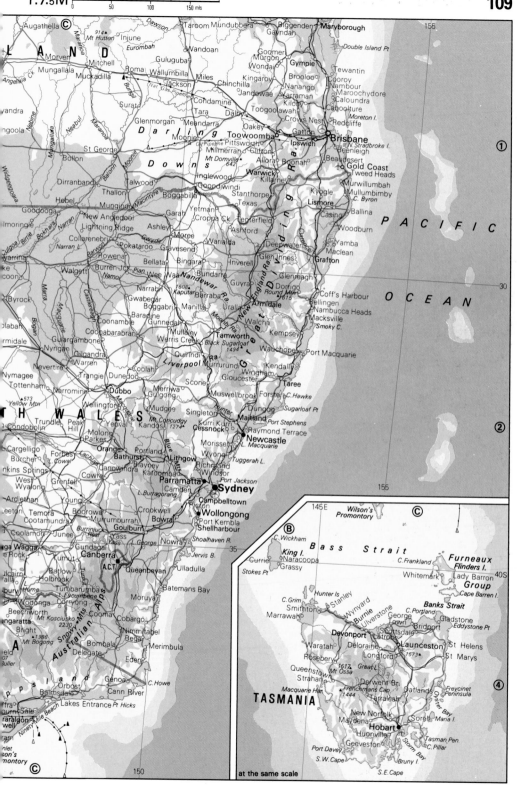

1:7.5M

100   200   300 km
50   100   150 mls

Augathella C
Taroom Mundubbera
LAND
Morven
Mitchell
Injune
Eurombah
Wandoan
Goomeri
Murgon
Wondai
Gympie
Brooloo
Nanango
Yarraman
Kilcoy
Toogoolawah
Crows Nest
Oakey
Gatton
Toowoomba
Ipswich
Pittsworth
Millmerran
Clifton
Mt Domville
642
Alloora
Warwick
Killarney
Inglewood
Goondiwindi
Stanthorpe
Texas
Tenterfield
Deepwater
Glen Innes
Glencoe
Guyra
Dorrigo
Round Mtn
1615
Armidale
Walcha
Kempsey
Wauchope
Port Macquarie
Kendall
Wingham
Gloucester
Taree
C. Hawke
Forster
Sugarloaf Pt
Port Stephens
Raymond Terrace
Newcastle
L. Macquarie
Tuggerah L.
Wyong
Gosford
Richmond
Windsor
Port Jackson
Parramatta
Sydney
Campbelltown
Picton
Wollongong
Port Kembla
Shellharbour
Nowra
Shoalhaven R.
Jervis B.
Ulladulla
Batemans Bay
Moruya

Maryborough
Double Island Pt
Tewantin
Cooroy
Nambour
Maroochydore
Caloundra
Caboolture
Moreton I.
Redcliffe
N. Stradbroke I.
Brisbane
Beenleigh
Beaudesert
Gold Coast
Tweed Heads
Murwillumbah
Mullumbimby
C. Byron
Lismore
Ballina
Casino
Woodburn
Yamba
Maclean
Grafton
Coff's Harbour
Bellingen
Nambucca Heads
Macksville
Smoky C.

PACIFIC

OCEAN

155

30

155

1
2

Currie
Naracoopa
Grassy
Stokes Pt
King I.
C. Wickham
Hunter Is
Marrawah
C. Grim
Smithton
Stanley
Wynyard
Burnie
Ulverstone
Devonport
Deloraine
Longford
Waratah
Rosebery
Queenstown
Strahan
Mt Ossa
1617
Frenchmans Cap
1444
Macquarie Har
New Norfolk
Maydena
Port Davey
S.W. Cape
Geeveston
Huonville
Hobart
S.E. Cape
Bruny I.
Storm Bay
C. Pillar
Tasman Pen.
Sorell
Maria I.
Oyster Bay
Freycinet
Peninsula
Oatlands
Derwent Br.
Tarraleah
Campbell Town
Ross
Launceston
St Marys
St Helens
Eddystone Pt
Gladstone
St Portland
Bridport
Scottsdale
George Town
Banks Strait
C. Portland
Whitemark
Lady Barron
Cape Barren I.
Flinders I.
Furneaux
Group
C. Frankland
Bass   Strait
Wilson's
Promontory
145E
B
C
40S

TASMANIA

at the same scale

4

Wilson's
Promontory
C

150

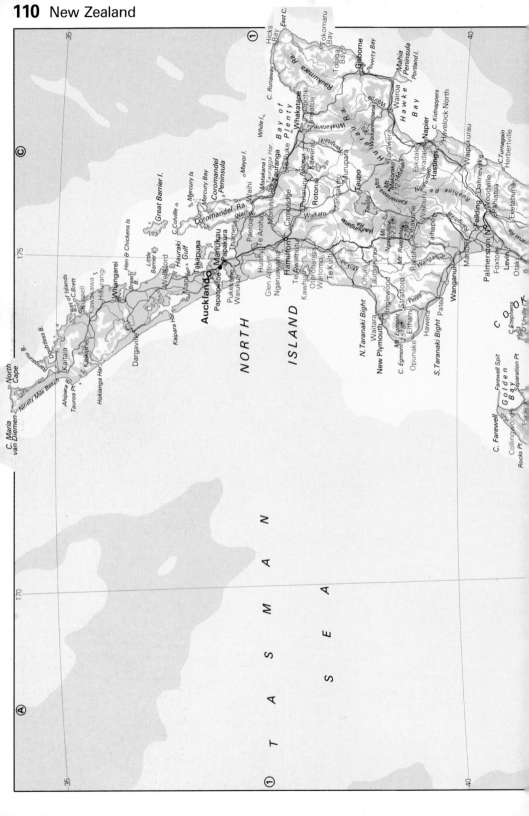

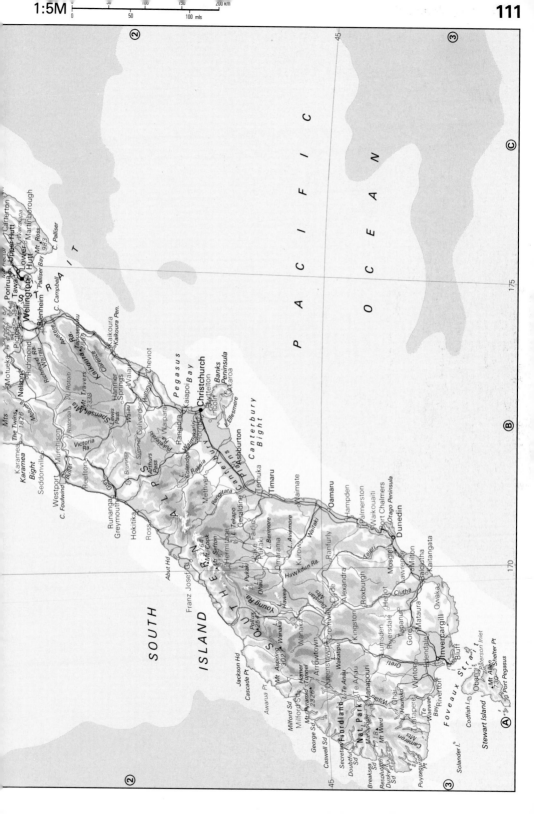

1:40M

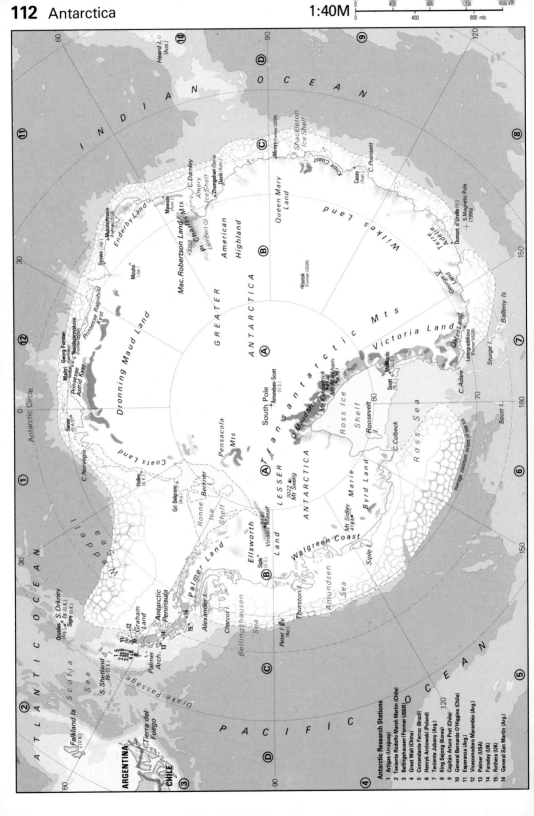

Antarctic Research Stations
1 Artigas (Uruguay)
2 Teniente Rodolfo Marsh Martin (Chile)
3 Bellingshausen (Former USSR)
4 Great Wall (China)
5 Comandante Ferraz (Brazil)
6 Henryk Arctowski (Poland)
7 Teniente Jubany (Arg.)
8 King Sejong (Korea)
9 General Bernardo O'Higgins (Chile)
10 Capitan Arturo Prat (Chile)
11 Esperanza (Arg.)
12 Vicecomodoro Marambio (Arg.)
13 Palmer (USA)
14 Faraday (UK)
15 Rothera (UK)
16 General San Martin (Arg.)

Index

In the index, the first number refers to the page, and the following letter and number to the section of the map in which the index entry can be found. For example, 48C2 **Paris** means that Paris can be found on page 48 where column C and row 2 meet.

Abbreviations used in the index

Although the maps in this edition have been revised to take account of the change of name from Zaire to Congo this index reflects the previous situation

Adrar

96A2	**Adrar** Region, Maur
96C2	**Adrar** *Mts* Alg
96A2	**Adrar Soutouf** Region, Mor
98C1	**Adré** Chad
95A2	**Adri** Libya
47E2	**Adria** Italy
14B2	**Adrian** Michigan, USA
52B2	**Adriatic S** S Europe
99D1	**Adwa** Eth
61F5	**Adygeya** Division, Russian Fed
97B4	**Adzopé** Côte d'Ivoire
55B3	**Aegean** *S* Greece
80E2	**Afghanistan** Republic, Asia
99E2	**Afgooye** Somalia
97C4	**Afikpo** Nig
38G6	**Afjord** Nor
96C1	**Aflou** Alg
99E2	**Afmadu** Somalia
97A3	**Afollé** Region, Maur
94B2	**Afula** Israel
92B2	**Afyon** Turk
95A3	**Agadem** Niger
97C3	**Agadez** Niger
96B1	**Agadir** Mor
85D4	**Agar** India
86C2	**Agartala** India
20B1	**Agassiz** Can
97B4	**Agboville** Côte d'Ivoire
93E1	**Agdam** Azerbaijan
75B1	**Agematsu** Japan
48C3	**Agen** France
90A3	**Agha Jārī** Iran
96A2	**Aghwinit** *Well* Mor
47D2	**Agno** *R* Italy
47E1	**Agordo** Italy
48C3	**Agout** *R* France
85D3	**Agra** India
93D2	**Ağri** Turk
53C2	**Agri** *R* Italy
53B3	**Agrigento** Italy
55B3	**Agrínion** Greece
34A3	**Agrio** *R* Chile
53B2	**Agropoli** Italy
61H2	**Agryz** Russian Fed
6E3	**Agto** Greenland
27D3	**Aguadilla** Puerto Rico
24B1	**Agua Prieta** Mexico
24B2	**Aguascalientes** Mexico
23A1	**Aguascalientes** State, Mexico
35C1	**Aguas Formosas** Brazil
50A1	**Agueda** Port
96C3	**Aguelhok** Mali
50B2	**Aguilas** Spain
23A2	**Aguililla** Mexico
100B4	**Agulhas,C** S Africa
79C4	**Agusan** *R* Phil
	Ahaggar = Hoggar
93E2	**Ahar** Iran
110B1	**Ahipara B** NZ
85C4	**Ahmadābād** India
87A1	**Ahmadnagar** India
99E2	**Ahmar** *Mts* Eth
46D1	**Ahr** *R* Germany
46D1	**Ahrgebirge** Region, Germany
23A1	**Ahuacatlán** Mexico
23A1	**Ahualulco** Mexico
39G7	**Åhus** Sweden
90B2	**Ahuvān** Iran
90A3	**Ahvāz** Iran
26A4	**Aiajuela** Costa Rica
47B1	**Aigle** Switz
47B2	**Aiguille d'Arves** *Mt* France
47B2	**Aiguille de la Grand Sassière** *Mt* France
75B1	**Aikawa** Japan
17B1	**Aiken** USA
73A5	**Ailao Shan** *Upland* China
35C1	**Aimorés** Brazil
96B1	**Ain Beni Mathar** Mor
95B2	**Ain Dalla** *Well* Egypt
51C2	**Ain el Hadjel** Alg
95A3	**Aïn Galakka** Chad
96B1	**Aïn Sefra** Alg
92B4	**'Ain Sukhna** Egypt
75A2	**Aioi** Japan
96B2	**Aioun Abd el Malek** *Well* Maur
97B3	**Aïoun El Atrouss** Maur
30C2	**Aiquile** Bol
97C3	**Aïr** *Desert Region* Niger
13E2	**Airdrie** Can
46B1	**Aire** France
42D3	**Aire** *R* Eng
46C2	**Aire** *R* France
6C3	**Airforce I** Can
47C1	**Airolo** Switz
4E3	**Aishihik** Can
12G2	**Aishihik L** Can
46B2	**Aisne** Department, France
49C2	**Aisne** *R* France
71F4	**Aitape** PNG
58D1	**Aiviekste** *R* Latvia
72B2	**Aixa Zuogi** China
49D3	**Aix-en-Provence** France
47A2	**Aix-les-Bains** France
86B2	**Aiyar Res** India
55B3	**Aiyion** Greece
55B3	**Aíyna** *I* Greece
86C2	**Aïzawl** India
100A3	**Aizeb** *R* Namibia
74E3	**Aizu-Wakamatsu** Japan
52A2	**Ajaccio** Corse
23B2	**Ajalpan** Mexico
65F5	**Ajaria** Division, Georgia
95B1	**Ajdābiyā** Libya
74E2	**Ajigasawa** Japan
94B2	**Ajlūn** Jordan
91C4	**Ajman** UAE
85C3	**Ajmer** India
9B3	**Ajo** USA
23A2	**Ajuchitan** Mexico
55C3	**Ak** *R* Turk
75B1	**Akaishi-sanchi** *Mts* Japan
87B1	**Akalkot** India
111B2	**Akaroa** NZ
75A2	**Akashi** Japan
61J3	**Akbulak** Russian Fed
93C2	**Akçakale** Turk
96A2	**Akchar** *Watercourse* Maur
55C3	**Akdağ** *Mt* Turk
98C2	**Aketi** Zaire
93D1	**Akhalkalaki** Georgia
93D1	**Akhalsikhe** Georgia
55B3	**Akharnaí** Greece
12D3	**Akhiok** USA
92A2	**Akhisar** Turk
58D1	**Akhiste** Latvia
95C2	**Akhmîm** Egypt
61G4	**Akhtubinsk** Russian Fed
60D4	**Akhtyrka** Ukraine
75A2	**Aki** Japan
7B4	**Akimiski I** Can
74E3	**Akita** Japan
96A3	**Akjoujt** Maur
94B2	**'Akko** Israel
4E3	**Aklavik** USA
97B3	**Aklé Aouana** *Desert Region* Maur
99D2	**Akobo** Sudan
99D2	**Akobo** *R* Sudan
84B1	**Akoha** Afghan
85D4	**Akola** India
85D4	**Akot** India
6D3	**Akpatok I** Can
55B3	**Ákra Kafirévs** *C* Greece
55B3	**Ákra Maléa** *C* Greece
38A2	**Akranes** Iceland
55C3	**Ákra Sídheros** *C* Greece
55B3	**Ákra Spátha** *C* Greece
55B3	**Ákra Taínaron** *C* Greece
10B2	**Akron** USA
94A1	**Akrotiri B** Cyprus
84D1	**Aksai Chin** *Mts* China
92B2	**Aksaray** Turk
61H3	**Aksay** Kazakhstan
84D1	**Aksayquin Hu** *L* China
92B2	**Akşehir** Turk
92B2	**Akseki** Turk
63D2	**Aksenovo Zilovskoye** Russian Fed
68D1	**Aksha** Russian Fed
82C1	**Aksu** China
61H5	**Aktau** Kazakhstan
65J5	**Aktogay** Kazakhstan
61J4	**Aktumsyk** Kazakhstan
65G4	**Aktyubinsk** Kazakhstan
38B1	**Akureyri** Iceland
	Akyab = Sittwe
65K5	**Akzhal** Kazakhstan
11B3	**Alabama** State, USA
11B3	**Alabama** *R* USA
17A1	**Alabaster** USA
92C2	**Ala Dağlari** *Mts* Turk
61F5	**Alagir** Russian Fed
47B2	**Alagna** Italy
31D3	**Alagoas** State, Brazil
31D4	**Alagoinhas** Brazil
51B1	**Alagón** Spain
93E4	**Al Ahmadi** Kuwait
25D3	**Alajuela** Costa Rica
12B2	**Alakanuk** USA
38L5	**Alakurtti** Russian Fed
93E3	**Al Amārah** Iraq
21A2	**Alameda** USA
23B1	**Alamo** Mexico
9C3	**Alamogordo** USA
9C3	**Alamosa** USA
39H6	**Aland** *I* Fin
92B2	**Alanya** Turk
17B1	**Alapaha** *R* USA
65H4	**Alapayevsk** Russian Fed
92A2	**Alaşehir** Turk
68C3	**Ala Shan** *Mts* China
4C3	**Alaska** State, USA
4D4	**Alaska,G of** USA
12C3	**Alaska Pen** USA
4C3	**Alaska Range** *Mts* USA
52A2	**Alassio** Italy
12D1	**Alatna** *R* USA
61G3	**Alatyr** Russian Fed
108B2	**Alawoona** Aust
91C5	**Al'Ayn** UAE
82B2	**Alayskiy Khrebet** *Mts* Tajikistan
49D3	**Alba** Italy
92C2	**Al Bāb** Syria
51B2	**Albacete** Spain
50A1	**Alba de Tormes** Spain
93D2	**Al Badi** Iraq
54B1	**Alba Iulia** Rom
54A2	**Albania** Republic, Europe
106A4	**Albany** Aust
17B1	**Albany** Georgia, USA
15D2	**Albany** New York, USA
8A2	**Albany** Oregon, USA
7B4	**Albany** *R* Can
34B2	**Albardón** Arg
91C5	**Al Batinah** Region, Oman
71F5	**Albatross B** Aust
95B1	**Al Baydā** Libya
11C3	**Albemarle Sd** USA
50B1	**Alberche** *R* Spain
108A1	**Alberga** Aust
46B1	**Albert** France
5G4	**Alberta** Province, Can
99D2	**Albert,L** Uganda/Zaïre
10A2	**Albert Lea** USA
99D2	**Albert Nile** *R* Uganda
49D2	**Albertville** France
48C3	**Albi** France
18B1	**Albia** USA
33G2	**Albina** Suriname
14B2	**Albion** Michigan, USA
15C2	**Albion** New York, USA
92C4	**Al Bi'r** S Arabia
91A5	**Al Biyadh** Region, S Arabia
50B2	**Alborán** *I* Spain
39G7	**Alborg** Den
93D3	**Al Bū Kamāl** Syria
47C1	**Albula** *R* Switz
9C3	**Albuquerque** USA
91C5	**Al Buraymi** Oman
95A1	**Al Burayqah** Libya
95B1	**Al Burdī** Libya
107D4	**Albury** Aust
93E3	**Al Buşayyah** Iraq
50B1	**Alcalá de Henares** Spain
53B3	**Alcamo** Italy
51B1	**Alcaniz** Spain
31C2	**Alcântara** Brazil
50B2	**Alcaraz** Spain
50B2	**Alcázar de San Juan** Spain
51B2	**Alcira** Spain
35D1	**Alcobaça** Brazil
50B1	**Alcolea de Pinar** Spain
51B2	**Alcoy** Spain
51C2	**Alcudia** Spain
89J8	**Aldabra** *Is* Indian O
63E2	**Aldan** Russian Fed
63E2	**Aldanskoye Nagor'ye** *Upland* Russian Fed
43E3	**Aldeburgh** Eng
48B2	**Alderney** *I* UK
43D4	**Aldershot** Eng
97A3	**Aleg** Maur
30E4	**Alegrete** Brazil
34C2	**Alejandro Roca** Arg
30H6	**Alejandro Selkirk** *I* Chile
63G2	**Aleksandrovsk Sakhalinskiy** Russian Fed
65J4	**Alekseyevka** Kazakhstan
60E3	**Aleksin** Russian Fed
58B1	**Alem** Sweden
35C2	**Além Paraíba** Brazil
49C2	**Alençon** France
21C4	**Alenuihaha Chan** Hawaiian Is
	Aleppo = Ḥalab
6D1	**Alert** Can
49C3	**Alès** France
52A2	**Alessandria** Italy
64B3	**Ålesund** Nor
12C3	**Aleutian Range** *Mts* USA
4E4	**Alexander Arch** USA
100A3	**Alexander Bay** S Africa
17A1	**Alexander City** USA
112C3	**Alexander I** Ant
111A3	**Alexandra** NZ
29G8	**Alexandra,C** South Georgia
6C2	**Alexandra Fjord** Can
95B1	**Alexandria** Egypt
11A3	**Alexandria** Louisiana, USA
10A2	**Alexandria** Minnesota, USA
10C3	**Alexandria** Virginia, USA
55C2	**Alexandroúpolis** Greece
13C2	**Alexis Creek** Can
94B2	**Aley** Leb
65K4	**Aleysk** Russian Fed
93D3	**Al Fallūjah** Iraq
51B1	**Alfaro** Spain
54C2	**Alfatar** Bulg
93E3	**Al Fāw** Iraq
35B2	**Alfenas** Brazil
55B3	**Alfiós** *R* Greece
47D2	**Alfonsine** Italy
35C2	**Alfonzo Cláudio** Brazil
35C2	**Alfredo Chaves** Brazil
61J4	**Alga** Kazakhstan
34B3	**Algarrobo del Aguila** Arg
50A2	**Algeciras** Spain

96C1 Alger Alg
96B2 Algeria Republic, Africa
53A2 Alghero Sardegna
Algiers = Alger
15C1 Algonquin Park Can
91C5 Al Hadd Oman
93D3 Al Hadithah Iraq
92C3 Al Hadithah S Arabia
93D2 Al Hadr Iraq
91C5 Al Hajar al Gharbi Mts Oman
91C5 Al Hajar ash Sharqi Mts Oman
93C3 Al Hamad Desert Region Jordan/ S Arabia
93E4 Al Haniyah Desert Region Iraq
91A5 Al Hariq S Arabia
93C3 Al Harrah Desert Region S Arabia
95A2 Al Haruj al Aswad Upland Libya
91A4 Al Hasa Region, S Arabia
93D2 Al Hasakah Syria
93C4 Al Hawja' S Arabia
93E3 Al Hayy Iraq
94C2 Al Hijanah Syria
93D3 Al Hillah Iraq
91A5 Al Hillah S Arabia
96B1 Al Hoceima Mor
91A4 Al Hufuf S Arabia
91B5 Al Humrah Region, UAE
91C5 Al Huwatsah Oman
90A2 Aliabad Iran
91C4 Aliabad Iran
55B2 Aliakmon R Greece
93E3 Ali al Gharbi Iraq
87A1 Alibag India
51B2 Alicante Spain
9D4 Alice USA
106C3 Alice Springs Aust
53B3 Alicudi I Italy
84D3 Aligarh India
90A3 Aligudarz Iran
84B2 Ali-Khel Afghan
55C3 Alimnia I Greece
86B1 Alipur Duar India
14B2 Aliquippa USA
22B2 Alisal USA
93C3 Al' Isawiyah S Arabia
100B4 Aliwal North S Africa
95B2 Al Jaghbub Libya
93D3 Al Jalamid S Arabia
95B2 Al Jawf Libya
93C4 Al Jawf S Arabia
93D2 Al Jazirah Desert Region Syria/Iraq
50A2 Aljezur Port
91A4 Al Jubayl S Arabia
91C5 Al Kamil Oman
93D2 Al Khabur R Syria
91C5 Al Khaburah Oman
93D3 Al Khalis Iraq
91C4 Al Khasab Oman
91B4 Al Khawr Qatar
95A1 Al Khums Libya
91B5 Al Kidan Region, S Arabia
94C2 Al Kiswah Syria
56A2 Alkmaar Neth
95B2 Al Kufrah Oasis Libya
93E3 Al Kut Iraq
92C2 Al Ladhiqiyah Syria
86A1 Allahabad India
94C2 Al Lajah Mt Syria
12D1 Allakaket USA
76B2 Allanmyo Myan
95C2 'Allaqi Watercourse Egypt
17B1 Allatoona L USA
15C2 Allegheny R USA
10C3 Allegheny Mts USA
17B1 Allendale USA
111A3 Allen,Mt NZ
15C2 Allentown USA
87B3 Alleppey India
49C2 Aller R France
47D1 Allgäu Mts Germany
8C2 Alliance USA
81C3 Al Lith S Arabia

91B5 Al Liwa Region, UAE
109D1 Allora Aust
14B2 Alma Michigan, USA
Alma Ata = Almaty
50A2 Almada Port
Al Madinah = Medina
71F2 Almagan I Pacific O
91B4 Al Manamah Bahrain
93D3 Al Ma'niyah Iraq
21A1 Almanor,L USA
51B2 Almansa Spain
13B1 Alma Peak Mt Can
91B5 Al Mariyyah UAE
95B1 Al Marj Libya
82B1 Almaty Kazakhstan
93D2 Al Mawsil Iraq
50B1 Almazán Spain
35C1 Almenara Brazil
50B2 Almeria Spain
61H3 Al'met'yevsk Russian Fed
56C1 Almhult Sweden
93E3 Al Miqdadiyah Iraq
112C3 Almirante Brown Base Ant
34A1 Almirante Latorre Chile
55B3 Almirós Greece
91A4 Al Mish'ab S Arabia
50A2 Almodôvar Port
84D3 Almora India
91A4 Al Mubarraz S Arabia
92C4 Al Mudawwara Jordan
91C5 Al Mudaybi Oman
91B4 Al Muharraq Bahrain
81C4 Al Mukalla Yemen
81C4 Al Mukha Yemen
93D3 Al Musayyib Iraq
44B3 Alness Scot
93E3 Al Nu'maniyah Iraq
42D2 Alnwick Eng
71D4 Alor I Indon
77C4 Alor Setar Malay
Alost = Aalst
107E2 Alotau PNG
106B3 Aloysius,Mt Aust
34C3 Alpachiri Arg
14B1 Alpena USA
47B2 Alpes du Valais Mts Switz
52B1 Alpi Dolomitiche Mts Italy
47B2 Alpi Graie Mts Italy
9C3 Alpine Texas, USA
47C1 Alpi Orobie Mts Italy
47B2 Alpi Pennine Mts Italy
47C1 Alpi Retiche Mts Switz
47D1 Alpi Venoste Mts Italy
52A1 Alps Mts Europe
95A1 Al Qaddahiyah Libya
94C1 Al Qadmus Syria
93D3 Al Qa'im Iraq
93C4 Al Qalibah S Arabia
93D2 Al Qamishli Syria
95A1 Al Qaryah Ash Sharqiyah Libya
92C3 Al Qaryatayn Syria
91A4 Al Qatif S Arabia
95A2 Al Qatrun Libya
91A4 Al Qaysamah S Arabia
94C2 Al Quatayfah Syria
50A2 Alqueva R Port
92C3 Al Qunaytirah Syria
81C4 Al Qunfidhah S Arabia
93E3 Al Qurnah Iraq
94C1 Al Qusayr Syria
92C3 Al Qutayfah Syria
56B1 Als I Den
49D2 Alsace Region, France
57B2 Alsfeld Germany
42C2 Alston Eng
38J5 Alta Nor
29D2 Alta Gracia Arg
27D5 Altagracia de Orituco Ven
68A2 Altai Mts Mongolia
17B1 Altamaha R USA

33G4 Altamira Brazil
23B1 Altamira Mexico
53C2 Altamura Italy
68C1 Altanbulag Mongolia
71F4 Altape PNG
24B2 Altata Mexico
63A3 Altay China
63B3 Altay Mongolia
63A2 Altay Mts Russian Fed
47C1 Altdorf Switz
46D1 Altenkirchen Germany
34B3 Altiplanicie del Payún Plat Arg
47B1 Altkirch France
101C2 Alto Molócue Mozam
10A3 Alton USA
15C2 Altoona USA
34B2 Alto Pencoso Mts Arg
35A1 Alto Sucuriú Brazil
23B2 Altotonga Mexico
23A2 Altoyac de Alvarez Mexico
82C2 Altun Shan Mts China
20B2 Alturas USA
9D3 Altus USA
91B5 Al'Ubaylah S Arabia
93C4 Al Urayq Desert Region S Arabia
91B5 Al'Uruq al Mu'taridah Region, S Arabia
9D2 Alva USA
23B2 Alvarado Mexico
19A3 Alvarado USA
39G6 Alvdalen Sweden
19A4 Alvin USA
38J5 Alvsbyn Sweden
80B3 Al Wajh S Arabia
85D3 Alwar India
93D3 Al Widyan Desert Region Iraq/S Arabia
72A2 Alxa Yougi China
93E2 Alyat Azerbaijan
39J8 Alytus Lithuania
46E2 Alzey Germany
23B2 Amacuzac R Mexico
99D2 Amadi Sudan
93D2 Amadiyah Iraq
6C3 Amadjuak L Can
74B4 Amakusa-shotô I Japan
39G7 Amål Sweden
63D2 Amalat R Russian Fed
55B3 Amaliás Greece
85D4 Amalner India
69E4 Amami I Japan
69E4 Amami gunto Arch Japan
100C4 Amanzimtoti S Africa
33G3 Amapá Brazil
33G3 Amapá State, Brazil
9C3 Amarillo USA
60E5 Amasya Turk
23A1 Amatitan Mexico
Amazonas = Solimões
32D4 Amazonas State, Brazil
28C3 Amazonas R Brazil
84D2 Ambala India
87C3 Ambalangoda Sri Lanka
101D3 Ambalavao Madag
98B2 Ambam Cam
101D2 Ambanja Madag
1C7 Ambarchik Russian Fed
32B4 Ambato Ecuador
101D2 Ambato-Boeny Madag
101D2 Ambatolampy Madag
101D2 Ambatondrazaka Madag
57C3 Amberg Germany
25D3 Ambergris Cay I Belize
86A2 Ambikápur India
101D2 Ambilobe Madag

101D3 Amboasary Madag
101D2 Ambodifototra Madag
101D3 Ambohimahasoa Madag
71D4 Ambon Indon
101D3 Ambositra Madag
101D3 Ambovombe Madag
98B3 Ambriz Angola
98C1 Am Dam Chad
64H3 Amderma Russian Fed
24B2 Ameca Mexico
23B2 Amecacameca Mexico
34C2 Ameghino Arg
56B2 Ameland I Neth
16C2 Amenia USA
112B10 American Highland Upland Ant
105H4 American Samoa Is Pacific O
17B1 Americus USA
101G1 Amersfoort S Africa
112C10 Amery Ice Shelf Ant
55B3 Amfilokhía Greece
55B3 Amfissa Greece
63F1 Amga Russian Fed
63F1 Amgal R Russian Fed
69F2 Amgu Russian Fed
69F1 Amgun' R Russian Fed
99D1 Amhara Region Eth
7D5 Amherst Can
16C1 Amherst Massachusetts, USA
Amherst = Kyaikkami
87B2 Amhür India
48C2 Amiens France
75B1 Amino Japan
94B1 Amioune Leb
89K8 Amirante Is Indian O
86B1 Amlekhgan Nepal
92C3 Amman Jordan
38K6 Ämmänsaario Fin
56B2 Ammersfoort Neth
90B2 Amol Iran
55C3 Amorgós I Greece
7C5 Amos Can
Amoy = Xiamen
101D3 Ampanihy Madag
35B2 Amparo Brazil
51C1 Amposta Spain
85D4 Amrávati India
85C4 Amreli India
84C2 Amritsar India
56A2 Amsterdam Neth
101H1 Amsterdam S Africa
15D2 Amsterdam USA
98C1 Am Timan Chad
88L3 Amu Darya R Uzbekistan
6A2 Amund Ringes I Can
4F2 Amundsen G Can
112B4 Amundsen S Ant
80E Amundsen-Scott Base Ant
78D3 Amuntai Indon
63E2 Amur R Russian Fed
33E2 Anaco Ven
8B2 Anaconda USA
20B1 Anacortes USA
55C3 Anáfi I Greece
93D3 'Anah Iraq
21B3 Anaheim USA
87B2 Anaimalai Hills India
83C4 Anakapalle India
12E1 Anaktuvuk P USA
101D2 Analalaya Madag
92B2 Anamur Turk
75A2 Anan Japan
87B2 Anantapur India
84D2 Anantnag India
31B5 Anápolis Brazil
90C3 Anär Iran
90B3 Anárak Iran
71F2 Anatahan I Pacific O
30D4 Añatuya Arg
74B3 Anbyŏn N Korea
22C4 Anacpa Is USA
4D3 Anchorage USA
30C2 Ancohuma Mt Bol
32B6 Ancón Peru

Ancona

52B2 **Ancona** Italy
16C1 **Ancram** USA
29B4 **Ancud** Chile
34A3 **Andacollo** Arg
108A1 **Andado** Aust
32C6 **Andahuaylas** Peru
38F6 **Andalsnes** Nor
50A2 **Andalucia** Region, Spain
17A1 **Andalusia** USA
83D4 **Andaman Is** Myan
83D4 **Andaman S** Myan
108A2 **Andamooka** Aust
38H5 **Andenes** Nor
47C1 **Andermatt** Switz
57B2 **Andernach** Germany
14A2 **Anderson** Indiana, USA
18B2 **Anderson** Missouri, USA
17B1 **Anderson** S Carolina, USA
4F3 **Anderson** *R* Can
87B1 **Andhra Pradesh** State, India
55B3 **Andikithira** *I* Greece
65J5 **Andizhan** Uzbekistan
65H6 **Andkhui** Afghan
74B3 **Andong** S Korea
51C1 **Andorra** Principality, SW Europe
51C1 **Andorra-La-Vella** Andorra
43D4 **Andover** Eng
35A2 **Andradina** Brazil
12B2 **Andreafsky** USA
92B2 **Andreas,C** Cyprus
53C2 **Andria** Italy
11C4 **Andros** *I* The Bahamas
55B3 **Ándros** *I* Greece
87A2 **Androth** *I* India
50B2 **Andújar** Spain
100A2 **Andulo** Angola
97C4 **Anécho** Togo
97C3 **Anéfis** Mali
34B3 **Añelo** Arg
63C2 **Angarsk** Russian Fed
38H6 **Ånge** Sweden
24A2 **Angel de la Guarda** *I* Mexico
79B2 **Angeles** Phil
39G7 **Angelholm** Sweden
109C1 **Angellala Creek** *R* Aust
22B1 **Angels Camp** USA
71E4 **Angemuk** *Mt* Indon
48B2 **Angers** France
76C3 **Angkor** *Hist Site* Camb
41C3 **Anglesey** County Wales
41C3 **Anglesey** *I* Wales
19A4 **Angleton** USA
6G3 **Angmagssalik** Greenland
101D2 **Angoche** Mozam
29B3 **Angol** Chile
14B2 **Angola** Indiana, USA
100A2 **Angola** Republic, Africa
103H6 **Angola Basin** Atlantic O
12H3 **Angoon** USA
48C2 **Angoulême** France
96A1 **Angra do Heroismo** Açores
35C2 **Angra dos Reis** Brazil
34C3 **Anguil** Arg
27E3 **Anguilla** *I* Caribbean S
26B2 **Anguilla Cays** *Is* Caribbean S
86B2 **Angul** India
99C3 **Angumu** Zaire
44C3 **Angus** Division, Scot
56C1 **Anholt** *I* Den
73C4 **Anhua** China
72D3 **Anhui** Province, China
12C2 **Aniak** USA
35B1 **Anicuns** Brazil
46B2 **Anizy-le-Château** France

4C3 **Anjak** USA
48B2 **Anjou** Region, France
101D2 **Anjouan** *I* Comoros
101D2 **Anjozorobe** Madag
74B3 **Anju** N Korea
72B3 **Ankang** China
92B2 **Ankara** Turk
101D2 **Ankaratra** *Mt* Madag
101D3 **Akazoabo** Madag
101D2 **Ankazobe** Madag
56C2 **Anklam** Germany
76D3 **An Loc** Viet
73B4 **Anlong** China
73C3 **Anlu** China
18C2 **Anna** USA
96C1 **'Annaba** Alg
92C3 **An Nabk** S Arabia
92C3 **An Nabk** Syria
108A1 **Anna Creek** Aust
80C3 **An Nafūd** *Desert* S Arabia
93D3 **An Najaf** Iraq
42C2 **Annan** Scot
15C3 **Annapolis** USA
86A1 **Annapurna** *Mt* Nepal
14B2 **Ann Arbor** USA
94C1 **An Nāsirah** Syria
93E3 **An Nāsirīyah** Iraq
47B2 **Annecy** France
47B1 **Annemasse** France
76D3 **An Nhon** Viet
73A5 **Anning** China
17A1 **Anniston** USA
89E8 **Annobon** *I* Eq Guinea
49C2 **Annonay** France
27J1 **Annotto Bay** Jamaica
73D3 **Anqing** China
72B2 **Ansai** China
57C3 **Ansbach** Germany
26C3 **Anse d'Hainault** Haiti
72E1 **Anshan** China
73B4 **Anshun** China
97C3 **Ansongo** Mali
14B3 **Ansted** USA
92C2 **Antakya** Turk
101E2 **Antalaha** Madag
92B2 **Antalya** Turk
92B2 **Antalya Körfezi** *B* Turk
101D2 **Antananarivo** Madag
112C1 **Antarctic Circle** Ant
112C3 **Antarctic Pen** Ant
50B2 **Antequera** Spain
96B2 **Anti-Atlas** *Mts* Mor
7D5 **Anticosti, Î. d'** Can
27E3 **Antigua** *I* Caribbean S
Anti Lebanon = Jebel esh Sharqi
21A2 **Antioch** USA
19A3 **Antlers** USA
30B3 **Antofagasta** Chile
45C1 **Antrim** County, N Ire
45C1 **Antrim** N Ire
45C1 **Antrim Hills** N Ire
101D2 **Antseranana** Madag
101D2 **Antsirabe** Madag
101D2 **Antsohiny** Madag
76D3 **An Tuc** Viet
46C1 **Antwerpen** Belg
45C2 **An Uaimh** Irish Rep
84C3 **Anupgarh** India
87C3 **Anuradhapura** Sri Lanka
Anvers = Antwerpen
4B3 **Anvik** USA
63B3 **Anxi** China
72C2 **Anyang** China
72A3 **A'nyêmaqên Shan** *Upland* China
47C2 **Anza** *R* Italy
13E1 **Anzac** Can
65K4 **Anzhero-Sudzhensk** Russian Fed
53B2 **Anzio** Italy
74E2 **Aomori** Japan
52A1 **Aosta** Italy
97B3 **Aoukar** *Desert Region* Maur
96C2 **Aoulef** Alg
95A2 **Aozou** Chad
30E3 **Apa** *R* Brazil/Par

11B4 **Apalachee B** USA
17B2 **Apalachicola** USA
17A2 **Apalachicola B** USA
23B2 **Apan** Mexico
64E3 **Apatity** Russian Fed
32C3 **Apaporis** *R* Colombia
35A2 **Aparecida do Taboado** Brazil
79B2 **Aparri** Phil
54A1 **Apatin** Croatia
64E3 **Apatity** Russian Fed
24B3 **Apatzingan** Mexico
56B2 **Apeldoorn** Neth
35B2 **Apiai** Brazil
33F2 **Apoera** Surinam
108B3 **Apollo Bay** Aust
79C4 **Apo,Mt** *Mt* Phil
17B2 **Apopka,L** USA
30F2 **Aporé** *R* Brazil
10A2 **Apostle Is** USA
10A2 **Apostle L** USA
23A1 **Apozol** Mexico
11B3 **Appalachian Mts** USA
52B2 **Appennino Abruzzese** *Mts* Italy
52A2 **Appennino Ligure** *Mts* Italy
53C2 **Appennino Lucano** *Mts* Italy
53B2 **Appennino Napoletano** *Mts* Italy
52B2 **Appennino Tosco-Emilliano** *Mts* Italy
52B2 **Appennino Umbro-Marchigiano** *Mts* Italy
47C1 **Appenzell** Switz
42C2 **Appleby** Eng
14A2 **Appleton** Wisconsin, USA
30F3 **Apucarana** Brazil
23B1 **Apulco** Mexico
32D2 **Apure** *R* Ven
32C6 **Apurimac** *R* Peru
92C4 **'Aqaba** Jordan
92B4 **'Aqaba,G of** Egypt/ S Arabia
90B3 **'Aqdā** Iran
30E3 **Aquidauana** Brazil
23A2 **Aquila** Mexico
86A1 **Ara** India
17A1 **Arab** USA
81D4 **Arabian S** Asia/ Arabian Pen
31D4 **Aracajú** Brazil
30E3 **Aracanguy, Mts de** Par
31D2 **Aracati** Brazil
30F3 **Araçatuba** Brazil
50A2 **Aracena** Spain
31C5 **Araçuai** Brazil
94B3 **Arad** Israel
60B4 **Arad** Rom
98C1 **Arada** Chad
91B5 **'Arādah** UAE
106C1 **Arafura S** Indon/Aust
30F2 **Aragarças** Brazil
51B1 **Aragón** Region, Spain
50B1 **Aragon** *R* Spain
33G6 **Araguaia** *R* Brazil
31B3 **Araguaina** Brazil
31B5 **Araguari** Brazil
35B1 **Araguari** *R* Brazil
75B1 **Arai** Japan
96C2 **Arak** Alg
90A3 **Arāk** Iran
76A2 **Arakan Yoma** *Mts* Myan
87B2 **Arakkonam** India
65G5 **Aral Sea** Kazakhstan/ Uzbekistan
80E1 **Aral'sk** Kazakhstan
Aral'skoye More = Aral S
40B2 **Aran** *I* Irish Rep
50B1 **Aranda de Duero** Spain
23A1 **Arandas** Mexico
50B1 **Aranjuez** Spain
75A2 **Arao** Japan

97B3 **Araouane** Mali
29E2 **Arapey** *R* Urug
31D4 **Arapiraca** Brazil
35A2 **Araporgas** Brazil
30G4 **Ararangua** Brazil
31B6 **Araraquara** Brazil
35B2 **Araras** Brazil
107D4 **Ararat** Aust
93D2 **Ararat** Armenia
93E2 **Aras** *R* Azerbaijan
75C1 **Arato** Japan
32D2 **Arauca** *R* Ven
34A3 **Arauco** Chile
32C2 **Arauea** Colombia
85C4 **Arávalli Range** *Mts* India
31B5 **Araxá** Brazil
99D2 **Arba Minch** Eth
53A3 **Arbatax** Sardegna
93D2 **Arbil** Iraq
47A1 **Arbois** France
39H6 **Arbrå** Sweden
44C3 **Arbroath** Scot
47A1 **Arc** France
47B2 **Arc** *R* France
48B3 **Arcachon** France
17B2 **Arcadia** USA
20B2 **Arcata** USA
23A2 **Arcelia** Mexico
26B2 **Archipiélago de Camaguey** *Arch* Cuba
29B6 **Archipiélago de la Reina Adelaida** *Arch* Chile
29B4 **Archipiélago de las Chones** *Arch* Chile
32B2 **Archipiélago de las Perlas** *Arch* Panama
35B2 **Arcos** Brazil
50A2 **Arcos de la Frontera** Spain
6B2 **Arctic Bay** Can
1C1 **Arctic Circle**
4E3 **Arctic Red** Can
4E3 **Arctic Red R** Can
4D3 **Arctic Village** USA
54C2 **Arda** *R* Bulg
65F6 **Ardabil** Iran
93D1 **Ardahan** Turk
39F6 **Ardal** Nor
96C2 **Ardar des Iforas** *Upland* Alg/Mali
45C2 **Ardee** Irish Rep
90B3 **Ardekān** Iran
46C2 **Ardennes** Department, France
57A2 **Ardennes** Region, Belg
90B3 **Ardestan** Iran
92C3 **Ardh es Suwwan** *Desert Region* Jordan
50A2 **Ardila** *R* Port
109C2 **Ardlethan** Aust
9D3 **Ardmore** USA
44A3 **Ardnamurchan** *Pt* Scot
46A1 **Ardres** France
44B3 **Ardrishaig** Scot
42B2 **Ardrossan** Scot
27D3 **Arecibo** Puerto Rico
31D2 **Areia Branca** Brazil
21A2 **Arena,Pt** USA
39F7 **Arendal** Nor
30B2 **Arequipa** Peru
52B2 **Arezzo** Italy
52B2 **Argenta** Italy
49C2 **Argentan** France
46B2 **Argenteuil** France
28C7 **Argentina** Republic, S America
103F7 **Argentine Basin** Atlantic O
48C2 **Argenton-sur-Creuse** France
54C2 **Argeş** *R* Rom
84B2 **Arghardab** *R* Afghan
55B3 **Argolikós Kólpos** *G* Greece
46C2 **Argonne** Region, France
55B3 **Árgos** Greece
55B3 **Argostólion** Greece

Auvergne

Auxerre

45B2 **Ballyvaghan**
Irish Rep
108B3 **Balmoral** Aust
34C2 **Balnearia** Arg
84B3 **Balochistān** Region,
Pak
100A2 **Balombo** Angola
109C1 **Balonn** R Aust
85C3 **Balotra** India
86A1 **Balrāmpur** India
107D4 **Balranald** Aust
31B3 **Balsas** Brazil
23B2 **Balsas** Mexico
24B3 **Balsas** R Mexico
60C4 **Balta** Ukraine
39H7 **Baltic S** N Europe
92B3 **Baltīm** Egypt
45B3 **Baltimore** Irish Rep
10C3 **Baltimore** USA
86B1 **Bālurghāt** India
61H4 **Balykshi** Kazakhstan
91C4 **Bam** Iran
98B1 **Bama** India
97B3 **Bamako** Mali
98C2 **Bambari** CAR
17B1 **Bamberg** USA
57C3 **Bamberg** Germany
98C2 **Bambili** Zaïre
35B2 **Bambui** Brazil
98B2 **Bamenda** Cam
13C3 **Bamfield** Can
98B2 **Bamingui** R CAR
98B2 **Bamingui Bangoran**
National Park CAR
84B2 **Bamiyan** Afghan
91D4 **Bampur** Iran
91D4 **Bampur** R Iran
98C2 **Banalia** Zaïre
97B3 **Banamba** Mali
76C3 **Ban Aranyaprathet**
Thai
76C2 **Ban Ban** Laos
77C4 **Ban Betong** Thai
45C1 **Banbridge** N Ire
43D3 **Banbury** Eng
44C3 **Banchory** Scot
25D3 **Banco Chinchorro** Is
Mexico
15C1 **Bancroft** Can
86A1 **Bānda** India
70A3 **Banda Aceh** Indon
97B4 **Bandama** R Côte
d'Ivoire
91C4 **Bandar Abbās** Iran
90A2 **Bandar Anzali** Iran
99F2 **Bandarbeyla** Somalia
91B4 **Bandar-e Daylam**
Iran
91B4 **Bandar-e Lengheh**
Iran
91B4 **Bandar-e Māqām**
Iran
91B4 **Bandar-e Rig** Iran
90B2 **Bandar-e Torkoman**
Iran
91A3 **Bandar Khomeynī**
Iran
78C2 **Bandar Seri Begawan**
Brunei
71D4 **Banda S** Indon
91C4 **Band Boni** Iran
35C2 **Bandeira** Mt Brazil
97B3 **Bandiagara** Mali
60C5 **Bandirma** Turk
45B3 **Bandon** Irish Rep
98B3 **Bandundu** Zaïre
78B4 **Bandung** Indon
25E2 **Banes** Cuba
13D2 **Banff** Can
44C3 **Banff** Scot
5G4 **Banff** R Can
13D2 **Banff Nat Pk** Can
87B2 **Bangalore** India
98C2 **Bangassou** CAR
70C3 **Banggi** / Malay
95B1 **Banghāzī** Libya
76D2 **Bang Hieng** R Laos
78B3 **Bangka** / Indon
78A3 **Bangko** Indon
76C3 **Bangkok** Thai
82C3 **Bangladesh**
Republic, Asia
84D2 **Bangong Co** L China
10D2 **Bangor** Maine, USA

45D1 **Bangor** N Ire
16B2 **Bangor**
Pennsylvania, USA
42B3 **Bangor** Wales
78D3 **Bangsalsembera**
Indon
76B3 **Bang Saphan Yai**
Thai
79B2 **Bangued** Phil
98B2 **Bangui** CAR
100C2 **Bangweulu** L
Zambia
77C4 **Ban Hat Yai** Thai
76C2 **Ban Hin Heup** Laos
76C1 **Ban Houei Sai** Laos
76B3 **Ban Hua Hin** Thai
97B3 **Bani** R Mali
97C3 **Bani Bangou** Niger
95A1 **Bani Walid** Libya
92C2 **Bāniyās** Syria
94B2 **Baniyas** Syria
52C2 **Banja Luka** Bosnia-
Herzegovina
78C3 **Banjarmasin** Indon
97A3 **Banjul** The Gambia
77B4 **Ban Kantang** Thai
76D2 **Ban Khemmarat**
Laos
77B4 **Ban Khok Kloi** Thai
71F5 **Banks I** Aust
5E4 **Banks I** British
Columbia, Can
4F2 **Banks I** Northwest
Territories, Can
20C1 **Banks L** USA
111B2 **Banks Pen** NZ
109C4 **Banks Str** Aust
86B2 **Bankura** India
76B2 **Ban Mae Sariang**
Thai
76B2 **Ban Mae Sot** Thai
76D3 **Ban Me Thuot** Viet
45C1 **Bann** R N Ire
77B4 **Ban Na San** Thai
84C2 **Bannu** Pak
34A3 **Baños Maule** Chile
76C2 **Ban Pak Neun** Laos
77C4 **Ban Pak Phanang**
Thai
76D3 **Ban Ru Kroy** Camb
76B3 **Ban Sai Yok** Thai
76C3 **Ban Sattahip** Thai
59B3 **Banská Bystrica**
Slovakia
85C4 **Bānswāra** India
77B4 **Ban Tha Kham** Thai
76D2 **Ban Thateng** Laos
76C2 **Ban Tha Tum** Thai
41B3 **Bantry** Irish Rep
41A3 **Bantry** B Irish Rep
76D3 **Ban Ya Soup** Viet
78C4 **Banyuwangi** Indon
72C3 **Baofeng** China
76C1 **Bao Ha** Viet
72B3 **Baoji** China
76D3 **Bao Loc** Viet
68B4 **Baoshan** China
72C1 **Baotou** China
87C1 **Bāpatla** India
46B1 **Bapaume** France
93D3 **Ba'Qūbah** Iraq
32J7 **Baquerizo Morena**
Ecuador
54A2 **Bar** Montenegro,
Yugos
99D1 **Bara** Sudan
99E2 **Baraawe** Somalia
78D3 **Barabai** Indon
86A1 **Bāra Banki** India
65J4 **Barabinsk**
Russian Fed
65J4 **Barabinskaya Step**
Steppe Kazakhstan/
Russian Fed
50B1 **Baracaldo** Spain
26C2 **Baracoa** Cuba
94C2 **Baradá** R Syria
109C2 **Baradine** Aust
87A1 **Bārāmati** India
84C2 **Baramula** Pak
85D3 **Bārān** India
79B3 **Barangas** Phil
4E4 **Baranof I** USA
60C3 **Baranovichi** Belarus

108A2 **Baratta** Aust
86B1 **Barauni** India
31C6 **Barbacena** Brazil
27F4 **Barbados** /
Caribbean S
51C1 **Barbastro** Spain
101H1 **Barberton** S Africa
48B2 **Barbezieux** France
32C2 **Barbòsa** Colombia
27E3 **Barbuda** /
Caribbean S
107D3 **Barcaldine** Aust
Barce = Al Marj
53C3 **Barcellona** Italy
51C1 **Barcelona** Spain
33E1 **Barcelona** Ven
107D3 **Barcoo** R Aust
34B3 **Barda del Medio** Arg
95A2 **Bardai** Chad
29C3 **Bardas Blancas** Arg
86B2 **Barddhamān** India
59C3 **Bardejov** Slovakia
47C2 **Bardi** Italy
47B2 **Bardonecchia** Italy
43B3 **Bardsey** / Wales
84D3 **Bareilly** India
64D2 **Barentsøya** /
Barents S
64E2 **Barents S**
Russian Fed
95C3 **Barentu** Eritrea
86A2 **Bargarh** India
47B2 **Barge** Italy
63D2 **Barguzin**
Russian Fed
63D2 **Barguzin** R
Russian Fed
86B2 **Barhi** India
53C2 **Bari** Italy
51D2 **Barika** Alg
32C2 **Barinas** Ven
86B2 **Baripāda** India
85C4 **Bari Sādri** India
86C2 **Barisal** Bang
78C3 **Barito** R Indon
95A2 **Barjuj** Watercourse
Libya
73A3 **Barkam** China
18C2 **Barkley,L** USA
13B3 **Barkley Sd** Can
100B4 **Barkly East** S Africa
106C2 **Barkly Tableland** Mts
Aust
46C2 **Bar-le-Duc** France
106A3 **Barlee,L** Aust
106A3 **Barlee Range** Mts
Aust
53C2 **Barletta** Italy
85C3 **Barmer** India
108B2 **Barmera** Aust
43B3 **Barmouth** Wales
42D2 **Barnard Castle** Eng
65K4 **Barnaul** Russian Fed
16B3 **Barnegat** USA
16B3 **Barnegat B** USA
6C2 **Barnes Icecap** Can
17B1 **Barnesville** Georgia,
USA
14B3 **Barnesville** Ohio,
USA
42D3 **Barnsley** Eng
43B4 **Barnstaple** Eng
97C4 **Baro** Nig
86C1 **Barpeta** India
32D1 **Barquisimeto** Ven
31C4 **Barra** Brazil
44A3 **Barra** / Scot
109D2 **Barraba** Aust
23A2 **Barra de Navidad**
Mexico
35C2 **Barra de Pirai** Brazil
35A1 **Barragem de São**
Simão Res Brazil
35A1 **Barra do Garças**
Brazil
35B1 **Barragem Agua**
Vermelha Res Brazil
50A2 **Barragem do Castelo**
do Bode Res Port
50A2 **Barragem do**
Maranhão Res Port
35A2 **Barragem Três**
Irmãos Res Brazil
44A3 **Barra Head** Pt Scot

31C6 **Barra Mansa** Brazil
32B6 **Barranca** Peru
32C2 **Barrancabermeja**
Colombia
33E2 **Barrancas** Ven
30E4 **Barranqueras** Arg
32C1 **Barranquilla**
Colombia
44A3 **Barra,Sound of** Chan
Scot
16C1 **Barre** USA
34B2 **Barreal** Arg
31C4 **Barreiras** Brazil
50A2 **Barreiro** Port
31D3 **Barreiros** Brazil
107D5 **Barren,C** Aust
12D3 **Barren Is** USA
31B6 **Barretos** Brazil
13E2 **Barrhead** Can
14C2 **Barrie** Can
13C2 **Barrière** Can
108B2 **Barrier Range** Mts
Aust
107E4 **Barrington,Mt** Aust
27N2 **Barrouaillie**
St Vincent and the
Grenadines
4C2 **Barrow** USA
45C2 **Barrow** R Irish Rep
106C3 **Barrow Creek** Aust
106A3 **Barrow I** Aust
42C2 **Barrow-in-Furness**
Eng
4C2 **Barrow,Pt** USA
6A2 **Barrow Str** Can
15C1 **Barry's Bay** Can
87B1 **Barsi** India
9B3 **Barstow** USA
49C2 **Bar-sur-Aube** France
33F2 **Bartica** Guyana
92B1 **Bartın** Turk
107D2 **Bartle Frere,Mt** Aust
9D3 **Bartlesville** USA
101C3 **Bartolomeu Dias**
Mozam
58C2 **Bartoszyce** Pol
78C4 **Barung** / Indon
85D4 **Barwah** India
85C4 **Barwāni** India
109C1 **Barwon** R Aust
61G3 **Barysh** Russian Fed
98B2 **Basankusu** Zaïre
34D2 **Basavilbas** Arg
79B1 **Basco** Phil
52A1 **Basel** Switz
53C2 **Basento** R Italy
13E2 **Bashaw** Can
79B1 **Bashi Chan** Phil
61H3 **Bashkortostan**
Division, Russian Fed
79B4 **Basilan** / Phil
43E4 **Basildon** Eng
43D4 **Basingstoke** Eng
8B2 **Basin Region** USA
93E3 **Basra** Iraq
46D2 **Bas-Rhin**
Department, France
76D3 **Bassac** R Camb
13E2 **Bassano** Can
52B1 **Bassano** Italy
47D2 **Bassano del Grappa**
Italy
97C4 **Bassari** Togo
101C3 **Bassas da India** /
Mozam Chan
76A2 **Bassein** Myan
27E3 **Basse Terre**
Guadeloupe
97C4 **Bassila** Benin
22C2 **Bass Lake** USA
107D4 **Bass Str** Aust
39G7 **Båstad** Sweden
91B4 **Bastak** Iran
86A1 **Basti** India
52A2 **Bastia** Corse
57B3 **Bastogne** Belg
19B3 **Bastrop** Louisiana,
USA
19A3 **Bastrop** Texas, USA
98A2 **Bata** Eq Guinea
78C3 **Batakan** Indon
84D2 **Batala** India
68B3 **Batang** China
98B2 **Batangafo** CAR

Batan Is

5J4 **Berens** *R* Can
5J4 **Berens River** Can
108A1 **Beresford** Aust
59C3 **Berettyoújfalu** Hung
58D2 **Bereza** Belarus
59C3 **Berezhany** Ukraine
65G4 **Berezniki**
 Russian Fed
60D4 **Berezovka** Ukraine
64H3 **Berezovo**
 Russian Fed
92A2 **Bergama** Turk
52A1 **Bergamo** Italy
39F6 **Bergen** Nor
46C1 **Bergen op Zoom**
 Neth
48C3 **Bergerac** France
46D1 **Bergisch-Gladbach**
 Germany
12F2 **Bering GI** USA
1C6 **Bering Str** USA/
 Russian Fed
91C4 **Berizak** Iran
50B2 **Berja** Spain
8A3 **Berkeley** USA
112B2 **Berkner I** Ant
54B2 **Berkovitsa** Bulg
43D4 **Berkshire** County,
 Eng
16C1 **Berkshire Hills** USA
13D2 **Berland** *R* Can
56C2 **Berlin** Germany
56C2 **Berlin** State, Germany
15D2 **Berlin** New
 Hampshire, USA
30D3 **Bermejo** Bol
30D4 **Bermejo** *R* Arg
3M5 **Bermuda** *I* Atlantic O
52A1 **Bern** Switz
16B2 **Bernardsville** USA
34C3 **Bernasconi** Arg
56C2 **Bernburg** Germany
47B1 **Berner Oberland** *Mts*
 Switz
6B2 **Bernier B** Can
57C3 **Berounka** *R*
 Czech Republic
108B2 **Berri** Aust
96C1 **Berriane** Alg
48C2 **Berry** Region, France
22A1 **Berryessa,L** USA
11C4 **Berry Is** The
 Bahamas
98B2 **Bertoua** Cam
45B2 **Bertraghboy B**
 Irish Rep
15C2 **Berwick** USA
42C2 **Berwick-upon-Tweed**
 Eng
43C3 **Berwyn** *Mts* Wales
101D2 **Besalampy** Madag
49D2 **Besançon** France
59C3 **Beskidy Zachodnie**
 Mts Pol
93C2 **Besni** Turk
94B3 **Besor** *R* Israel
11B3 **Bessemer** USA
101D2 **Betafo** Madag
50A1 **Betanzos** Spain
94B3 **Bet Guvrin** Israel
101G1 **Bethal** S Africa
100A3 **Bethanie** Namibia
18B1 **Bethany** Missouri,
 USA
18A2 **Bethany** Oklahoma,
 USA
4B3 **Bethel** Alaska, USA
16C2 **Bethel** Connecticut,
 USA
14B2 **Bethel Park** USA
15C3 **Bethesda** USA
94B3 **Bethlehem** Israel
101G1 **Bethlehem** S Africa
15C2 **Bethlehem** USA
48C1 **Bethune** France
101D3 **Betioky** Madag
108B1 **Betoota** Aust
98B2 **Betou** Congo
82A1 **Betpak Dala** *Steppe*
 Kazakhstan
101D3 **Betroka** Madag
7D5 **Betsiamites** Can
86A1 **Bettiah** India
12D1 **Bettles** USA

47C2 **Béttola** Italy
85D4 **Bétul** India
85D3 **Betwa** *R* India
46D1 **Betzdorf** Germany
12C3 **Beverley,L** USA
16D1 **Beverly** USA
21B3 **Beverly Hills** USA
97B4 **Beyla** Guinea
87B2 **Beypore** India
 Beyrouth = Beirut
92B2 **Beyşehir** Turk
92B2 **Beyşehir Gölü** *L* Turk
94B2 **Beyt Shean** Israel
47C1 **Bezau** Austria
60E2 **Bezhetsk**
 Russian Fed
49C3 **Béziers** France
90C2 **Bezmein**
 Turkmenistan
63C2 **Beznosova**
 Russian Fed
86B1 **Bhadgaon** Nepal
87C1 **Bhadrāchalam** India
86B2 **Bhadrakh** India
87B2 **Bhadra Res** India
87B2 **Bhadrāvati** India
84B3 **Bhag** Pak
86B1 **Bhāgalpur** India
84C2 **Bhakkar** Pak
82D3 **Bhamo** Myan
85D4 **Bhandāra** India
85D3 **Bharatpur** India
85C4 **Bharūch** India
86B2 **Bhātiāpāra Ghat**
 Bang
84C2 **Bhatinda** India
87A2 **Bhatkal** India
86B2 **Bhātpāra** India
85C4 **Bhāvnagar** India
84C2 **Bhera** Pak
86A1 **Bheri** *R* Nepal
86A2 **Bhilai** India
85C3 **Bhilwāra** India
87C1 **Bhimavaram** India
85D3 **Bhind** India
84D3 **Bhiwāni** India
87B1 **Bhongir** India
85D4 **Bhopāl** India
86B2 **Bhubaneshwar** India
85B4 **Bhuj** India
85D4 **Bhusāwal** India
82C3 **Bhutan** Kingdom,
 Asia
71E4 **Biak** *I* Indon
58C2 **Biala Podlaska** Pol
58B2 **Bialograd** Pol
58C2 **Bialystok** Pol
38A1 **Biargtangar** *C*
 Iceland
90C2 **Biārjmand** Iran
48B3 **Biarritz** France
47C1 **Biasca** Switz
92B4 **Biba** Egypt
74E2 **Bibai** Japan
100A2 **Bibala** Angola
57B3 **Biberach** Germany
97B4 **Bibiani** Ghana
54C1 **Bicaz** Rom
97C4 **Bida** Nig
87B1 **Bidar** India
91C5 **Bidbid** Oman
43B4 **Bideford** Eng
43B4 **Bideford B** Eng
96C2 **Bidon 5** Alg
58C2 **Biebrza** Pol
52A1 **Biel** Switz
59B2 **Bielawa** Pol
56B2 **Bielefeld** Germany
47B1 **Bieler See** *L* Switz
52A1 **Biella** Italy
58C2 **Bielsk Podlaski** Pol
76D3 **Bien Hoa** Viet
53B2 **Biferno** *R* Italy
92A1 **Biga** Turk
55C3 **Bigadiç** Turk
19C3 **Big Black** *R* USA
18A1 **Big Blue** *R* USA
17B2 **Big Cypress Swamp**
 USA
4D3 **Big Delta** USA
49D2 **Bigent** Germany
13F2 **Biggar** Can
5H4 **Biggar Kindersley**
 Can

109D1 **Biggenden** Aust
12G3 **Bigger,Mt** Can
8C2 **Bighorn** *R* USA
76C3 **Bight of Bangkok** *B*
 Thai
97C4 **Bight of Benin** *B* W
 Africa
97C4 **Bight of Biafra** *B*
 Cam
6C3 **Big I** Can
47C1 **Bignasco** Switz
97A3 **Bignona** Sen
21B2 **Big Pine** USA
17B2 **Big Pine Key** USA
22C3 **Big Pine Mt** USA
14A2 **Big Rapids** USA
5H4 **Big River** Can
9C3 **Big Spring** USA
7A4 **Big Trout L** Can
7B4 **Big Trout Lake** Can
52C2 **Bihać** Bosnia-
 Herzegovina
86B1 **Bihār** India
86B2 **Bihar** State, India
99D3 **Biharamulo** Tanz
60B4 **Bihor** *Mt* Rom
87B1 **Bijāpur** India
87C1 **Bijapur** India
90A2 **Bījar** Iran
86A1 **Bijauri** Nepal
54A2 **Bijeljina** Bosnia-
 Herzegovina
73B4 **Bijie** China
84D3 **Bijnor** India
84C3 **Bijnot** Pak
84C3 **Bikaner** India
94B2 **Bikfaya** Leb
69F2 **Bikin** Russian Fed
98B3 **Bikoro** Zaïre
85C3 **Bilara** India
84D2 **Bilaspur** India
86A2 **Bilāspur** India
76B3 **Bilauktaung Range**
 Mts Thai
50B1 **Bilbao** Spain
 Bilbo = Bilbao
59B3 **Bilé** *R*
 Czech Republic
54A2 **Bileća** Bosnia-
 Herzegovina
92B1 **Bilecik** Turk
98C2 **Bili** *R* Zaïre
79B3 **Biliran** *I* Phil
8C2 **Billings** USA
95A3 **Bilma** Niger
11B3 **Biloxi** USA
98C1 **Biltine** Chad
85D4 **Bina-Etawa** India
79B3 **Binalbagan** Phil
101C2 **Bindura** Zim
100B2 **Binga** Zim
101C2 **Binga** *Mt* Zim
109D1 **Bingara** Aust
57B3 **Bingen** Germany
10C2 **Binghamton** USA
78D1 **Bingkor** Malay
93D2 **Bingöl** Turk
72D3 **Binhai** China
78A2 **Bintan** *I* Indon
78A3 **Bintuhan** Indon
78C2 **Bintulu** Malay
29B3 **Bió Bió** *R* Chile
102J4 **Bioco** *I* Atlantic O
87B1 **Bir** India
95B2 **Bir Abu Husein** *Well*
 Egypt
95B2 **Bi'r al Harash** *Well*
 Libya
98C1 **Birao** CAR
86B1 **Biratnagar** Nepal
12E1 **Birch Creek** USA
108B3 **Birchip** Aust
5G4 **Birch Mts** Can
7A4 **Bird** Can
106C3 **Birdsville** Aust
106C2 **Birdum** Aust
86A1 **Birganj** Nepal
94A3 **Bir Gifgâfa** *Well*
 Egypt
94A3 **Bir Hasana** *Well*
 Egypt
35A2 **Birigui** Brazil
90C3 **Birjand** Iran
92B4 **Birkat Qarun** *L* Egypt

46D2 **Birkenfeld** Germany
42C3 **Birkenhead** Eng
60C4 **Birlad** Rom
94A3 **Bir Lahfân** *Well*
 Egypt
43C3 **Birmingham** Eng
11B3 **Birmingham** USA
95B2 **Bir Misâha** *Well*
 Egypt
96A2 **Bir Moghrein** Maur
97C3 **Birnin Kebbi** Nig
97C3 **Birni N'Konni** Nig
69F2 **Birobidzhan**
 Russian Fed
45C2 **Birr** Irish Rep
51C2 **Bir Rabalou** Alg
109C1 **Birrie** *R* Aust
44C2 **Birsay** Scot
61J2 **Birsk** Russian Fed
95B2 **Bir Tarfâwi** *Well*
 Egypt
63B2 **Biryusa** Russian Fed
39J7 **Biržai** Lithuania
96B2 **Bir Zreigat** *Well*
 Maur
48A2 **Biscay,B of** France/
 Spain
17B2 **Biscayne B** USA
46D2 **Bischwiller** France
73B4 **Bishan** China
82B1 **Bishkek** Kyrgyzstan
8B3 **Bishop** USA
42D2 **Bishop Auckland** Eng
43E4 **Bishop's Stortford**
 Eng
86A2 **Bishrāmpur** India
96C1 **Biskra** Alg
79C4 **Bislig** Phil
8C2 **Bismarck** USA
90A3 **Bisotūn** Iran
97A3 **Bissau** Guinea-
 Bissau
10A1 **Bissett** Can
5G4 **Bistcho L** Can
54C1 **Bistrita** *R* Rom
98B2 **Bitam** Gabon
57B3 **Bitburg** Germany
46D2 **Bitche** France
93D2 **Bitlis** Turk
55B2 **Bitola** Macedonia
56C2 **Bitterfeld** Germany
100A4 **Bitterfontein** S Africa
92B3 **Bitter Lakes** Egypt
8B2 **Bitteroot Range** *Mts*
 USA
74D3 **Biwa-ko** *L* Japan
99E1 **Biyo Kaboba** Eth
65K4 **Biysk** Russian Fed
96C1 **Bizerte** Tunisia
51C2 **Bj bou Arréridj** Alg
52C1 **Bjelovar** Croatia
96B2 **Bj Flye Ste Marie** Alg
64C2 **Bjørnøya** *I* Barents S
12F1 **Black** *R* USA
18B2 **Black** *R* USA
107D3 **Blackall** Aust
42C3 **Blackburn** Eng
4D3 **Blackburn,Mt** USA
13E2 **Black Diamond** Can
5H5 **Black Hills** USA
44B3 **Black Isle** *Pen* Scot
27R3 **Blackman's**
 Barbados
43C4 **Black Mts** Wales
43C3 **Blackpool** Eng
27H1 **Black River** Jamaica
8B2 **Black Rock Desert**
 USA
65E5 **Black S** Asia/Europe
45A1 **Blacksod B** Irish Rep
109D2 **Black Sugarloaf** *Mt*
 Aust
97B3 **Black Volta** *R* Ghana
41B3 **Blackwater** *R*
 Irish Rep
18A2 **Blackwell** USA
54B2 **Blagoevgrad** Bulg
63E2 **Blagoveshchensk**
 Russian Fed
20B1 **Blaine** USA
44C3 **Blair Atholl** Scot
44C3 **Blairgowrie** Scot
17B1 **Blakely** USA
108A1 **Blanche,L** Aust

10

Blanco

34A2 **Blanco** *R* Arg
34B1 **Blanco** *R* Arg
8A2 **Blanco,C** USA
7E4 **Blanc Sablon** Can
43C4 **Blandford Forum** Eng
43C4 **Blaneau Gwent** County Wales
46A2 **Blangy-sur-Bresle** France
46B1 **Blankenberge** Belg
101C2 **Blantyre** Malawi
48B2 **Blaye** France
109C2 **Blayney** Aust
111B2 **Blenheim** NZ
96C1 **Blida** Alg
14B1 **Blind River** Can
108A2 **Blinman** Aust
78C4 **Blitar** Indon
15D2 **Block I** USA
16D2 **Block Island Sd** USA
101G1 **Bloemfontein** S Africa
101G1 **Bloemhof** S Africa
101G1 **Bloemhof Dam** *Res* S Africa
33F3 **Blommesteinmeer** *L* Surinam
38A1 **Blonduós** Iceland
45B1 **Bloody Foreland** *C* Irish Rep
14A3 **Bloomfield** Indiana, USA
18B1 **Bloomfield** Iowa, USA
10B2 **Bloomington** Illinois, USA
14A3 **Bloomington** Indiana, USA
16A2 **Bloomsburg** USA
78C4 **Blora** Indon
6H3 **Blosseville Kyst** *Mts* Greenland
57B3 **Bludenz** Austria
11B3 **Bluefield** USA
32A1 **Bluefields** Nic
26B3 **Blue Mountain Peak** *Mt* Jamaica
16A2 **Blue Mt** USA
109D2 **Blue Mts** Aust
27J1 **Blue Mts** Jamaica
8A2 **Blue Mts** USA
Blue Nile = Bahr el Azraq
99D1 **Blue Nile** *R* Sudan
4G3 **Bluenose L** Can
11B3 **Blue Ridge Mts** USA
13D2 **Blue River** Can
45B1 **Blue Stack** *Mt* Irish Rep
111A3 **Bluff** NZ
106A4 **Bluff Knoll** *Mt* Aust
30G4 **Blumenau** Brazil
49D2 **Blundez** Austria
20B2 **Bly** USA
12E3 **Blying Sd** USA
42D2 **Blyth** Eng
9B3 **Blythe** USA
11B3 **Blytheville** USA
97A4 **Bo** Sierra Leone
79B3 **Boac** Phil
72D2 **Boading** China
14B2 **Boardman** USA
63C3 **Boatou** China
33E3 **Boa Vista** Brazil
97A4 **Boa Vista** *I* Cape Verde
76E1 **Bobai** China
47C2 **Bóbbio** Italy
97B3 **Bobo Dioulasso** Burkina
60C3 **Bobruysk** Belarus
17B2 **Boca Chica Key** *I* USA
32D5 **Bôca do Acre** Brazil
35C1 **Bocaiúva** Brazil
98B2 **Bocaranga** CAR
17B2 **Boca Raton** USA
59C3 **Bochnia** Pol
56B2 **Bocholt** Germany
46D1 **Bochum** Germany
100A2 **Bocoio** Angola
98B2 **Boda** CAR
63D2 **Bodaybo** Russian Fed

21A2 **Bodega Head** *Pt* USA
95A3 **Bodélé** *Region* Chad
38J5 **Boden** Sweden
47C1 **Bodensee** *L* Switz/Germany
87B1 **Bodhan** India
87B2 **Bodināyakkanūr** India
43B4 **Bodmin** Eng
43B4 **Bodmin Moor** *Upland* Eng
38G5 **Bodø** Nor
55C3 **Bodrum** Turk
98C3 **Boende** Zaïre
97A3 **Boffa** Guinea
76B2 **Bogale** Myan
19C3 **Bogalusa** USA
109C2 **Bogan** *R* Aust
97B3 **Bogandé** Burkina
6H3 **Bogarnes** Iceland
92C2 **Bogazlıyan** Turk
61K2 **Bogdanovich** Russian Fed
68A2 **Bogda Shan** *Mt* China
100A3 **Bogenfels** Namibia
109D1 **Boggabilla** Aust
109C2 **Boggabri** Aust
45B2 **Boggeragh Mts** Irish Rep
79B3 **Bogo** Phil
109C3 **Bogong,Mt** Aust
78B4 **Bogor** Indon
61H2 **Bogorodskoye** Russian Fed
32C3 **Bogotá** Colombia
63A2 **Bogotol** Russian Fed
86B2 **Bogra** Bang
72D2 **Bo Hai** *B* China
46B2 **Bohain-en-Vermandois** France
72D2 **Bohai Wan** *B* China
57C3 **Böhmer-Wald** *Upland* Germany
79B4 **Bohol** *I* Phil
79B4 **Bohol S** Phil
35A1 **Bois** *R* Brazil
14B1 **Bois Blanc I** USA
8B2 **Boise** USA
96A2 **Bojador,C** Mor
79B2 **Bojeador,C** Phil
90C2 **Bojnürd** Iran
97A3 **Boké** Guinea
109C1 **Bokhara** *R* Aust
39F7 **Boknafjord** *Inlet* Nor
98B3 **Boko** Congo
76C3 **Bokor** Camb
98C3 **Bokungu** Zaïre
98B1 **Bol** Chad
23A1 **Bolaānos** Mexico
97A3 **Bolama** Guinea-Bissau
23A1 **Bolanos** *R* Mexico
48C2 **Bolbec** France
97B4 **Bole** Ghana
59B2 **Boleslawiec** Pol
97B3 **Bolgatanga** Ghana
60C4 **Bolgrad** Ukraine
34C3 **Bolívar** Arg
18B2 **Bolivar** Missouri, USA
18C2 **Bolivar** Tennessee, USA
30C2 **Bolivia** Republic, S America
38H6 **Bollnas** Sweden
109C1 **Bollon** Aust
32C2 **Bollvar** *Mt* Ven
52B2 **Bologna** Italy
60D2 **Bologoye** Russian Fed
69F2 **Bolon'** Russian Fed
61G3 **Bol'shoy Irgiz** *R* Russian Fed
74C2 **Bol'shoy Kamen** Russian Fed
Bol'shoy Kavkaz =Caucasus
61G4 **Bol'shoy Uzen** *R* Kazakhstan
9C4 **Bolson de Mapimi** *Desert* Mexico
43C3 **Bolton** Eng

92B1 **Bolu** Turk
38A1 **Bolungarvik** Iceland
92B2 **Bolvadin** Turk
52B1 **Bolzano** Italy
98B3 **Boma** Zaïre
107D4 **Bombala** Aust
87A1 **Bombay** India
99D2 **Bombo** Uganda
35B1 **Bom Despacho** Brazil
86C1 **Bomdila** India
97A4 **Bomi Hills** Lib
31C4 **Bom Jesus da Lapa** Brazil
63E2 **Bomnak** Russian Fed
99C2 **Bomokandi** *R* Zaïre
98C2 **Bomu** *R* CAR/Zaïre
27D4 **Bonaire** *I* Caribbean S
12F2 **Bona,Mt** USA
25D3 **Bonanza** Nic
7E5 **Bonavista** Can
108A2 **Bon Bon** Aust
98C2 **Bondo** Zaïre
97B4 **Bondoukou** Côte d'Ivoire
Bône = 'Annaba
33E3 **Bonfim** Guyana
98C2 **Bongandanga** Zaïre
98B1 **Bongor** Chad
19A3 **Bonham** USA
53A2 **Bonifacio** Corse
52A2 **Bonifacio,Str of** *Chan* Medit S
Bonin Is = Ogasawara Gunto
17B2 **Bonita Springs** USA
57B2 **Bonn** Germany
20C1 **Bonners Ferry** USA
12H1 **Bonnet Plume** *R* Can
13E2 **Bonnyville** Can
97A4 **Bonthe** Sierra Leone
99E1 **Booaaso** Somalia
108B2 **Booligal** Aust
109D1 **Boonah** Aust
15C2 **Boonville** USA
109C2 **Boorowa** Aust
6A2 **Boothia,G of** Can
6A2 **Boothia Pen** Can
98B3 **Booué** Gabon
108A1 **Bopeechee** Aust
99D2 **Bor** Sudan
92B2 **Bor** Turk
54B2 **Bor** Serbia, Yugos
8B2 **Borah Peak** *Mt* USA
39G7 **Borås** Sweden
91B4 **Borāzjān** Iran
108A3 **Borda,C** Aust
48B3 **Bordeaux** France
4G2 **Borden I** Can
6B2 **Borden Pen** Can
16B2 **Bordentown** USA
108B3 **Bordertown** Aust
96C2 **Bordj Omar Dris** Alg
8D1 **Borens River** Can
38A2 **Borgarnes** Iceland
9C3 **Borger** USA
39H7 **Borgholm** Sweden
47C2 **Borgosia** Italy
47D1 **Borgo Valsugana** Italy
59C3 **Borislav** Ukraine
61F3 **Borisoglebsk** Russian Fed
60C3 **Borisov** Belarus
60E3 **Borisovka** Russian Fed
95A3 **Borkou** *Region* Chad
39H6 **Borlänge** Sweden
47C2 **Bormida** Italy
47D1 **Bormio** Italy
67F5 **Borneo** *I* Malay/Indon
39H7 **Bornholm** *I* Den
55C3 **Bornova** Turk
98C2 **Boro** *R* Sudan
97B3 **Boromo** Burkina
60D2 **Borovichi** Russian Fed
106C2 **Borroloola** Aust
54B1 **Borsa** Rom
90A3 **Borūjed** Iran
90B3 **Borūjen** Iran
58B2 **Bory Tucholskie** Region, Pol

63D2 **Borzya** Russian Fed
73B5 **Bose** China
101G1 **Boshof** S Africa
54A2 **Bosna** *R* Bosnia-Herzegovina
37E4 **Bosnia-Herzegovina** Republic, Europe
75C1 **Bōsō-hantō** *B* Japan
Bosporus = Karadeniz Boğazi
51C2 **Bosquet** Alg
98B2 **Bossangoa** CAR
98B2 **Bossèmbélé** CAR
19B3 **Bossier City** USA
65K5 **Bosten Hu** *L* China
43D3 **Boston** Eng
10C2 **Boston** USA
11A3 **Boston Mts** USA
85C4 **Botād** India
54B2 **Botevgrad** Bulg
101G1 **Bothaville** S Africa
64C3 **Bothnia,G of** Sweden/Fin
100B3 **Botletli** *R* Botswana
60C4 **Botosani** Rom
100B3 **Botswana** Republic, Africa
53C3 **Botte Donato** *Mt* Italy
46D1 **Bottrop** Germany
35B2 **Botucatu** Brazil
7E5 **Botwood** Can
89D7 **Bouaké** Côte d'Ivoire
98B2 **Bouar** CAR
96B1 **Bouârfa** Mor
98B2 **Bouca** CAR
51C2 **Boufarik** Alg
Bougie = Bejaïa
97B3 **Bougouni** Mali
46C2 **Bouillon** France
96B2 **Bou Izakarn** Mor
46D2 **Boulay-Moselle** France
8C2 **Boulder** Colorado, USA
9B3 **Boulder City** USA
22A2 **Boulder Creek** USA
48C1 **Boulogne** France
98B2 **Boumba** *R* CAR
97B4 **Bouna** Côte d'Ivoire
8B3 **Boundary Peak** *Mt* USA
97B4 **Boundiali** Côte d'Ivoire
107F3 **Bourail** Nouvelle Calédonie
97B3 **Bourem** Mali
49D2 **Bourg** France
49D2 **Bourg de Péage** France
49C2 **Bourgogne** Region, France
48C2 **Bourges** France
48C3 **Bourg-Madame** France
49C2 **Bourgogne** Region, France
47B2 **Bourg-St-Maurice** France
108C2 **Bourke** Aust
43D4 **Bournemouth** Eng
96C1 **Bou Saâda** Alg
98B1 **Bousso** Chad
97A3 **Boutilimit** Maur
103J7 **Bouvet** *I* Atlantic O
34D2 **Bovril** Arg
13E2 **Bow** *R* Can
107D2 **Bowen** Aust
19A3 **Bowie** Texas, USA
13E2 **Bow Island** Can
11B3 **Bowling Green** Kentucky, USA
18B2 **Bowling Green** Missouri, USA
14B2 **Bowling Green** Ohio, USA
15C3 **Bowling Green** Virginia, USA
15C2 **Bowmanville** Can
109D2 **Bowral** Aust
13C2 **Bowron** *R* Can
72D3 **Bo Xian** China
72D2 **Boxing** China
92B1 **Boyabat** Turk
98B2 **Boyali** CAR
5J4 **Boyd** Can

Bunguran

Code	Name
16B2	Boyertown USA
13E2	Boyle Can
41B3	Boyle Irish Rep
45C2	Boyne R Irish Rep
17B2	Boynoton Beach USA
98C2	Boyoma Falls Zaïre
55C3	Bozca Ada I Turk
55C3	Boz Dağlari Mts Turk
8B2	Bozeman USA
	Bozen = Bolzano
98B2	Bozene Zaire
98B2	Bozoum CAR
47B2	Bra Italy
52C2	Brač I Croatia
15C1	Bracebridge Can
95A2	Brach Libya
38H6	Bräcke Sweden
17B2	Bradenton USA
42D3	Bradford Eng
44E1	Brae Scot
44C3	Braemar Scot
50A1	Braga Port
34C3	Bragado Arg
50A1	Bragana Port
31B2	Bragança Brazil
35B2	Bragança Paulista Brazil
86C2	Brahman-Baria Bang
86B2	Brāhmani R India
86C1	Brahmaputra R India
7E5	Braie Verte Can
60C4	Brăila Rom
10A2	Brainerd USA
97A3	Brakna Region, Maur
5F4	Bralorne Can
14C2	Brampton Can
33E3	Branco R Brazil
100A3	Brandberg Mt Namibia
56C2	Brandenburg Germany
56C2	Brandenburg State, Germany
101G1	Brandfort S Africa
8D2	Brandon Can
100B4	Brandvlei S Africa
57C2	Brandys nad Lebem Czech Republic
58B2	Braniewo Pol
10B2	Brantford Can
108B3	Branxholme Aust
7D5	Bras D'Or L Can
35C1	Brasila de Minas Brazil
32D6	Brasiléia Brazil
31B5	Brasilia Brazil
54C1	Brasov Rom
78D1	Brassay Range Mts Malay
59B3	Bratislava Slovakia
63C2	Bratsk Russian Fed
15D2	Brattleboro USA
56C2	Braunschweig Germany
97A4	Brava I Cape Verde
9B3	Brawley USA
45C2	Bray Irish Rep
6C3	Bray I Can
13D2	Brazeau R Can
13D2	Brazeau,Mt Can
28D4	Brazil Republic, S America
103G5	Brazil Basin Atlantic O
9D3	Brazos R USA
98B3	Brazzaville Congo
57C3	Brdy Upland Czech Republic
111A3	Breaksea Sd NZ
110B1	Bream B NZ
78B4	Brebes Indon
44C3	Brechin Scot
46C1	Brecht Belg
59B3	Břeclav Czech Republic
43C4	Brecon Wales
43C4	Brecon Beacons Mts Wales
43B3	Brecon Beacons Nat Pk Wales
56A2	Breda Neth
100B4	Bredasdorp S Africa
38H6	Bredbyn Sweden

Code	Name
61J3	Bredy Russian Fed
15C2	Breezewood USA
47C1	Bregenz Austria
47C1	Bregenzer Ache R Austria
38A1	Breiðafjörður B Iceland
47C2	Brembo R Italy
17A1	Bremen USA
56B2	Bremen Germany
56B2	Bremerhaven Germany
20B1	Bremerton USA
19A3	Brenham USA
57C3	Brenner P Austria/Italy
47D2	Breno Italy
47D2	Brenta R Italy
22B2	Brentwood USA
52B1	Brescia Italy
	Breslau = Wrocław
47D1	Bressanone Italy
44E1	Bressay I Scot
48B2	Bressuire France
58C2	Brest Belarus
48B2	Brest France
48B2	Bretagne Region, France
46B2	Breteuil France
16B2	Breton Woods USA
110B1	Brett,C NZ
109C1	Brewarrina Aust
16C2	Brewster New York, USA
20C1	Brewster Washington, USA
101G1	Breyten S Africa
52C1	Brežice Slovenia
98C2	Bria CAR
49D3	Briancon France
49C2	Briare France
43C4	Bridgend County Wales
21B2	Bridgeport California, USA
15D2	Bridgeport Connecticut, USA
19A3	Bridgeport Texas, USA
22C1	Bridgeport Res USA
16B3	Bridgeton USA
27F4	Bridgetown Barbados
7D5	Bridgewater Can
16D2	Bridgewater USA
43C4	Bridgwater Eng
43C4	Bridgwater B Eng
42D2	Bridlington Eng
109C4	Bridport Aust
47B1	Brienzer See L Switz
46C2	Briey France
52A1	Brig Switz
8B2	Brigham City USA
109C3	Bright Aust
43D4	Brighton Eng
46E1	Brilon Germany
55A2	Brindisi Italy
19B3	Brinkley USA
107E3	Brisbane Aust
15D2	Bristol Connecticut, USA
43C4	Bristol County Eng
43C4	Bristol Eng
15D2	Bristol Pennsylvania, USA
16D2	Bristol Rhode Island, USA
11B3	Bristol Tennessee, USA
12B3	Bristol B USA
43B4	Bristol Chan Eng/Wales
4D3	British Mts USA
5F4	British Columbia Province, Can
6B1	British Empire Range Mts Can
101G1	Brits S Africa
100B4	Britstown S Africa
48C2	Brive France
59B3	Brno Czech Republic
17B1	Broad R USA
7C4	Broadback R Can
44A2	Broad Bay Inlet Scot

Code	Name
44B3	Broadford Scot
5H4	Brochet Can
4G2	Brock I Can
15C2	Brockport USA
16D1	Brockton USA
15C2	Brockville Can
6B2	Brodeur Pen Can
42B2	Brodick Scot
58B2	Brodnica Pol
60C3	Brody Ukraine
19B3	Broken Bow Oklahoma, USA
19B3	Broken Bow L USA
107D4	Broken Hill Aust
47C2	Broni Italy
38G5	Brønnøysund Nor
16C2	Bronx Borough, New York, USA
79A4	Brooke's Point Phil
18B2	Brookfield Missouri, USA
11A3	Brookhaven USA
20B2	Brookings Oregon, USA
8D2	Brookings South Dakota, USA
16D1	Brookline USA
16C2	Brooklyn Borough, New York, USA
5G4	Brooks Can
12C3	Brooks,L USA
12A1	Brooks Mt USA
4C3	Brooks Range Mts USA
17B2	Brooksville USA
109D1	Brooloo Aust
106B2	Broome Aust
44C2	Brora Scot
20B2	Brothers USA
95A3	Broulkou Chad
13E3	Browning USA
9D4	Brownsville USA
9D3	Brownwood USA
46B1	Bruay-en-Artois France
106A3	Bruce,Mt Aust
14B1	Bruce Pen Can
59B3	Brück an der Mur Austria
	Bruges = Brugge
46B1	Brugge Belg
46D1	Brühl Germany
78C2	Brunei Sultanate, S E Asia
52B1	Brunico Italy
111B2	Brunner,L NZ
11B3	Brunswick Georgia, USA
18B2	Brunswick Mississippi, USA
29B6	Brunswick,Pen de Chile
109C4	Bruny I Aust
61F1	Brusenets Russian Fed
26A3	Brus Laguna Honduras
	Brüssel = Bruxelles
56A2	Bruxelles Belg
9D3	Bryan USA
108A2	Bryan,Mt Aust
60D3	Bryansk Russian Fed
60D3	Bryansk Division, Russian Fed
19B3	Bryant USA
59B2	Brzeg Pol
93E4	Bübiyan I Kuwait/Iraq
99D3	Bubu R Tanz
32C2	Bucaramanga Colombia
44D3	Buchan Oilfield N Sea
97A4	Buchanan Lib
44D3	Buchan Deep N Sea
6C2	Buchan G Can
40C2	Buchan Ness Pen Scot
7E5	Buchans Can
34C2	Bucharado Arg
	Bucharest = Bucureşti
47C1	Buchs Switz
43D3	Buckingham Eng
12B1	Buckland USA

Code	Name
12B1	Buckland R USA
108A2	Buckleboo Aust
98B3	Buco Zau Congo
54C2	Bucureşti Rom
59B3	Budapest Hung
84D3	Budaun India
43B4	Bude Eng
19B3	Bude USA
61F5	Budennovsk Russian Fed
54A2	Budva Montenegro, Yugos
98A2	Buéa Cam
22B3	Buellton USA
34B2	Buena Esperanza Arg
32B3	Buenaventura Colombia
23A2	Buenavista Mexico
29E2	Buenos Aires Arg
29D3	Buenos Aires State, Arg
18B2	Buffalo Mississipi, USA
10C2	Buffalo New York, USA
8C2	Buffalo South Dakota, USA
19A3	Buffalo Texas, USA
8C2	Buffalo Wyoming, USA
101H1	Buffalo R S Africa
13E2	Buffalo L Alberta, Can
5G3	Buffalo L Northwest Territories, Can
5H4	Buffalo Narrows Can
17B1	Buford USA
54C2	Buftea Rom
59C2	Bug R Pol/Ukraine
32B3	Buga Colombia
90B2	Bugdayli Turkmenistan
61H3	Bugulma Russian Fed
61H3	Buguruslan Russian Fed
93C2	Buhayrat al Asad Res Syria
41C3	Builth Wells Wales
34A2	Buin Chile
99C3	Bujumbura Burundi
98C3	Bukama Zaïre
99C3	Bukavu Zaïre
80E2	Bukhara Uzbekistan
78C2	Bukit Batubrok Mt Indon
70B4	Bukittinggi Indon
99D3	Bukoba Tanz
78D3	Buku Gandadiwata Mt Indon
71E4	Bula Indon
79B3	Bulan Phil
84D3	Bulandshahr India
100B3	Bulawayo Zim
55C3	Buldan Turk
85D4	Buldāna India
68C2	Bulgan Mongolia
54B2	Bulgaria Republic, Europe
47B1	Bulle Switz
111B2	Buller R NZ
109C3	Buller,Mt Aust
106A4	Bullfinch Aust
108B1	Bulloo R Aust
108B1	Bulloo Downs Aust
108B1	Bulloo L Aust
18B2	Bull Shoals Res USA
34A3	Bulnes Chile
71F4	Bulolo PNG
101G1	Bultfontein S Africa
98C2	Bumba Zaire
76B2	Bumphal Dam Thai
99D2	Buna Kenya
106A4	Bunbury Aust
45C1	Buncrana Irish Rep
107E3	Bundaberg Aust
109D2	Bundarra Aust
85D3	Bündi India
45B1	Bundoran Irish Rep
109C1	Bungil R Aust
98B3	Bungo Angola
75A2	Bungo-suidō Str Japan
70B3	Bunguran I Ind

Bunia

99D2 Bunia Zaïre
18B2 Bunker USA
19B3 Bunkie USA
17B2 Bunnell USA
78C3 Buntok Indon
71D3 Buol Indon
94C2 Buräg Syria
98C1 Buram Sudan
99E2 Burao Somalia
79B3 Burauen Phil
80C3 Buraydah S Arabia
21B3 Burbank USA
109C2 Burcher Aust
92B2 Burdur Turk
63F3 Bureinskiy Khrebet Mts Russian Fed
56C2 Burg Germany
54C2 Burgas Bulg
17C1 Burgaw USA
47B1 Burgdorf Switz
100B4 Burgersdorp S Africa
50B1 Burgos Spain
58B1 Burgsvik Sweden
55C3 Burhaniye Turk
85D4 Burhänpur India
79B3 Burias I Phil
76C2 Buriram Thai
35B1 Buritis Brazil
13B2 Burke Chan Can
106C2 Burketown Aust
97B3 Burkina Republic, Africa
15C1 Burks Falls Can
8B2 Burley USA
10A2 Burlington Iowa, USA
16B2 Burlington New Jersey, USA
10C2 Burlington Vermont, USA
20B1 Burlington Washington, USA
Burma = Myanmar
20B2 Burney USA
16A2 Burnham USA
107D5 Burnie Aust
42C3 Burnley Eng
20C2 Burns USA
5F4 Burns Lake Can
82C1 Burqin China
108A2 Burra Aust
109D2 Burragorang,L Aust
44C2 Burray I Scot
109C2 Burren Junction Aust
109C2 Burrinjuck Res Aust
60C5 Bursa Turk
80B3 Bur Safâga Egypt
Bûr Sa'îd = Port Said
14B2 Burton USA
43D3 Burton upon Trent Eng
38J6 Burtrask Sweden
108B2 Burtundy Aust
71D4 Buru Indon
99C3 Burundi Republic, Africa
78A2 Burung Indon
99D1 Burye Eth
61H4 Burynshik Kazakhstan
43E3 Bury St Edmunds Eng
91B4 Büshehr Iran
98B3 Busira R Zaire
58C2 Buskozdroj Pol
94C2 Busrà ash Shäm Syria
106A4 Busselton Aust
49D2 Busto Italy
52A1 Busto Arsizio Italy
79A3 Busuanga I Phil
98C2 Buta Zaire
34B3 Buta Ranquil Arg
99C3 Butare Rwanda
42B2 Bute I Scot
69E2 Butha Qi China
14C2 Butler USA
8B2 Butte USA
77C4 Butterworth Malay
40B2 Butt of Lewis C Scot
6D3 Button Is Can
79C4 Butuan Phil
71D4 Butung I Indon

61F3 Buturlinovka Russian Fed
86A1 Butwal Nepal
99E2 Buulo Barde Somalia
99E2 Buur Hakaba Somalia
61F2 Buy Russian Fed
72B1 Buyant Ovvo Mongolia
61G5 Buynaksk Russian Fed
63D3 Buyr Nuur L Mongolia
93D2 Büyük Ağri Mt Turk
92A2 Büyük Menderes R Turk
54C1 Buzău Rom
54C1 Buzau R Rom
61H3 Buzuluk Russian Fed
16D2 Buzzards B USA
54C2 Byala Bulg
54B2 Byala Slatina Bulg
4H2 Byam Martin Chan Can
4H2 Byam Martin I Can
Byblos = Jubail
94B1 Byblos Hist Site, Leb
58B2 Bydgoszcz Pol
39F7 Bygland Nor
6C2 Bylot I Can
109C2 Byrock Aust
22B2 Byron USA
109D1 Byron,C Aust
59B2 Bytom Pol

C

30E4 Caacupé Par
100A2 Caála Angola
13B2 Caamano Sd Can
30E4 Caazapá Par
79B2 Cabanatuan Phil
31E3 Cabedelo Brazil
50A2 Cabeza del Buey Spain
34C3 Cabildo Arg
34A2 Cabildo Chile
32C1 Cabimas Ven
98B3 Cabinda Angola
98B3 Cabinda Province, Angola
27C3 Cabo Beata Dom Rep
51C2 Cabo Binibeca C Spain
53A3 Cabo Carbonara C Sardegna
34A3 Cabo Carranza C Chile
50A2 Cabo Carvoeiro C Port
9B3 Cabo Colnett C Mexico
32B2 Cabo Corrientes C Colombia
24B2 Cabo Corrientes C Mexico
26B3 Cabo Cruz C Cuba
50B1 Cabo de Ajo C Spain
51C1 Cabo de Caballeria C Spain
51C1 Cabo de Creus C Spain
50B2 Cabo de Gata C Spain
29C7 Cabo de Hornos C Chile
51C2 Cabo de la Nao C Spain
50A1 Cabo de Peñas C Spain
50A2 Cabo de Roca C Port
51C2 Cabo de Salinas C Spain
35C2 Cabo de São Tomé C Brazil
50A2 Cabo de São Vicente C Port
50A2 Cabo de Sines C Port
51C1 Cabo de Tortosa C Spain
29C4 Cabo Dos Bahias C Arg
50A2 Cabo Espichel C Port
9B4 Cabo Falso C Mexico

51B2 Cabo Ferrat C Alg
50A1 Cabo Finisterre C Spain
51C1 Cabo Formentor C Spain
35C2 Cabo Frio Brazil
35C2 Cabo Frio C Brazil
26A4 Cabo Gracias à Dios Honduras
31B2 Cabo Maguarinho C Brazil
50A2 Cabo Negro C Mor
109D1 Caboolture Aust
33G3 Cabo Orange C Brazil
21B3 Cabo Punta Banda C Mexico
101C2 Cabora Bassa Dam Mozam
24A1 Caborca Mexico
24C2 Cabo Rojo C Mexico
23B1 Cabos Mexico
29C6 Cabo San Diego C Arg
32A4 Cabo San Lorenzo C Ecuador
53A3 Cabo Teulada C Sardegna
50A2 Cabo Trafalgar C Spain
50B2 Cabo Tres Forcas C Mor
29C5 Cabo Tres Puntas C Arg
7D5 Cabot Str Can
50B2 Cabra Spain
50A1 Cabreira Mt Port
51C2 Cabrera I Spain
34A3 Cabrero Chile
51B2 Cabriel R Spain
23B2 Cacahuamilpa Mexico
54B2 Čačak Serbia, Yugos
23B2 C A Carillo Mexico
30E2 Cáceres Brazil
50A2 Caceres Spain
18B2 Cache R USA
13C2 Cache Creek Can
30C4 Cachi Arg
33G5 Cachimbo Brazil
31D4 Cachoeira Brazil
35A1 Cachoeira Alta Brazil
31D3 Cachoeira de Paulo Alfonso Waterfall Brazil
29F2 Cachoeira do Sul Brazil
31C6 Cachoeiro de Itapemirim Brazil
22C3 Cachuma,L USA
100A2 Cacolo Angola
100A2 Caconda Angola
35A1 Caçu Brazil
100A2 Cacuiluvar R Angola
59B3 Čadca Slovakia
43C3 Cader Idris Mts Wales
10B2 Cadillac USA
79B3 Cadiz Phil
50A2 Cadiz Spain
48B2 Caen France
42B3 Caernarfon Wales
43B3 Caernarfon B Wales
43C3 Caernarfonshire and Merionethshire County Wales
43C4 Caerphilly County Wales
94B2 Caesarea Hist Site Israel
31C4 Caetité Brazil
30C4 Cafayate Arg
92B2 Caga Tepe Turk
79B2 Cagayan R Phil
79B4 Cagayan de Oro Phil
79B4 Cagayan Is Phil
53A3 Cagliari Sardegna
27D3 Caguas Puerto Rico
45B3 Caha Mts Irish Rep
45A3 Cahersiveen Irish Rep
45C2 Cahir Irish Rep
45C2 Cahone Pt Irish Rep
48C3 Cahors France

101C2 Caia Mozam
100B2 Caianda Angola
35A1 Caiapó R Brazil
35A1 Caiapônia Brazil
31D3 Caicó Brazil
26C2 Caicos Is Caribbean S
11C4 Caicos Pass The Bahamas
12C2 Cairn Mt USA
44C3 Cairngorms Mts Scot
107D2 Cairns Aust
92B3 Cairo Egypt
11B3 Cairo USA
108B1 Caiwarro Aust
32B5 Cajabamba Peru
32B5 Cajamarca Peru
27D5 Calabozo Ven
54B2 Calafat Rom
29B6 Calafate Arg
79B3 Calagua Is Phil
51B1 Calahorra Spain
48C1 Calais France
30C3 Calama Chile
32C3 Calamar Colombia
79A3 Calamian Group Is Phil
98B3 Calandula Angola
70A3 Calang Indon
95B2 Calanscio Sand Sea Libya
79B3 Calapan Phil
54C2 Calarasi Rom
51B1 Calatayud Spain
22B2 Calaveras Res USA
79B3 Calbayog Phil
19B4 Calcasieu L USA
86B2 Calcutta India
50A2 Caldas da Rainha Port
31B5 Caldas Novas Brazil
30B4 Caldera Chile
8B2 Caldwell USA
29C5 Caleta Olivia Arg
9B3 Calexico USA
5G4 Calgary Can
17B1 Calhoun USA
17B1 Calhoun Falls USA
32B3 Cali Colombia
87B2 Calicut India
8B3 Caliente Nevada, USA
8A3 California State, USA
22C3 California Aqueduct USA
87B2 Calimera,Pt India
34B2 Calingasta Arg
22A1 Calistoga USA
108B1 Callabonna R Aust
108A1 Callabonna,L Aust
15C1 Callander USA
44B3 Callander Scot
108A1 Callanna Aust
32B6 Callao Peru
13E1 Calling L Can
23B1 Calnali Mexico
17B2 Caloosahatchee R USA
109D1 Caloundra Aust
23B2 Calpulalpan Mexico
53B3 Caltanissetta Italy
98B3 Caluango Angola
100A2 Calulo Angola
100A2 Caluquembe Angola
99F1 Caluula Somalia
13B2 Calvert I Can
52A2 Calvi Corse
23A1 Calvillo Mexico
100A4 Calvinia S Africa
25E2 Camagüey Cuba
25E2 Camagüey,Arch de Is Cuba
30B2 Camaná Peru
30C3 Camargo Bol
22C3 Camarillo USA
29C4 Camarones Arg
20B1 Camas USA
98B3 Camaxilo Angola
98B3 Cambatela Angola
76C3 Cambodia Republic, S E Asia
43B4 Camborne Eng
49C1 Cambrai France

Casilda

14

34C2 **Casilda** Arg
107E3 **Casino** Aust
32B5 **Casma** Peru
51B1 **Caspe** Spain
8C2 **Casper** USA
61G4 **Caspian Lowland** *Region* Kazakhstan
65G6 **Caspian S** Asia/ Europe
14C3 **Cass** USA
100B2 **Cassamba** Angola
46B1 **Cassel** France
12J3 **Cassiar** Can
4E3 **Cassiar Mts** Can
35A1 **Cassilândia** Brazil
53B2 **Cassino** Italy
22C3 **Castaic** USA
34B2 **Castaño** *R* Arg
47D2 **Castelfranco** Italy
49D3 **Castellane** France
34D3 **Castelli** Arg
51B2 **Castellon de la Plana** Spain
31C3 **Castelo** Brazil
50A2 **Castelo Branco** Port
48C3 **Castelsarrasin** France
53B3 **Castelvetrano** Italy
108B3 **Casterton** Aust
50B2 **Castilla La Nueva** *Region,* Spain
50B1 **Castilla La Vieja** *Region,* Spain
41B3 **Castlebar** Irish Rep
44A3 **Castlebay** Scot
42C2 **Castle Douglas** Scot
20C1 **Castlegar** Can
45B2 **Castleisland** Irish Rep
108B3 **Castlemain** Aust
45B2 **Castlerea** Irish Rep
109C2 **Castlereagh** Aust
48C3 **Castres-sur-l'Agout** France
27E4 **Castries** St Lucia
29B4 **Castro** Arg
30F3 **Castro** Brazil
31D4 **Castro Alves** Brazil
53C3 **Castrovillari** Italy
22B2 **Castroville** USA
111A2 **Caswell Sd** NZ
25E2 **Cat** *I* The Bahamas
79B3 **Catabalogan** Phil
32A5 **Catacaos** Peru
35C2 **Cataguases** Brazil
19B3 **Catahoula L** USA
35B1 **Catalão** Brazil
51C1 **Cataluña** *Region,* Spain
30C4 **Catamarca** Arg
30C4 **Catamarca** State, Arg
101C2 **Catandica** Mozam
79B3 **Catanduanes** *I* Phil
31B6 **Catanduva** Brazil
53C3 **Catania** Italy
53C3 **Catanzaro** Italy
79B3 **Catarman** Phil
108A2 **Catastrophe,C** Aust
26C5 **Catatumbo** *R* Ven
16A2 **Catawissa** USA
23B2 **Catemaco** Mexico
49D3 **Cater** Corse
52A2 **Cateraggio** Corse
98B3 **Catete** Angola
97A3 **Catio** Guinea-Bissau
7A4 **Cat Lake** Can
13D3 **Catlegar** Can
107E3 **Cato** *I* Aust
25D2 **Catoche,C** Mexico
16A3 **Catoctin Mt** USA
15C3 **Catonsville** USA
34C3 **Catrilo** Arg
15D2 **Catskill** USA
15D2 **Catskill Mts** USA
32C2 **Cauca** *R* Colombia
31D2 **Caucaia** Brazil
32B2 **Caucasia** Colombia
65F5 **Caucasus** *Mts* Georgia
46B1 **Caudry** France
98B3 **Caungula** Angola
29B3 **Cauquenes** Chile
87B2 **Cauvery** *R* India
49D3 **Cavaillon** France
47D1 **Cavalese** Italy
97B4 **Cavally** *R* Lib

45C2 **Cavan** County, Irish Rep
45C2 **Cavan** Irish Rep
79B3 **Cavite** Phil
31C2 **Caxias** Brazil
32C4 **Caxias** Brazil
30F4 **Caxias do Sul** Brazil
98B3 **Caxito** Angola
17B1 **Cayce** USA
93D1 **Çayeli** Turk
33G3 **Cayenne** French Guiana
46A1 **Cayeux-sur-Mer** France
25E3 **Cayman Brac** *I* Caribbean S
26A3 **Cayman Is** Caribbean S
26A3 **Cayman Trench** Caribbean S
99E2 **Caynabo** Somalia
25E2 **Cayo Romana** *I* Cuba
25D3 **Cayos Miskitos** *Is* Nic
26A2 **Cay Sal** *I* Caribbean S
100B2 **Cazombo** Angola
Ceará = Fortaleza
31C3 **Ceara** State, Brazil
79B3 **Cebu** Phil
79B3 **Cebu** *I* Phil
16B3 **Cecilton** USA
52B2 **Cecina** Italy
8B3 **Cedar City** USA
19A3 **Cedar Creek Res** USA
5J4 **Cedar L** Can
10A2 **Cedar Rapids** USA
17A1 **Cedartown** USA
24A2 **Cedros** *I* Mexico
106C4 **Ceduna** Aust
99E2 **Ceelbuur** Somalia
99E1 **Ceerigaabo** Somalia
53B3 **Cefalù** Italy
59B3 **Cegléd** Hung
100A2 **Cela** Angola
24B2 **Celaya** Mexico
Celebes = Sulawesi
70C3 **Celebes S** S E Asia
14B2 **Celina** USA
52C1 **Celje** Slovenia
56C2 **Celle** Germany
71E4 **Cendrawasih** *Pen* Indon
47C2 **Ceno** *R* Italy
19B3 **Center** USA
16C2 **Center Moriches** USA
17A1 **Center Point** USA
47D2 **Cento** Italy
98B2 **Central African Republic** Africa
16D2 **Central Falls** USA
18C2 **Centralia** Illinois, USA
8A2 **Centralia** Washington, USA
20B2 **Central Point** USA
71F4 **Central Range** *Mts* PNG
16A3 **Centreville** Maryland, USA
78C4 **Cepu** Indon
Ceram = Seram
71D4 **Ceram Sea** Indon
34C3 **Cereales** Arg
31B5 **Ceres** Brazil
100A4 **Ceres** S Africa
22B2 **Ceres** USA
48C2 **Cergy-Pontoise** France
53C2 **Cerignola** Italy
60C5 **Cernavodă** Rom
9C4 **Cerralvo** *I* Mexico
23A1 **Cerritos** Mexico
34B2 **Cerro Aconcagua** *Mt* Arg
23B1 **Cerro Azul** Mexico
34A3 **Cerro Campanario** *Mt* Chile
34C2 **Cerro Champaqui** *Mt* Arg
23A2 **Cerro Cuachaia** *Mt* Mexico

23B1 **Cerro de Astillero** Mexico
34B2 **Cerro de Olivares** *Mt* Arg
32B6 **Cerro de Pasco** Peru
27D3 **Cerro de Punta** *Mt* Puerto Rico
23A2 **Cerro El Cantado** *Mt* Mexico
34B3 **Cerro El Nevado** *Mt* Arg
23A2 **Cerro Grande** *Mts* Mexico
34A2 **Cerro Juncal** *Mt* Arg/ Chile
23A1 **Cerro la Ardilla** *Mts* Mexico
34B1 **Cerro las Tortolas** *Mt* Chile
23A2 **Cerro Laurel** *Mt* Mexico
34A2 **Cerro Mercedario** *Mt* Arg
34A3 **Cerro Mora** *Mt* Chile
27C4 **Cerron** *Mt* Ven
34B3 **Cerro Payún** *Mt* Arg
23B2 **Cerro Penón del Rosario** *Mt* Mexico
34B2 **Cerro Sosneado** *Mt* Arg
23A2 **Cerro Teotepec** *Mt* Mexico
34B2 **Cerro Tupungato** *Mt* Arg
23B2 **Cerro Yucuyacau** *Mt* Mexico
47C2 **Cervo** *R* Italy
52B2 **Cesena** Italy
60B2 **Cēsis** Latvia
57C3 **České Budejovice** Czech Republic
59B3 **Českomoravská Vysocina** *Mts* Czech Republic
55C3 **Çeşme** Turk
107E4 **Cessnock** Aust
52C2 **Cetina** *R* Croatia
96B1 **Ceuta** N W Africa
92C2 **Ceyham** Turk
92C2 **Ceyhan** *R* Turk
93C2 **Ceylanpınar** Turk
Ceylon = Sri Lanka
63B2 **Chaa-Khol** Russian Fed
47B1 **Chablais** *Region,* France
34C2 **Chacabuco** Arg
32B5 **Chachapoyas** Peru
34B3 **Chacharramendi** Arg
84C3 **Chachran** Pak
30D4 **Chaco** State, Arg
98B1 **Chad** Republic, Africa
98B1 **Chad** *L* C Africa
34B3 **Chadileuvu** *R* Arg
8C2 **Chadron** USA
18C2 **Chaffee** USA
85A3 **Chagai** Pak
63F2 **Chagda** Russian Fed
84B2 **Chaghcharan** Afghan
104B4 **Chagos Arch** Indian O
27L1 **Chaguanas** Trinidad
91D4 **Chāh Bahār** Iran
76C2 **Chai Badan** Thai
76C3 **Chaine des Cardamomes** *Mts* Camb
98C4 **Chaine des Mitumba** *Mts* Zaire
76C2 **Chaiyaphum** Thai
34D2 **Chajari** Arg
84C2 **Chakwal** Pak
30B2 **Chala** Peru
100C2 **Chalabesa** Zambia
84A2 **Chalap Dalam** *Mts* Afghan
73C4 **Chaling** China
85C4 **Chālisgaon** India
12F1 **Chalkyitsik** USA
46C2 **Challerange** France
46C2 **Châlons en Champagne** France
49C2 **Chalon sur Saône** France

57C3 **Cham** Germany
84B2 **Chaman** Pak
84D2 **Chamba** India
85D3 **Chambal** *R* India
15C3 **Chambersburg** USA
49D2 **Chambéry** France
46B2 **Chambly** France
85A3 **Chambor Kalat** Pak
90B3 **Chamgordan** Iran
34B2 **Chamical** Arg
47B2 **Chamonix** France
86A2 **Champa** India
49C2 **Champagne** Region, France
101G1 **Champagne Castle** *Mt* Lesotho
47A1 **Champagnole** France
10B2 **Champaign** USA
76D3 **Champassak** Laos
10C2 **Champlain,L** USA
87B2 **Chāmrājnagar** India
30B4 **Chañaral** Chile
34A3 **Chanco** Chile
4D3 **Chandalar** USA
4D3 **Chandalar** *R* USA
84D2 **Chandigarh** India
86C2 **Chandpur** Bang
85D5 **Chandrapur** India
91D4 **Chānf** Iran
101C2 **Changara** Mozam
74B2 **Changbai** China
69E2 **Changchun** China
73C4 **Changde** China
68E4 **Chang-hua** Taiwan
76D2 **Changjiang** China
73D3 **Chang Jiang** *R* China
74B2 **Changjin** N Korea
73C4 **Changsha** China
72E3 **Changshu** China
74A2 **Changtu** China
72B2 **Changwu** China
74B3 **Changyön** N Korea
72C2 **Changzhi** China
73E3 **Changzhou** China
48B2 **Channel Is** Europe
9B3 **Channel Is** USA
7E5 **Channel Port-aux-Basques** Can
76C3 **Chanthaburi** Thai
46B2 **Chantilly** France
18A2 **Chanute** USA
73D5 **Chaoàn** China
73D5 **Chao'an** China
73D3 **Chao Hu** *L* China
76C3 **Chao Phraya** *R* Thai
72E1 **Chaoyang** China
31C4 **Chapada Diamantina** *Mts* Brazil
31C2 **Chapadinha** Brazil
23A1 **Chapala** Mexico
23A1 **Chapala,Lac de** *L* Mexico
61H3 **Chapayevo** Kazakhstan
30F4 **Chapecó** Brazil
27H1 **Chapeltown** Jamaica
7B5 **Chapleau** Can
61E3 **Chaplygin** Russian Fed
112C3 **Charcot I** Ant
80E2 **Chardzhou** Turkmenistan
48C2 **Charente** *R* France
98B1 **Chari** *R* Chad
98B1 **Chari Baguirmi** Region, Chad
84B1 **Charikar** Afghan
18B1 **Chariton** *R* USA
33F2 **Charity** Guyana
85D3 **Charkhāri** India
46C1 **Charleroi** Belg
18C2 **Charleston** Illinois, USA
18C2 **Charleston** Missouri, USA
11C3 **Charleston** S Carolina, USA
10B3 **Charleston** W Virginia, USA
98C3 **Charlesville** Zaïre
107D3 **Charleville** Aust
49C2 **Charleville-Mézières** France
14A1 **Charlevoix** USA

14B2 **Charlotte** Michigan, USA
11B3 **Charlotte** N Carolina, USA
17B2 **Charlotte Harbor** *B* USA
10C3 **Charlottesville** USA
7D5 **Charlottetown** Can
27K1 **Charlotteville** Tobago
108B3 **Charlton** Aust
10C1 **Charlton I** Can
84C2 **Charsadda** Pak
107D3 **Charters Towers** Aust
48C2 **Chartres** France
29E3 **Chascomús** Arg
13D2 **Chase** Can
48B2 **Châteaubriant** France
48C2 **Châteaudun** France
48B2 **Châteaulin** France
48C2 **Châteauroux** France
46D2 **Châteu-Salins** France
49C2 **Cháteau-Thierry** France
46C1 **Châtelet** Belg
48C2 **Châtellerault** France
43E4 **Chatham** Eng
7D5 **Chatham** New Brunswick, Can
16C1 **Chatham** New York, USA
14B2 **Chatham** Ontario, Can
13A2 **Chatham Sd** Can
12H3 **Chatham Str** USA
49C2 **Châtillon** France
47B2 **Châtillon** Italy
16B3 **Chatsworth** USA
17B1 **Chattahoochee** USA
17A1 **Chattahoochee** *R* USA
11B3 **Chattanooga** USA
76A1 **Chauk** Myan
49D2 **Chaumont** France
46B2 **Chauny** France
77D3 **Chau Phu** Viet
50A1 **Chaves** Port
61H2 **Chaykovskiy** Russian Fed
50B2 **Chazaouet** Alg
34C2 **Chazón** Arg
32C2 **Chcontá** Colombia
57C2 **Cheb** Czech Republic
65F4 **Cheboksary** Russian Fed
10B2 **Cheboygan** USA
61G5 **Chechnya** Division, Russian Fed
74B3 **Chech'on** S Korea
85C3 **Chechro** Pak
18A2 **Checotah** USA
76A2 **Cheduba** *I* Myan
108B1 **Cheepie** Aust
96B2 **Chegga** Maur
100C2 **Chegutu** Zim
20B1 **Chehalis** USA
74B4 **Cheju** S Korea
74B4 **Cheju do** *I* S Korea
74B4 **Cheju-haehyöp** *Str* S Korea
63F2 **Chekunda** Russian Fed
20B1 **Chelan,L** USA
90B2 **Cheleken** Turkmenistan
34B3 **Chelforo** Arg
80D1 **Chelkar** Kazakhstan
59C2 **Chelm** Pol
58B2 **Chelmno** Pol
43E4 **Chelmsford** Eng
43C4 **Cheltenham** Eng
61K2 **Chelyabinsk** Russian Fed
61K3 **Chelyabinsk** Division, Russian Fed
101C2 **Chemba** Mozam
57C2 **Chemnitz** Germany
84D2 **Chenab** *R* India/Pak
96B2 **Chenachane** Alg
20C1 **Cheney** USA
18A2 **Cheney Res** USA

72D1 **Chengda** China
73A3 **Chengdu** China
72E2 **Chengshan Jiao** *Pt* China
73C4 **Chenxi** China
73C4 **Chen Xian** China
73D3 **Cheo Xian** China
32B5 **Chepén** Peru
34B2 **Chepes** Arg
48C2 **Cher** *R* France
23A2 **Cheran** Mexico
17C1 **Cheraw** USA
48B2 **Cherbourg** France
96C1 **Cherchell** Alg
63C2 **Cheremkhovo** Russian Fed
60E2 **Cherepovets** Russian Fed
60D4 **Cherkassy** Ukraine
61F5 **Cherkessk** Russian Fed
60D3 **Chernigov** Ukraine
60D3 **Chernobyl** Ukraine
60C4 **Chernovtsy** Ukraine
61J2 **Chernushka** Russian Fed
60B3 **Chernyakhovsk** Russian Fed
61G4 **Chernyye Zemli** Region, Russian Fed
18A2 **Cherokees,L o'the** USA
34A3 **Cherquenco** Chile
86C1 **Cherrapunji** India
60C3 **Cherven'** Belarus
59C2 **Chervonograd** Ukraine
10C3 **Chesapeake** *B* USA
42C3 **Cheshire** County, Eng
16C1 **Cheshire** USA
64F3 **Chëshskaya Guba** *B* Russian Fed
21A1 **Chester** California, USA
42C3 **Chester** Eng
18C2 **Chester** Illinois, USA
16C1 **Chester** Massachusets, USA
15C3 **Chester** Pennsylvania, USA
17B1 **Chester** S Carolina, USA
16A3 **Chester** *R* USA
42D3 **Chesterfield** Eng
6A3 **Chesterfield Inlet** Can
16A3 **Chestertown** USA
25D3 **Chetumal** Mexico
13C1 **Chetwynd** Can
12A2 **Chevak** USA
111B2 **Cheviot** NZ
40C2 **Cheviots** *Hills* Eng/Scot
13D3 **Chewelah** USA
8C2 **Cheyenne** USA
86A1 **Chhapra** India
86C1 **Chhātak** Bang
85D4 **Chhatarpur** India
85D4 **Chhindwāra** India
86B1 **Chhuka** Bhutan
73E5 **Chia'i** Taiwan
100A2 **Chiange** Angola
76C2 **Chiang Kham** Thai
76B2 **Chiang Mai** Thai
47C1 **Chiavenna** Italy
74E3 **Chiba** Japan
86B2 **Chibāsa** India
100A2 **Chibia** Angola
7C4 **Chibougamou** Can
75A1 **Chiburi-jima** *I* Japan
101C3 **Chibuto** Mozam
10B2 **Chicago** USA
14A2 **Chicago Heights** USA
12G3 **Chichagof I** USA
43D4 **Chichester** Eng
75B1 **Chichibu** Japan
69G4 **Chichi-jima** *I* Japan
11B3 **Chickamauga L** USA
19C3 **Chickasawhay** *R* USA
9D3 **Chickasha** USA
12F2 **Chicken** USA
32A5 **Chiclayo** Peru

8A3 **Chico** USA
29C4 **Chico** *R* Arg
101C2 **Chicoa** Mozam
15D2 **Chicopee** USA
7C5 **Chicoutimi** Can
101C3 **Chicualacuala** Mozam
87B2 **Chidambaram** India
6D3 **Chidley,C** Can
17B2 **Chiefland** USA
99C3 **Chiengi** Zambia
47B2 **Chieri** Italy
46C2 **Chiers** *R* France
47C1 **Chiesa** Italy
47D2 **Chiese** *R* Italy
52B2 **Chieti** Italy
72D1 **Chifeng** China
12C3 **Chiginigak,Mt** USA
4C3 **Chigmit Mts** USA
23B2 **Chignahuapán** Mexico
12C3 **Chignik** USA
24B2 **Chihuahua** Mexico
87B2 **Chik Ballapur** India
87B2 **Chikmagalūr** India
12C2 **Chikuminuk L** USA
101C2 **Chikwawa** Malawi
76A1 **Chi-kyaw** Myan
87C1 **Chilakalūrupet** India
23B2 **Chilapa** Mexico
87B3 **Chilaw** Sri Lanka
28B6 **Chile** Republic
34B2 **Chilecito** Mendoza, Arg
100B2 **Chililabombwe** Zambia
86B2 **Chilka** *L* India
13C2 **Chilko** *R* Can
5F4 **Chilko L** Can
13C2 **Chilkotin** *R* Can
34A3 **Chillán** Chile
34D3 **Chillar** Arg
18B2 **Chillicothe** Missouri, USA
14B3 **Chillicothe** Ohio, USA
13C3 **Chilliwack** Can
86B1 **Chilmari** India
101C2 **Chilongozi** Zambia
20B2 **Chiloquin** USA
24C3 **Chilpancingo** Mexico
43D4 **Chiltern Hills** *Upland* Eng
14A2 **Chilton** USA
101C2 **Chilumba** Malawi
69E4 **Chi-lung** Taiwan
101C2 **Chilwa** *L* Malawi
100C2 **Chimanimani** Zim
46C1 **Chimay** Belg
65G5 **Chimbay** Uzbekistan
32B4 **Chimborazo** *Mt* Ecuador
32B5 **Chimbote** Peru
65H5 **Chimkent** Kazakhstan
101C2 **Chimoio** Mozam
67E3 **China** Republic, Asia
   China National Republic = Taiwan
25D3 **Chinandega** Nic
32B6 **Chincha Alta** Peru
109D1 **Chinchilla** Aust
101C2 **Chinde** Mozam
86C2 **Chindwin** *R* Myan
100B2 **Chingola** Zambia
100A2 **Chinguar** Angola
96A2 **Chinguetti** Maur
74B3 **Chinhae** S Korea
100C2 **Chinhoyi** Zim
12D3 **Chiniak,C** USA
84C2 **Chiniot** Pak
74B3 **Chinju** S Korea
98C2 **Chinko** *R* CAR
75B1 **Chino** Japan
101C2 **Chinsali** Zambia
52B1 **Chioggia** Italy
101C2 **Chipata** Zambia
101C3 **Chipinge** Zim
87A1 **Chiplūn** India
43C4 **Chippenham** Eng
10A2 **Chippewa Falls** USA
32A4 **Chira** *R* Peru
87C1 **Chirāla** India
101C3 **Chiredzi** Zim

95A2 **Chirfa** Niger
32A2 **Chiriqui** *Mt* Panama
54C2 **Chirpan** Bulg
32A2 **Chirripo Grande** *Mt* Costa Rica
100B2 **Chirundu** Zim
100B2 **Chisamba** Zambia
7C4 **Chisasibi** Can
73B4 **Chishui He** *R* China
   Chişināu = Kishinev
47B2 **Chisone** *R* Italy
61H2 **Chistopol** Russian Fed
68D1 **Chita** Russian Fed
100A2 **Chitado** Angola
100A2 **Chitembo** Angola
12F2 **Chitina** USA
12F2 **Chitina** *R* USA
87B2 **Chitradurga** India
84C1 **Chitral** Pak
32A2 **Chitré** Panama
86C2 **Chittagong** Bang
85C4 **Chittaurgarh** India
87B2 **Chittoor** India
100B2 **Chiume** Angola
47D1 **Chiusa** Italy
47B2 **Chivasso** Italy
100C2 **Chivhu** Zim
29D2 **Chivilcoy** Arg
100C2 **Chivu** Zim
75A1 **Chizu** Japan
29C3 **Choele Choel** Arg
34C3 **Choique** Arg
24B2 **Choix** Mexico
58B2 **Chojnice** Pol
99D1 **Choke** *Mts* Eth
48B2 **Cholet** France
23B2 **Cholula** Mexico
100B2 **Choma** Zambia
86B1 **Chomo Yummo** *Mt* China/India
57C2 **Chomutov** Czech Republic
63C1 **Chona** *R* Russian Fed
74B3 **Ch'ŏnan** S Korea
76C3 **Chon Buri** Thai
32A4 **Chone** Ecuador
74B2 **Ch'ŏngjin** N Korea
74B3 **Chongju** N Korea
74B3 **Ch'ŏngju** S Korea
100A2 **Chongoroi** Angola
73B4 **Chongqing** China
74B3 **Chŏngŭp** S Korea
74B3 **Chŏnju** S Korea
86B1 **Chooyu** *Mt* China/Nepal
59D3 **Chortkov** Ukraine
74B3 **Ch'ŏrwŏn** N Korea
59B2 **Chorzow** Pol
74E3 **Choshi** Japan
34A3 **Chos-Malal** Arg
58B2 **Choszczno** Pol
86A2 **Chotanāgpur** Region, India
96C1 **Chott Melrhir** Alg
22B2 **Chowchilla** USA
63D3 **Choybalsan** Mongolia
6A3 **Chrantrey Inlet** *B* Can
111B2 **Christchurch** NZ
101G1 **Christiana** S Africa
6D2 **Christian,C** Can
12H3 **Christian Sd** USA
6E3 **Christianshab** Greenland
104D4 **Christmas I** Indian O
65J5 **Chu** Kazakhstan
65J5 **Chu** *R* Kazakhstan
29C4 **Chubut** State, Arg
29C4 **Chubut** *R* Arg
60D2 **Chudovo** Russian Fed
   Chudskoye Ozero = Peipus, Lake
4D3 **Chugach Mts** USA
12E2 **Chugiak** USA
75A1 **Chūgoku-sanchi** *Mts* Japan
29F2 **Chuí** Brazil
29B3 **Chuillán** Chile
77C5 **Chukai** Malay
76D2 **Chu Lai** Viet

34D2 **Colonia del Sacramento** Urug
34B3 **Colonia 25 de Mayo** Arg
29C5 **Colonia Las Heras** Arg
44A3 **Colonsay** *I* Scot
23A1 **Colontlán** Mexico
27E5 **Coloradito** Ven
8C3 **Colorado** State, USA
9B3 **Colorado** *R* Arizona, USA
29D3 **Colorado** *R* Buenos Aires, Arg
9D3 **Colorado** *R* Texas, USA
9B3 **Colorado Plat** USA
8C3 **Colorado Springs** USA
22D3 **Colton** USA
16A3 **Columbia** Maryland, USA
19C3 **Columbia** Mississippi, USA
10A3 **Columbia** Missouri, USA
15C2 **Columbia** Pennsylvania, USA
11B3 **Columbia** S Carolina, USA
11B3 **Columbia** Tennessee, USA
13D2 **Columbia** *R* Can
8A2 **Columbia** *R* USA
5G4 **Columbia,Mt** Can
20C1 **Columbia Plat** USA
11B3 **Columbus** Georgia, USA
14A3 **Columbus** Indiana, USA
11B3 **Columbus** Mississippi, USA
8D2 **Columbus** Nebraska, USA
10B2 **Columbus** Ohio, USA
19A4 **Columbus** Texas, USA
20C1 **Colville** USA
4C3 **Colville** *R* USA
110C1 **Colville,C** NZ
4F3 **Colville L** Can
42C3 **Colwyn Bay** Wales
47E2 **Comacchio** Italy
22B1 **Comanche Res** USA
112C2 **Comandante Ferraz** *Base* Ant
25D3 **Comayagua** Honduras
34A2 **Combarbalá** Chile
45C2 **Comeragh** *Mts* Irish Rep
86C2 **Comilla** Bang
25C3 **Comitán** Mexico
46C2 **Commercy** France
6B3 **Committees B** Can
52A1 **Como** Italy
29C5 **Comodoro Rivadavia** Arg
23A1 **Comonfort** Mexico
87B3 **Comorin,C** India
101D2 **Comoros** *Is* Indian O
49C2 **Compiègne** France
23A1 **Compostela** Mexico
34B2 **Comte Salas** Arg
86C1 **Cona** China
97A4 **Conakry** Guinea
34B2 **Concarán** Arg
48B2 **Concarneau** France
35D1 **Conceiçao da Barra** Brazil
31B3 **Conceição do Araguaia** Brazil
35C1 **Conceiçao do Mato Dentro** Brazil
29B3 **Concepción** Chile
30E3 **Concepción** Par
29E2 **Concepción** *R* Arg
24B2 **Concepcion del Oro** Mexico
34D2 **Concepcion del Uruguay** Arg
9A3 **Conception,Pt** Can
35B2 **Conchas** Brazil
9C4 **Conchos** *R* Mexico

21A2 **Concord** California, USA
10C2 **Concord** New Hampshire, USA
29E2 **Concordia** Arg
8D3 **Concordia** USA
20B1 **Concrete** USA
109D1 **Condamine** Aust
107D4 **Condobolin** Aust
20B1 **Condon** USA
46C1 **Condroz** *Mts* Belg
17A1 **Conecuh** *R* USA
47E2 **Conegliano** Italy
89F8 **Congo** Republic, Africa
89F8 **Congo** *R* Congo
98C3 **Congo, Democratic Republic of** Africa
14B1 **Coniston** Can
45B2 **Connaught** Region, Irish Rep
14B2 **Conneaut** USA
10C2 **Connecticut** State, USA
15D2 **Connecticut** *R* USA
15C2 **Connellsville** USA
45B2 **Connemara,Mts of** Irish Rep
14A3 **Connersville** USA
108B2 **Conoble** Aust
19A3 **Conroe** USA
35C2 **Conselheiro Lafaiete** Brazil
77D4 **Con Son** *Is* Viet
Constance,L =
Bodensee
60C5 **Constanta** Rom
96C1 **Constantine** Alg
12C3 **Constantine,C** USA
29B3 **Constitución** Chile
13F3 **Consul** Can
47E2 **Contarina** Italy
31C4 **Contas** *R* Brazil
23B2 **Contreras** Mexico
4H3 **Contuoyto L** Can
11A3 **Conway** Arkansas, USA
15D2 **Conway** New Hampshire, USA
17C1 **Conway** South Carolina, USA
108A1 **Conway,L** Aust
42C3 **Conwy** Wales
106C3 **Cooer Pedy** Aust
110B2 **Cook** *Str* NZ
13B2 **Cook,C** Can
4C3 **Cook Inlet** *B* USA
105H4 **Cook Is** Pacific O
111B2 **Cook,Mt** NZ
107D2 **Cooktown** Aust
109C2 **Coolabah** Aust
108C1 **Cooladdi** Aust
109C2 **Coolah** Aust
109C2 **Coolamon** Aust
106B4 **Coolgardie** Aust
109C3 **Cooma** Aust
109C2 **Coonabarabran** Aust
109C2 **Coonamble** Aust
108B2 **Coonbah** Aust
108A2 **Coondambo** Aust
108C1 **Coongoola** Aust
87B2 **Coonoor** Aust
108B1 **Cooper Basin** Aust
106C3 **Cooper Creek** Aust
108B1 **Cooper Creek** *R* Aust
108A3 **Coorong,The** Aust
109D1 **Cooroy** Aust
20B2 **Coos B** USA
20B2 **Coos Bay** USA
107D4 **Cootamundra** Aust
45C1 **Cootehill** Irish Rep
23B2 **Copala** Mexico
23B2 **Copalillo** Mexico
Copenhagen =
København
30B4 **Copiapó** Chile
47D2 **Copparo** Italy
12F2 **Copper** *R* USA
4D3 **Copper Centre** USA
14B1 **Copper Cliff** Can
Coppermine =
Qurlurtuuk
4G3 **Coppermine** *R* Can

30B4 **Coquimbo** Chile
54B2 **Corabia** Rom
17B2 **Coral Gables** USA
6B3 **Coral Harbour** Can
107D2 **Coral S** Aust/PNG
104F4 **Coral Sea Basin** Pacific O
107E2 **Coral Sea Island Territories** Aust
108B3 **Corangamite,L** Aust
33F3 **Corantijn** *R* Surinam/Guyana
46B2 **Corbeil-Essonnes** France
50A1 **Corcubion** Spain
11B3 **Cordele** USA
50A1 **Cordillera Cantabrica** *Mts* Spain
26C3 **Cordillera Central** *Mts* Dom Rep
79B2 **Cordillera Central** *Mts* Phil
34B2 **Cordillera de Ansita** *Mts* Arg
32B5 **Cordillera de los Andes** *Mts* Peru
30C4 **Cordillera del Toro** *Mt* Arg
32C2 **Cordillera de Mérida** Ven
34A3 **Cordillera de Viento** *Mts* Arg
25D3 **Cordillera Isabelia** *Mts* Nic
32B3 **Cordillera Occidental** *Mts* Colombia
32B3 **Cordillera Oriental** *Mts* Colombia
108B1 **Cordillo Downs** Aust
29D2 **Córdoba** Arg
24C3 **Córdoba** Mexico
50B2 **Córdoba** Spain
29D2 **Córdoba** State, Arg
4D3 **Cordova** USA
Corfu = Kérkira
109D2 **Coricudgy,Mt** Aust
53C3 **Corigliano Calabro** Italy
11B3 **Corinth** Mississippi, USA
31C5 **Corinto** Brazil
45B2 **Cork** County, Irish Rep
41B3 **Cork** Irish Rep
92A1 **Çorlu** Turk
31C5 **Cornel Fabriciano** Brazil
35A2 **Cornelio Procópio** Brazil
7E5 **Corner Brook** Can
109C3 **Corner Inlet** *B* Aust
15C2 **Corning** USA
7C5 **Cornwall** Can
43B4 **Cornwall** County, Eng
43B4 **Cornwall,C** Eng
4H2 **Cornwall I** Can
6A2 **Cornwallis I** Can
32D1 **Coro** Ven
31C2 **Coroatá** Brazil
30C2 **Coroico** Bol
35B1 **Coromandel** Brazil
87C2 **Coromandel Coast** India
110C1 **Coromandel Pen** NZ
110C1 **Coromandel Range** *Mts* NZ
22D4 **Corona** California, USA
13E2 **Coronation** Can
4G3 **Coronation G** Can
34C2 **Coronda** Arg
29B3 **Coronel** Chile
34D3 **Coronel Brandsen** Arg
34C3 **Coronel Dorrego** Arg
35C1 **Coronel Fabriciano** Brazil
30E4 **Coronel Oviedo** Par
29D3 **Coronel Pringles** Arg
34C3 **Coronel Suárez** Arg
34D3 **Coronel Vidal** Arg
30B2 **Coropuna** *Mt* Peru
109C3 **Corowa** Aust
49D3 **Corps** France

9D4 **Corpus Christi** USA
9D4 **Corpus Christi,L** USA
79B3 **Corregidor** *I* Phil
35A1 **Corrente** *R* Mato Grosso, Brazil
30E4 **Corrientes** Arg
30E4 **Corrientes** State, Arg
19B3 **Corrigan** USA
106A4 **Corrigin** Aust
107E2 **Corringe Is** Aust
109C3 **Corryong** Aust
52A2 **Corse** *I* Medit S
42B2 **Corsewall** *Pt* Scot
Corsica = Corse
9D3 **Corsicana** USA
52A2 **Corte** Corse
9C3 **Cortez** USA
52B1 **Cortina d'Ampezzo** Italy
15C2 **Cortland** USA
23A2 **Coruca de Catalan** Mexico
93D1 **Çoruh** *R* Turk
60E5 **Çorum** Turk
30E2 **Corumbá** Brazil
35B1 **Corumba** *R* Brazil
35B1 **Corumbaiba** Brazil
20B2 **Corvallis** USA
96A1 **Corvo** *I* Açores
43C3 **Corwen** Wales
23B2 **Coscomatopec** Mexico
53C3 **Cosenza** Italy
101D1 **Cosmoledo** *Is* Seychelles
34C2 **Cosquín** Arg
51B2 **Costa Blanca** Region, Spain
51C1 **Costa Brava** Region, Spain
50B2 **Costa de la Luz** Region, Spain
50B2 **Costa del Sol** Region, Spain
22D4 **Costa Mesa** USA
25D3 **Costa Rica** Republic, Cent America
79B4 **Cotabato** Phil
30C3 **Cotagaita** Bol
49D3 **Côte d'Azur** Region, France
97B4 **Côte d'Ivoire** Republic, Africa
46C2 **Côtes de Meuse** *Mts* France
97C4 **Cotonou** Benin
32B4 **Cotopaxi** *Mt* Ecuador
43C4 **Cotswold Hills** *Upland* Eng
20B2 **Cottage Grove** USA
56C2 **Cottbus** Germany
108A3 **Couedic,C du** Aust
20C1 **Couer d'Alene L** USA
46B2 **Coulommiers** France
15C1 **Coulonge** *R* Can
22B2 **Coulterville** USA
4B3 **Council** USA
8D2 **Council Bluffs** USA
58C1 **Courland Lagoon** *Lg* Lithuania/Russian Fed
47B2 **Courmayeur** Italy
13B3 **Courtenay** Can
Courtrai = Kortrijk
48B2 **Coutances** France
43D3 **Coventry** Eng
50A1 **Covilhã** Spain
17B1 **Covington** Georgia, USA
19B3 **Covington** Louisiana, USA
109C2 **Cowal,L** Aust
108B3 **Cowangie** Aust
15D1 **Cowansville** Can
108A1 **Coward Springs** Aust
108A2 **Cowell** Aust
108C3 **Cowes** Aust
20B1 **Cowichan L** Can
20B1 **Cowiltz** *R* USA
109C2 **Cowra** Aust
30F2 **Coxim** Brazil
16C1 **Coxsackie** USA
86C2 **Cox's Bazar** Bang
22B2 **Coyote** USA

Coyuca de Benitez

60C2	**Daugavpils** Latvia
6D1	**Dauguard Jensen Land** Greenland
84A1	**Daulatabad** Afghan
85D3	**Daulpur** India
46D1	**Daun** Germany
87A1	**Daund** India
5H4	**Dauphin** Can
16A2	**Dauphin** USA
49D2	**Dauphiné** Region, France
97C3	**Daura** Nig
85D3	**Dausa** India
87B2	**Dāvangere** India
79C4	**Davao** Phil
79C4	**Davao G** Phil
22A2	**Davenport** California, USA
10A2	**Davenport** Iowa, USA
32A2	**David** Panama
4D3	**Davidson Mts** USA
21A2	**Davis** USA
112C10	**Davis** *Base* Ant
7D4	**Davis Inlet** Can
6E3	**Davis Str** Greenland/ Can
61J3	**Davlekanovo** Russian Fed
47C1	**Davos** Switz
99E2	**Dawa** *R* Eth
73A4	**Dawan** China
84B2	**Dawat Yar** Afghan
	Dawei = Tavoy
91B4	**Dawhat Salwah** *B* Qatar/S Arabia
76B2	**Dawna Range** *Mts* Myan
4E3	**Dawson** Can
17B1	**Dawson** Georgia, USA
107D3	**Dawson** *R* Aust
5F4	**Dawson Creek** Can
13D2	**Dawson,Mt** Can
12G2	**Dawson Range** *Mts* Can
73A3	**Dawu** China
73C3	**Dawu** China
48B3	**Dax** France
73B3	**Daxian** China
73B5	**Daxin** China
73A3	**Daxue Shan** *Mts* China
73C4	**Dayong** China
94C2	**Dayr'Ali** Syria
94C1	**Dayr'Atiyah** Syria
93D2	**Dayr az Zawr** Syria
10B3	**Dayton** Ohio, USA
19B4	**Dayton** Texas, USA
20C1	**Dayton** Washington, USA
11B4	**Daytona Beach** USA
73C4	**Dayu** China
78D3	**Dayu** Indon
72D2	**Da Yunhe** *R* China
20C2	**Dayville** USA
73B3	**Dazhu** China
100B4	**De Aar** S Africa
26C2	**Deadman's Cay** The Bahamas
92C3	**Dead S** Israel/Jordan
46A1	**Deal** Eng
101G1	**Dealesville** S Africa
13B2	**Dean** *R* Can
13B2	**Dean Chan** Can
34C2	**Deán Funes** Arg
14B2	**Dearborn** USA
4F3	**Dease Arm** *B* Can
4E4	**Dease Lake** Can
9B3	**Death V** USA
48C2	**Deauville** France
97B4	**Debakala** Côte d'Ivoire
12B2	**Debauch Mt** USA
27L1	**Débé** Trinidad
59C2	**Debica** Pol
58C2	**Deblin** Pol
97B3	**Débo,L** Mali
59C3	**Debrecen** Hung
99D2	**Debre Birhan** Eth
99D1	**Debre Markos** Eth
99D1	**Debre Tabor** Eth
11B3	**Decatur** Alabama, USA

17B1	**Decatur** Georgia, USA
10B3	**Decatur** Illinois, USA
14B2	**Decatur** Indiana, USA
48C3	**Decazeville** France
73A4	**Dechang** China
97B3	**Dédougou** Burkina
101C2	**Dedza** Malawi
42B2	**Dee** *R* Dumfries and Galloway, Scot
42C3	**Dee** *R* Eng/Wales
44C3	**Dee** *R* Grampian, Scot
15C1	**Deep River** Can
16C2	**Deep River** USA
109D1	**Deepwater** Aust
7E5	**Deer Lake** Can
8B2	**Deer Lodge** USA
34D3	**Defferrari** Arg
17A1	**De Funiak Springs** USA
68B3	**Dêgê** China
99E1	**Degeh Bur** Eth
106A3	**De Grey** *R* Aust
91B3	**Deh Bid** Iran
84B1	**Dehi** Afghan
96D1	**Dehibat** Tunisia
87B3	**Dehiwala-Mt Lavinia** Sri Lanka
90A3	**Dehlorān** Iran
84D2	**Dehra Dün** India
86A2	**Dehri** India
98C2	**Deim Zubeir** Sudan
94B2	**Deir Abu Sa'id** Jordan
94C1	**Deir el Ahmar** Leb
60B4	**Dej** Rom
19B3	**De Kalb** Texas, USA
63G2	**De Kastri** Russian Fed
98C3	**Dekese** Zaïre
98B2	**Dekoa** CAR
106B1	**Dekusi** Indon
9B3	**Delano** USA
10C3	**Delaware** State, USA
14B2	**Delaware** USA
15C2	**Delaware** *R* USA
10C3	**Delaware B** USA
109C3	**Delegate** Aust
47B1	**Delemont** Switz
101D2	**Delgado** *C* Mozam
84D3	**Delhi** India
15D2	**Delhi** New York, USA
92B1	**Delice** Turk
24B2	**Delicias** Mexico
90B3	**Delijan** Iran
47B1	**Delle** France
22D4	**Del Mar** USA
39F8	**Delmenhorst** Germany
4E3	**De Long** *Mts* USA
109C4	**Deloraine** Aust
5H5	**Deloraine** Can
17B2	**Delray Beach** USA
9C4	**Del Rio** USA
8B3	**Delta** USA
12E2	**Delta** *R* USA
12E2	**Delta Junction** USA
99D2	**Dembi Dolo** Eth
46C1	**Demer** *R* Belg
9C3	**Deming** USA
54C2	**Demirköy** Turk
49C1	**Denain** France
82A2	**Denau** Uzbekistan
42C3	**Denbigh** Wales
12B2	**Denbigh,C** USA
43C3	**Denbighshire** County Wales
78B3	**Dendang** Indon
46C1	**Dendermond** Belg
99D2	**Dendi** *Mt* Eth
46B1	**Dèndre** *R* Belg
72B1	**Dengkou** China
72C3	**Deng Xian** China
	Den Haag = 's-Gravenhage
27H1	**Denham,Mt** Jamaica
56A2	**Den Helder** Neth
51C2	**Denia** Spain
107D4	**Deniliquin** Aust
20C2	**Denio** USA
9D3	**Denison** Texas, USA
12D3	**Denison,Mt** USA

92A2	**Denizli** Turk
39F7	**Denmark** Kingdom, Europe
1C1	**Denmark Str** Greenland/Iceland
27P2	**Dennery** St Lucia
78D4	**Denpasar** Indon
16B3	**Denton** Maryland, USA
9D3	**Denton** Texas, USA
107E1	**D'Entrecasteaux Is** PNG
47B1	**Dents du Midi** *Mt* Switz
8C3	**Denver** USA
98B2	**Déo** *R* Cam
86B2	**Deoghar** India
85C5	**Deolāli** India
84D1	**Deosai Plain** India
95B3	**Dépression du Mourdi** Chad
19B3	**De Queen** USA
84C3	**Dera** Pak
84B3	**Dera Bugti** Pak
84C2	**Dera Ismail Khan** Pak
106B2	**Derby** Aust
16C2	**Derby** Connecticut, USA
43D3	**Derby** County, Eng
43D3	**Derby** Eng
18A2	**Derby** Kansas, USA
60E3	**Dergachi** Ukraine
19B3	**De Ridder** USA
	Derna = Darnah
95C3	**Derudeb** Sudan
109C4	**Derwent Bridge** Aust
34B2	**Desaguadero** *R* Arg
34B2	**Desaguadero** *R* Arg
30C2	**Désaguadero** *R* Bol
21B3	**Descanso** Mexico
20B2	**Deschutes** *R* USA
99D1	**Desē** Eth
29C5	**Deseado** Arg
29C5	**Deseado** *R* Arg
47D2	**Desenzano** Italy
96A1	**Deserta Grande** *I* Medeira
30C4	**Desierto de Atacama** *Desert* Chile
18B2	**Desloge** USA
10A2	**Des Moines** Iowa, USA
60D3	**Desna** *R* Russian Fed
29B6	**Desolación** *I* Chile
14A2	**Des Plaines** USA
56C2	**Dessau** Germany
12G2	**Destruction Bay** Can
46A1	**Desvres** France
54B1	**Deta** Rom
100B2	**Dete** Zim
10B2	**Detroit** USA
76D3	**Det Udom** Thai
54B1	**Deva** Rom
56B2	**Deventer** Neth
44C3	**Deveron** *R* Scot
85C3	**Devikot** India
22C2	**Devil Postpile Nat Mon** USA
22C1	**Devils Gate** *P* USA
	Devil's Island = Isla du Diable
8D2	**Devils Lake** USA
12H3	**Devils Paw** *Mt* Can
43D4	**Devizes** Eng
85D3	**Devli** India
55B2	**Devoll** *R* Alb
43B4	**Devon** County, Eng
6A2	**Devon I** Can
107D5	**Devonport** Aust
86C1	**Dewangiri** Bhutan
85D4	**Dewās** India
101G1	**Dewetsdorp** S Africa
11B3	**Dewey Res** USA
19B3	**De Witt** USA
18C2	**Dexter** Missouri, USA
73A3	**Deyang** China
90C3	**Deyhuk** Iran
90A3	**Dezfül** Iran
72D2	**Dezhou** China
90A2	**Dezh Shāhpür** Iran
91B4	**Dhahran** S Arabia
86C2	**Dhākā** Bang
87B2	**Dhamavaram** India

86A2	**Dhamtari** India
86B2	**Dhanbād** India
86A1	**Dhangarhi** Nepal
86B1	**Dhankuta** Nepal
85D4	**Dhār** India
87B2	**Dharmapuri** India
84D2	**Dharmshala** India
97B3	**Dhar Oualata** *Desert Region* Maur
86A1	**Dhaulagiri** *Mt* Nepal
86B2	**Dhenkānāi** India
94B3	**Dhibah** Jordan
55C3	**Dhíkti Óri** *Mt* Greece
55C3	**Dhodhekánisos** *Is* Greece
55B3	**Dhomokós** Greece
87B1	**Dhone** India
85C4	**Dhoraji** India
85C4	**Dhrāngadhra** India
86B1	**Dhuburi** India
85C4	**Dhule** India
22B2	**Diablo,Mt** USA
21A2	**Diablo Range** *Mts* USA
34C2	**Diamante** Arg
34B2	**Diamante** *R* Arg
31C5	**Diamantina** Brazil
107D3	**Diamantina** *R* Aust
86B2	**Diamond Harbours** India
22B1	**Diamond Springs** USA
91C4	**Dibā** UAE
98C3	**Dibaya** Zaïre
86C1	**Dibrugarh** India
8C2	**Dickinson** USA
15C2	**Dickson City** USA
93D2	**Dicle** *R* Turk
13E2	**Didsbury** Can
85C3	**Didwāna** India
97B3	**Diebougou** Burkina
46D2	**Diekirch** Lux
97B3	**Diéma** Mali
76C1	**Dien Bien Phu** Viet
56B2	**Diepholz** Germany
48C2	**Dieppe** France
46C1	**Diest** Belg
46D2	**Dieuze** France
7D5	**Digby** Can
49D3	**Digne-les-Bains** France
49C2	**Digoin** France
79C4	**Digos** Phil
71E4	**Digul** *R* Indon
86C1	**Dihang** *R* India
	Dijlah = Tigris
49C2	**Dijon** France
98B2	**Dik** Chad
99E1	**Dikhil** Djibouti
46B1	**Diksmuide** Belg
18I0	**Dikson** Russian Fed
82A2	**Dilaram** Afghan
106B1	**Dili** Indon
76D3	**Di Linh** Viet
46E1	**Dillenburg** Germ
99C1	**Dilling** Sudan
12C3	**Dillingham** USA
8B2	**Dillon** USA
16A2	**Dillsburg** USA
100B2	**Dilolo** Zaïre
	Dimashq = Damascus
98C3	**Dimbelenge** Zaïre
97B4	**Dimbokro** Côte d'Ivoire
54C2	**Dimitrovgrad** Bulg
61G2	**Dimitrovgrad** Russian Fed
94B3	**Dimona** Israel
86C1	**Dimāpur** India
79C3	**Dinagat** *I* Phil
86B1	**Dinajpur** India
48B2	**Dinan** France
46C1	**Dinant** Belg
92B2	**Dinar** Turk
99D1	**Dinder** *R* Sudan
87B2	**Dindigul** India
72B2	**Dingbian** China
86B1	**Dinggyê** China
41A3	**Dingle** Irish Rep
41A3	**Dingle** *B* Irish Rep
97A3	**Dinguiraye** Guinea
44B3	**Dingwall** Scot
72A2	**Dingxi** China
72D2	**Ding Xian** China

El Milagro

El Mīna

94B1 El Mīna Leb	20C2 Emmett USA	92A1 Ergene R Turk	48C2 Etampes France
92B4 El Minya Egypt	16A3 Emmitsburg USA	96B2 Erg Iguidi Region Alg	108A1 Etamunbanie,L Aust
22B1 Elmira California, USA	12B2 Emmonak USA	58D1 Ergli Latvia	46A1 Etaples France
10C2 Elmira New York, USA	9C4 Emory Peak Mt USA	98B1 Erguig R Chad	85D3 Etâwah India
96B2 El Mreitl Well Maur	24A2 Empalme Mexico	68D1 Ergun' R China/Russian Fed	99D2 Ethiopia Republic, Africa
56B2 Elmshorn Germany	101H1 Empangeni S Africa	63E2 Ergun Zuoqi China	23B2 Etla Mexico
98C1 El Muglad Sudan	30E4 Empedrado Arg	95C3 Eriba Sudan	53B3 Etna Mt Italy
96B2 El Mzereb Well Mali	105G1 Emperor Seamount Chain Pacific O	10C2 Erie USA	12H3 Etolin I USA
79A3 El Nido Phil	18A2 Emporia Kansas, USA	10B2 Erie,L Can/USA	12A2 Etolin Str USA
99D1 El Obeid Sudan	56B2 Ems R Germany	42B2 Erin Port Eng	6C2 Eton Can
23A2 El Oro Mexico	44B2 Enard B Scot	44A3 Eriskay I Scot	100A2 Etosha Nat Pk Namibia
96C1 El Oued Alg	23A1 Encarnacion Mexico	99D1 Eritrea Republic,Africa	100A2 Etosha Pan Salt L Namibia
9C3 El Paso USA	30E4 Encarnación Par	46D1 Erkelenz Germany	17B1 Etowah R USA
21A2 El Porta USA	97B4 Enchi Ghana	57C3 Erlangen Germany	46D2 Ettelbruck Lux
22C2 El Portal USA	22D4 Encinitas USA	19B3 Erling,L USA	109C2 Euabalong Aust
50A2 El Puerto del Sta Maria Spain	35C1 Encruzilhada Brazil	101G1 Ermelo S Africa	14B2 Euclid USA
El Qâhira = Cairo	106B1 Endeh Indon	87B3 Ernâkulam India	109C3 Eucumbene,L Aust
El Quds = Jerusalem	13D2 Enderby Can	87B2 Erode India	108A2 Eudunda Aust
94B3 El Quseima Egypt	112C11 Enderby Land Region, Ant	108B1 Eromanga Aust	19A2 Eufala L USA
9D3 El Reno USA	15C2 Endicott USA	96B1 Er Rachidia Mor	17A1 Eufaula USA
4E3 Elsa Can	12D1 Endicott Mts USA	99D1 Er Rahad Sudan	8A2 Eugene USA
25D3 El Salvador Republic, Cent America	47D1 Engadin Mts Switz	101C2 Errego Mozam	108C1 Eulo Aust
22D4 Elsinore L USA	79B2 Engaño,C Phil	40B2 Errigal Mt Irish Rep	19B3 Eunice Louisiana, USA
34B3 El Sosneade Arg	94B3 En Gedi Israel	41A3 Erris Head Pt Irish Rep	46D1 Eupen Germany
57C2 Elsterwerde Germany	47C1 Engelberg Switz	99D1 Er Roseires Sudan	93D3 Euphrates R Iraq
El Suweis = Suez	78A4 Enggano I Indon	94B2 Er Rummân Jordan	19C3 Eupora USA
50A1 El Teleno Mt Spain	41C3 England Country, UK	57C2 Erzgebirge Upland Germany	48C2 Eure R France
110B1 Eltham NZ	7E4 Englee Can	93C2 Erzincan Turk	20B2 Eureka California, USA
33E2 El Tigre Ven	41C3 English Channel Eng/France	65F6 Erzurum Turk	6B1 Eureka Can
92B4 El Tih Desert Region Egypt	97B3 Enji Well Maur	48C3 Esara R Spain	8B3 Eureka Nevada, USA
34C2 El Tio Arg	39H7 Enkoping Sweden	56B1 Esbjerg Den	6B2 Eureka Sd Can
20C1 Eltopia USA	53B3 Enna Italy	9C4 Escalón Mexico	108C3 Euroa Aust
92B4 El Tûr Egypt	99C1 En Nahud Sudan	10B2 Escanaba USA	109C1 Eurombah R Aust
87C1 Elūru India	95B3 Ennedi Region Chad	25C3 Escárcega Mexico	101D3 Europa I Mozam Chan
50A2 Elvas Port	109C1 Enngonia Aust	46C2 Esch Lux	57B2 Euskirchen Germany
32C5 Elvira Brazil	41B3 Ennis Irish Rep	21B3 Escondido USA	13B2 Eutsuk L Can
34A2 El Volcán Chile	19A3 Ennis Texas, USA	24B2 Escuinapa Mexico	13D2 Evansburg Can
14A2 Elwood USA	45C2 Enniscorthy Irish Rep	25C3 Escuintla Guatemala	6B1 Evans,C Can
43E3 Ely Eng	45C1 Enniskillen N Ire	98B2 Eséka Cam	7C4 Evans,L Can
10A2 Ely Minnesota, USA	45B2 Ennistimon Irish Rep	51C1 Esera R Spain	6B3 Evans Str Can
8B3 Ely Nevada, USA	94B2 Enn Nâqoûra Leb	90B3 Eşfahân Iran	14A2 Evanston Illinois, USA
14B2 Elyria USA	57C3 Enns R Austria	101H1 Eshowe S Africa	8B2 Evanston Wyoming, USA
90B2 Emāmrūd Iran	39F8 Enschede Neth	110C1 Eskdale NZ	11B3 Evansville Indiana, USA
84B1 Emām Sāheb Afghan	24A1 Ensenada Mexico	38C1 Eskifjörður Iceland	101G1 Evaton S Africa
58B1 Eman R Sweden	73B3 Enshi China	39H7 Eskilstuna Sweden	106C4 Everard,L Aust
61J4 Emba Kazakhstan	99D2 Entebbe Uganda	4E3 Eskimo L Can	82C3 Everest,Mt China/Nepal
61J4 Emba R Kazakhstan	17A1 Enterprise Alabama, USA	7A3 Eskimo Point Can	8A2 Everett Washington, USA
29C3 Embalse Cerros Colorados L Arg	20C1 Enterprise Oregon, USA	92B2 Eskisehir Turk	16C1 Everett,Mt USA
51B2 Embalse de Alarcón Res Spain	97C4 Enugu Nig	50A1 Esla R Spain	11B4 Everglades,The Swamp USA
50A2 Embalse de Alcántarà Res Spain	75B1 Enzan Japan	29A5 Esmeralda I Chile	43D3 Evesham Eng
50A1 Embalse de Almendra Res Spain	49C2 Epernay France	32B3 Esmeraldas Ecuador	98B2 Evinayong Eq Guinea
50A2 Embalse de Garcia de Sola Res Spain	16A2 Ephrata Pennsylvania, USA	26B2 Esmerelda Cuba	39F7 Evje Nor
33E2 Embalse de Guri L Ven	20C1 Ephrata Washington, USA	49C3 Espalion France	47B1 Evolène Switz
51B1 Embalse de Mequinenza Res Spain	49D2 Épinal France	14B1 Espanola Can	50A2 Évora Port
50A1 Embalse de Ricobayo Res Spain	46A2 Epte R France	32J7 Española I Ecuador	48C2 Evreux France
29E2 Embalse de Rio Negro Res Urug	100A3 Epukiro Namibia	106B4 Esperance Aust	55B3 Évvoia I Greece
29C3 Embalse El Chocón L Arg	34C3 Epu pel Arg	34C2 Esperanza Arg	98B3 Ewo Congo
29C4 Embalse Florentine Ameghino L Arg	90B3 Eqlid Iran	112C2 Esperanza Base Ant	22C1 Excelsior Mt USA
50A1 Embalse Gabriel y Galan Res Spain	89D7 Equator	35C1 Espírito Santo State, Brazil	18B2 Excelsior Springs USA
30D3 Embarcación Arg	98A2 Equatorial Guinea Republic, Africa	101C3 Espungabera Mozam	21B2 Exeter California, USA
5G4 Embarras Portage Can	47C2 Erba Italy	29B4 Esquel Arg	43C4 Exeter Eng
47B2 Embrun France	46D2 Erbeskopf Mt Germany	20B1 Esquimalt Can	15D2 Exeter New Hampshire, USA
99D3 Embu Kenya	34A3 Ercilla Chile	34D2 Esquina Arg	43C4 Exmoor Nat Pk Eng
56B2 Emden Germany	93D2 Erciş Turk	94C2 Es Samra Jordan	43C4 Exmouth Eng
73A4 Emei China	92C2 Erciyas Daglari Mt Turk	96B1 Essaouira Mor	50A2 Extremadura Region, Spain
107D3 Emerald Aust	74B2 Erdaobaihe China	96A2 Es Semara Mor	25E2 Exuma Sd The Bahamas
7D4 Emeri Can	72C1 Erdene Mongolia	56B2 Essen Germany	99D3 Eyasi L Tanz
5J5 Emerson Can	68C2 Erdenet Mongolia	33F3 Essequibo R Guyana	42C2 Eyemouth Scot
21B1 Emigrant P USA	95B3 Erdi Region Chad	43E4 Essex County, Eng	99E2 Eyl Somalia
95A3 Emi Koussi Mt Chad	30F4 Erechim Brazil	14B2 Essexville USA	106B4 Eyre Aust
34B3 Emilo Mitre Arg	92B1 Ereğli Turk	57B3 Esslingen Germany	106C3 Eyre Creek R Aust
92B2 Emirdağ Turk	92B2 Ereğli Turk	46B2 Essonne France	106C3 Eyre,L Aust
16B2 Emmaus USA	68D2 Erenhot China	31D4 Estância Brazil	106C4 Eyre Pen Aust
56B2 Emmen Neth	50B1 Eresma R Spain	101G1 Estcourt S Africa	79B3 Eyte I Phil
	46D1 Erft R Germany	47D2 Este Italy	23A1 Ezatlan Mexico
	57C2 Erfurt Germany	46B2 Esternay France	55C3 Ezine Turk
	93C2 Ergani Turk	30D3 Esteros Par	
	96B2 Erg Chech Desert Region Alg	5H5 Estevan Can	
	95A3 Erg du Djourab Desert Chad	17B1 Estill USA	
	97D3 Erg Du Ténéré Desert Region Niger	60B2 Estonia Republic, Europe	
		29B6 Estrecho de Magallanes Str Chile	
		50A2 Estremoz Port	
		59B3 Esztergom Hung	
		108A1 Etadunna Aust	
		46C2 Etam France	

F

4G3 **Faber L** Can
39G7 **Fåborg** Den
52B2 **Fabriano** Italy
95A3 **Fachi** Niger
95B3 **Fada** Chad
97C3 **Fada N'Gourma** Burkina
52B2 **Faenza** Italy
6E3 **Faeringehavn** Greenland
98B2 **Fafa** R CAR
99E2 **Fafan** R Eth
54B1 **Fägäras** Rom
46C1 **Fagnes** Region, Belg
97B3 **Faguibine,L** L Mali
91C5 **Fahud** Oman
96A1 **Faiol** I Açores
4D3 **Fairbanks** USA
14B3 **Fairborn** USA
8D2 **Fairbury** USA
16A3 **Fairfax** USA
21A2 **Fairfield** California, USA
16C2 **Fairfield** Connecticut, USA
14B3 **Fairfield** Ohio, USA
45C1 **Fair Head** Pt N Ire
40C2 **Fair Isle** I Scot
111B2 **Fairlie** NZ
14B3 **Fairmont** W Virginia, USA
13D1 **Fairview** Can
4E4 **Fairweather,Mt** USA
71F3 **Fais** I Pacific O
84C2 **Faisalabad** Pak
8C2 **Faith** USA
44E1 **Faither,The** Pen Scot
86A1 **Faizäbäd** India
43E3 **Fakenham** Eng
39G7 **Faköping** Sweden
86C2 **Falam** Myan
24C2 **Falcon Res** Mexico/ USA
97A3 **Falémé** R Mali/Sen
39G7 **Falkenberg** Sweden
42C2 **Falkirk** Scot
44C3 **Falkirk** Division, Scot
29D6 **Falkland Is** Dependency, S Atlantic
29E6 **Falkland Sd** Falkland Is
22D4 **Fallbrook** USA
8B3 **Fallon** USA
15D2 **Fall River** USA
18A1 **Falls City** USA
43B4 **Falmouth** Eng
27H1 **Falmouth** Jamaica
16D2 **Falmouth** Massachusetts, USA
100A4 **False B** S Africa
24A2 **Falso,C** Mexico
56C2 **Falster** I Den
54C1 **Fälticeni** Rom
39H6 **Falun** Sweden
92B2 **Famagusta** Cyprus
46C1 **Famenne** Region, Belg
76B2 **Fang** Thai
99D2 **Fangak** Sudan
73E5 **Fang liao** Taiwan
52B2 **Fano** Italy
112C3 **Faraday** Base Ant
99C2 **Faradje** Zaïre
101D3 **Farafangana** Madag
95B2 **Farafra Oasis** Egypt
80E2 **Farah** Afghan
71F2 **Farallon de Medinilla** I Pacific O
97A3 **Faranah** Guinea
71F3 **Faraulep** I Pacific O
43D4 **Fareham** Eng
Farewell,C = Kap Farvel
107G5 **Farewell,C** NZ
110B2 **Farewell Spit** Pt NZ
8D2 **Fargo** USA
94B2 **Fari'a** R Israel
10A2 **Faribault** USA
86B2 **Faridpur** Bang
90C2 **Farimän** Iran

18B2 **Farmington** Missouri, USA
9C3 **Farmington** New Mexico, USA
22B2 **Farmington Res** USA
42D2 **Farne Deep** N Sea
13D2 **Farnham,Mt** Can
12H2 **Faro** Can
50A2 **Faro** Port
39H7 **Fåro** I Sweden
89K9 **Farquhar** Is Indian O
44B3 **Farrar** R Scot
14B2 **Farrell** USA
55B3 **Fársala** Greece
91B4 **Fasä** Iran
45B3 **Fastnet Rock** Irish Rep
60C3 **Fastov** Ukraine
86A1 **Fatehpur** India
13D1 **Father** Can
30F2 **Fatima du Sul** Brazil
101G1 **Fauresmith** S Africa
47B2 **Faverges** France
7B4 **Fawn** R Can
38H6 **Fax** R Sweden
38A2 **Faxaflói** B Iceland
95A3 **Faya** Chad
11A3 **Fayetteville** Arkansas, USA
11C3 **Fayetteville** N Carolina, USA
93E4 **Faylakah** I Kuwait
84C2 **Fäzilka** India
96A2 **Fdérik** Maur
11C3 **Fear,C** USA
21A2 **Feather Middle Fork** R USA
48C2 **Fécamp** France
34D2 **Federación** Arg
34D2 **Federal** Arg
71F3 **Federated States of Micronesia** Is Pacific O
56C2 **Fehmarn** I Germany
32C5 **Feijó** Brazil
73C5 **Feilai Xai Bei Jiang** R China
110C2 **Feilding** NZ
100C2 **Feira** Zambia
31D4 **Feira de Santan** Brazil
92C2 **Feke** Turk
57B3 **Feldkirch** Austria
34D2 **Feliciano** R Arg
41D3 **Felixstowe** Eng
47D1 **Feltre** Italy
38G6 **Femund** L Nor
74A2 **Fengcheng** China
73B4 **Fengdu** China
72D1 **Fenging** China
73B3 **Fengjie** China
72B3 **Feng Xian** China
72C1 **Fengzhen** China
72C2 **Fen He** R China
101D2 **Fenoarivo Atsinanana** Madag
60E5 **Feodosiya** Ukraine
90C3 **Ferdow** Iran
46B2 **Fère-Champenoise** France
82B2 **Fergana** Uzbekistan
45C1 **Fermanagh** County, N Ire
45B2 **Fermoy** Irish Rep
47D1 **Fern** Mt Austria
32J7 **Fernandina** I Ecuador
17B1 **Fernandina Beach** USA
103G5 **Fernando de Noronha** I Atlantic O
35A2 **Fernandópolis** Brazil
20B1 **Ferndale** USA
21B2 **Fernley** USA
52B2 **Ferrara** Italy
32B5 **Ferreñafe** Peru
19B3 **Ferriday** USA
96B1 **Fès** Mor
18B2 **Festus** USA
54C2 **Fetești** Rom
92A2 **Fethiye** Turk
61H5 **Fetisovo** Kazakhstan
44E1 **Fetlar** I Scot
84C1 **Feyzabad** Afghan

101D3 **Fianarantsoa** Madag
99D2 **Fichè** Eth
101G1 **Ficksburg** S Africa
47D2 **Fidenza** Italy
55A2 **Fier** Alb
47D1 **Fiera Di Primeiro** Italy
44C3 **Fife** Region, Scot
44C3 **Fife Ness** Pen Scot
48C3 **Figeac** France
50A1 **Figueira da Foz** Port
51C1 **Figueras** Spain
Figueres = Figueras
96B1 **Figuig** Mor
105G4 **Fiji** Is Pacific O
30D3 **Filadelfia** Par
54B2 **Filiaşi** Rom
55B3 **Filiatrá** Greece
53B3 **Filicudi** I Italy
21B3 **Fillmore** California, USA
44B3 **Findhorn** R Scot
10B2 **Findlay** USA
13D2 **Findlay,Mt** Can
15C2 **Finger Lakes** USA
101C2 **Fingoè** Mozam
92B2 **Finike** Turk
106C3 **Finke** R Aust
108A1 **Finke Flood Flats** Aust
64D3 **Finland** Republic, N Europe
39J7 **Finland,G of** N Europe
5F4 **Finlay** R Can
5F4 **Finlay Forks** Can
108C3 **Finley** Aust
38H5 **Finnsnes** Nor
71F4 **Finschhafen** PNG
47C1 **Finsteraarhorn** Mt Switz
56C2 **Finsterwalde** Germany
45C1 **Fintona** N Ire
111A3 **Fiordland Nat Pk** NZ
94B2 **Fiq** Syria
93C2 **Firat** R Turk
22B2 **Firebaugh** USA
52B2 **Firenze** Italy
34C2 **Firmat** Arg
85D3 **Firozäbäd** India
84C2 **Firozpur** India
39H7 **Firspång** Sweden
42B2 **Firth of Clyde** Estuary Scot
44C3 **Firth of Forth** Estuary Scot
44A3 **Firth of Lorn** Estuary Scot
40C2 **Firth of Tay** Estuary Scot
91B4 **Firüzäbäd** Iran
100A3 **Fish** R Namibia
22C2 **Fish Camp** USA
16C2 **Fishers I** USA
6B3 **Fisher Str** Can
43B4 **Fishguard** Wales
6E3 **Fiskenaesset** Greenland
46B2 **Fismes** France
15D2 **Fitchburg** USA
44E2 **Fitful Head** Pt Scot
17B1 **Fitzgerald** USA
106B2 **Fitzroy** R Aust
106B2 **Fitzroy Crossing** Aust
14B1 **Fitzwilliam I** Can
Fiume = Rijeka
99C3 **Fizi** Zaïre
9B3 **Flagstaff** USA
42D2 **Flamborough Head** C Eng
8C2 **Flaming Gorge Res** USA
44A2 **Flannan Isles** Is Scot
12J2 **Flat** R Can
13E3 **Flathead** R USA
8B2 **Flathead L** USA
18B2 **Flat River** USA
8A2 **Flattery,C** USA
42C3 **Fleetwood** Eng
39F7 **Flekkefjord** Nor
69G4 **Fleming Deep** Pacific O
16B2 **Flemington** USA
56B2 **Flensburg** Germany

47B1 **Fleurier** Switz
106C4 **Flinders** I Aust
107D4 **Flinders** I Aust
107D2 **Flinders** R Aust
106C4 **Flinders Range** Mts Aust
5H4 **Flin Flon** Can
10B2 **Flint** USA
42C3 **Flint** Wales
11B3 **Flint** R USA
42C3 **Flintshire** County Wales
46B1 **Flixecourt** France
17A1 **Florala** USA
Florence = Firenze
11B3 **Florence** Alabama, USA
18A2 **Florence** Kansas, USA
20B2 **Florence** Oregon, USA
11C3 **Florence** S Carolina, USA
32B3 **Florencia** Colombia
46C2 **Florenville** Belg
25D3 **Flores** Guatemala
96A1 **Flores** I Açores
106B1 **Flores** I Indon
34D3 **Flores** R Arg
70C4 **Flores S** Indon
31C3 **Floriano** Brazil
30G4 **Florianópolis** Brazil
25D2 **Florida** State, USA
29E2 **Florida** Urug
17B2 **Florida B** USA
17B2 **Florida City** USA
107E1 **Florida Is** Solomon Is
11B4 **Florida Keys** Is USA
11B4 **Florida,Strs of** USA
55B2 **Flórina** Greece
38F6 **Florø** Nor
47D1 **Fluchthorn** Mt Austria
54C1 **Focsani** Rom
53C2 **Foggia** Italy
97A4 **Fogo** I Cape Verde
48C3 **Foix** France
6C3 **Foley I** Can
52B2 **Foligno** Italy
43E4 **Folkestone** Eng
17B1 **Folkston** USA
52B2 **Follonica** Italy
22B1 **Folsom** USA
22B1 **Folsom L** L USA
5H4 **Fond-du-Lac** Can
10B2 **Fond du Lac** USA
48C2 **Fontainebleau** France
18B2 **Fontenac** USA
48B2 **Fontenay-le-Comte** France
52C1 **Fonyód** Hung
Foochow = Fuzhou
12D2 **Foraker,Mt** USA
46D2 **Forbach** France
109C2 **Forbes** Aust
97C4 **Forcados** Nig
38F6 **Forde** Nor
108C1 **Fords Bridge** Aust
19B3 **Fordyce** USA
97A4 **Forécariah** Guinea
6G3 **Forel,Mt** Greenland
14B2 **Forest** Can
17B1 **Forest Park** USA
22A1 **Forestville** USA
44C3 **Forfar** Scot
46A2 **Forges-les-Eaux** France
20B1 **Forks** USA
52B2 **Forlì** Italy
51C2 **Formentera** I Spain
53B2 **Formia** Italy
96A1 **Formigas** I Açores
Formosa = Taiwan
30E4 **Formosa** Arg
31B5 **Formosa** Brazil
30D3 **Formosa** State, Arg
73D5 **Formosa Str** Taiwan/ China
47D2 **Forotto di Taro** Italy
38D3 **Føroyar** Is N Atlantic O
44C3 **Forres** Scot
106B4 **Forrest** Aust

86C2 **Gangaw** Myan
72A2 **Gangca** China
82C2 **Gangdise Shan** *Mts* China
Ganges = Ganga
86B1 **Gangtok** India
72B3 **Gangu** China
8C2 **Gannett Peak** *Mt* USA
72B2 **Ganquan** China
108A3 **Gantheaume** *C* Aust
39K8 **Gantsevichi** Belarus
73D4 **Ganzhou** China
97C3 **Gao** Mali
72A2 **Gaolan** China
72C2 **Gaoping** China
97B3 **Gaoua** Burkina
97A3 **Gaoual** Guinea
72D3 **Gaoyou Hu** *L* China
73C5 **Gaozhou** China
49D3 **Gap** France
79B2 **Gapan** Phil
84D2 **Gar** China
109C1 **Garah** Aust
31D3 **Garanhuns** Brazil
21A1 **Garberville** USA
35B2 **Garça** Brazil
35A2 **Garcias** Brazil
47D2 **Garda** Italy
9C3 **Garden City** USA
14A1 **Garden Pen** USA
34D3 **Gardey** Arg
84B2 **Gardez** Afghan
16C2 **Gardiners I** USA
16D1 **Gardner** USA
47D2 **Gardone** Italy
47D2 **Gargano** Italy
85D4 **Garhākota** India
61K2 **Gari** Russian Fed
100A4 **Garies** S Africa
99D3 **Garissa** Kenya
19A3 **Garland** USA
57C3 **Garmisch-Partenkirchen** Germany
90B2 **Garmsar** Iran
18A2 **Garnett** USA
8B2 **Garnett Peak** *Mt* USA
48C3 **Garonne** *R* France
44B3 **Garry** *R* Scot
78B4 **Garut** Indon
86A2 **Garwa** India
14A2 **Gary** USA
82C2 **Garyarsa** China
4H3 **Gary L** Can
19A3 **Garza-Little Elm** *Res* USA
90B2 **Gasan Kuli** Turkmenistan
48B3 **Gascogne** Region, France
18B2 **Gasconade** *R* USA
106A3 **Gascoyne** *R* Aust
98B2 **Gashaka** Nig
97D3 **Gashua** Nig
10D2 **Gaspé** Can
10D2 **Gaspé,C. de** Can
94A1 **Gata,C** Cyprus
60C2 **Gatchina** Russian Fed
42D2 **Gateshead** Eng
19A3 **Gatesville** USA
15C1 **Gatineau** Can
15C1 **Gatineau** *R* Can
109D1 **Gatton** Aust
86C1 **Gauháti** India
58C1 **Gauja** *R* Latvia
86A1 **Gauri Phanta** India
100B3 **Gauteng** Province, S Africa
22B3 **Gaviota** USA
39H6 **Gävle** Sweden
108A2 **Gawler Ranges** *Mts* Aust
72A1 **Gaxun Nur** *L* China
86A2 **Gaya** India
97C3 **Gaya** Niger
14B1 **Gaylord** USA
109D1 **Gayndah** Aust
61H1 **Gayny** Russian Fed
60C4 **Gaysin** Ukraine
94B3 **Gaza** Israel

94B3 **Gaza** Autonomous Region S W Asia
92C2 **Gaziantep** Turk
97B4 **Gbaringa** Lib
58B2 **Gdańsk** Pol
58B2 **Gdańsk,G of** Pol
39K7 **Gdov** Russian Fed
58B2 **Gdynia** Pol
94A3 **Gebel Halāl** *Mt* Egypt
92B4 **Gebel Katherina** *Mt* Egypt
94A3 **Gebel Libni** *Mt* Egypt
94A3 **Gebel Maghâra** *Mt* Egypt
99D1 **Gedaref** Sudan
55C3 **Gediz** *R* Turk
56C2 **Gedser** Den
46C1 **Geel** Belg
108B3 **Geelong** Aust
109C4 **Geeveston** Aust
97D3 **Geidam** Nig
46D1 **Geilenkirchen** Germany
99D3 **Geita** Tanz
73A5 **Gejiu** China
53B3 **Gela** Italy
99E2 **Geladi** Eth
46D1 **Geldern** Germany
55C2 **Gelibolu** Turk
92B2 **Gelidonya Burun** Turk
46D1 **Gelsenkirchen** Germany
39F8 **Gelting** Germany
77C5 **Gemas** Malay
46C1 **Gembloux** Belg
98B2 **Gemena** Zaire
92C2 **Gemerek** Turk
92A1 **Gemlik** Turk
52B1 **Gemona** Italy
100B3 **Gemsbok** *Nat Pk* Botswana
98C1 **Geneina** Sudan
34C3 **General Acha** Arg
34C3 **General Alvear** Buenos Aires, Arg
34B2 **General Alvear** Mendoza, Arg
34C2 **General Arenales** Arg
34D3 **General Belgrano** Arg
112B2 **General Belgrano** *Base* Ant
112C2 **General Bernardo O'Higgins** *Base* Ant
34D3 **General Conesa** Buenos Aires, Arg
30D3 **General Eugenio A Garay** Par
34D3 **General Guido** Arg
34C3 **General La Madrid** Arg
34C2 **General Levalle** Arg
30C4 **General Manuel Belgrano** *Mt* Arg
34D3 **General Paz** Buenos Aires, Arg
34C3 **General Pico** Arg
34D3 **General Pirán** Arg
29C3 **General Roca** Arg
112C3 **General San Martin** *Base* Ant
79C4 **General Santos** Phil
34C3 **General Viamonte** Arg
34C3 **General Villegas** Arg
15C2 **Genesee** *R* USA
15C2 **Geneseo** USA
Geneva = Genève
18A1 **Geneva** Nebraska, USA
15C2 **Geneva** New York, USA
Geneva,L of = LacLéman
52A1 **Genève** Switz
50B2 **Genil** *R* Spain
Genoa = Genova
109C3 **Genoa** Aust
52A2 **Genova** Italy

32J7 **Genovesa** *I* Ecuador
46B1 **Gent** Belg
78B4 **Genteng** Indon
56C2 **Genthin** Germany
93E1 **Geokchay** Azerbaijan
100B4 **George** S Africa
7D4 **George** *R* Can
109C2 **George,L** Aust
17B2 **George,L** Florida, USA
15D2 **George,L** New York, USA
111A2 **George Sd** NZ
109C4 **George Town** Aust
15C3 **Georgetown** Delaware, USA
33F2 **Georgetown** Guyana
14B3 **Georgetown** Kentucky, USA
77C4 **George Town** Malay
27N2 **Georgetown** St Vincent and the Grenadines
17C1 **Georgetown** S Carolina, USA
19A3 **Georgetown** Texas, USA
97A3 **Georgetown** The Gambia
112C8 **George V Land** Region, Ant
65F5 **Georgia** Republic, Europe
112C12 **Georg Forster** *Base* Ant
17B1 **Georgia** State, USA
14B1 **Georgian B** Can
13C3 **Georgia,Str of** Can
106C3 **Georgina** *R* Aust
61F5 **Georgiyevsk** Russian Fed
57C2 **Gera** Germany
46B1 **Geraardsbergen** Belg
111B2 **Geraldine** NZ
106A3 **Geraldton** Aust
10B2 **Geraldton** Can
94B3 **Gerar** *R* Israel
4C3 **Gerdine,Mt** USA
12E2 **Gerdova Peak** *Mt* USA
77C4 **Gerik** Malay
60B4 **Gerlachovský Štit** *Mt* Pol
13C1 **Germanson Lodge** Can
56C2 **Germany** Republic, Europe
101G1 **Germiston** S Africa
46D1 **Gerolstein** Germany
51C1 **Gerona** Spain
46E1 **Geseke** Germany
99E2 **Gestro** *R* Eth
50B1 **Getafe** Spain
16A3 **Gettysburg** Pennsylvania, USA
93D2 **Gevaş** Turk
55B2 **Gevgelija** Macedonia
47B1 **Gex** France
94C2 **Ghabāghib** Syria
96C1 **Ghadamis** Libya
90B2 **Ghaem Shahr** Iran
86A1 **Ghāghara** *R* India
97B4 **Ghana** Republic, Africa
100B3 **Ghanzi** Botswana
96C1 **Ghardaïa** Alg
95A1 **Gharyan** Libya
95A2 **Ghāt** Libya
84D3 **Ghāziābād** India
84C3 **Ghazi Khan** Pak
84B2 **Ghazni** Afghan
54C1 **Gheorgheni** Rom
88E4 **Ghudamis** Alg
90D3 **Ghurian** Afghan
95B2 **Gialo** Libya
99E2 **Giamame** Somalia
53C3 **Giarre** Italy
100A3 **Gibeon** Namibia
50A2 **Gibraltar** Colony, SW Europe
50A2 **Gibraltar,Str of** Spain/Africa
106B3 **Gibson Desert** Aust
20B1 **Gibsons** Can

87B1 **Giddalūr** India
99D2 **Gidolē** Eth
57B2 **Giessen** Germany
17B2 **Gifford** USA
74D3 **Gifu** Japan
42B2 **Gigha** *I* Scot
52B2 **Giglio** *I* Italy
50A1 **Gijón** Spain
107D2 **Gilbert** *R* Aust
13C2 **Gilbert,Mt** Can
101C2 **Gilé** Mozam
94B2 **Gilead** Region, Jordan
95B2 **Gilf Kebir Plat** Egypt
109C2 **Gilgandra** Aust
84C1 **Gilgit** Pak
84C1 **Gilgit** *R* Pak
108C2 **Gilgunnia** Aust
7A4 **Gillam** Can
108A2 **Gilles** *L* Aust
13B2 **Gill I** Can
14A1 **Gills Rock** USA
14A2 **Gilman** USA
22B2 **Gilroy** USA
8D1 **Gimli** Can
101H1 **Gingindlovu** S Africa
79C4 **Gingoog** Phil
99E2 **Ginir** Eth
55B3 **Gióna** *Mt* Greece
109C3 **Gippsland** *Mts* Aust
14B2 **Girard** USA
32C3 **Girardot** Colombia
44C3 **Girdle Ness** *Pen* Scot
93C1 **Giresun** Turk
85C4 **Gir Hills** India
98B2 **Giri** *R* Zaire
86B2 **Girīdīh** India
Girona = Gerona
48B2 **Gironde** *R* France
42B2 **Girvan** Scot
111C2 **Gisborne** NZ
46A2 **Gisors** France
99C3 **Gitega** Burundi
Giuba,R = Juba,R
54C2 **Giurgiu** Rom
46C1 **Givet** Belg
58C2 **Gizycko** Pol
55B2 **Gjirokastër** Alb
4J3 **Gjoatlaven** Can
39G6 **Gjovik** Nor
7D5 **Glace Bay** Can
12G3 **Glacier Bay Nat Mon** USA
13E3 **Glacier Nat Pk** USA/Can
20B1 **Glacier Peak** *Mt* USA
6B2 **Glacier Str** Can
107E3 **Gladstone** Queensland, Aust
108A2 **Gladstone** S Aust, Aust
109C4 **Gladstone** Tasmania, Aust
14A1 **Gladstone** USA
38A1 **Glama** *Mt* Iceland
39G6 **Glåma** *R* Nor
46D2 **Glan** *R* Germany
47C1 **Glarner** *Mts* Switz
47C1 **Glarus** Switz
18A2 **Glasco** USA
8C2 **Glasgow** Montana, USA
42B2 **Glasgow** Scot
42B2 **Glasgow, City of** Division, Scot
16B3 **Glassboro** USA
43C4 **Glastonbury** Eng
61H2 **Glazov** Russian Fed
59B3 **Gleisdorf** Austria
110C1 **Glen Afton** NZ
16A3 **Glen Burnie** USA
101H1 **Glencoe** S Africa
9B3 **Glendale** Arizona, USA
22C3 **Glendale** California, USA
12E2 **Glenhallen** USA
109D1 **Glen Innes** Aust
109C1 **Glenmorgan** Aust
109D2 **Glenreagh** Aust
16A3 **Glen Rock** USA
19A3 **Glen Rose** USA

Glenrothes

44C3	Glenrothes UK
15D2	Glens Falls USA
45B1	Glenties Irish Rep
19B3	Glenwood Arkansas, USA
8C3	Glenwood Springs USA
39F6	Glittertind Mt Nor
59B2	Gliwice Pol
9B3	Globe USA
58B2	Głogów Pol
38G5	Glomfjord Nor
109D2	Gloucester Aust
43C4	Gloucester Eng
16D1	Gloucester USA
58D1	Glubokoye Belarus
60D3	Glukhov Russian Fed
59B3	Gmünd Austria
57C3	Gmunden Austria
58B2	Gniezno Pol
100A3	Goabeg Namibia
87A1	Goa, Daman and Diu Union Territory, India
86C1	Goälpära India
99D2	Goba Eth
100A3	Gobabis Namibia
34C2	Gobernador Crespo Arg
34B3	Gobernador Duval Arg
72B1	Gobi Desert China/ Mongolia
75B2	Gobo Japan
87B1	Godag India
87C1	Godävari R India
14B2	Goderich Can
6E3	Godhavn Greenland
85C4	Godhra India
34B2	Godoy Cruz Arg
7A4	Gods L Can
6E3	Godthab Greenland
	Godwin Austen = K2
35B1	Goiandira Brazil
35B1	Goianésia Brazil
35B1	Goiânia Brazil
35A1	Goiás Brazil
31B4	Goiás State, Brazil
35A2	Goio-Erê Brazil
99D2	Gojab R Eth
55C2	Gökçeada I Turk
55C3	Gökova Körfezi B Turk
92C2	Göksun Turk
63C3	Gol R Mongolia
86C1	Goläghät India
93C2	Gölbaşi Turk
20C2	Golconda USA
20B2	Gold Beach USA
109D1	Gold Coast Aust
13D2	Golden Can
110B2	Golden B NZ
20B1	Goldendale USA
22A2	Golden Gate Chan USA
19B4	Golden Meadow USA
21B2	Goldfield USA
13B3	Gold River Can
56C2	Goleniów Pol
22C3	Goleta USA
52A2	Golfe d'Ajaccio G Corse
96D1	Golfe de Gabes G Tunisia
	Golfe de Gascogne = Biscay,Bay of
52A2	Golfe de St Florent G Corse
48B2	Golfe de St-Malo B France
49C3	Golfe du Lion G France
29B4	Golfo Corcovado G Chile
50B2	Golfo de Almeira G Spain
29B4	Golfo de Ancud G Chile
25D2	Golfo de Batabano G Cuba
50A2	Golfo de Cadiz G Spain
53A3	Golfo de Cagliari G Sardegna

24A1	Golfo de California G Mexico
25D4	Golfo de Chiriqui G Panama
25D3	Golfo de Fonseca Honduras
26B2	Golfo de Guacanayabo G Cuba
32A4	Golfo de Guayaquil G Ecuador
26B5	Golfo del Darien G Colombia/Panama
32A2	Golfo de los Mosquitos G Panama
25D3	Golfo del Papagaya G Nic
51B2	Golfo de Mazarrón G Spain
25D4	Golfo de Nicoya G Costa Rica
53A3	Golfo de Oristano G Sardegna
25E4	Golfo de Panamá G Panama
25D3	Golfo de Papagayo G Costa Rica
27E4	Golfo de Paria G Ven
29B5	Golfo de Penas G Chile
49D3	Golfo de St Florent Corse
51C1	Golfo de San Jorge G Spain
24C3	Golfo de Tehuantepec G Mexico
32B3	Golfo de Torugas G Colombia
32B2	Golfo de Uraba G Colombia
51C2	Golfo de Valencia G Spain
27C4	Golfo de Venezuela G Ven
52A2	Golfo di Genova G Italy
53C3	Golfo di Policastro G Italy
53C3	Golfo di Squillace G Italy
53C2	Golfo di Taranto G Italy
52B1	Golfo di Venezia G Italy
25D4	Golfo Dulce G Costa Rica
29C5	Golfo San Jorge G Arg
29D4	Golfo San Matías G Arg
68B3	Golmud China
99E2	Golocha Eth
12B2	Golovin B USA
74F2	Golovnino Russian Fed
99C3	Goma Zaire
97D3	Gombe Nig
60D3	Gomel Belarus
96A2	Gomera I Canary Is
24B2	Gómez Palacio Mexico
63E2	Gonam R Russian Fed
90C2	Gonbad-e Kävüs Iran
86A1	Gonda India
85C4	Gondal India
99D1	Gonder Eth
92A1	Gönen Turk
55C3	Gonen R Turk
73A4	Gongga Shan Mt China
72A2	Gonghe China
97D3	Gongola R Nig
22B2	Gonzales California, USA
19A4	Gonzales Texas, USA
34C3	Gonzalez Chaves Arg
13C2	Good Hope Mt Can
8C2	Goodland USA
12B3	Goodnews Bay USA
109C1	Goodooga R Aust
42D3	Goole Eng

108C2	Goolgowi Aust
108A3	Goolwa Aust
106A4	Goomalling Aust
108C2	Goombalie Aust
109D1	Goomer Aust
109D1	Goomeri Aust
109D1	Goondiwindi Aust
7E4	Goose Bay Can
17C1	Goose Creek USA
20B2	Goose L USA
87B1	Gooty India
63C2	Gora Munku Sardyk Mt Mongolia/ Russian Fed
64H3	Gora Narodnaya Mt Russian Fed
64G3	Gora Tel'pos-iz Russian Fed
54A2	Goražde Bosnia-Herzegovina
4D3	Gordon USA
13E1	Gordon L Can
15C3	Gordonsville USA
98B2	Goré Chad
99D2	Gorē Eth
111A3	Gore NZ
63F2	Gore Topko Mt Russian Fed
45C2	Gorey Irish Rep
90B2	Gorgän Iran
93E2	Goris Armenia
52B1	Gorizia Italy
	Gor'kiy = Nizniy Novgorod
61F2	Gor'kovskoye Vodokhranilishche Res Russian Fed
57C2	Görlitz Germany
60E4	Gorlovka Ukraine
22C3	Gorman USA
54C2	Gorna Orjahovica Bulg
68A1	Gorno-Altaysk Russian Fed
69G2	Gornozavodsk Russian Fed
61F2	Gorodets Russian Fed
59C3	Gorodok Ukraine
59D3	Gorodok Ukraine
71F4	Goroka PNG
86A1	Gorokhpur India
101C2	Gorongosa Mozam
71D3	Gorontalo Indon
61K2	Goro Yurma Mt Russian Fed
45B2	Gort Irish Rep
63C2	Goryachinsk Russian Fed
59D3	Goryn' R Ukraine
59C2	Góry Świetokrzyskie Upland Pol
64G3	Gory Tel'pos-iz' Mt Russian Fed
39H8	Gorzów Wielkopolski Pol
74E2	Goshogawara Japan
52C2	Gospić Croatia
54B2	Gostivar Macedonia
58B2	Gostynin Pol
39G7	Göteborg Sweden
98B2	Gotel Mts Nig
39H7	Gotland I Sweden
74B4	Gotō-retto I Japan
39H7	Gotska Sandön I Sweden
74C3	Götsu Japan
98B1	Goudoumaria Niger
103H7	Gough I Atlantic O
109C2	Goulburn Aust
97B3	Goumbou Mali
97B3	Goundam Mali
98B1	Gouré Niger
97B3	Gourma Rharous Mali
46A2	Gournay-en-Bray France
95A3	Gouro Chad
71E5	Gove Pen Aust
60B4	Goverla Mt Ukraine
35C1	Governador Valadares Brazil
86A2	Govind Ballabh Paht Sägar L India

15C2	Gowanda USA
84B3	Gowärän Afghan
30E4	Goya Arg
98C1	Goz-Beida Chad
53B3	Gozo I Medit S
95C3	Goz Regeb Sudan
100B4	Graaff-Reinet S Africa
15C1	Gracefield Can
109D1	Grafton Aust
8D2	Grafton N Dakota, USA
14B3	Grafton W Virginia, USA
5E4	Graham I Can
13C1	Graham R Can
13E1	Graham L Can
100B4	Grahamstown S Africa
31B3	Grajaú Brazil
58C2	Grajewo Pol
55B2	Grámmos Mt Greece/Alb
44B3	Grampian Mts Scot
32C3	Granada Colombia
25D3	Granada Nic
50B2	Granada Spain
15D1	Granby Can
96A2	Gran Canaria I Canary Is
30D4	Gran Chaco Region Arg
14A2	Grand R Michigan, USA
18B1	Grand R Missouri, USA
27Q2	Grand B Dominica
11C4	Grand Bahama I The Bahamas
7E5	Grand Bank Can
102F2	Grand Banks Atlantic O
97B4	Grand Bassam Côte d'Ivoire
9B3	Grand Canyon USA
26A3	Grand Cayman I Caribbean S
13E2	Grand Centre Can
20C1	Grand Coulee USA
34B3	Grande R Arg
31C4	Grande R Bahia, Brazil
35B1	Grande R Minas Gerais/São Paulo, Brazil
13D2	Grande Cache Can
47A2	Grande Chartreuse Region, France
101D2	Grande Comore I Comoros
13D1	Grande Prairie Can
19A3	Grande Prairie USA
95A3	Grand Erg de Bilma Desert Niger
96B2	Grand erg Occidental Mts Alg
96C2	Grand erg Oriental Mts Alg
7C4	Grande Rivière de la Baleine R Can
20C1	Grande Ronde R USA
7D5	Grand Falls New Brunswick, Can
7E5	Grand Falls Newfoundland, Can
20C1	Grand Forks Can
8D2	Grand Forks USA
16B1	Grand Gorge USA
14A2	Grand Haven USA
19C3	Grand Isle USA
19B4	Grand L USA
15D1	Grand Mère Can
50A2	Gràndola Port
5J4	Grand Rapids Can
14A2	Grand Rapids Michigan, USA
10A2	Grand Rapids Minnesota, USA
47B2	Grand St Bernard P Italy/Switz
8B2	Grand Teton Mt USA

Gunung Besar

Gunung Bulu

110C1	Hastings NZ
108B2	Hatfield Aust
12B1	Hatham Inlet USA
85D3	Häthras India
76D2	Ha Tinh Viet
108B2	Hattah Aust
11C3	Hatteras,C USA
19C3	Hattiesburg USA
59B3	Hatvan Hung
76D3	Hau Bon Viet
99E2	Haud Region, Eth
39F7	Haugesund Nor
110C1	Hauhungaroa Range Mts NZ
13F1	Haultain R Can
110B1	Hauraki G NZ
111A3	Hauroko,L NZ
47C1	Hausstock Mt Switz
96B1	Haut Atlas Mts Mor
98C2	Haute Kotto Region, CAR
46C1	Hautes Fagnes Mts Belg
46B1	Hautmont Belg
96B1	Hauts Plateaux Mts Alg
90D3	Hauzdar Iran
18B1	Havana USA
	Havana = Habana
87B3	Havankulam Sri Lanka
110C1	Havelock North NZ
43B4	Haverfordwest Wales
16D1	Haverhill USA
87B2	Häveri India
16C2	Haverstraw USA
59B3	Havlíčkův Brod Czech Republic
8C2	Havre USA
16A3	Havre de Grace USA
7D4	Havre-St-Pierre Can
54C2	Havsa Turk
21C4	Hawaii I Hawaiian Is
21C4	Hawaii Volcanoes Nat Pk Hawaiian Is
111A2	Hawea,L NZ
110B1	Hawera NZ
42C2	Hawick Scot
111A2	Hawkdun Range Mts NZ
110C1	Hawke B NZ
109D2	Hawke,C Aust
108A2	Hawker Aust
76B1	Hawng Luk Myan
93D3	Hawr al Habbaniyah L Iraq
93E3	Hawr al Hammár L Iraq
21B2	Hawthorne USA
108B2	Hay Aust
5G3	Hay R Can
46D2	Hayange France
4B3	Haycock USA
7A4	Hayes R Can
6D2	Hayes Halvø Region Greenland
12E2	Hayes,Mt USA
5G3	Hay River Can
18A2	Haysville USA
22A2	Hayward California, USA
86B2	Hazärïbäg India
46B1	Hazebrouck France
19B3	Hazelhurst USA
4G2	Hazel Str Can
5F4	Hazelton Can
13B1	Hazelton Mts Can
6C1	Hazen L Can
94B3	Hazeva Israel
16B2	Hazleton USA
22A1	Healdsburg USA
108C3	Healesville Aust
12E2	Healy USA
104B6	Heard I Indian O
19A3	Hearne USA
10B2	Hearst Can
72D2	Hebei Province, China
109C1	Hebel Aust
72C2	Hebi China
72C2	Hebian China
7D4	Hebron Can
94B3	Hebron Israel
18A1	Hebron Nebraska, USA
5E4	Hecate Str Can
12H3	Heceta I USA
73B5	Hechi China
4G2	Hecla and Griper B Can
111C2	Hector,Mt NZ
38G6	Hede Sweden
39H6	Hedemora Sweden
20C1	He Devil Mt USA
56B2	Heerenveen Neth
46C1	Heerlen Neth
	Hefa = Haifa
73D3	Hefei China
73B4	Hefeng China
69F2	Hegang China
75B1	Hegura-jima I Japan
94B3	Heidan R Jordan
56B2	Heide Germany
101G1	Heidelberg Transvaal, S Africa
57B3	Heidelberg Germany
63E2	Heihe China
101G1	Heilbron S Africa
57B3	Heilbronn Germany
56C2	Heiligenstadt Germany
38K6	Heinola Fin
73B4	Hejiang China
6J3	Hekla Mt Iceland
76C1	Hekou Viet
73A5	Hekou Yaozou Zizhixian China
72B2	Helan China
72B2	Helan Shan Mt China
19B3	Helena Arkansas, USA
8B2	Helena Montana, USA
22D3	Helendale USA
71E3	Helen Reef I Pacific O
44B3	Helensburgh Scot
91B4	Helleh R Iran
51B2	Hellin Spain
20C1	Hells Canyon R USA
46D1	Hellweg Region, Germany
22B2	Helm USA
80E2	Helmand R Afghan
100A3	Helmeringhausen Namibia
46C1	Helmond Neth
44C2	Helmsdale Scot
74B2	Helong China
39G7	Helsingborg Sweden
	Helsingfors = Helsinki
56C1	Helsingør Den
38J6	Helsinki Fin
43B4	Helston Eng
92B4	Helwân Egypt
19A3	Hempstead USA
39H7	Hemse Sweden
72A3	Henan China
72C3	Henan Province, China
110B1	Hen and Chicken Is NZ
14A3	Henderson Kentucky, USA
9B3	Henderson Nevada, USA
19B3	Henderson Texas, USA
73E5	Heng-ch'un Taiwan
68B4	Hengduan Shan Mts China
56B2	Hengelo Neth
72B2	Hengshan China
72D2	Hengshui China
76D1	Heng Xian China
73C4	Hengyang China
77A4	Henhoaha Nicobar Is
43D4	Henley-on-Thames Eng
16B3	Henlopen,C USA
7B4	Henrietta Maria,C Can
18A2	Henryetta USA
112C2	Henryk Arctowski Base Ant
6D3	Henry Kater Pen Can
68C2	Hentiyn Nuruu Mts Mongolia
76B2	Henzada Myan
73B5	Hepu China
80E2	Herat Afghan
5H4	Herbert Can
110C2	Herbertville NZ
46E1	Herborn Germany
26A4	Heredia Costa Rica
43C3	Hereford Eng
43C3	Hereford & Worcester County, Eng
46C1	Herentals Belg
47B1	Héricourt France
18A2	Herington USA
111A3	Heriot NZ
47C1	Herisau Switz
15D2	Herkimer USA
44E1	Herma Ness Pen Scot
109C2	Hermidale Aust
111B2	Hermitage NZ
	Hermon,Mt = Jebel ash Shaykh
24A2	Hermosillo Mexico
16A2	Herndon Pennsylvania, USA
22C2	Herndon California, USA
46D1	Herne Germany
56B1	Herning Den
90A2	Herowäbad Iran
50A2	Herrera del Duque Spain
16A2	Hershey USA
43D4	Hertford County, Eng
94B2	Herzliyya Israel
46C1	Hesbaye Region, Belg
46B1	Hesdin France
72B2	Heshui China
22D3	Hesperia USA
12H2	Hess R Can
57B2	Hessen State, Germ
22C2	Hetch Hetchy Res USA
42C2	Hexham Eng
73C5	He Xian China
73C5	Heyuan China
108B3	Heywood Aust
72D2	Heze China
17B2	Hialeah USA
10A2	Hibbing USA
110C1	Hicks Bay NZ
109C3	Hicks,Pt Aust
23B1	Hidalgo State, Mexico
24B2	Hidalgo del Parral Mexico
35B1	Hidrolândia Brazil
96A2	Hierro I Canary Is
75C1	Higashine Japan
74B4	Higashi-suidō Str Japan
20B2	High Desert USA
19B4	High Island USA
44B3	Highland Division, Scot
22D3	Highland USA
22C1	Highland Peak Mt USA
16B2	Highlands Falls USA
11B3	High Point USA
13D1	High Prairie Can
5G4	High River Can
17B2	High Springs USA
16B2	Hightstown USA
43D4	High Wycombe Eng
39J7	Hiiumaa I Estonia
80B3	Hijaz Region, S Arabia
75B2	Hikigawa Japan
75B1	Hikone Japan
110B1	Hikurangi NZ
9C4	Hildago Mexico
9C4	Hildago del Parral Mexico
56B2	Hildesheim Germany
27R3	Hillaby,Mt Barbados
56C1	Hillerød Den
14B3	Hillsboro Ohio, USA
20B1	Hillsboro Oregon, USA
19A3	Hillsboro Texas, USA
108C2	Hillston Aust
44E1	Hillswick Scot
21C4	Hilo Hawaiian Is
93C2	Hilvan Turk
56B2	Hilversum Neth
84D2	Himachal Pradesh State, India
82B3	Himalaya Mts Asia
85C4	Himatnagar India
74C4	Himeji Japan
74D3	Himi Japan
92C3	Hims Syria
12E2	Hinchinbrook Entrance USA
12E2	Hinchinbrook I USA
85D3	Hindaun India
84B1	Hindu Kush Mts Afghan
87B2	Hindupur India
13D1	Hines Creek Can
85D4	Hinganghät India
69E2	Hinggan Ling Upland China
85B3	Hingol R Pak
85D5	Hingoli India
38H5	Hinnøya I Nor
16C1	Hinsdale USA
13D2	Hinton Can
34B2	Hipolito Itrogoyen Arg
86A2	Hirakud Res India
92B2	Hirfanli Baraji Res Turk
87B2	Hirihar India
74E2	Hirosaki Japan
74C4	Hiroshima Japan
46C2	Hirson France
54C2	Hirşova Rom
56B1	Hirtshals Den
84D3	Hisär India
26C3	Hispaniola I Caribbean S
94C1	Hisyah Syria
93D3	Hit Iraq
74E3	Hitachi Japan
75C1	Hitachi-Ota Japan
43D4	Hitchin Eng
38F6	Hitra I Nor
75A2	Hiuchi-nada B Japan
75A2	Hiwasa Japan
56B1	Hjørring Den
76B1	Hka R Myan
97C4	Ho Ghana
76D1	Hoa Binh Viet
76D3	Hoa Da Viet
109C4	Hobart Aust
9C3	Hobbs USA
56B1	Hobro Den
13C2	Hobson L Can
99E2	Hobyo Somalia
76D3	Ho Chi Minh Viet
57C3	Hochkonig Mt Austria
54B1	Hódmező'hely Hung
59B3	Hodonin Czech Republic
74B2	Hoeryong N Korea
57C2	Hof Germany
38B2	Hofsjökull Mts Iceland
74C4	Höfu Japan
96C2	Hoggar Upland Alg
46D1	Hohe Acht Mt Germany
72C1	Hohhot China
6J3	Höhn Iceland
68B3	Hoh Sai Hu L China
82C2	Hoh Xil Shan Mts China
99D2	Hoima Uganda
86C1	Hojai India
75A2	Hojo Japan
110B1	Hokianga Harbour B NZ
111B2	Hokitika NZ
74E2	Hokkaido Japan
90C2	Hokmābād Iran
109C3	Holbrook Aust
9B3	Holbrook USA
19A2	Holdenville USA
87B2	Hole Narsipur India
27R3	Holetown Barbados
26B2	Holguin Cuba
111B2	Holitika NZ
12C2	Holitna R USA

Hollabrunn

59B3 Hollabrunn Austria
14A2 Holland USA
22B2 Hollister USA
19C3 Holly Springs USA
22C3 Hollywood California, USA
17B2 Hollywood Florida, USA
4G2 Holman Island Can
38J6 Holmsund Sweden
94B2 Holon Israel
56B1 Holstebro Den
6E3 Holsteinborg Greenland
14B2 Holt USA
18A2 Holton USA
12C2 Holy Cross USA
42B3 Holyhead Wales
42D2 Holy I Eng
43B3 Holy I Wales
16C1 Holyoke Massachusetts, USA
86C2 Homalin Myan
6D3 Home B Can
12D3 Homer Alaska, USA
19B3 Homer Louisiana, USA
111A2 Homer Tunnel NZ
17B1 Homerville USA
17B2 Homestead USA
17A1 Homewood USA
87B1 Homnābād India
101C3 Homoine Mozam
25D3 Hondo R Mexico
25D3 Honduras Republic, Cent America
25D3 Honduras,G of Honduras
39G6 Hønefoss Nor
15C2 Honesdale USA
21A1 Honey L USA
76C1 Hong R Viet
76D1 Hon Gai Viet
73A4 Hongguo China
73C4 Hong Hu L China
72B2 Honghui China
73C4 Hongjiang China
73C5 Hong Kong China, S E Asia
68D2 Hongor Mongolia
73B5 Hongshui He R China
72A3 Hongyuan China
72D3 Hongze Hu L China
107E1 Honiara Solomon Is
77C4 Hon Khoai I Camb
76D3 Hon Lan I Viet
38K4 Honningsvåg Nor
21C4 Honolulu Hawaiian Is
77C4 Hon Panjang I Viet
74D3 Honshu I Japan
20B1 Hood,Mt USA
20B1 Hood River USA
45C2 Hook Head C Irish Rep
12G3 Hoonah USA
12A2 Hooper Bay USA
101G1 Hoopstad S Africa
56A2 Hoorn Neth
9B3 Hoover Dam USA
12E2 Hope Alaska, USA
19B3 Hope Arkansas, USA
13C3 Hope Can
7D4 Hopedale Can
64D2 Hopen I Barents S
6D3 Hopes Advance,C Can
108B3 Hopetoun Aust
100B3 Hopetown S Africa
18C2 Hopkinsville USA
20B1 Hoquiam USA
93D1 Horasan Turk
99F1 Hordiyo Somalia
47C1 Horgen Switz
105H5 Horizon Depth Pacific O
91C4 Hormuz,Str of Oman/ Iran
59B3 Horn Austria
6H3 Horn C Iceland
38H5 Hornavan L Sweden
19B3 Hornbeck USA
20B2 Hornbrook USA
111B2 Hornby NZ

7B5 Hornepayne Can
4F3 Horn Mts Can
42D3 Hornsea Eng
72B1 Horn Uul Mt Mongolia
30E3 Horqueta Par
15C2 Horseheads USA
56C1 Horsens Den
20B1 Horseshoe Bay Can
108B3 Horsham Aust
43D4 Horsham Eng
39G7 Horten Nor
4F3 Horton R Can
78C2 Hose Mts Malay
85D4 Hoshangābād India
84D2 Hoshiārpur India
87B1 Hospet India
29C7 Hoste I Chile
82B2 Hotan China
19B3 Hot Springs Arkansas, USA
8C2 Hot Springs S. Dakota, USA
4G3 Hottah Can
46A2 Houdan France
72C2 Houma China
19B4 Houma USA
16C2 Housatonic R USA
13B2 Houston Can
19C3 Houston Mississippi, USA
19A4 Houston Texas, USA
106A3 Houtman Is Aust
68B2 Hovd Mongolia
68C1 Hövsgol Nuur L Mongolia
14A2 Howard City USA
12C1 Howard P USA
109C3 Howe,C Aust
101H1 Howick S Africa
44C2 Hoy I Scot
39F6 Høyanger Nor
59B2 Hradeç-Králové Czech Republic
59B3 Hranice Czech Republic
59B3 Hron R Slovakia
73E5 Hsin-chu Taiwan
73E5 Hsüeh Shan Mt Taiwan
72B2 Huachi China
32B6 Huacho Peru
72C1 Huade China
72D3 Huaibei China
72D3 Huaibin China
72D3 Huai He R China
73C4 Huaihua China
73C5 Huaiji China
72D3 Huainan China
69E4 Hua-lien Taiwan
32B5 Huallaga R Peru
32B5 Huallanca Peru
32B5 Huamachuco Peru
100A2 Huambo Angola
30C2 Huanay Bol
32B5 Huancabamba Peru
32B6 Huancavelica Peru
32B6 Huancayo Peru
73D3 Huangchuan China
Huang Hai = Yellow S
72D2 Huang He R China
72B2 Huangiing China
76D2 Huangliu China
73C3 Huangpi China
73D4 Huangshan China
73D3 Huangshi China
34C3 Huanguelén Arg
73E4 Huangyan China
74B2 Huanren China
32B5 Huānuco Peru
30C2 Huanuni Bol
72B2 Huan Xian China
32B5 Huaráz Peru
32B6 Huarmey Peru
32B5 Huascarán Mt Peru
30B4 Huasco Chile
23B2 Huatusco Mexico
23B1 Huauchinango Mexico
23B2 Huautla Mexico
72C2 Hua Xian China
24B2 Huayapan R Mexico
73C3 Hubei Province, China

87B1 Hubli India
34C3 Hucal Arg
74B2 Huch'ang N Korea
42D3 Huddersfield Eng
39H6 Hudiksvall Sweden
17B2 Hudson Florida, USA
14B2 Hudson Michigan, USA
16C1 Hudson New York, USA
16C1 Hudson R USA
7B4 Hudson B Can
5H4 Hudson Bay Can
13C1 Hudson's Hope Can
6C3 Hudson Str Can
76D2 Hue Viet
23B1 Huejutla Mexico
50A2 Huelva Spain
23A2 Hueramo Mexico
51B2 Húercal Overa Spain
51B1 Huesca Spain
23B2 Huexotla Hist Site Mexico
107D3 Hughenden Aust
12D1 Hughes USA
86B2 Hugli R India
19A3 Hugo USA
73D4 Hui'an China
110C1 Huiarau Range Mts NZ
74B2 Huich'ŏn N Korea
74B2 Huifa He R China
32B3 Huila Mt Colombia
73D5 Huilai China
73A4 Huili China
74B2 Huinan China
34C2 Huinca Renancó Arg
25C3 Huixtla Mexico
73A4 Huize China
73C5 Huizhou China
23B2 Hujuápan de Léon Mexico
69F2 Hulin China
15C1 Hull Can
42D3 Hull Eng
58B1 Hultsfred Sweden
63D3 Hulun Nur L China
69E1 Huma China
33E5 Humaita Brazil
100B4 Humansdorp S Africa
42D3 Humber R Eng
5H4 Humboldt Can
20C2 Humboldt R USA
20B2 Humboldt B USA
6D2 Humboldt Gletscher Gl Greenland
21B2 Humboldt L USA
108C1 Humeburn Aust
109C3 Hume,L Aust
100A2 Humpata Angola
22C2 Humphreys USA
38A1 Húnaflóri B Iceland
73C4 Hunan Province, China
74C2 Hunchun China
13C2 Hundred Mile House Can
54B1 Hunedoara Rom
59B3 Hungary Republic, Europe
108B1 Hungerford Aust
74B3 Hŭngnam N Korea
74B2 Hunjiang China
46D2 Hunsrück Mts, Germany
109D2 Hunter R Aust
13B2 Hunter I Can
109C4 Hunter Is Aust
12D2 Hunter,Mt USA
14A3 Huntingburg USA
43D3 Huntingdon Eng
14A2 Huntingdon Indiana, USA
14B3 Huntington W Virginia, USA
22C4 Huntington Beach USA
22C2 Huntington L USA
110C1 Huntly NZ
44C3 Huntly Scot
12J2 Hunt,Mt Can
108A1 Hunt Pen Aust
17A1 Huntsville Alabama, USA

15C1 Huntsville Can
19A3 Huntsville Texas, USA
76D2 Huong Khe Viet
71F4 Huon Peninsula Pen PNG
109C4 Huonville Anst
14B1 Hurd,C Can
80B3 Hurghada Egypt
8D2 Huron S. Dakota, USA
14B1 Huron,L Can/USA
34A2 Hurtado Chile
111B2 Hurunui R NZ
38B1 Husavik Iceland
54C1 Huşi Rom
39G7 Huskvarna Sweden
12C1 Huslia USA
94B2 Husn Jordan
56B2 Husum Germany
109C1 Hutton,Mt Aust
72D2 Hutuo He R China
46C1 Huy Belg
72A2 Huzhu China
52C2 Hvar I Croatia
100B2 Hwange Zim
100B2 Hwange Nat Pk Zim
15D2 Hyannis USA
68B2 Hyaryas Nuur L Mongolia
5E4 Hydaburg Can
16C2 Hyde Park USA
87B1 Hyderābād India
85B3 Hyderabad Pak
49D3 Hyères France
12J2 Hyland R Can
8B2 Hyndman Peak Mt USA
38K6 Hyrynsalmi Fin
13D1 Hythe Can
74C4 Hyūga Japan
39J6 Hyvikää Fin

I

31C4 Iaçu Brazil
54C2 Ialomiţa R Rom
54C1 Iaşi Rom
97C4 Ibadan Nig
32B3 Ibagué Colombia
54B2 Ibar R Montenegro/ Serbia, Yugos
32B3 Ibarra Ecuador
35B1 Ibiá Brazil
30E4 Ibicuí R Brazil
34D2 Ibicuy Arg
51C2 Ibiza Spain
51C2 Ibiza I Spain
101D2 Ibo Mozam
31C4 Ibotirama Brazil
91C5 'Ibrī Oman
32B6 Ica Peru
32D4 Icá R Brazil
32D3 Icana Brazil
38A1 Iceland Republic, N Atlantic O
13C2 Ice Mt Can
87A1 Ichalkaranji India
74E3 Ichihara Japan
75B1 Ichinomiya Japan
74E3 Ichinoseki Japan
12F3 Icy B USA
4B2 Icy C USA
19B3 Idabell USA
8B2 Idaho Falls USA
20B2 Idanha USA
46D2 Idar Oberstein Germany
95A2 Idehan Marzūg Desert Libya
95A2 Idehan Ubari Desert Libya
96C2 Idelés Alg
68B2 Iderlym Gol R Mongolia
95C2 Idfu Egypt
55B3 Idhi Óros Mt Greece
55B3 Idhra I Greece
98B3 Idiofa Zaire
12C2 Iditarod R USA
92C2 Idlib Syria
39K7 Idritsa Russian Fed
100B4 Idutywa S Africa
55C3 Ierápetra Greece
46B1 Ieper Belg

63D2	Iet Oktyobr'ya Russian Fed
99D3	Ifakara Tanz
71F3	Ifalik I Pacific O
101D3	Ifanadiana Madag
97C4	Ife Nig
97C3	Iférouane Niger
78C2	Igan Malay
35B2	Igaranava Brazil
93E2	Igdir Iran
39H6	Iggesund Sweden
34B2	Iglesia Arg
53A3	Iglesias Sardegna
6B3	Igloolik Can
10A2	Ignace Can
55B3	Igoumenítsa Greece
61H2	Igra Russian Fed
23B2	Iguala Mexico
35B2	Iguape Brazil
35B2	Iguatama Brazil
31D3	Iguatu Brazil
98A3	Iguéla Gabon
101D3	Ihosy Madag
74D3	Iida Japan
75B1	Iide-san Mt Japan
38K6	Iisalmi Fin
75A2	Iizuka Japan
97C4	Ijebu Ode Nig
56B2	Ijsselmeer S Neth
55C3	Ikaría I Greece
74E2	Ikeda Japan
98C3	Ikela Zaïre
54B2	Ikhtiman Bulg
12D3	Ikolik,C USA
101D2	Ikopa R Madag
79B2	Ilagan Phil
90A3	Ilām Iran
47C1	Ilanz Switz
13F1	Ile à la Crosse Can
13F1	Ile à la Crosse,L Can
89G8	Ilebo Zaïre
96D1	Ile de Jerba I Tunisia
48B2	Ile de Noirmoutier I France
48B2	Ile de Ré I France
107F3	Ile des Pins I Nouvelle Calédonie
48A2	Ile d'Ouessant I France
48B2	Ile d'Yeu I France
61J3	Ilek R Russian Fed
107F2	Iles Bélèp Nouvelle Calédonie
107E2	Iles Chesterfield Nouvelle Calédonie
49D3	Iles d'Hyères Is France
43B4	Ilfracombe Eng
92B1	Ilgaz Dağları Mts Turk
101C3	Ilha Bazaruto I Mozam
33G3	Ilha De Maracá I Brazil
33G4	Ilha de Marajó I Brazil
35B2	Ilha de São Sebastião I Brazil
33G6	Ilha do Bananal Region Brazil
35C2	Ilha Grande I Brazil
35B2	Ilha Santo Amaro I Brazil
96A1	Ilhas Selvegens I Atlantic O
35A2	Ilha Solteira Dam Brazil
31D4	Ilhéus Brazil
12C3	Iliamna L USA
12D2	Iliamna V USA
79B4	Iligan Phil
63C2	Ilim R Russian Fed
63C2	Ilim Russian Fed
63G3	Il'inskiy Russian Fed
55B3	Iliodhrómia I Greece
79B4	Illana B Phil
34A2	Illapel Chile
34A2	Illapel R Chile
97C3	Illéla Niger
47D1	Iller R Germany
4C4	Illiamna L USA
10A2	Illinois State, USA
18B2	Illinois R USA
96C2	Illizi Alg

30B2	Ilo Peru
79B3	Iloilo Phil
38L6	Ilomantsi Fin
97C4	Ilorin Nig
75A2	Imabari Japan
75B1	Imalchi Japan
60C1	Imatra Fin
30G4	Imbituba Brazil
99E2	Imi Eth
20C2	Imlay USA
47D1	Immenstadt Germany
52B2	Imola Italy
31B3	Imperatriz Brazil
52A2	Imperia Italy
98B2	Impfondo Congo
86C2	Imphäl India
47D1	Imst Austria
12B1	Imuruk L USA
75B1	Ina Japan
96C2	In Afahleleh Well Alg
75B2	Inamba-jima I Japan
96C2	In Amenas Alg
38K5	Inari Fin
38K5	Inarijärvi L Fin
75C1	Inawashiro-ko L Japan
96C2	In Belbel Alg
60E5	Ince Burun Pt Turk
92B2	Incekum Burun Pt Turk
74B3	Inch'ŏn S Korea
96B2	In Dagouber Well Mali
35B1	Indaia R Brazil
38H6	Indals R Sweden
21B2	Independence California, USA
18A2	Independence Kansas, USA
18B2	Independence Missouri, USA
78A3	Inderagiri R Indon
61H4	Inderborskly Kazakhstan
83B3	India Federal Republic, Asia
14A2	Indiana State, USA
15C2	Indiana USA
104C6	Indian-Antarctic Ridge Indian O
14A3	Indianapolis USA
	Indian Desert = Thar Desert
7E4	Indian Harbour Can
104B4	Indian O
18B1	Indianola Iowa, USA
19B3	Indianola Mississippi, USA
35B1	Indianópolis Brazil
76D2	Indo China Region, S E Asia
70C4	Indonesia Republic, S E Asia
85D4	Indore India
78B4	Indramayu Indon
48C2	Indre R France
85B3	Indus R Pak
60D5	Inebulu Turk
96C2	In Ebeggi Well Alg
96C2	In Ecker Alg
92A1	Inegöl Turk
96D2	In Ezzane Alg
97C3	Ingal Niger
14B2	Ingersoll Can
107D2	Ingham Aust
6D2	Inglefield Land Region Can
110B1	Inglewood NZ
109D1	Inglewood Queensland, Aust
22C4	Inglewood USA
108B3	Inglewood Victoria, Aust
38B2	Ingólfshöfdi I Iceland
57C3	Ingolstadt Germany
86B2	Ingrãj Bázâr India
96C3	In-Guezzam Well Alg
101C3	Inhambane Mozam
101C3	Inharrime Mozam
35B1	Inhumas Brazil
32D3	Inirida R Colombia
45A2	Inishbofin I Irish Rep

45A1	Inishkea I Irish Rep
45B2	Inishmaan I Irish Rep
45B2	Inishmore I Irish Rep
45B1	Inishmurray I Irish Rep
45C1	Inishowen District, Irish Rep
45A2	Inishshark I Irish Rep
45A2	Inishturk I Irish Rep
109C1	Injune Aust
12H3	Inklin Can
12H3	Inklin R Can
12C1	Inland L USA
47D1	Inn R Austria
108B1	Innamincka Aust
68C2	Inner Mongolia Autonomous Region, China
107D2	Innisfail Aust
12C2	Innoko R USA
57C3	Innsbruck Austria
98B3	Inongo Zaïre
58B2	Inowrocław Pol
96C2	In Salah Alg
47B1	Interlaken Switz
24C3	Intexpec Mexico
47C2	Intra Italy
78D3	Intu Indon
75C1	Inubo-saki C Japan
7C4	Inukjuak Can
4E3	Inuvik Can
4F3	Inuvik Region Can
44B3	Inveraray Scot
111A3	Invercargill NZ
44B4	Inverclyde Division, Scot
109D1	Inverell Aust
13D2	Invermere Can
44B3	Inverness Scot
44C3	Inverurie Scot
108A3	Investigator Str Aust
68A1	Inya Russian Fed
21B2	Inyokern USA
98B3	Inzia R Zaïre
55B3	Ioánnina Greece
18A2	Iola USA
44A3	Iona I Scot
100A2	Iôna Nat Pk Angola
20C1	Ione USA
	Ionian Is = Iónioi Nísoi
55A3	Ionian S Italy/Greece
55B3	Iónioi Nísoi Is Greece
55C3	Íos I Greece
10A2	Iowa R USA
10A2	Iowa City USA
35B1	Ipameri Brazil
35C1	Ipanema Brazil
61F4	Ipatovo Russian Fed
32B3	Ipiales Colombia
77C5	Ipoh Malay
30F2	Iporá Brazil
55C2	Ipsala Turk
109D1	Ipswich Aust
43E3	Ipswich Eng
16D1	Ipswich USA
30B3	Iquique Chile
32C4	Iquitos Peru
55C3	Iráklion Greece
80D2	Iran Republic, S W Asia
91D4	Iränshahr Iran
23A1	Irapuato Mexico
93D3	Iraq Republic, S W Asia
95A2	Irã Wan Watercourse Libya
94B2	Irbid Jordan
61K2	Irbit Russian Fed
36C3	Ireland Republic, NW Europe
33F3	Ireng R Guyana
74B3	Iri S Korea
71E4	Irian Jaya Province, Indon
95B3	Iriba Chad
79B3	Iriga Phil
99D3	Iringa Tanz
69E4	Iriomote I Japan
33G5	Iriri R Brazil
42B3	Irish S Eng/Irish Rep
12D1	Irkillik R USA

63C2	Irkutsk Russian Fed
65J4	Irlysh R Kazakhstan
108A2	Iron Knob Aust
14A1	Iron Mountain USA
107D2	Iron Range Aust
14A1	Iron River USA
14B3	Irontown USA
10A2	Ironwood USA
10B2	Iroquois Falls Can
75B2	Iro-zaki C Japan
76A2	Irrawaddy,Mouths of the Myan
65H4	Irtysh R Russian Fed
51B1	Irun Spain
42B2	Irvine Scot
19A3	Irving USA
79B4	Isabela Phil
32J7	Isabela I Ecuador
4H2	Isachsen Can
4H2	Isachsen,C Can
6H3	Isafjördur Iceland
74C4	Isahaya Japan
98C2	Isangi Zaïre
47D1	Isar R Germany
47D1	Isarco R Italy
44E1	Isbister Scot
47D1	Ischgl Austria
53B2	Ischia I Italy
75B2	Ise Japan
47D2	Iseo Italy
46D1	Iserlohn Germany
53B2	Isernia Italy
75B2	Ise-wan B Japan
69E4	Ishigaki I Japan
74E2	Ishikari R Japan
74E2	Ishikari-wan B Japan
65H4	Ishim Russian Fed
65H4	Ishim R Kazakhstan
74E3	Ishinomaki Japan
75C1	Ishioka Japan
84C1	Ishkashim Afghan
14A1	Ishpeming USA
65J4	Isil'kul Russian Fed
99D2	Isiolo Kenya
98C2	Isiro Zaïre
92C2	Iskenderun Turk
92C2	Iskenferun Körfezi B Turk
92B1	Iskilip Turk
65K4	Iskitim Russian Fed
54B2	Iskur R Bulg
12H3	Iskut R Can/USA
23B2	Isla Mexico
34C3	Isla Bermejo I Arg
27E4	Isla Blanquilla Ven
32A2	Isla Coiba I Panama
9B4	Isla de Cedros I Mexico
29B4	Isla de Chiloé I Chile
25D2	Isla de Cozumel I Mexico
26C3	Isla de la Gonâve Cuba
26A2	Isla de la Juventud I Cuba
34D2	Isla de las Lechiguanas I Arg
3K8	Isla del Coco I Costa Rica
25D3	Isla del Maíz I Caribbean S
23B1	Isla de Lobos I Mexico
29D6	Isla de los Estados I Arg
28E2	Isla de Marajó I Brazil
105L5	Isla de Pascua I Pacific O
26A4	Isla de Providencia I Caribbean S
26A4	Isla de San Andres I Caribbean S
30G4	Isla de Santa Catarina I Brazil
33G2	Isla du Diable I French Guiana
31E2	Isla Fernando de Noronha I Brazil
29C6	Isla Grande de Tierra del Fuego I Arg/Chile
27D4	Isla la Tortuga I Ven
84C2	Islamabad Pak

Isla Magdalena

24A2	Isla Magdalena / Mexico
27E4	Isla Margarita Ven
34A3	Isla Mocha Chile
17B2	Islamorada USA
10A1	Island L Can
108A2	Island Lg Aust
110B1	Islands,B of NZ
32A4	Isla Puná / Ecuador
103D6	Isla San Ambrosia / Pacific O
103D6	Isla San Felix / Pacific O
24A2	Isla Santa Margarita / Mexico
34A3	Isla Santa Maria / Chile
51C2	Islas Baleares Is Spain
96A2	Islas Canarias Is Atlantic O
51C2	Islas Columbretes Is Spain
25D3	Islas de la Bahia Is Honduras
26A4	Islas del Maiz Is Caribbean S
33E1	Islas de Margarita Is Ven
29C7	Islas Diego Ramírez Is Chile
32J7	Islas Galapagos Is Pacific O
30H6	Islas Juan Fernández Chile
32D1	Islas los Roques Is Ven
	Islas Malvinas = Falkland Is
105L3	Islas Revilla Gigedo Is Pacific O
29C7	Islas Wollaston Is Chile
97A3	Isla Tidra / Maur
29B5	Isla Wellington / Chile
48C2	Isle R France
104B5	Isle Amsterdam / Indian O
43D4	Isle of Wight / Eng
10B2	Isle Royale / USA
104B5	Isle St Paul / Indian O
104A6	Isles Crozet / Indian O
105J4	Isles de la Société Pacific O
105K5	Isles Gambier Is Pacific O
101D2	Isles Glorieuses Is Madag
104B6	Isles Kerguelen Is Indian O
105K4	Isles Marquises Is Pacific O
105J4	Isles Tuamotu Is Pacific O
105J5	Isles Tubai Is Pacific O
22B1	Isleton USA
92B3	Ismâ'iliya Egypt
101D3	Isoanala Madag
101C2	Isoka Zambia
53B3	Isola Egadi / Italy
52B2	Isola Ponziane / Italy
53B3	Isole Lipari Is Italy
52C2	Isoles Tremiti Is Italy
75B1	Isosaki Japan
92B2	Isparta Turk
94B2	Israel Republic, S W Asia
51C2	Isser R Alg
48C2	Issoire France
49C2	Issoudun France
92A1	Istanbul Turk
55B3	Istiáia Greece
25C3	Istmo de Tehuantepec Isthmus Mexico
17B2	Istokpoga,L USA
52B1	Istra Pen Croatia
35B1	Itaberai Brazil
35C1	Itabira Brazil
35C2	Itabirito Brazil

31D4	Itabuna Brazil
33F4	Itacoatiara Brazil
32B2	Itagui Colombia
33F4	Itaituba Brazil
30G4	Itajai Brazil
35B2	Itajuba Brazil
52B2	Italy Repubic, Europe
35D1	Itamaraju Brazil
35C1	Itamarandiba Brazil
35C1	Itambacuri Brazil
35C1	Itambé Mt Brazil
86C1	Itânagar India
35B2	Itanhaém Brazil
35C1	Itanhém Brazil
35C1	Itanhém R Brazil
35C1	Itaobim Brazil
35B2	Itapecerica Brazil
35C2	Itaperuna Brazil
31C5	Itapetinga Brazil
35B2	Itapetininga Brazil
35B2	Itapeva Brazil
31D2	Itapipoca Brazil
35B1	Itapuranga Brazil
30E4	Itaquí Brazil
35C1	Itarantim Brazil
35B2	Itararé Brazil
35B2	Itararé R Brazil
35C2	Itaúna Brazil
33E6	Iténez R Brazil/Bol
15C2	Ithaca USA
98C2	Itimbiri R Zaïre
35C1	Itinga Brazil
6E3	Itivdleg Greenland
75B2	Ito Japan
74D3	Itoigawa Japan
33E6	Itonomas R Bol
35B2	Itu Brazil
35B1	Itumbiara Brazil
35A1	Iturama Brazil
30C3	Iturbe Arg
35B1	Itururtaba Brazil
56B2	Itzehoe Germany
58D2	Ivacevichi Belarus
35A2	Ivai R Brazil
38K5	Ivalo Fin
54A2	Ivangrad Montenegro, Yugos
108B2	Ivanhoe Aust
59C3	Ivano-Frankovsk Ukraine
61F2	Ivanovo Russian Fed
61F2	Ivanovo Division, Russian Fed
65H3	Ivdel' Russian Fed
98B2	Ivindo R Gabon
101D3	Ivohibe Madag
101D2	Ivongo Soanierana Madag
	Ivory Coast = Côte d'Ivoire
52A1	Ivrea Italy
6C3	Ivujivik Can
74E3	Iwaki Japan
74C4	Iwakuni Japan
74E2	Iwanai Japan
97C4	Iwo Nig
69G4	Iwo Jima / Japan
23B1	Ixmiquilpan Mexico
23A2	Ixtapa Mexico
23A1	Ixtlán Mexico
75A2	Iyo Japan
75A2	Iyo-nada B Japan
65G4	Izhevsk Russian Fed
64G3	Izhma Russian Fed
91C5	Izki Oman
60C4	Izmail Ukraine
92A2	Izmir Turk
55C3	Izmir Körfezi B Turk
92A1	Izmit Turk
92A1	Iznik Turk
55C2	Iznik Golü L Turk
94C2	Izra' Syria
23B2	Izúcar de Matamoros Mexico
75B2	Izumi-sano Japan
75A1	Izumo Japan
74D4	Izu-shotó Is Japan

J

95B1	Jabal al Akhdar Mts Libya
94C2	Jabal al 'Arab Syria
95A2	Jabal as Sawdá Mts Libya

91B5	Jabal az Zannah UAE
94C1	Jabal Halimah Mt Leb/Syria
83B3	Jabalpur India
59B2	Jablonec nad Nisou Czech Republic
31D3	Jaboatão Brazil
35B2	Jaboticabal Brazil
51B1	Jaca Spain
23B1	Jacala Mexico
33F5	Jacareacanga Brazil
35B2	Jacarei Brazil
30F3	Jacarezinho Brazil
29C2	Jáchal Arg
35C1	Jacinto Brazil
13F2	Jackfish L Can
109C1	Jackson Aust
22B1	Jackson California, USA
14B2	Jackson Michigan, USA
19B3	Jackson Mississippi, USA
18C2	Jackson Missouri, USA
14B3	Jackson Ohio, USA
11B3	Jackson Tennessee, USA
111B2	Jackson,C NZ
111A2	Jackson Head Pt NZ
19B3	Jacksonville Arkansas, USA
17B1	Jacksonville Florida, USA
18B2	Jacksonville Illinois, USA
17C1	Jacksonville N Carolina, USA
19A3	Jacksonville Texas, USA
17B1	Jacksonville Beach USA
26C3	Jacmel Haiti
84B3	Jacobabad Pak
31C4	Jacobina Brazil
23A2	Jacona Mexico
	Jadotville = Likasi
32B5	Jaén Peru
50B2	Jaén Spain
	Jaffa = Tel Aviv Yafo
108A3	Jaffa,C Aust
87B3	Jaffna Sri Lanka
86B2	Jagannathganj Ghat Bang
87C1	Jagdalpur India
91C4	Jagin R Iran
87B1	Jagtial India
29F2	Jaguarão R Brazil
35B2	Jahrom Iran
85D5	Jäina India
72A2	Jainca China
85D3	Jaipur India
85C3	Jaisalmer India
90C2	Jajarm Iran
52C2	Jajce Bosnia-Herzegovina
78B4	Jakarta Indon
6E3	Jakobshavn Greenland
38J6	Jakobstad Fin
23B2	Jalaca Mexico
84B2	Jalal-Kut Afghan
84D2	Jalandhar India
23B2	Jalapa Mexico
35A2	Jales Brazil
86B1	Jaleswar Nepal
85D4	Jalgaon India
97D4	Jalingo Nig
51B1	Jalón R Spain
85C3	Jálor India
23A1	Jalostotitlan Mexico
86B1	Jalpäiguri India
23B1	Jalpan Mexico
95B2	Jälu Oasis Libya
32A4	Jama Ecuador
26B3	Jamaica / Caribbean S
26B3	Jamaica Chan Caribbean S
86B2	Jamalpur Bang
78A3	Jambi Indon
85C4	Jambusar India
7B4	James B Can
5J5	Jameston USA

108A2	Jamestown Aust
8D2	Jamestown N. Dakota, USA
15C2	Jamestown New York, USA
16D2	Jamestown Rhode Island, USA
23B2	Jamiltepec Mexico
87B1	Jamkhandi India
84C2	Jammu India
84D2	Jammu and Kashmir State, India
85B4	Jamnagar India
84C3	Jampur Pak
38K6	Jämsä Fin
86B2	Jamshedpur India
86B1	Janakpur Nepal
35C1	Janaúba Brazil
90B3	Jandaq Iran
109D1	Jandowae Aust
1B1	Jan Mayen / Norwegian S
35C1	Januária Brazil
85D4	Jaora India
51	Japan Empire, E Asia
74C3	Japan,S of S E Asia
104F2	Japan Trench Pacific O
32D4	Japurá R Brazil
93C2	Jarābulus Syria
35B1	Jaraguá Brazil
50B1	Jarama R Spain
94B2	Jarash Jordan
30E3	Jardim Brazil
51B2	Jardin R Spain
26B2	Jardines de la Reina Is Cuba
	Jargalant = Hovd
33G3	Jari R Brazil
86C1	Jaria Jhänjail Bang
46C2	Jarny France
58B2	Jarocin Pol
59C2	Jaroslaw Pol
38G6	Järpen Sweden
72B2	Jartai China
85C4	Jasdan India
97C4	Jasikan Ghana
91C4	Jäsk Iran
59C3	Jaslo Pol
29D6	Jason Is Falkland Is
18B2	Jasper Arkansas, USA
13D2	Jasper Can
17B1	Jasper Florida, USA
14A3	Jasper Indiana, USA
19B3	Jasper Texas, USA
13D2	Jasper Nat Pk Can
58B2	Jastrowie Pol
35A1	Jataí Brazil
51B2	Játiva Spain
35B2	Jau Brazil
32B6	Jauja Peru
86A1	Jaunpur India
	Java = Jawa
87B2	Javadi Hills India
	Javari = Yavari
70B4	Java S Indon
106A2	Java Trench Indon
78B4	Jawa / Indon
71F4	Jayapura Indon
94C2	Jayrūd Syria
96B2	Jbel Ouarkziz Mts Mor
96B1	Jbel Sarhro Mt Mor
19B4	Jeanerette USA
97C4	Jebba Nig
93D2	Jebel 'Abd al 'Aziz Mt Syria
95B3	Jebel Abyad Sudan
91C5	Jebel Akhdar Mt Oman
92C4	Jebel al Lawz Mt S Arabia
94B2	Jebel ash Shaykh Mt Syria
95C2	Jebel Asoteriba Mt Sudan
94B3	Jebel Ed Dabab Mt Jordan
94B3	Jebel el Ata'ita Mt Jordan
92C3	Jebel esh Sharqi Mts Leb/Syria

Kaiwi Chan

Kai Xian

34

73B3 **Kai Xian** China
73A5 **Kaiyuan** Liaoning, China
74A2 **Kaiyuan** Yunnan, China
12C2 **Kaiyuh Mts** USA
38K6 **Kajaani** Fin
84B2 **Kajaki** Afghan
99D3 **Kajiado** Kenya
84B2 **Kajrān** Afghan
99D1 **Kaka** Sudan
99D2 **Kakamega** Kenya
75A2 **Kake** Japan
12H3 **Kake** USA
12D3 **Kakhonak** USA
65E5 **Kakhovskoye Vodokhranilishche** Res Ukraine
91B4 **Kākī** Iran
87C1 **Kākināda** India
75A2 **Kakogawa** Japan
4D2 **Kaktovik** USA
75C1 **Kakuda** Japan
Kalaallit Nunaat = Greenland
55B3 **Kalabáka** Greece
78D1 **Kalabakan** Malay
100B2 **Kalabo** Zambia
61F3 **Kalach** Russian Fed
61F4 **Kalach-na-Donu** Russian Fed
86C2 **Kaladan** R Myan
21C4 **Ka Lae** C Hawaiian Is
100B3 **Kalahari Desert** Botswana
38J6 **Kalajoki** Fin
63D2 **Kalakan** Russian Fed
70A3 **Kalakepen** Indon
84C1 **Kalam** Pak
55B3 **Kalámai** Greece
10B2 **Kalamazoo** USA
84B3 **Kalat** Pak
92B1 **Kalecik** Turk
78D3 **Kalembau** I Indon
99C3 **Kalémié** Zaïre
38L5 **Kalevala** Russian Fed
86C2 **Kalewa** Myan
12D2 **Kalgin I** USA
106B4 **Kalgoorlie** Aust
78B4 **Kalianda** Indon
79B3 **Kalibo** Phil
98C3 **Kalima** Zaïre
78C3 **Kalimantan** Province, Indon
55C3 **Kálimnos** I Greece
86B1 **Kālimpang** India
60B3 **Kaliningrad** Russian Fed
60C3 **Kalinkovichi** Belarus
8B2 **Kalispell** USA
58B2 **Kalisz** Pol
99D3 **Kaliua** Tanz
38J5 **Kalix** R Sweden
100A3 **Kalkfeld** Namibia
100A3 **Kalkrand** Namibia
108A1 **Kallakoopah** R Aust
38K6 **Kallávesi** L Fin
55C3 **Kallonis Kólpos** B Greece
39H7 **Kalmar** Sweden
61G4 **Kalmykia-Khalmg Tangch** Division, Russian Fed
100B2 **Kalomo** Zambia
18B1 **Kalona** USA
13B2 **Kalone Peak** Mt Can
87A2 **Kalpeni** I India
85D3 **Kālpi** India
53A3 **Kalsat Khasba** Tunisia
12B2 **Kalskag** USA
12C2 **Kaltag** USA
60E3 **Kaluga** Russian Fed
60E3 **Kaluga** Division, Russian Fed
39G7 **Kalundborg** Den
59C3 **Kalush** Ukraine
87B2 **Kalyandurg** India
60E2 **Kalyazin** Russian Fed
61H1 **Kama** R Russian Fed
74E3 **Kamaishi** Japan
84C2 **Kamalia** Pak
110C1 **Kamanawa Mts** NZ
100A2 **Kamanjab** Namibia

84D2 **Kamat** Mt India
87B3 **Kamban** India
61H2 **Kambarka** Russian Fed
97A4 **Kambia** Sierra Leone
59D3 **Kamenets Podolskiy** Ukraine
61F3 **Kamenka** Russian Fed
65K4 **Kamen-na-Obi** Russian Fed
61K2 **Kamensk-Ural'skiy** Russian Fed
5H3 **Kamilukuak L** Can
98C3 **Kamina** Zaïre
7A3 **Kaminak L** Can
75C1 **Kaminoyama** Japan
5F4 **Kamloops** Can
93E1 **Kamo** Armenia
75C1 **Kamogawa** Japan
99D2 **Kampala** Uganda
77C5 **Kampar** Malay
78A2 **Kampar** R Indon
56B2 **Kampen** Neth
76B2 **Kamphaeng Phet** Thai
77C3 **Kampot** Camb
91D4 **Kamsaptar** Iran
61J2 **Kamskoye Vodokhranilishche** Res Russian Fed
85D4 **Kāmthi** India
61G3 **Kamyshin** Russian Fed
61K2 **Kamyshlov** Russian Fed
7C4 **Kanaaupscow** R Can
98C3 **Kananga** Zaïre
61G2 **Kanash** Russian Fed
75B1 **Kanayama** Japan
74D3 **Kanazawa** Japan
4C3 **Kanbisha** USA
87B2 **Kānchipuram** India
84B2 **Kandahar** Afghan
64E3 **Kandalaksha** Russian Fed
38L5 **Kandalakshskaya Guba** B Russian Fed
97C3 **Kandi** Benin
109C2 **Kandos** Aust
87C3 **Kandy** Sri Lanka
15C2 **Kane** USA
6C1 **Kane Basin** B Can
98B1 **Kanem** Desert Region Chad
97B3 **Kangaba** Mali
92C2 **Kangal** Turk
6E3 **Kangâmiut** Greenland
91B4 **Kangān** Iran
77C4 **Kangar** Malay
106C4 **Kangaroo I** Aust
6E3 **Kangâtsiaq** Greenland
90A3 **Kangavar** Iran
72C1 **Kangbao** China
82C3 **Kangchenjunga** Mt Nepal
73A4 **Kangding** China
6G3 **Kangerdlugssuaq** B Greenland
6G3 **Kangerdlugssvatsaiq** B Greenland
99D2 **Kangetet** Kenya
74B2 **Kanggye** N Korea
7D4 **Kangiqsualujjuaq** Can
6C3 **Kangiqsujuaq** Can
7C3 **Kangirsuk** Can
74B3 **Kangnŭng** S Korea
98B2 **Kango** Gabon
68B4 **Kangto** Mt China
72B3 **Kang Xian** China
77D4 **Kanh Hung** Viet
98C3 **Kaniama** Zaïre
87B1 **Kani Giri** India
39J6 **Kankaanpää** Fin
14A2 **Kankakee** USA
14A2 **Kankakee** R USA
97B3 **Kankan** Guinea
86A2 **Kānker** India
87B3 **Kanniyākuman** India
97C3 **Kano** Nig

74C4 **Kanoya** Japan
86A1 **Kānpur** India
9D3 **Kansas** State, USA
18A2 **Kansas** R USA
10A3 **Kansas City** USA
73D5 **Kanshi** China
63B2 **Kansk** Russian Fed
97C3 **Kantchari** Burkina
86B2 **Kanthi** India
12D2 **Kantishna** USA
12D2 **Kantishna** R USA
100B3 **Kanye** Botswana
68D4 **Kao-hsiung** Taiwan
100A2 **Kaoka Veld** Plain Namibia
97A3 **Kaolack** Sen
100B2 **Kaoma** Zambia
21C4 **Kapaau** Hawaiian Is
98C3 **Kapanga** Zaïre
6F3 **Kap Cort Adelaer** C Greenland
6H3 **Kap Dalton** C Greenland
39H7 **Kapellskär** Sweden
6F3 **Kap Farvel** C Greenland
6G3 **Kap Gustav Holm** C Greenland
100B2 **Kapiri** Zambia
78C2 **Kapit** Malay
19B3 **Kaplan** USA
57C3 **Kaplice** Czech Republic
77B4 **Kapoe** Thai
99C3 **Kapona** Zaïre
52C1 **Kaposvár** Hung
6C2 **Kap Parry** C Can
6H3 **Kap Ravn** C Greenland
78B3 **Kapuas** R Indon
108A2 **Kapunda** Aust
84D2 **Kapurthala** India
7B5 **Kapuskasing** Can
109D2 **Kaputar** Mt Aust
93E2 **Kapydzhik** Mt Armenia
6D2 **Kap York** C Greenland
92B1 **Karabük** Turk
55C2 **Karacabey** Turk
61F5 **Karachevo-Cherkesiya** Division, Russian Fed
85B4 **Karachi** Pak
87A1 **Karād** India
60E5 **Kara Daglari** Mt Turk
54C5 **Karadeniz Boğazi** Sd Turk
68D1 **Karaftit** Russian Fed
65J5 **Karaganda** Kazakhstan
65J5 **Karagayly** Kazakhstan
87B2 **Kāraikāl** India
90B2 **Karaj** Iran
92C3 **Karak** Jordan
65G5 **Kara Kalpakskaya Respublika,** Uzbekistan
84D1 **Karakax He** R China
71D3 **Karakelong** I Indon
84D1 **Karakoram** Mts India
84D1 **Karakoram** P India/China
97A3 **Karakoro** R Maur/Sen
65G6 **Karakumy** Desert Russian Fed
94B3 **Karama** Jordan
92B2 **Karaman** Turk
65K5 **Karamay** China
111B2 **Karamea** NZ
111B2 **Karamea Bight** B NZ
85D4 **Kāranja** India
92B2 **Karapinar** Turk
64H2 **Kara S** Russian Fed
100A3 **Karasburg** Namibia
38K5 **Karasjok** Nor
65J4 **Karasuk** Russian Fed
92C2 **Karataş** Turk
65H5 **Kara Tau** Mts Kazakhstan
76B3 **Karathuri** Myan
74B4 **Karatsu** Japan

91B4 **Karāz** Iran
93D3 **Karbalā'** Iraq
59C3 **Karcag** Hung
55B3 **Kardhitsa** Greece
38J5 **Karesvando** Sweden
96B2 **Karet** Desert Region Maur
65K4 **Kargasok** Russian Fed
97D3 **Kari** Nig
100B2 **Kariba** Zim
100B2 **Kariba** L Zim/Zambia
100B2 **Kariba Dam** Zim/Zambia
95C3 **Karima** Sudan
78B3 **Karimata** I Indon
86C2 **Karimganj** Bang
87B1 **Karīmnagar** India
99E1 **Karin** Somalia
39J6 **Karis** Fin
99C3 **Karishimbe** Mt Zaïre
55B3 **Káristos** Greece
87A2 **Kārkal** India
71F4 **Karkar** I PNG
90A3 **Karkheh** R Iran
60D4 **Karkinitskiy Zaliv** B Ukraine
63B3 **Karlik Shan** Mt China
58B2 **Karlino** Pol
52C2 **Karlobag** Croatia
52C1 **Karlovac** Croatia
54B2 **Karlovo** Bulg
57C2 **Karlovy Vary** Czech Republic
39G7 **Karlshamn** Sweden
39G7 **Karlskoga** Sweden
39H7 **Karlskrona** Sweden
57B3 **Karlsruhe** Germany
39G7 **Karlstad** Sweden
12D3 **Karluk** USA
86C2 **Karnafuli Res** Bang
84D3 **Karnal** India
87A1 **Karnataka** State, India
54C2 **Karnobat** Bulg
100B2 **Karoi** Zim
99D3 **Karonga** Malawi
95C3 **Karora** Sudan
78D3 **Karossa** Indon
55C3 **Kárpathos** I Greece
6E2 **Karrats Fjord** Greenland
93D1 **Kars** Turk
65H4 **Karsakpay** Kazakhstan
58D1 **Kārsava** Latvia
80E2 **Karshi** Uzbekistan
38J6 **Karstula** Fin
94B1 **Kartaba** Leb
54C2 **Kartal** Turk
61K3 **Kartaly** Russian Fed
90A3 **Kārūn** R Iran
86A1 **Karwa** India
87A2 **Kārwār** India
68D1 **Karymskoye** Russian Fed
98B3 **Kasai** R Zaïre
100B2 **Kasaji** Zaïre
101C2 **Kasama** Zambia
99D3 **Kasanga** Tanz
87A2 **Kāsaragod** India
5H3 **Kasba L** Can
100B2 **Kasempa** Zambia
100B2 **Kasenga** Zaïre
99D2 **Kasese** Uganda
90B3 **Kāshān** Iran
12C2 **Kashegelok** USA
82B2 **Kashi** China
84D3 **Kāshipur** India
74D3 **Kashiwazaki** Japan
90C2 **Kashmar** Iran
66D3 **Kashmir** State, India
61F3 **Kasimov** Russian Fed
18C2 **Kaskaskia** R USA
38J6 **Kaskinen** Fin
61K2 **Kasli** Russian Fed
5G5 **Kaslo** Can
98C3 **Kasonga** Zaïre
98B3 **Kasongo-Lunda** Zaïre
55C3 **Kásos** I Greece
Kaspiyskiy = Lagan'
95C3 **Kassala** Sudan
56B2 **Kassel** Germany

96C1	**Kasserine** Tunisia
100A2	**Kassinga** Angola
92B1	**Kastamonou** Turk
55B3	**Kastélli** Greece
92A2	**Kastellorizon** *I* Greece
55B2	**Kastoría** Greece
55C3	**Kástron** Greece
74D3	**Kasugai** Japan
75A1	**Kasumi** Japan
101C2	**Kasungu** Malawi
84C2	**Kasur** Pak
100B2	**Kataba** Zambia
98C3	**Katako-kombe** Zaïre
4D3	**Katalla** USA
63G2	**Katangli** Russian Fed
106A4	**Katanning** Aust
55B2	**Katerini** Greece
5E4	**Kates Needle** *Mt* Can/USA
82D3	**Katha** Myan
106C2	**Katherine** Aust
85C4	**Kāthiāwār** *Pen* India
86B1	**Kathmandu** Nepal
84D2	**Kathua** India
86B1	**Katihār** India
100B2	**Katima Mulilo** Namibia
4C4	**Katmai,Mt** USA
12D3	**Katmai Nat Mon** USA
86A2	**Katni** India
109D2	**Katoomba** Aust
59B2	**Katowice** Pol
39H7	**Katrineholm** Sweden
97C3	**Katsina** Nig
97C4	**Katsina Ala** Nig
75C1	**Katsuta** Japan
75C1	**Katsuura** Japan
75B1	**Katsuy** Japan
65H6	**Kattakurgan** Uzbekistan
39G7	**Kattegat** *Str* Den/Sweden
21C4	**Kauai** *I* Hawaiian Is
21C4	**Kauai Chan** Hawaiian Is
21C4	**Kaulakahi Chan** Hawaiian Is
21C4	**Kaunakaki** Hawaiian Is
60B3	**Kaunas** Lithuania
97C3	**Kaura Namoda** Nig
38J5	**Kautokeino** Nor
55B2	**Kavadarci** Macedonia
55A2	**Kavajë** Alb
87B2	**Kavali** India
55B2	**Kaválla** Greece
85B4	**Kāvda** India
75B1	**Kawagoe** Japan
75B1	**Kawaguchi** Japan
110B1	**Kawakawa** NZ
99C3	**Kawambwa** Zambia
86A2	**Kawardha** India
15C2	**Kawartha Lakes** Can
74D3	**Kawasaki** Japan
110C1	**Kawerau** NZ
110B1	**Kawhia** NZ
97B3	**Kaya** Burkina
12F3	**Kayak I** USA
78D2	**Kayan** *R* Indon
87B3	**Kāyankulam** India
97A3	**Kayes** Mali
92C2	**Kayseri** Turk
1B8	**Kazach'ye** Russian Fed
93E1	**Kazakh** Azerbaijan
65G5	**Kazakhstan** Republic, Asia
61G2	**Kazan'** Russian Fed
54C2	**Kazanlŭk** Bulg
69G4	**Kazan Retto** *Is* Japan
91B4	**Kāzerūn** Iran
61H1	**Kazhim** Russian Fed
93E1	**Kazi Magomed** Azerbaijan
59C3	**Kazincbarcika** Hung
55B3	**Kéa** *I* Greece
21C4	**Kealaikahiki Chan** Hawaiian Is
8D2	**Kearney** USA
93C2	**Keban Baraji** *Res* Turk

97A3	**Kébémer** Sen
96C1	**Kebili** Tunisia
94C1	**Kebīr** *R* Leb/Syria
38H5	**Kebrekaise** *Mt* Sweden
59B3	**Kecskemét** Hung
58C1	**Kedainiai** Lithuania
97A3	**Kédougou** Sen
12J2	**Keele** *R* Can
12H2	**Keele Pk** *Mt* Can
21B2	**Keeler** USA
15D2	**Keene** New Hampshire, USA
100A3	**Keetmanshoop** Namibia
18C1	**Keewanee** USA
6A3	**Keewatin** *Region* Can
55B3	**Kefallinía** *I* Greece
94B2	**Kefar Sava** Israel
97C4	**Keffi** Nig
38A2	**Keflavik** Iceland
5G4	**Keg River** Can
76B1	**Kehsi Mansam** Myan
108B3	**Keith** Aust
44C3	**Keith** Scot
4F3	**Keith Arm** *B* Can
6D3	**Kekertuk** Can
85D3	**Kekri** India
77C5	**Kelang** Malay
77C4	**Kelantan** *R* Malay
84B1	**Kelif** Turkmenistan
92C1	**Kelkit** *R* Turk
98B3	**Kellé** Congo
4F2	**Kellet,C** Can
20C1	**Kellogg** USA
64D3	**Kelloselka** Fin
45C2	**Kells** Irish Rep
42B2	**Kells Range** *Hills* Scot
58C1	**Kelme** Lithuania
5G5	**Kelowna** Can
5F4	**Kelsey Bay** Can
42C2	**Kelso** Scot
20B1	**Kelso** USA
64E3	**Kem'** Russian Fed
38L6	**Kem'** *R* Russian Fed
97B3	**Ke Macina** Mali
13B2	**Kemano** Can
65K4	**Kemerovo** Russian Fed
38J5	**Kemi** Fin
38K5	**Kemi** *R* Fin
38K5	**Kemijärvi** Fin
46C1	**Kempen** Region, Belg
26B2	**Kemps Bay** The Bahamas
109D2	**Kempsey** Aust
57C3	**Kempten** Germany
12D2	**Kenai** USA
12D3	**Kenai Mts** USA
12D2	**Kenai Pen** USA
99D2	**Kenamuke Swamp** Sudan
42C2	**Kendal** Eng
109D2	**Kendall** Aust
71D4	**Kendari** Indon
78C3	**Kendawangan** Indon
86B2	**Kendrāpāra** India
20C1	**Kendrick** USA
97A4	**Kenema** Sierra Leone
98B3	**Kenge** Zaïre
76B1	**Kengtung** Myan
100B3	**Kenhardt** S Africa
97A3	**Kéniéba** Mali
96B1	**Kenitra** Mor
45B3	**Kenmare** Irish Rep
45B3	**Kenmare** *R* Irish Rep
19B4	**Kenner** USA
18C2	**Kennett** USA
16B3	**Kennett Square** USA
20C1	**Kennewick** USA
5F4	**Kenny Dam** Can
7A5	**Kenora** Can
10B2	**Kenosha** USA
43E4	**Kent** County, Eng
20B1	**Kent** Washington, USA
14A2	**Kentland** USA
14B2	**Kenton** USA
4H3	**Kent Pen** Can
11B3	**Kentucky** State, USA
11B3	**Kentucky L** USA

19B3	**Kentwood** Louisiana, USA
14A2	**Kentwood** Michigan, USA
99D2	**Kenya** Republic, Africa
	Kenya,Mt = Kirinyaga
18B1	**Keokuk** USA
86A2	**Keonchi** India
86B2	**Keonjhargarh** India
71E4	**Kepaluan Tanimbar** *Arch* Indon
6H3	**Keplavik** Iceland
59B2	**Kepno** Pol
78B2	**Kepulauan Anambas** *Arch* Indon
71E4	**Kepulauan Aru** *Arch* Indon
78B2	**Kepulauan Badas** *Is* Indon
71E4	**Kepulauan Banda** *Arch* Indon
71D4	**Kepulauan Banggai** *I* Indon
78B2	**Kepulauan Bunguran Seletan** *Arch* Indon
71E4	**Kepulauan Kai** *Arch* Indon
71D4	**Kepulauan Leti** *I* Indon
78A3	**Kepulauan Lingga** *Is* Indon
70A4	**Kepulauan Mentawi** *Arch* Indon
78A2	**Kepulauan Riau** *Arch* Indon
78D4	**Kepulauan Sabalana** *Arch* Indon
71D3	**Kepulauan Sangihe** *Arch* Indon
71D4	**Kepulauan Sula** *I* Indon
71D3	**Kepulauan Talaud** *Arch* Indon
78B2	**Kepulauan Tambelan** *Is* Indon
71E4	**Kepulauan Tanimbar** *I* Indon
71D4	**Kepulauan Togian** *I* Indon
71D4	**Kepulauan Tukambesi** *Is* Indon
87B2	**Kerala** State, India
108B3	**Kerang** Aust
39K6	**Kerava** Fin
60E4	**Kerch'** Ukraine
71F4	**Kerema** PNG
20C1	**Keremeps** Can
95C3	**Keren** Eritrea
104B6	**Kerguelen Ridge** Indian O
99D3	**Kericho** Kenya
70B4	**Kerinci** *Mt* Indon
99D2	**Kerio** *R* Kenya
80E2	**Kerki** Turkmenistan
55A3	**Kérkira** Greece
55A3	**Kérkira** *I* Greece
91C3	**Kerman** Iran
22B2	**Kerman** USA
90A3	**Kermānshāh** Iran
21B2	**Kern** *R* USA
13F2	**Kerrobert** Can
45B2	**Kerry** County, Irish Rep
17B1	**Kershaw** USA
78B3	**Kertamulia** Indon
63D3	**Kerulen** *R* Mongolia
96B2	**Kerzaz** Alg
55C2	**Keşan** Turk
74E3	**Kesennuma** Japan
38L5	**Kesten 'ga** Russian Fed
42C2	**Keswick** Eng
65K4	**Ket** *R* Russian Fed
97C4	**Kéta** Ghana
78C3	**Ketapang** Indon
5E4	**Ketchikan** USA
97C3	**Ketia** Niger
85B4	**Keti Bandar** Pak
58C2	**Kętrzyn** Pol
43D3	**Kettering** Eng
14B3	**Kettering** USA
20C1	**Kettle** *R* Can

20C1	**Kettle River Range** *Mts* USA
7C3	**Kettlestone B** Can
90C3	**Kevir-i Namak** *Salt Flat* Iran
14A2	**Kewaunee** USA
14B1	**Key Harbour** Can
17B2	**Key Largo** USA
11B4	**Key West** USA
63C2	**Kezhma** Russian Fed
54A1	**K'fetegháza** Hung
12B2	**Kgun L** USA
94C2	**Khabab** Syria
62H3	**Khabarovsk** Russian Fed
85B3	**Khairpur** Pak
85B3	**Khairpur** Region, Pak
100B3	**Khakhea** Botswana
55C3	**Khálki** *I* Greece
55B2	**Khalkidhíki** *Pen* Greece
55B3	**Khalkís** Greece
61G2	**Khalturin** Russian Fed
85C4	**Khambhāt,G of** India
85D4	**Khāmgaon** India
76C2	**Kham Keut** Laos
87C1	**Khammam** India
90A2	**Khamseh** *Mts* Iran
76C2	**Khan** *R* Laos
84B1	**Khanabad** Afghan
93E3	**Khānaqin** Iraq
85D4	**Khandwa** India
84C2	**Khanewal** Pak
94C3	**Khan ez Zabib** Jordan
77D4	**Khanh Hung** Viet
55B3	**Khaniá** Greece
84C3	**Khanpur** Pak
65H3	**Khanty-Mansiysk** Russian Fed
94B3	**Khan Yunis** Egypt
84D1	**Khapalu** India
68C2	**Khapcheranga** Russian Fed
61G4	**Kharabali** Russian Fed
86B2	**Kharagpur** India
91C4	**Khāran** Iran
84B3	**Bharan** Pak
90B3	**Kharānaq** Iran
91B4	**Khārg** *Is* Iran
95C2	**Khârga Oasis** Egypt
85D4	**Khargon** India
60E4	**Khar'kov** Ukraine
54C2	**Kharmanli** Bulg
61F2	**Kharovsk** Russian Fed
95C3	**Khartoum** Sudan
95C3	**Khartoum North** Sudan
74C2	**Khasan** Russian Fed
95C3	**Khashm el Girba** Sudan
86C1	**Khasi-Jaīntīa Hills** India
54C2	**Khaskovo** Bulg
1B9	**Khatanga** Russian Fed
76B3	**Khawsa** Myan
76C2	**Khe Bo** Viet
85C4	**Khed Brahma** India
51C2	**Khemis** Alg
96B1	**Khenifra** Mor
51D2	**Kherrata** Alg
60D4	**Kherson** Ukraine
63D2	**Khilok** Russian Fed
55C3	**Khios** Greece
55C3	**Khíos** *I* Greece
60C4	**Khmel'nitskiy** Ukraine
59C3	**Khodorov** Ukraine
84B1	**Kholm** Afghan
76D3	**Khong** Laos
91B4	**Khonj** Iran
69F2	**Khor** Russian Fed
91A3	**Khorramshahr** Iran
91B5	**Khōr Duwayhin** *B* UAE
84C1	**Khorog** Tajikistan
90A3	**Khorramābad** Iran
90C3	**Khosf** Iran
84B2	**Khost** Pak

Khotin

60C4 **Khotin** Ukraine
12C2 **Khotol** *Mt* USA
60C3 **Khoyniki** Belarus
63F2 **Khrebet Dzhugdzhur**
    Mts Russian Fed
90C2 **Khrebet Kopet Dag**
    Mts Turkmenistan
64H3 **Khrebet Pay-khoy**
    Mts Russian Fed
82C1 **Khrebet Tarbagatay**
    Mts Kazakhstan
63E2 **Khrebet Tukuringra**
    Mts Russian Fed
82A1 **Khudzhand**
    Tajikistan
86B2 **Khulna** Bang
84D1 **Khunjerab** *P* China/
    India
90B3 **Khunsar** Iran
91A4 **Khurays** S Arabia
86B2 **Khurda** India
84D3 **Khurja** India
84C2 **Khushab** Pak
94B2 **Khushniyah** Syria
59C3 **Khust** Ukraine
99C1 **Khuwei** Sudan
85B3 **Khuzdar** Pak
90D3 **Khvāf** Iran
61G3 **Khvalynsk**
    Russian Fed
90C3 **Khvor** Iran
91B4 **Khvormūj** Iran
93D2 **Khvoy** Iran
84C1 **Khwaja Muhammad**
    Mts Afghan
84C2 **Khyber P** Afghan/Pak
99C3 **Kiambi** Zaire
19A3 **Kiamichi** *R* USA
12B1 **Kiana** USA
98B3 **Kibangou** Congo
99D3 **Kibaya** Tanz
98C3 **Kibombo** Zaire
99D3 **Kibondo** Tanz
99D3 **Kibungu** Rwanda
55B2 **Kičevo** Macedonia
5G4 **Kicking Horse P** Can
97C3 **Kidal** Mali
43C3 **Kidderminster** Eng
97A3 **Kidira** Sen
110C1 **Kidnappers,C** NZ
56C2 **Kiel** Germany
59C2 **Kielce** Pol
56C2 **Kieler Bucht** *B*
    Germany
Kiev = Kiyev
80E2 **Kifab** Uzbekistan
97A3 **Kiffa** Maur
89H8 **Kigali** Rwanda
12A2 **Kigluaik Mts** USA
99C3 **Kigoma** Tanz
75B2 **Kii-sanchi** *Mts* Japan
74C4 **Kii-suido** *B* Japan
54B1 **Kikinda** Serbia,
    Yugos
55B3 **Kikládhes** *Is* Greece
71F4 **Kikori** PNG
98B3 **Kikwit** Zaire
21C4 **Kilauea Crater** *Mt*
    Hawaiian Is
4C3 **Kilbuck Mts** USA
74B2 **Kilchu** N Korea
109D1 **Kilcoy** Aust
45C2 **Kildare** County,
    Irish Rep
45C2 **Kildare** Irish Rep
19B3 **Kilgore** USA
99D3 **Kilifi** Kenya
99D3 **Kilimanjaro** *Mt* Tanz
99D3 **Kilindoni** Tanz
92C2 **Kilis** Turk
45B2 **Kilkee** Irish Rep
45C2 **Kilkenny** County,
    Irish Rep
45C2 **Kilkenny** Irish Rep
45B2 **Kilkieran B** Irish Rep
55B2 **Kilkis** Greece
45B1 **Killala B** Irish Rep
45B2 **Killaloe** Irish Rep
109D1 **Killarney** Aust
41B3 **Killarney** Irish Rep
19A3 **Killeen** USA
12D1 **Killik** *R* USA
44B3 **Killin** Scot
55B3 **Killíni** *Mt* Greece

45B1 **Killybegs** Irish Rep
42B2 **Kilmarnock** Scot
61H2 **Kil'mez** Russian Fed
99D3 **Kilosa** Tanz
41B3 **Kilrush** Irish Rep
99C3 **Kilwa** Zaire
99D3 **Kilwa Kisiwani** Tanz
99D3 **Kilwa Kivinje** Tanz
108A2 **Kimba** Aust
12F2 **Kimball,Mt** USA
13D3 **Kimberley** Can
101F1 **Kimberley** S Africa
106B2 **Kimberley Plat** Aust
74B2 **Kimch'aek** N Korea
74B3 **Kimch'ŏn** S Korea
55B3 **Kími** Greece
60E2 **Kimry** Russian Fed
70C3 **Kinabalu** *Mt* Malay
78D1 **Kinabatangan** *R*
    Malay
14B2 **Kincardine** Can
13B1 **Kincolith** Can
19B3 **Kinder** USA
13F2 **Kindersley** Can
97A3 **Kindia** Guinea
98C3 **Kindu** Zaire
61H3 **Kinel'** Russian Fed
61F2 **Kineshma**
    Russian Fed
109D1 **Kingaroy** Aust
21A2 **King City** USA
5F4 **Kingcome Inlet** Can
7C4 **King George Is** Can
107D4 **King I** Aust
13B2 **King I** Can
106B2 **King Leopold Range**
    Mts Aust
9B3 **Kingman** USA
98C3 **Kingombe** Zaire
108A2 **Kingoonya** Aust
22C2 **Kingsburg** USA
21B2 **Kings Canyon Nat Pk**
    USA
108A3 **Kingscote** Aust
106B2 **King Sd** Aust
112C2 **King Sejong** *Base*
    Ant
14A1 **Kingsford** USA
17B1 **Kingsland** USA
43E3 **King's Lynn** Eng
16C2 **Kings Park** USA
8B2 **Kings Peak** *Mt* USA
107C4 **Kingston** Aust
7C5 **Kingston** Can
25E3 **Kingston** Jamaica
15D2 **Kingston** New York,
    USA
111A3 **Kingston** NZ
42D3 **Kingston upon Hull**
    County Eng
27E4 **Kingstown**
    St Vincent and the
    Grenadines
9D4 **Kingsville** USA
44B3 **Kingussie** Scot
4J3 **King William I** Can
100B4 **King William's Town**
    S Africa
98B3 **Kinkala** Congo
39G7 **Kinna** Sweden
44D3 **Kinnairds Head** *Pt*
    Scot
75B1 **Kinomoto** Japan
44C3 **Kinross** Scot
45B3 **Kinsale** Irish Rep
98B3 **Kinshasa** Zaire
78D3 **Kintap** Indon
42B2 **Kintyre** *Pen* Scot
13D1 **Kinuso** Can
99D2 **Kinyeti** *Mt* Sudan
55B3 **Kiparissía** Greece
55B3 **Kiparissiakós Kólpos**
    G Greece
15C1 **Kipawa,L** Can
99D3 **Kipili** Tanz
12B3 **Kipnuk** USA
45C2 **Kippure** *Mt* Irish Rep
100B2 **Kipushi** Zaire
63C2 **Kirensk** Russian Fed
Kirghizia =
    Kyrgyzstan
82B1 **Kirgizskiy Khrebet**
    Mts Kyrgyzstan
98B3 **Kiri** Zaire

105G4 **Kiribati** *Is* Pacific O
92B2 **Kırıkkale** Turk
99D3 **Kirinyaga** *Mt* Kenya
60D2 **Kirishi** Russian Fed
85B3 **Kirithar Range** *Mts*
    Pak
55C3 **Kirkağaç** Turk
90A2 **Kirk Bulāg Dāgh** *Mt*
    Iran
42C2 **Kirkby** Eng
44C3 **Kirkcaldy** Scot
42B2 **Kirkcudbright** Scot
38K5 **Kirkenes** Nor
7B5 **Kirkland Lake** Can
112A **Kirkpatrick,Mt** Ant
10A2 **Kirksville** USA
93D2 **Kirkūk** Iraq
44C2 **Kirkwall** Scot
18B2 **Kirkwood** USA
60D3 **Kirov** Russian Fed
61G2 **Kirov** Russian Fed
61G2 **Kirov** Division,
    Russian Fed
93D1 **Kirovakan** Armenia
61J2 **Kirovgrad**
    Russian Fed
60D4 **Kirovograd** Ukraine
61H2 **Kirs** Russian Fed
92B2 **Kirşehir** Turk
56C2 **Kiruna** Sweden
75B1 **Kiryū** Japan
98C2 **Kisangani** Zaire
75B1 **Kisarazu** Japan
86B1 **Kishanganj** India
85C3 **Kishangarh** India
60C4 **Kishinev** Moldova
75B2 **Kishiwada** Japan
99D3 **Kisii** Kenya
99D3 **Kisiju** Tanz
59B3 **Kiskunhalas** Hung
65F5 **Kislovodsk**
    Russian Fed
99E3 **Kismaayo** Somalia
75B1 **Kiso-sammyaku** *Mts*
    Japan
97A4 **Kissidougou** Guinea
17B2 **Kissimmee,L** USA
99D3 **Kisumu** Kenya
59C3 **Kisvárda** Hung
97B3 **Kita** Mali
65H6 **Kitab** Uzbekistan
75C1 **Kitakata** Japan
74C4 **Kita-Kyūshū** Japan
99D2 **Kitale** Kenya
69G4 **Kitalo** *I* Japan
74E2 **Kitami** Japan
7B5 **Kitchener** Can
99D2 **Kitgum** Uganda
55B3 **Kíthira** *I* Greece
55B3 **Kíthnos** *I* Greece
94A1 **Kiti,C** Cyprus
4H3 **Kitikmeot** *Region*
    Can
5F4 **Kitimat** Can
38K5 **Kitnen** *R* Fin
75A2 **Kitsuki** Japan
15C2 **Kittanning** USA
38J5 **Kittilä** Fin
99D3 **Kitunda** Tanz
13B1 **Kitwanga** Can
100B2 **Kitwe** Zambia
57C3 **Kitzbühel** Austria
47E1 **Kitzbühler Alpen** *Mts*
    Austria
57C3 **Kitzingen** Germany
98C3 **Kiumbi** Zaire
12B1 **Kivalina** USA
59D2 **Kivercy** Ukraine
99C3 **Kivu,L** Zaire/Rwanda
4B3 **Kiwalik** USA
60D3 **Kiyev** Ukraine
61J2 **Kizel** Russian Fed
92C2 **Kizil** *R* Turk
80D2 **Kizyl-Arvat**
    Turkmenistan
90B2 **Kizyl-Atrek**
    Turkmenistan
57C2 **Kladno**
    Czech Republic
57C3 **Klagenfurt** Austria
60B2 **Klaipėda** Lithuania
8A2 **Klamath** USA
20B2 **Klamath** USA
8A2 **Klamath Falls** USA

20B2 **Klamath Mts** USA
57C3 **Klatovy**
    Czech Republic
12H3 **Klawak** USA
94B1 **Kleiat** Leb
101G1 **Klerksdorp** S Africa
60E2 **Klin** Russian Fed
58B1 **Klintehamn** Sweden
60D3 **Klintsy** Russian Fed
52C2 **Ključ** Bosnia-
    Herzegovina
59B2 **Klodzko** Pol
12G2 **Klondike** *R* Can/USA
4D3 **Klondike Plat** Can/
    USA
59B3 **Klosterneuburg**
    Austria
12G2 **Kluane** *R* Can
12G2 **Kluane L** Can
12G2 **Kluane Nat Pk** Can
59B2 **Kluczbork** Pol
12G3 **Klukwan** USA
12E2 **Klutina L** USA
12E2 **Knight I** USA
43C3 **Knighton** Wales
52C2 **Knin** Croatia
106A4 **Knob,C** Aust
46B1 **Knokke-Heist** Belg
112C9 **Knox Coast** Ant
11B3 **Knoxville** Tennessee,
    USA
6H3 **Knud Ramsussens**
    Land *Region*
    Greenland
78B3 **Koba** Indon
6F3 **Kobbermirebugt**
    Greenland
74D4 **Kobe** Japan
56C1 **København** Den
57B2 **Koblenz** Germany
60B3 **Kobrin** Russian Fed
71E4 **Kobroör** *I* Indon
12C1 **Kobuk** *R* USA
54B2 **Kočani** Macedonia
76C3 **Ko Chang** *I* Thai
86B1 **Koch Bihār** India
47D1 **Kochel** Germany
6C3 **Koch I** Can
Kochi = Cochin
74C4 **Kōchi** Japan
12D3 **Kodiak** USA
12D3 **Kodiak I** USA
87B2 **Kodiyakkari** India
99D2 **Kodok** Sudan
100A3 **Koes** Namibia
101G1 **Koffiefontein** S Africa
97B4 **Koforidua** Ghana
74D3 **Kōfu** Japan
75B1 **Koga** Japan
39G7 **Køge** Den
84C2 **Kohat** Pak
84B2 **Koh-i-Baba** *Mts*
    Afghan
84B1 **Koh-i-Hisar** *Mts*
    Afghan
84B2 **Koh-i-Khurd** *Mt*
    Afghan
86C1 **Kohima** India
84B1 **Koh-i-Mazar** *Mt*
    Afghan
84B3 **Kohlu** Pak
60C2 **Kohtla Järve** Estonia
75B1 **Koide** Japan
12F2 **Koidern** Can
77A4 **Koihoa** *Is* Nicobar Is
74B4 **Kŏje-do** *I* S Korea
65H4 **Kokchetav**
    Kazakhstan
39J6 **Kokemaki** *L* Fin
38J6 **Kokkola** Fin
107D1 **Kokoda** PNG
14A2 **Kokomo** USA
71E4 **Kokonau** Indon
65K5 **Kokpekty** Kazakhstan
7D4 **Koksoak** *R* Can
100B4 **Kokstad** S Africa
76C3 **Ko Kut** *I* Thai
38L5 **Kola** Russian Fed
71D4 **Kolaka** Indon
77B4 **Ko Lanta** *I* Thai
Kollam = Quilon
87B2 **Kolār** India
87B2 **Kolār Gold Fields**
    India

23B1	Laguna de Pueblo Viejo *L* Mexico
24C2	Laguna de Tamiahua *Lg* Mexico
25C3	Laguna de Términos *Lg* Mexico
23A1	Laguna de Yuriria *L* Mexico
23B1	Laguna le Altamira Mexico
24C2	Laguna Madre *Lg* Mexico
34C2	Laguna Mar Chiquita *L* Arg
29B4	Laguna Nahuel Huapi *L* Arg
34C2	Laguna Paiva Arg
29B4	Laguna Ranco Chile
9C4	Laguna Seca Mexico
23B1	Laguna Tortugas *L* Mexico
70C3	Lahad Datu Malay
78A3	Lahat Indon
38J6	Lahia Fin
90B2	Lāhijān Iran
46D1	Lahn *R* Germany
46D1	Lahnstein Germany
84C2	Lahore Pak
39K6	Lahti Fin
23A2	La Huerta Mexico
98B2	Lai Chad
73B5	Laibin China
76C1	Lai Chau Viet
100B4	Laingsburg S Africa
44B2	Lairg Scot
78A3	Lais Indon
79C4	Lais Phil
72E2	Laiyang China
72D2	Laizhou Wan *B* China
34A3	Laja *R* Chile
30F4	Lajes Brazil
22D4	La Jolla USA
9C3	La Junta USA
109C2	Lake Cargelligo Aust
11A3	Lake Charles USA
17B1	Lake City Florida, USA
17C1	Lake City S Carolina, USA
42C2	Lake District Region, Eng
22D4	Lake Elsinore USA
106C3	Lake Eyre Basin Aust
15C2	Lakefield Can
6D3	Lake Harbour Can
22C3	Lake Hughes USA
16B2	Lakehurst USA
19A4	Lake Jackson USA
13E2	Lake la Biche Can
17B2	Lakeland USA
7A5	Lake of the Woods Can
20B1	Lake Oswego USA
21A2	Lakeport USA
19B3	Lake Providence USA
111B2	Lake Pukaki NZ
109C3	Lakes Entrance Aust
22C2	Lakeshore USA
108B1	Lake Stewart Aust
15C1	Lake Traverse Can
8A2	Lakeview USA
20B1	Lakeview Mt Can
19B3	Lake Village USA
17B2	Lake Wales USA
22C4	Lakewood California, USA
16B2	Lakewood New Jersey, USA
14B2	Lakewood Ohio, USA
17B2	Lake Worth USA
86A1	Lakhimpur India
85B4	Lakhpat India
84C2	Lakki Pak
55B3	Lakonikós Kólpos *G* Greece
97B4	Lakota Côte d'Ivoire
38K4	Laksefjord *Inlet* Nor
38K4	Lakselv Nor
34C2	La Laguna Arg
32A4	La Libertad Ecuador
34A2	La Ligua Chile

50A2	La Linea Spain
85D4	Lalitpur India
5H4	La Loche Can
13F1	la Loche,L Can
46C1	La Louvière Belg
26A4	La Luz Nic
7C5	La Malbaie Can
23B2	La Malinche *Mt* Mexico
50B2	La Mancha Region, Spain
9C3	Lamar Colorado, USA
18B2	Lamar Missouri, USA
19A4	La Marque USA
98B3	Lambaréné Gabon
32A5	Lambayeque Peru
112B10	Lambert Gl Ant
16B2	Lambertville USA
4F2	Lamblon,C Can
47C2	Lambro *R* Italy
76C2	Lam Chi *R* Thai
50A1	Lamego Port
47B2	La Meije *Mt* France
32B6	La Merced Peru
21B3	La Mesa USA
55B3	Lamia Greece
42C2	Lammermuir Hills Scot
39G7	Lammhult Sweden
79B3	Lamon B Phil
18B1	Lamoni USA
71F3	Lamotrek *I* Pacific O
43B3	Lampeter Wales
99E3	Lamu Kenya
47D1	Lana Italy
21C4	Lanai *I* Hawaiian Is
21C4	Lanai City Hawaiian Is
42C2	Lanark Scot
76B3	Lanbi *I* Myan
76C1	Lancang *R* China
42C3	Lancashire County, Eng
21B3	Lancaster California, USA
42C2	Lancaster Eng
18B1	Lancaster Mississippi, USA
15D2	Lancaster New Hampshire, USA
14B3	Lancaster Ohio, USA
10C3	Lancaster Pennsylvania, USA
17B1	Lancaster S Carolina, USA
6B2	Lancaster Sd Can
78B3	Landak *R* Indon
46E2	Landan Germany
57C3	Landeck Austria
8C2	Lander USA
34C2	Landeta Arg
57C3	Landsberg Germany
4F2	Lands End *C* Can
43B4	Land's End *Pt* Eng
57C3	Landshut Germany
39G7	Landskrona Sweden
17A1	Lanett USA
56B2	Langenhagen Germany
47B1	Langenthal Switz
42C2	Langholm Scot
38A2	Langjökull *Mts* Iceland
77B4	Langkawi *I* Malay
13C3	Langley Can
108C1	Langlo *R* Aust
47B1	Langnau Switz
49D2	Langres France
70A3	langsa Indon
68C2	Lang Shan *Mts* China
76D1	Lang Son Viet
48C3	Languedoc Region, France
29B3	Lanin *Mt* Arg
79B4	Lanoa,L *L* Phil
16B2	Lansdale USA
7B4	Lansdowne House Can
16B2	Lansford USA
10B2	Lansing USA
47B2	Lanslebourg France

96A2	Lanzarote *I* Canary Is
72A2	Lanzhou China
47B2	Lanzo Torinese Italy
79B2	Laoag Phil
76C1	Lao Cai Viet
72D1	Laoha He *R* China
45C2	Laois County, Irish Rep
46B2	Laon France
32B6	La Oroya Peru
76C2	Laos Republic, S E Asia
49C2	Lapalisse France
32B2	La Palma Panama
96A2	La Palma *I* Canary Is
34B3	La Pampa State, Arg
33E2	La Paragua Ven
29E2	La Paz Arg
34B2	La Paz Arg
30C2	La Paz Bol
24A2	La Paz Mexico
69G2	La Perouse Str Japan/Russian Fed
23A1	La Piedad Mexico
20B2	La Pine USA
19B3	Laplace USA
23A2	la Placita Mexico
29E2	La Plata Arg
13F1	La Plonge,L Can
14A2	La Porte USA
39K6	Lappeenranta Fin
38H5	Lappland Region Sweden/Fin
34C3	Laprida Arg
1B8	Laptev S Russian Fed
38J6	Lapua Fin
79B3	Lapu-Lapu Phil
9B4	La Purisma Mexico
95B2	Laqiya Arba'in Well Sudan
30C3	La Quiaca Arg
52B2	L'Aquila Italy
91B4	Lār Iran
96B1	Larache Mor
8C2	Laramie USA
8C2	Laramie Range *Mts* USA
50B2	Larca Spain
9D4	Laredo USA
91B4	Larestan Region, Iran
	Largeau = Faya
47B2	L'Argentière France
17B2	Largo USA
42B2	Largs Scot
90A2	Lāri Iran
30C4	La Rioja Arg
30C4	La Rioja State, Arg
55B3	Lárisa Greece
85B3	Larkana Pak
92B3	Larnaca Cyprus
94A1	Larnaca B Cyprus
45D1	Larne N Ire
50A1	La Robla Spain
46C1	La Roche-en-Ardenne Belg
48B2	La Rochelle France
47B1	La Roche-sur-Foron France
48B2	La Roche-sur-Yon France
51B2	La Roda Spain
27D3	La Romana Dom Rep
5H4	La Ronge Can
5H4	La Ronge,L Can
39F7	Larvik Nor
65J3	Laryak Russian Fed
50B2	La Sagra *Mt* Spain
15D1	La Salle Can
18C1	La Salle USA
7C5	La Sarre Can
34C1	Las Avispas Arg
34A2	Las Cabras Chile
5G4	Lascombe Can
9C3	Las Cruces USA
26C3	La Selle *Mt* Haiti
72B2	Lasengmia China
30B4	La Serena Chile
29E3	Las Flores Arg
76B1	Lashio Myan
53C3	La Sila *Mts* Italy
90B2	Lāsjerd Iran
34A3	Las Lajas Chile

50A2	Las Marismas Marshland Spain
96A2	Las Palmas de Gran Canaria Canary Is
52A2	La Spezia Italy
29C4	Las Plumas Arg
34C2	Las Rosas Arg
20B2	Lassen Peak *Mt* USA
20B2	Lassen Volcanic Nat Pk USA
23B2	las Tinai Mexico
98B3	Lastoursville Gabon
52C2	Lastovo *I* Croatia
24B2	Las Tres Marias *Is* Mexico
34C2	Las Varillas Arg
9C3	Las Vegas USA
	Latakia = Al Lādhiqiyah
53B2	Latina Italy
34B2	La Toma Arg
32D1	La Tortuga *I* Ven
79B2	La Trinidad Phil
109C4	Latrobe Aust
94B3	Latrun Israel
7C5	La Tuque Can
87B1	Lātūr India
60B2	Latvia Republic, Europe
107D5	Launceston Aust
43B4	Launceston Eng
29B4	La Unión Chile
25D3	La Union El Salvador
23A2	La Union Mexico
32B5	La Unión Peru
107D2	Laura Aust
15C3	Laurel Delaware, USA
16A3	Laurel Maryland, USA
11B3	Laurel Mississippi, USA
17B1	Laurens USA
17C1	Laurinburg USA
52A1	Lausanne Switz
78D3	Laut *I* Indon
29B5	Lautaro *Mt* Chile
46D2	Lauterecken Germany
15D1	Laval Can
48B2	Laval France
22B2	Laveaga Peak *Mt* USA
47C2	Laveno Italy
31B6	Lavras Brazil
4A3	Lavrentiya Russian Fed
101H1	Lavumisa Swaziland
78D1	Lawas Malay
76B1	Lawksawk Myan
18A2	Lawrence Kansas, USA
15D2	Lawrence Massachusetts, USA
111A3	Lawrence NZ
14A3	Lawrenceville Illinois, USA
9D3	Lawton USA
91A5	Layla S Arabia
99D2	Laylo Sudan
23A2	Lázaro Cárdenas Mexico
99E1	Laz Daua Somalia
79B4	Lazi Phil
8C2	Lead USA
13F2	Leader Can
18A2	Leavenworth USA
58B2	Leba Pol
18B2	Lebanon Missouri, USA
20B2	Lebanon Oregon, USA
15C2	Lebanon Pennsylvania, USA
92C3	Lebanon Republic, S W Asia
101C3	Lebombo *Mts* Mozam/S Africa/ Swaziland
58B2	Lebork Pol
47A2	Le Bourg-d'Oisans France
47B1	Le Brassus Switz
29B3	Lebu Chile

Le Buet

47B1 **Le Buet** Mt France	16C1 **Lenox** USA	8C2 **Lewistown** Montana, USA	13C2 **Lillooet** R Can
46B1 **Le Cateau** France	46B1 **Lens** France	15C2 **Lewistown** Pennsylvania, USA	101C2 **Lilongwe** Malawi
55A2 **Lecce** Italy	63D1 **Lensk** Russian Fed	19B3 **Lewisville** USA	79B4 **Liloy** Phil
52A1 **Lecco** Italy	53B3 **Lentini** Italy	11B3 **Lexington** Kentucky, USA	54A2 **Lim** R Montenegro/Serbia, Yugos
47D1 **Lech** R Austria	76B3 **Lenya** R Myan	18B2 **Lexington** Missouri, USA	32B6 **Lima** Peru
47D1 **Lechtaler Alpen** Mts Austria	52B1 **Leoben** Austria	15C3 **Lexington Park** USA	50A1 **Lima** Spain
49C2 **Le Creusot** France	43C3 **Leominster** Eng	79C3 **Leyte G** Phil	10B2 **Lima** USA
43C3 **Ledbury** Eng	16D1 **Leominster** USA	54A2 **Lezhe** Alb	92B3 **Limassol** Cyprus
13E2 **Leduc** Can	24B2 **Leon** Mexico	82D3 **Lhasa** China	45C1 **Limavady** N Ire
16C1 **Lee** USA	25D3 **León** Nic	86B1 **Lhazê** China	34B3 **Limay** R Arg
45B3 **Lee** R Irish Rep	50A1 **Leon** Region, Spain	70A3 **Lhokseumawe** Indon	34B3 **Limay Mahuida** Arg
41C3 **Leeds** Eng	50A1 **León** Spain	86C1 **Lhozhag** China	98A2 **Limbe** Cam
43C3 **Leek** Eng	100A3 **Leonardville** Namibia	68B4 **Lhunze** China	101C2 **Limbe** Malawi
56B2 **Leer** Germany	106B3 **Leonora** Aust	**Liancourt Rocks** = Tok-do	57B2 **Limburg** W Gem
17B2 **Leesburg** Florida, USA	35C2 **Leopoldina** Brazil	79C4 **Lianga** Phil	31B6 **Limeira** Brazil
16A3 **Leesburg** Virginia, USA	**Léopoldville** = Kinshasa	72B3 **Liangdang** China	45B2 **Limerick** County, Irish Rep
19B3 **Leesville** USA	60C3 **Lepel** Belarus	73C5 **Lianjiang** China	41B3 **Limerick** Irish Rep
109C2 **Leeton** Aust	73D4 **Leping** China	73C5 **Lianping** China	56B1 **Limfjorden** L Den
56B2 **Leeuwarden** Neth	49C2 **Le Puy-en-Velay** France	73C5 **Lian Xian** China	106C2 **Limmen Bight** B Aust
106A4 **Leeuwin,C** Aust	98B2 **Léré** Chad	72D3 **Lianyungang** China	55C3 **Límnos** I Greece
22C2 **Lee Vining** USA	101G1 **Leribe** Lesotho	72E1 **Liaoding Bandao** Pen China	31D3 **Limoeiro** Brazil
27E3 **Leeward Is** Caribbean S	47C2 **Lerici** Italy	72E1 **Liaodong Wan** B China	48C2 **Limoges** France
94A1 **Lefkara** Cyprus	51C1 **Lérida** Spain	72E1 **Liao He** R China	25D4 **Limón** Costa Rica
79B3 **Legazpi** Phil	23A1 **Lerma** R Mexico	72E1 **Liaoning** Province, China	8C3 **Limon** USA
47D2 **Legnago** Italy	47D1 **Lermoos** Austria	72E1 **Liaoyang** China	48C2 **Limousin** Region, France
59B2 **Legnica** Pol	55C3 **Léros** I Greece	72E1 **Liaoyuan** China	79A3 **Linapacan Str** Phil
33F2 **Leguan Inlet** Guyana	44E1 **Lerwick** Scot	74B2 **Liaoyuang** China	29B3 **Linares** Chile
32C4 **Leguizamo** Colombia	46A2 **Les Andelys** France	4F3 **Liard** R Can	9D4 **Linares** Mexico
84D2 **Leh** India	26C3 **Les Cayes** Haiti	4F4 **Liard River** Can	50B2 **Linares** Spain
48C2 **Le havre** France	47B2 **Les Ecrins** Mt France	46C2 **Liart** France	68B4 **Lincang** China
16B2 **Lehigh** R USA	73A4 **Leshan** China	98B2 **Libenge** Zaire	29D2 **Lincoln** Arg
16B2 **Lehighton** USA	54B2 **Leskovac** Serbia, Yugos	9C3 **Liberal** USA	18A1 **Lincoln** California, USA
84C2 **Leiah** Pak	48B3 **Les Landes** Region, France	57C2 **Liberec** Czech Republic	42D3 **Lincoln** County, Eng
59B3 **Leibnitz** Austria	101G1 **Leslie** S Africa	97A4 **Liberia** Republic, Africa	42D3 **Lincoln** Eng
43D3 **Leicester** County, Eng	61H2 **Lesnoy** Russian Fed	18B2 **Liberty** Missouri, USA	18C1 **Lincoln** Illinois, USA
43D3 **Leicester** Eng	63B2 **Lesosibirsk** Russian Fed	15D2 **Liberty** New York, USA	8D2 **Lincoln** Nebraska, USA
107C2 **Leichhardt** R Aust	101G1 **Lesotho** Kingdom, S Africa	19B3 **Liberty** Texas, USA	15D2 **Lincoln** New Hampshire, USA
56A2 **Leiden** Neth	69F2 **Lesozavodsk** Russian Fed	48B3 **Libourne** France	111B2 **Lincoln** NZ
46B1 **Leie** R Belg	48B2 **Les Sables-d'Olonne** France	23B2 **Libres** Mexico	80A **Lincoln** S Greenland
106C4 **Leigh Creek** Aust	112A **Lesser Antarctica** Region, Ant	98A2 **Libreville** Gabon	20B2 **Lincoln City** USA
43D4 **Leighton Buzzard** Eng	27D4 **Lesser Antilles** Is Caribbean S	95A2 **Libya** Republic, Africa	14B2 **Lincoln Park** USA
56B2 **Leine** R Germany	65F5 **Lesser Caucasus** Mts Azerbaijan/Georgia	95B2 **Libyan Desert** Libya	52A2 **L'Incudina** Mt Corse
45C2 **Leinster** Region, Irish Rep	13E1 **Lesser Slave L** Can	95B1 **Libyan Plat** Egypt	57B3 **Lindau** Germany
57C2 **Leipzig** Germany	55C3 **Lésvos** I Greece	53B3 **Licata** Italy	33F2 **Linden** Guyana
50A2 **Leiria** Port	58B2 **Leszno** Pol	43D3 **Lichfield** Eng	39F7 **Lindesnes** C Nor
39F7 **Leirvik** Nor	86C2 **Letha Range** Mts Myan	101C2 **Lichinga** Mozam	99D3 **Lindi** Tanz
45B1 **Leitrim** County, Irish Rep	5G5 **Lethbridge** Can	101G1 **Lichtenburg** S Africa	98C2 **Lindi** R Zaire
73C4 **Leiyang** China	33F3 **Lethem** Guyana	14B3 **Licking** R USA	101G1 **Lindley** S Africa
73B5 **Leizhou Bandao** Pen China	59D3 **Letichev** Ukraine	22B2 **Lick Observatory** USA	55C3 **Lindos** Greece
73C5 **Leizhou Wan** B China	63D2 **Let Oktyobr'ya** Russian Fed	60C3 **Lida** Belarus	15C2 **Lindsay** Can
56A2 **Lek** R Neth	78B2 **Letong** Indon	39G7 **Lidköping** Sweden	105J3 **Line Is** Pacific O
96C1 **Le Kef** Tunisia	46A1 **Le Touquet-Paris-Plage** France	53B2 **Lido di Ostia** Italy	72C2 **Linfen** China
19B3 **Leland** USA	76B2 **Letpadan** Myan	52A1 **Liechtenstein** Principality, Europe	76D2 **Lingao** China
54A2 **Lelija** Mt Bosnia-Herzegovina	48C1 **Le Tréport** France	57B2 **Liège** Belg	79B2 **Lingayen** Phil
47B1 **Le Locle** France	47B1 **Leuk** Switz	58C1 **Lielupe** R Latvia	56B2 **Lingen** Germany
48C2 **Le Mans** France	57A2 **Leuven** Belg	98C2 **Lienart** Zaire	73C4 **Lingling** China
6D3 **Lemicux Is** Can	55B3 **Levádhia** Greece	57C3 **Lienz** Austria	73B5 **Lingshan** China
8C2 **Lemmon** USA	38G6 **Levanger** Nor	60B2 **Liepäja** Latvia	72C2 **Lingshi** China
21B2 **Lemoore** USA	47B2 **Levanna** Mt Italy	46C1 **Lier** Belg	97A3 **Linguère** Sen
49C2 **Lempdes** France	71D5 **Lévêque,C** Aust	47B1 **Liestal** Switz	73E4 **Linhai** Rhejiang, China
86C2 **Lemro** R Myan	46D1 **Leverkusen** Germany	15C1 **Lièvre** R Can	31D5 **Linhares** Brazil
52C2 **Le Murge** Region, Italy	59B3 **Levice** Slovakia	57C3 **Liezen** Austria	72B1 **Linhe** China
63C2 **Lena** R Russian Fed	47D1 **Levico** Italy	45C2 **Liffey** R Irish Rep	74B2 **Linjiang** China
38L6 **Lendery** Russian Fed	110C2 **Levin** NZ	45C1 **Lifford** Irish Rep	39H7 **Linköping** Sweden
73C4 **Lengshujiang** China	7C5 **Lévis** Can	107F3 **Lifu** I Nouvelle Calédonie	72D2 **Linqing** China
Leningrad = Sankt-Peterburg	15D2 **Levittown** USA	109C1 **Lightning Ridge** Aust	35B2 **Lins** Brazil
60C2 **Leningrad** Division, Russian Fed	55B3 **Lévka Óri** Mt Greece	46C2 **Ligny-en-Barrois** France	72A2 **Lintao** China
112B7 **Leningradskaya** Base Ant	55B3 **Levkás** Greece	101C2 **Ligonha** R Mozam	47C1 **Linthal** Switz
61H3 **Leninogorsk** Tatarstan, Russian Fed	106B2 **Lévêque,C** Aust	47C2 **Liguria** Region, Italy	68D2 **Linxi** China
68A1 **Leninogorsk** Kazakhstan	54C2 **Levski** Bulg	52A2 **Ligurian S** Italy	72A2 **Linxia** China
65K4 **Leninsk-Kuznetskiy** Russian Fed	43E4 **Lewes** Eng	21C4 **Lihue** Hawaiian Is	57C3 **Linz** Austria
69F2 **Leninskoye** Russian Fed	40B2 **Lewis** I Scot	100B2 **Likasi** Zaire	79B3 **Lipa** Phil
65F6 **Lenkoran'** Azerbaijan	16A2 **Lewisburg** USA	49C1 **Lille** France	53B3 **Lipari** I Italy
46E1 **Lenne** R Germany	111B2 **Lewis P** NZ	39G6 **Lillehammer** Nor	61E3 **Lipetsk** Russian Fed
	8B2 **Lewis Range** Mts USA	46B1 **Lillers** France	60E3 **Lipetsk** Division, Russian Fed
	8B2 **Lewiston** Idaho, USA	39G7 **Lillestom** Nor	54B1 **Lipova** Rom
	10C2 **Lewiston** Maine, USA	13C2 **Lillooet** Can	56B2 **Lippe** R Germany
			46E1 **Lippstadt** Germany
			99D2 **Lira** Uganda
			98B3 **Liranga** Congo
			98C2 **Lisala** Zaire
			50A2 **Lisboa** Port
			Lisbon = Lisboa
			45C1 **Lisburn** N Ire
			45B2 **Liscannor B** Irish Rep

73D4 **Lishui** China
73C4 **Li Shui** *R* China
60E4 **Lisichansk** Ukraine
48C2 **Lisieux** France
60E3 **Liski** Russian Fed
46B2 **L'Isle-Adam** France
47B1 **L'Isle-sur-le-Doubs** France
107E3 **Lismore** Aust
45B2 **Listowel** Irish Rep
73B5 **Litang** China
94B2 **Litani** *R* Leb
33G3 **Litani** *R* Surinam
18C2 **Litchfield** USA
107E4 **Lithgow** Aust
60B2 **Lithuania** Republic, Europe
16A2 **Lititz** USA
69F2 **Litovko** Russian Fed
19A3 **Little** *R* USA
11C4 **Little Abaco** *I* The Bahamas
110C1 **Little Barrier I** NZ
13E2 **Little Bow** *R* Can
25D3 **Little Cayman** *I* Caribbean S
16B3 **Little Egg Harbor** *B* USA
26C2 **Little Inagua** *I* Caribbean S
77A4 **Little Nicobar** *I* Nicobar Is
11A3 **Little Rock** USA
22D3 **Littlerock** USA
13D2 **Little Smoky** Can
13D2 **Little Smoky** *R* Can
16A3 **Littlestown** USA
15D2 **Littleton** New Hampshire, USA
74B2 **Liuhe** China
73B5 **Liuzhou** China
55B3 **Livanátais** Greece
58D1 **Līvani** Latvia
12E1 **Livengood** USA
17B1 **Live Oak** USA
21A2 **Livermore** USA
7D5 **Liverpool** Can
42C3 **Liverpool** Eng
4E2 **Liverpool B** Can
42C3 **Liverpool B** Eng
6C2 **Liverpool,C** Can
109D2 **Liverpool Range** *Mts* Aust
8B2 **Livingston** Montana, USA
19B3 **Livingston** Texas, USA
44C4 **Livingston** UK
Livingstone = **Maramba**
19A3 **Livingston,L** USA
52C2 **Livno** Bosnia-Herzegovina
60E3 **Livny** Russian Fed
14B2 **Livonia** USA
52B2 **Livorno** Italy
99D3 **Liwale** Tanz
52B1 **Ljubljana** Slovenia
38G6 **Ljungan** *R* Sweden
39G7 **Ljungby** Sweden
39H6 **Ljusdal** Sweden
38H6 **Ljusnan** *R* Sweden
43C4 **Llandeilo** Wales
43C4 **Llandovery** Wales
43C3 **Llandrindod Wells** Wales
42C3 **Llandudno** Wales
43B4 **Llanelli** Wales
43C3 **Llangollen** Wales
9C3 **Llano Estacado** *Plat* USA
32C2 **Llanos** Region, Colombia/Ven
30D2 **Llanos de Chiquitos** Region, Bol
Lleida = Lérida
50A2 **Llerena** Spain
43B3 **Lleyn** *Pen* Wales
89E7 **Llorin** Nig
5H4 **Lloydminster** Can
30C3 **Llullaillaco** *Mt* Arg/Chile
30C3 **Loa** *R* Chile
49C2 **Loan** France

98B3 **Loange** *R* Zaïre
100B3 **Lobatse** Botswana
98B2 **Lobaye** *R* CAR
34D3 **Loberia** Arg
100A2 **Lobito** Angola
34D3 **Lobos** Arg
47B2 **Locano** Italy
47C1 **Locarno** Switz
44B3 **Loch Awe** *L* Scot
44A3 **Lochboisdale** Scot
44A3 **Loch Bracadale** *Inlet* Scot
44B3 **Loch Broom** *Estuary* Scot
42B2 **Loch Doon** *L* Scot
44B3 **Loch Earn** *L* Scot
44B2 **Loch Eriboll** *Inlet* Scot
44B3 **Loch Ericht** *L* Scot
48C2 **Loches** France
44B3 **Loch Etive** *Inlet* Scot
44B3 **Loch Ewe** *Inlet* Scot
44B3 **Loch Fyne** *Inlet* Scot
44B3 **Loch Hourn** *Inlet* Scot
44B2 **Lochinver** Scot
44B3 **Loch Katrine** *L* Scot
44C3 **Loch Leven** *L* Scot
44B3 **Loch Linnhe** *Inlet* Scot
44B3 **Loch Lochy** *L* Scot
44B3 **Loch Lomond** *L* Scot
44B3 **Loch Long** *Inlet* Scot
44A3 **Lochmaddy** Scot
44B3 **Loch Maree** *L* Scot
44B3 **Loch Morar** *L* Scot
44C3 **Lochnagar** *Mt* Scot
44B3 **Loch Ness** *L* Scot
44B3 **Loch Rannoch** *L* Scot
44A2 **Loch Roag** *Inlet* Scot
44B3 **Loch Sheil** *L* Scot
44B2 **Loch Shin** *L* Scot
44A3 **Loch Snizort** *Inlet* Scot
44B3 **Loch Sunart** *Inlet* Scot
44B3 **Loch Tay** *L* Scot
44B3 **Loch Torridon** *Inlet* Scot
108A2 **Lock** Aust
42C2 **Lockerbie** Scot
15C2 **Lock Haven** USA
15C2 **Lockport** USA
76D3 **Loc Ninh** Viet
53C3 **Locri** Italy
94B3 **Lod** Israel
108B3 **Loddon** *R* Aust
60D1 **Lodeynoye Pole** Russian Fed
84C3 **Lodhran** Pak
52A1 **Lodi** Italy
21A2 **Lodi** USA
98C3 **Lodja** Zaïre
47B1 **Lods** France
99D2 **Lodwar** Kenya
58B2 **Łódź** Pol
38G5 **Lofoten** *Is* Nor
8B2 **Logan** Utah, USA
4D3 **Logan,Mt** Can
14A2 **Logansport** Indiana, USA
19B3 **Logansport** Louisiana, USA
50B1 **Logroño** Spain
86A2 **Lohärdaga** India
39J6 **Lohja** Fin
76B2 **Loikaw** Myan
39J6 **Loimaa** Fin
48C2 **Loir** *R* France
49C2 **Loire** *R* France
32B4 **Loja** Ecuador
50B2 **Loja** Spain
38K5 **Lokan Tekojärvi** *Res* Fin
46B1 **Lokeren** Belg
99D2 **Lokitaung** Kenya
58D1 **Loknya** Russian Fed
98C3 **Lokolo** *R* Zaïre
98C3 **Lokoro** *R* Zaïre
6D3 **Loks Land** *I* Can
56C2 **Lolland** *I* Den
54C2 **Lom** Bulg
98C3 **Lomami** *R* Zaïre

97A4 **Loma Mts** Sierra Leone/Guinea
47C2 **Lombardia** Region, Italy
71D4 **Lomblen** *I* Indon
78D4 **Lombok** *I* Indon
97C4 **Lomé** Togo
98C3 **Lomela** Zaïre
98C3 **Lomela** *R* Zaïre
60C2 **Lomonosov** Russian Fed
47B1 **Lomont** Region, France
21A3 **Lompoc** USA
58C2 **Łomza** Pol
87A1 **Lonävale** India
29B3 **Loncoche** Chile
7B5 **London** Can
43D4 **London** Eng
45C1 **Londonderry** County, N Ire
45C1 **Londonderry** N Ire
29B7 **Londonderry** *I* Chile
106B2 **Londonderry,C** Aust
30C4 **Londres** Arg
30F3 **Londrina** Brazil
21B2 **Lone Pine** USA
11C4 **Long** *I* The Bahamas
71F4 **Long** *I* PNG
78C2 **Long Akah** Malay
47E1 **Longarone** Italy
34A3 **Longavi** *Mt* Chile
27H2 **Long B** Jamaica
17C1 **Long B** USA
9B3 **Long Beach** California, USA
15D2 **Long Beach** New York, USA
15D2 **Long Branch** USA
73D5 **Longchuan** China
20C2 **Long Creek** USA
109C4 **Longford** Aust
45C2 **Longford** County, Irish Rep
45C2 **Longford** Irish Rep
44D3 **Long Forties** *Region* N Sea
72D1 **Longhua** China
7C4 **Long I** Can
10C2 **Long I** USA
16C2 **Long Island Sd** USA
7B4 **Longlac** Can
73B5 **Longlin** China
8C2 **Longmont** USA
78D2 **Longnawan** Indon
29B3 **Longquimay** Chile
107D3 **Longreach** Aust
72A2 **Longshou Shan** *Upland* China
42C2 **Longtown** Eng
15D1 **Longueuil** Can
34A3 **Longuimay** Chile
46C2 **Longuyon** France
11A3 **Longview** Texas, USA
8A2 **Longview** Washington, USA
46C2 **Longwy** France
72A3 **Longxi** China
77D3 **Long Xuyen** Viet
73D4 **Longyan** China
73B5 **Longzhou** China
47D2 **Lonigo** Italy
49D2 **Lons-le-Saunier** France
11C3 **Lookout,C** USA
99D3 **Loolmalasin** *Mt* Tanz
13D1 **Loon** *R* Can
45B2 **Loop Hd** *C* Irish Rep
76C3 **Lop Buri** Thai
98A3 **Lopez** *C* Gabon
68B2 **Lop Nur** *L* China
50A2 **Lora del Rio** Spain
10B2 **Lorain** USA
84B2 **Loralai** Pak
90B3 **Lordegán** Iran
107E4 **Lord Howe** *I* Aust
105G5 **Lord Howe Rise** Pacific O
6A3 **Lord Mayor B** Can
9C3 **Lordsburg** USA
35B2 **Lorena** Brazil
47E2 **Loreo** Italy
23A1 **Loreto** Mexico

48B2 **Lorient** France
108B3 **Lorne** Aust
57B3 **Lörrach** Germany
49D2 **Lorraine** *Region* France
9C3 **Los Alamos** USA
34A2 **Los Andes** Chile
29B3 **Los Angeles** Chile
9B3 **Los Angeles** USA
21A2 **Los Banos** USA
34B2 **Los Cerrillos** Arg
21A2 **Los Gatos** USA
52B2 **Lošinj** *I* Croatia
29B3 **Los Lagos** Chile
24B2 **Los Mochis** Mexico
22B3 **Los Olivos** USA
34A3 **Los Sauces** Chile
44C3 **Lossiemouth** Scot
27E4 **Los Testigos** *Is* Ven
29B2 **Los Vilos** Chile
48C3 **Lot** *R* France
34A3 **Lota** Chile
42C2 **Lothian** Region, Scot
99D2 **Lotikipi Plain** Sudan/Kenya
98C3 **Loto** Zaïre
47B1 **Lötschberg Tunnel** Switz
38K5 **Lotta** *R* Fin/Russian Fed
48B2 **Loudéac** France
97A3 **Louga** Sen
41B3 **Lough Allen** *L* Irish Rep
45C2 **Lough Boderg** *L* Irish Rep
43D3 **Loughborough** Eng
45C2 **Lough Bowna** *L* Irish Rep
45C1 **Lough Carlingford** *L* N Ire
41B3 **Lough Conn** *L* Irish Rep
41B3 **Lough Corrib** *L* Irish Rep
41B3 **Lough Derg** *L* Irish Rep
45C2 **Lough Derravaragh** *L* Irish Rep
4H2 **Loughead I** Can
45C2 **Lough Ennell** *L* Irish Rep
41B3 **Lough Erne** *L* N Ire
40B2 **Lough Foyle** *Estuary* N Ire/Irish Rep
40B3 **Lough Neagh** *L* N Ire
45C1 **Lough Oughter** *L* Irish Rep
45B2 **Loughrea** Irish Rep
45C2 **Lough Ree** *L* Irish Rep
45C2 **Lough Sheelin** *L* Irish Rep
42B2 **Lough Strangford** *L* Irish Rep
45C1 **Lough Swilly** *Estuary* Irish Rep
14B2 **Louisa** USA
70C3 **Louisa Reef** *I* S E Asia
12E2 **Louise,L** Can
107E2 **Louisiade Arch** Solomon Is
11A3 **Louisiana** State, USA
17B1 **Louisville** Georgia, USA
11B3 **Louisville** Kentucky, USA
38L5 **Loukhi** Russian Fed
48B3 **Lourdes** France
108C2 **Louth** Aust
45C2 **Louth** County, Irish Rep
42D3 **Louth** Eng
Louvain = Leuven
48C2 **Louviers** France
60D2 **Lovat** *R* Russian Fed
54B2 **Lovech** Bulg
21B1 **Lovelock** USA
52B1 **Lóvere** Italy
9C3 **Lovington** USA
38L5 **Lovozero** Russian Fed
6B3 **Low,C** Can

78C4	**Madiun** Indon
99D2	**Mado Gashi** Kenya
47D1	**Madonna Di Campiglio** Italy
87C2	**Madras** India
20B2	**Madras** USA
29A6	**Madre de Dios** / Chile
32D6	**Madre de Dios** R Bol
50B1	**Madrid** Spain
50B2	**Madridejos** Spain
78C4	**Madura** / Indon
87B3	**Madurai** India
75B1	**Maebashi** Japan
76B3	**Mae Khlong** R Thai
77B4	**Mae Nam Lunang** R Thai
76C2	**Mae Nam Mun** R Thai
76B2	**Mae Nam Ping** R Thai
101D2	**Maevatanana** Madag
101G1	**Mafeteng** Lesotho
109C3	**Maffra** Aust
99D3	**Mafia** / Tanz
101G1	**Mafikeng** S Africa
30G4	**Mafra** Brazil
92C3	**Mafraq** Jordan
32C2	**Maganguê** Colombia
34D3	**Magdalena** Arg
24A1	**Magdalena** Mexico
26C4	**Magdalena** R Colombia
78D1	**Magdalena,Mt** Malay
56C2	**Magdeburg** Germany
31C6	**Magé** Brazil
78C4	**Magelang** Indon
47C1	**Maggia** R Switz
92B4	**Maghâgha** Egypt
45C1	**Magherafelt** N Ire
55A2	**Maglie** Italy
61J3	**Magnitogorsk** Russian Fed
19B3	**Magnolia** USA
101C2	**Magoé** Mozam
15D1	**Magog** Can
23B1	**Magosal** Mexico
13E2	**Magrath** Can
7A3	**Maguse River** Can
76B1	**Magwe** Myan
90A2	**Mahābād** Iran
86B1	**Mahabharat Range** Mts Nepal
87A1	**Mahād** India
85D4	**Mahadeo Hills** India
101D2	**Mahajanga** Madag
100B3	**Mahalapye** Botswana
86A2	**Mahānadi** R India
101D2	**Mahanoro** Madag
16A2	**Mahanoy City** USA
87A1	**Maharashtra** State, India
86A2	**Mahāsamund** India
76C2	**Maha Sarakham** Thai
101D2	**Mahavavy** R Madag
87B1	**Mahbübnagar** India
96D1	**Mahdia** Tunisia
87B2	**Mahe** India
85D4	**Mahekar** India
101D2	**Mahéli** / Comoros
86A2	**Mahendragarh** India
99D3	**Mahenge** Tanz
85C4	**Mahesāna** India
110C1	**Mahia Pen** NZ
85D3	**Mahoba** India
51C2	**Mahón** Spain
12J1	**Mahony L** Can
96D1	**Mahrés** Tunisia
85C4	**Mahuva** India
32C1	**Maicao** Colombia
47B1	**Maiche** France
43E4	**Maidstone** Eng
98B1	**Maiduguri** Nig
86A2	**Maihar** India
86C2	**Maijdi** Bang
76B3	**Mail Kyun** / Myan
84A1	**Maimana** Afghan
14B1	**Main Chan** Can
98B3	**Mai-Ndombe** L Zaïre
10D2	**Maine** State, USA
48B2	**Maine** Region France
44C2	**Mainland** / Scot
85D3	**Mainpuri** India
46A2	**Maintenon** France
101D2	**Maintirano** Madag
57B2	**Mainz** Germany
97A4	**Maio** / Cape Verde
29C2	**Maipó** Mt Arg/Chile
34D3	**Maipú** Arg
32D1	**Maiquetía** Ven
47B2	**Maira** R Italy
86C1	**Mairābāri** India
86C2	**Maiskhal I** Bang
107E4	**Maitland** New South Wales, Aust
108A2	**Maitland** S Australia, Aust
112C12	**Maitri** Base Ant
74D3	**Maizuru** Japan
70C4	**Majene** Indon
30B2	**Majes** R Peru
99D2	**Maji** Eth
72D2	**Majia He** R China
	Majunga = Mahajanga
70C4	**Makale** Indon
86B1	**Makalu** Mt China/ Nepal
98B2	**Makanza** Zaïre
52C2	**Makarska** Croatia
61F2	**Makaryev** Russian Fed
	Makassar = Ujung Pandang
78D3	**Makassar Str** Indon
61H4	**Makat** Kazakhstan
97A4	**Makeni** Sierra Leone
60E4	**Makeyevka** Ukraine
100B3	**Makgadikgadi** Salt Pan Botswana
61G5	**Makhachkala** Russian Fed
99D3	**Makindu** Kenya
88H5	**Makkah** S Arabia
7E4	**Makkovik** Can
59C3	**Makó** Hung
98B2	**Makokou** Gabon
110C1	**Makorako,Mt** NZ
98B2	**Makoua** Congo
85C3	**Makrāna** India
85A3	**Makran Coast Range** Mts Pak
96C1	**Makthar** Tunisia
93D2	**Mākū** Iran
98C3	**Makumbi** Zaïre
74C4	**Makurazaki** Japan
97C4	**Makurdi** Nig
79B4	**Malabang** Phil
87A2	**Malabar Coast** India
89E7	**Malabo** Bioko
77C5	**Malacca,Str of** S E Asia
32C2	**Málaga** Colombia
50B2	**Malaga** Spain
101D3	**Malaimbandy** Madag
107F1	**Malaita** / Solomon Is
99D2	**Malakal** Sudan
84C2	**Malakand** Pak
78C4	**Malang** Indon
98B3	**Malange** Angola
97C3	**Malanville** Benin
39H7	**Mälaren** L Sweden
34B3	**Malargüe** Arg
12F3	**Malaspina Gl** USA
93C2	**Malatya** Turk
101C2	**Malawi** Republic, Africa
	Malawi,L = Nyasa,L
79C4	**Malaybalay** Phil
90A3	**Malāyer** Iran
70B3	**Malaysia** Federation, S E Asia
93D2	**Malazgirt** Turk
58B2	**Malbork** Pol
56C2	**Malchin** Germany
18C2	**Malden** USA
83B5	**Maldives Is** Indian O
104B4	**Maldives Ridge** Indian O
29F2	**Maldonado** Urug
47D1	**Male** Italy
85C4	**Malegaon** India
59B3	**Malé Karpaty** Upland Slovakia
101C2	**Malema** Mozam
84B2	**Mālestān** Afghan
38H5	**Malgomaj** L Sweden
95B3	**Malha** Well Sudan
20C2	**Malheur L** USA
97B3	**Mali** Republic, Africa
78D1	**Malinau** Indon
99E3	**Malindi** Kenya
	Malines = Mechelen
40B2	**Malin Head** Pt Irish Rep
86A2	**Malkala Range** Mts India
85D4	**Malkāpur** India
55C2	**Malkara** Turk
54C2	**Malko Tŭrnovo** Bulg
44B3	**Mallaig** Scot
95C2	**Mallawi** Egypt
47D1	**Málles Venosta** Italy
51C2	**Mallorca** / Spain
45B2	**Mallow** Irish Rep
38G6	**Malm** Nor
38J5	**Malmberget** Sweden
46D1	**Malmédy** Germany
43C4	**Malmesbury** Eng
100A4	**Malmesbury** S Africa
39G7	**Malmö** Sweden
61G2	**Malmyzh** Russian Fed
79B3	**Malolos** Phil
15D2	**Malone** USA
101G1	**Maloti Mts** Lesotho
38F6	**Måløy** Nor
28A2	**Malpelo** / Colombia
34A2	**Malpo** R Chile
85D3	**Mālpura** India
8C2	**Malta** Montana, USA
53B3	**Malta Chan** Malta/ Italy
53B3	**Malta** / Medit S
100A3	**Maltahöhe** Namibia
42D2	**Malton** Eng
39G6	**Malung** Sweden
87A1	**Mālvan** India
19B3	**Malvern** USA
85D4	**Malwa Plat** India
61G4	**Malyy Uzen'** R Kazakhstan
63D2	**Mama** Russian Fed
61H2	**Mamadysh** Russian Fed
99C2	**Mambasa** Zaïre
71E4	**Mamberamo** R Indon
98B2	**Mambéré** R CAR
98A2	**Mamfé** Cam
33D6	**Mamoré** R Bol
97A3	**Mamou** Guinea
101D2	**Mampikony** Madag
97B4	**Mampong** Ghana
94B3	**Mamshit** Hist Site Israel
100B3	**Mamuno** Botswana
97B4	**Man** Côte d'Ivoire
21C4	**Mana** Hawaiian Is
101D3	**Manabo** Madag
33E4	**Manacapuru** Brazil
51C2	**Manacor** Spain
71D3	**Manado** Indon
25D3	**Managua** Nic
101D3	**Manakara** Madag
101D2	**Mananara** Madag
101D3	**Mananjary** Madag
111A3	**Manapouri** NZ
111A3	**Manapouri,L** NZ
86C1	**Manas** Bhutan
82C1	**Manas** China
65K5	**Manas Hu** L China
86A1	**Manaslu** Mt Nepal
16B2	**Manasquan** USA
33F4	**Manaus** Brazil
92B2	**Manavgat** Turk
93C2	**Manbij** Syria
42B2	**Man,Calf of** / Eng
87B1	**Mancheral** India
15D2	**Manchester** Connecticut, USA
42C3	**Manchester** Eng
10C2	**Manchester** New Hampshire, USA
16A2	**Manchester** Pennsylvania, USA
69E2	**Manchuria** Hist Region, China
91B4	**Mand** R Iran
101C2	**Manda** Tanz
35A2	**Mandaguari** Brazil
39F7	**Mandal** Nor
76B1	**Mandalay** Myan
68C2	**Mandalgovi** Mongolia
8C2	**Mandan** USA
14A2	**Mandelona** USA
99E2	**Mandera** Eth
26B3	**Mandeville** Jamaica
101C2	**Mandimba** Mozam
86A2	**Mandla** India
101D2	**Mandritsara** Madag
85D4	**Mandsaur** India
53C2	**Manduria** Italy
85B4	**Māndvi** India
87B2	**Mandya** India
58D2	**Manevichi** Ukraine
42D3	**Manfield** Eng
53C2	**Manfredonia** Italy
98B1	**Manga** Desert Region Niger
110C1	**Mangakino** NZ
54C2	**Mangalia** Rom
98B1	**Mangalmé** Chad
87A2	**Mangalore** India
78B3	**Manggar** Indon
68B3	**Mangnia** China
101C2	**Mangoche** Malawi
101D3	**Mangoky** R Madag
71D4	**Mangole** / Indon
85B4	**Māngral** India
63E2	**Mangui** China
8D3	**Manhattan** USA
31C6	**Manhuacu** Brazil
101D2	**Mania** R Madag
101C2	**Manica** Mozam
7D5	**Manicouagan** R Can
91A4	**Manifah** S Arabia
79B3	**Manila** Phil
109D2	**Manilla** Aust
97B3	**Maninian** Côte d'Ivoire
86C2	**Manipur** State, India
86C2	**Manipur** R Myan
92A2	**Manisa** Turk
41C3	**Man,Isle of** Irish S
14A2	**Manistee** USA
14A2	**Manistee** R USA
14A1	**Manistique** USA
5H4	**Manitoba** Province, Can
5J4	**Manitoba,L** Can
13F2	**Manito L** Can
14A1	**Manitou Is** USA
7B5	**Manitoulin** / Can
14A2	**Manitowoc** USA
15C1	**Maniwaki** Can
32B2	**Manizales** Colombia
101D3	**Manja** Madag
106A4	**Manjimup** Aust
87B1	**Mānjra** R India
10A2	**Mankato** USA
97B4	**Mankono** Côte d'Ivoire
12D2	**Manley Hot Springs** USA
110B1	**Manly** NZ
85C4	**Manmād** India
78A3	**Manna** Indon
108A2	**Mannahill** Aust
87B3	**Mannar** Sri Lanka
87B3	**Mannār,G of** India
87B2	**Mannārgudi** India
57B3	**Mannheim** Germany
13D1	**Manning** Can
17B1	**Manning** USA
108A2	**Mannum** Aust
97A4	**Mano** Sierra Leone
71E4	**Manokwari** Indon
98C3	**Manono** Zaïre
76B3	**Manoron** Myan
75B1	**Mano-wan** B Japan
74B2	**Manp'o** N Korea
84D3	**Mānsa** India
100B2	**Mansa** Zambia
6B3	**Mansel I** Can
19B2	**Mansfield** Arkansas, USA
108C3	**Mansfield** Aust
19B3	**Mansfield** Louisiana, USA
16D1	**Mansfield** Massachusetts, USA
10B2	**Mansfield** Ohio, USA

Mansfield

21C4	**Mauna Kea** *Mt* Hawaiian Is
21C4	**Mauna Loa** *Mt* Hawaiian Is
4F3	**Maunoir** *L* Can
4F3	**Maunoir,L** Can
48C2	**Mauriac** France
96A2	**Mauritania** Republic, Africa
100E3	**Mauritius** *I* Indian O
100B2	**Mavinga** Angola
86C2	**Mawlaik** Myan
	Mawlamyine = Moulmein
112C10	**Mawson** *Base* Ant
78B3	**Maya** *I* Indon
63F2	**Maya** *R* Russian Fed
93D2	**Mayādīn** Syria
11C4	**Mayaguana** *I* The Bahamas
27D3	**Mayagüez** Puerto Rico
97C3	**Mayahi** Niger
98B3	**Mayama** Congo
90C2	**Mayamey** Iran
42B2	**Maybole** Scot
10C3	**May,C** USA
109C4	**Maydena** Aust
46D1	**Mayen** Germany
48B2	**Mayenne** France
13D2	**Mayerthorpe** Can
18C2	**Mayfield** USA
61E5	**Maykop** Russian Fed
65H6	**Maymaneh** Afghan
76B1	**Maymyo** Myan
4E3	**Mayo** Can
45B2	**Mayo** County, Irish Rep
16A3	**Mayo** USA
45B1	**Mayo,Mts of** Irish Rep
79B3	**Mayon** *Mt* Phil
51C2	**Mayor** *Mt* Spain
34C3	**Mayor Buratovich** Arg
110C1	**Mayor I** NZ
30D2	**Mayor P Lagerenza** Par
101D2	**Mayotte** *I* Indian O
27H2	**May Pen** Jamaica
16B3	**May Point,C** USA
47D1	**Mayrhofen** Austria
16B3	**Mays Landing** USA
14B3	**Maysville** USA
98B3	**Mayumba** Gabon
100B2	**Mazabuka** Zambia
84D1	**Mazar** China
94B3	**Mazar** Jordan
53B3	**Mazara del Vallo** Italy
84B1	**Mazar-i-Sharif** Afghan
24B2	**Mazatlán** Mexico
60B2	**Mazeikiai** Lithuania
94B3	**Mazra** Jordan
101C3	**Mbabane** Swaziland
98B2	**Mbaïki** CAR
99D3	**Mbala** Zambia
100B3	**Mbalabala** Zim
99D2	**Mbale** Uganda
98B2	**Mbalmayo** Cam
98B2	**Mbam** *R* Cam
101C2	**Mbamba Bay** Tanz
98B2	**Mbandaka** Zaïre
98B3	**Mbanza Congo** Angola
98B3	**Mbanza-Ngungu** Zaïre
99D3	**Mbarara** Uganda
98B2	**Mbènza** Congo
98B2	**Mbére** *R* Cam
99D3	**Mbeya** Tanz
98B3	**Mbinda** Congo
97A3	**Mbout** Maur
98C3	**Mbuji-Mayi** Zaïre
99D3	**Mbulu** Tanz
96B2	**Mcherrah** Region, Alg
101C2	**Mchinji** Malawi
76D3	**Mdrak** Viet
9B3	**Mead,L** USA
5H4	**Meadow Lake** Can
14B2	**Meadville** USA
7E4	**Mealy Mts** Can
109C1	**Meandarra** Aust
5G4	**Meander River** Can
45C2	**Meath** County, Irish Rep
49C2	**Meaux** France
16C1	**Mechanicville** USA
56A2	**Mechelen** Belg
96B1	**Mecheria** Alg
56C2	**Mecklenburg-Vorpommern** *State* Germany
56C2	**Mecklenburger Bucht** *B* Germany
101C2	**Meconta** Mozam
101C2	**Mecuburi** Mozam
101D2	**Mecufi** Mozam
101C2	**Mecula** Mozam
70A3	**Medan** Indon
34C3	**Medanos** Arg
34D2	**Médanos** Arg
13E2	**Medecine Hat** Can
32B2	**Medellín** Colombia
96D1	**Medenine** Tunisia
8A2	**Medford** USA
54C2	**Medgidia** Rom
34B2	**Media Agua** Arg
54B1	**Mediaş** Rom
20C1	**Medical Lake** USA
5G5	**Medicine Hat** Can
35C1	**Medina** Brazil
80B3	**Medina** S Arabia
50B1	**Medinaceli** Spain
50B1	**Medina del Campo** Spain
50A1	**Medina de Rio Seco** Spain
86B2	**Medinipur** India
88E4	**Mediterranean S** Europe
13F2	**Medley** Can
61J3	**Mednogorsk** Russian Fed
86D1	**Mêdog** China
98B2	**Medouneu** Gabon
61F3	**Medvedista** *R* Russian Fed
64E3	**Medvezh'yegorsk** Russian Fed
106A3	**Meekatharra** Aust
84D3	**Meerut** India
99D2	**Mēga** Eth
55B3	**Megalópolis** Greece
55B3	**Mégara** Greece
86C1	**Meghālaya** State, India
86C2	**Meghna** *R* Bang
94B2	**Megiddo** *Hist Site* Israel
91B4	**Mehran** *R* Iran
90B3	**Mehriz** Iran
35B1	**Meia Ponte** *R* Brazil
98B2	**Meiganga** Cam
76B1	**Meiktila** Myan
47C1	**Meiringen** Switz
73A4	**Meishan** China
57C2	**Meissen** Germany
73D5	**Mei Xian** China
73D5	**Meizhou** China
30B3	**Mejillones** Chile
98B2	**Mekambo** Gabon
99D1	**Mek'elē** Eth
96B1	**Meknès** Mor
76D3	**Mekong** *R* Camb
97C3	**Mekrou** *R* Benin
77C5	**Melaka** Malay
104F4	**Melanesia** *Region* Pacific O
78C3	**Melawi** *R* Indon
107D4	**Melbourne** Aust
11B4	**Melbourne** USA
9C4	**Melchor Muzquiz** Mexico
61J3	**Meleuz** Russian Fed
98B1	**Melfi** Chad
5H4	**Melfort** Can
96B1	**Melilla** N W Africa
29B4	**Melimoyu** *Mt* Chile
34C2	**Melincué** Arg
34A2	**Melipilla** Chile
60E4	**Melitopol'** Ukraine
6D2	**Meliville Bugt** *B* Greenland
99D2	**Melka Guba** Eth
101H1	**Melmoth** S Africa
34C2	**Melo** Arg
29F2	**Melo** Urug
22B2	**Melones Res** USA
12D1	**Melozitna** *R* USA
47C1	**Mels** Switz
43D3	**Melton Mowbry** Eng
49C2	**Melun** France
5H4	**Melville** Can
27Q2	**Melville,C** Dominica
4F3	**Melville Hills** *Mts* Can
106C2	**Melville I** Aust
4G2	**Melville I** Can
7E4	**Melville,L** Can
6B3	**Melville Pen** Can
45B1	**Melvin,L** Irish Rep
101D2	**Memba** Mozam
106A1	**Memboro** Indon
57C3	**Memmingen** Germany
78B2	**Mempawah** Indon
11B3	**Memphis** Tennessee, USA
19B3	**Mena** USA
43B3	**Menai Str** Wales
97C3	**Ménaka** Mali
14A2	**Menasha** USA
78C3	**Mendawai** *R* Indon
49C3	**Mende** France
99D2	**Mendebo** *Mts* Eth
43C4	**Mendip Hills** *Upland* Eng
20B2	**Mendocino,C** USA
105J2	**Mendocino Seascarp** Pacific O
22B2	**Mendota** California, USA
29C2	**Mendoza** Arg
29C3	**Mendoza** State, Arg
55C3	**Menemen** Turk
46B1	**Menen** Belg
72D3	**Mengcheng** China
78B3	**Menggala** Indon
76B1	**Menghai** China
73A5	**Mengla** China
76B1	**Menglian** China
73A5	**Mengzi** China
107D4	**Menindee** Aust
108B2	**Menindee L** Aust
108A3	**Meningie** Aust
14A1	**Menominee** USA
14A2	**Menomonee Falls** USA
100A2	**Menongue** Angola
51C1	**Menorca** *I* Spain
12F2	**Mentasta Mts** USA
78B3	**Mentok** Indon
14B2	**Mentor** USA
46B2	**Ménu** France
72A2	**Menyuan** China
61H2	**Menzelinsk** Russian Fed
56B2	**Meppen** Germany
78D2	**Merah** Indon
18B2	**Meramec** *R* USA
52B1	**Merano** Italy
71F4	**Merauke** Indon
8A3	**Merced** USA
22B2	**Merced** *R* USA
29B2	**Mercedario** *Mt* Chile
29C2	**Mercedes** Arg
29E2	**Mercedes** Buenos Aires, Arg
30E4	**Mercedes** Corrientes, Arg
29E2	**Mercedes** Urug
110C1	**Mercury B** NZ
110C1	**Mercury Is** NZ
4F2	**Mercy B** Can
6D3	**Mercy,C** Can
99E2	**Mereeg** Somalia
76B3	**Mergui** Myan
76B3	**Mergui Arch** Myan
25D2	**Mérida** Mexico
50A2	**Mérida** Spain
32C2	**Mérida** Ven
11B3	**Meridian** USA
109C3	**Merimbula** Aust
108B2	**Meringur** Aust
95C3	**Merowe** Sudan
106A4	**Merredin** Aust
42B2	**Merrick** *Mt* Scot
14A2	**Merrillville** USA
13C2	**Merritt** Can
17B2	**Merritt Island** USA
109D2	**Merriwa** Aust
99E1	**Mersa Fatma** Eritrea
51B2	**Mers el Kebir** Alg
42C3	**Mersey** *R* Eng
42C3	**Merseyside** Metropolitan County, Eng
92B2	**Mersin** Turk
77C5	**Mersing** Malay
85C3	**Merta** India
43C4	**Merthyr Tydfil** Wales
43C4	**Merthyr Tydfil** County Wales
50A2	**Mertola** Port
99D3	**Meru** *Mt* Tanz
60E5	**Merzifon** Turk
46D2	**Merzig** Germany
9B3	**Mesa** USA
46E1	**Meschede** Germany
93D1	**Mescit Dağ** *Mt* Turk
12C3	**Meshik** USA
99C2	**Meshra Er Req** Sudan
47C1	**Mesocco** Switz
55B3	**Mesolóngion** Greece
19A3	**Mesquite** Texas, USA
101C2	**Messalo** *R* Mozam
53C3	**Messina** Italy
100B3	**Messina** S Africa
55B3	**Messini** Greece
55B3	**Messiniakós Kólpos** *G* Greece
54B2	**Mesta** *R* Bulg
52B1	**Mestre** Italy
32C3	**Meta** *R* Colombia
60D2	**Meta** *R* Russian Fed
32D2	**Meta** *R* Ven
6C3	**Meta Incognito Pen** Can
19B4	**Metairie** USA
20C1	**Metaline Falls** USA
30D4	**Metán** Arg
101C2	**Metangula** Mozam
53C2	**Metaponto** Italy
44C3	**Methil** Scot
16D1	**Methuen** USA
111B2	**Methven** NZ
12H3	**Metlakatla** USA
18C2	**Metropolis** USA
87B2	**Mettür** India
49D2	**Metz** France
70A3	**Meulaboh** Indon
46A2	**Meulan** France
46C2	**Meuse** Department, France
49D2	**Meuse** *R* France
19A3	**Mexia** USA
24A1	**Mexicali** Mexico
24B2	**Mexico** Federal Republic, Cent America
24C3	**México** Mexico
23A2	**México** State, Mexico
18B2	**Mexico** USA
24C2	**Mexico,G of** Cent America
94B3	**Mezada** *Hist Site* Israel
23B2	**Mezcala** Mexico
64F3	**Mezen'** Russian Fed
64G2	**Mezhdusharskiy, Ostrov** *I* Russian Fed
85D4	**Mhow** India
23B2	**Miahuatlán** Mexico
11B4	**Miami** Florida, USA
18B2	**Miami** Oklahoma, USA
11B4	**Miami Beach** USA
90A2	**Miandowāb** Iran
101D2	**Miandrivazo** Madag
90A2	**Miäneh** Iran
84C2	**Mianwali** Pak
73A3	**Mianyang** China
73C3	**Mianyang** China
73A3	**Mianzhu** China
72E2	**Miaodao Qundao** *Arch* China
73B4	**Miao Ling** *Upland* China
61K3	**Miass** Russian Fed
59C3	**Michalovce** Slovakia
27D3	**Miches** Dom Rep
10B2	**Michigan** State, USA
14A2	**Michigan City** USA

Michigan,L

10B2 **Michigan,L** USA
7B5 **Michipicoten I** Can
23A2 **Michoacan** State, Mexico
54C2 **Michurin** Bulg
61F3 **Michurinsk** Russian Fed
104F3 **Micronesia** *Region* Pacific O
78B2 **Midai** *I* Indon
102F4 **Mid Atlantic Ridge** Atlantic O
46B1 **Middelburg** Neth
20B2 **Middle Alkali L** USA
16D2 **Middleboro** USA
100B4 **Middleburg** Cape Province, S Africa
16A2 **Middleburg** Pennsylvania, USA
101G1 **Middleburg** Transvaal, S Africa
16B1 **Middleburgh** USA
15D2 **Middlebury** USA
11B3 **Middlesboro** USA
42D2 **Middlesbrough** Eng
42D2 **Middlesbrough** County Eng
16C2 **Middletown** Connecticut, USA
16B3 **Middletown** Delaware, USA
15D2 **Middletown** New York, USA
14B3 **Middletown** Ohio, USA
16A2 **Middletown** Pennsylvania, USA
96B1 **Midelt** Mor
104B4 **Mid Indian Basin** Indian O
104B4 **Mid Indian Ridge** Indian O
7C5 **Midland** Can
14B2 **Midland** Michigan, USA
9C3 **Midland** Texas, USA
101D3 **Midongy Atsimo** Madag
105G2 **Mid Pacific Mts** Pacific O
20C2 **Midvale** USA
105H2 **Midway Is** Pacific O
18A2 **Midwest City** USA
93D2 **Midyat** Turk
54B2 **Midžor** *Mt* Serbia, Yugos
59B2 **Mielec** Pol
54C1 **Miercurea-Ciuc** Rom
50A1 **Mieres** Spain
16A2 **Mifflintown** USA
75A2 **Mihara** Japan
72D1 **Mijun Shuiku** *Res* China
54B2 **Mikhaylovgrad** Bulg
61F3 **Mikhaylovka** Russian Fed
65J4 **Mikhaylovskiy** Russian Fed
38K6 **Mikkeli** Fin
55C3 **Mikonos** *I* Greece
59B3 **Mikulov** Czech Republic
99D3 **Mikumi** Tanz
74D3 **Mikuni-sammyaku** *Mts* Japan
75B2 **Mikura-jima** *I* Japan
32B4 **Milagro** Ecuador
Milan = Milano
51C2 **Milana** Alg
101C2 **Milange** Mozam
52A1 **Milano** Italy
92A2 **Milas** Turk
107D4 **Mildura** Aust
73A5 **Mile** China
93D3 **Mileh Tharthār** *L* Iraq
107E3 **Miles** Aust
8C2 **Miles City** USA
16C2 **Milford** Connecticut, USA
15C3 **Milford** Delaware, USA
15D2 **Milford** Massachusetts, USA

18A1 **Milford** Nebraska, USA
16B2 **Milford** Pennsylvania, USA
43B4 **Milford Haven** Wales
43B4 **Milford Haven** *Sd* Wales
18A2 **Milford L** USA
111A2 **Milford Sd** NZ
13E2 **Milk River** Can
49C3 **Millau** France
16C2 **Millbrook** USA
17B1 **Milledgeville** USA
12F2 **Miller,Mt** USA
61F4 **Millerovo** Russian Fed
16A2 **Millersburg** USA
108A1 **Millers Creek** Aust
16C1 **Millers Falls** USA
16C2 **Millerton** USA
22C2 **Millerton L** USA
108B3 **Millicent** Aust
109D1 **Millmerran** Aust
45B2 **Milltown Malbay** Irish Rep
22A2 **Mill Valley** USA
15D3 **Millville** USA
6H2 **Milne Land** *I* Greenland
21C4 **Mililii** Hawaiian Is
55B3 **Milos** *I* Greece
107D3 **Milparinka** Aust
16A2 **Milroy** USA
111A3 **Milton** NZ
16A2 **Milton** Pennsylvania, USA
10B2 **Milwaukee** USA
51C2 **Mina** *R* Alg
93E4 **Mina' al Ahmadī** Kuwait
91C4 **Mināb** Iran
74C4 **Minamata** Japan
78A2 **Minas** Indon
29E2 **Minas** Urug
31B5 **Minas Gerais** State, Brazil
35C1 **Minas Novas** Brazil
25C3 **Minatitlan** Mexico
76A1 **Minbu** Myan
76A1 **Minbya** Myan
34A2 **Mincha** Chile
44A3 **Minch,Little** *Sd* Scot
44A2 **Minch,North** *Sd* Scot
40B2 **Minch,The** *Sd* Scot
12D2 **Minchumina,L** USA
47D2 **Mincio** *R* Italy
79B4 **Mindanao** *I* Phil
19B3 **Minden** Louisiana, USA
56B2 **Minden** Germany
108B2 **Mindona L** Aust
79B3 **Mindoro** *I* Phil
79B3 **Mindoro Str** Phil
45C3 **Mine Hd** *C* Irish Rep
43C4 **Minehead** Eng
30F2 **Mineiros** Brazil
19A3 **Mineola** USA
23B1 **Mineral de Monte** Mexico
16A2 **Minersville** USA
108B2 **Mingary** Aust
72A2 **Minhe** China
87A3 **Minicoy** *I* India
73D4 **Min Jiang** *R* Fujian, China
73A4 **Min Jiang** *R* Sichuan, China
22C2 **Minkler** USA
108A2 **Minlaton** Aust
72A2 **Minle** China
97C4 **Minna** Nig
10A2 **Minneapolis** USA
5J4 **Minnedosa** Can
10A2 **Minnesota** State, USA
50A1 **Miño** *R* Spain
8C2 **Minot** USA
72A2 **Minqin** China
72A3 **Min Shan** *Upland* China
60C3 **Minsk** Belarus
58C2 **Mińsk Mazowiecki** Pol

12E2 **Minto** USA
4G2 **Minto Inlet** *B* Can
7C4 **Minto,L** Can
63B2 **Minusinsk** Russian Fed
72A3 **Min Xian** China
7E5 **Miquelon** Can
22D3 **Mirage L** USA
87A1 **Miraj** India
29E3 **Miramar** Arg
84B2 **Miram Shah** Pak
50B1 **Miranda de Ebro** Spain
47D2 **Mirandola** Italy
84B2 **Mir Bachchen Küt** Afghan
78D1 **Miri** Malay
96A3 **Mirik,C** Maur
63A1 **Mirnoye** Russian Fed
63D1 **Mirnyy** Russian Fed
112C9 **Mirnyy** *Base* Ant
84C2 **Mirpur** Pak
85B3 **Mirpur Khas** Pak
55B3 **Mirtoan S** Greece
74B3 **Miryang** S Korea
86A1 **Mirzāpur** India
23B2 **Misantla** Mexico
84C1 **Misgar** Pak
14A2 **Mishawaka** USA
12B1 **Misheguk Mt** USA
75A2 **Mi-shima** *I* Japan
107E2 **Misima** *I* Solomon Is
30F4 **Misiones** State, Arg
59C3 **Miskolc** Hung
94C2 **Mismiyah** Syria
71E4 **Misoöl** *I* Indon
95A1 **Misrātah** Libya
7B5 **Missinaibi** *R* Can
20B1 **Mission** City USA
15C2 **Mississauga** Can
11A3 **Mississippi** State, USA
11A3 **Mississippi** *R* USA
19C3 **Mississippi Delta** USA
8B2 **Missoula** USA
96B1 **Missour** Mor
11A3 **Missouri** State, USA
10A2 **Missouri** *R* USA
10C1 **Mistassini,L** USA
30B2 **Misti** *Mt* Peru
109C1 **Mitchell** Aust
8D2 **Mitchell** USA
107D2 **Mitchell** *R* Aust
11B3 **Mitchell,Mt** USA
45B2 **Mitchelstown** Irish Rep
84C3 **Mithankot** Pak
55C3 **Mitilíni** Greece
23B2 **Mitla** Mexico
95C3 **Mits'iwa** Eritrea
32C3 **Mitu** Colombia
99C3 **Mitumbar** *Mts* Zaïre
98C3 **Mitwaba** Zaïre
98B2 **Mitzic** Gabon
75B1 **Miura** Japan
72C3 **Mi Xian** China
69F3 **Miyake** *I* Japan
75B2 **Miyake-jima** *I* Japan
69E4 **Miyako** *I* Japan
74C4 **Miyakonojō** Japan
74C4 **Miyazaki** Japan
75B1 **Miyazu** Japan
74C4 **Miyoshi** Japan
72D1 **Miyun** China
99D2 **Mizan Teferi** Eth
95A1 **Mizdah** Libya
45B3 **Mizen Hd** *C* Irish Rep
54C1 **Mizil** Rom
86C2 **Mizo Hills** India
86C2 **Mizoram** Union Territory, India
94B3 **Mizpe Ramon** Israel
112B11 **Mizuho** *Base* Ant
74E3 **Mizusawa** Japan
39H7 **Mjolby** Sweden
100B2 **Mkushi** Zambia
101H1 **Mkuzi** S Africa
57C2 **Mladá Boleslav** Czech Republic
58C2 **Mława** Pol
52C2 **Mljet** *I* Croatia
100B3 **Mmabatho** S Africa
84D2 **Mnadi** India

97A4 **Moa** *R* Sierra Leone
94B3 **Moab** Region, Jordan
9C3 **Moab** USA
98B3 **Moanda** Congo
98B3 **Moanda** Gabon
99C3 **Moba** Zaïre
75C1 **Mobara** Japan
98C2 **Mobaye** CAR
98C2 **Mobayi** Zaïre
10A3 **Moberly** USA
11B3 **Mobile** USA
11B3 **Mobile B** USA
8C2 **Mobridge** USA
101D2 **Moçambique** Mozam
76C1 **Moc Chau** Viet
100B3 **Mochudi** Botswana
101D2 **Mocimboa da Praia** Mozam
32B3 **Mocoa** Colombia
35B2 **Mococa** Brazil
34D2 **Mocoreta** *R* Arg
23B1 **Moctezuma** *R* Mexico
101C2 **Mocuba** Mozam
47B2 **Modane** France
101G1 **Modder** *R* S Africa
52B2 **Modena** Italy
46D2 **Moder** *R* France
8A3 **Modesto** USA
22B2 **Modesto Res** USA
53B3 **Modica** Italy
59B3 **Mödling** Austria
107D4 **Moe** Aust
47C1 **Moesa** *R* Switz
42C2 **Moffat** Scot
84D2 **Moga** India
35B2 **Mogi das Cruzes** Brazil
60C3 **Mogilev** Belarus
60C4 **Mogilev Podolskiy** Ukraine
35B2 **Mogi-Mirim** Brazil
101D2 **Mogincual** Mozam
47E2 **Mogliano** Italy
34B2 **Mogna** Arg
68D1 **Mogocha** Russian Fed
65K4 **Mogochin** Russian Fed
50A2 **Moguer** Spain
110C1 **Mohaka** *R* NZ
86C2 **Mohanganj** Bang
15D2 **Mohawk** *R* USA
99D3 **Mohoro** Tanz
65J5 **Mointy** Kazakhstan
38G5 **Mo i Rana** Nor
48C3 **Moissac** France
21B2 **Mojave** USA
22D3 **Mojave** *R* USA
9B3 **Mojave Desert** USA
78C4 **Mojokerto** Indon
86B1 **Mokama** India
110B1 **Mokau** *R* NZ
22B1 **Mokelumne Aqueduct** USA
22B1 **Mokelumne Hill** USA
22B1 **Mokelumne North Fork** *R* USA
101G1 **Mokhotlong** Lesotho
96D1 **Moknine** Tunisia
86C1 **Mokokchüng** India
98B1 **Mokolo** Cam
74B4 **Mokp'o** S Korea
61F3 **Moksha** *R* Russian Fed
23B1 **Molango** Mexico
55B3 **Moláoi** Greece
Moldavia = Moldova
38F6 **Molde** Nor
60C4 **Moldova** Republic, Europe
54B1 **Moldoveanu** *Mt* Rom
100B3 **Molepolole** Botswana
53C2 **Molfetta** Italy
34A3 **Molina** Chile
30B2 **Mollendo** Peru
60C3 **Molodechno** Belarus
112C11 **Molodezhnaya** *Base* Ant

21C4 **Molokai** / Hawaiian Is
61G2 **Moloma** R Russian Fed
109C2 **Molong** Aust
100B3 **Molopo** R Botswana
98B2 **Molounddu** Cam
8D1 **Molson L** Can
71D4 **Molucca** S Indon
71D4 **Moluccas** Is Indon
101C2 **Moma** Mozam
31C3 **Mombaca** Brazil
99D3 **Mombasa** Kenya
98C2 **Mompono** Zaïre
56C2 **Mon** / Den
44A3 **Monach** Is Scot
49D3 **Monaco** Principality, Europe
44B3 **Monadhliath** Mts Scot
45C1 **Monaghan** County, Irish Rep
45C1 **Monaghan** Irish Rep
27D3 **Mona Pass** Caribbean S
13B2 **Monarch Mt** Can
5G4 **Monashee Mts** Can
41B3 **Monastereven** Irish Rep
47B2 **Moncalieri** Italy
31B2 **Monção** Brazil
38L5 **Monchegorsk** Russian Fed
56B2 **Mönchen-gladbach** Germany
24B2 **Monclova** Mexico
7D5 **Moncton** Can
9C4 **Monctova** Mexico
50A1 **Mondego** R Port
52A2 **Mondovi** Italy
27H1 **Moneague** Jamaica
14C2 **Monessen** USA
18B2 **Monett** USA
52B1 **Monfalcone** Italy
50A1 **Monforte de Lemos** Spain
98C2 **Monga** Zaïre
98C2 **Mongala** R Zaïre
99D2 **Mongalla** Sudan
76D1 **Mong Cai** Viet
98B1 **Mongo** Chad
68B2 **Mongolia** Republic, Asia
100B2 **Mongu** Zambia
21B2 **Monitor Range** Mts USA
98C3 **Monkoto** Zaïre
43C4 **Monmouth** Wales
18B1 **Monmouth** USA
13C2 **Monmouth,Mt** Can
43C4 **Monmouthshire** County Wales
97C4 **Mono** R Togo
21B2 **Mono L** USA
53C2 **Monopoli** Italy
51B1 **Monreal del Campo** Spain
19B3 **Monroe** Louisiana, USA
14B2 **Monroe** Michigan, USA
20B1 **Monroe** Washington, USA
18B2 **Monroe City** USA
97A4 **Monrovia** Lib
20D3 **Monrovia** USA
56A2 **Mons** Belg
47D2 **Monselice** Italy
16C1 **Monson** USA
58B1 **Mönsterås** Sweden
101D2 **Montagne d'Ambre** Mt Madag
96C1 **Montagnes des Ouled Naïl** Mts Alg
12E3 **Montague I** USA
49C3 **Mont Aigoual** Mt France
48B2 **Montaigu** France
53C3 **Montallo** Mt Italy
8B2 **Montana** State, USA
50A1 **Montañas de León** Mts Spain
49C2 **Montargis** France
48C3 **Montauban** France

15D2 **Montauk** USA
15D2 **Montauk Pt** USA
49D2 **Montbéliard** France
52A1 **Mont Blanc** Mt France/Italy
49C2 **Montceau les Mines** France
51C1 **Montceny** Mt Spain
49D3 **Mont Cinto** Mt Corse
46C2 **Montcornet** France
48B3 **Mont-de-Marsan** France
48C2 **Montdidier** France
30D2 **Monteagudo** Bol
33G4 **Monte Alegre** Brazil
52B2 **Monte Amiata** Mt Italy
47D2 **Monte Baldo** Mt Italy
15C1 **Montebello** Can
106A3 **Monte Bello Is** Aust
47E2 **Montebelluna** Italy
49D3 **Monte Carlo** Monaco
35B1 **Monte Carmelo** Brazil
34D2 **Monte Caseros** Arg
52B2 **Monte Cimone** Mt Italy
52A2 **Monte Cinto** Mt Corse
34B2 **Monte Coman** Arg
52B2 **Monte Corno** Mt Italy
27C3 **Montecristi** Dom Rep
52B2 **Montecristo** / Italy
23A1 **Monte Escobedo** Mexico
53C2 **Monte Gargano** Mt Italy
26B3 **Montego Bay** Jamaica
47D2 **Monte Grappa** Mt Italy
47C2 **Monte Lesima** Mt Italy
49C3 **Montélimar** France
53B2 **Monte Miletto** Mt Italy
50A2 **Montemo-o-Novo** Port
24C2 **Montemorelos** Mexico
26B5 **Montená** Colombia
54A2 **Montenegro** Republic, Yugos
35D1 **Monte Pascoal** Mt Brazil
34A2 **Monte Patria** Chile
53C3 **Monte Pollino** Mt Italy
101C2 **Montepuez** Mozam
8A3 **Monterey** California, USA
15C3 **Monterey** Virginia, USA
8A3 **Monterey B** USA
32B2 **Montería** Colombia
30D2 **Montero** Bol
47B2 **Monte Rosa** Mt Italy/Switz
24B2 **Monterrey** Mexico
31C5 **Montes Claros** Brazil
50B2 **Montes de Toledo** Mts Spain
29E2 **Montevideo** Urug
52A2 **Monte Viso** Mt Italy
27P2 **Mont Gimie** Mt St Lucia
11B3 **Montgomery** Alabama, USA
96C2 **Mont Gréboun** Niger
46C2 **Montherme** France
47B1 **Monthey** Switz
19B3 **Monticello** Arkansas, USA
16B2 **Monticello** New York, USA
9C3 **Monticello** Utah, USA
53A2 **Monti del Gennargentu** Mt Sardegna
47D2 **Monti Lessini** Mts Italy

53B3 **Monti Nebrodi** Mts Italy
7C5 **Mont-Laurier** Can
48C2 **Montluçon** France
7C5 **Montmagny** Can
46C2 **Montmédy** France
49C3 **Mont Mézenc** Mt France
46B2 **Montmirail** France
50B2 **Montoro** Spain
49D3 **Mont Pelat** Mt France
14B2 **Montpelier** Ohio, USA
10C2 **Montpelier** Vermont, USA
49C3 **Montpellier** France
7C5 **Montréal** Can
48C1 **Montreuil** France
52A1 **Montreux** Switz
47B1 **Mont Risoux** Mt France
8C3 **Montrose** Colorado, USA
40C2 **Montrose** Scot
48B2 **Mont-St-Michel** France
96B1 **Monts des Ksour** Mts Alg
51C3 **Monts des Ouled Neil** Mts Alg
51C2 **Monts du Hodna** Mts Alg
27E3 **Montserrat** / Caribbean S
10C1 **Monts Otish** Mts Can
12B1 **Monument Mt** USA
9B3 **Monument V** USA
98C2 **Monveda** Zaïre
76B1 **Monywa** Myan
52A1 **Monza** Italy
100B2 **Monze** Zambia
101H1 **Mooi** R S'Africa
101G1 **Mooi River** S Africa
108B1 **Moomba** Aust
109D2 **Moonbi Range** Mts Aust
108B1 **Moonda L** Aust
109D1 **Moonie** Aust
109C1 **Moonie** R Aust
108A2 **Moonta** Aust
106A4 **Moora** Aust
106A3 **Moore,L** Aust
42C2 **Moorfoot Hills** Scot
8D2 **Moorhead** USA
22C3 **Moorpark** USA
7B4 **Moose** R Can
5H4 **Moose Jaw** Can
5H4 **Moosomin** Can
7B4 **Moosonee** Can
16D2 **Moosup** USA
101C2 **Mopeia** Mozam
97B3 **Mopti** Mali
30B2 **Moquegua** Peru
39G6 **Mora** Sweden
31D3 **Morada** Brazil
84D3 **Morādābād** India
35B1 **Morada Nova de Minas** L Brazil
101D2 **Morafenobe** Madag
101D2 **Moramanga** Madag
27J2 **Morant Bay** Jamaica
27J2 **Morant Pt** Jamaica
87B3 **Moratuwa** Sri Lanka
59B3 **Morava** R Austria/ Slovakia
54B2 **Morava** R Serbia, Yugos
90C2 **Moraveh Tappeh** Iran
44C3 **Moray** Division, Scot
40C2 **Moray Firth** Estuary Scot
47C1 **Morbegno** Italy
85C4 **Morbi** India
93D2 **Mor Dağ** Mt Turk
5J5 **Morden** Can
61F3 **Mordoviya** Division, Russian Fed
42C2 **Morecambe** Eng
42C2 **Morecambe B** Eng
107D3 **Moree** Aust
14B3 **Morehead** USA
47C1 **Mörel** Switz

24B3 **Morelia** Mexico
23B2 **Morelos** State, Mexico
85D3 **Morena** India
5E4 **Moresby I** Can
109D1 **Moreton I** Aust
46B2 **Moreuil** France
47B1 **Morez** France
19B4 **Morgan City** USA
22B2 **Morgan Hill** USA
14C3 **Morgantown** USA
101G1 **Morgenzon** S Africa
47B1 **Morges** Switz
46D2 **Morhange** France
74E2 **Mori** Japan
27K1 **Moriatio** Tobago
13B2 **Morice L** Can
13E2 **Morinville** Can
74E3 **Morioka** Japan
109D2 **Morisset** Aust
63D1 **Morkoka** R Russian Fed
48B2 **Morlaix** France
27Q2 **Morne Diablotin** Mt Dominica
106C2 **Mornington** / Aust
85B3 **Moro** Pak
96B2 **Morocco** Kingdom, Africa
79B4 **Moro G** Phil
99D3 **Morogoro** Tanz
23A1 **Moroleon** Mexico
101D3 **Morombe** Madag
26B2 **Morón** Cuba
101D3 **Morondava** Madag
50A2 **Moron de la Frontera** Spain
101D2 **Moroni** Comoros
71D3 **Morotai** / Indon
99D2 **Moroto** Uganda
61F4 **Morozovsk** Russian Fed
42D2 **Morpeth** Eng
19B2 **Morrilton** USA
35B1 **Morrinhos** Brazil
110C1 **Morrinsville** NZ
16B2 **Morristown** New Jersey, USA
15C2 **Morristown** New York, USA
16B2 **Morrisville** Pennsylvania, USA
21A2 **Morro Bay** USA
23A2 **Morro de Papanoa** Mexico
23A2 **Morro de Petatlán** Mexico
101C2 **Morrumbala** Mozam
101C3 **Morrumbene** Mozam
61F3 **Morshansk** Russian Fed
47C2 **Mortara** Italy
34C2 **Morteros** Arg
33G6 **Mortes** R Mato Grosso, Brazil
35C2 **Mortes** R Minas Gerais, Brazil
108B3 **Mortlake** Aust
27L1 **Moruga** Trinidad
109D3 **Moruya** Aust
109C1 **Morven** Aust
44B3 **Morvern** Pen Scot
109C3 **Morwell** Aust
76B3 **Moscos Is** Myan
20C1 **Moscow** Idaho, USA
56B2 **Mosel** R Germany
46D2 **Moselle** Department, France
46D2 **Moselle** R France
20C1 **Moses Lake** USA
111B3 **Mosgiel** NZ
99D3 **Moshi** Tanz
38G5 **Mosjøen** Nor
63G2 **Moskal'vo** Russian Fed
60E2 **Moskva** Russian Fed
60E2 **Moskva** Division, Russian Fed
35C1 **Mosquito** R Brazil
39G7 **Moss** Nor
98B3 **Mossaka** Congo
100B4 **Mossel Bay** S Africa
98B3 **Mossendjo** Congo

Mossgiel

86D2 **Myingyan** Myan
76B1 **Myingyao** Myan
76B3 **Myinmoletkat** *Mt*
Myan
82D3 **Myitkyina** Myan
76B3 **Myitta** Myan
86C2 **Mymensingh** Bang
69F3 **Myojin** *I* Japan
39F6 **Myrdal** Nor
38B2 **Myrdalsjökur** *Ice Cap*
Iceland
17C1 **Myrtle Beach** USA
20B2 **Myrtle Creek** USA
39G7 **Mysen** Nor
56C2 **Mysíloborz** Pol
64F3 **Mys Kanin Nos** *C*
Russian Fed
59B3 **Myslenice** Pol
69H1 **Mys Lopatka** *C*
Russian Fed
87B2 **Mysore** India
60D5 **Mys Sarych** *C*
Ukraine
16D2 **Mystic** USA
61H5 **Mys Tyub-Karagan** *Pt*
Kazakhstan
63G2 **Mys Yelizavety** *C*
Russian Fed
64H2 **Mys Zhelaniya** *C*
Russian Fed
77D3 **My Tho** Viet
20B2 **Mytle Point** USA
101C2 **Mzimba** Malawi
101C2 **Mzuzú** Malawi

N

21C4 **Naalehu** Hawaiian Is
39J6 **Naantali** Fin
45C2 **Naas** Irish Rep
75B2 **Nabari** Japan
61H2 **Naberezhnye Chelny**
Russian Fed
12F2 **Nabesna** *R* USA
96D1 **Nabeul** Tunisia
94B2 **Nablus** Israel
101D2 **Nacala** Mozam
20B1 **Naches** USA
101C2 **Nachingwea** Tanz
19B3 **Nacogdoches** USA
76A3 **Nacondam** *I*
Indian O
24B1 **Nacozari** Mexico
85C4 **Nadiād** India
50B2 **Nador** Mor
90B3 **Nadüshan** Iran
59C3 **Nadvornaya** Ukraine
56C1 **Naestved** Den
95B2 **Nafürah** Libya
75A2 **Nagahama** Japan
82D3 **Naga Hills** Myan
75B1 **Nagai** Japan
86C1 **Nāgāland** State,
India
74D3 **Nagano** Japan
74D3 **Nagaoka** Japan
86C1 **Nagaon** India
87B2 **Nāgappattinam** India
85C4 **Nagar Parkar** Pak
74B4 **Nagasaki** Japan
75B2 **Nagashima** Japan
75A2 **Nagato** Japan
85C3 **Nāgaur** India
87B3 **Nāgercoil** India
85B3 **Nagha Kalat** Pak
84D3 **Nagina** India
74D3 **Nagoya** Japan
85D4 **Nāgpur** India
82D2 **Nagqu** China
59B3 **Nagykanizsa** Hung
59B3 **Nagykörös** Hung
69E4 **Naha** Japan
8A2 **Nahaimo** Can
84D2 **Nāhan** India
4F3 **Nahanni Butte** Can
94B2 **Nahariya** Israel
90A3 **Nahāvand** Iran
46D2 **Nahe** *R* Germany
72D2 **Nahpu** China
72E1 **Naimen Qi** China
7D4 **Nain** Can
90B3 **Nā'in** Iran
84D3 **Naini Tai** India
44C3 **Nairn** Scot
99D3 **Nairobi** Kenya

90B3 **Najafābād** Iran
74C2 **Najin** N Korea
75A2 **Nakama** Japan
74E3 **Nakaminato** Japan
75A2 **Nakamura** Japan
75B1 **Nakano** Japan
75A1 **Nakano-shima** *I*
Japan
74C4 **Nakatsu** Japan
75B1 **Nakatsu-gawa** Japan
95C3 **Nak' fa** Eritrea
93E2 **Nakhichevan**
Azerbaijan
93E2 **Nakhichevan**
Division, Azerbaijan
92B4 **Nakhl** Egypt
74C2 **Nakhodka**
Russian Fed
76C3 **Nakhon Pathom**
Thai
76C3 **Nakhon Ratchasima**
Thai
77C4 **Nakhon Si**
Thammarat Thai
12H3 **Nakina** Can
7B4 **Nakina** Ontario, Can
12C3 **Naknek** USA
12C3 **Naknek L** USA
4C4 **Nakrek** USA
39G8 **Nakskov** Den
99D3 **Nakuru** Kenya
13D2 **Nakusp** Can
61F5 **Nal'chik** Russian Fed
87B1 **Nalgonda** India
87B1 **Nallamala Range** *Mts*
India
95A1 **Nālūt** Libya
101H1 **Namaacha** Mozam
65G6 **Namak** *L* Iran
90C3 **Namakzar-e Shadad**
Salt Flat Iran
65J5 **Namangan**
Uzbekistan
101C2 **Namapa** Mozam
100A4 **Namaqualand**
Region, S Africa
109D1 **Nambour** Aust
109D2 **Nambucca Heads**
Aust
77D4 **Nam Can** Viet
82D2 **Nam Co** *L* China
76D1 **Nam Dinh** Viet
101C2 **Nametil** Mozam
74B4 **Namhae-do** *I* S
Korea
100A2 **Namib Desert**
Namibia
100A2 **Namibe** Angola
100A3 **Namibia** Republic,
Africa
82D3 **Namjagbarwa Feng**
Mt China
71D4 **Namlea** Indon
109C2 **Namoi** *R* Aust
13D1 **Nampa** Can
20C2 **Nampa** USA
97B3 **Nampala** Mali
76C2 **Nam Phong** Thai
74B3 **Namp'o** N Korea
101C2 **Nampula** Mozam
38G6 **Namsos** Nor
76B1 **Namton** Myan
86D2 **Namtu** Myan
13B2 **Namu** Can
101C2 **Namuno** Mozam
46C1 **Namur** Belg
100A2 **Namutoni** Namibia
74B3 **Namwön** S Korea
13C3 **Nanaimo** Can
74B2 **Nanam** N Korea
109D1 **Nanango** Aust
74D3 **Nanao** Japan
75B1 **Nanatsu-jima** *I*
Japan
73B3 **Nanbu** China
73D4 **Nanchang** China
73B3 **Nanchong** China
49D2 **Nancy** France
87B1 **Nānded** India
109D2 **Nandewar Range**
Mts Aust
85C4 **Nandurbar** India
87B1 **Nandyāl** India
98B2 **Nanga Eboko** Cam

84C1 **Nanga Parbat** *Mt*
Pak
78C3 **Nangapinoh** Indon
78C3 **Nangatayap** Indon
74B2 **Nangnim Sanmaek**
Mts N Korea
86C1 **Nang Xian** China
67F3 **Nangzhou** China
87B2 **Nanjangüd** India
72D3 **Nanjing** China
Nanking = Nanjing
75A2 **Nankoku** Japan
73C4 **Nan Ling** Region,
China
76D1 **Nanliu** *R* China
73B5 **Nanning** China
6F3 **Nanortalik**
Greenland
73A5 **Nanpan Jiang** *R*
China
86A1 **Nānpāra** India
73D4 **Nanping** China
6A1 **Nansen Sd** Can
99D3 **Nansio** Tanz
48B2 **Nantes** France
13E2 **Nanton** Can
72E3 **Nantong** China
10C2 **Nantucket** *I* USA
35C1 **Nanuque** Brazil
72C3 **Nanyang** China
72D2 **Nanyang Hu** *L* China
99D2 **Nanyuki** Kenya
74D3 **Naoetsu** Japan
85B4 **Naokot** Pak
22A1 **Napa** USA
12B2 **Napaiskak** USA
15C2 **Napanee** Can
65K4 **Napas** Russian Fed
6E3 **Napassoq** Greenland
76D2 **Nape** Laos
110C1 **Napier** NZ
Naples = Napoli
17B2 **Naples** Florida, USA
19B3 **Naples** Texas, USA
73B5 **Napo** China
32C4 **Napo** *R* Peru/
Ecuador
53B2 **Napoli** Italy
90A2 **Naqadeh** Iran
92C4 **Naqb Ishtar** Jordan
75B2 **Nara** Japan
97B3 **Nara** Mali
107D4 **Naracoorte** Aust
23B1 **Naranjos** Mexico
87C1 **Narasaraopet** India
77C4 **Narathiwat** Thai
86C2 **Narayanganj** Bang
87B1 **Nārāyenpet** India
49C3 **Narbonne** France
84D2 **Narendranagar** India
6C2 **Nares Str** Can
58C2 **Narew** *R* Pol
75C1 **Narita** Japan
85C4 **Narmada** *R* India
84D3 **Nārnaul** India
60E2 **Naro Fominsk**
Russian Fed
99D3 **Narok** Kenya
84C2 **Narowal** Pak
107D4 **Narrabri** Aust
109C1 **Narran** *L* Aust
109C1 **Narran** *R* Aust
109C2 **Narrandera** Aust
106A4 **Narrogin** Aust
109C2 **Narromine** Aust
85D4 **Narsimhapur** India
87C1 **Narsipatnam** India
6F3 **Narssalik** Greenland
6F3 **Narssaq** Greenland
6F3 **Narssarssuaq**
Greenland
75C1 **Narugo** Japan
75A2 **Naruto** Japan
60C2 **Narva** Russian Fed
38H5 **Narvik** Nor
84D3 **Narwāna** India
64G3 **Nar'yan Mar**
Russian Fed
108B1 **Narylico** Aust
65J5 **Naryn** Kyrgyzstan
97C4 **Nasarawa** Nig
103D5 **Nasca Ridge**
Pacific O
16D1 **Nashua** USA

19B3 **Nashville** Arkansas,
USA
11B3 **Nashville** Tennessee,
USA
54A1 **Našice** Croatia
85D4 **Nāsik** India
99D2 **Nasir** Sudan
13B1 **Nass** *R* Can
26B1 **Nassau**
The Bahamas
16C1 **Nassau** USA
95C2 **Nasser,L** Egypt
39G7 **Nässjö** Sweden
7C4 **Nastapoka Is** Can
100B3 **Nata** Botswana
31D3 **Natal** Brazil
70A3 **Natal** Indon
90B3 **Natanz** Iran
7D4 **Natashquan** Can
7D4 **Natashquan** *R* Can
19B3 **Natchez** USA
19B3 **Natchitoches** USA
108C3 **Nathalia** Aust
6H2 **Nathorsts Land**
Region Greenland
13C1 **Nation** *R* Can
21B3 **National City** USA
75C1 **Natori** Japan
99D3 **Natron** *L* Tanz
106A4 **Naturaliste,C** Aust
47D1 **Nauders** Austria
56C2 **Nauen** Germany
16C2 **Naugatuck** USA
57C2 **Naumburg** Germany
94B3 **Naur** Jordan
105G4 **Nauru** *I* Pacific O
63C2 **Naushki** Russian Fed
23B1 **Nautla** Mexico
9C3 **Navajo Res** USA
50A2 **Navalmoral de la**
Mata Spain
29C7 **Navarino** *I* Chile
51B1 **Navarra** Province,
Spain
34D3 **Navarro** Arg
19A3 **Navasota** USA
19A3 **Navasota** *R* USA
50A1 **Navia** *R* Spain
34A2 **Navidad** Chile
85C4 **Navlakhi** India
60D3 **Navlya** Russian Fed
24B2 **Navojoa** Mexico
55B3 **Návpaktos** Greece
55B3 **Návplion** Greece
85C4 **Navsāri** India
94C2 **Nawá** Syria
86B2 **Nawāda** India
84B2 **Nawah** Afghan
85B3 **Nawrabshah** Pak
73B4 **Naxi** China
55C3 **Náxos** *I* Greece
23A1 **Nayar** Mexico
90C3 **Nay Band** Iran
91B4 **Nāy Band** Iran
74E2 **Nayoro** Japan
94B2 **Nazareth** Israel
48B2 **Nazay** France
32C6 **Nazca** Peru
92A2 **Nazilli** Turk
63B2 **Nazimovo**
Russian Fed
13C2 **Nazko** *R* Can
99D2 **Nazret** Eth
91C5 **Nazwa** Oman
65J4 **Nazyvayevsk**
Russian Fed
98B3 **Ndalatando** Angola
98C2 **Ndélé** CAR
98B3 **Ndendé** Gabon
98B1 **Ndjamena** Chad
98B3 **Ndjolé** Gabon
100B2 **Ndola** Zambia
109C1 **Neabul** Aust
108A1 **Neales** *R* Aust
55B3 **Neápolis** Greece
43C4 **Neath** Wales
43C4 **Neath and Port**
Talbot County Wales
109C1 **Nebine** *R* Aust
65G6 **Nebit Dag**
Turkmenistan
8C2 **Nebraska** State, USA
18A1 **Nebraska City** USA
13C2 **Nechako** *R* Can

Neches

Nowa Sól

58B2 **Nowa Sól** Pol
18A2 **Nowata** USA
Nowgong = Nagaon
12D2 **Nowitna** *R* USA
109D2 **Nowra** Aust
90B2 **Now Shahr** Iran
84C2 **Nowshera** Pak
59C3 **Nowy Sącz** Pol
12H3 **Noyes** *I* USA
46B2 **Noyon** France
97B4 **Nsawam** Ghana
99D1 **Nuba** *Mts* Sudan
81B3 **Nubian Desert** Sudan
34A3 **Nuble** *R* Chile
9D4 **Nueces** *R* USA
5J3 **Nueltin** *L* Can
26A2 **Nueva Gerona** Cuba
34A3 **Nueva Imperial** Chile
9C4 **Nueva Laredo** Mexico
34D2 **Nueva Palmira** Urug
24B2 **Nueva Rosita** Mexico
26B2 **Nuevitas** Cuba
24B1 **Nuevo Casas Grandes** Mexico
24C2 **Nuevo Laredo** Mexico
99E2 **Nugaal** Region, Somalia
6E2 **Nûgâtsiaq** Greenland
6E2 **Nugssuag** *Pen* Greenland
6E2 **Nûgussaq** *I* Greenland
108A2 **Nukey Bluff** *Mt* Aust
93D3 **Nukhayb** Iraq
65G5 **Nukus** Uzbekistan
12C2 **Nulato** USA
106B4 **Nullarbor Plain** Aust
97D4 **Numan** Nig
75B1 **Numata** Japan
98C2 **Numatinna** *R* Sudan
74D3 **Numazu** Japan
71E4 **Numfoor** *I* Indon
108C3 **Numurkah** Aust
12B2 **Nunapitchuk** USA
84D2 **Nunkun** *Mt* India
53A2 **Nuoro** Sardegna
91B3 **Nurābād** Iran
47C2 **Nure** *R* Italy
108A2 **Nuriootpa** Aust
84C1 **Nuristan** *Upland* Afghan
61H3 **Nurlat** Russian Fed
38K6 **Nurmes** Fin
57C3 **Nürnberg** Germany
108C2 **Nurri** *Mt* Aust
92D2 **Nusaybin** Turk
12C3 **Nushagak** *R* USA
12C3 **Nushagak** *B* USA
12C3 **Nushagak Pen** USA
84B3 **Nushki** Pak
7D4 **Nutak** Can
12F2 **Nutzotin Mts** USA
Nuuk = Godthåb
86A1 **Nuwakot** Nepal
87C3 **Nuwara-Eliya** Sri Lanka
6C3 **Nuyujukjuak** Can
16C2 **Nyack** USA
99D2 **Nyahururu** Kenya
108B3 **Nyah West** Aust
4C3 **Nyai** USA
68B3 **Nyainqentanglha Shan** *Mts* China
99D3 **Nyakabindi** Tanz
98C1 **Nyala** Sudan
86B1 **Nyalam** China
98C2 **Nyamlell** Sudan
64F3 **Nyandoma** Russian Fed
100C2 **Nyanga** Zim
98B3 **Nyanga** *R* Gabon
101C2 **Nyasa L** Malawi/Mozam
76B2 **Nyaunglebin** Myan
61J2 **Nyazepetrovsk** Russian Fed
39G7 **Nyborg** Den
39H7 **Nybro** Sweden
64J3 **Nyda** Russian Fed
6D1 **Nyeboes Land** *Region* Can
99D3 **Nyeri** Kenya

101C2 **Nyimba** Zambia
82D3 **Nyingchi** China
59C3 **Nyiregyháza** Hung
99D2 **Nyiru,Mt** Kenya
38J6 **Nykarleby** Fin
39F7 **Nykøbing** Den
39G8 **Nykøbing** Den
39H7 **Nyköbing** Sweden
100B3 **Nylstroom** S Africa
109C2 **Nymagee** Aust
39H7 **Nynäshamn** Sweden
109C2 **Nyngan** Aust
47B1 **Nyon** Switz
98B2 **Nyong** *R* Cam
49D3 **Nyons** France
59B2 **Nysa** Pol
20C2 **Nyssa** USA
63D1 **Nyurba** Russian Fed
99D3 **Nzega** Tanz
97B4 **Nzérékore** Guinea
98B3 **N'zeto** Angola

O

6F3 **Oaggsimiut** Greenland
8C2 **Oahe Res** USA
21C4 **Oahu** *I* Hawaiian Is
108B2 **Oakbank** Aust
22B2 **Oakdale** USA
109D1 **Oakey** Aust
21A2 **Oakland** California, USA
20B2 **Oakland** Oregon, USA
14A3 **Oakland City** USA
14A2 **Oak Lawn** USA
22B2 **Oakley** California, USA
20B2 **Oakridge** USA
14C2 **Oakville** Can
111B3 **Oamaru** NZ
112B7 **Oates Land** Region, Ant
109C4 **Oatlands** Aust
23B2 **Oaxaca** Mexico
23B2 **Oaxaca** State, Mexico
65J3 **Ob'** *R* Russian Fed
75B1 **Obama** Japan
111A3 **Oban** NZ
44B3 **Oban** Scot
75C1 **Obanazawa** Japan
47D1 **Oberammergau** Germany
46D1 **Oberhausen** Germany
47D1 **Oberstdorf** Germany
71D4 **Obi** *I* Indon
33F4 **Obidos** Brazil
74E2 **Obihiro** Japan
98C2 **Obo** CAR
99E1 **Obock** Djibouti
58B2 **Oborniki** Pol
60E3 **Oboyan** Russian Fed
20B2 **O'Brien** USA
61H3 **Obshchiy Syrt** *Mts* Russian Fed
64J3 **Obskava Guba** *B* Russian Fed
97B4 **Obuasi** Ghana
17B2 **Ocala** USA
32C2 **Ocana** Colombia
50B2 **Ocaño** Spain
12G3 **Ocean C** USA
15C3 **Ocean City** Maryland, USA
16B3 **Ocean City** New Jersey, USA
5F4 **Ocean Falls** Can
22D4 **Oceanside** USA
19C3 **Ocean Springs** USA
61H2 **Ocher** Russian Fed
44C3 **Ochil Hills** Scot
17B1 **Ochlockonee** *R* USA
27H1 **Ocho Rios** Jamaica
17B1 **Ocmulgee** *R* USA
17B1 **Oconee** *R* USA
14A2 **Oconto** USA
23A1 **Ocotlán** Jalisco, Mexico
23B2 **Ocotlán** Oaxaca, Mexico
97B4 **Oda** Ghana
75A1 **Oda** Japan

38B2 **Ódáðahraun** Region, Iceland
74E2 **Odate** Japan
74D3 **Odawara** Japan
39F6 **Odda** Nor
50A2 **Odemira** Port
55C3 **Ödemiş** Turk
101G1 **Odendaalsrus** S Africa
39G7 **Odense** Den
56C2 **Oder** *R* Pol/Germany
9C3 **Odessa** Texas, USA
60D4 **Odessa** Ukraine
20C1 **Odessa** Washington, USA
97B4 **Odienné** Côte d'Ivoire
59B2 **Odra** *R* Pol
31C3 **Oeiras** Brazil
53C2 **Ofanto** *R* Italy
94B3 **Ofaqim** Israel
45C2 **Offaly** County, Irish Rep
49D1 **Offenbach** Germany
49D2 **Offenburg** Germany
74D3 **Oga** Japan
99E2 **Ogaden** Region, Eth
74D3 **Ogaki** Japan
8C2 **Ogallala** USA
69G4 **Ogasawara Gunto** *Is* Japan
97C4 **Ogbomosho** Nig
8B2 **Ogden** Utah, USA
15C2 **Ogdensburg** USA
17B1 **Ogeechee** *R* USA
12G1 **Ogilvie** Can
4E3 **Ogilvie Mts** Can
17B1 **Oglethorpe,Mt** USA
47D2 **Oglio** *R* Italy
47B1 **Ognon** *R* France
97C4 **Ogoja** Nig
98A3 **Ogooué** *R* Gabon
58C1 **Ogre** Latvia
96B2 **Oguilet Khenachich** *Well* Mali
52C1 **Ogulin** Croatia
111A3 **Ohai** NZ
110C1 **Ohakune** NZ
96C2 **Ohanet** Alg
111A2 **Ohau,L** NZ
10B2 **Ohio** State, USA
14A3 **Ohio** *R* USA
100A2 **Ohopoho** Namibia
57C2 **Ohre** *R* Czech Republic
55B2 **Ohrid** Macedonia
55B2 **Ohridsko Jezero** *L* Macedonia/Alb
110B1 **Ohura** NZ
33G3 **Oiapoque** French Guiana
68B2 **Oijiaojing** China
14C2 **Oil City** USA
21B2 **Oildale** USA
46B2 **Oise** Department, France
49C2 **Oise** *R* France
74C4 **Oita** Japan
22C3 **Ojai** USA
24B2 **Ojinaga** Mexico
23B2 **Ojitlán** Mexico
75B1 **Ojiya** Japan
30C4 **Ojos del Salado** *Mt* Arg
23A1 **Ojueloz** Mexico
60E3 **Oka** *R* Russian Fed
100A3 **Okahandja** Namibia
20C1 **Okanagan Falls** Can
13D2 **Okanagan L** Can
20C1 **Okanogan** USA
20C1 **Okanogan** *R* USA
20B1 **Okanogan Range** *Mts* Can/USA
84C2 **Okara** Pak
100A2 **Okavango** *R* Angola/Namibia
100B2 **Okavango Delta** *Marsh* Botswana
74D3 **Okaya** Japan
74C4 **Okayama** Japan
75B2 **Okazaki** Japan
17B2 **Okeechobee** USA
17B2 **Okeechobee,L** USA

17B1 **Okefenokee Swamp** USA
97C4 **Okene** Nig
85B4 **Okha** India
69G1 **Okha** Russian Fed
86B1 **Okhaldunga** Nepal
62J3 **Okhotsk,S of** Russian Fed
69E4 **Okinawa** *I* Japan
69E4 **Okinawa gunto** *Arch* Japan
74C3 **Oki-shoto** *Is* Japan
9D3 **Oklahoma** State, USA
18A2 **Oklahoma City** USA
18A2 **Okmulgee** USA
98B3 **Okondja** Gabon
98B3 **Okoyo** Congo
97C4 **Okpara** *R* Nig
61J4 **Oktyabr'sk** Kazakhstan
61H3 **Oktyabr'skiy** Russian Fed
74D2 **Okushiri-tō** *I* Japan
38A2 **Olafsvik** Iceland
39H7 **Oland** *I* Sweden
108B2 **Olary** Aust
18B2 **Olathe** USA
29D3 **Olavarria** Arg
53A2 **Olbia** Sardegna
12G1 **Old Crow** Can
56B2 **Oldenburg** Niedersachsen, Germany
56C2 **Oldenburg** Schleswig-Holstein, Germany
15C2 **Old Forge** USA
42C3 **Oldham** Eng
12D3 **Old Harbor** USA
41B3 **Old Head of Kinsale** *C* Scot
16C2 **Old Lyme** USA
13E2 **Olds** Can
72B1 **Oldziyt** Mongolia
15C2 **Olean** USA
63E2 **Olekma** *R* Russian Fed
63D1 **Olekminsk** Russian Fed
38L5 **Olenegorsk** Russian Fed
58D2 **Olevsk** Ukraine
69F2 **Ol'ga** Russian Fed
100A3 **Olifants** *R* Namibia
55B2 **Ólimbos** *Mt* Greece
35B2 **Olimpia** Brazil
23B2 **Olinala** Mexico
31E3 **Olinda** Brazil
34C2 **Oliva** Arg
29C2 **Olivares** *Mt* Arg
35C2 **Oliveira** Brazil
13D3 **Oliver** Can
30C3 **Ollague** Chile
30C3 **Ollagüe** *Mt* Bol
18C2 **Olney** USA
68E1 **Olochi** Russian Fed
39G7 **Olofstrom** Sweden
98B3 **Olombo** Congo
59B3 **Olomouc** Czech Republic
60D1 **Olonets** Russian Fed
79B3 **Olongapo** Phil
48B3 **Oloron Ste Marie** France
68D1 **Olovyannaya** Russian Fed
46D1 **Olpe** Germany
58C2 **Olsztyn** Pol
54B2 **Olt** *R* Rom
47B1 **Olten** Switz
20B1 **Olympia** USA
20B1 **Olympic Nat Pk** USA
Olympus = Ólimbos
20B1 **Olympus,Mt** USA
65J4 **Om'** *R* Russian Fed
75B1 **Omachi** Japan
75B2 **Omae-zaki** *C* Japan
45C1 **Omagh** N Ire
18A1 **Omaha** USA
20C1 **Omak** USA
91C5 **Oman** Sultanate, Arabian Pen
91C4 **Oman,G of** UAE
98A3 **Omboué** Gabon

99D1	**Omdurman** Sudan
23B2	**Ometepec** Mexico
99D1	**Om Hajer** Eritrea
13B1	**Omineca** *R* Can
13B1	**Omineca Mts** Can
75B1	**Omiya** Japan
12H3	**Ommaney,C** USA
4H2	**Ommanney B** Can
99D2	**Omo** *R* Eth
65J4	**Omsk** Russian Fed
74B4	**Omura** Japan
74C4	**Omuta** Japan
61H2	**Omutninsk** Russian Fed
78D3	**Onang** Indon
14B1	**Onaping L** Can
100A2	**Oncócua** Angola
100A2	**Ondangua** Namibia
59C3	**Ondava** *R* Slovakia
68D2	**Ondörhaan** Molgolia
83B5	**One and Half Degree Chan** Indian O
64E3	**Onega** Russian Fed
64E3	**Onega** *R* Russian Fed
15C2	**Oneida L** USA
8D2	**O'Neill** USA
69H2	**Onekotan** *I* Russian Fed
98C3	**Onema** Zaïre
15D2	**Oneonta** USA
54C1	**Onești** Rom
64E3	**Onezhskoye Ozero** *L* Russian Fed
100A2	**Ongiva** Angola
74B3	**Ongjin** N Korea
72D1	**Ongniud Qi** China
87C1	**Ongole** India
15C2	**Onieda L** USA
101D3	**Onilahy** *R* Madag
97C4	**Onitsha** Nig
68C2	**Onjüül** Mongolia
75B1	**Ono** Japan
75B2	**Onohara-jima** *I* Japan
74C4	**Onomichi** Japan
106A3	**Onslow** Aust
17C1	**Onslow B** USA
75B1	**Ontake-san** *Mt* Japan
22D3	**Ontario** California, USA
20C2	**Ontario** Oregon, USA
7A4	**Ontario** Province, Can
15C2	**Ontario,L** Can/USA
51B2	**Onteniente** Spain
106C3	**Oodnadatta** Aust
106C4	**Ooldea** Aust
18A2	**Oologah L** USA
46B1	**Oostende** Belg
46B1	**Oosterschelde** *Estuary* Neth
87B2	**Ootacamund** India
13B2	**Ootsa L** Can
69H1	**Opala** Russian Fed
98C3	**Opala** Zaïre
87C3	**Opanake** Sri Lanka
61G2	**Oparino** Russian Fed
59B3	**Opava** Czech Republic
17A1	**Opelika** USA
19B3	**Opelousas** USA
12C2	**Ophir** USA
58D1	**Opochka** Russian Fed
59B2	**Opole** Pol
	Oporto = Porto
110C1	**Opotiki** NZ
17A1	**Opp** USA
38F6	**Oppdal** Nor
110B1	**Opunake** NZ
54B1	**Oradea** Rom
38B2	**Oraefajökull** *Mts* Iceland
85D3	**Orai** India
96B1	**Oran** Alg
30D3	**Orán** Arg
109C2	**Orange** Aust
22D4	**Orange** California, USA
49C3	**Orange** France
19B3	**Orange** Texas, USA
100A3	**Orange** *R* S Africa
17B1	**Orangeburg** USA
17B1	**Orange Park** USA
14B2	**Orangeville** Can
56C2	**Oranienburg** Germany
79C3	**Orăstie** Rom
54B1	**Oravita** Rom
52B2	**Orbetello** Italy
109C3	**Orbost** Aust
46B1	**Orchies** France
47B2	**Orco** *R* Italy
106B2	**Ord** *R* Aust
106B2	**Ord,Mt** Aust
93C1	**Ordu** Turk
39H7	**Örebro** Sweden
8A2	**Oregon** State, USA
14B2	**Oregon** USA
20B1	**Oregon City** USA
39H6	**Oregrund** Sweden
60E2	**Orekhovo Zuyevo** Russian Fed
60E3	**Orel** Russian Fed
60E3	**Orel** Division Russian Fed
61H3	**Orenburg** Russian Fed
61H3	**Orenburg** Division Russian Fed
34D3	**Orense** Arg
50A1	**Orense** Spain
56C1	**Oresund** *Str* Den/ Sweden
111A3	**Oreti** *R* NZ
55C3	**Orhaneli** *R* Turk
68C2	**Orhon Gol** *R* Mongolia
23B2	**Oriental** Mexico
108B1	**Orientos** Aust
51B2	**Orihuela** Spain
15C2	**Orillia** Can
33E2	**Orinoco** *R* Ven
86A2	**Orissa** State, India
53A3	**Oristano** Sardegna
38K6	**Orivesi** *L* Fin
33F4	**Oriximina** Brazil
23B2	**Orizaba** Mexico
35B1	**Orizona** Brazil
44C2	**Orkney** *I* Scot
35B2	**Orlândia** Brazil
17B2	**Orlando** USA
48C2	**Orléanais** *Region* France
48C2	**Orléans** France
63B2	**Orlik** Russian Fed
82A3	**Ormara** Pak
79B3	**Ormoc** Phil
17B2	**Ormond Beach** USA
46C2	**Ornain** *R* France
47B1	**Ornans** France
48B2	**Orne** *R* France
38H6	**Örnsköldsvik** Sweden
32C3	**Orocué** Colombia
94B3	**Oron** Israel
	Orontes = 'Aşi
79B4	**Oroquieta** Phil
59C3	**Oroscháza** Hung
21A2	**Oroville** California, USA
20C1	**Oroville** Washington, USA
47B1	**Orsières** Switz
65G4	**Orsk** Russian Fed
38F6	**Ørsta** Nor
48B3	**Orthez** France
50A1	**Ortigueira** Spain
47D1	**Ortles** *Mts* Italy
27L1	**Ortoire** *R* Trinidad
93E2	**Orümiyeh** Iran
30C2	**Oruro** Bol
61J2	**Osa** Russian Fed
18B2	**Osage** *R* USA
75B1	**Osaka** Japan
25D4	**Osa,Pen de** Costa Rica
18C2	**Osceola** Arkansas, USA
18B1	**Osceola** Iowa, USA
20C2	**Osgood Mts** USA
15C2	**Oshawa** Can
75B2	**O-shima** *I* Japan
10B2	**Oshkosh** USA
97C4	**Oshogbo** Nig
7B5	**Oshosh** USA
98B3	**Oshwe** Zaïre
54A1	**Osijek** Croatia
65K5	**Osinniki** Russian Fed
58D2	**Osipovichi** Belarus
18B1	**Oskaloosa** USA
60A2	**Oskarshamn** Sweden
39G7	**Oslo** Nor
92C2	**Osmaniye** Turk
56B2	**Osnabrück** Germany
30F4	**Osório** Brazil
29B4	**Osorno** Chile
50B1	**Osorno** Spain
20C1	**Osoyoos** Can
13C1	**Ospika** *R* Can
107D5	**Ossa,Mt** Aust
16C2	**Ossining** USA
60D2	**Ostashkov** Russian Fed
	Ostend = Oostende
38G6	**Østerdalen** *V* Nor
38G6	**Ostersund** Sweden
56B2	**Ostfriesische Inseln** *Is* Germany
39H6	**Östhammär** Sweden
53B2	**Ostia** Italy
47D2	**Ostiglia** Italy
59B3	**Ostrava** Czech Republic
58B2	**Ostróda** Pol
58B2	**Ostroleka** Pol
60C2	**Ostrov** Russian Fed
64J2	**Ostrov Belyy** *I* Russian Fed
64H1	**Ostrov Greem Bell** *I* Barents S
64F3	**Ostrov Kolguyev** *I* Russian Fed
74F2	**Ostrov Kunashir** *I* Russian Fed
64F2	**Ostrov Mechdusharskiy** *I* Barents S
90B2	**Ostrov Ogurchinskiy** *I* Turkmenistan
64G1	**Ostrov Rudol'fa** *I* Barents S
64G2	**Ostrov Vaygach** *I* Russian Fed
1B7	**Ostrov Vrangelya** *I* Russian Fed
58B2	**Ostrów Wlkp.** Pol
59C2	**Ostrowiec** Pol
58C2	**Ostrów Mazowiecka** Pol
50A2	**Osuna** Spain
15C2	**Osweg** USA
15C2	**Oswego** USA
43C3	**Oswestry** Eng
59B2	**Oświęcim** Pol
75B1	**Ota** Japan
111B3	**Otago Pen** NZ
110C2	**Otaki** NZ
74E2	**Otaru** Japan
32B3	**Otavalo** Ecuador
100A2	**Otavi** Namibia
75C1	**Otawara** Japan
20C1	**Othello** USA
55B3	**Othris** *Mt* Greece
16C1	**Otis** Massachusetts, USA
16B2	**Otisville** USA
100A3	**Otjiwarongo** Namibia
72B2	**Otog Qi** China
110C1	**Otorohanga** NZ
55A2	**Otranto** Italy
55A2	**Otranto,Str of** *Chan* Italy/Alb
14A2	**Otsego** USA
75B1	**Otsu** Japan
39F6	**Otta** Nor
39F7	**Otta** *R* Nor
15C1	**Ottawa** Can
18A2	**Ottawa** Kansas, USA
15C1	**Ottawa** *R* Can
7B4	**Ottawa Is** Can
7B4	**Otter Rapids** Can
6B1	**Otto Fjord** Can
101G1	**Ottosdal** S Africa
18B1	**Ottumwa** USA
46D2	**Ottweiler** Germany
97C4	**Oturkpo** Nig
32B5	**Otusco** Peru
108B3	**Otway,C** Aust
58C2	**Otwock** Pol
47D1	**Ötz** Austria
47D1	**Ötzal** *Mts* Austria
76C1	**Ou** *R* Laos
19B3	**Ouachita** *R* USA
19B3	**Ouachita,L** USA
19B3	**Ouachita Mts** USA
96A2	**Ouadane** Maur
98C2	**Ouadda** CAR
98C1	**Ouaddai** *Desert Region* Chad
97B3	**Ouagadougou** Burkina
97B3	**Ouahigouya** Burkina
98C2	**Ouaka** CAR
97C3	**Oualam** Niger
98C2	**Ouanda Djallé** CAR
96A2	**Ouarane** Region, Maur
96C1	**Ouargla** Alg
98C2	**Ouarra** *R* CAR
96B1	**Ouarzazate** Mor
51C2	**Ouassel** *R* Alg
98B2	**Oubangui** *R* Congo
46B1	**Oudenaarde** Belg
100B4	**Oudtshoorn** S Africa
51B2	**Oued Tlélat** Alg
96B1	**Oued Zem** Mor
98B2	**Ouesso** Congo
96B1	**Ouezzane** Mor
98B2	**Ouham** *R* Chad
97C4	**Ouidah** Benin
96B1	**Oujda** Mor
38J6	**Oulainen** Fin
38K5	**Oulu** Fin
38K6	**Oulu** *R* Fin
38K6	**Oulujärvi** *L* Fin
95B3	**Oum Chalouba** Chad
98B1	**Oum Hadjer** Chad
95B3	**Oum Haouach** *Watercourse* Chad
38K5	**Ounas** *R* Fin
95B3	**Ounianga Kébir** Chad
46D1	**Our** *R* Germany
46B2	**Ourcq** *R* France
	Ourense = Orense
31C3	**Ouricurí** Brazil
35B2	**Ourinhos** Brazil
35C2	**Ouro Prêto** Brazil
46C1	**Ourthe** *R* Belg
42D2	**Ouse** *R* Eng
43E3	**Ouse** *R* Eng
40B2	**Outer Hebrides** *Is* Scot
22C4	**Outer Santa Barbara** *Chan* USA
100A3	**Outjo** Namibia
38K6	**Outokumpu** Fin
108B3	**Ouyen** Aust
47C2	**Ovada** Italy
34A2	**Ovalle** Chile
100A2	**Ovamboland** Region, Namibia
61H5	**Ova Tyuleni** *Is* Kazakhstan
38J5	**Övertorneå** Sweden
50A1	**Oviedo** Spain
60C3	**Ovruch** Ukraine
63E2	**Ovsyanka** Russian Fed
111A3	**Owaka** NZ
75B2	**Owase** Japan
11B3	**Owensboro** USA
21B2	**Owens L** USA
14B2	**Owen Sound** Can
107D1	**Owen Stanley Range** *Mts* PNG
97C4	**Owerri** Nig
97C4	**Owo** Nig
14B2	**Owosso** USA
20C2	**Owyhee** *R* USA
20C2	**Owyhee Mts** USA
32B6	**Oxapampa** Peru
39H7	**Oxelösund** Sweden
43D4	**Oxford** County, Eng
43D4	**Oxford** Eng
16D1	**Oxford** Massachusetts, USA
19C3	**Oxford** Mississippi, USA
45B1	**Ox Mts** Irish Rep

Oxnard

22C3 **Oxnard** USA
74D3 **Oyama** Japan
13E2 **Oyen** Can
98B2 **Oyem** Gabon
44B3 **Oykel** *R* Scot
39F6 **Øyre** Nor
109C4 **Oyster B** Aust
79B4 **Ozamiz** Phil
17A1 **Ozark** USA
18B2 **Ozark Plat** USA
18B2 **Ozarks,L of the** USA
59C3 **Ozd** Hung
65K5 **Ozero Alakol** *L* Kazakhstan/ Russian Fed
65J5 **Ozero Balkhash** *L* Kazakhstan
63C2 **Ozero Baykal** *L* Kazakhstan
65J4 **Ozero Chany** *L* Russian Fed
69F1 **Ozero Chukchagirskoye** Russian Fed
69F1 **Ozero Evoron** Russian Fed
Ozero Chudskoye = Peipus,L
60D2 **Ozero Il'men** *L* Russian Fed
38L5 **Ozero Imandra** *L* Russian Fed
82B1 **Ozero Issyk Kul'** *L* Kyrgyzstan
69F2 **Ozero Khanka** *L* China/Russian Fed
38L5 **Ozero Kovdozero** *L* Russian Fed
38L5 **Ozero Kuyto** *L* Russian Fed
38L5 **Ozero Pyaozero** *L* Russian Fed
65H4 **Ozero Tengiz** *L* Kazakhstan
38L5 **Ozero Topozero** *L* Russian Fed
65K5 **Ozero Zaysan** Kazakhstan
23B1 **Ozuluama** Mexico

P

100A4 **Paarl** S Africa
44A3 **Pabbay** *I* Scot
58B2 **Pabianice** Pol
86B2 **Pabna** Bang
58D2 **Pabrade** Lithuania
32B5 **Pacasmayo** Peru
23B1 **Pachuca** Mexico
105K6 **Pacific-Antarctic Ridge** Pacific O
22B2 **Pacific Grove** USA
78C4 **Pacitan** Indon
35C1 **Pacuí** *R* Brazil
70B4 **Padang** Indon
56B2 **Paderborn** Germany
5J3 **Padlei** Can
86C2 **Padma** *R* Bang
47D2 **Padova** Italy
9D4 **Padre I** USA
43B4 **Padstow** Eng
108B3 **Padthaway** Aust
Padua = Padova
14A3 **Paducah** Kentucky, USA
11B3 **Paducah** USA
38L5 **Padunskoye More** *L* Russian Fed
74A3 **Paengnyŏng-do** *I* S Korea
110C1 **Paeroa** NZ
100C3 **Pafuri** Mozam
52B2 **Pag** *I* Croatia
79B4 **Pagadian** Phil
70B4 **Pagai Selatan** *I* Indon
70B4 **Pagai Utara** *I* Indon
71F2 **Pagan** *I* Pacific O
78D3 **Pagatan** Indon
55C3 **Pagondhas** Greece
110C2 **Pahiatua** NZ
21C4 **Pahoa** Hawaiian Is
17B2 **Pahokee** USA
39K6 **Päijänne** *L* Fin
21C4 **Pailola Chan** Hawaiian Is

14B2 **Painesville** USA
9B3 **Painted Desert** USA
42B2 **Paisley** Scot
32A5 **Paita** Peru
38J5 **Pajala** Sweden
80E3 **Pakistan** Republic, Asia
76C2 **Pak Lay** Laos
86D2 **Pakokku** Myan
13E2 **Pakowki L** Can
52C1 **Pakrac** Croatia
54A1 **Paks** Hung
76C2 **Pak Sane** Laos
76D2 **Pakse** Laos
99D2 **Pakwach** Uganda
98B2 **Pala** Chad
52C2 **Palagruža** *I* Croatia
46B2 **Palaiseau** France
Palakhat = Palghat
78C3 **Palangkaraya** Indon
87B2 **Palani** India
85C4 **Palanpur** India
100B3 **Palapye** Botswana
17B2 **Palatka** USA
71E3 **Palau Is** Pacific O
76B3 **Palaw** Myan
79A4 **Palawan** *I* Phil
79A4 **Palawan Pass** Phil
87B3 **Palayankottai** India
39J7 **Paldiski** Estonia
78A3 **Palembang** Indon
50B1 **Palencia** Spain
94A1 **Paleokhorio** Cyprus
53B3 **Palermo** Italy
19A3 **Palestine** USA
86C2 **Paletwa** Myan
87B2 **Pālghāt** India
85C3 **Pali** India
85C4 **Pālitāna** India
87B3 **Palk Str** India/ Sri Lanka
61G3 **Pallasovka** Russian Fed
38J5 **Pallastunturi** *Mt* Fin
111B2 **Palliser B** NZ
111C2 **Palliser,C** NZ
101D2 **Palma** Mozam
51C2 **Palma de Mallorca** Spain
31D3 **Palmares** Brazil
26A5 **Palmar Sur** Costa Rica
31B4 **Palmas** Brazil
97B4 **Palmas,C** Lib
26B2 **Palma Soriano** Cuba
17B2 **Palm Bay** USA
17B2 **Palm Beach** USA
22C3 **Palmdale** USA
31D3 **Palmeira dos Indos** Brazil
12E2 **Palmer** USA
112C3 **Palmer** *Base* Ant
112C3 **Palmer Arch** Ant
112B3 **Palmer Land** *Region* Ant
111B3 **Palmerston** NZ
110C2 **Palmerston North** NZ
16B2 **Palmerton** USA
17B2 **Palmetto** USA
53C3 **Palmi** Italy
32B3 **Palmira** Colombia
107D2 **Palm Is** Aust
21B3 **Palm Springs** USA
18B2 **Palmyra** Missouri, USA
16A2 **Palmyra** Pennsylvania, USA
86B2 **Palmyras Pt** India
22A2 **Palo Alto** USA
78B2 **Paloh** Indon
99D1 **Paloich** Sudan
21B3 **Palomar Mt** USA
70D4 **Palopo** Indon
70C4 **Palu** Indon
92C2 **Palu** Turk
84D3 **Palwal** India
97C3 **Pama** Burkina
78C4 **Pamekasan** Indon
78B4 **Pameungpeuk** Indon
48C3 **Pamiers** France
82B2 **Pamir** *Mts* China
65J6 **Pamir** *R* Russian Fed
11C3 **Pamlico Sd** USA
9C3 **Pampa** USA

34B2 **Pampa de la Salinas** *Salt pan* Arg
34B3 **Pampa de la Varita** *Plain* Arg
32C2 **Pamplona** Colombia
50B1 **Pamplona** Spain
18C2 **Pana** USA
54B2 **Panagyurishte** Bulg
87A1 **Panaji** India
32B2 **Panamá** Panama
32A2 **Panama** Republic, Cent America
26B5 **Panama Canal** Panama
17A1 **Panama City** USA
21B2 **Panamint Range** *Mts* USA
21B2 **Panamint V** USA
47D2 **Panaro** *R* Italy
79B3 **Panay** *I* Phil
54B2 **Pancevo** Serbia, Yugos
79B3 **Pandan** Phil
87B1 **Pandharpur** India
108A1 **Pandie Pandie** Aust
58C1 **Panevežys** Lithuania
65K5 **Panfilov** Kazakhstan
76B1 **Pang** *R* Myan
99D3 **Pangani** Tanz
99D3 **Pangani** *R* Tanz
98C3 **Pangi** Zaïre
78B3 **Pangkalpinang** Indon
6D3 **Pangnirtung** Can
76B1 **Pangtara** Myan
79B4 **Pangutaran Group** *Is* Phil
84D3 **Panipat** India
84B2 **Panjao** Afghan
74B3 **P'anmunjŏm** N Korea
86A2 **Panna** India
35A2 **Panorama** Brazil
53B3 **Pantelleria** *I* Medit S
23B1 **Pantepec** Mexico
23B1 **Pánuco** Mexico
23B1 **Pánuco** *R* Mexico
73A4 **Pan Xian** China
53C3 **Paola** Italy
18B2 **Paola** USA
14A3 **Paoli** USA
59B3 **Pápa** Hung
110B1 **Papakura** NZ
23B2 **Papaloapan** *R* Mexico
23B1 **Papantla** Mexico
44E1 **Papa Stour** *I* Scot
110B1 **Papatoetoe** NZ
44C2 **Papa Westray** *I* Scot
107D1 **Papua,G of** PNG
107D1 **Papua New Guinea** Republic, S E Asia
34A2 **Papudo** Chile
76B2 **Papun** Myan
33G4 **Para** State, Brazil
31B2 **Pará** *R* Brazil
106A3 **Paraburdoo** Aust
32B6 **Paracas,Pen de** Peru
35B1 **Paracatu** Brazil
35B1 **Paracatu** *R* Brazil
108A2 **Parachilna** Aust
84C2 **Parachinar** Pak
54B2 **Paracin** Serbia, Yugos
35C1 **Pará de Minas** Brazil
21A2 **Paradise** California, USA
18B2 **Paragould** USA
33E6 **Paraguá** *R* Bol
33E2 **Paragua** *R* Ven
30E2 **Paraguai** *R* Brazil
30E4 **Paraguari** Par
30E3 **Paraguay** Republic, S America
30E3 **Paraguay** *R* Par
31D3 **Paraiba** State, Brazil
35B2 **Paraiba** *R* Brazil
35C2 **Paraiba do Sul** *R* Brazil
97C4 **Parakou** Benin
108A2 **Parakylia** Aust
87B3 **Paramakkudi** India
33F2 **Paramaribo** Surinam
69H1 **Paramushir** *I* Russian Fed
30F3 **Paraná** State, Brazil

34C2 **Paraná** Urug
29E2 **Paraná** *R* Arg
31B4 **Paraná** *R* Brazil
35A2 **Paraná** *R* Brazil
30G4 **Paranaguá** Brazil
35A1 **Paranaiba** Brazil
35A1 **Paranaiba** *R* Brazil
35A2 **Paranapanema** *R* Brazil
35A2 **Paranavai** Brazil
79B4 **Parang** Phil
35C1 **Paraope** *R* Brazil
110B2 **Paraparaumu** NZ
87B1 **Parbhani** India
94B2 **Pardes Hanna** Israel
34D3 **Pardo** Arg
35D1 **Pardo** *R* Bahia, Brazil
35A2 **Pardo** *R* Mato Grosso do Sul, Brazil
35B1 **Pardo** *R* Minas Gerais, Brazil
35B2 **Pardo** *R* Sao Paulo, Brazil
59B2 **Pardubice** Czech Republic
69F4 **Parece Vela** *Reef* Pacific O
10C2 **Parent** Can
70C4 **Parepare** Indon
34C3 **Parera** Arg
70B4 **Pariaman** Indon
33E1 **Paria,Pen de** Ven
48C2 **Paris** France
14B3 **Paris** Kentucky, USA
19A3 **Paris** Texas, USA
14B3 **Parkersburg** USA
109C2 **Parkes** Aust
16B3 **Parkesburg** USA
14A2 **Park Forest** USA
20B1 **Parksville** Can
87B1 **Parli** India
47D2 **Parma** Italy
14B2 **Parma** USA
31C2 **Parnaiba** Brazil
31C2 **Parnaiba** *R* Brazil
55B3 **Párnon Óros** *Mts* Greece
60B2 **Pärnu** Estonia
86B1 **Paro** Bhutan
108B1 **Paroo** *R* Aust
108B2 **Paroo Channel** *R* Aust
55C3 **Páros** *I* Greece
47B2 **Parpaillon** *Mts* France
34A3 **Parral** Chile
109D2 **Parramatta** Aust
9C4 **Parras** Mexico
6B3 **Parry B** Can
4G2 **Parry Is** Can
7C5 **Parry Sd** Can
14B1 **Parry Sound** Can
57C3 **Parsberg** Germany
5F4 **Parsnip** *R* Can
18A2 **Parsons** Kansas, USA
14C3 **Parsons** West Virginia, USA
48B2 **Parthenay** France
53B3 **Partinico** Italy
74C2 **Partizansk** Russian Fed
33G4 **Paru** *R* Brazil
101G1 **Parys** S Africa
19A4 **Pasadena** Texas, USA
22C3 **Pasadena** California, USA
78D3 **Pasangkayu** Indon
76B2 **Pasawing** Myan
19C3 **Pascagoula** USA
54C1 **Pascani** Rom
20C1 **Pasco** USA
46B1 **Pas-de-Calais** Department, France
39G8 **Pasewalk** Germany
91C4 **Pashū'īyeh** Iran
106B4 **Pasley,C** Aust
29E2 **Paso de los Toros** Urug
29B4 **Paso Limay** Arg
21A2 **Paso Robles** USA
45B3 **Passage West** Irish Rep
16B2 **Passaic** USA

57C3 **Passau** Germany
30E4 **Passo de los Libres** Arg
47D1 **Passo di Stelvio** *Mt* Italy
30F4 **Passo Fundo** Brazil
35B2 **Passos** Brazil
47B2 **Passy** France
32B4 **Pastaza** *R* Peru
34C3 **Pasteur** Arg
5H4 **Pas,The** Can
32B3 **Pasto** Colombia
12B2 **Pastol B** USA
47D2 **Pasubio** *Mt* Italy
78C4 **Pasuruan** Indon
58C1 **Pasvalys** Lithuania
85C4 **Pātan** India
86B1 **Patan** Nepal
108B3 **Patchewollock** Aust
110B1 **Patea** NZ
111B2 **Patea** *R* NZ
53B3 **Paterno** Italy
16B2 **Paterson** USA
111A3 **Paterson Inlet** *B* NZ
84D2 **Pathankot** India
 Pathein = Bassein
84D2 **Patiāla** India
32B6 **Pativilca** Peru
55C3 **Pátmos** *I* Greece
86B1 **Patna** India
93D2 **Patnos** Turk
63D2 **Patomskoye Nagor'ye** *Upland* Russian Fed
31D3 **Patos** Brazil
35B1 **Patos de Minas** Brazil
34B2 **Patquia** Arg
55B3 **Pátrai** Greece
35B1 **Patrocinio** Brazil
99E3 **Patta** *I* Kenya
78D4 **Pattallasang** Indon
77C4 **Pattani** Thai
22B2 **Patterson** California, USA
19B4 **Patterson** Louisiana, USA
12H2 **Patterson,Mt** Can
22C2 **Patterson Mt** USA
13B1 **Pattullo,Mt** Can
31D3 **Patu** Brazil
86C2 **Patuakhali** Bang
25D3 **Patuca** *R* Honduras
23A2 **Patzcuaro** Mexico
48B3 **Pau** France
4F3 **Paulatuk** Can
31C3 **Paulistana** Brazil
101H1 **Paulpietersburg** S Africa
19A3 **Pauls Valley** USA
76B2 **Paungde** Myan
84D2 **Pauri** India
38H5 **Pauskie** Nor
35C1 **Pavão** Brazil
47C2 **Pavia** Italy
65J4 **Pavlodar** Kazakhstan
61J2 **Pavlovka** Russian Fed
61F2 **Pavlovo** Russian Fed
61F3 **Pavlovsk** Russian Fed
78C3 **Pawan** *R* Indon
18A2 **Pawhuska** USA
16D2 **Pawtucket** USA
47B1 **Payerne** Switz
20C2 **Payette** USA
7C4 **Payne,L** Can
34D2 **Paysandu** Urug
46A2 **Pays-de-Bray** Region, France
54B2 **Pazardzhik** Bulg
13D1 **Peace** *R* Can
17B2 **Peace** *R* USA
13D1 **Peace River** Can
43D3 **Peak District Nat Pk** Eng
108A1 **Peake** *R* Aust
109C2 **Peak Hill** Aust
71E4 **Peak Mandala** *Mt* Indon
42D3 **Peak,The** *Mt* Eng
19B3 **Pearl** *R* USA
21C4 **Pearl City** Hawaiian Is

21C4 **Pearl Harbor** Hawaiian Is
4H2 **Peary Chan** Can
101C2 **Pebane** Mozam
54B2 **Peć** Serbia, Yugos
35C1 **Peçanha** Brazil
19B4 **Pecan Island** USA
38L5 **Pechenga** Russian Fed
64F3 **Pechora** *R* Russian Fed
64G3 **Pechorskoye More** *S* Russian Fed
53C3 **Pecoraro** *Mt* Italy
9C3 **Pecos** USA
9C3 **Pecos** *R* USA
59B3 **Pécs** Hung
108A1 **Pedirka** Aust
35C1 **Pedra Azul** Brazil
35B2 **Pedregulho** Brazil
26B3 **Pedro Cays** *Is* Caribbean S
30C3 **Pedro de Valdivia** Chile
30E3 **Pedro Juan Caballero** Par
34C3 **Pedro Luro** Arg
23B1 **Pedro Mentova** Mexico
87C3 **Pedro,Pt** Sri Lanka
108B2 **Peebinga** Aust
42C2 **Peebles** Scot
17C1 **Pee Dee** *R* USA
16C2 **Peekskill** USA
42B2 **Peel** Eng
12H1 **Peel** *R* Can
4J2 **Peel Sd** Can
108A1 **Peera Peera Poolanna L** Aust
13E1 **Peerless L** Can
71E4 **Peg Arfak** *Mt* Indon
111B2 **Pegasus B** NZ
83D4 **Pegu** Myan
78A3 **Pegunungan Barisan** *Mts* Indon
78C2 **Pegunungan Iran** *Mts* Malay/Indon
71E4 **Pegunungan Maoke** *Mts* Indon
78D3 **Pegunungan Meratus** *Mts* Indon
78C2 **Pegunungan Muller** *Mts* Indon
78C3 **Pegunungan Schwaner** *Mts* Indon
78A3 **Pegunungan Tigapuluh** *Mts* Indon
76B2 **Pegu Yoma** *Mts* Myan
34C3 **Pehuajó** Arg
 Péipsi Järve = Peipus,L
39K7 **Peipus, Lake** Estonia/ Russian Fed
35A2 **Peixe** *R* Sao Paulo, Brazil
72D3 **Pei Xian** China
78B4 **Pekalongan** Indon
77C5 **Pekan** Malay
78A2 **Pekanbaru** Indon
18C1 **Pekin** USA
 Peking = Beijing
77C5 **Pelabohan Kelang** Malay
78D4 **Pelau Pelau Kangean** *Is* Indon
78C4 **Pelau Pelau Karimunjawa** *Arch* Indon
78D4 **Pelau Pelau Postilyon** *Is* Indon
54B1 **Peleaga** *Mt* Rom
63D2 **Peleduy** Russian Fed
14B2 **Pelee I** Can
71D4 **Peleng** *I* Indon
12G3 **Pelican** USA
69F1 **Peliny Osipenko** Russian Fed
34C3 **Pellegrini** Arg
38J5 **Pello** Fin
12H2 **Pelly** *R* Can
6A3 **Pelly Bay** Can
12G2 **Pelly Crossing** Can
12H2 **Pelly Mts** Can

30F5 **Pelotas** Brazil
30F4 **Pelotas** *R* Brazil
47B2 **Pelvoux** Region, France
78B4 **Pemalang** Indon
78A3 **Pematang** Indon
101D2 **Pemba** Mozam
99D3 **Pemba** *I* Tanz
13C2 **Pemberton** Can
13D2 **Pembina** *R* Can
15C1 **Pembroke** Can
17B1 **Pembroke** USA
43B4 **Pembroke** Wales
43B4 **Pembrokeshire** County Wales
34A3 **Pemuco** Chile
78D2 **Penambo Range** *Mts* Malay
35A2 **Penápolis** Brazil
50A2 **Peñarroya** Spain
51B1 **Penarroya** *Mt* Spain
50A1 **Peña Trevina** *Mt* Spain
98B2 **Pende** *R* Chad
12J3 **Pendelton,Mt** Can
20C1 **Pendleton** USA
20C1 **Pend Oreille** *R* USA
31D4 **Penedo** Brazil
85D5 **Penganga** *R* India
73D5 **P'eng-hu Lieh-tao** *Is* Taiwan
72E2 **Penglai** China
73B4 **Pengshui** China
71E4 **Pengunungan Maoke** *Mts* Indon
26C4 **Península de la Guajiri** *Pen* Colombia
27E4 **Península de Paria** *Pen* Ven
77C5 **Peninsular Malaysia** Malay
10D2 **Peninsule de Gaspé** *Pen* Can
23A1 **Penjamo** Mexico
87B2 **Penner** *R* India
42C2 **Pennine Chain** *Mts* Eng
16B3 **Penns Grove** USA
10C2 **Pennsylvania** State, USA
6D3 **Penny Highlands** *Mts* Can
108B3 **Penola** Aust
106C4 **Penong** Aust
42C2 **Penrith** Eng
11B3 **Pensacola** USA
112A **Pensacola Mts** Ant
78D1 **Pensiangan** Malay
13D3 **Penticton** Can
44C2 **Pentland Firth** *Chan* Scot
42C2 **Pentland Hills** Scot
61G3 **Penza** Russian Fed
61G3 **Penza** Division, Russian Fed
43B4 **Penzance** Eng
10B2 **Peoria** USA
78A3 **Perabumulih** Indon
77C5 **Perak** *R* Malay
78A2 **Perawang** Indon
32B3 **Pereira** Colombia
35A2 **Pereira Barreto** Brazil
61F4 **Perelazovskiy** Russian Fed
12D3 **Perenosa B** USA
34C2 **Pergamino** Arg
7C4 **Peribonca** *R* Can
48C2 **Périqueux** France
25E4 **Perlas Arch de** *Is* Panama
61J2 **Perm'** Russian Fed
61J2 **Perm' Division** Russian Fed
 Pernambuco = Recife
31D3 **Pernambuco** State, Brazil
108A2 **Pernatty Lg** Aust
54B2 **Pernik** Bulg
46B2 **Péronne** France
23B2 **Perote** Mexico
49C3 **Perpignan** France
22D4 **Perris** USA
17B1 **Perry** Florida, USA

17B1 **Perry** Georgia, USA
18A2 **Perry** Oklahoma, USA
4H3 **Perry River** Can
14B2 **Perrysburg** USA
12C3 **Perryville** Alaska, USA
18C2 **Perryville** Missouri, USA
106A4 **Perth** Aust
15C2 **Perth** Can
44C3 **Perth** Scot
16B2 **Perth Amboy** USA
44C3 **Perthshire and Kinross** Division, Scot
32C6 **Peru** Republic, S America
18C1 **Peru** USA
103E5 **Peru-Chile Trench** Pacific O
52B2 **Perugia** Italy
52C2 **Perušic** Croatia
93D2 **Pervari** Turk
61F3 **Pervomaysk** Russian Fed
60D4 **Pervomaysk** Ukraine
61J2 **Pervoural'sk** Russian Fed
52B2 **Pesaro** Italy
22A2 **Pescadero** USA
 Pescadores = P'eng-hu Lieh-tao
52B2 **Pescara** Italy
47D2 **Peschiera** Italy
84C2 **Peshawar** Pak
54B2 **Peshkopi** Alb
14A1 **Peshtigo** USA
60E2 **Pestovo** Russian Fed
94B2 **Petah Tiqwa** Israel
21A2 **Petaluma** USA
46C2 **Pétange** Lux
23A2 **Petatlán** Mexico
101C2 **Petauke** Zambia
108A2 **Peterborough** Aust
15C2 **Peterborough** Can
43D3 **Peterborough** Eng
44D3 **Peterhead** Scot
6D1 **Petermann Gletscher** *Gl* Greenland
106B3 **Petermann Range** *Mts* Aust
29B3 **Peteroa** *Mt* Arg/Chile
13F1 **Peter Pond L** Can
12H3 **Petersburg** Alaska, USA
85C4 **Petlād** India
23B2 **Petlalcingo** Mexico
25D2 **Peto** Mexico
63D2 **Petomskoye Nagor'ye** *Upland* Russian Fed
34A2 **Petorca** Chile
14B1 **Petoskey** USA
31C3 **Petrolina** Brazil
65H4 **Petropavlovsk** Kazakhstan
35C2 **Petrópolis** Brazil
61G3 **Petrovsk** Russian Fed
68C1 **Petrovsk Zabaykal'skiy** Russian Fed
64E3 **Petrozavodsk** Russian Fed
101G1 **Petrus** S Africa
101G1 **Petrusburg** S Africa
1B7 **Pevek** Russian Fed
46D2 **Pfälzer Wald** Region, Germany
57B3 **Pforzheim** Germany
84D2 **Phagwara** India
85C3 **Phalodi** India
46D2 **Phalsbourg** France
87A1 **Phaltan** India
77B4 **Phangnga** Thai
76C3 **Phanom Dang** *Mts* Camb
76D3 **Phan Rang** Viet
76D3 **Phan Thiet** Viet
17A1 **Phenix City** USA
76B3 **Phet Buri** Thai
76D3 **Phiafay** Laos
19C3 **Philadelphia** Mississippi, USA

1B8 **Polyarnyy**
Yakutskaya,
Russian Fed
105H3 **Polynesia** *Region*
Pacific O
32B5 **Pomabamba** Peru
35C2 **Pomba** *R* Brazil
22D3 **Pomona** USA
18A2 **Pomona Res** USA
17B2 **Pompano Beach**
USA
16B2 **Pompton Lakes**
USA
18A2 **Ponca City** USA
27D3 **Ponce** Puerto Rico
17B2 **Ponce de Leon B**
USA
87B2 **Pondicherry** India
6C2 **Pond Inlet** Can
50A1 **Ponferrade** Spain
98C2 **Pongo** *R* Sudan
101H1 **Pongola** *R* S Africa
87B2 **Ponnāni** India
86C2 **Ponnyadoung Range**
Mts Myan
13E2 **Ponoka** Can
64F3 **Ponoy** Russian Fed
48B2 **Pons** France
35D1 **Ponta da Baleia** *Pt*
Brazil
96A1 **Ponta Delgada**
Açores
98B3 **Ponta do Padrão** *Pt*
Angola
35C2 **Ponta dos Búzios** *Pt*
Brazil
30F4 **Ponta Grossa** Brazil
35B2 **Pontal** Brazil
46D2 **Pont-à-Mousson**
France
30E3 **Ponta Pora** Brazil
49D2 **Pontarlier** France
19B3 **Pontchartrain,L** USA
52B2 **Pontedera** Italy
52A2 **Ponte Leccia** Corse
50A1 **Pontevedra** Spain
18C1 **Pontiac** Illinois,
USA
14B2 **Pontiac** Michigan,
USA
78B3 **Pontianak** Indon
48B2 **Pontivy** France
46B2 **Pontoise** France
19C3 **Pontotoc** USA
43C4 **Pontypool** Wales
43C4 **Pontypridd** Wales
43D4 **Poole** Eng
Poona = Pune
108B2 **Pooncarie** Aust
108B2 **Poopelloe,L** *L* Aust
12C2 **Poorman** USA
32B3 **Popayán** Colombia
46B1 **Poperinge** Belg
108B2 **Popilta L** Aust
18B2 **Poplar Bluff** USA
19C3 **Poplarville** USA
107D1 **Popndetta** PNG
23B2 **Popocatepetl** *Mt*
Mexico
98B3 **Popokabaka** Zaïre
71F4 **Popondetta** PNG
54C2 **Popovo** Bulg
85B4 **Porbandar** India
13A2 **Porcher I** Can
12F1 **Porcupine** *R* Can/
USA
52B1 **Poreč** Croatia
35A2 **Porecatu** Brazil
39J6 **Pori** Fin
111B2 **Porirua** NZ
38H5 **Porjus** Sweden
69G2 **Poronaysk**
Russian Fed
47B1 **Porrentruy** Switz
38K4 **Porsangen** *Inlet* Nor
39F7 **Porsgrunn** Nor
45C1 **Portadown** N Ire
8D2 **Portage la Prairie**
Can
13C3 **Port Alberni** Can
50A2 **Portalegre** Port
9C3 **Portales** USA
100B4 **Port Alfred** S Africa
13B2 **Port Alice** Can

19B3 **Port Allen** USA
20B1 **Port Angeles** USA
26B3 **Port Antonio**
Jamaica
45C2 **Portarlington**
Irish Rep
19B4 **Port Arthur** USA
108A2 **Port Augusta** Aust
26C3 **Port-au-Prince** Haiti
14B2 **Port Austin** USA
108B3 **Port Campbell** Aust
86B2 **Port Canning** India
7D5 **Port Cartier** Can
111B3 **Port Chalmers** NZ
17B2 **Port Charlotte** USA
16C2 **Port Chester** USA
15C2 **Port Colborne** Can
15C2 **Port Credit** Can
109C4 **Port Davey** Aust
26C3 **Port-de-Paix** Haiti
77C5 **Port Dickson** Malay
100C4 **Port Edward** S Africa
35C1 **Porteirinha** Brazil
14B2 **Port Elgin** Can
100B4 **Port Elizabeth**
S Africa
27N2 **Porter Pt** St Vincent
and the Grenadines
21B2 **Porterville** USA
107D4 **Port Fairy** Aust
98A3 **Port Gentil** Gabon
19B3 **Port Gibson** USA
12D3 **Port Graham** USA
20B1 **Port Hammond** Can
89E7 **Port Harcourt** Nig
13B2 **Port Hardy** Can
7D5 **Port Hawkesbury**
Can
106A3 **Port Hedland** Aust
Port Heiden = Meshik
43B3 **Porthmadog** Wales
7E4 **Port Hope Simpson**
Can
22C3 **Port Hueneme** USA
14B2 **Port Huron** USA
50A2 **Portimão** Port
109D2 **Port Jackson** *B* Aust
16C2 **Port Jefferson** USA
16B2 **Port Jervis** USA
109D2 **Port Kembla** Aust
14B2 **Portland** Indiana,
USA
10C2 **Portland** Maine, USA
109C2 **Portland** New South
Wales, Aust
20B1 **Portland** Oregon,
USA
108B3 **Portland** Victoria,
Aust
27H2 **Portland Bight** *B*
Jamaica
43C4 **Portland Bill** *Pt* Eng
109C4 **Portland,C** Aust
13A1 **Portland Canal** Can/
USA
110C1 **Portland I** NZ
27H2 **Portland Pt** Jamaica
45C2 **Port Laoise** Irish Rep
108A2 **Port Lincoln** Aust
97A4 **Port Loko** Sierra
Leone
101E3 **Port Louis** Mauritius
108B3 **Port MacDonnell**
Aust
13B2 **Port McNeill** Can
109D2 **Port Macquarie** Aust
12B3 **Port Moller** USA
107D1 **Port Moresby** PNG
100A3 **Port Nolloth** S Africa
16B3 **Port Norris** USA
89E7 **Port Novo** Benin
50A1 **Porto** Port
30F5 **Pôrto Alegre** Brazil
33F6 **Pôrto Artur** Brazil
30F3 **Pôrto E Cunha** Brazil
52B2 **Portoferraio** Italy
27E4 **Port of Spain**
Trinidad
47D2 **Portomaggiore** Italy
97C4 **Porto Novo** Benin
20B1 **Port Orchard** USA
20B2 **Port Orford** USA
96A1 **Porto Santo** *I*
Medeira

31D5 **Pôrto Seguro** Brazil
53A2 **Porto Torres**
Sardegna
53A2 **Porto Vecchio** Corse
33E5 **Pôrto Velho** Brazil
111A3 **Port Pegasus** *B* NZ
108B3 **Port Phillip B** Aust
108A2 **Port Pirie** Aust
44A3 **Portree** Scot
20B1 **Port Renfrew** Can
27J2 **Port Royal** Jamaica
17B1 **Port Royal Sd** USA
45C1 **Portrush** N Ire
92B3 **Port Said** Egypt
17A2 **Port St Joe** USA
100B4 **Port St Johns**
S Africa
7E4 **Port Saunders** Can
100C4 **Port Shepstone**
S Africa
13A2 **Port Simpson** Can
27Q2 **Portsmouth**
Dominica
43D4 **Portsmouth** Eng
14B3 **Portsmouth** Ohio,
USA
11C3 **Portsmouth** Virginia,
USA
109D2 **Port Stephens** *B*
Aust
95C3 **Port Sudan** Sudan
19C3 **Port Sulphur** USA
38K5 **Porttipahdan**
Tekojärvi *Res* Fin
50A2 **Portugal**
Republic, Europe
14A2 **Port Washington**
USA
77C5 **Port Weld** Malay
32D6 **Porvenir** Bol
39K6 **Porvoo** Fin
30E4 **Posadas** Arg
50A2 **Posadas** Spain
47D1 **Poschiavo** Switz
6B2 **Posheim Pen** Can
90C3 **Posht-e Badam** Iran
71D4 **Poso** Indon
58D1 **Postavy** Belarus
14B2 **Post Clinton** USA
100B3 **Postmasburg**
S Africa
52B1 **Postojna** Slovenia
74C2 **Pos'yet** Russian Fed
101G1 **Potchetstroom**
S Africa
19B2 **Poteau** USA
53C2 **Potenza** Italy
100B3 **Potgietersrus**
S Africa
97D3 **Potiskum** Nig
20C1 **Potlatch** USA
15C3 **Potomac** *R* USA
30C2 **Potosi** Bol
30C4 **Potrerillos** Chile
56C2 **Potsdam** Germany
16B2 **Pottstown** USA
16A2 **Pottsville** USA
16C2 **Poughkeepsie** USA
35B2 **Pouso Alegre** Brazil
110C1 **Poverty B** NZ
61F3 **Povorino**
Russian Fed
7C4 **Povungnituk** Can
8C2 **Powder** *R* USA
106C2 **Powell Creek** Aust
9B3 **Powell,L** USA
13C3 **Powell River** Can
8C2 **Power** *R* USA
43C3 **Powys** County,
Wales
73D4 **Poyang Hu** *L* China
92B2 **Pozantı** Turk
23B1 **Poza Rica** Mexico
58B2 **Poznań** Pol
30E3 **Pozo Colorado** Par
53B2 **Pozzuoli** Italy
97B4 **Pra** *R* Ghana
76C3 **Prachin Buri** Thai
76B3 **Prachuap Khiri Khan**
Thai
59B2 **Pradĕd** *Mt*
Czech Republic
49C3 **Pradelles** France
35D1 **Prado** Brazil

Prague = Praha
57C2 **Praha** Czech Republic
97A4 **Praia** Cape Verde
33E5 **Prainha** Brazil
18B2 **Prairie Village** USA
76C3 **Prakhon Chai** Thai
35B1 **Prata** Brazil
35B1 **Prata** *R* Brazil
**Prates = Dongsha
Qundao**
49E3 **Prato** Italy
16B1 **Prattsville** USA
17A1 **Prattville** USA
48B1 **Prawle Pt** Eng
78D4 **Praya** Indon
47D1 **Predazzo** Italy
63B2 **Predivinsk**
Russian Fed
58C2 **Pregolyu** *R*
Russian Fed
76D3 **Prek Kak** Camb
56C2 **Prenzlau** Germany
76A3 **Preparis** *I* Myan
76A2 **Preparis North Chan**
Myan
59B3 **Přerov**
Czech Republic
23A2 **Presa del Infiernillo**
Mexico
9B3 **Prescott** Arizona,
USA
19B3 **Prescott** Arkansas,
USA
15C2 **Prescott** Can
30D4 **Presidencia Roque**
Sáenz Peña Arg
35A2 **Presidente Epitácio**
Brazil
112C2 **Presidente Frei** *Base*
Ant
23B2 **Presidente Migúel**
Aleman *L* Mexico
35A2 **Presidente Prudente**
Brazil
35A2 **Presidente Venceslau**
Brazil
59C3 **Prešov** Slovakia
55B2 **Prespansko Jezero** *L*
Macedonia, Yugos
10D2 **Presque Isle** USA
42C3 **Preston** Eng
8B2 **Preston** Idaho, USA
18B2 **Preston** Missouri,
USA
42B2 **Prestwick** Scot
31B6 **Prêto** Brazil
35B1 **Prêto** *R* Brazil
101G1 **Pretoria** S Africa
55B3 **Préveza** Greece
76D3 **Prey Veng** Camb
8B3 **Price** USA
13B2 **Price I** Can
60D4 **Prichernomorskaya**
Nizmennost'
Lowland Ukraine
27M2 **Prickly Pt** Grenada
58C1 **Priekule** Lithuania
100B3 **Prieska** S Africa
20C1 **Priest L** USA
20C1 **Priest River** USA
55B2 **Prilep** Macedonia,
Yugos
60D3 **Priluki** Ukraine
34C2 **Primero** *R* Arg
39K6 **Primorsk**
Russian Fed
60E4 **Primorsko-Akhtarsk**
Russian Fed
13F2 **Primrose L** Can
5H4 **Prince Albert** Can
4F2 **Prince Albert,C** Can
4G2 **Prince Albert Pen**
Can
4G2 **Prince Albert Sd**
Can
6C3 **Prince Charles I** Can
112B10 **Prince Charles Mts**
Ant
7D5 **Prince Edward I** Can
13C2 **Prince George** Can
4H2 **Prince Gustaf Adolp**
S Can
5E4 **Prince of Wales** *I*
USA

Prince of Wales I

73B5	**Qinzhou** China
76E2	**Qionghai** China
73A3	**Qionglai Shan** *Upland* China
76D1	**Qiongzhou Haixia** *Str* China
69E2	**Qiqihar** China
94B2	**Qiryat Ata** Israel
94B3	**Qiryat Gat** Israel
94B2	**Qiryat Shemona** Israel
94B2	**Qiryat Yam** Israel
94B2	**Qishon** *R* Israel
63A3	**Qitai** China
73C4	**Qiyang** China
72B1	**Qog Qi** China
90B2	**Qolleh-ye Damavand** *Mt* Iran
90B3	**Qom** Iran
90B3	**Qomisheh** Iran
	Qomolangma Feng = Everest,Mt
94C1	**Qornet es Saouda** *Mt* Leb
6E3	**Qôrnoq** Greenland
90A2	**Qorveh** Iran
91C4	**Qotābad** Iran
16C1	**Quabbin Res** USA
16B2	**Quakertown** USA
77C3	**Quam Phu Quoc** *I* Viet
76D2	**Quang Ngai** Viet
76D2	**Quang Tri** Viet
77D4	**Quan Long** Viet
73D5	**Quanzhou** Fujian, China
73C4	**Quanzhou** Guangxi, China
5H4	**Qu' Appelle** *R* Can
91C5	**Quarayyāt** Oman
13B2	**Quatsino Sd** Can
90C2	**Quchan** Iran
109C3	**Queanbeyan** Aust
15D1	**Québec** Can
7C4	**Quebec** Province, Can
35B1	**Quebra-Anzol** *R* Brazil
34D2	**Quebracho** Urug
30F4	**Quedas do Iguaçu** Brazil/Arg
16A3	**Queen Anne** USA
13B2	**Queen Bess,Mt** Can
5E4	**Queen Charlotte Is** Can
13B2	**Queen Charlotte Sd** Can
13B2	**Queen Charlotte Str** Can
4H1	**Queen Elizabeth Is** Can
112B9	**Queen Mary Land** Region, Ant
4H3	**Queen Maud G** Can
112A	**Queen Maud Mts** Ant
16C2	**Queens** Borough, New York, USA
108B3	**Queenscliff** Aust
107D3	**Queensland** State, Aust
109C4	**Queenstown** Aust
111A3	**Queenstown** NZ
100B4	**Queenstown** S Africa
16A3	**Queenstown** USA
98B3	**Quela** Angola
101C2	**Quelimane** Mozam
34C3	**Quemuquemú** Arg
13C2	**Quensel L** Can
34D3	**Quequén** Arg
34D3	**Quequén** *R* Arg
23A1	**Querétaro** Mexico
23A1	**Queretaro** *State* Mexico
13C2	**Quesnel** Can
84B2	**Quetta** Pak
25C3	**Quezaltenango** Guatemala
79B3	**Quezon City** Phil
100A2	**Quibala** Angola
98B3	**Quibaxe** Angola
32B2	**Quibdó** Colombia
48B2	**Quiberon** France
98B3	**Quicama Nat Pk** Angola
73A4	**Quijing** China
34A2	**Quilima** Chile
34C2	**Quilino** Arg
32C6	**Quillabamba** Peru
30C2	**Quillacollo** Bol
48C3	**Quillan** France
5H4	**Quill L** Can
5H4	**Quill Lakes** Can
34A2	**Quillota** Chile
87B3	**Quilon** India
108B1	**Quilpie** Aust
34A2	**Quilpué** Chile
98B3	**Quimbele** Angola
48B2	**Quimper** France
48B2	**Quimperlé** France
21A2	**Quincy** California, USA
10A3	**Quincy** Illinois, USA
16D1	**Quincy** Massachusetts, USA
34B2	**Quines** Arg
12B3	**Quinhagak** USA
76D3	**Qui Nhon** Viet
50B2	**Quintanar de la Orden** Spain
34A2	**Quintero** Chile
34C2	**Quinto** *R* Arg
34A3	**Quirihue** Chile
100A2	**Quirima** Angola
109D2	**Quirindi** Aust
101D2	**Quissanga** Mozam
101C3	**Quissico** Mozam
32B4	**Quito** Ecuador
31D2	**Quixadá** Brazil
108A2	**Quorn** Aust
4G3	**Qurlurtuuk** Can
95C2	**Quseir** Egypt
6E3	**Qutdligssat** Greenland
	Quthing = Moyeni
73B3	**Qu Xian** Sichuan, China
73D4	**Qu Xian** Zhejiang, China
76D2	**Quynh Luu** Viet
72C2	**Quzhou** China
86C1	**Qüzü** China

R

38J6	**Raahe** Fin
44A3	**Raasay** *I* Scot
44A3	**Raasay,Sound of** *Chan* Scot
99F1	**Raas Caseyr** *C* Somalia
52B2	**Rab** *I* Croatia
78D4	**Raba** Indon
59B3	**Rába** *R* Hung
96B1	**Rabat** Mor
94B3	**Rabba** Jordan
80B3	**Rabigh** S Arabia
47B2	**Racconigi** Italy
7E5	**Race,C** Can
94B2	**Rachaya** Leb
57C3	**Rachel** *Mt* Germany
76D3	**Rach Gia** Viet
14A2	**Racine** USA
59D3	**Rădăuţi** Rom
85C4	**Radhanpur** India
27L1	**Radix,Pt** Trinidad
58C2	**Radom** Pol
59B2	**Radomsko** Pol
58C1	**Radviliškis** Lithuania
4G3	**Rae** Can
86A1	**Rãe Bareli** India
6B3	**Rae Isthmus** Can
4G3	**Rae L** Can
110C1	**Raetihi** NZ
34C2	**Rafaela** Arg
94B3	**Rafah** Egypt
98C2	**Rafai** CAR
93D3	**Rafha Al Jumaymah** S Arabia
91C3	**Rafsanjān** Iran
98C2	**Raga** Sudan
27R3	**Ragged Pt** Barbados
53B3	**Ragusa** Italy
99D1	**Rahad** *R* Sudan
84C3	**Rahimyar Khan** Pak
90B3	**Rāhjerd** Iran
34D2	**Raíces** Arg
87B1	**Rāichur** India
86A2	**Raigarh** India
108B3	**Rainbow** Aust
17A1	**Rainbow City** USA
20B1	**Rainier** USA
20B1	**Rainier,Mt** USA
10A2	**Rainy L** Can
12D2	**Rainy P** USA
10A2	**Rainy River** Can
86A2	**Raipur** India
87C1	**Rājahmundry** India
78C2	**Rajang** *R* Malay
84C3	**Rajanpur** Pak
87B3	**Rājapālaiyam** India
85C3	**Rājasthan** State, India
84D3	**Rājgarh** India
85D4	**Rājgarh** State, India
85C4	**Rājkot** India
86B2	**Rājmahāl Hills** India
86A2	**Raj Nāndgaon** India
85C4	**Rājpipla** India
86B2	**Rajshahi** Bang
85D4	**Rajur** India
111B2	**Rakaia** *R* NZ
78B4	**Rakata** *I* Indon
82C3	**Raka Zangbo** *R* China
59C3	**Rakhov** Ukraine
100B3	**Rakops** Botswana
58D2	**Rakov** Belarus
11C3	**Raleigh** USA
7A5	**Ralny L** Can
94B2	**Rama** Israel
94B3	**Ramallah** Israel
87B3	**Rāmanāthapuram** India
69G3	**Ramapo Deep** Pacific O
94B2	**Ramat Gan** Israel
46A2	**Rambouillet** France
86B2	**Rāmgarh** Bihar, India
85C3	**Rāmgarh** Rajasthan, India
90A3	**Rāmhormoz** Iran
94B3	**Ramla** Israel
91C5	**Ramlat Al Wahibah** Region, Oman
21B3	**Ramona** USA
84D3	**Rāmpur** India
85D4	**Rāmpura** India
90B2	**Rāmsar** Iran
42B2	**Ramsey** Eng
16B2	**Ramsey** USA
43B4	**Ramsey I** Wales
43E4	**Ramsgate** Eng
94C2	**Ramtha** Jordan
71F4	**Ramu** *R* PNG
34A2	**Rancagua** Chile
86B2	**Rānchi** India
86A2	**Rānchi Plat** India
101G1	**Randburg** S Africa
39G7	**Randers** Den
101G1	**Randfontein** S Africa
15D2	**Randolph** Vermont, USA
111B3	**Ranfurly** NZ
86C2	**Rangamati** Bang
111B2	**Rangiora** NZ
110C1	**Rangitaiki** *R* NZ
111B2	**Rangitata** *R* NZ
110C1	**Rangitikei** *R* NZ
	Rangoon = Yangon
86B1	**Rangpur** India
87B2	**Rānibennur** India
8A2	**Ranier,Mt** *Mt* USA
86B2	**Rāniganj** India
109C2	**Rankins Springs** Aust
6A3	**Ranklin Inlet** Can
85B4	**Rann of Kachchh** *Flood Area* India
77B4	**Ranong** Thai
70A3	**Rantauparapat** Indon
18C1	**Rantoul** USA
49D3	**Rapallo** Italy
34A2	**Rapel** *R* Chile
6D3	**Raper,C** Can
8C2	**Rapid City** USA
14A1	**Rapid River** USA
15C3	**Rappahannock** *R* USA
47C1	**Rapperswil** Switz
16B2	**Raritan B** USA
95C2	**Ras Abu Shagara** *C* Sudan
93D2	**Ra's al 'Ayn** Syria
91C5	**Ra's al Hadd** *C* Oman
91C4	**Ras al Kaimah** UAE
91C4	**Ras-al-Kuh** *C* Iran
81D4	**Ra's al Madrakah** *C* Oman
91A4	**Ra's az Zawr** *C* S Arabia
95C2	**Räs Bânas** *C* Egypt
94A3	**Ras Burûn** *C* Egypt
99D1	**Ras Dashan** *Mt* Eth
90A3	**Ra's-e-Barkan** *Pt* Iran
92A3	**Rás el Kenâyis** *Pt* Egypt
81D4	**Ra's Fartak** *C* Yemen
95C2	**Rás Ghârib** Egypt
99D1	**Rashad** Sudan
94B3	**Rashādīya** Jordan
92B3	**Rashīd** Egypt
90A2	**Rasht** Iran
91C5	**Ra's Jibish** *C* Oman
99E1	**Ras Khanzira** *C* Somalia
84B3	**Ras Koh** *Mt* Pak
95C2	**Rás Muhammad** *C* Egypt
96A2	**Ras Nouadhibou** *C* Maur
69H2	**Rasshua** *I* Russian Fed
61F3	**Rasskazovo** Russian Fed
91A4	**Ra's Tanāqib** *C* S Arabia
91B4	**Ra's Tannūrah** *C* S Arabia
57B3	**Rastatt** Germany
	Ras Uarc = Cabo Tres Forcas
99F1	**Ras Xaafuun** *C* Somalia
84C3	**Ratangarh** India
76B3	**Rat Buri** Thai
85D3	**Rath** India
56C2	**Rathenow** Germany
45B2	**Rathkeale** Irish Rep
45C1	**Rathlin** *I* N Ire
45B2	**Ráth Luirc** Irish Rep
85D4	**Ratlām** India
87A1	**Ratnāgiri** India
87C3	**Ratnapura** Sri Lanka
58C2	**Ratno** Ukraine
47D1	**Rattenberg** Austria
39H6	**Rättvik** Sweden
12H3	**Ratz,Mt** Can
34D3	**Rauch** Arg
110C1	**Raukumara Range** *Mts* NZ
35C2	**Raul Soares** Brazil
39J6	**Rauma** Fin
86A2	**Raurkela** India
90A3	**Ravānsar** Iran
90C3	**Rāvar** Iran
59C2	**Rava Russkaya** Ukraine
16C1	**Ravena** USA
52B2	**Ravenna** Italy
57B3	**Ravensburg** Germany
107D2	**Ravenshoe** Aust
42E2	**Ravenspurn** *Oilfield* N Sea
84C2	**Ravi** *R* Pak
84C2	**Rawalpindi** Pak
93D2	**Rawāndiz** Iraq
58B2	**Rawicz** Pol
106B4	**Rawlinna** Aust
8C2	**Rawlins** USA
29C4	**Rawson** Arg
78C3	**Raya** *Mt* Indon
87B2	**Rāyadurg** India
94C2	**Rayak** Leb
7E5	**Ray,C** Can
91C4	**Rāyen** Iran
22C2	**Raymond** California, USA
20B1	**Raymond** Washington, USA
109D2	**Raymond Terrace** Aust
12D1	**Ray Mts** USA
23B1	**Rayon** Mexico
90A2	**Razan** Iran
54C2	**Razgrad** Bulg

Razim

10B2 **Rockford** USA	27Q2 **Rosalie** Dominica	48B2 **Royan** France	60E3 **Ryazan'** Russian Fed
11B3 **Rock Hill** USA	22C3 **Rosamond L** USA	46B2 **Roye** France	60E3 **Ryazan'** Division, Russian Fed
10A2 **Rock Island** USA	34C2 **Rosario** Arg	43D3 **Royston** Eng	61F3 **Ryazhsk** Russian Fed
108B3 **Rocklands Res** Aust	31C2 **Rosário** Brazil	59C3 **Rožňava** Slovakia	60E2 **Rybinsk** Russian Fed
17B2 **Rockledge** USA	34D2 **Rosario del Tala** Arg	46B2 **Rozoy** France	60E2 **Rybinskoye**
8C2 **Rock Springs** Wyoming, USA	48B2 **Roscoff** France	61F3 **Rtishchevo** Russian Fed	**Vodokhranilishche** Res Russian Fed
110B2 **Rocks Pt** NZ	45B2 **Roscommon** County, Irish Rep	99D3 **Ruaha Nat Pk** Tanz	13D1 **Rycroft** Can
109C3 **Rock,The** Aust	41B3 **Roscommon** Irish Rep	110C1 **Ruahine Range** Mts NZ	43D4 **Ryde** Eng
16C2 **Rockville** Connecticut, USA	45C2 **Roscrea** Irish Rep	110C1 **Ruapehu,Mt** NZ	43E4 **Rye** Eng
14A3 **Rockville** Indiana, USA	27E3 **Roseau** Dominica	65D3 **Rub al Khālī** Desert S Arabia	20C2 **Rye Patch Res** USA
16A3 **Rockville** Maryland, USA	109C4 **Rosebery** Aust	44A3 **Rubha Hunish** Scot	60D3 **Ryl'sk** Russian Fed
14B1 **Rocky Island L** Can	20B2 **Roseburg** USA	35A2 **Rubinéia** Brazil	61G4 **Ryn Peski** Desert Kazakhstan
13E2 **Rocky Mountain House** Can	19A4 **Rosenberg** USA	65K4 **Rubtsovsk** Russian Fed	74D3 **Ryōtsu** Japan
8B1 **Rocky Mts** Can/USA	57C3 **Rosenheim** Germany	12C2 **Ruby** USA	59D3 **Ryskany** Moldova
12B2 **Rocky Pt** USA	13F2 **Rosetown** Can	91C4 **Rudan** Iran	69E4 **Ryūkyū Retto** Arch Japan
56C2 **Rødbyhavn** Den	54B2 **Roşiori de Vede** Rom	90A2 **Rūdbār** Iran	59C2 **Rzeszów** Pol
34B2 **Rodeo** Arg	39G7 **Roskilde** Den	69F2 **Rudnaya Pristan'** Russian Fed	60D2 **Rzhev** Russian Fed
49C3 **Rodez** France	60D3 **Roslavl'** Russian Fed	54B2 **Rudoka Planina** Mt Macedonia	
55C3 **Ródhos** Greece	61E2 **Roslyatino** Russian Fed	72E3 **Rudong** China	**S**
55C3 **Ródhos** r Greece	111B2 **Ross** NZ	14B1 **Rudyard** USA	91B3 **Sa'ādatābād** Iran
52C2 **Rodi Garganico** Italy	12H2 **Ross** r Can	46A1 **Rue** France	56C2 **Saale** r Germany
54B2 **Rodopi Planina** Mts Bulg	40B3 **Rossan** Pt Irish Rep	48C2 **Ruffec** France	47B1 **Saanen** Switz
106A3 **Roebourne** Aust	53C3 **Rossano** Italy	99D3 **Rufiji** r Tanz	46D2 **Saar** r Germany
46C1 **Roermond** Neth	19C3 **Ross Barnet Res** USA	34C2 **Rufino** Arg	46D2 **Saarbrücken** Germany
46B1 **Roeselare** Belg	15C1 **Rosseau L** L Can	97A3 **Rufisque** Sen	46D2 **Saarburg** Germany
6B3 **Roes Welcome Sd** Can	107E2 **Rossel I** Solomon Is	100B2 **Rufunsa** Zambia	39J7 **Saaremaa** I Estonia
18B2 **Rogers** USA	112A **Ross Ice Shelf** Ant	43D3 **Rugby** Eng	46D2 **Saarland** State, Germany
14B1 **Rogers City** USA	20B1 **Ross L** USA	39G8 **Rügen** I Germany	46D2 **Saarlouis** Germany
20B2 **Rogue** r USA	13D3 **Rossland** Can	56B2 **Ruhr** r Germany	34C3 **Saavedra** Arg
85B3 **Rohn** Pak	45C2 **Rosslare** Irish Rep	73D4 **Ruijin** China	54A2 **Šabac** Serbia, Yugos
84D3 **Rohtak** India	111C2 **Ross,Mt** NZ	54B2 **Rujen** Mt Bulg/ Macedonia	51C1 **Sabadell** Spain
58C1 **Roja** Latvia	97A3 **Rosso** Maur	99D3 **Rukwa** L Tanz	75B1 **Sabae** Japan
35A2 **Rolândia** Brazil	43C4 **Ross-on-Wye** Eng	44A3 **Rum** I Scot	78D1 **Sabah** State, Malay
18B2 **Rolla** USA	60E4 **Rossosh** Russian Fed	54A1 **Ruma** Serbia, Yugos	26C4 **Sabanalarga** Colombia
109C1 **Roma** Aust	4E3 **Ross River** Can	91A4 **Rumãh** S Arabia	70A3 **Sabang** Indon
52B2 **Roma** Italy	112B6 **Ross S** Ant	98C2 **Rumbek** Sudan	87C1 **Sabari** r India
47C2 **Romagnano** Italy	91B4 **Rostãq** Iran	26C2 **Rum Cay** I Caribbean S	94B2 **Sabastiya** Israel
17C1 **Romain,C** USA	56C2 **Rostock** Germany	47A2 **Rumilly** France	30C2 **Sabaya** Bol
54C1 **Roman** Rom	**Rostov = Rostov-na-Donu**	106C2 **Rum Jungle** Aust	93C3 **Sab'Bi'ãr** Syria
103H5 **Romanche Gap** Atlantic O	61E4 **Rostov-na-Donu** Russian Fed	101C2 **Rumphi** Malawi	94C2 **Sabhã** Jordan
71D4 **Romang** I Indon	17B1 **Roswell** Georgia, USA	111B2 **Runanga** NZ	95A2 **Sabhã** Libya
60B4 **Romania** Republic, E Europe	9C3 **Roswell** New Mexico, USA	110C1 **Runaway,C** NZ	24B2 **Sabinas** Mexico
17B2 **Romano,C** USA	71F2 **Rota** Pacific O	100C3 **Rundi** r Zim	24B2 **Sabinas Hidalgo** Mexico
49D2 **Romans sur Isère** France	56B2 **Rotenburg** Niedersachsen, Germany	100A2 **Rundu** Namibia	19A3 **Sabine** r USA
79B3 **Romblon** Phil	46E1 **Rothaar-Geb** Region Germany	99D3 **Runga** Tanz	19B4 **Sabine L** USA
Rome = Roma	112C3 **Rothera** Base Ant	99D3 **Rungwa** r Tanz	91B5 **Sabkhat Matti** Salt Marsh UAE
17A1 **Rome** Georgia, USA	42D3 **Rotherham** Eng	99D3 **Rungwe** Mt Tanz	94A3 **Sabkhet El Bardawil** Lg Egypt
15C2 **Rome** New York, USA	42B2 **Rothesay** Scot	82C2 **Ruoqiang** China	79B3 **Sablayan** Phil
49C2 **Romilly-sur-Seine** France	71D5 **Roti** I Indon	68C2 **Ruo Shui** r China	7D5 **Sable,C** Can
15C3 **Romney** USA	108C2 **Roto** Aust	54C1 **Rupea** Rom	17B2 **Sable,C** USA
60D3 **Romny** Ukraine	111B2 **Rotoiti,L** NZ	7C4 **Rupert** r Can	7D5 **Sable I** Can
56B1 **Rømø** I Den	111B2 **Rotoroa,L** NZ	46D1 **Rur** r Germany	90C2 **Sabzevār** Iran
47B1 **Romont** Switz	110C1 **Rotorua** NZ	32D6 **Rurrenabaque** Bol	20C1 **Sacajawea Peak** USA
48C2 **Romorantin** France	110C1 **Rotorua,L** NZ	101C2 **Rusape** Zim	10A1 **Sachigo** r Can
50A2 **Ronda** Spain	56A2 **Rotterdam** Neth	54C2 **Ruse** Bulg	57C2 **Sachsen** State, Germany
33E6 **Rondônia** Brazil	46B1 **Roubaix** France	18B1 **Rushville** Illinois, USA	56C2 **Sachsen-Anhalt** State, Germany
24F6 **Rondônia** State, Brazil	48C2 **Rouen** France	108B3 **Rushworth** Aust	4F2 **Sachs Harbour** Can
30F2 **Rondonópolis** Brazil	42E3 **Rough** Oilfield N Sea	19A3 **Rusk** USA	47B1 **Säckingen** Germany
73B4 **Rong'an** China	**Roulers = Roeselare**	17B2 **Ruskin** USA	22B1 **Sacramento** USA
73B4 **Rongchang** China	101E3 **Round I** Mauritius	110B1 **Russell** NZ	22B1 **Sacramento** r USA
72E2 **Rongcheng** China	109D2 **Round Mt** Aust	18B2 **Russellville** Arkansas, USA	21A1 **Sacramento** V USA
73B4 **Rongjiang** China	8C2 **Roundup** USA	18C2 **Russellville** Kentucky, USA	9C3 **Sacramento Mts** USA
73B4 **Rong Jiang** r China	44C2 **Rousay** I Scot	21A2 **Russian** r USA	81C4 **Sa'dah** Yemen
76A1 **Rongklang Range** Mts Myan	48C3 **Roussillon** Region, France	62C3 **Russian Fed** Asia/ Europe	54B2 **Sadanski** Bulg
39G7 **Rønne** Den	10C2 **Rouyn** Can	93E1 **Rustavi** Georgia	82D3 **Sadiya** India
39H7 **Ronneby** Sweden	38K5 **Rovaniemi** Fin	101G1 **Rustenburg** S Africa	50A2 **Sado** r Port
112B2 **Ronne Ice Shelf** Ant	47D2 **Rovereto** Italy	19B3 **Ruston** USA	74D3 **Sado-shima** I Japan
46B1 **Ronse** Belg	47D2 **Rovigo** Italy	99C3 **Rutana** Burundi	85C3 **Sādri** India
46A1 **Ronthieu** Region, France	52B1 **Rovinj** Croatia	46E1 **Rüthen** Germany	**Safad = Zefat**
9C3 **Roof Butte** Mt USA	59D2 **Rovno** Ukraine	23B2 **Rutla** Mexico	84A2 **Safed Koh** Mts Afghan
84D3 **Roorkee** India	90A2 **Row'ãn** Iran	15D2 **Rutland** USA	39G7 **Saffle** Sweden
46C1 **Roosendaal** Neth	109C1 **Rowena** Aust	84D2 **Rutog** China	92C3 **Safi** Jordan
112B6 **Roosevelt I** Ant	6C3 **Rowley I** Can	**Ruvu = Pangani**	96B1 **Safi** Mor
106C2 **Roper** r Aust	106A2 **Rowley Shoals** Aust	101D2 **Ruvuma** r Tanz/ Mozam	90D3 **Safidabeh** Iran
33E3 **Roraima** State, Brazil	79A3 **Roxas** Palawan, Phil	99D2 **Ruwenzori Range** Mts Uganda/Zaire	94C1 **Sãfitã** Syria
33E2 **Roraima** Mt Ven	79B3 **Roxas** Panay, Phil	101C2 **Ruya** r Zim	93E3 **Safwãn** Iraq
38G6 **Røros** Nor	111A3 **Roxburgh** NZ	59B3 **Ružomberok** Slovakia	75A2 **Saga** Japan
47C1 **Rorschach** Switz	45C2 **Royal Canal** Irish Rep	99C3 **Rwanda** Republic, Africa	76B1 **Sagaing** Myan
38G6 **Rørvik** Nor	43D3 **Royal Leamington Spa** Eng		75B2 **Sagami-nada** B Japan
	14B2 **Royal Oak** USA		
	43E4 **Royal Tunbridge Wells** Eng		

Sāgar

68B1 **Samagaltay** Russian Fed
79B4 **Samales Group** *Is* Phil
27D3 **Samaná** Dom Rep
92C2 **Samandaği** Turk
84B1 **Samangan** Afghan
79C3 **Samar** *I* Phil
61H3 **Samara** Russian Fed
61G3 **Samara** Division, Russian Fed
107E2 **Samarai** PNG
78D3 **Samarinda** Indon
80E2 **Samarkand** Uzbekistan
93D3 **Sāmarrā'** Iraq
79B3 **Samar S** Phil
86A2 **Sambalpur** India
78B2 **Sambas** Indon
101E2 **Sambava** Madag
84D3 **Sambhal** India
78D3 **Samboja** Indon
59C3 **Sambor** Ukraine
46B1 **Sambre** *R* France
74B3 **Samch'ŏk** S Korea
99D3 **Same** Tanz
47C1 **Samedan** Switz
46A1 **Samer** France
100B2 **Samfya** Zambia
76B1 **Samka** Myan
76C1 **Sam Neua** Laos
55C3 **Sámos** *I* Greece
55C2 **Samothráki** *I* Greece
34C2 **Sampacho** Arg
78D3 **Sampaga** Indon
78C3 **Sampit** Indon
78C3 **Sampit** *R* Indon
19B3 **Sam Rayburn Res** USA
76C3 **Samrong** Camb
56C1 **Samsø** *I* Den
92C1 **Samsun** Turk
97B3 **San** Mali
76D3 **San** *R* Camb
59C2 **San** *R* Pol
81C4 **Şan'ā'** Yemen
98B2 **Sanaga** *R* Cam
29C2 **San Agustín** Arg
79C4 **San Agustin,C** Phil
90A2 **Sanandaj** Iran
22B1 **San Andreas** USA
25C3 **San Andrés Tuxtla** Mexico
9C3 **San Angelo** USA
53A3 **San Antioco** Sardegna
53A3 **San Antioco** *I* Medit S
34A2 **San Antonio** Chile
9C3 **San Antonio** New Mexico, USA
79B2 **San Antonio** Phil
9D4 **San Antonio** *R* Texas, USA
51C2 **San Antonio Abad** Spain
25D2 **San Antonio,C** Cuba
26A2 **San Antonio de los Banos** Cuba
22D3 **San Antonio,Mt** USA
29C4 **San Antonio Oeste** Arg
34D3 **San Augustin** Arg
34B2 **San Augustin de Valle Féril** Arg
85D4 **Sanawad** India
23A1 **San Bartolo** Mexico
24A3 **San Benedicto** *I* Mexico
22B2 **San Benito** *R* USA
22B2 **San Benito Mt** USA
22D3 **San Bernardino** USA
34A2 **San Bernardo** Chile
17A2 **San Blas,C** USA
34A3 **San Carlos** Chile
32A1 **San Carlos** Nic
79B2 **San Carlos** Phil
29B4 **San Carlos de Bariloche** Arg
69E4 **San-chung** Taiwan
61G2 **Sanchursk** Russian Fed
34A3 **San Clemente** Chile
22D4 **San Clemente** USA

21B3 **San Clemente I** USA
34C2 **San Cristóbal** Arg
25C3 **San Cristóbal** Mexico
32C2 **San Cristóbal** Ven
32J7 **San Cristóbal** *I* Ecuador
107F2 **San Cristobal** *I* Solomon Is
25E2 **Sancti Spíritus** Cuba
78C3 **Sandai** Indon
70C3 **Sandakan** Malay
44C2 **Sanday** *I* Scot
9C3 **Sanderson** USA
13F1 **Sandfly L** Can
21B3 **San Diego** USA
92B2 **Sandıklı** Turk
86A1 **Sandīla** India
39F7 **Sandnes** Nor
38G5 **Sandnessjøen** Nor
98C3 **Sandoa** Zaïre
59C2 **Sandomierz** Pol
38D3 **Sandoy** Føroyar
20C1 **Sandpoint** USA
49D2 **Sandrio** Italy
18A2 **Sand Springs** USA
106A3 **Sandstone** Aust
73C4 **Sandu** China
14B2 **Sandusky** USA
39H6 **Sandviken** Sweden
7A4 **Sandy L** Can
34C2 **San Elcano** Arg
9B3 **San Felipe** Baja Cal, Mexico
34A2 **San Felipe** Chile
23A1 **San Felipe** Guanajuato, Mexico
27D4 **San Felipe** Ven
51C1 **San Feliu de Guixols** Spain
28A5 **San Felix** *I* Pacific O
34A2 **San Fernando** Chile
79B2 **San Fernando** Phil
79B2 **San Fernando** Phil
50A2 **San Fernando** Spain
27E4 **San Fernando** Trinidad
22C3 **San Fernando** USA
32D2 **San Fernando** Ven
17B2 **Sanford** Florida, USA
12F2 **Sanford,Mt** USA
34C2 **San Francisco** Arg
27C3 **San Francisco** Dom Rep
22A2 **San Francisco** USA
22A2 **San Francisco** USA
24B2 **San Francisco del Oro** Mexico
23A1 **San Francisco del Rincon** Mexico
22D3 **San Gabriel Mts** USA
85C5 **Sangamner** India
18C2 **Sangamon** *R* USA
71F2 **Sangan** *I* Pacific O
87B1 **Sangāreddi** India
78D4 **Sangeang** *I* Indon
22C2 **Sanger** USA
72C2 **Sanggan He** *R* China
78C2 **Sanggau** Indon
98B2 **Sangha** *R* Congo
85B3 **Sanghar** Pak
76B2 **Sangkhla Buri** Thai
78D2 **Sangkulirang** Indon
87A1 **Sāngli** India
98B2 **Sangmélima** Cam
9B3 **San Gorgonio Mt** USA
9C3 **Sangre de Cristo** *Mts* USA
34C2 **San Gregorio** Arg
22A2 **San Gregorio** USA
84D2 **Sangrür** India
30E4 **San Ignacio** Arg
79B3 **San Isidro** Phil
32B2 **San Jacinto** Colombia
21B3 **San Jacinto Peak** *Mt* USA
34A3 **San Javier** Chile
34D2 **San Javier** Sante Fe, Arg
74D3 **Sanjō** *I* Japan
31C6 **São João del Rei** Brazil
22B2 **San Joaquin** *R* USA

22B2 **San Joaquin Valley** USA
32A1 **San José** Costa Rica
25C3 **San José** Guatemala
79B2 **San Jose** Luzon, Phil
79B3 **San Jose** Mindoro, Phil
22B2 **San Jose** USA
9B4 **San José** *I* Mexico
30D2 **San José de Chiquitos** Bol
34D2 **San José de Feliciano** Arg
34B2 **San José de Jachal** Arg
34C2 **San José de la Dormida** Arg
31B6 **San José do Rio Prêto** Brazil
24B2 **San José del Cabo** Mexico
34B2 **San Juan** Arg
27D3 **San Juan** Puerto Rico
34B2 **San Juan** State, Arg
27L1 **San Juan** Trinidad
32D2 **San Juan** Ven
26B2 **San Juan** *Mt* Cuba
8C3 **San Juan** *Mts* USA
34B2 **San Juan** *R* Arg
23B2 **San Juan** *R* Mexico
25D3 **San Juan** *R* Nic/ Costa Rica
23B2 **San Juan Bautista** Mexico
30E4 **San Juan Bautista** Par
22B2 **San Juan Bautista** USA
25D3 **San Juan del Norte** Nic
27D4 **San Juan de los Cayos** Ven
23A1 **San Juan de loz Lagoz** Mexico
23A1 **San Juan del Rio** Mexico
25D3 **San Juan del Sur** Nic
20B1 **San Juan Is** USA
23B2 **San Juan Tepozcolula** Mexico
29C5 **San Julián** Arg
34C2 **San Justo** Arg
60D2 **Sankt-Peterburg** Russian Fed
98C3 **Sankuru** *R* Zaïre
22A2 **San Leandro** USA
93C2 **Şanlıurfa** Turk
32B3 **San Lorenzo** Ecuador
34C2 **San Lorenzo** Arg
22B2 **San Lucas** USA
34B2 **San Luis** Arg
34B2 **San Luis** State, Arg
23A1 **San Luis de la Paz** Mexico
21A2 **San Luis Obispo** USA
23A1 **San Luis Potosi** Mexico
22B2 **San Luis Res** USA
53A3 **Sanluri** Sardegna
33D2 **San Maigualida** *Mts* Ven
34D3 **San Manuel** Arg
34A2 **San Marcos** Chile
23B2 **San Marcos** Mexico
52B2 **San Marino** Republic, Europe
34B2 **San Martin** Mendoza, Arg
112C3 **San Martin** *Base* Ant
47D1 **San Martino di Castroza** Italy
23B2 **San Martin Tuxmelucan** Mexico
22A2 **San Mateo** USA
30E2 **San Matias** Bol
72C3 **Sanmenxia** China
25D3 **San Miguel** El Salvador
22B3 **San Miguel** *I* USA
23A1 **San Miguel del Allende** Mexico
34D3 **San Miguel del Monte** Arg

30C4 **San Miguel de Tucumán** Arg
73D4 **Sanming** China
9B3 **San Nicolas** *I* USA
34C2 **San Nicolás de los Arroyos** Arg
101G1 **Sannieshof** S Africa
97B4 **Sanniquellie** Lib
59C3 **Sanok** Pol
26B5 **San Onofore** Colombia
22D4 **San Onofre** USA
79B3 **San Pablo** Phil
22A1 **San Pablo B** USA
34D2 **San Pedro** Buenos Aires, Arg
97B4 **San Pédro** Côte d'Ivoire
30D3 **San Pedro** Jujuy, Arg
30E3 **San Pedro** Par
22C4 **San Pedro Chan** USA
9C4 **San Pedro de los Colonias** Mexico
25D3 **San Pedro Sula** Honduras
53A3 **San Pietro** *I* Medit S
24A1 **San Quintin** Mexico
34B2 **San Rafael** Arg
22A2 **San Rafael** USA
22C3 **San Rafael Mts** USA
49D3 **San Remo** Italy
34D2 **San Salvador** Arg
26C2 **San Salvador** *I* Caribbean S
32J7 **San Salvador** *I* Ecuador
30C3 **San Salvador de Jujuy** Arg
97C3 **Sansanné - Mango** Togo
51B1 **San Sebastian** Spain
53C2 **San Severo** Italy
30C2 **Santa Ana** Bol
25C3 **Santa Ana** Guatemala
22D4 **Santa Ana** USA
22D4 **Santa Ana Mts** USA
34A3 **Santa Bárbara** Chile
24B2 **Santa Barbara** Mexico
22C3 **Santa Barbara** USA
22C4 **Santa Barbara** *I* USA
22B3 **Santa Barbara Chan** USA
22C3 **Santa Barbara Res** USA
22C4 **Santa Catalina** *I* USA
22C4 **Santa Catalina,G of** USA
30F4 **Santa Catarina** State, Brazil
26B2 **Santa Clara** Cuba
22B2 **Santa Clara** USA
22C3 **Santa Clara** *R* USA
29C6 **Santa Cruz** Arg
30D2 **Santa Cruz** Bol
34A2 **Santa Cruz** Chile
79B3 **Santa Cruz** Phil
29B5 **Santa Cruz** State, Arg
22A2 **Santa Cruz** USA
22C4 **Santa Cruz** *I* USA
35D1 **Santa Cruz Cabrália** Brazil
22C3 **Santa Cruz Chan** USA
96A2 **Santa Cruz de la Palma** Canary Is
26B2 **Santa Cruz del Sur** Cuba
96A2 **Santa Cruz de Tenerife** Canary Is
100B2 **Santa Cruz do Cuando** Angola
35B2 **Santa Cruz do Rio Pardo** Brazil
22A2 **Santa Cruz Mts** USA
34D2 **Santa Elena** Arg
33E3 **Santa Elena** Ven
34C2 **Santa Fe** Arg
34C2 **Santa Fe** State, Arg
9C3 **Santa Fe** USA
35A1 **Santa Helena de Goiás** Brazil
73B3 **Santai** China

Santa Inés

29B6 **Santa Inés** / Chile
34B3 **Santa Isabel** La Pampa, Arg
34C2 **Santa Isabel** Sante Fe, Arg
107E1 **Santa Isabel** / Solomon Is
21A2 **Santa Lucia** Ra USA
21A2 **Santa Lucia Range** Mts USA
97A4 **Santa Luzia** / Cape Verde
9B4 **Santa Margarita** / Mexico
22D4 **Santa Margarita** R USA
30F4 **Santa Maria** Brazil
26C4 **Santa Maria** Colombia
21A3 **Santa Maria** USA
96A1 **Santa Maria** / Açores
23B1 **Santa Maria** R Queretaro, Mexico
23A1 **Santa Maria del Rio** Mexico
32C1 **Santa Marta** Colombia
22C3 **Santa Monica** USA
22C4 **Santa Monica B** USA
29E2 **Santana do Livramento** Brazil
32B3 **Santander** Colombia
50B1 **Santander** Spain
51C2 **Santañy** Spain
22C3 **Santa Paula** USA
31C2 **Santa Quitéria** Brazil
33G4 **Santarem** Brazil
50A2 **Santarém** Port
22A1 **Santa Rosa** California, USA
25D3 **Santa Rosa** Honduras
34C3 **Santa Rosa** La Pampa, Arg
34B2 **Santa Rosa** Mendoza, Arg
34B2 **Santa Rosa** San Luis, Arg
22B3 **Santa Rosa** / USA
24A2 **Santa Rosalía** Mexico
20C2 **Santa Rosa Range** Mts USA
31D3 **Santa Talhada** Brazil
35C1 **Santa Teresa** Brazil
53A2 **Santa Teresa di Gallura** Sardegna
22B3 **Santa Ynez** R USA
22B3 **Santa Ynez Mts** USA
17C1 **Santee** R USA
47C2 **Santhia** Italy
34A2 **Santiago** Chile
27C3 **Santiago** Dom Rep
32A2 **Santiago** Panama
79B2 **Santiago** Phil
32B4 **Santiago** R Peru
50A1 **Santiago de Compostela** Spain
26B2 **Santiago de Cuba** Cuba
30D4 **Santiago del Estero** Arg
30D4 **Santiago del Estero** State, Arg
22D4 **Santiago Peak** Mt USA
31C5 **Santo** State, Brazil
35A2 **Santo Anastatácio** Brazil
30F4 **Santo Angelo** Brazil
97A4 **Santo Antão** / Cape Verde
35A2 **Santo Antonio da Platina** Brazil
27D3 **Santo Domingo** Dom Rep
35B2 **Santos** Brazil
35C2 **Santos Dumont** Brazil
30E4 **Santo Tomé** Arg
29B5 **San Valentin** Mt Chile
34A2 **San Vicente** Chile
98B3 **Sanza Pomba** Angola

30E4 **São Borja** Brazil
35B2 **São Carlos** Brazil
33G5 **São Félix** Mato Grosso, Brazil
35C2 **São Fidélis** Brazil
35C1 **São Francisco** Brazil
31D3 **São Francisco** R Brazil
30G4 **São Francisco do Sul** Brazil
35B1 **São Gotardo** Brazil
99D3 **Sao Hill** Tanz
35C2 **São João da Barra** Brazil
35B2 **São João da Boa Vista** Brazil
35C1 **São João da Ponte** Brazil
35C2 **São João del Rei** Brazil
35B2 **São Joaquim da Barra** Brazil
96A1 **São Jorge** / Açores
35B2 **São José do Rio Prêto** Brazil
35B2 **São José dos Campos** Brazil
31C2 **São Luis** Brazil
35B1 **São Marcos** R Brazil
35C1 **São Maria do Suaçui** Brazil
35D1 **São Mateus** Brazil
35C1 **São Mateus** R Brazil
96A1 **São Miguel** / Açores
49C2 **Saône** R France
97A4 **São Nicolau** / Cape Verde
35B2 **São Paulo** Brazil
35A2 **São Paulo** State, Brazil
31C3 **São Raimundo Nonato** Brazil
35B1 **São Romão** Brazil
35B2 **São Sebastia do Paraiso** Brazil
35A1 **São Simão** Goias, Brazil
35B2 **São Simão** Sao Paulo, Brazil
97A4 **São Tiago** / Cape Verde
97C4 **São Tomé** / W Africa
97C4 **São Tomé and Principe** Republic, W Africa
96B2 **Saoura** Watercourse Alg
35B2 **São Vicente** Brazil
97A4 **São Vincente** / Cape Verde
55C2 **Sápai** Greece
78D4 **Sape** Indon
97C4 **Sapele** Nig
74E2 **Sapporo** Japan
53C2 **Sapri** Italy
18A2 **Sapulpa** USA
90A2 **Saqqez** Iran
10C2 **Saquenay** R Can
90A2 **Satengar** Is Indon
54A2 **Sarajevo** Bosnia-Herzegovina
90D2 **Sarakhs** Iran
61J3 **Saraktash** Russian Fed
63A2 **Sarala** Russian Fed
15D2 **Saranac L** USA
15D2 **Saranac Lake** USA
55B3 **Sarandë** Alb
79C4 **Sarangani Is** Phil
61G3 **Saransk** Russian Fed
61H2 **Sarapul** Russian Fed
17B2 **Sarasota** USA
54C1 **Sarata** Ukraine
15D2 **Saratoga Springs** USA
78C2 **Saratok** Malay
61G3 **Saratov** Division, Russian Fed
61G3 **Saratov** Russian Fed
61G3 **Saratovskoye Vodokhranilishche** Res Russian Fed
67F4 **Sarawak** State, Malay

92A2 **Saraykoy** Turk
90C3 **Sarbisheh** Iran
47D1 **Sarca** R Italy
95A2 **Sardalas** Libya
90A2 **Sar Dasht** Iran
52A2 **Sardegna** / Medit S
 Sardinia = Sardegna
38H5 **Sarektjåkkå** Mt Sweden
84C2 **Sargodha** Pak
98B2 **Sarh** Chad
90B2 **Sārī** Iran
94B2 **Sarida** R Isreal
93D1 **Sarikamiş** Turk
107D3 **Sarina** Aust
47B1 **Sarine** R Switz
84B1 **Sar-i-Pul** Afghan
95B2 **Sarir** Libya
95A2 **Sarir Tibesti** Desert Libya
74B3 **Sariwŏn** N Korea
48B2 **Sark** / UK
92C2 **Sarkišla** Turk
71E4 **Sarmi** Indon
29C5 **Sarmiento** Arg
39G6 **Särna** Sweden
47C1 **Sarnen** Switz
14B2 **Sarnia** Can
58D2 **Sarny** Ukraine
6E2 **Saroaq** Greenland
84B2 **Sarobi** Afghan
78A3 **Sarolangun** Indon
55B3 **Saronikós Kólpos** G Greece
47C2 **Saronno** Italy
55C2 **Saros Körfezi** B Turk
39G7 **Sarpsborg** Nor
46D2 **Sarralbe** France
46D2 **Sarrebourg** France
46D2 **Sarreguemines** France
46D2 **Sarre-Union** France
51B1 **Sarrion** Spain
85B3 **Sartanahu** Pak
53A2 **Sartène** Corse
48B2 **Sarthe** R France
61H4 **Sarykamys** Kazakhstan
65H5 **Sarysu** R Kazakhstan
86A2 **Sasarām** India
74B4 **Sasebo** Japan
5H4 **Saskatchewan** Province, Can
5H4 **Saskatchewan** R Can
13F2 **Saskatoon** Can
101G1 **Sasolburg** S Africa
61F3 **Sasovo** Russian Fed
97B4 **Sassandra** Côte d'Ivoire
97B4 **Sassandra** R Côte d'Ivoire
53A2 **Sassari** Sardegna
56C2 **Sassnitz** Germany
47D2 **Sassuolo** Italy
34C2 **Sastre** Arg
87A1 **Satāra** India
4G2 **Satellite B** Can
78D4 **Satengar** Is Indon
39H6 **Säter** Sweden
17B1 **Satilla** R USA
61J2 **Satka** Russian Fed
84D2 **Satluj** R India
86A2 **Satna** India
85C4 **Sātpura Range** Mts India
54B1 **Satu Mare** Rom
34D2 **Sauce** Arg
39F7 **Sauda** Nor
80C3 **Saudi Arabia** Kingdom, Arabian Pen
46D2 **Sauer** R Germany/ Lux
46D1 **Sauerland** Region, Germany
38B1 **Sauðárkrókur** Iceland
14A2 **Saugatuck** USA
16C1 **Saugerties** USA
13B2 **Saugstad,Mt** Can
7B5 **Sault Sainte Marie** Can
14B1 **Sault Ste Marie** Can
14B1 **Sault Ste Marie** USA

71E4 **Saumlaki** Indon
48B2 **Saumur** France
98C3 **Saurimo** Angola
27M2 **Sauteurs** Grenada
54A2 **Sava** R Serbia, Yugos
97C4 **Savalou** Benin
17B1 **Savannah** Georgia, USA
17B1 **Savannah** R USA
76C2 **Savannakhet** Laos
26B3 **Savanna la Mar** Jamaica
7A4 **Savant Lake** Can
76D2 **Savarane** Laos
97C4 **Savé** Benin
101C3 **Save** R Mozam
90B3 **Sāveh** Iran
46D2 **Saverne** France
47B2 **Savigliano** Italy
46B2 **Savigny** France
49D2 **Savoie** Region France
49D3 **Savona** Italy
38K6 **Savonlinna** Fin
4A3 **Savoonga** USA
38K5 **Savukoski** Fin
71D4 **Savu S** Indon
76A1 **Saw** Myan
85D3 **Sawai Mādhopur** India
78A2 **Sawang** Indon
76B2 **Sawankhalok** Thai
75C1 **Sawara** Japan
12E1 **Sawtooth Mt** USA
106B2 **Sawu** / Indon
97C3 **Say** Niger
84B1 **Sayghan** Afghan
91B5 **Sayhūt** Yemen
61G4 **Saykhin** Kazakhstan
68D2 **Saynshand** Mongolia
61H5 **Say-Utes** Kazakhstan
16C2 **Sayville** USA
13B2 **Sayward** Can
57C3 **Sázava** R Czech Republic
51C2 **Sbisseb** R Alg
42C2 **Scafell Pike** Mt Eng
44E1 **Scalloway** Scot
44C2 **Scapa Flow** Sd Scot
15C2 **Scarborough** Can
42D2 **Scarborough** Eng
27E4 **Scarborough** Tobago
44A2 **Scarp** / Scot
45B2 **Scarriff** Irish Rep
52A1 **Schaffhausen** Switz
57C3 **Scharding** Austria
46D1 **Scharteberg** Mt Germany
7D4 **Schefferville** Can
46B1 **Schelde** R Belg
10C2 **Schenectady** USA
47D2 **Schio** Italy
46D1 **Schleiden** Germany
56B2 **Schleswig** Germany
56B2 **Schleswig Holstein** State, Germany
16B1 **Schoharie** USA
71F4 **Schouten** Is PNG
7B5 **Schreiber** Can
21B2 **Schurz** USA
16A2 **Schuykill Haven** USA
16B2 **Schuylkill** R USA
57B3 **Schwabische Alb** Upland Germany
57B3 **Schwarzwald** Upland Germany
12C1 **Schwatka Mts** USA
47D1 **Schwaz** Austria
57C2 **Schweinfurt** Germany
101G1 **Schweizer Reneke** S Africa
56C2 **Schwerin** Germany
47C1 **Schwyz** Switz
53B3 **Sciacca** Italy
14B3 **Scioto** R USA
109D2 **Scone** Aust
6H2 **Scoresby Sd** Greenland
103F7 **Scotia Ridge** Atlantic O
103F7 **Scotia S** Atlantic O

44B3 **Scotland** Country, UK
112B7 **Scott** *Base* Ant
13B2 **Scott,C** Can
9C2 **Scott City** USA
112C6 **Scott I** Ant
6C2 **Scott Inlet** *B* Can
42C2 **Scotish Borders** Division Scot
20B2 **Scott,Mt** USA
106B2 **Scott Reef** Timor S
8C2 **Scottsbluff** USA
17A1 **Scottsboro** USA
109C4 **Scottsdale** Aust
10C2 **Scranton** USA
47D1 **Scuol** Switz
Scutari = Shkodër
5J4 **Seal** *R* Can
108B3 **Sea Lake** Aust
18B2 **Searcy** USA
22B2 **Seaside** California, USA
20B1 **Seaside** Oregon, USA
16B3 **Seaside Park** USA
20B1 **Seattle** USA
22A1 **Sebastopol** USA
58D1 **Sebez** Russian Fed
17B2 **Sebring** USA
111A3 **Secretary I** NZ
18B2 **Sedalia** USA
46C2 **Sedan** France
111B2 **Seddonville** NZ
94B3 **Sede Boqer** Israel
94B3 **Sederot** Israel
97A3 **Sédhiou** Sen
94B3 **Sedom** Israel
100A3 **Seeheim** Namibia
111B2 **Sefton,Mt** NZ
77C5 **Segamat** Malay
51B2 **Segorbe** Spain
97B3 **Ségou** Mali
Segovia = Coco
50B1 **Segovia** Spain
51C1 **Segre** *R* Spain
97B4 **Séguéla** Côte d'Ivoire
96A2 **Seguia el Hamra** *Watercourse* Mor
34C2 **Segundo** *R* Arg
78D2 **Seguntur** Indon
50B2 **Segura** *R* Spain
85B3 **Sehwan** Pak
46D2 **Seille** *R* France
38J6 **Seinäjoki** Fin
48C2 **Seine** *R* France
46B2 **Seine-et-Marne** Department, France
99D3 **Sekenke** Tanz
99D1 **Sek'ot'a** Eth
20B1 **Selah** USA
71E4 **Selaru** *I* Indon
78D4 **Selat Alas** *Str* Indon
78B3 **Selat Bangka** *Str* Indon
78A3 **Selat Berhala** *B* Indon
71E4 **Selat Dampier** *Str* Indon
78B3 **Selat Gaspar** *Str* Indon
78D4 **Selat Lombok** *Str* Indon
78D4 **Selat Sape** *Str* Indon
78B4 **Selat Sunda** *Str* Indon
71D4 **Selat Wetar** *Chan* Indon
12B1 **Selawik** USA
12C1 **Selawik** *R* USA
12B1 **Selawik L** USA
42D3 **Selby** Eng
55C3 **Selçuk** Turk
12D3 **Seldovia** USA
100B3 **Selebi Pikwe** Botswana
6H3 **Selfoss** Iceland
95B2 **Selima Oasis** Sudan
5J4 **Selkirk** Can
42C2 **Selkirk** Scot
13D2 **Selkirk Mts** Can
22C2 **Selma** California, USA
50B2 **Selouane** Mor
12H2 **Selous,Mt** Can

78B3 **Selta Karimata** *Str* Indon
32C5 **Selvas** Region, Brazil
107D3 **Selwyn** Aust
4E3 **Selwyn Mts** Can
78C4 **Semarang** Indon
61E2 **Semenov** Russian Fed
12C3 **Semidi Is** USA
60E3 **Semiluki** Russian Fed
19A2 **Seminole** Oklahoma, USA
17B1 **Seminole,L** USA
65K4 **Semipalatinsk** Kazakhstan
79B3 **Semirara Is** Phil
90B3 **Semirom** Iran
78C2 **Semitau** Indon
90B2 **Semnän** Iran
46C2 **Semois** *R* Belg
23B2 **Sempoala** Hist Site, Mexico
32D5 **Sena Madureira** Brazil
100B2 **Senanga** Zambia
19C3 **Senatobia** USA
74E3 **Sendai** Honshū, Japan
74C4 **Sendai** Kyūshū, Japan
85D4 **Sendwha** India
15C2 **Seneca Falls** USA
97A3 **Senegal** Republic, Africa
97A3 **Sénégal** *R* Maur Sen
101G1 **Senekal** S Africa
31D4 **Senhor do Bonfim** Brazil
52B2 **Senigallia** Italy
52C2 **Senj** Croatia
69E4 **Senkaku Gunto** *Is* Japan
46B2 **Senlis** France
99D1 **Sennar** Sudan
7C5 **Senneterre** Can
49C2 **Sens** France
54A1 **Senta** Serbia, Yugos
98C3 **Sentery** Zaïre
13C2 **Sentinel Peak** *Mt* Can
85D4 **Seoni** India
Seoul = Soul
110B2 **Separation Pt** NZ
76D2 **Sepone** Laos
7D4 **Sept-Iles** Can
95A2 **Séquédine** Niger
21B2 **Sequoia** Nat Pk, USA
71D4 **Seram** *I* Indon
78B4 **Serang** Indon
78B2 **Serasan** *I* Indon
54A2 **Serbia** Republic, Yugos
61F3 **Serdobsk** Russian Fed
77C5 **Seremban** Malay
99D3 **Serengeti Nat Pk** Tanz
100C2 **Serenje** Zambia
59D3 **Seret** *R* Ukraine
61G2 **Sergach** Russian Fed
65H3 **Sergino** Russian Fed
31D4 **Sergipe** State, Brazil
60E2 **Segiyev Posad** Russian Fed
78C2 **Seria** Brunei
78C2 **Serian** Malay
55B3 **Sérifos** *I* Greece
47C2 **Serio** *R* Italy
95B2 **Serir Calanscio** *Desert* Libya
46C2 **Sermaize-les-Bains** France
71D4 **Sermata** *I* Indon
61H3 **Sernovodsk** Russian Fed
65H4 **Serov** Russian Fed
100B3 **Serowe** Botswana
50A2 **Serpa** Port
60E3 **Serpukhov** Russian Fed
35B2 **Serra da Canastra** *Mts* Brazil
50A1 **Serra da Estrela** *Mts* Port

35B2 **Serra da Mantiqueira** *Mts* Brazil
35A1 **Serra da Mombuca** Brazil
35C1 **Serra do Cabral** *Mt* Brazil
33F5 **Serra do Cachimbo** *Mts* Brazil
35A1 **Serra do Caiapó** *Mts* Brazil
35A2 **Serra do Cantu** *Mts* Brazil
35C2 **Serra do Caparaó** *Mts* Brazil
31C5 **Serra do Chifre** Brazil
35C1 **Serra do Espinhaço** *Mts* Brazil
35B2 **Serra do Mar** *Mts* Brazil
35A2 **Serra do Mirante** *Mts* Brazil
33G3 **Serra do Navio** Brazil
35B2 **Serra do Paranapiacaba** *Mts* Brazil
33F6 **Serra dos Caiabis** *Mts* Brazil
35A2 **Serra dos Dourados** *Mts* Brazil
33E6 **Serra dos Parecis** *Mts* Brazil
35B1 **Serra dos Pilões** *Mts* Brazil
35A1 **Serra Dourada** *Mts* Brazil
33F6 **Serra Formosa** *Mts* Brazil
55B2 **Sérrai** Greece
25D3 **Serrana Bank** *Is* Caribbean S
51B1 **Serrana de Cuenca** *Mts* Spain
35A1 **Serranópolis** Brazil
33E3 **Serra Pacaraima** *Mts* Brazil/Ven
33E3 **Serra Parima** *Mts* Brazil
33G3 **Serra Tumucumaque** Brazil
46B2 **Serre** *R* France
34B2 **Serrezuela** Arg
31D4 **Serrinha** Brazil
6G3 **Serrmilik** Greenland
35C1 **Serro** Brazil
35A2 **Sertanópolis** Brazil
72A3 **Sêrtar** China
78C3 **Seruyan** *R* Indon
100A2 **Sesfontein** Namibia
100B2 **Sesheke** Zambia
47B2 **Sestriere** Italy
74D2 **Setana** Japan
49C3 **Sète** France
35C1 **Sete Lagoas** Brazil
96C1 **Sétif** Alg
75B1 **Seto** Japan
75A2 **Seto Naikai** *S* Japan
96B1 **Settat** Mor
42C2 **Settle** Eng
5G4 **Settler** Can
50A2 **Sêtubal** Port
93E1 **Sevan,Oz** *L* Armenia
60D5 **Sevastopol'** Ukraine
7B4 **Severn** *R* Can
43C3 **Severn** *R* Eng
61F5 **Severnaya Osetiya** Division Russian Fed
1B9 **Severnaya Zemlya** *I* Russian Fed
63C2 **Severo-Baykalskoye Nagorye** *Mts* Russian Fed
60E4 **Severo Donets** Ukraine
64E3 **Severodvinsk** Russian Fed
64H3 **Severo Sos'va** *R* Russian Fed
8B3 **Sevier** *R* USA
8B3 **Sevier L** USA
50A2 **Seville = Sevilla**
Seville = Sevilla
54C2 **Sevlievo** Bulg
97A4 **Sewa** *R* Sierra Leone

12E2 **Seward** Alaska, USA
18A1 **Seward** Nebraska, USA
12A1 **Seward Pen** USA
13D1 **Sexsmith** Can
89K8 **Seychelles** *Is* Indian O
38C1 **Seyðisfjörður** Iceland
92C2 **Seyhan** Turk
60E3 **Seym** *R* Russian Fed
108C3 **Seymour** Aust
16C2 **Seymour** Connecticut, USA
14A3 **Seymour** Indiana, USA
46B2 **Sézanne** France
96D1 **Sfax** Tunisia
54C1 **Sfinto Gheorghe** Rom
56A2 **'s-Gravenhage** Neth
72B3 **Shaanxi** Province, China
98C3 **Shabunda** Zaïre
82B2 **Shache** China
112C9 **Shackleton Ice Shelf** Ant
85B3 **Shadadkot** Pak
91B3 **Shādhām** *R* Iran
43C4 **Shaftesbury** Eng
29G8 **Shag Rocks** *Is* South Georgia
90A3 **Shāhabād** Iran
94C2 **Shahbā** Syria
91C3 **Shahdap** Iran
86A2 **Shahdol** India
90A2 **Shāhīn Dezh** Iran
90C3 **Shāh Kūh** Iran
91C3 **Shahr-e Bābak** Iran
Shahresa = Qomisheh
90B3 **Shahr Kord** Iran
87B1 **Shājābād** India
84D3 **Shajahānpur** India
85D4 **Shājāpur** India
61F4 **Shakhty** Russian Fed
61G2 **Shakhun'ya** Russian Fed
97C4 **Shaki** Nig
12B2 **Shaktoolik** USA
61J2 **Shamary** Russian Fed
99D2 **Shambe** Sudan
16A2 **Shamokin** USA
16B1 **Shandaken** USA
72D2 **Shandong** Province, China
73C5 **Shangchuan Dao** *I* China
72C1 **Shangdu** China
73E3 **Shanghai** China
72C3 **Shangnan** China
100B2 **Shangombo** Zambia
73D4 **Shangra** China
73B5 **Shangsi** China
72C3 **Shang Xian** China
41B3 **Shannon** *R* Irish Rep
72D3 **Shanqiu** China
74B2 **Shansonggang** China
63F2 **Shantarskiye Ostrova** *I* Russian Fed
73D5 **Shantou** China
72C2 **Shanxi** Province, China
72D3 **Shan Xian** China
73C5 **Shaoguan** China
73E4 **Shaoxing** China
73C4 **Shaoyang** China
44C2 **Shapinsay** *I* Scot
94C2 **Shaqqā** Syria
72A1 **Sharhulsan** Mongolia
90C2 **Sharīfābād** Iran
91C4 **Sharjah** UAE
106A3 **Shark B** Aust
90C2 **Sharlauk** Turkmenistan
94B2 **Sharon,Plain of** Israel
61G2 **Sharya** Russian Fed
99D2 **Shashemanē** Eth
73C3 **Shashi** China
20B2 **Shasta L** USA
20B2 **Shasta,Mt** USA
93E3 **Shaṭṭ al Gharrat** *R* Iraq
94B3 **Shaubak** Jordan
13F3 **Shaunavon** Can

Shaver L

Sorsatunturi

Sorsele

71D3	**Tahuna** Indon
72D2	**Tai'an** China
72B3	**Taibai Shan** *Mt* China
72D1	**Taibus Qi** China
73E5	**T'ai-chung** Taiwan
111B3	**Taieri** *R* NZ
72C2	**Taihang Shan** China
110C1	**Taihape** NZ
72E3	**Tai Hu** *L* China
108A3	**Tailem Bend** Aust
44B3	**Tain** Scot
73E5	**T'ai-nan** Taiwan
35C1	**Taiobeiras** Brazil
73E5	**T'ai pei** Taiwan
77C5	**Taiping** Malay
75C1	**Taira** Japan
78A3	**Tais** Indon
75A1	**Taisha** Japan
29B5	**Taitao,Pen de** Chile
73E5	**T'ai-tung** Taiwan
38K5	**Taivelkoski** Fin
69E4	**Taiwan** Republic, China
	Taiwan Haixia = Formosa Str
72C2	**Taiyuan** China
72D3	**Taizhou** China
81C4	**Ta'izz** Yemen
82A2	**Tajikistan** Republic, Asia
50B1	**Tajo** *R* Spain
76B2	**Tak** Thai
74D3	**Takada** Japan
75A2	**Takahashi** Japan
110B2	**Takaka** NZ
74C4	**Takamatsu** Japan
74D3	**Takaoka** Japan
110B1	**Takapuna** NZ
74D3	**Takasaki** Japan
75B1	**Takayama** Japan
74D3	**Takefu** Japan
70A3	**Takengon** Indon
76C3	**Takeo** Camb
75A2	**Takeo** Japan
	Take-shima = Tok-do
90A2	**Takestān** Iran
75A2	**Taketa** Japan
4G3	**Takjvak L** Can
99D1	**Takkaze** *R* Eritrea/Eth
13B1	**Takla L** Can
13B1	**Takla Landing** Can
12B2	**Takslesluk L** USA
12H2	**Taku Arm** *R* Can
23A1	**Tala** Mexico
59B3	**Talabanya** Hung
84C2	**Talagang** Pak
34A2	**Talagante** Chile
87B3	**Talaimannar** Sri Lanka
97C3	**Talak** *Desert* Region, Niger
78A3	**Talangbetutu** Indon
32A4	**Talara** Peru
50B2	**Talavera de la Reina** Spain
34A3	**Talca** Chile
34A3	**Talcahuano** Chile
86B2	**Tālcher** India
82B1	**Taldy Kurgan** Kazakhstan
71D4	**Taliabu** Indon
84B1	**Taligan** Afghan
99D2	**Tali Post** Sudan
78D4	**Taliwang** Indon
12D2	**Talkeetna** USA
12E2	**Talkeetna Mts** USA
17A1	**Talladega** USA
93D2	**Tall 'Afar** Iraq
17B1	**Tallahassee** USA
94C1	**Tall Bisah** Syria
60B2	**Tallinn** Estonia
92C3	**Tall Kalakh** Syria
19B3	**Tallulah** USA
60D4	**Tal'noye** Ukraine
58C2	**Talpaki** Russian Fed
30B4	**Taltal** Chile
109C1	**Talwood** Aust
78D1	**Tamabo Range** *Mts* Malay
97B4	**Tamale** Ghana
96C2	**Tamanrasset** Alg
96C2	**Tamanrasset** *Watercourse* Alg
16B2	**Tamaqua** USA
	Tamatave = Toamasina
23A2	**Tamazula** Jalisco, Mexico
23B2	**Tamazulapán** Mexico
23B1	**Tamazunchale** Mexico
97A3	**Tambacounda** Sen
61F3	**Tambov** Division, Russian Fed
61F3	**Tambov** Russian Fed
50A1	**Tambre** *R* Spain
98C2	**Tambura** Sudan
97A3	**Tamchaket** Maur
50A1	**Tamega** *R* Port
23B1	**Tamiahua** Mexico
87B2	**Tamil Nādu** State, India
76D2	**Tam Ky** Viet
17B2	**Tampa** USA
17B2	**Tampa B** USA
39J6	**Tampere** Fin
23B1	**Tampico** Mexico
68D2	**Tamsagbulag** Mongolia
86C2	**Tamu** Myan
23B1	**Tamuis** Mexico
109D2	**Tamworth** Aust
43D3	**Tamworth** Eng
38K4	**Tana** Nor
99D1	**Tana** *L* Eth
99E3	**Tana** *R* Kenya
38K5	**Tana** *R* Nor/Fin
75B2	**Tanabe** Japan
38K4	**Tanafjord** *Inlet* Nor
78D3	**Tanahgrogot** Indon
71E4	**Tanahmerah** Indon
12D1	**Tanana** USA
12E2	**Tanana** *R* USA
	Tananarive = Antananarivo
47C2	**Tanaro** *R* Italy
74B2	**Tanch'ŏn** N Korea
34D3	**Tandil** Arg
78B2	**Tandjong Datu** *Pt* Indon
71E4	**Tandjung d'Urville** *C* Indon
78D3	**Tandjung Layar** *C* Indon
78B3	**Tandjung Lumut** *C* Indon
78D2	**Tandjung Mangkalihet** *C* Indon
78C3	**Tandjung Sambar** *C* Indon
78C2	**Tandjung Sirik** *C* Malay
71E4	**Tandjung Vals** *C* Indon
85B3	**Tando Adam** Pak
85B3	**Tando Muhammad Khan** Pak
108B2	**Tandou L** Aust
87B1	**Tāndūr** India
110C1	**Taneatua** NZ
76B2	**Tanen Range** *Mts* Myan/Thai
96B2	**Tanezrouft** *Desert Region* Alg
91C4	**Tang** Iran
99D3	**Tanga** Tanz
60E4	**Tanganrog** Russian Fed
99C3	**Tanganyika,L** Tanz/Zaire
96B1	**Tanger** Mor
82C2	**Tanggula Shan** *Mts* China
	Tangier = Tanger
78A2	**Tangjungpinang** Indon
82C2	**Tangra Yumco** *L* China
72D2	**Tangshan** China
79B4	**Tangub** Phil
63C2	**Tanguy** Russian Fed
	Tanintharyi = Tenasserim
79B4	**Tanjay** Phil
101D3	**Tanjona Ankaboa** *C* Madag
101D2	**Tanjona Babaomby** *C* Madag
101D2	**Tanjona Vilanandro** *C* Madag
101D3	**Tanjona Vohimena** *C* Madag
78C4	**Tanjong Bugel** *C* Indon
78B4	**Tanjong Cangkuang** *C* Indon
78C3	**Tanjong Puting** *C* Indon
78C3	**Tanjong Selatan** *C* Indon
78D3	**Tanjung** Indon
70A3	**Tanjungbalai** Indon
78A3	**Tanjung Jabung** *Pt* Indon
78B3	**Tanjungpandan** Indon
78B4	**Tanjung Priok** Indon
78D2	**Tanjungredeb** Indon
78D2	**Tanjungselor** Indon
84C2	**Tank** Pak
68B1	**Tannu Ola** *Mts* Russian Fed
97B4	**Tano** *R* Ghana
97C3	**Tanout** Niger
23B1	**Tanquián** Mexico
73E4	**Tan-shui** Taiwan
86A1	**Tansing** Nepal
95C1	**Tanta** Egypt
96A2	**Tan-Tan** Mor
4B3	**Tanunak** USA
99D3	**Tanzania** Republic, Africa
72A3	**Tao He** *R* China
72B2	**Taole** China
96B1	**Taourirt** Mor
60C2	**Tapa** Estonia
25C3	**Tapachula** Mexico
33F4	**Tapajós** *R* Brazil
34C3	**Tapalquén** Arg
70B4	**Tapan** Indon
111A3	**Tapanui** NZ
32D5	**Tapauá** *R* Brazil
85D4	**Tapi** *R* India
86B1	**Taplejung** Nepal
111B2	**Tapuaeniku** *Mt* NZ
35B2	**Tapuaritinga** Brazil
79B4	**Tapul Group** *Is* Phil
33E4	**Tapurucuara** Brazil
109D1	**Tara** Aust
65J4	**Tara** Russian Fed
65J4	**Tara** *R* Russian Fed
54A2	**Tara** *R* Bosnia-Herzegovina/Montenegro, Yugos
97D4	**Taraba** *R* Nig
30D2	**Tarabuco** Bol
	Tarābulus = Tripoli
50B1	**Taracón** Spain
110C1	**Taradale** NZ
78D2	**Tarakan** Indon
110B1	**Taranaki, Mt** NZ
44A3	**Taransay** *I* Scot
53C2	**Taranto** Italy
32B5	**Tarapoto** Peru
49C2	**Tarare** France
110C2	**Tararua Range** *Mts* NZ
96C2	**Tarat** Alg
110C1	**Tarawera** NZ
51B1	**Tarazona** Spain
44C3	**Tarbat Ness** *Pen* Scot
84C2	**Tarbela Res** Pak
42B2	**Tarbert** Strathclyde, Scot
44A3	**Tarbert** Western Isles, Scot
48C3	**Tarbes** France
106C4	**Tarcoola** Aust
109C2	**Tarcoon** Aust
109D2	**Taree** Aust
96A2	**Tarfaya** Mor
95A1	**Tarhūnah** Libya
91B5	**Tarif** UAE
30D3	**Tarija** Bol
87B2	**Tarikere** India
81C4	**Tarim** Yemen
99D3	**Tarime** Tanz
82C1	**Tarim He** *R* China
82C2	**Tarim Pendi** *Basin* China
84B2	**Tarin Kut** Afghan
18A1	**Tarkio** USA
79B2	**Tarlac** Phil
32B6	**Tarma** Peru
49C3	**Tarn** *R* France
59C2	**Tarnobrzeg** Pol
59C3	**Tarnów** Pol
107D3	**Taroom** Aust
51C1	**Tarragona** Spain
109C4	**Tarraleah** Aust
51C1	**Tarrasa** Spain
16C2	**Tarrytown** USA
92B2	**Tarsus** Turk
44D2	**Tartan** *Oilfield* N Sea
47D2	**Tartaro** *R* Italy
60C2	**Tartu** Estonia
92C3	**Tartūs** Syria
35C1	**Tarumirim** Brazil
70A3	**Tarutung** Indon
52B1	**Tarvisio** Italy
80D1	**Tashauz** Turkmenistan
86C1	**Tashigang** Bhutan
82A1	**Tashkent** Uzbekistan
65K4	**Tashtagol** Russian Fed
63A2	**Tashtyp** Russian Fed
78B4	**Tasikmalaya** Indon
94B2	**Tasil** Syria
6E2	**Tasiussaq** Greenland
95A3	**Tasker** *Well* Niger
110B2	**Tasman B** NZ
107D5	**Tasmania** *I* Aust
111B2	**Tasman Mts** NZ
109C4	**Tasman Pen** Aust
107E4	**Tasman S** NZ Aust
92C1	**Taşova** Turk
96C2	**Tassili du Hoggar** *Desert* Region, Alg
96C2	**Tassili N'jjer** *Desert* Region, Alg
96B2	**Tata** Mor
96D1	**Tataouine** Tunisia
65J4	**Tatarsk** Russian Fed
69G2	**Tatarskiy Proliv** *Str* Russian Fed
61G2	**Tatarstan** Russian Fed
75B1	**Tateyama** Japan
5G3	**Tathlina L** Can
12E2	**Tatitlek** USA
13C2	**Tatla Lake** Can
59B3	**Tatry** *Mts* Pol/Slovakia
75A2	**Tatsuno** Japan
85B4	**Tatta** Pak
35B2	**Tatui** Brazil
93D2	**Tatvan** Turk
31C3	**Tauá** Brazil
35B2	**Taubaté** Brazil
110C1	**Taumarunui** NZ
101F1	**Taung** S Africa
76B2	**Taungdwingyi** Myan
76B1	**Taung-gyi** Myan
76A2	**Taungup** Myan
84C2	**Taunsa** Pak
43C4	**Taunton** Eng
16D2	**Taunton** USA
46E1	**Taunus** Region, Germany
110C1	**Taupo** NZ
110C1	**Taupo,L** NZ
58C1	**Taurage** Lithuania
110C1	**Tauranga** NZ
110C1	**Tauranga Harbour** *B* NZ
110B1	**Tauroa Pt** NZ
7A3	**Tavani** Can
7A3	**Tavani** Can
65H4	**Tavda** *R* Russian Fed
43B4	**Tavistock** Eng
76B3	**Tavoy** Myan
76B3	**Tavoy Pt** Myan
92A2	**Tavsanli** Turk
111B2	**Tawa** NZ
19A3	**Tawakoni,L** USA
14B2	**Tawas City** USA
70C3	**Tawau** Malay
98C1	**Taweisha** Sudan
79B4	**Tawitawi** *I* Phil
79B4	**Tawitawi Group** *Is* Phil
23B2	**Taxco** Mexico

29C6	**Tierra del Fuego** Territory, Arg
28C8	**Tierra del Fuego** / Arg/Chile
35B2	**Tietê** Brazil
35A2	**Tiete** *R* Brazil
14B2	**Tiffin** USA
17B1	**Tifton** USA
32B4	**Tigre** *R* Peru
33E2	**Tigre** *R* Ven
93E3	**Tigris** *R* Iraq
23B1	**Tihuatlán** Mexico
21B3	**Tijuana** Mexico
85D4	**Tikamgarh** India
60D2	**Tikhin** Russian Fed
61F4	**Tikhoretsk** Russian Fed
93D3	**Tikrît** Iraq
1B8	**Tiksi** Russian Fed
46C1	**Tilburg** Neth
43E4	**Tilbury** Eng
30C3	**Tilcara** Arg
108B1	**Tilcha** Aust
76A1	**Tilin** Myan
97C3	**Tillabéri** Niger
20B1	**Tillamook** USA
97C3	**Tillia** Niger
55C3	**Tilos** / Greece
108B2	**Tilpa** Aust
32B3	**Tiluá** Colombia
64G3	**Timanskiy Kryazh** *Mts* Russian Fed
111B2	**Timaru** NZ
60E4	**Timashevsk** Russian Fed
55B3	**Timbákion** Greece
19B4	**Timbalier B** USA
97B3	**Timbédra** Maur
	Timbuktu = **Tombouctou**
97B3	**Timétrine Monts** *Mts* Mali
97C3	**Timia** Niger
96C2	**Timiș** *R* Rom
54B1	**Timișoara** Rom
10B2	**Timmins** Can
106B1	**Timor** / Indon
106B2	**Timor S** Aust/Indon
34C3	**Timote** Arg
79C4	**Tinaca Pt** Phil
27D5	**Tinaco** Ven
87B2	**Tindivanam** India
96B2	**Tindouf** Alg
96B2	**Tinfouchy** Alg
96C2	**Tin Fouye** Alg
6F3	**Tingmiarmiut** Greenland
32B5	**Tingo Maria** Peru
97B3	**Tingrela** Côte d'Ivoire
86B1	**Tingri** China
71F2	**Tinian** Pacific O
30C4	**Tinogasta** Arg
55C3	**Tinos** / Greece
43B4	**Tintagel Head** *Pt* Eng
96C2	**Tin Tarabine** *Watercourse* Alg
108B3	**Tintinara** Aust
96C2	**Tin Zaouaten** Alg
2‹C2	**Tioga P** USA
77C5	**Tioman** / Malay
47D1	**Tione** Italy
45C2	**Tipperary** County, Irish Rep
41B3	**Tipperary** Irish Rep
18B2	**Tipton** Missouri, USA
87B2	**Tiptür** India
23A2	**Tiquicheo** Mexico
55A2	**Tiranë** Alb
47D1	**Tirano** Italy
60C4	**Tiraspol** Moldova
87B2	**Tirchchiráppalli** India
55C3	**Tire** Turk
93C1	**Tirebolu** Turk
44A3	**Tiree** / Scot
54C2	**Tîrgoviște** Rom
54B1	**Tîrgu Jiu** Rom
54B1	**Tîrgu Mureș** Rom
84C1	**Tirich Mir** *Mt* Pak
96A2	**Tiris** Region, Mor
61J3	**Tirlyanskiy** Russian Fed
54B1	**Tîrnăveni** Rom
55B3	**Tírnavos** Greece
85D4	**Tirodi** India
47D1	**Tirol** Province, Austria
53A2	**Tirso** *R* Sardegna
87B3	**Tiruchchendûr** India
87B3	**Tirunelveli** India
87B2	**Tirupati** India
87B2	**Tiruppattür** India
87B2	**Tiruppur** India
87B2	**Tiruvannamalai** India
19A3	**Tishomingo** USA
94C2	**Tisiyah** Syria
59C3	**Tisza** *R* Hung
86A2	**Titlagarh** India
54B2	**Titov Veles** Macedonia
98C2	**Titule** Zaire
17B2	**Titusville** USA
43C4	**Tiverton** Eng
52B2	**Tivoli** Italy
23B2	**Tixtla** Mexico
99E2	**Tiyeglow** Somalia
23B2	**Tizayuca** Mexico
25D2	**Tizimin** Mexico
96C1	**Tizi Ouzou** Alg
96B2	**Tiznit** Mor
23A1	**Tizpan el Alto** Mexico
23B2	**Tlacolula** Mexico
23B2	**Tlacotalpan** Mexico
23A2	**Tlalchana** Mexico
23B2	**Tlalnepantla** Mexico
23B2	**Tlalpan** Mexico
23A1	**Tlaltenango** Mexico
23B2	**Tlancualpicán** Mexico
23B2	**Tlapa** Mexico
23B2	**Tlapacoyan** Mexico
23A1	**Tlaquepaque** Mexico
23B2	**Tlaxcala** Mexico
23B2	**Tlaxcala** State, Mexico
23B2	**Tlaxiaco** Mexico
96B1	**Tlemcem** Alg
101D2	**Toamasina** Madag
34C3	**Toay** Arg
75B2	**Toba** Japan
84B2	**Toba and Kakar Ranges** *Mts* Pak
27E4	**Tobago** / Caribbean S
13C2	**Toba Inlet** *Sd* Can
71D3	**Tobelo** Indon
14B1	**Tobermory** Can
44A3	**Tobermory** Scot
71E3	**Tobi** / Pacific O
21B1	**Tobin,Mt** USA
65H4	**Tobol** *R* Kazakhstan
70D4	**Toboli** Indon
65H4	**Tobol'sk** Russian Fed
	Tobruk = Tubruq
31B2	**Tocantins** *R* Brazil
31B3	**Tocantins** State, Brazil
17B1	**Toccoa** USA
47C1	**Toce** *R* Italy
30B3	**Tocopilla** Chile
30C3	**Tocorpuri** *Mt* Chile
32D1	**Tocuyo** *R* Ven
85D3	**Toda** India
47C1	**Tödi** *Mt* Switz
75A1	**Todong** S Korea
9B4	**Todos Santos** Mexico
13E2	**Tofield** Can
13B3	**Tofino** Can
12B3	**Togiak** USA
12B3	**Togiak B** USA
97C4	**Togo** Republic, Africa
72C1	**Togtoh** China
12F2	**Tok** USA
74E2	**Tokachi** *R* Japan
75B1	**Tokamachi** Japan
95C3	**Tokar** Egypt
69E4	**Tokara Retto** *Arch* Japan
92C1	**Tokat** Turk
74B3	**Tôkchôk-kundo** *Arch* S Korea
82B1	**Tokmak** Kyrgyzstan
110C1	**Tokomaru Bay** NZ
75A1	**Tok-to** / S Korea
12H3	**Toku** *R* Can/USA
78C3	**Tokung** Indon
69E4	**Tokuno** / Japan
74C4	**Tokushima** Japan
75A2	**Tokuyama** Japan
74D3	**Tôkyô** Japan
110C1	**Tolaga Bay** NZ
101D3	**Tôlañaro** Madag
30F3	**Toledo** Brazil
50B2	**Toledo** Spain
14B2	**Toledo** USA
19B3	**Toledo Bend Res** USA
101D3	**Toliara** Madag
23B1	**Toliman** Mexico
32B3	**Tolina** *Mt* Colombia
51B1	**Tolosa** Spain
29B3	**Toltén** Chile
23B2	**Toluca** Mexico
61G3	**Tol'yatti** Russian Fed
74E2	**Tomakomai** Japan
78D1	**Tomani** Malay
58C2	**Tomaszów Mazowiecka** Pol
11B3	**Tombigbee** *R* USA
98B3	**Tomboco** Angola
35C2	**Tombos** Brazil
97B3	**Tombouctou** Mali
100A2	**Tombua** Angola
34A3	**Tomé** Chile
50B2	**Tomelloso** Spain
50A2	**Tomer** Port
106B3	**Tomkinson Range** *Mts* Aust
63E2	**Tommot** Russian Fed
55B2	**Tomorrit** *Mt* Alb
65K4	**Tomsk** Russian Fed
16B3	**Toms River** USA
25C3	**Tonalá** Mexico
20C1	**Tonasket** USA
15C2	**Tonawanda** USA
105H4	**Tonga** *Is* Pacific O
101H1	**Tongaat** S Africa
73D3	**Tongcheng** China
72B2	**Tongchuan** China
72A2	**Tongde** China
46C1	**Tongeren** Belg
76E2	**Tonggu Jiao** / China
73A5	**Tonghai** China
74B2	**Tonghua** China
74B3	**Tongjosôn-man** N Korea
76D1	**Tongkin,G of** China/Viet
72E1	**Tonglia** China
73D3	**Tongling** China
108B2	**Tongo** Aust
34A2	**Tongoy** Chile
73B4	**Tongren** Guizhou, China
72A2	**Tongren** Qinghai, China
86C1	**Tongsa** Bhutan
76B1	**Tongta** Myan
68B3	**Tongtian He** *R* China
44B2	**Tongue** Scot
72D2	**Tong Xian** China
72B2	**Tongxin** China
73B4	**Tongzi** China
9C4	**Tonichi** Mexico
99C2	**Tonj** Sudan
85D3	**Tonk** India
18A2	**Tonkawa** USA
76C3	**Tonle Sap** *L* Camb
21B2	**Tonopah** USA
12E2	**Tonsina** USA
8B2	**Tooele** USA
109D1	**Toogoolawah** Aust
108B1	**Toompine** Aust
109D1	**Toowoomba** Aust
22C1	**Topaz L** USA
18A2	**Topeka** USA
9C4	**Topolobampo** Mexico
20B1	**Toppenish** USA
99D2	**Tor** Eth
55C3	**Torbali** Turk
90C2	**Torbat-e-Heydarîyeh** Iran
90D2	**Torbat-e Jâm** Iran
12D2	**Torbert,Mt** USA
50A1	**Tordesillas** Spain
43C4	**Torfaen** County Wales
56C2	**Torgau** Germany
46B1	**Torhout** Belg
69G3	**Tori** / Japan
47B2	**Torino** Italy
99D2	**Torit** Sudan
35A1	**Torixoreu** Brazil
50A1	**Tormes** *R* Spain
13E2	**Tornado Mt** Can
38J5	**Torne** *L* Sweden
38H5	**Torneträsk** Sweden
7D4	**Torngat** *Mts* Can
38J5	**Tornio** Fin
34C3	**Tornquist** Arg
15C2	**Toronto** Can
60D2	**Toropets** Russian Fed
99D2	**Tororo** Uganda
92B2	**Toros Dağlari** *Mts* Turk
43C4	**Torquay** Eng
22C4	**Torrance** USA
50A2	**Torrão** Port
51C1	**Torreblanca** Spain
53B2	**Torre del Greco** Italy
50B1	**Torrelavega** Spain
50B2	**Torremolinos** Spain
108A2	**Torrens,L** Aust
24B2	**Torreón** Mexico
47B2	**Torre Pellice** Italy
107D2	**Torres Str** Aust
50A2	**Torres Vedras** Port
16C2	**Torrington** Connecticut, USA
8C2	**Torrington** Wyoming, USA
9C4	**Torrón** Mexico
38D3	**Tórshavn** Føroyar
47C2	**Tortona** Italy
51C1	**Tortosa** Spain
90C2	**Torüd** Iran
58B2	**Toruń** Pol
40B2	**Tory** / Irish Rep
60D2	**Torzhok** Russian Fed
75A2	**Tosa** Japan
74C4	**Tosa-shimizu** Japan
74C4	**Tosa-wan** *B* Japan
75B2	**To-shima** / Japan
	Toshkent = Tashkent
60D2	**Tosno** Russian Fed
75A2	**Tosu** Japan
92B1	**Tosya** Turk
61F1	**Tot'ma** Russian Fed
43C4	**Totnes** Eng
33F2	**Totness** Surinam
23B2	**Totolapan** Mexico
51B2	**Totona** Spain
109C2	**Tottenham** Aust
74C3	**Tottori** Japan
97B4	**Touba** Côte d'Ivoire
97A3	**Touba** Sen
96B1	**Toubkal** *Mt* Mor
97B3	**Tougan** Burkina
96C1	**Touggourt** Alg
97A3	**Tougué** Guinea
46C2	**Toul** France
49D3	**Toulon** France
48C3	**Toulouse** France
97B4	**Toumodi** Côte d'Ivoire
76B2	**Toungoo** Myan
46B1	**Tourcoing** France
96A2	**Tourine** Maur
46B1	**Tournai** Belg
48C2	**Tours** France
74E2	**Towada** Japan
74E2	**Towada-ko** *L* Japan
15C2	**Towanda** USA
107D2	**Townsville** Aust
16A3	**Towson** USA
43C4	**Towy** *R* Wales
74D3	**Toyama** Japan
75B1	**Toyama-wan** *B* Japan
75B2	**Toyohashi** Japan
75B2	**Toyonaka** Japan
75A1	**Toyooka** Japan
74D3	**Toyota** Japan
96C1	**Tozeur** Tunisia
46D2	**Traben-Trarbach** Germany
93C1	**Trabzon** Turk
22B2	**Tracy** California, USA
34A3	**Traiguén** Chile

13D3 Trail Can
41B3 Tralee Irish Rep
45B2 Tralee B Irish Rep
45C2 Tramore Irish Rep
39G7 Tranås Sweden
77B4 Trang Thai
71E4 Trangan I Indon
109C2 Trangie Aust
12E2 Transalaskan Pipeline USA
Transylvanian Alps = Muntii Carpaţii Meridionali
53B3 Trapani Italy
109C3 Traralgon Aust
97A3 Trarza Region, Maur
76C3 Trat Thai
108B2 Traveller's L Aust
56C2 Travemünde Germ
14A2 Traverse City USA
12C1 Traverse Peak Mt USA
111B2 Travers,Mt NZ
47C2 Trebbia R Italy
59B3 Třebíč Czech Republic
54A2 Trebinje Bosnia-Herzegovina
57C3 Trebon Czech Republic
29F2 Treinta y Tres Urug
29C4 Trelew Arg
39G7 Trelleborg Sweden
43B3 Tremadog B Wales
15D1 Tremblant,Mt Can
13C2 Trembleur L Can
16A2 Tremont USA
59B3 Trenčin Slovakia
34C3 Trenque Lauquén Arg
43D3 Trent R Eng
47D1 Trentino Region, Italy
47D1 Trento Italy
15C2 Trenton Can
18B1 Trenton Missouri, USA
16B2 Trenton New Jersey, USA
7E5 Trepassey Can
34C3 Tres Arroyos Arg
35B2 Tres Corações Brazil
30F3 Três Lagoas Brazil
34C3 Tres Lomas Arg
22B2 Tres Pinos USA
35C2 Três Rios Brazil
47C2 Treviglio Italy
47E2 Treviso Italy
47C2 Trezzo Italy
87B2 Trichūr India
108C2 Trida Aust
46D2 Trier Germany
52B1 Trieste Italy
45C2 Trim Irish Rep
87C3 Trincomalee Sri Lanka
33E6 Trinidad Bol
29E2 Trinidad Urug
9C3 Trinidad USA
34C3 Trinidad I Arg
27E4 Trinidad I Caribbean S
103G6 Trindade I Atlantic O
27E4 Trinidad & Tobago Republic Caribbean S
19A3 Trinity USA
9D3 Trinity R USA
7E5 Trinity B Can
12D3 Trinity Is USA
17A1 Trion USA
94B1 Tripoli Leb
95A1 Tripoli Libya
55B3 Tripolis Greece
86C2 Tripura State, India
103H6 Tristan da Cunha Is Atlantic O
87B3 Trivandrum India
59B3 Trnava Slovakia
107E1 Trobriand Is PNG
15D1 Trois-Riviéres Can
65H4 Troitsk Russian Fed
39G7 Trollhättan Sweden
38F6 Trollheimen Mt Nor
89K9 Tromelin I Indian O

38H5 Tromsø Nor
38G6 Trondheim Nor
38G6 Trondheimfjord Inlet Nor
42B2 Troon Scot
102J3 Tropic of Cancer
103J6 Tropic of Capricorn
96B2 Troudenni Mali
7A4 Trout L Ontario, Can
17A1 Troy Alabama, USA
16C1 Troy New York, USA
14B2 Troy Ohio, USA
54B2 Troyan Bulg
49C2 Troyes France
91B5 Trucial Coast Region, UAE
21A2 Truckee R USA
25D3 Trujillo Honduras
32B5 Trujillo Peru
50A2 Trujillo Spain
32C2 Trujillo Ven
109C2 Trundle Aust
7D5 Truro Can
43B4 Truro Eng
68B2 Tsagaan Nuur L Mongolia
68B1 Tsagan-Tologoy Russian Fed
101D2 Tsaratanana Madag
100B3 Tsau Botswana
99D3 Tsavo Kenya
99D3 Tsavo Nat Pk Kenya
65J4 Tselinograd Kazakhstan
100A3 Tses Namibia
68C2 Tsetserleg Mongolia
97C4 Tsévié Togo
100B3 Tshabong Botswana
100B3 Tshane Botswana
98B3 Tshela Zaïre
98C3 Tshibala Zaïre
98C3 Tshikapa Zaïre
98C3 Tshuapa R Zaïre
101D3 Tsihombe Madag
61F4 Tsimlyanskoye Vodokhranilishche Res Russian Fed
Tsinan = Jinan
Tsingtao = Qingdao
101D2 Tsiroanomandidy Madag
13B2 Tsitsutl Peak Mt Can
58D2 Tsna R Belarus
72B1 Tsogt Ovoo Mongolia
68C2 Tsomog Mongolia
75B2 Tsu Japan
75B1 Tsubata Japan
74E3 Tsuchira Japan
74E2 Tsugaru-kaikyō Str Japan
100A2 Tsumeb Namibia
100A3 Tsumis Namibia
75B1 Tsunugi Japan
74D3 Tsuruga Japan
74D3 Tsuruoka Japan
75B1 Tsushima Japan
74B4 Tsushima I Japan
74C3 Tsuyama Japan
50A1 Tua R Port
45B2 Tuam Irish Rep
60E5 Tuapse Russian Fed
111A3 Tuatapere NZ
30G4 Tubarão Brazil
94B2 Tubas Israel
79A4 Tubbataha Reefs Is Phil
57B3 Tübingen Germany
95B1 Tubruq Libya
16B3 Tuckerton USA
9B3 Tucson USA
30C4 Tucumán State, Arg
34B2 Tucunuco Arg
33E2 Tucupita Ven
51B1 Tudela Spain
93C3 Tudmur Syria
101H1 Tugela R S Africa
109D2 Tuggerah L Aust
12D3 Tugidak I USA
79B2 Tuguegarao Phil
63F2 Tugur Russian Fed
72D2 Tuhai He R China
4E3 Tuktoyaktuk USA
58C1 Tukums Latvia

99D3 Tukuyu Tanz
84B1 Tukzar Afghan
60E3 Tula Russian Fed
60E3 Tula Division Russian Fed
23B1 Tulancingo Mexico
78A3 Tulangbawang R Indon
32B3 Tulcán Colombia
60C5 Tulcea Rom
100B3 Tuli Zim
94B2 Tulkarm Israel
48C2 Tulle France
19B3 Tullos USA
45C2 Tullow Irish Rep
18A2 Tulsa USA
93C3 Tulūl ash Shāmīyah Desert Region Syria/ S Arabia
63C2 Tulun Russian Fed
78C4 Tulungagung Indon
32B3 Tumaco Colombia
109C3 Tumbarumba Aust
32A4 Tumbes Ecuador
108A2 Tumby Bay Aust
74B2 Tumen China
87B2 Tumkūr India
77C4 Tumpat Malay
85D4 Tumsar India
97B3 Tumu Ghana
109C3 Tumut Aust
109C3 Tumut R Aust
27L1 Tunapuna Trinidad
93C2 Tunceli Turk
99D3 Tunduma Zambia
101C2 Tunduru Tanz
54C2 Tundzha R Bulg
87B1 Tungabhadra R India
68D4 Tung-Chiang Taiwan
38B2 Tungnafellsjökull Mts Iceland
12J2 Tungsten Can
63B1 Tunguska R Russian Fed
87C1 Tuni India
96D1 Tunis Tunisia
88E4 Tunisia Republic, N Africa
32C2 Tunja Colombia
12B2 Tuntutuliak USA
12B2 Tununak USA
34B2 Tunuyán Arg
34B2 Tunuyán R Arg
22C2 Tuolumne Meadows USA
35A2 Tupã Brazil
35B1 Tupaciguara Brazil
19C3 Tupelo USA
30C3 Tupiza Bol
15D2 Tupper Lake USA
34B2 Tupungato Arg
29C2 Tupungato Mt Arg
86C1 Tura India
63C1 Tura Russian Fed
61K2 Tura R Russian Fed
90C2 Turān Iran
63B2 Turan Russian Fed
93C3 Turayf S Arabia
80E3 Turbat Pak
32B2 Turbo Colombia
54B1 Turda Rom
63A3 Turfan Depression China
65H4 Turgay Kazakhstan
63B3 Turgen Uul Mt Mongolia
54C2 Turgovishte Bulg
92A2 Turgutlu Turk
92C1 Turhal Turk
39K7 Tūri Estonia
51B2 Turia R Spain
Turin = Torino
61K2 Turinsk Russian Fed
69F2 Turiy Rog Russian Fed
99D2 Turkana,L Kenya/Eth
80E1 Turkestan Region, C Asia
82A1 Turkestan Kazakhstan
92C2 Turkey Republic, W Asia
80D1 Turkmenistan Republic, Asia

90B2 Turkmenskiy Zaliv B Turkmenistan
27C2 Turks Is Caribbean S
39J6 Turku Fin
99D2 Turkwel R Kenya
22B2 Turlock USA
22B2 Turlock L USA
110C2 Turnagain,C NZ
25D3 Turneffe I Belize
16C1 Turners Falls USA
46C1 Turnhout Belg
13F1 Turnor L Can
54B2 Turnu Măgurele Rom
63A3 Turpan China
26B2 Turquino Mt Cuba
80E1 Turtkul' Uzbekistan
18A2 Turtle Creek Res USA
13F2 Turtle L Can
63A1 Turukhansk Russian Fed
68C1 Turuntayevo Russian Fed
35A1 Turvo R Goias, Brazil
35B2 Turvo R São Paulo, Brazil
58C2 Tur'ya R Ukraine
19C3 Tuscaloosa USA
18C2 Tuscola USA
90C3 Tusharik Iran
Tutera = Tudela
87B3 Tuticorin India
54C2 Tutrakan Bulg
57B3 Tuttlingen Germany
68C2 Tuul Gol R Mongolia
105G4 Tuvalu Is Pacific O
63B2 Tuvinskaya Respublika, Russian Fed
23A2 Tuxpan Jalisco, Mexico
24B2 Tuxpan Nayarit, Mexico
23B1 Tuxpan Veracruz, Mexico
23B2 Tuxtepec Mexico
25C3 Tuxtla Gutiérrez Mexico
50A1 Túy Spain
76D3 Tuy Hoa Viet
92B2 Tuz Gölü Salt L Turk
93D3 Tuz Khurmātū Iraq
54A2 Tuzla Bosnia-Herzegovina
60E2 Tver' Russian Fed
60D2 Tver' Division Russian Fed
42C2 Tweed R Eng/Scot
109D1 Tweed Heads Aust
42C2 Tweedsmuir Hills Scot
7E5 Twillingate Can
8B2 Twin Falls USA
111B2 Twins,The Mt NZ
14A2 Two Rivers USA
63E2 Tygda Russian Fed
19A3 Tyler USA
65K3 Tym R Russian Fed
69G1 Tymovskoye Russian Fed
42D2 Tyne R Eng
42D2 Tynemouth Eng
38G6 Tynset Nor
12D3 Tyonek USA
94B2 Tyr USA
Tyre = Tyr
45C1 Tyrone County, N Ire
108B3 Tyrrell,L Aust
53B2 Tyrrhenian S Italy
65H4 Tyumen' Russian Fed
43B3 Tywyn Wales
55B3 Tzoumérka Mt Greece

U

99E2 Uarsciek Somalia
35C2 Ubá Brazil
35C1 Ubai Brazil
98B2 Ubangi R CAR
47B2 Ubaye R France
75A2 Ube Japan
50B2 Ubeda Spain

Ubekendt Ejland

58D1	**Valmiera** Latvia	
35A2	**Valparaíso** Brazil	
34A2	**Valparaíso** Chile	
23A1	**Valparaíso** Mexico	
17A1	**Valparaiso** USA	
101G1	**Vals** R S Africa	
85C4	**Valsād** India	
60E3	**Valuyki** Russian Fed	
50A2	**Valverde del Camino** Spain	
38J6	**Vammala** Fin	
93D2	**Van** Turk	
63C1	**Vanavara** Russian Fed	
18B2	**Van Buren** Arkansas, USA	
13C1	**Vancouver** Can	
20B1	**Vancouver** USA	
5F5	**Vancouver I** Can	
12G2	**Vancouver,Mt** Can	
18C2	**Vandalia** Illinois, USA	
14B3	**Vandalia** Ohio, USA	
13C2	**Vanderhoof** Can	
106C2	**Van Diemen G** Gulf Aust	
39G7	**Vänern** L Sweden	
39G7	**Vänersborg** Sweden	
101D3	**Vangaindrano** Madag	
93D2	**Van Gölü** Salt L Turk	
76C2	**Vang Vieng** Laos	
9C3	**Van Horn** USA	
15C1	**Vanier** Can	
1C6	**Vankarem** Russian Fed	
38H6	**Vännäs** Sweden	
48B2	**Vannes** France	
47B2	**Vanoise** Mts France	
100A4	**Vanrhynsdorp** S Africa	
6B3	**Vansittart I** Can	
105G4	**Vanuatu** Is Pacific O	
14B2	**Van Wert** USA	
47C2	**Varallo** Italy	
90B2	**Varāmīn** Iran	
86A1	**Vārānasi** India	
38K4	**Varangerfjord** Inlet Nor	
38K4	**Varangerhalvøya** Pen Nor	
52C1	**Varazdin** Croatia	
39G7	**Varberg** Sweden	
39F7	**Varde** Den	
38L4	**Vardø** Nor	
58C2	**Varéna** Lithuania	
47C2	**Varenna** Italy	
47C2	**Varese** Italy	
35B2	**Varginha** Brazil	
38K6	**Varkaus** Fin	
54C2	**Varna** Bulg	
39G7	**Värnamo** Sweden	
17B1	**Varnville** USA	
35C1	**Várzea da Palma** Brazil	
47C2	**Varzi** Italy	
50B1	**Vascongadas** Region, Spain	
60D3	**Vasil'kov** Ukraine	
14B2	**Vassar** USA	
39H7	**Västerås** Sweden	
39H7	**Västervik** Sweden	
52B2	**Vasto** Italy	
65J4	**Vasyugan** R Russian Fed	
38B2	**Vatnajökull** Mts Iceland	
38A1	**Vatneyri** Iceland	
54C1	**Vatra Dornei** Rom	
39G7	**Vättern** L Sweden	
9C3	**Vaughn** USA	
32C3	**Vaupés** R Colombia	
13E2	**Vauxhall** Can	
87C3	**Vavunija** Sri Lanka	
39G7	**Växjö** Sweden	
64G2	**Vaygach, Ostrov** I Russian Fed	
34C2	**Vedia** Arg	
38G5	**Vega** I Nor	
13E2	**Vegreville** Can	
50A2	**Vejer de la Frontera** Spain	
39F7	**Vejle** Den	
52C2	**Velebit** Mts Croatia	

52C1	**Velenje** Slovenia	
35C1	**Velhas** R Brazil	
39K7	**Velikaya** R Russian Fed	
60D2	**Velikiye Luki** Russian Fed	
61G1	**Velikiy Ustyug** Russian Fed	
54C2	**Veliko Tǔrnovo** Bulg	
97A3	**Vélingara** Sen	
87B2	**Vellore** India	
61F1	**Vel'sk** Russian Fed	
87B3	**Vembanad L** India	
34C2	**Venado Tuerto** Arg	
35B2	**Vençeslau Braz** Brazil	
49C2	**Vendôme** France	
12E1	**Venetie** USA	
47D2	**Veneto** Region, Italy	
47E2	**Venezia** Italy	
32D2	**Venezuela** Republic, S America	
87A1	**Vengurla** India	
12C3	**Veniaminof V** USA	
	Venice = Venezia	
87B2	**Venkatagiri** India	
56B2	**Venlo** Neth	
58C1	**Venta** R Latvia	
101G1	**Ventersburg** S Africa	
58C1	**Ventspils** Latvia	
32D3	**Ventuari** R Ven	
22C3	**Ventura** USA	
60D1	**Vepsovskaya Vozvyshennost'** Upland Russian Fed	
30D4	**Vera** Arg	
51B2	**Vera** Spain	
23B2	**Veracruz** Mexico	
23B1	**Veracruz** State, Mexico	
85C4	**Verāval** India	
47C2	**Verbania** Italy	
47C2	**Vercelli** Italy	
35A1	**Verde** R Goias, Brazil	
23A1	**Verde** R Jalisco, Mexico	
35A1	**Verde** R Mato Grosso do Sul, Brazil	
23B2	**Verde** R Oaxaca, Mexico	
	Verde,C = Cap Vert	
35C1	**Verde Grande** R Brazil	
34C3	**Verde,Pen** Arg	
49D3	**Verden** R France	
46C2	**Verdun** France	
101G1	**Vereeniging** S Africa	
61H2	**Vereshchagino** Russian Fed	
97A3	**Verga,C** Guinea	
34D3	**Vergara** Arg	
50A1	**Verín** Spain	
63D2	**Verkh Angara** R Russian Fed	
61J3	**Verkhneural'sk** Russian Fed	
63E1	**Verkhnevilyuysk** Russian Fed	
1C8	**Verkhoyansk** Russian Fed	
35A1	**Vermelho** R Brazil	
13E2	**Vermilion** Can	
10C2	**Vermont** State, USA	
22B2	**Vernalis** USA	
13D2	**Vernon** Can	
46A2	**Vernon** France	
9D3	**Vernon** USA	
17B2	**Vero Beach** USA	
54B2	**Veroia** Greece	
47D2	**Verolanuova** Italy	
47D2	**Verona** Italy	
46B2	**Versailles** France	
101H1	**Verulam** S Africa	
46C1	**Verviers** Belg	
46B2	**Vervins** France	
46C2	**Vesle** R France	
49D2	**Vesoul** France	
38G5	**Vesterålen** Is Nor	
38G5	**Vestfjorden** Inlet Nor	
38A2	**Vestmannaeyjar** Iceland	
53B2	**Vesuvio** Mt Italy	
59B3	**Veszprém** Hung	
39H7	**Vetlanda** Sweden	

61F2	**Vetluga** R Russian Fed	
46B1	**Veurne** Belg	
47B1	**Vevey** Switz	
46A2	**Vexin** Region, France	
47A2	**Veynes** France	
50A1	**Viana do Castelo** Port	
	Viangchan = Vientiane	
49E3	**Viareggio** Italy	
39F7	**Viborg** Den	
53C3	**Vibo Valentia** Italy	
	Vic = Vich	
112C2	**Vicecomodoro Marambio** Base Ant	
52B1	**Vicenza** Italy	
51C1	**Vich** Spain	
32D3	**Vichada** R Colombia	
61F2	**Vichuga** Russian Fed	
49C2	**Vichy** France	
19B3	**Vicksburg** USA	
35C2	**Vicosa** Brazil	
106C4	**Victor Harbour** Aust	
34C2	**Victoria** Arg	
13C3	**Victoria** Can	
34A3	**Victoria** Chile	
108B3	**Victoria** State, Aust	
9D4	**Victoria** USA	
106C2	**Victoria** R Aust	
26B2	**Victoria de las Tunas** Cuba	
100B2	**Victoria Falls** Zambia/Zim	
4G2	**Victoria I** Can	
108B2	**Victoria,L** Aust	
99D3	**Victoria,L** C Africa	
112B7	**Victoria Land** Region, Ant	
86C2	**Victoria,Mt** Myan	
99D2	**Victoria Nile** R Uganda	
111B2	**Victoria Range** Mts NZ	
106C2	**Victoria River Downs** Aust	
4H3	**Victoria Str** Can	
15D1	**Victoriaville** Can	
100B4	**Victoria West** S Africa	
34B3	**Victorica** Arg	
21B3	**Victorville** USA	
34A2	**Vicuña** Chile	
34C2	**Vicuña Mackenna** Arg	
17B1	**Vidalia** USA	
54C2	**Videle** Rom	
54B2	**Vidin** Bulg	
85D4	**Vidisha** India	
58D1	**Vidzy** Belarus	
29D4	**Viedma** Arg	
26A4	**Viéjo** Costa Rica	
	Vielha = Viella	
51C1	**Viella** Spain	
	Vienna = Wien	
18C2	**Vienna** Illinois, USA	
14B3	**Vienna** W Virginia, USA	
49C2	**Vienne** France	
48C2	**Vienne** R France	
76C2	**Vientiane** Laos	
47C1	**Vierwaldstätter See** L Switz	
48C2	**Vierzon** France	
53C2	**Vieste** Italy	
70B2	**Vietnam** Republic, S E Asia	
76D1	**Vietri** Viet	
27P2	**Vieux Fort** St Lucia	
79B2	**Vigan** Phil	
47C2	**Vigevano** Italy	
48B3	**Vignemale** Mt France	
50A1	**Vigo** Spain	
87C1	**Vijayawāda** India	
55A2	**Vijosë** R Alb	
38B2	**Vik** Iceland	
54B2	**Vikhren** Mt Bulg	
13E2	**Viking** Can	
38G6	**Vikna** I Nor	
101C2	**Vila da Maganja** Mozam	
101C2	**Vila Machado** Mozam	
101C3	**Vilanculos** Mozam	

	Vilanova i la Geltrú = Villanueva-y-Geltrú	
50A1	**Vila Real** Port	
101C2	**Vila Vasco da Gama** Mozam	
35C2	**Vila Velha** Brazil	
58D2	**Vileyka** Belarus	
38H6	**Vilhelmina** Sweden	
33E6	**Vilhena** Brazil	
60C2	**Viljandi** Estonia	
101G1	**Viljoenskroon** S Africa	
9C3	**Villa Ahumada** Mexico	
34B2	**Villa Atuel** Arg	
50A1	**Villaba** Spain	
23A2	**Villa Carranza** Mexico	
52B1	**Villach** Austria	
34B2	**Villa Colon** Arg	
34C2	**Villa Constitución** Arg	
34C1	**Villa de Maria** Arg	
23A1	**Villa de Reyes** Mexico	
34B2	**Villa Dolores** Arg	
47D2	**Villafranca di Verona** Italy	
34C2	**Villa General Mitre** Arg	
34B2	**Villa General Roca** Arg	
34D2	**Villaguay** Arg	
25C3	**Villahermosa** Mexico	
23A1	**Villa Hidalgo** Mexico	
34C2	**Villa Huidobro** Arg	
34C3	**Villa Iris** Arg	
34C2	**Villa Maria** Arg	
30D3	**Villa Montes** Bol	
23A1	**Villaneuva** Mexico	
50A1	**Vila Nova de Gaia** Port	
50A2	**Villanueva de la Serena** Spain	
51C1	**Villanueva-y-Geltrú** Spain	
34B3	**Villa Regina** Arg	
51B2	**Villarreal** Spain	
29B3	**Villarrica** Chile	
30E4	**Villarrica** Par	
50B2	**Villarrobledo** Spain	
51B2	**Villena** Spain	
46B2	**Villeneuve-St-Georges** France	
48C3	**Villeneuve-sur-Lot** France	
19B3	**Ville Platte** USA	
46B2	**Villers-Cotterêts** France	
49C2	**Villeurbanne** France	
101G1	**Villiers** S Africa	
87B2	**Villupuram** India	
58D2	**Vilnius** Lithuania	
63D1	**Vilyuy** R Russian Fed	
63E1	**Vilyuysk** Russian Fed	
34A2	**Viña del Mar** Chile	
51C1	**Vinaroz** Spain	
14A3	**Vincennes** USA	
38H5	**Vindel** R Sweden	
85D4	**Vindhya Range** Mts India	
16B3	**Vineland** USA	
16D2	**Vineyard Haven** USA	
76D2	**Vinh** Viet	
76D3	**Vinh Cam Ranh** B Viet	
77D4	**Vinh Loi** Viet	
77D3	**Vinh Long** Viet	
18A2	**Vinita** USA	
54A1	**Vinkovci** Croatia	
60C4	**Vinnitsa** Ukraine	
112B3	**Vinson Massif** Upland Ant	
100A3	**Vioolsdrift** S Africa	
47D1	**Vipiteno** Italy	
79B3	**Virac** Phil	
87B2	**Virddhāchalam** India	

73B3 **Wanxian** China
73B3 **Wanyuan** China
13D2 **Wapiti** R Can
18B2 **Wappapello,L** USA
16C2 **Wappingers Falls** USA
87B1 **Warangal** India
109C4 **Waratah** Aust
108C3 **Waratah B** Aust
108C3 **Warburton** Aust
108A1 **Warburton R** Aust
109C1 **Ward** R Aust
101G1 **Warden** S Africa
99E2 **Warder** Eth
85D4 **Wardha** India
111A3 **Ware** Can
16C1 **Ware** USA
16D2 **Wareham** USA
109D1 **Warialda** Aust
76C2 **Warin Chamrap** Thai
100B3 **Warmbad** S Africa
16B2 **Warminster** USA
21B2 **Warm Springs** USA
56C2 **Warnemünde** Germany
20B2 **Warner Mts** USA
17B1 **Warner Robins** USA
108B3 **Warracknabeal** Aust
108A1 **Warrandirinna,L** Aust
107D3 **Warrego** R Aust
19B3 **Warren** Arkansas, USA
109C2 **Warren** Aust
16D2 **Warren** Massachusetts, USA
14B2 **Warren** Ohio, USA
15C2 **Warren** Pennsylvania, USA
45C1 **Warrenpoint** N Ire
18B2 **Warrensburg** USA
101F1 **Warrenton** S Africa
15C3 **Warrenton** USA
97C4 **Warri** Nig
108A1 **Warrina** Aust
42C3 **Warrington** Eng
108B3 **Warrnambool** Aust
Warsaw = Warszawa
58C2 **Warszawa** Pol
59B2 **Warta** R Pol
109D1 **Warwick** Aust
43D3 **Warwick** County, Eng
43D3 **Warwick** Eng
16B2 **Warwick** New York, USA
16D2 **Warwick** Rhode Island, USA
8B3 **Wasatch Range** Mts USA
101H1 **Wasbank** S Africa
21B2 **Wasco** USA
4H2 **Washburn L** Can
85D4 **Washīm** India
10C3 **Washington** District of Columbia, USA
17B1 **Washington** Georgia, USA
14A3 **Washington** Indiana, USA
18B2 **Washington** Missouri, USA
16B2 **Washington** New Jersey, USA
14B2 **Washington** Pennsylvania, USA
8A2 **Washington** State, USA
14B3 **Washington Court House** USA
6D1 **Washington Land** Can
15D2 **Washington,Mt** USA
43E3 **Wash,The** Eng
85A3 **Washuk** Pak
12E2 **Wasilla** USA
7C4 **Waskaganish** Can
26A4 **Waspán** Nic
70D4 **Watampone** Indon
16C2 **Waterbury** USA
45C2 **Waterford** County, Irish Rep
41B3 **Waterford** Irish Rep
45C2 **Waterford Harbour** Irish Rep

46C1 **Waterloo** Belg
10A2 **Waterloo** USA
15C2 **Watertown** New York, USA
101H1 **Waterval-Boven** S Africa
10D2 **Waterville** Maine, USA
16C1 **Watervliet** USA
5G4 **Waterways** Can
43D4 **Watford** Eng
15C2 **Watkins Glen** USA
8C1 **Watrous** Can
99C2 **Watsa** Zaïre
12J2 **Watson Lake** Can
22B2 **Watsonville** USA
71F4 **Wau** PNG
99C2 **Wau** Sudan
7B5 **Waua** Can
109D2 **Wauchope** Aust
17B2 **Wauchula** USA
14A2 **Waukegan** USA
10B2 **Wausau** USA
14A2 **Wauwatosa** USA
106C2 **Wave Hill** Aust
43E3 **Waveney** R Eng
14B3 **Waverly** Ohio, USA
46C1 **Wavre** Belg
10B2 **Wawa** Can
95A2 **Wāw Al Kabīr** Libya
95A2 **Wāw an Nāmūs** Well Libya
22C2 **Wawona** USA
19A3 **Waxahachie** USA
17B1 **Waycross** USA
17B1 **Waynesboro** Georgia, USA
19C3 **Waynesboro** Mississippi, USA
16A3 **Waynesboro** Pennsylvania, USA
15C3 **Waynesboro** Virginia, USA
18B2 **Waynesville** Missouri, USA
84B2 **Wazi Khwa** Afghan
43E4 **Weald,The** Upland Eng
42C2 **Wear** R Eng
19A3 **Weatherford** Texas, USA
20B2 **Weaverville** USA
14B1 **Webbwood** Can
16D1 **Webster** USA
18B2 **Webster Groves** USA
29D6 **Weddell I** Falkland Is
112C2 **Weddell S** Ant
13C2 **Wedge Mt** Can
20B2 **Weed** USA
101H1 **Weenen** S Africa
109C2 **Wee Waa** Aust
72D1 **Weichang** China
57C3 **Weiden** Germany
72D2 **Weifang** China
72E2 **Weihai** China
72C3 **Wei He** R Henan, China
72C2 **Wei He** R Shaanxi, China
109C1 **Weilmoringle** Aust
73A4 **Weining** China
107D2 **Weipa** Aust
14B2 **Weirton** USA
20C2 **Weiser** USA
72D3 **Weishan Hu** L China
57C2 **Weissenfels** Germ
17A1 **Weiss L** USA
99D1 **Weldiya** Eth
101G1 **Welkom** S Africa
15C2 **Welland** Can
43D3 **Welland** R Eng
106C2 **Wellesley Is** Aust
12G2 **Wellesley L** Can
43D3 **Wellingborough** Eng
109C2 **Wellington** Aust
18A2 **Wellington** Kansas, USA
111B2 **Wellington** NZ
6A2 **Wellington Chan** Can
13C2 **Wells** Can
43C4 **Wells** Eng
110B1 **Wellsford** NZ
106B3 **Wells,L** Aust
57C3 **Wels** Austria

43C3 **Welshpool** Wales
13D1 **Wembley** Can
7C4 **Wemindji** Can
20B1 **Wenatchee** USA
20C1 **Wenatchee** R USA
97B4 **Wenchi** Ghana
72E2 **Wenden** China
73E4 **Wenling** China
32J7 **Wenman** I Ecuador
73A5 **Wenshan** China
107D4 **Wenthaggi** Aust
108B2 **Wentworth** Aust
72A3 **Wen Xian** China
73E4 **Wenzhou** China
73C4 **Wenzhu** China
101G1 **Wepener** S Africa
12G1 **Wernecke Mts** Can
57C2 **Werra** R Germany
109D2 **Werris Creek** Aust
56B2 **Wesel** Germany
56B2 **Weser** R Germany
106C2 **Wessel Is** Aust
14A2 **West Allis** USA
104C4 **West Australian Basin** Indian O
104C5 **West Australian Ridge** Indian O
94B2 **West Bank** Territory, S E Asia
19C3 **West B** USA
86B2 **West Bengal** State, India
43D3 **West Bromwich** Eng
16B3 **West Chester** USA
44B4 **West Dunbartonshire** Division, Scot
46D1 **Westerburg** Germ
56B2 **Westerland** Germany
16D2 **Westerly** USA
106A3 **Western Australia** State, Aust
100A4 **Western Cape** Province, S Africa
87A1 **Western Ghats** Mts India
44A3 **Western Isles** Division, Scot
96A2 **Western Sahara** Region, Mor
105H4 **Western Samoa** Is Pacific O
46B1 **Westerschelde** Estuary Neth
46D1 **Westerwald** Region, Germany
49D1 **Westfalen** Region, Germany
29D6 **West Falkland** I Falkland Is
16C1 **Westfield** Massachusetts, USA
15C2 **Westfield** New York, USA
18C2 **West Frankfort** USA
109C1 **Westgate** Aust
102E3 **West Indies** Is Caribbean S
13E2 **Westlock** Can
14B2 **West Lorne** Can
44C4 **West Lothian** Division, Scot
45C2 **Westmeath** County, Irish Rep
18B2 **West Memphis** USA
43D3 **West Midlands** County, Eng
43D4 **Westminster** Eng
16A3 **Westminster** Maryland, USA
17B1 **Westminster** S Carolina, USA
100B3 **West Nicholson** Zim
78D1 **Weston** Malay
14B3 **Weston** USA
43C4 **Weston-super-Mare** Eng
17B2 **West Palm Beach** USA
18B2 **West Plains** USA
22B1 **West Point** California, USA
19C3 **West Point** Mississippi, USA

16C2 **West Point** New York, USA
12F2 **West Point** Mt USA
45B2 **Westport** Irish Rep
111B2 **Westport** NZ
40C2 **Westray** I Scot
13C2 **West Road** R Can
42E3 **West Sole** Oilfield N Sea
11B3 **West Virginia** State, USA
22C1 **West Walker** R USA
109C2 **West Wyalong** Aust
42D3 **West Yorkshire** County, Eng
71D4 **Wetar** I Indon
13E2 **Wetaskiwin** Can
99D3 **Wete** Tanz
46E1 **Wetzlar** Germany
Wevok = Cape Lisburne
71F4 **Wewak** PNG
19A2 **Wewoka** USA
45C2 **Wexford** County, Irish Rep
45C2 **Wexford** Irish Rep
5H5 **Weyburn** Can
43C4 **Weymouth** Eng
16D1 **Weymouth** USA
110C1 **Whakatane** NZ
110C1 **Whakatane** R NZ
44E1 **Whalsay** I Scot
110B1 **Whangarei** NZ
42D3 **Wharfe** R Eng
19A4 **Wharton** USA
111B2 **Whataroa** NZ
16A3 **Wheaton** Maryland, USA
8B3 **Wheeler Peak** Mt Nevada, USA
9C3 **Wheeler Peak** Mt New Mexico, USA
14B2 **Wheeling** USA
13C3 **Whistler** Can
15C2 **Whitby** Can
42D2 **Whitby** Eng
18B2 **White** R Arkansas, USA
12F2 **White** R Can
14A3 **White** R Indiana, USA
8C2 **White** R S Dakota, USA
7E4 **White B** Can
108B2 **White Cliffs** Aust
40C2 **White Coomb** Mt Scot
13D2 **Whitecourt** Can
14A1 **Whitefish Pt** USA
7D4 **Whitegull L** Can
15D2 **Whitehall** New York, USA
16B2 **Whitehall** Pennsylvania, USA
42C2 **Whitehaven** Eng
12G2 **Whitehorse** Can
110C1 **White I** NZ
19B4 **White L** USA
109C4 **Whitemark** Aust
21B2 **White Mountain Peak** Mt USA
12E1 **White Mts** Alaska, USA
15D2 **White Mts** New Hampshire, USA
99D1 **White Nile** R Sudan
16C2 **White Plains** USA
7B5 **White River** Can
15D2 **White River Junction** USA
White S = Beloye More
13B2 **Whitesail L** Can
20B1 **White Salmon** USA
17C1 **Whiteville** USA
97B4 **White Volta** R Ghana
42B2 **Whithorn** Scot
17B1 **Whitmire** USA
21B2 **Whitney,Mt** USA
12E2 **Whittier** Alaska, USA
22C4 **Whittier** California, USA
5H3 **Wholdia L** Can

94C2 **Yabrūd** Syria
20B2 **Yachats** USA
30D3 **Yacuiba** Bol
87B1 **Yādgir** India
95A1 **Yafran** Libya
23A1 **Yahualica** Mexico
98C2 **Yahuma** Zaïre
75B1 **Yaita** Japan
75B2 **Yaizu** Japan
73A4 **Yajiang** China
20B1 **Yakima** USA
20B1 **Yakima** R USA
97B3 **Yako** Burkina
98C2 **Yakoma** Zaïre
74E2 **Yakumo** Japan
12G3 **Yakutat** USA
12G3 **Yakutat B** USA
63E1 **Yakutsk** Russian Fed
77C4 **Yala** Thai
23B2 **Yalalag** Mexico
98C2 **Yalinga** CAR
109C3 **Yallourn** Aust
68B3 **Yalong** R China
73A4 **Yalong Jiang** R China
54C2 **Yalova** Turk
60D5 **Yalta** Ukraine
74B2 **Yalu Jiang** R China
74D3 **Yamagata** Japan
74C4 **Yamaguchi** Japan
68D1 **Yamarovka** Russian Fed
109D1 **Yamba** New S Wales, Aust
108B2 **Yamba** S Australia, Aust
99C2 **Yambio** Sudan
54C2 **Yambol** Bulg
71E4 **Yamdena** I Indon
Yam Kinneret = Tiberias,L
108B1 **Yamma Yamma,L** Aust
97B4 **Yamoussoukro** Côte d'Ivoire
85D3 **Yamuna** R India
86C1 **Yamzho Yumco** L China
63F1 **Yana** R Russian Fed
108B3 **Yanac** Aust
75A2 **Yanagawa** Japan
87C1 **Yanam** India
72B2 **Yan'an** China
80B3 **Yanbu'al Bahr** S Arabia
108B2 **Yancannia** Aust
72E3 **Yancheng** China
72B2 **Yanchi** China
108B1 **Yandama** R Aust
98C2 **Yangambi** Zaïre
72C1 **Yang He** R China
73C5 **Yangjiang** China
76B2 **Yangon** Myan
72C2 **Yangquan** China
73C5 **Yangshan** China
73C3 **Yangtze Gorges** China
72E3 **Yangtze,Mouths of the** China
72D3 **Yangzhou** China
73B4 **Yanhe** China
74B2 **Yanji** China
108C3 **Yanko** R Aust
8D2 **Yankton** USA
68A2 **Yanqqi** China
72D1 **Yan Shan** Hills
108B1 **Yantabulla** Aust
72E2 **Yantai** China
72D2 **Yanzhou** China
98B2 **Yaoundé** Cam
71E4 **Yapen** I Indon
71E3 **Yap Is** Pacific O
24B2 **Yaqui** R Mexico
61G2 **Yaransk** Russian Fed
32C3 **Yari** R Colombia
74D3 **Yariga-dake** Mt Japan
82B2 **Yarkant He** R China
86C1 **Yarlung Zangbo Jiang** R China
7D5 **Yarmouth** Can
94B2 **Yarmük** R Syria/Jordan
61E2 **Yaroslavl'** Russian Fed

94B2 **Yarqon** R Israel
109C3 **Yarram** Aust
109D1 **Yarraman** Aust
109C3 **Yarrawonga** Aust
60D2 **Yartsevo** Russian Fed
63B1 **Yartsevo** Russian Fed
32B2 **Yarumal** Colombia
97C3 **Yashi** Nig
97C4 **Yashikera** Nig
61F4 **Yashkul'** Russian Fed
84C1 **Yasin** Pak
59C3 **Yasinya** Ukraine
109C2 **Yass** Aust
109C2 **Yass** R Aust
75A1 **Yasugi** Japan
18A2 **Yates Center** USA
98C2 **Yatolema** Zaïre
74C4 **Yatsushiro** Japan
94B3 **Yatta** Israel
32C4 **Yavari** Peru
85D4 **Yavatmāl** India
74C4 **Yawatahama** Japan
76D2 **Ya Xian** China
90B3 **Yazd** Iran
90B3 **Yazd-e Khvāst** Iran
19B3 **Yazoo** R USA
19B3 **Yazoo City** USA
76B2 **Ye** Myan
59D3 **Yedintsy** Moldova
108A2 **Yeelanna** Aust
60E3 **Yefremov** Russian Fed
61F4 **Yegorlyk** R Russian Fed
99D2 **Yei** Sudan
65H4 **Yekaterinburg** Russian Fed
60E3 **Yelets** Russian Fed
44E1 **Yell** I Scot
87C1 **Yellandu** India
Yellow = Huang He
8B1 **Yellowhead P** Can
4G3 **Yellowknife** Can
5G4 **Yellowmead P** Can
109C2 **Yellow Mt** Aust
69E3 **Yellow Sea** China/Korea
8C2 **Yellowstone** R USA
8B2 **Yellowstone L** USA
6B1 **Yelverton B** Can
97C3 **Yelwa** Nig
81C4 **Yemen Republic,** Arabian Pen
76C1 **Yen Bai** Viet
97B4 **Yendi** Ghana
76B1 **Yengan** Myan
63B2 **Yeniseysk** Russian Fed
63B1 **Yeniseyskiy Kryazh** Ridge Russian Fed
64J2 **Yeniseyskiy Zal** B Russian Fed
12D2 **Yentna** R USA
43C4 **Yeo** R Eng
109C2 **Yeoval** Aust
43C4 **Yeovil** Eng
63C1 **Yerbogachen** Russian Fed
65F5 **Yerevan** Armenia
21B2 **Yerington** USA
21B3 **Yermo** USA
69E1 **Yerofey-Pavlovich** Russian Fed
94B3 **Yeroham** Israel
61G3 **Yershov** Russian Fed
Yerushalayim = Jerusalem
92C1 **Yeşil** R Turk
94B2 **Yesud Hama'ala** Israel
109D1 **Yetman** Aust
96B2 **Yetti** Maur
93E1 **Yevlakh** Azerbaijan
60D4 **Yevpatoriya** Ukraine
72E2 **Ye Xian** China
60E4 **Yeysk** Russian Fed
55B2 **Yiannitsá** Greece
73A4 **Yibin** China
73C3 **Yichang** China
69E2 **Yichun** China
72B2 **Yijun** China

54C2 **Yildiz Dağlari** Upland Turk
92C2 **Yildizeli** Turk
73A5 **Yiliang** China
72B2 **Yinchuan** China
72D3 **Ying He** R China
72E1 **Yingkou** China
73D3 **Yingshan** Hubei, China
72B3 **Yingshan** Sichuan, China
73D4 **Yingtan** China
82C1 **Yining** China
72B1 **Yin Shan** Upland China
99D2 **Yirga Alem** Eth
99D2 **Virol** Sudan
63D3 **Yirshi** China
73B5 **Yishan** China
72D2 **Yishui** China
55B3 **Yíthion** Greece
38J6 **Yivieska** Fin
73C4 **Yiyang** China
38K5 **Yli-Kitka** L Fin
38J5 **Ylilornio** Sweden
19A4 **Yoakum** USA
23B2 **Yogope** Mexico
78C4 **Yogyakarta** Indon
13D2 **Yoho Nat Pk** Can
98B2 **Yokadouma** Cam
75B2 **Yokkaichi** Japan
75B1 **Yokohama** Japan
75B1 **Yokosuka** Japan
74C3 **Yonago** Japan
74E3 **Yonezawa** Japan
73D4 **Yong'an** China
72A2 **Yongchang** China
74B3 **Yŏngch'on** S Korea
73B4 **Yongchuan** China
72A2 **Yongdeng** China
73D5 **Yongding** China
72D2 **Yongding He** R China
74B3 **Yŏngdŏk** S Korea
74B3 **Yŏnghŭng** N Korea
74B3 **Yongju** S Korea
72B2 **Yongning** China
16C2 **Yonkers** USA
49C2 **Yonne** R France
42D3 **York** Eng
42D3 **York County** Eng
18A1 **York** Nebraska, USA
16A3 **York** Pennsylvania, USA
107D2 **York,C** Aust
108A2 **Yorke Pen** Aust
108A3 **Yorketown** Aust
7A4 **York Factory** Can
41C3 **Yorkshire Moors** Moorland Eng
42D2 **Yorkshire Wolds** Upland Eng
5H4 **Yorkton** Can
22B2 **Yosemite L** USA
22C1 **Yosemite Nat Pk** USA
75A2 **Yoshii** R Japan
75A2 **Yoshino** R Japan
61G2 **Yoshkar Ola** Russian Fed
74B4 **Yŏsu** S Korea
41B3 **Youghal** Irish Rep
45C3 **Youghal Harb** Irish Rep
73B5 **You Jiang** R China
109C2 **Young** Aust
34D2 **Young** Urug
111A2 **Young Range** Mts NZ
13E2 **Youngstown** Can
14B2 **Youngstown** Ohio, USA
22A1 **Yountville** USA
73B4 **Youyang** China
92B2 **Yozgat** Turk
20B2 **Yreka** USA
39G7 **Ystad** Sweden
43C3 **Ystwyth** R Wales
44C3 **Ythan** R Scot
73C4 **Yuan Jiang** R Hunan, China
73A5 **Yuan Jiang** R Yunnan, China
73A4 **Yuanmu** China

72C2 **Yuanping** China
21A2 **Yuba City** USA
74E2 **Yūbari** Japan
25D3 **Yucatan** Pen Mexico
25D2 **Yucatan Chan** Mexico/Cuba
72C2 **Yuci** China
63F2 **Yudoma** R Russian Fed
73D4 **Yudu** China
73A4 **Yuexi** China
73C4 **Yueyang** China
54A2 **Yugoslavia** Republic, Europe
73B5 **Yu Jiang** R China
12C2 **Yukon** R Can/USA
4E3 **Yukon Territory** Can
76E1 **Yulin** Guangdong, China
73C5 **Yulin** Guangxi, China
72B2 **Yulin** Shaanxi, China
9B3 **Yuma** USA
68B3 **Yumen** China
72D2 **Yunan** China
34A3 **Yungay** Chile
73C5 **Yunkai Dashan** Hills China
108A2 **Yunta** Aust
72C3 **Yunxi** China
72C3 **Yun Xian** China
73B3 **Yunyang** China
32B5 **Yurimaguas** Peru
73E5 **Yu Shan** Mt Taiwan
38L6 **Yushkozero** Russian Fed
82D2 **Yushu** Tibet, China
73A5 **Yuxi** China
74F2 **Yuzhno-Kuril'sk** Russian Fed
69G2 **Yuzhno-Sakhalinsk** Russian Fed
61J3 **Yuzh Ural** Mts Russian Fed
46A2 **Yvelines** Department, France
47B1 **Yverdon** Switz

Z

56A2 **Zaandam** Neth
93D2 **Zāb al Babir** R Iraq
93D2 **Zāb as Şaghīr** R Iraq
68D2 **Zabaykal'sk** Russian Fed
59B3 **Zabreh** Czech Republic
59B2 **Zabrze** Pol
23A2 **Zacapu** Mexico
24B2 **Zacatecas** Mexico
23B2 **Zacatepec** Morelos, Mexico
23B2 **Zacatepec** Oaxaca, Mexico
23B2 **Zacatlan** Mexico
23A1 **Zacoalco** Mexico
23B1 **Zacualtipan** Mexico
52C2 **Zadar** Croatia
76B3 **Zadetkyi** I Myan
50A2 **Zafra** Spain
95C1 **Zagazig** Egypt
96B1 **Zagora** Mor
52C1 **Zagreb** Croatia
91D4 **Zāhedān** Iran
94B2 **Zahle** Leb
51C2 **Zahrez Chergui** Marshland Alg
61H2 **Zainsk** Russian Fed
Zaïre = Democratic Republic of Congo
98B3 **Zaïre** R Zaïre/Congo
54B2 **Zaječar** Yugos
68C1 **Zakamensk** Russian Fed
93D2 **Zakho** Iraq
55B3 **Zákinthos** I Greece
59B3 **Zakopane** Pol
59B3 **Zalaegerszeg** Hung
54B1 **Zalău** Rom
56C2 **Zalew Szczeciński** Lg Pol
98C1 **Zalingei** Sudan
63F2 **Zaliv Akademii** B Russian Fed
65G5 **Zaliv Kara-Bogaz Gol** B Turkmenistan

How to make a felt handbag
Lisa Slinn

Published by Morse-Brown Publishing
Series Editor: John Morse-Brown
Photography © Morse-Brown Design Limited
Design & Production: Morse-Brown Design Limited.
www.morsebrowndesign.co.uk
For more titles in this series, see www.how2crafts.com

ISBN: 0-9550241-5-3

Welcome to felt

This book is designed for the fledgling felt maker. It shows the rudimentary traditional steps to hand-felting. Using lightweight **Merino Wool Tops** (see page 2 for a description of felting terms) for colourful designs, felt can easily be made on a sturdy tabletop and the equipment needed is simple and easy to obtain.

We will be making a piece of flat felt in this book. Felt can also be made into 3D objects using a 'resist' and this method may be explored in a later publication.

Felt making is a craft that has been around in various cultures for over 7,000 years. Caps of thick, solid felt from the Early Bronze Age are preserved in the National Museum of Copenhagen.

As a process, hand-felting mats wool fibres together by using, moisture, soap and hand rolling.

An introduction to wool

To make this bag, you will need to buy **fine Merino wool tops**. I have explained each of these terms below:

Merino sheep are regarded as having the finest and softest wool of any sheep. Merino wool can also be dyed in fabulous colours and this also makes it ideal for bag and clothing designs. The wool in its raw state originates from Australian sheep.

Fine wool is wool of a low micron count (where the micron is the international unit of wool measurement).

Merino wool tops is wool that has been washed, carded, combed and formed into a soft rope called a sliver. For this project I have used Merino 64s (between 21 and 23 microns).

I bought the Merino wool for this book from **www.winghamwoolwork.co.uk**. You may also want to buy a 'shade set' (a small sample of each shade to help you choose suitable colours).

There are many wool suppliers worldwide – just make sure they supply Merino wool to the specifications listed above and in the colours you need.

Getting started

To make a piece of flat felt you will need the following:

- A piece of 1cm (½ inch) diameter wooden dowelling about 1m (40 inches) long from any large DIY store or home improvement centre.
- A piece of net curtain at least 90cm (35½ inches) square (from curtain stores, charity or thrift shops).
- A piece of bubble wrap 1m (40 inches) square from any large DIY store or home improvement centre.
- A plastic bottle (eg a 1 litre plastic milk bottle). With a needle, make some holes in the lid of this bottle so that you can evenly sprinkle water over your dry wool.
- Warm soapy water.

- Merino wool. I have used approximately 100g of purple, 100g of deep pink, 50g of yellow and 50g of black Merino. The wool is usually sold in packs of either 50 or 100g.
- A work table. Making felt is a very energetic job so it will need to be a sturdy table.
- A piece of paper 44cm x 85cm (17½ x 33½ inches). I have used parcel paper.
- Scissors, craft knife, pencil and ruler.
- A large towel.
- A white plastic carrier bag.
- A butter knife or flat ruler.
- Tailor's chalk or ordinary white chalk.
- Needle and pink thread.
- A simple sewing machine is advisable, but don't worry if you don't have one – you can finish the bag by hand.

Making the template

For the size of bag we are making it is a good idea to make a template (Fig 1). Take your brown parcel paper and cut a piece 44 x 85cm (17½ x 33½ inches). Place it flat on your work table.

Now lay the bubble wrap on top of the template, bubble side up (Fig 2). You should be able to see the template clearly underneath. Then lay the net on top of the bubble wrap in such a way so that half of it can be folded over on top of the template later on (see drawing on right).

Your wool will shrink in size by about a third throughout the felting process which is why your template is one third bigger in size than your finished piece.

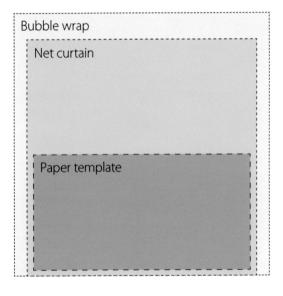

Bubble wrap

Net curtain

Paper template

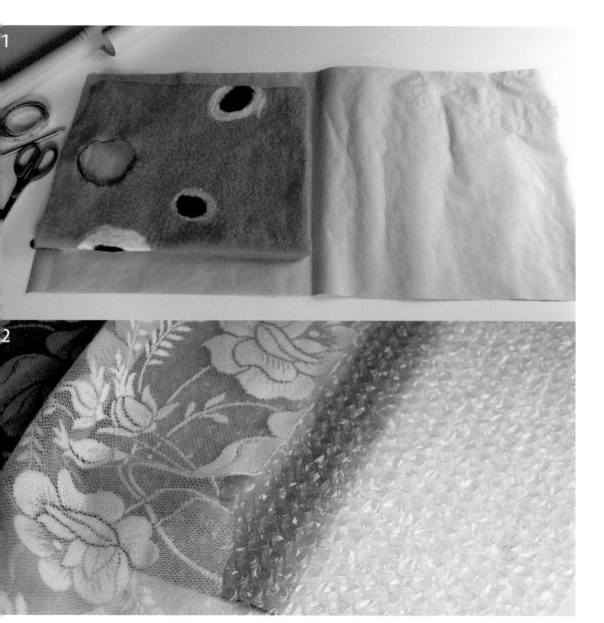

Laying out your wool

Take the end of the purple wool out of its bag and spread out the ends of the fibres by pulling them gently (Fig 3). Hold the wool with your left hand about 20cm (8 inches) back from the end. Now grasp the end with your right hand and gently pull a piece of wool about 10cm (4 inches) long from the main piece (Fig 4).

With the template laid out lengthwise in front of you, lay this piece of wool on top of the net in the far left hand corner of the template so that it lies width-ways across the paper template.

Now tease out a second piece of wool and place this overlapping the first piece by about half (Fig 5). Continue until you have created a line of overlapping wool width-ways right across the paper template. There should be no gaps. The neater you lay out your wool the more refined will be the piece of felt you'll produce. Any gaps will make the felt thin in places and in order to make a strong, sturdy bag, you need an evenly structured piece of felt.

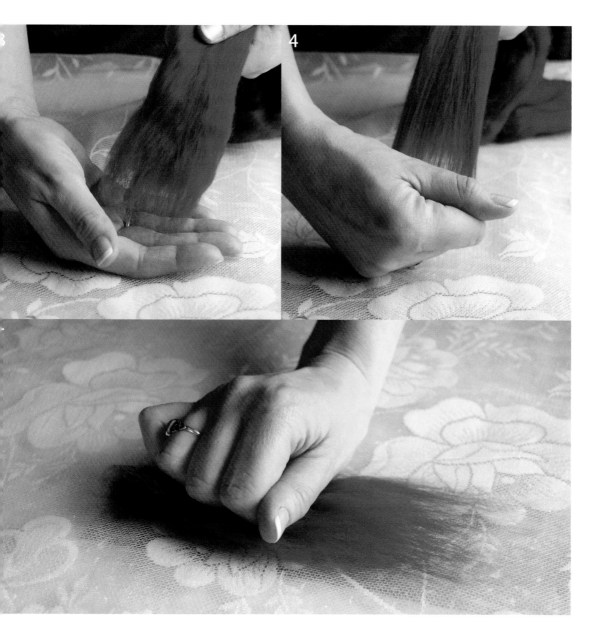

When you have got to the end of your first line, begin a second line alongside the first, overlapping the first line by about half the width of the line. Continue in this manner (Fig 6) until you have one complete layer of wool covering the paper template, with all the pieces overlapping each other by about half.

Now begin your second layer in exactly the same manner, but this time laying the pieces perpendicularly across the first layer (Fig 7). The aim is to have alternate horizontal and vertical layers of wool. Tuck any stray edges under to neaten your piece.

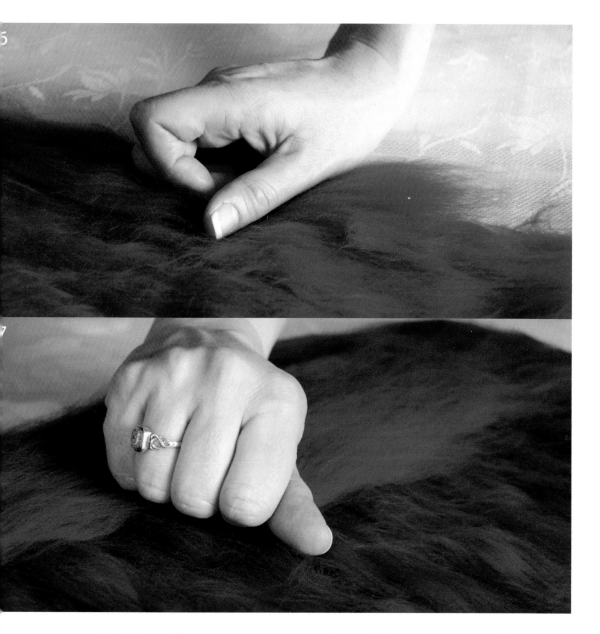

After you've completed two layers of purple wool take your pink wool and tease out the ends', as described on page 10. Lay out pieces of pink wool, beginning at the far left hand corner, as you did with the first layer of purple wool, overlapping each piece as before (Figs 8 & 9).

When you've finished the first layer of pink, lay out a second layer of pink perpendicularly across the first layer, as you did with the purple wool (Fig 10). Again, tuck under any stray edges to make the sides as straight as possible.

The final product should resemble a beautifully soft big pink cloud (Fig 11)!

You are now ready to create your pattern.

Creating your pattern

Take the yellow wool and tease out a piece that is about 20cm (8 inches) long. Separate the piece so that it is in strands of about 2cm in width. This should give you about 5 thinnish strands. Take one of the strands and make a circular shape on top of the wool (Fig 12). Take another strand to complete the circle (Fig 13).

Now tease out a piece of the black wool. Spread it across the inside of the circle (Fig 14).

I have laid out six circles across the piece (Fig 15).

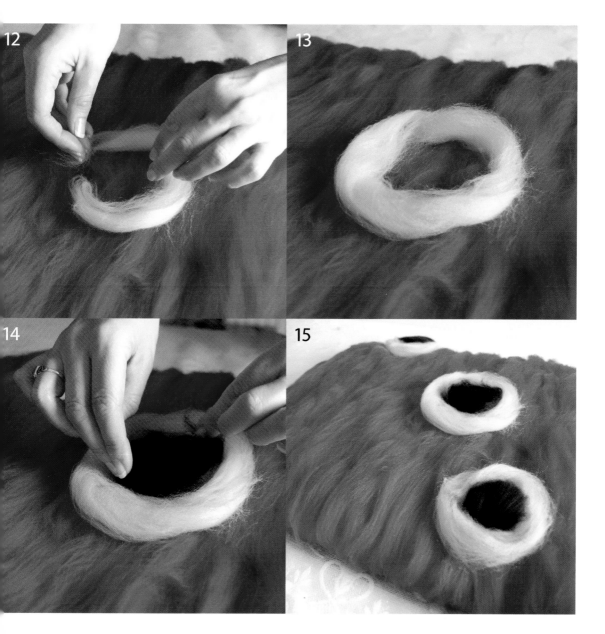

The pre-felting process

Lift the remaining half of the net curtain and lay it carefully over the whole piece (Fig 16). Make sure that you don't pull it too tight across the wool or it will wrinkle your work.

Squirt a teaspoon of washing up liquid into your plastic milk bottle. Now fill it two thirds full with tepid water. With the lid on (in which you previously made some holes with a needle), sprinkle the soapy water all over your piece (Fig 17). The aim is to wet it all over gradually.

Now take a plain white plastic bag and scrunch it up so that you can hold it firmly. If you don't have a plain white bag then take any plastic bag and turn it inside out. With the bag, begin to rub all over the net curtain, to spread out the water and flatten the wet wool (Fig 18). Rub side to side as well as up and down.

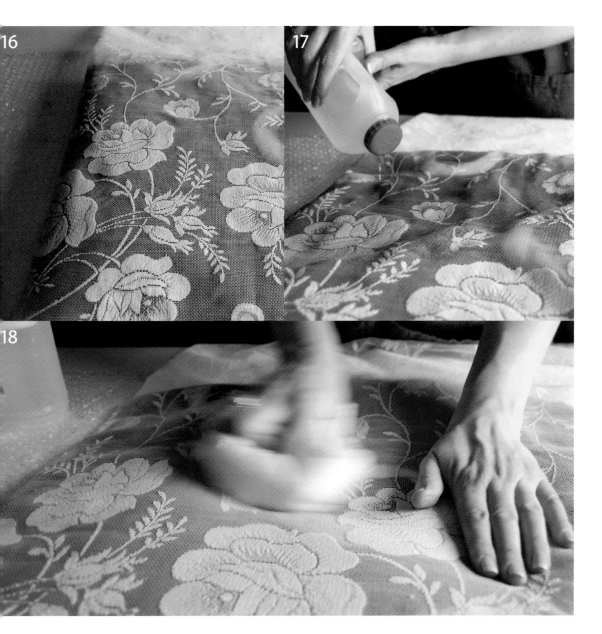

Rub the wool with the plastic bag until the fibres begin to stick together and begin to very slightly come through the net. If you gently peel back the net, the fibres should not pull away with the net but stay flat and firm (Fig 19). You can check to see if this is happening after about 5 minutes of hard rubbing. If the fibres are still loose and you can move them with your fingers, replace the net and carry on rubbing.

When you have rubbed the pink side flat and it is evenly wet but not dripping, turn the whole piece over and repeat the process on the purple side (Figs 20 & 21). Again, rub for about 5 minutes.

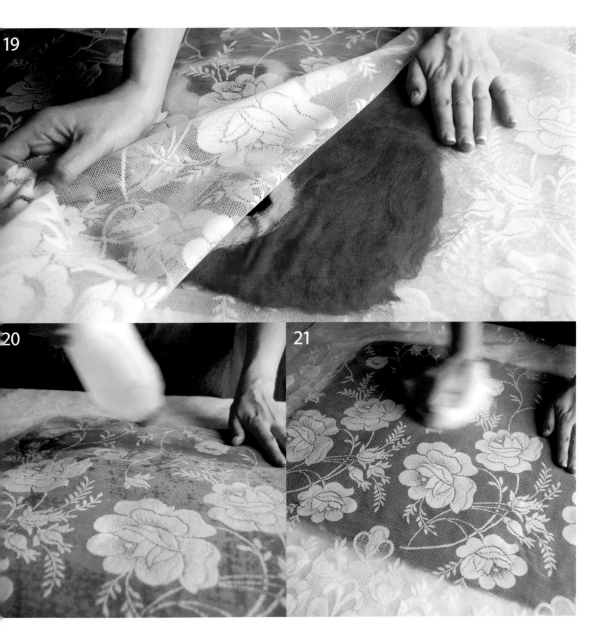

Peel back the netting and flatten the piece with your hand (Fig 22).

Take a butter knife or flat ruler and tuck under the edges of the piece (Figs 23 and 24). Work your way all round the piece so that you end up with a straight-edged rectangle of felt (Fig 25). Don't tuck more than about 1cm (½ inch) underneath.

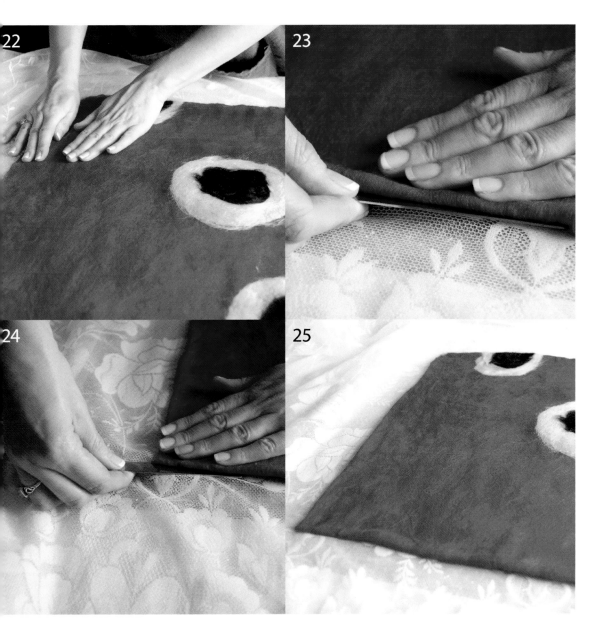

Replace the net and rub the edges of the work through the net in order to make them felt firmly into the piece. Wet the edges with the water as before and rub them hard for another 5 minutes (Fig 26).

Turn the piece over and rub the edges again for another 5 minutes (Fig 27).

The wool has now reached its 'pre-felting' stage, when all of the fibres are firm and attached to each other. To check that your felt is quite firm, pinch the edges as shown in Figure 28. If the fibres are firmly matted together you won't be able to easily pull them apart.

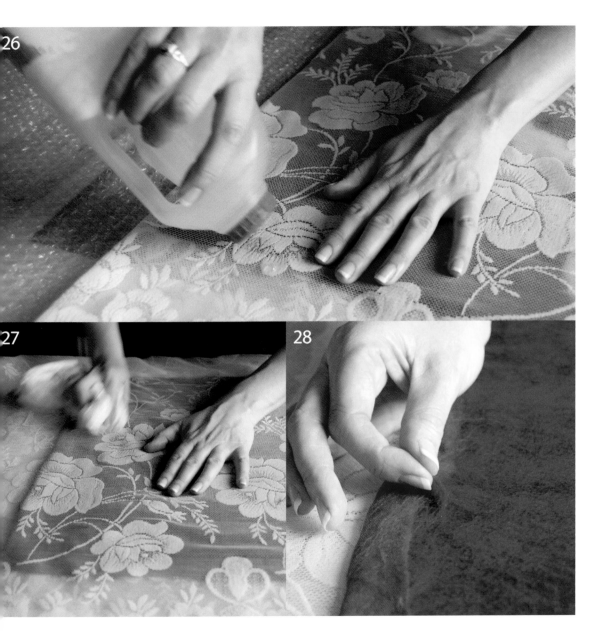

The felting process

Lay the felt inside the netting and place it on top of the bubble wrap. Fold the remaining bubble wrap over the top of the felt and netting.

Take the dowelling and lay it on top of the felt at the edge, as shown in Figure 29. Grasp the bubble wrap, felt and netting and firmly roll them around the dowelling, trying not to crease the felt as you go (Fig 30). Once it's all rolled up, put the roll on a dry towel, and roll it up inside the towel.

Place the roll on a sturdy tabletop, preferably at waist height. Because this next stage is a very energetic process, it's important to be able to stand comfortably when you roll or 'felt' the work.

The actual felting process begins now. Your aim is to roll the piece 1000 times. Place your forearms on top of the roll and push down with your arms. Then begin to rock backwards and forwards (Fig 31). Rolling it like this means you won't strain your hands. It also allows you to roll much faster than you would if you were just rolling with your hands.

Count the number of rolls in your head as you go, counting one roll as both the forward and backwards movement along your forearms.

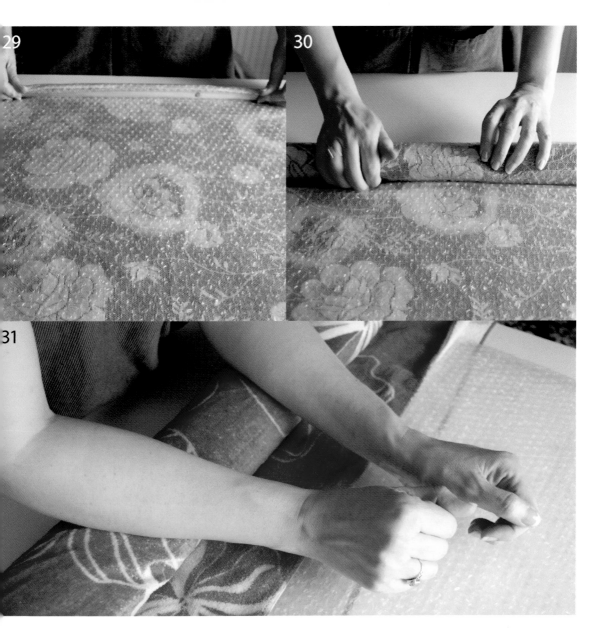

After 250 rolls take the felt out of the towel, bubble wrap and netting. Turn it through 90 degrees so that a new edge is nearest to you. Then turn it over and put it inside the bubble wrap. (At this point you can discard the netting, because if you continued to roll with the netting in place, the felt would begin to stick to it.) Wrap it around the dowelling again as before. Put the roll inside the towel and roll it another 250 times.

After these 500 rolls, take the felt out of the towel and bubble wrap and again turn it through 90 degrees. Turn it over and put it inside the bubble wrap again. By this stage you shouldn't need the towel (Fig 32). Roll it another 250 times (Fig 33). Then repeat this process once more. The aim is to roll from all four edges and to roll the front and back of the piece alternately so that the rectangular shape of the piece is maintained.

(It's a bit like rolling pastry where you have to keep turning it round and turning it over to make sure it stays the right shape for your pie dish.)

After about 1000 rolls the felt should be finished. To make sure, check that the fibres are solid and that you can't easily pull them apart with your fingers. You also need to check that the circular patterns on top of the felt have no loose fibres. If they do, continue rolling until they are firmly embedded into the felt.

Washing the felt

Your finished piece should resemble the felt in Fig 34. Don't worry if it's not completely rectangular and has slightly uneven edges – you can cut it to make it perfectly rectangular before you sew it.

Take your felt and rinse it first in warm water, then in cold (Fig 35). Do this alternately a couple of times until the water runs completely clear. By doing this you are washing out the washing-up liquid. You are also continuing the felting process. When you've finished, gently wring out the water (Fig 36).

34

35

36

Drying the felt

Lay out the felt and flatten it firmly on a sturdy table with the palms of your hands to ease it back into shape (Fig 37).

Roll the felt up inside the towel (Fig 38) and then bang it on the table a few times until the towel is quite wet to finish wringing it out (Fig 39).

Take the felt out of the towel and flatten it again with the palms of your hands. Leave it to dry completely on a flat surface for 24 to 36 hours (Fig 40).

When the felt is completely dry you can begin to make it into a bag.

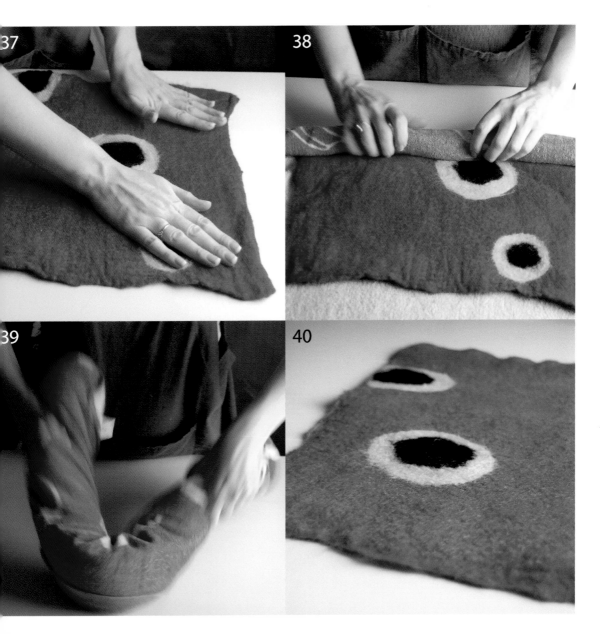

Making the felt into a bag

Fold the rectangle of felt in half to make a square shape, purple side up. Pin the two open sides of the bag together and, cutting through both pieces of felt, trim the edges straight (Fig 41). You can see when the felt is cut that it has different coloured layers (Fig 42).

Now we're going to make your felt into a sturdy, medium-sized shopper bag. The handles are made by cutting a circle into the felt on both sides of the bag and stitching around the edges.

Take a piece of brown paper and cut a circle about 9cm (3½ inches) in diameter. A good template for this is the base of a wine bottle. Pin the template onto the felt on one side, about 6cm (2½ inches) from the top of the bag in the middle. Draw around the template with some tailor's chalk (or ordinary chalk if you can't find tailor's chalk) (Fig 43) and then remove the paper.

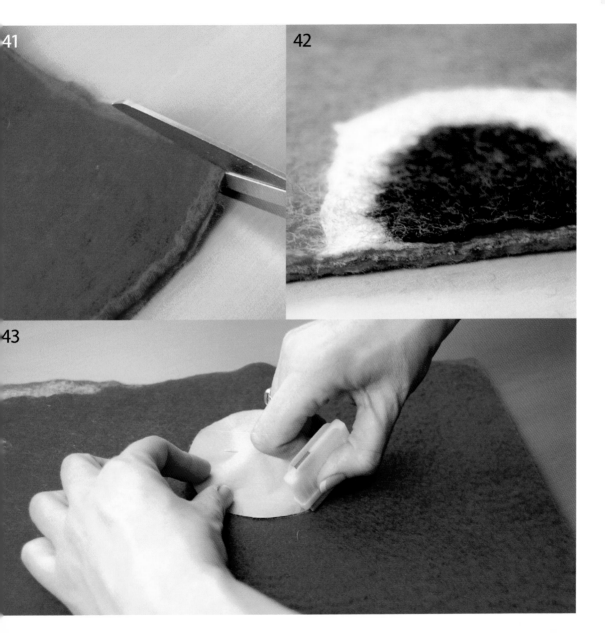

Completing the bag

Take a craft knife and cut from the edge of the circle into the centre (Fig 44). Then, with a sharp pair of scissors, cut out the circle (Fig 45).

Repeat the same process on the other side of the bag, making sure that the circles are directly above each other before cutting them out.

Take some pink thread to match the felt and zigzag stitch all around the edge of the sides of the two individual circles using a sewing machine (Fig 46). If you haven't got a sewing machine you can easily sew this by hand using a blanket stitch.

Now stitch the two sides of the bag together with a running stitch (Fig 47). Again, this can be done by hand if you don't have a sewing machine.

Turn the bag inside out.

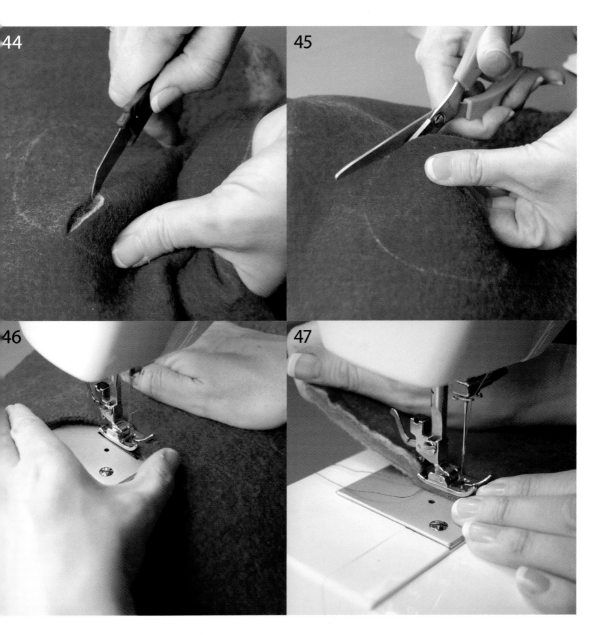

The completed bag

Here's the completed bag. A real head-turner, and all your own work!

Now that you know how to make felt you can experiment with other designs. For more inspiration, check back on the **how2crafts website** from time to time to see photos of bags made by other people who bought this book.

About the author

Lisa Slinn was born in Birmingham, England, and educated at Birmingham University. Since 2004/5, when she studied ceramics and textiles at the Midland Arts Centre, she has been making felt by hand. She has had her work exhibited at Bilston Craft Gallery in the West Midlands, and at local designer maker events.

She draws her inspiration from fashion and innovative product design, and her love of colour is evident in her work.